Option
Volatility
and
Pricing

Option Volatility and Pricing

ADVANCED TRADING STRATEGIES AND TECHNIQUES

SECOND EDITION

SHELDON NATENBERG

NEW YORK CHICAGO SAN FRANCISCO LISBON LONDON MADRID
MEXICO CITY MILAN NEW DELHI SAN JUAN SEOUL
SINGAPORE SYDNEY TORONTO

15   LCR   22

ISBN: 978-0-07-181877-3
MHID: 0-07-181877-4

e-ISBN: 978-0-07-181878-0
e-MHID: 0-07-181878-2

Library of Congress Cataloging-in-Publication Data

Natenberg, Sheldon.
  Option volatility and pricing : advanced trading strategies and techniques / by Sheldon Natenberg. — 2nd edition.
    pages cm
  Includes index.
  ISBN 978-0-07-181877-3 (alk. paper) — ISBN 0-07-181877-4 (alk. paper)
1. Options (Finance) I. Title.
  HG6042.N38 2015
  332.63'28—dc23

                                                          2014026216

McGraw-Hill Education books are available at special quantity discounts to use as premiums and sales promotions, or for use in corporate training programs. To contact a representative, please visit the Contact Us page at www.mhprofessional.com.

To Leona, for her support and encouragement throughout my career.

To Eddie, who continually makes me proud to be a father.

Contents

Preface

It probably seems strange for an author to wait 20 years to revise a professional publication, especially one that has been continuously in print over the entire period. To those of you who were hoping for at least one revision in the intervening years, I can only offer my apology and the excuse that other obligations prevented me from undertaking such a revision.

Much has changed in option markets over the last 20 years. Most markets are now fully electronic, and the days of floor trading are clearly numbered. Only in the United States do option-trading floors still exist, and even those are inevitably giving way to electronic trading. Twenty years ago, organized option markets existed only in the major industrialized nations. But as the importance of derivatives as both an investment vehicle and a risk-management tool has become widely recognized, new option markets have opened in countries around the world. Options are now traded not only on traditional products—stocks, interest rates, commodities, and foreign currencies—but also on a bewildering array of new products—real estate, pollution, weather, inflation, and insurance. Many exchanges have also added variations on traditional products—short-term and midcurve options, flex options, options on spreads, and implied and realized volatility contracts.

Not only has there been a dramatic increase in the number of option markets, but the traders in those markets have become increasingly sophisticated. When this text was first published, knowledgeable traders could only be found at firms that traded derivatives professionally—market-making firms, hedge funds, investment banks, and other proprietary trading firms. Now, many retail customers have a level of knowledge equal to that of a professional trader. At the same time, universities are adding or expanding programs in financial engineering. In many cases, those who choose a career in derivatives trading have already had in-depth exposure to the mathematics of option pricing.

While much has changed in the last 20 years, much has also remained the same. There is still a core body of material that a serious option trader needs to master, and this core material is much the same as it has always been. The previous edition of this text was an attempt to present this material in a manner that was easily accessible and that did not require a familiarity with advanced mathematics. This edition retains that approach. Although some presentations may have been changed in the interest of improving an explanation or clarifying a concept, all the major topics from the previous edition have been retained.

So what's new in this edition? As in the first edition, an attempt has been made to explain important concepts in the simplest possible manner using an intuitive rather than mathematical approach. However, it is also true that a full understanding of many option concepts requires a familiarity with more advanced mathematics. Consequently, some explanations have been expanded to include a discussion of the relevant mathematics. But even these discussions tend to avoid mathematical concepts with which many readers are unlikely to be familiar. Many chapters have also been expanded to include a more detailed discussion of the relevant topics. In addition, there are several completely new chapters covering forward pricing, risk dynamics, the Black-Scholes model, binomial option pricing, and volatility contracts.

As with any living language, market terminology, and more specifically, option terminology, has changed over time. Some terms that were common when the first edition appeared have gone out of favor or disappeared completely. Other terms that did not previously exist have gained wide acceptance. This is reflected in small changes to the vocabulary used in this text.

It is almost impossible to keep up with the amount of information that is available on options. Not only do new books appear with greater frequency, but the Internet has enabled traders to find relevant source material almost instantaneously. For this reason, the Bibliography has been eliminated. This should not be construed as an attempt to discourage readers from consulting other sources. This book represents only one approach to options—that of a professional trader. Many excellent option books are available, and any aspiring option trader will want to consult a broad range of texts in order to understand the many different ways one can approach option markets. For those who are interested in the mathematics of option pricing, this text is in no way meant to take the place of a good university textbook on financial engineering.

Nothing in this text is really new, and all the concepts will be familiar, in one form or another, to most experienced option traders. The presentation represents my best attempt, as an option educator, to present these concepts in a clear and easily accessible manner. The material is based not only on what I have personally learned throughout my career but also on the knowledge and experiences of many others with whom I have been privileged to work. In particular, my colleagues Tim Weithers and Samuel Kadziela offered many helpful comments and insights and in some cases rescued me from embarrassing errors. Any remaining errors, of which there are almost certainly a few, are strictly my own.

I make no claim to having found a magic secret to successful option trading. Anyone seeking such a formula will have to look elsewhere. The secret, if there is one, is in learning as much as possible, applying in the real world what has been learned, and analyzing both one's successes and one's failures.

Sheldon Natenberg

Option
Volatility
and
Pricing

Financial Contracts

My friend Jerry lives in a small town, the same town in which he was born and raised. Because Jerry's parents are no longer alive and many of his friends have left, he is seriously thinking of packing up and moving to a larger city. However, Jerry recently heard that there is a plan to build a major highway that will pass very close to his hometown. Because the highway is likely to bring new life to the town, Jerry is reconsidering his decision to move away. It has also occurred to Jerry that the highway may bring new business opportunities.

For many years, Jerry's family was in the restaurant business, and Jerry is thinking of building a restaurant at the main intersection leading from the highway into town. If Jerry does decide to build the restaurant, he will need to acquire land along the highway. Fortunately, Jerry has located a plot of land, currently owned by Farmer Smith, that is ideally suited for the restaurant. Because the land does not seem to be in use, Jerry is hoping that Farmer Smith might be willing to sell it.

If Farmer Smith is indeed willing to sell, how can Jerry acquire the land on which to build his restaurant? First, Jerry must find out how much Farmer Smith wants for the land. Let's say $100,000. If Jerry thinks that the price is reasonable, he can agree to pay this amount and, in return, take ownership of the land. In this case, Jerry and Farmer Smith will have entered into a *spot* or *cash transaction*.

In a cash transaction, both parties agree on terms, followed immediately by an exchange of money for goods. The trading of stock on an exchange is usually considered to be a cash transaction: the buyer and seller agree on the price, the buyer pays the seller, and the seller delivers the stock. The actions essentially take place simultaneously. (Admittedly, on most stock exchanges, there is a settlement period between the time the price is agreed on and the time the stock is actually delivered and payment is made. However, the settlement period is relatively short, so for practical purposes most traders consider this a cash transaction.)

However, it has also occurred to Jerry that it will probably take several years to build the highway. Because Jerry wants the opening of his restaurant to coincide with the opening of the highway, he doesn't need to begin construction on the restaurant for at least another year. There is no point in taking possession of the land right now—it will just sit unused for a year. Given his construction schedule, Jerry has decided to approach Farmer Smith with a slightly different proposition. Jerry will agree to Farmer Smith's price of $100,000, but he will propose to Farmer Smith that they complete the transaction in one year, at which time Farmer Smith will receive payment, and Jerry will take possession of the land. If both parties agree to this, Jerry and Farmer Smith will have entered into a *forward contract*. In a forward contract, the parties agree on the terms now, but the actual exchange of money for goods does not take place until some later date, the *maturity* or *expiration date*.

If Jerry and Farmer Smith enter into a forward contract, it's unlikely that the price Farmer Smith will want for his land in one year will be the same price that he is asking today. Because both the payment and the transfer of goods are deferred, there may be advantages or disadvantages to one party or the other. Farmer Smith may point out that if he receives full payment of $100,000 right now, he can deposit the money in his bank and begin to earn interest. In a forward contract, however, he will have to forego any interest earnings. As a result, Farmer Smith may insist that he and Jerry negotiate a one-year *forward price* that takes into consideration this loss of interest.

Forward contracts are common when a potential buyer requires goods in the future or when a potential seller knows that a supply of goods will be ready for sale in the future. A bakery may need a periodic supply of grain to support operations. Some grain may be required now, but the bakery also knows that additional grain will be required at regular intervals in the future. In order to eliminate the risk of rising grain prices, the bakery can buy grain in the forward market—agreeing on a price now but not taking delivery or making payment until some later date. In the same way, a farmer who knows that he will have grain ready for harvest at a later date can sell his crop in the forward market to insure against falling prices.

When a forward contract is traded on an organized exchange, it is usually referred to as a *futures contract*. On a futures exchange, the contract specifications for a forward contract are standardized to more easily facilitate trading. The exchange specifies the quantity and quality of goods to be delivered, the date and place of delivery, and the method of payment. Additionally, the exchange guarantees the integrity of the contract. Should either the buyer or the seller default, the exchange assumes the responsibility of fulfilling the terms of the forward contract.

The earliest futures exchanges enabled producers and users of physical commodities—grains, precious metals, and energy products—to protect themselves against price fluctuations. More recently, many exchanges have introduced futures contracts on financial instruments—stocks and stock indexes, interest-rate contracts, and foreign currencies. Although there is still significant trading in physical commodities, the total value of exchange-traded financial instruments now greatly exceeds the value of physical commodities.

Returning to Jerry, he finds that he has a new problem. The government has indicated its desire to build the highway, but the necessary funds have not yet been authorized. With many other public works projects competing for a limited amount of money, it's possible that the entire highway project could be canceled. If this happens, Jerry intends to return to his original plan and move away. In order to make an informed decision, Jerry needs time to see what the government will do. If the highway is actually built, Jerry wants to purchase Farmer Smith's land. If the highway isn't built, Jerry wants to be able to walk away without any obligation.

Jerry believes that he will know for certain within a year whether the highway project will be approved. As a result, Jerry approaches Farmer Smith with a new proposition. Jerry and Farmer Smith will negotiate a one-year forward price for the land, but Jerry will have one year to decide whether to go ahead with the purchase. One year from now, Jerry can either buy the land at the agreed-on forward price, or he can walk away with no obligation or penalty.

There is much that can happen over one year, and without some inducement Farmer Smith is unlikely to agree to this proposal. Someone may make a better offer for the land, but Farmer Smith will be unable to accept the offer because he must hold the land in the event that Jerry decides to buy. For the next year, Farmer Smith will be a hostage to Jerry's final decision.

Jerry understands Farmer Smith's dilemma, so he offers to negotiate a separate payment to compensate Farmer Smith for this uncertainty. In effect, Jerry is offering to buy the right to decide at a later date whether to purchase the land. Regardless of Jerry's final decision, Farmer Smith will get to keep this separate payment. If Jerry and Farmer Smith can agree on this separate payment, as well as the forward price, they will enter into an *option contract*. An option contract gives one party the right to make a decision at a later date. In this example, Jerry is the buyer of a *call option*, giving him the right to decide at a later date whether to buy. Farmer Smith is the seller of the call option.

Deciding whether to buy the land for his restaurant is not Jerry's only problem. He owns a house that he inherited from his parents and that he was planning to sell prior to moving away. Before hearing about the highway project, Jerry had put up a "For Sale" sign in front of the house, and a young couple, seeing the sign, showed enough interest in the house to make an offer. Jerry was seriously considering accepting the offer, but then the highway project came up. Now Jerry doesn't know what to do. If the government goes ahead with the highway and Jerry goes ahead with his restaurant, he wants to keep his house. If not, he wants to sell the house. Given the situation, Jerry might make a proposal to the couple similar to that which he made to Farmer Smith. Jerry and the couple will agree on a price for the house, but Jerry will have one year in which to decide whether to actually sell the house.

Like Farmer Smith, the couple's initial reaction is likely to be negative. If they agree to Jerry's proposal, they will have to make temporary housing arrangements for the next year. If they find another house they like better, they won't be able to buy it because they might eventually be required to purchase Jerry's house. They will spend the next year in housing limbo, a hostage to Jerry's final decision.

As with Farmer Smith, Jerry understands the couple's dilemma and offers to compensate them for their inconvenience by paying an agreed-on amount.

Regardless of Jerry's final decision, the couple will get to keep this amount. If Jerry and the couple can agree on terms, Jerry will have purchased a *put option* from the couple. A put option gives one party the right to decide whether to sell at a later date.

Perhaps the most familiar type of option contract is insurance. In many ways an insurance contract is analogous to a put option. A homeowner who purchases insurance has the right to sell all or part of the home back to the insurance company at a later date. If the home should burn to the ground, the homeowner will inform the insurance company that he now wishes to sell the home back to the insurance company for the insured amount. Even though the home no longer exists, the insurance company is paying the homeowner as if it were actually purchasing the home. Of course, if the house does not burn down, perhaps even appreciating in value, the homeowner is under no obligation to sell the property to the insurance company.

As with an insurance contract, the purchase of an option involves the payment of a *premium*. This amount is negotiated between the buyer and the seller, and the seller keeps the premium regardless of any subsequent decision on the part of the buyer.

Many terms of an insurance contract are similar to the terms of an option contract. An option, like an insurance contract, has an *expiration date*. Does a homeowner want a six-month insurance policy? A one-year policy? The insurance contract may also specify an *exercise price*, how much the holder will receive if certain events occur. This exercise price, which may also include a deductible amount, is analogous to an agreed-on forward price.

The logic used to price option contracts is also similar to the logic used to price insurance contracts. What is the probability that a house will burn down? What is the probability that someone will have an automobile accident? What is the probability that someone will die? By assigning probabilities to different occurrences, an insurance company will try to determine a fair value for the insurance contract. The insurance company hopes to generate a profit by selling the contract to the customer at a price greater than its fair value. In the same way, someone dealing with exchange-traded contracts may also ask, "What is the probability that this contract will go up in value? What is the probability that this contract will go down in value?" By assigning probabilities to different outcomes, it may be possible to determine the contract's fair value.

In later chapters we will take a closer look at how forwards, futures, and options are priced. For now, we can see that their values are likely to depend on or be derived from the value of some *underlying* asset. When my friend Jerry wanted to enter into a one-year forward contract to buy the land from Farmer Smith, the value of the forward contract derived from (among other things) the current value of the land. When Jerry was considering buying a call option from Farmer Smith, the value of that option derived from the value of the forward contract. When Jerry was considering selling his house, the value of the put option derived from the current value of the house. For this reason, forwards, futures, and options are commonly referred to as *derivative contracts* or, simply, *derivatives*.

There is one other common type of derivatives contract. A *swap* is an agreement to exchange cash flows. The most common type, a *plain-vanilla interest-rate swap*, is an agreement to exchange fixed interest-rate payments for floating interest-rate payments. But a swap can consist of almost any type of cash-flow agreement between two parties. Because swaps are not standardized and therefore most often traded off exchanges, in this text we will restrict our discussion to the most common derivatives—forwards, futures, and options.

Buying and Selling

We usually assume that in order to sell something, we must first own it. For most transactions, the normal order is to buy first and sell later. However, in derivative markets, the order can be reversed. Instead of buying first and selling later, we can sell first and buy later. The profit that results from a purchase and sale is usually independent of the order in which the transactions occur. We will show a profit if we either buy first at a low price and sell later at a high price or sell first at a high price and buy later at a low price.

Sometimes we may want to specify the order in which trades take place. The first trade to take place, either buying or selling, is an *opening trade*, resulting in an *open position*. A subsequent trade, reversing the initial trade, is a *closing trade*. A widely used measure of trading activity in exchange-traded derivative contracts is the amount of *open interest*, the number of contracts traded on an exchange that have not yet been closed out. Logically, the number of long and short contracts that have not been closed out must be equal because for every buyer there must be a seller.

If a trader first buys a contract (an opening trade), he is *long* the contract. If the trader first sells a contract (also an opening trade), he is *short* the contract. Long and short tend to describe a position once it has been taken, but traders also refer to the act of making an opening trade as either *going long* (buying) or *going short* (selling).

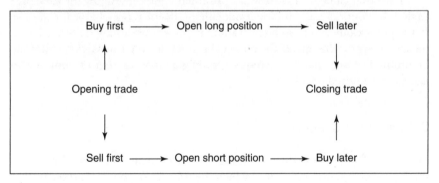

A long position will usually result in a debit (we must pay money when we buy), and a short position will usually result in a credit (we expect to receive money when we sell). We will see later that these terms are also used when trading multiple contracts, simultaneously buying some contracts and selling others. When the total trade results in a debit, it is a long position; when it results in a credit, it is a short position.

The terms *long* and *short* may also refer to whether a trader wants the market to rise or fall. A trader who has a long stock market position wants the stock market to rise. A trader who has a short position wants the market to fall. However, when referring to derivatives, the terms can be confusing because a trader who has bought, or is long, a derivative may in fact want the underlying market to fall in price. In order to avoid confusion, we will refer to either a long or short contract position (we have either bought or sold contracts) or a long or short market position (we want the underlying market to rise or fall).

Notional Value of a Forward Contract

Because a forward contract is an agreement to exchange money for goods at some later date, when a forward contract is initially traded, no money changes hands. Because no cash flow results, in a sense, there is no cash value associated with the contract. But a forward contract does have a *notional value* or *nominal value*. For physical commodities, the notional value of a forward contract is equal to the number of units to be delivered at maturity multiplied by the unit price. If a forward contract calls for the delivery of 1,000 units at a price of $75 per unit, the notional value of the contract is $75 × 1,000 = $75,000.

For some forward contracts, physical delivery is not practical. For example, many exchanges trade futures contracts on stock indexes. But it would be impractical to actually deliver a stock index because it would require the delivery of all stocks in the index in exactly the right proportion, which in some cases might mean delivering fractional shares. For financial futures, where the contract is not settled through physical delivery, the notional value is equal to the cash price of the index or instrument multiplied by a point value. A stock index that is trading at 825.00 and that has a point value of $200 has a notional value of 825.00 × $200 = $165,000.

The point value of a stock index or similar contract is set by the exchange so that the contract has a notional value that is deemed reasonable for trading. If the point value is set too high, trading in the contract may be too risky for most market participants. If the point value is set too low, transaction costs may be prohibitive because it may require trading a large number of contracts to achieve the desired result.

Settlement Procedures

What actually happens when a contract is traded on an exchange? The settlement procedure—the manner in which the transfer of money and ownership of a contract is facilitated—depends on the rules of the exchange and the type of contract traded.

Consider a trader who buys 100 shares of a $50 stock on an exchange. The total value of the stock is 100 × $50 = $5,000, and the buyer is required to pay the seller this amount. The exchange, acting as intermediary, collects $5,000 from the buyer and transfers this money to the seller. At the same time, the exchange takes delivery of the shares from the seller and transfers these to the buyer. This is essentially a cash transaction with the exchange making both delivery and payment.

Suppose that the stock that was originally purchased at $50 per share subsequently rises to $60. How will the buyer feel? He will certainly be happy and may mentally record a profit of $1,000 (100 shares times the $10 increase per share). But he can't actually spend this $1,000 because the profit is *unrealized* —it only appears on paper (hence the term *paper profit*). If the buyer wants to spend the $1,000, he will have to turn it into a *realized* profit by going back into the marketplace and selling his 100 shares to someone else at $60 per share. This *stock-type settlement* requires full and immediate payment, and all profits or losses are unrealized until the position is closed.

Now consider what happens when a futures contract is traded on an exchange. Because a futures contract is a forward contract, there is no immediate exchange of money for goods. The buyer pays no money, and the seller receives none. But by entering into a forward contract, both the buyer and the seller have taken on future obligations. At contract maturity, the seller is obligated to deliver, and the buyer is obligated to pay. The exchange wants to ensure that both parties live up to these obligations. To do this, the exchange collects a *margin deposit* from each party that it holds as security against possible default by the buyer or seller. The amount of margin is commensurate with the risk to the exchange and depends on the notional value of the contract, as well as the possibility of price fluctuations over the life of the futures contract. An exchange will try to set margin requirements high enough so that the exchange is reasonably protected against default but not so high that it inhibits trading.

For example, consider the futures contract calling for delivery of 1,000 units of a commodity at a unit price of $75. The notional value of the contract is $75,000. If the exchange has set a margin requirement for the contract at $3,000, when the contract is traded, both the buyer and seller must immediately deposit $3,000 with the exchange.

What happens if the price of the commodity subsequently rises to $80? Now the buyer has a profit of $5 × 1,000 = $5,000, whereas the seller has a loss of equal amount. As a result, the exchange will now transfer $5,000 from the seller's account to the buyer's account. This daily *variation* credit or debit results from fluctuations in the price of the futures contract as long as the position remains open. *Futures-type settlement*, where there is an initial margin deposit followed by daily cash transfers, is also known as *margin and variation settlement*.

A futures trader can close out a position in one of two ways. Prior to maturity of the futures contract, he can make an offsetting trade, selling out the futures contract he initially bought or buying back the futures contract he initially sold. If the position is closed through an offsetting purchase or sale, a final variation payment is made, and the margin deposit is returned to the trader.

Alternatively, a trader may choose to carry the position to maturity, at which time *physical settlement* will take place. The seller must make delivery, and the buyer must pay an amount equal to the current value of the commodity. After delivery and payment have been made, the margin deposits will be returned to the respective parties. In our example, the original trade price was $75. If the price of the commodity at maturity is $90, the buyer must pay $90 × 1,000 = $90,000.

It may seem that the buyer has paid $15 more per unit than the original trade price of $75. But recall that as the futures contract rose in price from $75 to $90, the buyer was credited with $15 in the form of variation. The total price paid, the $90 final price less the $15 variation, was indeed equal to the agreed-on price of $75 per unit.

Futures contracts such as stock indexes, which are not settled through physical delivery, can also be carried to maturity. In this case, there is one final variation payment based on the underlying index price at maturity. At that time, the margin deposits are also returned to the parties. These types of futures, where no physical delivery takes place at maturity, are said to be *cash-settled*.

A futures trader must always have sufficient funds to cover the margin requirements for any trade he intends to make. But he should also have sufficient funds to cover any variation requirements. If the position moves against him and he does not have sufficient funds, he may be forced to close the position earlier than intended.

There is an important distinction between margin and variation. Margin[1] is money collected by the exchange to ensure that a trader can fulfill future financial obligations should the market move against him. Even though deposited with the exchange, margin deposits still belong to the trader and can therefore earn interest for the trader. Variation is a credit or debit that results from fluctuations in the price of a futures contract. A variation payment can either earn interest, if the variation results in a credit, or lose interest, if the variation results in a debit.

Examples of the cash flows and profit or loss for a series of stock and futures trades are shown in Figures 1-1 and 1-2, respectively. In each example, we assume that the opening trade was made at the first day's settlement price so that there is no profit and loss (i.e., a P&L of zero) at the end of day 1. For simplicity, we have also ignored any interest earned on credits or interest paid on debits.

We make this very important distinction between stock-type settlement and futures-type settlement because some contracts are settled like stock and some contracts are settled like futures. It should come as no surprise that stock

Figure 1-1 Stock-type settlement.

	Stock price	Trade	Cash flow credit (+) debit (−)	Current stock position	Cumulative realized P&L	Unrealized P&L
Day 1 (opening trade)	$53	buy 1,200 shares	−$53 x 1,200 = −$63,600	long 1,200 shares	0	0
Day 2	$57	sell 500 shares	+$57 x 500 = +$28,500	long 700 shares	($57−$53) x 500 = +$2,000	($57−$53) x 700 = +$2,800
Day 3	$51	no trade	0	long 700 shares	+$2,000	($51−$53) x 700 = −$1,400
Day 4 (closing)	$54	sell 700 shares	+$54 x 700 = +37,800	0	+$2,000 + ($54−$53) x 700 = +$2,000 + $700 = +$2,700	0

---

[1] A margin requirement for a professional trader on an equity options exchange is sometimes referred to as a *haircut*.

Figure 1-2 Futures-type settlement.

contract size: 1,000 units	margin, per contract: $3,000					
	Futures price (per unit)	Trade	Current futures position	Margin requirement	Variation	Cumulative realized P&L
Day 1 (opening trade)	$75	sell 9 futures	short 9 futures	9 x $3,000 = $27,000	0	0
Day 2	$77	no trade	short 9 futures	9 x $3,000 = $27,000	($77–$75) x –9 x 1,000 = –$18,000	–$18,000
Day 3	$74	buy 2 futures	short 7 futures	7 x $3,000 = $21,000	($74–$77) x –9 x 1,000 = +$27,000	–$18,000 +$27,000 =+$9,000
Day 4	$70	buy 4 futures	short 3 futures	3 x $3,000 = $9,000	($70–$74) x –7 x 1,000 = +$28,000	+$9,000 +$28,000 =+$37,000
Day 5 (closing)	$80	buy 3 futures	0	0	($80–$70) x –3 x 1,000 = –$30,000	+$37,000 –$30,000 =+$7,000

is subject to stock-type settlement and futures are subject to futures-type settlement. But what about options? Currently, all exchange-traded options in North America, whether options on stock, stock indexes, futures, or foreign currencies, are settled like stock. Options must be paid for immediately and in full, and all profits or losses are unrealized until the position is liquidated. In stock option markets, this is both logical and consistent because both the underlying contract and options on that contract are settled using identical procedures. However, on U.S. futures options markets, the underlying contract is settled one way (futures-type settlement), while the options are settled in a different way (stock-type settlement). This can sometimes cause problems when a trader has bought or sold an option to hedge a futures position. Even if the profits from the option position exactly offset the losses from the futures position, the profits from the option position, because the options are settled like stock, are unrealized. But the losses from the futures position will require an immediate cash outlay to cover variation requirements. If a trader is unaware of the different settlement procedures, he can occasionally find himself with unexpected cash-flow problems.

The settlement situation on most exchanges outside North America has been simplified by making option and underlying settlement procedures identical. If the underlying is subject to stock-type settlement, then the options on the underlying are subject to stock-type settlement. If the underlying is subject to futures-type settlement, then the options are subject to futures-type settlement. Under this method, a trader is unlikely to have a surprise variation requirement on a position that he thinks is well hedged.

In this text, when presenting option examples, we will generally assume the settlement convention used in North America, where all options are subject to stock-type settlement.

Market Integrity

Anyone who enters into a contract to buy or sell wants to be confident that the *counterparty* will fulfill his responsibilities under the terms of the contract. A buyer wants to be sure that the seller will deliver; a seller wants to be sure that the buyer will pay. No one will want to trade in a marketplace if there is a real possibility that the counterparty might default on a contract. To guarantee the integrity of an exchange-traded contract, exchanges assume the responsibility for both delivery and payment. When a trade is made on an exchange, the link between buyer and seller is immediately broken and replaced with two new links. The exchange becomes the buyer from each seller. If the buyer defaults, the exchange will guarantee payment. The exchange also becomes the seller to each buyer. If the seller defaults, the exchange will guarantee delivery.

To protect itself against possible default, an exchange will establish a *clearinghouse*. The clearinghouse may be a division of the exchange or a completely independent entity and is responsible for processing and guaranteeing all trades made on the exchange.[2] The clearinghouse assumes the ultimate responsibility for ensuring the integrity of all exchange-traded contracts.[3]

Figure 1-3 The clearing process.

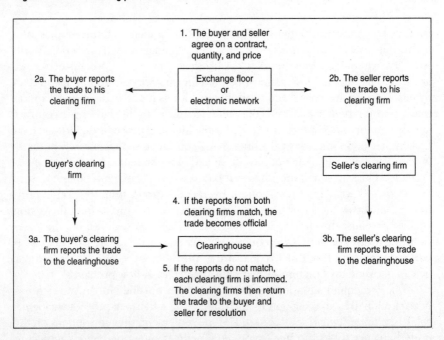

---

[2] In the United States, the two largest derivatives clearinghouses are the Options Clearing Corporation, responsible for processing all equity option trades, and the CME Clearing House, responsible for processing all trades made on exchanges falling within the CME Group. For instruments other than derivatives, such as stock and bonds, the Depository Trust and Clearing Corporation provides clearing services for many U.S. exchanges.
[3] Although the exchange and clearinghouse may be separate entities, for simplicity, we will occasionally use the terms interchangeably.

The clearinghouse is made up of member *clearing firms*. A clearing firm processes trades made by individual traders and agrees to fulfill any financial obligation arising from those trades. Should an individual trader default, the clearing firm guarantees fulfillment of that trader's responsibilities. No individual may trade on an exchange without first becoming associated with a clearing firm.

As part of its responsibilities, a clearing firm will collect the required margin from individual traders and deposit these funds with the clearinghouse.[4] In some cases, the clearinghouse may permit a clearing firm to aggregate the positions of all traders at the firm. Because some traders will have long positions while other traders will have short positions in the same contract, the clearinghouse may reduce the margin deposits required from the clearing firm. At its discretion, and depending on market conditions, a clearing firm may require an individual trader to deposit more money with the clearing firm than is required by the clearinghouse.

The current system of guarantees—individual trader, clearing firm, and clearinghouse—has proven effective in ensuring the integrity of exchange-traded contracts. Although individual traders and clearing firms occasionally fail, a clearinghouse has never failed in the United States.

---

[4] We noted earlier that, in theory, there is no loss of interest associated with a margin deposit. In practice, the amount of interest paid on margin deposits will vary by clearing firm and is typically negotiated between the clearing firm and the individual customer.

2

Forward Pricing

What should be the fair price for a forward contract? We can answer this question by considering the costs and benefits of buying now compared with buying on some future date. In a forward contract, the costs and benefits are not eliminated; they are simply deferred. They should therefore be reflected in the forward price.

forward price = current cash price + costs of buying now
− benefits of buying now

Let's return to our example from Chapter 1 where my friend Jerry wanted to acquire land on which to build a restaurant. He was considering both a cash purchase and a one-year forward contract. If he enters into a forward contract, what should be a fair one-year forward price for the land?

If Jerry wants to buy the land right now, he will have to pay Farmer Smith's asking price of $100,000. However, in researching the feasibility of a one-year forward contract, Jerry has learned the following:

1. The cost of money, whether borrowing or lending,[1] is currently 8.00 percent annually.

2. The owner of the land must pay $2,000 in real estate taxes; the taxes are due in nine months.

3. There is a small oil well on the land that pumps oil at the rate of $500 per month; the oil revenue is receivable at the end of each month.

If Jerry decides to buy the land now, what are the costs compared with buying the land one year from now? First, Jerry will have to borrow $100,000 from the local bank. At a rate of 8 percent, the one-year interest costs will be

$$8\% \times \$100,000 = \$8,000$$

---

[1] At this point, we will assume that the same interest rate applies to all transactions, whether borrowing or lending. Admittedly, for a trader, the interest cost of borrowing will almost always be higher than the interest earned when lending.

If Jerry buys the land now, he will also be liable for the $2,000 in property taxes due in nine months. In order to pay the taxes, he will need to borrow an additional $2,000 from the bank for the remaining three months of the forward contract

$$\$2,000 + (\$2,000 \times 8\% \times 3/12) = \$2,000 + \$40 = \$2,040$$

The total costs of buying now are the interest on the cash price, the real estate taxes, and the interest on the taxes

$$\$8,000 + \$2,040 = \$10,040$$

What are the benefits of buying now? If Jerry buys the land now, at the end of each month he will receive $500 worth of oil revenue. Over the 12-month life of the forward contract, he will receive

$$12 \times \$500 = \$6,000$$

Additionally, Jerry can earn interest on the oil revenue. At the end of the first month, he will be able to invest $500 for 11 months at 8 percent. At the end of the second month, he will be able to invest $500 for 10 months. The total interest on the oil revenue is

$$(\$500 \times 8\% \times 11/12) + (\$500 \times 8\% \times 10/12) + \cdots + (\$500 \times 8\% \times 1/12) = \$220$$

The total benefits of buying now are the oil revenue plus the interest on the oil revenue

$$\$6,000 + \$220 = \$6,220$$

If there are no other considerations, a fair one-year forward price for the land ought to be

The current cash price	$100,000
Plus the costs of buying now	+$ 10,040
Less the benefits of buying now	–$ 6,220
	$103,820

Assuming that Jerry and Farmer Smith agree on all these calculations, it should make no difference to either party whether Jerry purchases the land now at a price of $100,000 or enters into a forward contract to purchase the land one year from now at a price of $103,820. The transactions are essentially the same.

Traders in forward or futures contracts sometimes refer to the *basis*, the difference between the cash price and the forward price. In our example, the basis is

$$\$100,000 - \$103,820 = \textbf{-\$3,820}$$

In most cases, the basis will be a negative number—the costs of buying now will outweigh the benefits of buying now. However, in our example, the basis will turn positive if the price of oil rises enough. If one year's worth of oil revenue, together with the interest earned on the revenue, is greater than the $10,040 cost of buying now, the forward price will be less than the cash price. Consequently, the basis will be positive.

How should we calculate the fair forward price for exchange-traded futures contracts? This depends on the costs and benefits associated with a position in the underlying contract. The costs and benefits for some commonly traded futures are listed in the following table:

Instrument	Costs of Buying Now	Benefits of Buying Now
Physical commodity	Interest on cash price Storage costs Insurance costs	Convenience yield (to be discussed)
Stock	Interest on stock price	Dividends (if any) Interest on dividends
Bonds and notes	Interest on bond or note price	Coupon payments Interest on coupon payments
Foreign currency	Interest cost of borrowing the domestic currency	Interest earned on the foreign currency

Physical Commodities (Grains, Energy Products, Precious Metals, etc.)

If we buy a physical commodity now, we will have to pay the current price together with the interest on this amount. Additionally, we will have to store the commodity until maturity of the forward contract. When we store the commodity, we would also be wise to insure it against possible loss while in storage. If

C = commodity price[2]
t = time to maturity of the forward contract
r = interest rate
s = annual storage costs per commodity unit
i = annual insurance costs per commodity unit[3]

then the forward price F can be written as

$$F = C \times (1 + r \times t) + (s \times t) + (i \times t)$$

Initially, it may seem that there are no benefits to buying a physical commodity, so the basis should always be negative. A normal or *contango* commodity market is one in which long-term futures contracts trade at a premium to short-term contracts. But sometimes the opposite occurs—a futures contract will trade at a discount to cash. If the cash price of a commodity is greater than a futures price, the market is *backward* or in *backwardation*. This seems illogical because the interest

---

[2] In this chapter only, we will use a capital C to represent the price of a commodity. In all other chapters, C will refer to the price of a call option.

[3] For physical commodities, both storage and insurance costs usually are quoted together as one price.

and storage costs will always be positive. However, consider a company that needs a commodity to keep its factory running. If the company cannot obtain the commodity, it may have to take the very costly step of temporarily closing the factory. The cost of such drastic action may, in the company's view, be prohibitive. In order to avoid this, the company may be willing to pay an inflated price to obtain the commodity right now. If commodity supplies are tight, the price that the company may have to pay could result in a backward market—the cash price will be greater than the price of a futures contract. The benefit of being able to obtain a commodity right now is sometimes referred to as a *convenience yield*.

It can be difficult to assign an exact value to the convenience yield. However, if interest costs, storage costs, and insurance costs are known, a trader can infer the convenience yield by observing the relationship between the cash price and futures prices. For example, consider a three-month forward contract on a commodity

> Three-month forward price F = $77.40
> Interest rate r = 8 percent
> Annual storage costs s = $3.00
> Annual insurance costs i = $0.60

What should be the cash price C? If

$$F = C \times (1 + r \times t) + (s \times t) + (i \times t)$$

then

$$C = \frac{F - (s + i) \times t}{1 + r \times t}$$

$$= \frac{77.40 - (3.00 + 0.60) \times 3/12}{1 + 0.08 \times 3/12}$$

$$= \frac{76.50}{1.02} = \mathbf{\$75.00}$$

If the cash price in the marketplace is actually $76.25, the convenience yield ought to be $1.25. This is the additional amount users are willing to pay for the benefit of having immediate access to the commodity.

Stock

If we buy stock now, we will have to pay the current price together with the interest on this amount. In return, we will receive any dividends that the stock pays over the life of the forward contract together with the interest earned on the dividend payments. If

> S = stock price
> t = time to maturity of the forward contract
> r = interest rate over the life of the forward contract
> d_i = each dividend payment expected prior to maturity of the forward contract

t_i = time remaining to maturity after each dividend payment
r_i = the applicable interest rate (the *forward rate*[4]) from each dividend payment to maturity of the forward contract

then the forward price F can be written as

$$F = S + (S \times r \times t) - [d_1 \times (1 + r_1 \times t_1)] - \cdots - [d_n \times (1 + r_n \times t_n)]$$
$$= [S \times (1 + r \times t)] - \Sigma[d_n \times (1 + r_n \times t_n)]$$

Example

Stock price S = \$67.00
Time to maturity t = 8 months
Interest rate r = 6.00 percent
Semiannual dividend payment d = \$0.33
Time to next dividend payment = 1 month

From this, we know that

$$t_1 = 8 \text{ months} - 1 \text{ month} = 7 \text{ months}$$
$$t_2 = 8 \text{ months} - 1 \text{ month} - 6 \text{ months} = 1 \text{ month}$$

If

$$r_1 = 6.20\%$$
$$r_2 = 6.50\%$$

then a fair eight-month forward price for the stock should be

$$F = [67.00 \times (1 + 0.06 \times 8/12)] - [0.33 \times (1 + 0.062 \times 7/12)]$$
$$- [0.33 \times (1 + 0.065 \times 1/12)]$$
$$= 69.68 - 0.3419 - 0.3318 = \mathbf{69.0063}$$

Except for long-term stock forward contracts, there will usually be a limited number of dividend payments, and the amount of interest that can be earned on each payment will be small. For simplicity, we will aggregate all the dividends D expected over the life of the forward contract and ignore any interest that can be earned on the dividends. The forward price for a stock can then be written as

$$F = [S \times (1 + r \times t)] - D$$

---

[4] The *forward* rate is the rate of interest that is applicable beginning on some future date for a specified period of time. Forward rates are often expressed in months

1 × 5 forward rate   A four-month rate beginning in one month
3 × 9 forward rate   A six-month rate beginning in three months
4 × 12 forward rate   An eight-month rate beginning in four months

A *forward-rate agreement* (FRA) is an agreement to borrow or lend money for a fixed period, beginning on some future date. A 3 × 9 FRA is an agreement to borrow money for six months, but beginning three months from now.

An approximate eight-month forward price should be

$$67.00 \times (1 + 0.06 \times 8/12) - (2 \times 0.33) = \mathbf{69.02}$$

Bonds and Notes

If we treat the coupon payments as if they were dividends, we can evaluate bond and note forward contracts in a similar manner to stock forwards. We must pay the bond price together with the interest cost on that price. In return, we will receive fixed coupon payments on which we can earn interest. If

B = bond price
t = time to maturity of the forward contract
r = interest rate over the life of the forward contract
c_i = each coupon expected prior to maturity of the forward contract
t_i = time remaining to maturity after each coupon payment
r_i = applicable interest rate from each coupon payment to maturity of the forward contract

then the forward price F can be written as

$$F = B + (B \times r \times t) - [c_1 \times (1 + r_1 \times t_1)] - \cdots - [c_n \times (1 + r_n \times t_n)]$$
$$= [B \times (1 + r \times t)] - \Sigma[c_n \times (1 + r_n \times t_n)]$$

Example

Bond price B = $109.76
Time to maturity t = 10 months
Interest rate r = 8.00 percent
Semiannual coupon payment c = 5.25 percent
Time to next coupon payment = 2 months

From this, we know that

$$t_1 = 10 \text{ months} - 2 \text{ months} = 8 \text{ months}$$
$$t_2 = 10 \text{ months} - 2 \text{ months} - 6 \text{ months} = 2 \text{ months}$$

If

$$r_1 = 8.20\%$$
$$r_2 = 8.50\%$$

then a fair 10-month forward price for the bond should be

$$F = [109.76 \times (1 + 0.08 \times 10/12)] - [5.25 \times (1 + 0.082 \times 8/12)]$$
$$- [5.25 \times (1 + 0.085 \times 2/12)]$$
$$= 117.0773 - 5.5370 - 5.3244 = \mathbf{106.2159}$$

Foreign Currencies

With foreign-currency forward contracts, we must deal with two different rates—the domestic interest rate we must pay on the domestic currency to buy the foreign currency and the foreign interest rate we earn if we hold the foreign currency. Unfortunately, if we begin with the spot exchange rate, add the domestic interest costs, and subtract the foreign-currency benefits, we get an answer that is expressed in different units. To calculate a foreign-currency forward price, we must first express the spot exchange rate S as a fraction—the cost of one foreign-currency unit in terms of domestic-currency units C_d divided by one foreign-currency unit C_f

$$S = \frac{C_d}{C_f}$$

Suppose that we have a domestic rate r_d and a foreign rate r_f. What should be the forward exchange rate at the end of time t? If we invest C_f at r_f and we invest C_d at r_f, the exchange rate at time t ought to be

$$F = \frac{C_d \times (1 + r_d \times t)}{C_f \times (1 + r_f \times t)}$$

$$= \frac{C_d}{C_f} \times \frac{1 + r_d \times t}{1 + r_f \times t}$$

$$= S \times \frac{1 + r_d \times t}{1 + r_f \times t}$$

For example, suppose that €1.00 = $1.50. Then

$$S = \frac{1.50}{1.00} = 1.50$$

If

Dollar interest rate $r_\$ = 6.00\%$

Euro interest rate $r_€ = 4.00\%$

then the six-month forward price is

$$F = \frac{1.50 \times (1 + 0.06 \times 6/12)}{1.00 \times (1 + 0.04 \times 6/12)}$$

$$= \frac{1.50}{1.00} \times \frac{1 + 0.06 \times 6/12}{1.00 \times (1 + 0.04 \times 6/12)}$$

$$= \frac{1.50 \times 1.03}{1.02} = \mathbf{1.5147}$$

Stock and Futures Options

In this text we will focus primarily on the two most common classes of exchange-traded options—stock options and futures options.[5] Although there is some trading in options on physical commodities, bonds, and foreign currencies in the over-the-counter (OTC) market,[6] almost all exchange-traded options on these instruments are futures options. A trader in exchange-traded options on crude oil is really trading options on crude oil futures. A trader in exchange-traded bond options is really trading options on bond futures.

For both stock options and futures options, the value of the option will depend on the forward price for the underlying contract. We have already looked at the forward price for a stock. But what is the forward price for a futures contract? A futures contract is a forward contract. Therefore, the forward price for a futures contract is the futures price. If a three-month futures contract is trading at $75.00, the three-month forward price is $75.00. If a six-month futures contract is trading at $80.00, the six-month forward price is $80.00. In some ways, this makes options on futures easier to evaluate than options on stock because no additional calculation is required to determine the forward price.

Arbitrage

If asked to define the term *arbitrage*, a trader might describe it as "a trade that results in a riskless profit." Whether there is such a thing as a riskless profit is open for debate because there is almost always something that can go wrong. For our purposes, we will define arbitrage as the buying and selling of the same or very closely related instruments in different markets to profit from an apparent mispricing.

For example, consider a commodity that is trading in London at a price of $700 per unit and trading in New York at a price of $710 per unit. Ignoring transaction costs and any currency risk, there seems to be an arbitrage opportunity by purchasing the commodity in London and simultaneously selling it in New York. Will this yield an arbitrage profit of $10? Or are there other factors that must be considered? One consideration might be transportation costs. The buyer in New York will expect delivery of the commodity. If the commodity is purchased in London, and if it costs more than $10 per unit to ship the commodity from London to New York, any arbitrage profit will be offset by the transportation costs. Even if transportation costs are less than $10, there are also insurance costs because no one will want to risk loss of the commodity in transit, either by air or by sea, from London to New York. Of course, anyone trading a commodity professionally ought to know the transportation and insurance costs. Consequently, it will be immediately obvious whether an arbitrage profit is possible.

In a foreign-currency market, a trader may attempt to profit by borrowing a low-interest-rate domestic currency and using this to purchase a

---

[5] Later, in Chapter 22, we will also look at stock index futures and options.
[6] The OTC market, or *over-the-counter market*, is a term usually applied to trading that does not take place on an organized exchange.

high-interest-rate foreign currency. The trader hopes to pay a low interest rate and simultaneously earn a high interest rate. However, this type of *carry trade* is not without risk. The interest rates may not be fixed, and over the life of the strategy, the interest rate that must be paid on the domestic currency may rise while the interest rate that can be earned on the foreign currency may fall. Moreover, the exchange rate is not fixed. At some point, the trader will have to repay the domestic currency that he borrowed. He expects to do this with the foreign currency that he now owns. If the value of the foreign currency has declined with respect to the domestic currency, it will cost him more to repurchase the domestic currency and repay the loan. The carry trade is sometimes referred to as *arbitrage*, but in fact, it entails so many risks that the term is probably misapplied.

Because cash markets and futures markets are so closely related, a common type of *cash-and-carry arbitrage* involves buying in the cash market, selling in the futures market, and carrying the position to maturity.

Returning to our previous stock example:

Stock price S = \$67.00
Time to maturity t = 8 months
Interest rate r = 6.00 percent
Expected dividends D = 0.66

Ignoring interest on the dividend, the calculated eight-month forward price is

$$67.00 \times (1 + 0.06 \times 8/12) - 0.66 = 69.02$$

Suppose that there is a market in forward contracts on this stock and that the price of an eight-month forward contract is \$69.50. What will a trader do? If the trader believes that the contract is worth only \$69.02, he will sell the forward contract at \$69.50 and simultaneously buy the stock for \$67.00. The cash-and-carry arbitrage profit should be

$$69.50 - 69.02 = 0.48$$

To confirm this, we can list all the cash flows associated with the transaction, keeping in mind that at maturity the trader will deliver the stock and in return receive the agreed-on forward price of 69.50.

Cost of borrowing \$67.00 for eight months at 6 percent (67.00 × 0.06 × 8/12)	−2.68
Cost of buying the stock	−67.00
Dividend payment of 0.66	+0.66
Forward price received at maturity	+69.50
Total of all cash flows	+0.48

Fluctuations in the price of either the stock or the futures contract will not affect the results. Both the initial stock price (\$67.00) and the price to be paid for the stock at maturity (\$69.50) are fixed and cannot be changed.

Even though fluctuations in the stock or futures price do not represent a risk, other factors may affect the outcome of the strategy. If interest rates rise, the interest costs associated with buying the stock will rise, reducing the potential profit.[7] Moreover, unless the company has actually announced the amount of the dividend, the expected dividend payment might be an estimate based on the company's past dividend payments. If the company unexpectedly cuts the dividend, the arbitrage profit will be reduced.

Given the apparent mispricing of the futures contract, a trader might question his own evaluation. Is $69.02 an accurate forward price? Perhaps the interest rate of 6 percent is too low. Perhaps the dividend of $0.66 is too high.

We initially made our calculations by solving for F in terms of the spot price, time, interest rates, and dividends

$$F = [S \times (1 + r \times t)] - D$$

If we know the forward price F but are missing one of the other values, we can solve for that missing value. If we know the forward price, time to maturity, interest rate, and dividend, we can solve for S, the *implied spot price* of the underlying contract

$$S = \frac{F + D}{1 + r \times t}$$

If we know everything except the interest rate r, we can solve for the *implied interest rate*

$$r = \frac{[(F + D)/S] - 1}{t}$$

If we know everything except the dividend D, we can solve for the *implied dividend*

$$D = [S \times (1 + r \times t)] - F$$

Implied values are an important concept, one that we will return to frequently. If a trader believes that a contract is fairly priced, the implied value must represent the marketplace's consensus estimate of the missing value.

Returning to our eight-month forward contract, suppose that we believe that all values except the interest rate are accurate. What is the implied interest rate?

$$r = \frac{[(F + D)/S] - 1}{t}$$

$$= \frac{[(69.50 + 0.66)/67.00] - 1}{8/12} = 0.0707 \quad (7.07\%)$$

If we know all values except the dividend, the implied dividend is

$$D = [S \times (1 + r \times t)] - F = [67.00 \times (1 + 0.06 \times 8/12)] - 69.50 = 0.18$$

If two dividends are expected over the life of the forward contract, the marketplace seems to expect two payments of $0.09 each.

---

[7] If money has been borrowed or lent at a fixed rate, there is no interest-rate risk. However, most traders borrow and lend at a variable rate, resulting in interest-rate risk over the life of the forward contract.

Dividends

In order to evaluate derivative contracts on stock, a trader may be required to make an estimate of a stock's future dividend flow. A trader will usually need to estimate the amount of the dividend and the date on which the dividend will be paid. To better understand dividends, it may be useful to define some important terms in the dividend process.

Declared Date. The date on which a company announces both the amount of the dividend and the date on which the dividend will be paid. Once the company declares the dividend, the dividend risk is eliminated, at least until the next dividend payment.

Record Date. The date on which the stock must be owned in order to receive the dividend. Regardless of the date on which the stock is purchased, ownership of the stock does not become official until the *settlement date*, the date on which the purchaser of the stock officially takes possession. In the United States, the settlement date for stock is normally three business days after the trade is made (sometimes referred to as $T + 3$).

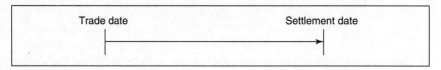

Ex-Dividend Date (Ex-Date). The first day on which a stock is trading without the rights to the dividend. In the United States, the last day on which a stock can be purchased in order to receive the dividend is three business days prior to the record date. The ex-dividend date is two business days prior to the record date.

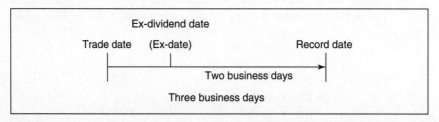

On the ex-dividend date, quotes for the stock will indicate that the stock is trading *ex-div*, and all quotes will be posted with the amount of the dividend deducted from the stock price. If a stock closes on the day prior to the ex-dividend date at a price of $67.50 and opens the following day (the ex-dividend date) at a price of $68.25, and the amount of the dividend is $0.40, the price of the stock will read

$$68.25 + 1.15 \text{ ex-div } 0.40$$

If the stock had opened unchanged, the price would have been the previous day's price of $67.50 less the dividend of $0.40, or $67.10. With the stock at $68.25, its price increase is $1.15.

Payable Date.   The date on which the dividend will be paid to qualifying shareholders (those owning shares on the record date).

The amount of the dividend can often be estimated from the company's past dividend payments. If a company pays quarterly dividends, as is common in the United States, and has paid a dividend of 25 cents for the last 10 quarters, then it is reasonable to assume that in the future the company will continue to pay 25 cents.

We have generally ignored the interest that can be earned on dividends, so it may seem that the date on which the dividend will be paid is not really important. If, however, the date on which the dividend will be paid is expected to fall close to the maturity date of a derivative contract, a slight miscalculation of the dividend date can significantly alter the value of the derivative.

Short Sales

Many derivatives strategies involve buying and selling either stock or futures contracts. Except for the situation when a market is *locked*,[8] there are no restrictions on the buying or selling of futures contracts. There are also no restrictions on the purchase of stock or on the sale of stock that is already owned. However, there may be situations in which a trader will want to *sell stock short*, that is, sell stock that he does not already own. The trader hopes to buy back the stock at a later date at a lower price.

Depending on the exchange or local regulatory authority, there may be special rules specifying the conditions under which stock can be sold short. In all cases, however, a trader who wants to sell stock short must first borrow the stock. This is possible because many institutions that hold stock may be willing to lend out the stock to facilitate a short sale. A brokerage firm holding a client's stock may be permitted under its agreement with the client to lend out the stock. This does not mean that one can always borrow stock. Sometimes it will be difficult or even impossible to borrow stock, resulting in a *short-stock squeeze*. But most actively traded stocks can be borrowed with relative ease, with the borrowing usually facilitated by the trader's clearing firm.

Consider a trader who borrows 900 shares of stock from a brokerage firm in order to sell the stock short at a price of $68 per share. The purchaser will pay the trader $68 × 900, or $61,200, and the trader will deliver the borrowed stock. The purchaser of the stock does not care whether the stock was sold short or long (whether the seller borrowed the stock or actually owned it). As far as the purchaser is concerned, he is now the owner of record of the stock.

---

[8] Some futures exchanges have daily price limits for futures contracts. When a futures contract reaches this limit, the market is said to be *locked* or *locked limit*. If the market is either *limit up* or *limit down*, no further trading may take place until the price comes off the limit (someone is willing to sell at a price equal to or less than the up limit or buy at a price equal to or higher than the down limit).

Borrowed stock must eventually be returned to the lender, in this case the brokerage firm. As security against this obligation, the brokerage firm will hold the $61,200 proceeds from the sale. Because the $61,200, in theory, belongs to the trader, the firm will pay the trader interest on this amount. At the same time, the trader is obligated to pay the brokerage firm any dividends that accrue over the short-sale period.

How does the brokerage firm as the lender profit from this transaction? The lending firm profits because it pays the trader only a portion of the full interest on the $61,200. The exact amount paid to the trader will depend on how difficult it is to borrow the stock. If the stock is easy to borrow, the trader may receive only slightly less than the rate he would expect to receive on any ordinary cash credit. However, if relatively few shares are available for lending, the trader may receive only a fraction of the normal rate. In the most extreme case, where the stock is very difficult to borrow, the trader may receive no interest at all. The rate that the trader receives on the short sale of stock is sometimes referred to as the *short-stock rebate*.

We can make a distinction between the *long rate* r_l that applies to ordinary borrowing and lending and the *short rate* r_s that applies to the short sale of stock. The difference between the long and short rates represents the *borrowing costs* r_{bc}

$$r_l - r_s = r_{bc}$$

In a previous example we determined the forward price for a stock

Stock price $S = \$67.00$
Time to maturity $t = 8$ months
Interest rate $r = 6.00$ percent
Expected dividend payment $D = \$0.66$

Ignoring interest on the dividends, the eight-month forward price is

$$67.00 \times (1 + 0.06 \times 8/12) - 0.66 = 69.02$$

If the price of an eight-month forward contract is $69.50, there is an arbitrage opportunity by selling the forward contract and purchasing the stock. Suppose that instead the eight-month forward contract is trading at a price of $68.75. Now there seems to be an arbitrage opportunity by purchasing the forward contract and selling the stock. Indeed, if a trader already owns the stock, this will result in a profit of $69.02 − $68.75 = $0.27. If, however, the trader does not own stock and must sell the stock short in order to execute the strategy, he will not receive the full interest of 6 percent. If the lending firm will retain 2 percent in borrowing costs, the trader will only receive the short rate of 4 percent. The forward price is now

$$67.00 \times (1 + 0.04 \times 8/12) - 0.66 = 68.13$$

If the trader attempts to execute the arbitrage by selling the stock short, he will lose money because

$$68.13 - 68.75 = -0.62$$

A trader who does not own the stock can only profit if the forward price is less than $68.13 or more than $69.02. Between these prices, no arbitrage is possible.

What interest rate should apply to option transactions? Unlike stock, an option is not a deliverable security. It is a contract that is created between a buyer and a seller. Even if a trader does not own a specific option, he need not "borrow" the option in order to sell it. For this reason, we always apply the ordinary long rate to the cash flow resulting from either the purchase or sale of an option.

3

Contract Specifications and Option Terminology

Every option market brings together traders and investors with different expectations and goals. Some enter the market with an opinion on which direction prices will move. Some intend to use options to protect existing positions against adverse price movement. Some hope to take advantage of price discrepancies between similar or related products. Some act as middlemen, buying and selling as an accommodation to other market participants and hoping to profit from the difference between the bid price and ask price.

Even though expectations and goals differ, every trader's education must include an understanding of option contract specifications and a mastery of the terminology used in option markets. Without a clear understanding of the terms of an option contract and the rights and responsibilities under that contract, a trader cannot hope to make the best use of options, nor will he be prepared for the very real risks of trading. Without a facility in the language of options, a trader will find it impossible to communicate his desire to buy or sell in the marketplace.

Contract Specifications

There are several aspects to contract specifications.

Type

In Chapter 1, we introduced the two types of options. A *call option* is the right to buy or take a long position in an asset at a fixed price on or before a specified date. A *put option* is the right to sell or take a short position in an asset.

Note the difference between an option and a futures contract. A futures contract requires delivery at a fixed price. The buyer and seller of a futures contract both have clearly defined obligations that they must meet. The seller must make delivery, and the buyer must take delivery. The buyer of an option, however, has a choice. He can choose to take delivery (a call) or make delivery (a put). If the buyer of an option chooses to either make or take delivery, the seller of the option is obligated to take the other side. In option trading, all rights lie with the buyer and all obligations with the seller.

Underlying

The *underlying asset* or, more simply, the *underlying* is the security or commodity to be bought or sold under the terms of the option contract. If an option is purchased directly from a bank or other dealer, the quantity of the underlying can be tailored to meet the buyer's individual requirements. If the option is purchased on an exchange, the quantity of the underlying is set by the exchange. On stock option exchanges, the underlying is typically 100 shares of stock.[1] The owner of a call has the right to buy 100 shares; the owner of a put has the right to sell 100 shares. If, however, the price of an underlying stock is either very low or very high, an exchange may adjust the number of shares in the underlying contract in order to create a contract size that is deemed reasonable for trading on the exchange.[2]

On all futures options exchanges, the underlying is uniformly one futures contract. The owner of a call has the right to buy one futures contract; the owner of a put has the right to sell one futures contract. Most often, the underlying for an option on a futures contract is the futures month that corresponds to the expiration month of the option. The underlying for an April futures option is an April futures contract; the underlying for a November futures option is a November futures contract. However, an exchange may also choose to list *serial options* on futures—option expirations where there is no corresponding futures month. When a futures option has no corresponding futures month, the underlying contract is the nearest futures contract beyond expiration of the option.

For example, many financial futures are listed on a quarterly cycle, with trading in March, June, September, and December futures. The underlying for a March option is a March futures contract; the underlying for a June option is a June futures contract. If there are also serial options, then

> The underlying for a January or February option is a March futures contract.
> The underlying for an April or May option is a June futures contract.
> The underlying for a July or August option is a September futures contract.
> The underlying for an October or November option is a December futures contract.

Some interest-rate futures markets [e.g., Eurodollars at the Chicago Mercantile Exchange, Short Sterling and Euribor at the London International Financial Futures Exchange], in addition to listing long-term options on a long-term futures contract, may also list short-term options on the same

---

[1] One hundred shares is sometimes referred to as a *round lot*. An order to buy or sell fewer than 100 shares is an *odd lot*.
[2] Many exchanges also permit trading in *flex options*, where the buyer and seller may negotiate the contract specifications, including the quantity of the underlying, the expiration date, the exercise price, and the exercise style.

long-term futures contract. A March futures contract maturing in two years may be the underlying for a March option expiring in two years. But the same futures contract may also be the underlying for a March option expiring in one year. Short-term options on long-term futures are listed as *midcurve options*. The options can be one-year midcurve (a short-term option on a futures contract with at least one year to maturity), two-year midcurve (a short-term option on a futures contract with at least two years to maturity), or five-year midcurve (a short-term option on a futures contract with at least five years to maturity).

Expiration Date or Expiry

The expiration date is the date on which the owner of an option must make the final decision whether to buy, in the case of a call, or to sell, in the case of a put. After expiration, all rights and obligations under the option contract cease to exist.

On many stock option exchanges, the expiration date for stock and stock index options is the third Friday of the expiration month.[3] Of more importance to most traders is the *last trading day*, the last business day prior to expiration on which an option can be bought or sold on an exchange. For most stock options, expiration day and the last trading day are the same, the third Friday of the month. However, Good Friday, a legal holiday in many countries, occasionally falls on the third Friday of April. When this occurs, the last trading day is the preceding Thursday.

When stock options were introduced in the United States, trading in expiring contracts ended at the close of business on the third Friday of the month. However, many derivative strategies require carrying an offsetting stock position to expiration, at which time the stock position is liquidated. Consequently, stock exchanges found that as the close of trading approached on expiration Friday, they were faced with large orders to buy or sell stock. These large orders often had the effect of disrupting trading or distorting prices at expiration.

To alleviate the problem of large order imbalances at expiration, some derivative exchanges, working with the stock exchanges on which the underlying stocks were traded, agreed to establish an expiration value for a derivatives contract based on the opening price of the underlying contract rather than the closing price on the last trading day. This *AM expiration* is commonly used for stock index contracts. Options on individual stocks are still subject to the traditional *PM expiration*, where the value of an option is determined by the underlying stock price at the close of trading on the last trading day.

Although the expiration date for stock options is relatively uniform, the expiration date for futures options can vary, depending on the underlying commodity or financial instrument. For futures on physical commodities, such as agricultural or energy products, delivery at maturity may take several days. As a consequence, options on futures for physical commodities will often expire several days or even weeks prior to the maturity of the futures contract, most commonly in the month prior to the futures month. An option on a March futures contract will expire in February; an option on a July futures contract will

---

[3] In the early days of option trading, exchange-traded options often expired on a nonbusiness day, typically on a Saturday. This gave the exchange an extra day to process the paperwork associated with expiring options.

expire in June; an option on a November futures contract will expire in October. A trader will need to consult the exchange calendar to determine the exact expiration date, which is set by each individual exchange.

Exercise Price or Strike Price

The exercise or strike price is the price at which the underlying will be delivered should the holder of an option choose to exercise his right to buy or sell. If the option is exercised, the owner of a call will pay the exercise price; the owner of a put will receive the exercise price.

The exercise prices available for trading on an option exchange are set by the exchange, usually at equal intervals and bracketing the current price of the underlying contract. If the price of the underlying contract is 62 when options are introduced, the exchange may set exercise prices of 50, 55, 60, 65, 70, and 75. At a later date, as the price of the underlying moves up or down, the exchange can add additional exercise prices. If the price of the underlying rises to 70, the exchange may add exercise prices of 80, 85, and 90. Additionally, if the exchange feels that it will further facilitate trading, it can introduce intermediate exercise prices—52½, 57½, 62½, 67½.

As an example of an exchange-traded option, the buyer of a crude oil October 90 call on the New York Mercantile Exchange has the right to take a long position in one October crude oil futures contract for 1,000 barrels of crude oil (the underlying) at a price of $90 per barrel (the exercise price) on or before the October expiration (the expiration date). The buyer of a General Electric March 30 put on the Chicago Board Options Exchange has the right to take a short position in 100 shares of General Electric stock (the underlying) at a price of $30 per share (the exercise price) on or before March expiration (the expiration date).

Option contract specifications are further outlined in Figure 3-1.

Exercise and Assignment

The buyer of a call or a put option has the right to exercise that option prior to its expiration date, thereby converting the option into a long underlying position in the case of a call or a short underlying position in the case of a put. A trader who exercises a crude oil October 90 call has chosen to take a long position in one October crude oil futures contract at $90 per barrel. A trader who

Figure 3-1 Option contract specifications.

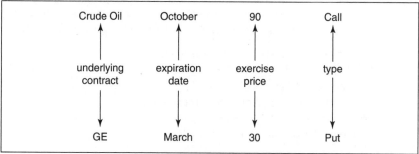

exercises a GE March 30 put has chosen to take a short position in 100 shares of GE stock at $30 per share. Once an option is exercised, the rights and obligations associated with the option cease to exist, just as if the option had been allowed to expire.

A trader who intends to exercise an option must submit an exercise notice to either the seller of the option, if purchased from a dealer, or to the exchange, if the option was purchased on an exchange. When a valid exercise notice is submitted, the seller of the option has been assigned. Depending on the type of option, the seller will be required to take a long or short position in the underlying contract at the option's exercise price.

Once a contract has been traded on an exchange, the link between buyer and seller is broken, with the exchange becoming the counterparty to all trades. Still, when a trader exercises an option, the exchange must assign someone to either buy or sell the underlying contract at the exercise price. How does the exchange make this decision? The party who is assigned must be someone who has sold the option and has not closed out the position through an offsetting trade. Beyond this, the exchange's decision on who will be assigned is essentially random, with no trader having either a greater or lesser probability of being assigned.

New traders sometimes become confused about whether the exercise and assignment result in a long position (buying the underlying contract) or a short position (selling the underlying contract). The following summary may help: if you

Exercise a call	You choose to *buy* at the exercise price.
Are assigned on a call	You are required to *sell* at the exercise price.
Exercise a put	You choose to *sell* at the exercise price.
Are assigned on a put	You are required to *buy* at the exercise price

Depending on the underlying contract, when an exchange-traded option is exercised, it can settle into

1. The physical underlying

2. A futures position

3. Cash

Settlement into the Physical Underlying

If a call option settles into the physical underlying, the exerciser pays the exercise price and in return receives the underlying. If a put option settles into the physical underlying, the exerciser receives the exercise price and in return must deliver the underlying. Stock options always settle into the physical underlying.

> You exercise one January 110 call on stock.
> You must pay $100 \times \$110 = \$11,000$.
> You receive 100 shares of stock.
> You are assigned on six April 40 calls on stock.
> You receive $600 \times \$40 = \$24,000$.
> You must deliver 600 shares of stock.

You exercise two July 60 puts on stock.
  You receive 200 × $60 = $12,000.
  You must deliver 200 shares of stock.
You are assigned on three October 95 puts on stock.
  You must pay 300 × $95 = $28,500.
  You receive 300 shares of stock.

Note that the cash flow resulting from settlement into the physical underlying depends only on the exercise price. In our examples, whether the price of the stock at exercise is $10 or $1,000, the exerciser of a call pays only the exercise price, not the stock price. The exerciser of a put receives only the exercise price. Of course, the profit or loss resulting from the option trade will depend on both the stock price and the price originally paid for the option. But the cash flow when the option is exercised is independent of these.

Settlement into a Futures Position

If an option settles into a futures position, it is just as if the exerciser is buying or selling the futures contract at the exercise price. The position is immediately subject to futures-type settlement, requiring a margin deposit and accompanied by a variation payment.

An underlying futures contract is currently trading at 85.00 with a point value of $1,000. Margin requirements are $3,000 per contract.

You exercise one February 80 call.
  You immediately become long one futures contract at a price of 80.
  You must deposit with the exchange the required margin of $3,000.
  You will receive a variation credit of (85 – 80) × $1,000 = $5,000.
You are assigned on six May 75 calls.
  You immediately become short six futures contracts at a price of 75.
  You must deposit with the exchange the required margin of 6 × $3,000 = $18,000.
  You will have a variation debit of (75 – 85) × $1,000 × 6 = –$60,000
You exercise four August 100 puts.
  You immediately become short four futures contracts at a price of 100.
  You must deposit with the exchange the required margin of 4 × $3,000 = $12,000.
  You will receive a variation credit of (100 – 85) × $1,000 × 4 = $60,000.
You are assigned on two November 95 puts.
  You immediately become long two futures contracts at a price of 95.
  You must deposit with the exchange the required margin of 2 × $3,000 = $6,000.
  You will have a variation debit of (85 – 95) × $1,000 × 2 = –$20,000.

Settlement into Cash

This type of settlement is used primarily for index contracts where delivery of the underlying contract is not practical. If exercise of an option settles into cash, no underlying position results. There is a cash payment equal to the difference between the exercise price and the underlying price at the end of the trading day.

An underlying index is fixed at the end of the trading day at 300. The exchange has assigned a value of $500 to each index point.

You exercise three March 250 calls.
You have no underlying position.
Your account will be credited with $(300 - 250) \times \$500 \times 3 = \$75,000$.
You are assigned on seven June 275 calls.
You have no underlying position.
Your account will be debited by $(275 - 300) \times \$500 \times 7 = \$87,500$.
You exercise two September 320 puts.
You have no underlying position.
Your account will be credited with $(320 - 300) \times \$500 \times 2 = \$20,000$.
You are assigned on four December 340 puts.
You have no underlying position.
Your account will be debited by $(300 - 340) \times \$500 \times 4 = \$80,000$.

Exercise Style

In addition to the underlying contract, exercise price, expiration date, and type, an option is further identified by its exercise style, either *European* or *American*. A European option can only be exercised at expiration. In practice, this means that the holder of a European option must make the final decision whether to exercise or not on the last business day prior to expiration. In contrast, an American option can be exercised on any business day prior to expiration.

The designation of an option's exercise style as either European or American has nothing to do with geographic location. Many options traded in the United States are European, and many options traded in Europe are American.[4] Generally, options on futures and options on individual stocks tend to be American. Options on indexes tend to be European.

Option Price Components

As in any competitive market, an option's price, or premium, is determined by supply and demand. Buyers and sellers make competitive bids and offers in the marketplace. When a bid and offer coincide, a trade is made.

The premium paid for an option can be separated into two components— the *intrinsic value* and the *time value*. An option has intrinsic value if it enables the holder of the option to buy low and sell high or sell high and buy low, with the intrinsic value being equal to the difference between the buying price and the selling price. With an underlying contract trading at $435, the intrinsic value of a 400 call is $35. By exercising the option, the holder of the 400 call can buy at $400. If he then sells at the market price of $435, $35 will be credited to his account. With an underlying contract trading at $62, the intrinsic value of a 70

---

[4] It does appear that the first options traded in the United States carried with them the right of early exercise— hence the term *American option*.

put is $8. By exercising the option, the holder of the put can sell at $70. If he then buys at the market price of $62, he will show a total credit of $8.

A call will only have intrinsic value if its exercise price is less than the current market price of the underlying contract because no one would choose to buy high and sell low. A put will only have intrinsic value if its exercise price is greater than the current market price of the underlying contract because no one would choose to sell low and buy high. The amount of intrinsic value is the amount by which the exercise price is less than the current underlying price in the case of a call or the amount by which the exercise price is greater than the current underlying price in the case of a put. No option can have an intrinsic value less than zero. If S is the spot price of the underlying contract and X is the exercise price, then

Call intrinsic value = maximum of either 0 or $S - X$.
Put intrinsic value = maximum of either 0 or $X - S$.

Note that the intrinsic value is independent of the expiration date. With the underlying contract at $83, a March 70 call and a September 70 call both have an intrinsic value of $13. A June 90 put and a December 90 put both have an intrinsic value of $7.

Usually, an option's price in the marketplace will be greater than its intrinsic value. The *time value*, sometimes also referred to as the option's *time premium* or *extrinsic value*, is the additional amount of premium beyond the intrinsic value that traders are willing to pay for an option. Market participants are willing to pay this additional amount primarily because of the protective characteristics afforded by an option over an outright long or short position in the underlying contract.

An option's premium is always composed of precisely its intrinsic value and its time value. Examples of intrinsic value and time value are shown in Figure 3-2. If a $400 call is trading at $50 with the underlying trading at $435, the time value of the call must be $15 because the intrinsic value is $35. The two components must add up to the option's total premium of $50. If a $70 put on a stock is trading for $11 with the stock trading at $62, the time value of the put must be $3 because the intrinsic value is $8. Again, the intrinsic value and the time value must add up to the option's premium of $11.

Even though an option's premium is always composed of its intrinsic value and its time value, one or both of these components can be zero. If the option has no intrinsic value, its price in the marketplace will consist solely of time value. If the option has no time value, its price will consist solely of intrinsic value. In the latter case, traders say that the option is trading at *parity*.

Although an option's intrinsic value can never be less than zero, it is possible for a European option to have a negative time value. (More about this in Chapter 16 when we look at the early exercise of American options.) When this happens, the option can trade for less than parity. Usually, however, an option's premium will reflect some nonnegative amount of time value.

In the Money, At the Money, and Out of the Money

Depending on the relationship between an option's exercise price and the price of the underlying contract, options are said to be in the money, at the

Figure 3-2 Intrinsic value and time value.

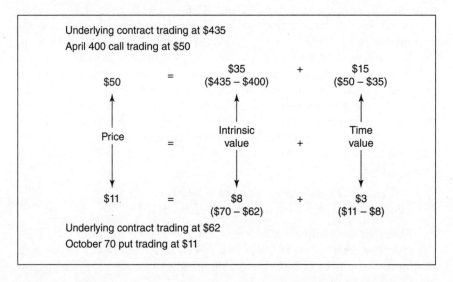

money, and out of the money. Any option that has a positive intrinsic value is said to be *in the money* by the amount of the intrinsic value. With a stock at $44, a $40 call is in the money by $4. A $55 put on the same stock is in the money by $11. An option with no intrinsic value is said to be *out of the money*, and its price consists solely of time value. In order to be in the money, a call must have an exercise price lower than the current price of the underlying contract, and a put must have an exercise price higher than the current price of the underlying contract. Note that if a call is in the money, a put with the same exercise price and underlying contract must be out of the money. Conversely, if the put is in the money, a call with the same exercise price must be out of the money. In our examples with the stock at $44, the $40 put is out of the money by $4 and the $55 call is out of the money by $11.

Finally, an option whose exercise price is equal to the current price of the underlying contract is said to be *at the money*. Technically, such an option is also out of the money because it has no intrinsic value. Traders make the distinction between at-the-money and out-of-the-money options because, as we shall see, at-the-money options often have very specific and desirable characteristics, and such options tend to be the most actively traded.

If we want to be very precise, for an option to be at the money, its exercise price must be exactly equal to the current price of the underlying contract. However, for exchange-traded options, the term is commonly applied to the call and put whose exercise price is closest to the current price of the underlying contract. With a stock at $74 and $5 between exercise prices ($65, $70, $75, $80, etc.), the $75 call and the $75 put are the at-the-money options. These are the call and put options with exercise prices closest to the current price of the underlying contract. In-, at-, and out-of-the-money options are outlined in Figure 3-3.

Figure 3-3 In-, at-, and out-of-the-money options.

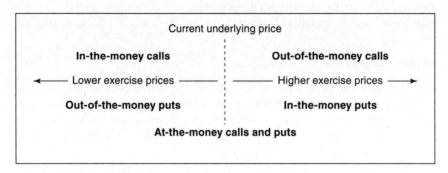

Current underlying price

In-the-money calls   **Out-of-the-money calls**

◄——— Lower exercise prices ——— ┆ ——— Higher exercise prices ——►

Out-of-the-money puts   **In-the-money puts**

At-the-money calls and puts

Automatic Exercise

At expiration an in-the-money option will always have some intrinsic value. A trader can capture this value by either selling the option in the marketplace prior to expiration or exercising the option and immediately closing the underlying position. When exchange-traded options were first introduced, anyone wishing to exercise an option was required to formally submit an *exercise notice* to the exchange. If someone forgot to submit an exercise notice for an in-the-money option, the option would expire unexercised, and the trader would lose the intrinsic value. This is an outcome that no rational person would accept. Unfortunately, in the early days of option trading, this occurred occasionally for various reasons: perhaps the trader was unaware that he was required to submit an exercise notice, perhaps the trader was out of communication with the exchange and was therefore unable to submit an exercise notice, or perhaps there was an error on the part of the clearing firm in processing the exercise notice.

To avoid a situation where an in-the-money option expires unexercised, which would be an embarrassment to both the individual trader and the exchange, most exchanges have instituted an *automatic exercise policy*. The exchange will exercise on behalf of the option holder any in-the-money option at expiration, even if an exercise notice has not been submitted. The criteria for automatic exercise may vary from one exchange to another and may also vary depending on who holds the option. For example, because of transaction costs, it may not be economically worthwhile to exercise an option that is only very slightly in the money. Therefore, the exchange may automatically exercise only options that are in the money by some predetermined amount. If the automatic exercise threshold is 0.05, then an option must be in the money by at least 0.05 in order for the exchange to exercise the option. If the option is in the money by 0.03, a trader may still exercise the option but must do so by submitting an exercise notice. On the opposite side, if the option is in the money by 0.06, a trader who feels that the option is not worth exercising may submit a *do not exercise notice*. Otherwise, the exchange will automatically exercise the option on the trader's behalf.

Because professional traders and retail customers have different cost structures, the exchange may have a different automatic exercise threshold for each party. The threshold may be 0.05 for retail customers but only 0.02 for professionals. To determine who is a professional trader and who is not, an exchange will usually specify the criteria necessary for inclusion in each category.

Option Margining

Depending on the exchange and the type of underlying contract, options can be subject to either stock-type settlement or futures-type settlement. However, once an option trade is made, there are additional risks that the clearinghouse must consider. Is the risk to an option position limited or unlimited? If unlimited, how should the clearinghouse protect itself?

When the risk of an option position is limited, the margin that must be deposited with the clearinghouse will never be greater than the maximum risk to the position. The buyer of an option can never have risk greater than the premium paid for the option, and the clearinghouse will never require a margin deposit greater than this amount. Even if an option position is very complex, as long as there is a maximum risk to the position, there will also be a maximum margin requirement.

Some option positions, however, have unlimited risk. For such positions, the clearinghouse must consider the risk associated with a wide variety of outcomes. Once this is done, the clearinghouse can require a margin deposit commensurate with the perceived risk of the position. Unlike futures margining, where the clearinghouse sets a fixed margin deposit for each open futures position, there is no single method of determining the margin for a complex option position. However, all methods are *risk-based*, requiring an analysis of the position's risk under a broad range of market conditions. In the United States, the Options Clearing Corporation has developed its own risked-based margining system for stock and index options. The most widely used margining system on futures exchanges is the *Standard Portfolio Analysis of Risk* (SPAN) system developed by the Chicago Mercantile Exchange. Both margining systems create an array of possible outcomes with respect to both the underlying price and the perceived speed with which the underlying price can change. The clearinghouse then uses this array to determine a reasonable margin requirement.[5]

---

[5] A description of SPAN margining can be found at http://www.cmegroup.com/clearing/risk-management. A description of the risk-based margining system used by the Options Clearing Corporation can be found at http://www.optionsclearing.com/risk-management/margins/.

4

Expiration Profit
and Loss

The trader who enters an option market for the first time may find himself subjected to a form of contract shock. Unlike a trader in equities or futures, whose choices are limited to a small number of instruments, an option trader must often deal with a bewildering assortment of contracts. With several expiration months, with multiple exercise prices available in each month, and with both calls and puts at each exercise price, it is not unusual for an option trader to be faced with what at first seems like an overwhelming number of different contracts. With so many choices available, a trader needs some logical method of deciding which options actually represent profit opportunities. Which should he buy? Which should he sell? Which should he avoid? The choices are so numerous that a prospective option trader might be inclined to give up in frustration.

To begin, a trader might ask a very obvious question: what is an option worth? The question may be obvious, but the answer, unfortunately, is not, because option prices can be affected by many different market forces. However, there is one time in an option's life when everyone ought to be able to agree on the option's value. At expiration, an option is worth exactly its intrinsic value: zero if it is out of the money or the difference between the underlying price and the exercise price if it is in the money.

Following is a series of underlying prices and the value at expiration for two options, a $95 call and $110 put:

Underlying Price	95 Call	110 Put
80	0	30
85	0	25
90	0	20
95	0	15
100	5	10

Underlying Price	95 Call	110 Put
105	10	5
110	15	0
115	20	0
120	25	0
125	30	0

For the 95 call, if the underlying price at expiration is 95 or below, the call is out of the money and therefore worthless. If, however, the underlying price rises above 95, the 95 call will go into the money, gaining one point in value for each point that the underlying price rises above 95. For the 110 put, if the underlying price is 110 or above, the put is out of the money and therefore worthless. But if the underlying price falls below 110, the 110 put goes into the money, gaining one point in value for each point decline in the underlying price.

Parity Graphs

For someone who has bought an option, the intrinsic value represents a credit, or positive value. The buyer of the option will be able to buy low and sell high. For someone who has sold an option, the intrinsic value represents a debit, or negative value. The seller of the option will be forced to buy high and sell low. We can use an option's intrinsic value to draw a graph of the value of an option position at expiration as a function of the price of the underlying contract. Figure 4-1 shows such a graph for a long call position. Below the exercise price, the option has no value. Above the exercise price, the option gains one point in value for each point increase in the underlying price.

Figure 4-1 Long call.

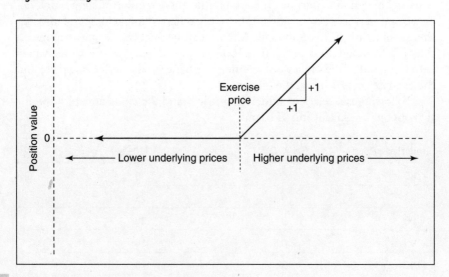

Figure 4-2 Short call.

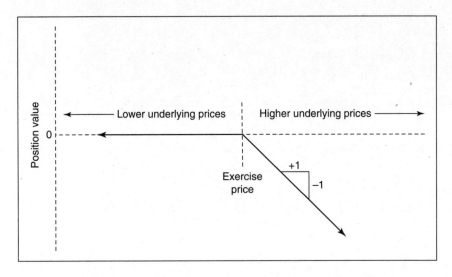

Figure 4-2 shows the value of a short call position at expiration. Now, if the option is in the money, the value of the position is negative. For every point the underlying rises above the exercise price, the position loses one point in value.

We can create the same type of expiration graphs for long and short put positions, as shown in Figures 4-3 and 4-4. For a long or short put, the value of the position is zero if the underlying price is above the exercise price. For a long put, the position gains one point for each point decline in the underlying price. For a short put, the position loses one point in value for each point decline in the underlying price.

A *parity graph* represents the value of an option position at expiration, *parity* being another name for *intrinsic value*. Because of their shapes, traders

Figure 4-3 Long put.

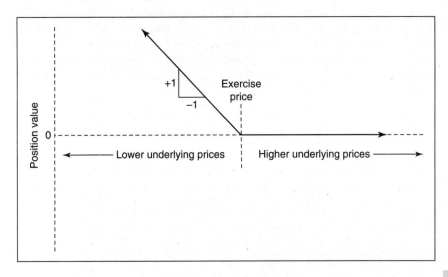

Figure 4-4 Short put.

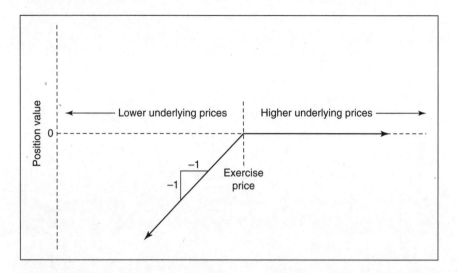

sometimes refer to the four basic parity graphs (long and short call and long and short put) as the *hockey-stick diagrams.*

The four basic parity graphs highlight one of the most important characteristics of option trading. Buyers of options have limited risk (they can never lose more than the price of the option) and unlimited profit potential. Sellers of options have limited profit potential (they can never make more than the price of the option) and unlimited risk.[1]

Given the apparently unbalanced risk-reward tradeoff, new option traders tend to have the same reaction: why would anyone do anything other than buy options? The purchase of an option results in a position with limited risk and unlimited profit, which certainly seems more desirable than the limited profit and unlimited risk that result from the sale of an option. Yet, in every option market, there are traders who are willing to sell options. Why are they willing to do this in the face of this apparently unbalanced risk-reward tradeoff? The answer has to do with not just the best and worst that can happen but also with the likelihood of those occurrences. It's true that someone who sells an option is exposed to unlimited risk, but if the amount received for the option is great enough and the perceived risk is low enough, a trader might be willing to take that risk. In later chapters we will see the very important role probability plays in option pricing.

Slope

From the parity graphs, we can see that if an option is out of the money, its value is unaffected by changes in the price of the underlying contract. If the option is in the money, it will either gain or lose value as the underlying price changes.

---

[1] Admittedly, in traditional stock and commodity markets, a put does not represent unlimited profit potential to the buyer nor unlimited risk to the seller because the underlying contract cannot fall below zero. But for practical purposes most traders think of both calls and puts as having unlimited potential value.

The slope of the graph is the change in value of the option position with respect to changes in the price of the underlying contract, often expressed as a fraction

$$\text{slope} = \frac{\text{change in position value}}{\text{change in underlying price}}$$

We can summarize the slopes of the basic positions as follows:

Position	Slope
Long or short any out-of-the-money option	0
Long an in-the-money call	+1
Short an in-the-money call	−1
Long an in-the-money put	−1
Short an in-the-money put	+1

In addition to parity graphs for individual options, we can also create parity graphs for positions consisting of multiple options by adding up the slopes of the individual options. Figure 4-5 is the parity graph of a position consisting of a long call and long put at the same exercise price. We can calculate the total slopes as follows:

Below the exercise price	Slope
Call is out of the money	0
Put is in the money	−1
Total slope below the exercise price	−1

Above the exercise price	Slope
Put is out of the money	0
Call is in the money	+1
Total slope above the exercise price	+1

The combined position will gain value if the underlying price moves in either direction away from the exercise price. The position is typical of many option strategies that may be sensitive to the magnitude of movement in the underlying contract rather than the direction of movement.

Many option strategies involve combining options with the underlying contract, so we will also want to consider the slope of an underlying position. As shown in Figure 4-6, the slope of a long underlying position is always +1, and the slope of a short underlying position is always −1. The slopes are constant regardless of the underlying price. This is an important distinction between an option position and an underlying position. Because of the insurance

Figure 4-5 (*a*) Long call and long put at the same exercise price. (*b*) Combined position.

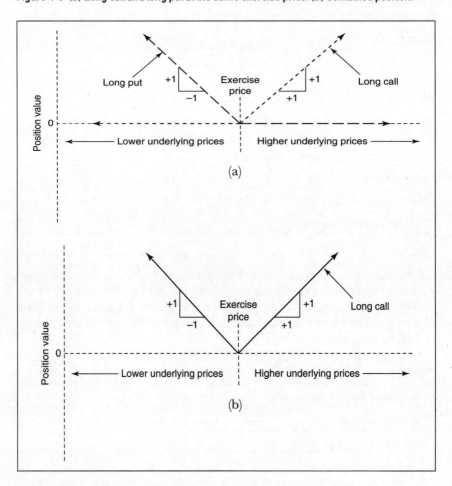

Figure 4-6 Long and short underlying position.

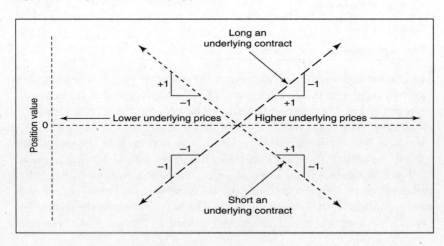

feature of an option, the parity graph of an option position will always bend at the exercise price.

Figure 4-7 shows the parity graph of a position that combines two long call options at the same exercise price and with a short underlying contract. Below the exercise price, the total slope is −1 (0 for the out-of-the-money calls, −1 for the short underlying). Above the exercise price, the total slope is +1 (+2 for the in-the-money calls, −1 for the short underlying contract). This parity graph is identical to the position in Figure 4-5, which must mean that the same option strategy can be constructed in more than one way. This is an important characteristic of options that we will look at in more detail in Chapter 14. Note also that the location of the underlying position is irrelevant to the parity graph. Regardless of the price of the underlying, the slope is always either +1 for a long underlying position or −1 for a short underlying position.

Figure 4-7 (*a*) Long two calls and short an underlying contract. (*b*) Combined position.

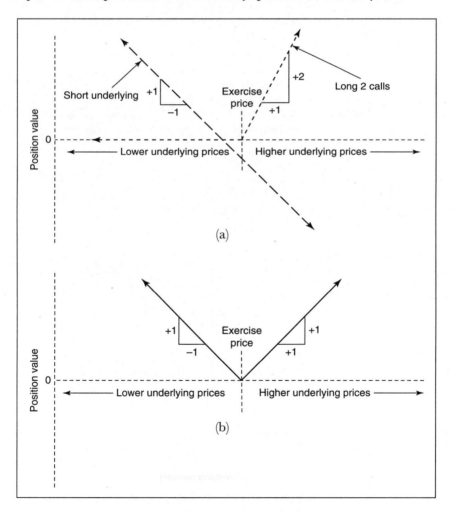

Figure 4-8 is the parity graph of a long call and short put at the same exercise price. Below the exercise price, the total slope is +1 (0 for the long out-of-the-money call, +1 for the short in-the-money put). Above the exercise price, the total slope is also +1 (+1 for the in-the-money call, 0 for the out-of-the-money put). The slope of the entire position is always +1, exactly the same as a long underlying contract.

If a position consists of many different contracts, including underlying contracts and calls and puts over a wide range of exercise prices, the parity graph for the position may be quite complex. But the procedure for constructing the graph is always the same: determine the slopes of the graph below the lowest exercise price, above the highest exercise price, and between all the intermediate exercise prices, and then connect all the line segments.

Figure 4-8 (*a*) Long call and short put at the same exercise price. (*b*) Combined position.

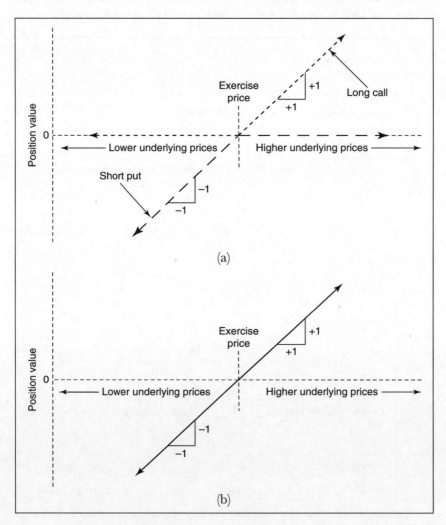

Consider this position:

−4   underlying contracts

+3	65 calls	+2	65 puts
+2	70 calls	−4	70 puts
−6	75 calls	+3	75 puts
+4	80 calls	−2	80 puts

What should the parity graph look like?

To determine the slopes of a complex position, it may be helpful to construct a table showing the slopes of the individual contracts over all intervals. We can then add up the individual slopes to get the total slope over each interval.

Contract	Below 65	65–70	70–75	75–80	Above 80
+3 65 calls	0	+3	+3	+3	+3
+2 65 puts	−2	0	0	0	0
+2 70 calls	0	0	+2	+2	+2
−4 70 puts	+4	+4	0	0	0
−6 75 calls	0	0	0	−6	−6
+3 75 puts	−3	−3	−3	0	0
+4 80 calls	0	0	0	0	+4
−2 80 puts	+2	+2	+2	+2	0
−4 Underlying contracts	−4	−4	−4	−4	−4
Total	−3	+2	0	−3	−1

The entire parity graph is shown in Figure 4-9. Note that for this graph there is no *y*-axis. For complex graphs where options are bought and sold at

Figure 4-9

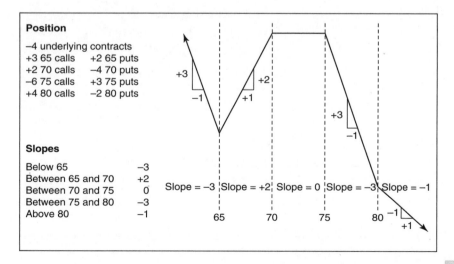

many different exercise prices, it may not be possible to position the graph along the *y*-axis. Nevertheless, the parity graph tells us something about the characteristics of the position. Here we can see that the potential profit on the downside, as well as the potential loss on the upside, is unlimited.

Expiration Profit and Loss

A parity graph may tell us the characteristics of an option position at expiration, but an equally important consideration will be the profit or loss that results from the position. Whether the position makes or loses money will depend on the prices at which the contracts are bought and sold. The purchase of options will create a debit, whereas the sale of options will create a credit. For a simple option position, the expiration profit and loss (P&L) graph will be the parity graph shifted downward by the amount of any debit or upward by the amount of any credit.

Consider the following option prices with the underlying contract trading at a price of 98.00:

	85	90	95	100	105	110	115
Calls	14.25	9.75	6.25	3.50	1.75	0.75	0.25
Puts	0.25	1.00	2.25	4.50	7.75	11.75	16.25

Figure 4-10 shows the parity graph of a long 100 call position. If the option is purchased at a price of 3.50, we can construct the expiration P&L

Figure 4-10 Long a 100 call at a price of 3.50.

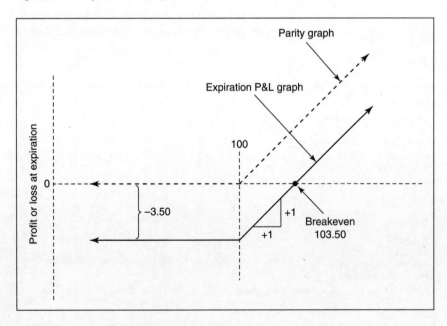

graph by shifting the entire parity graph down by this amount. If the underlying is anywhere below 100 at expiration, the option will be worthless, and the position will lose 3.50. With the underlying above 100, the slope of the graph is +1; the option will gain one point in value for each point increase in the price of the underlying. We can also see that there is a *breakeven price* at which the option position will be worth exactly 3.50. Logically, this must occur at an underlying price of 103.50.

Figure 4-11 shows the parity graph of a short 95 put position. If the option is sold at a price of 2.25, we can construct the expiration P&L graph by shifting the entire graph up by this amount. With an underlying price anywhere above 95 at expiration, the option will be worthless, and the position will show a profit of 2.25. With an underlying price below 95, the slope of the graph is +1; the position will lose one point for each point decline in the price of the underlying. The breakeven price for the position is 92.75, the price at which the 95 put will be worth exactly 2.25.

The relative expiration value of long option positions at different exercise prices—95, 100, and 105—is shown in Figure 4-12. The same relative value for long put positions is shown in Figure 4-13. Calls with lower exercise prices have greater values (i.e., they enable the holder to buy at a lower price), whereas puts with higher exercise prices have greater values (i.e., they enable the holder to sell at a higher price).

For more complex positions, it may not be immediately clear whether the position will result in a credit or debit. In this case, we can construct an expiration P&L graph by first determining the slopes of the graph over all the intervals. Then we can calculate the P&L at one point, and from this one P&L point, we can use the slopes to determine the P&L at all other points.

Figure 4-11 Short a 95 put at a price of 2.25.

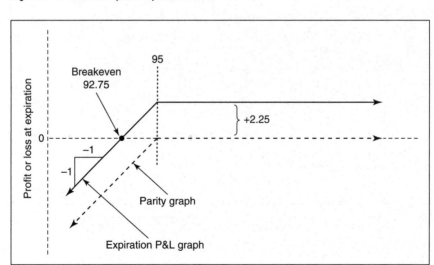

Figure 4-12 Long a 95 call –6.25; long a 100 call –3.50; long a 105 call –1.75.

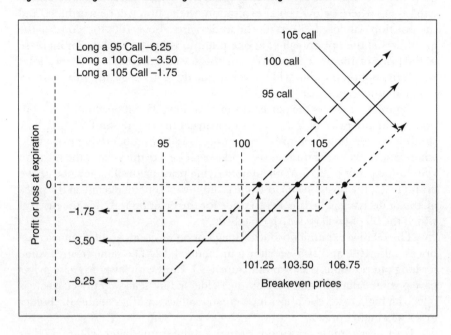

Figure 4-13 Long a 95 put –2.25; long a 100 put –4.50; long a 105 put –7.75.

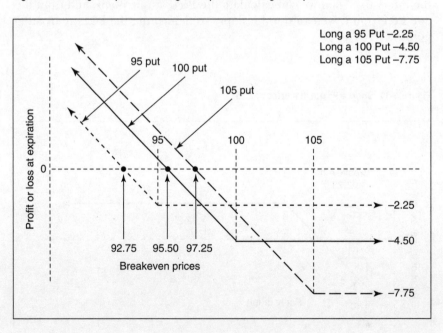

Consider the following position

Position		Contract Price
+1	95 call	6.25
−1	105 call	1.75
−2	105 puts	7.75
−2	Underlying contracts	98.00

The slopes of the position are

Contract		Below 95	95–105	Above 105
+1	95 call	0	+1	+1
−1	105 call	0	0	−1
−2	105 puts	+2	+2	0
−2	Underlying contracts	−2	−2	−2
Total		0	+1	−2

It is usually easiest to determine the P&L at an exercise price, so let's use 95. The P&L at an underlying price of 95 is

Position		Contract Price	Contract Value at 95	Contract P&L at 95	Total Contract P&L
+1	95 call	6.25	0	−6.25	−6.25
−1	105 call	1.75	0	+1.75	+1.75
−2	105 puts	7.75	10.00	−2.25	−4.50
−2	Underlying contracts	98.00	95.00	+3.00	+6.00
Total P&L at 95.00					−3.00

Figure 4-14 shows the entire expiration P&L graph for the position. Below 95, the slope of the graph is 0, so the P&L is always −3.00. Between 95 and 105, the slope is +1, so the P&L at 105 (10 points higher) is −3.00 + 10.00 = +7.00. Above 105, the slope is −2, with the position losing two points for each point increase in the price of the underlying.

The position has two breakeven prices, one between 95 and 105 and one above 105. With a P&L of −3.00 at 95 and a slope of +1 between 95 and 105, the first breakeven is

$$95.00 + (3.00/1) = 98.00$$

Figure 4-14

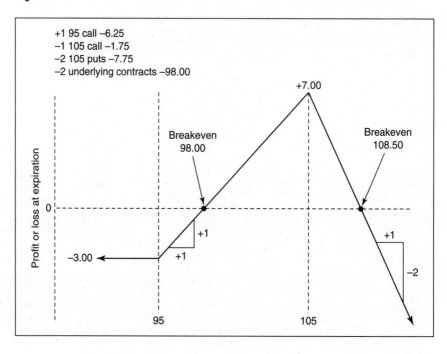

+1 95 call −6.25
−1 105 call −1.75
−2 105 puts −7.75
−2 underlying contracts −98.00

With a P&L of +7.00 at 105 and a slope above 105 of −2, the second breakeven is

$$105.00 + (7.00/2) = 108.50$$

Finally, let's go back to the parity-graph position shown in Figure 4-9. Suppose that we are told that at expiration with an underlying price of 62.00 the position will show a profit of 2.10. What will be the P&L at expiration if the underlying price is 81.50? Using the slopes, we can work our way from 62.00 to 81.50

Interval	Beginning P&L	Slope	Ending P&L
62.00–65.00	+2.10	−3	+2.10 − (3 × 3) = **−6.90**
65.00–70.00	−6.90	+2	−6.90 + (2 × 5) = **+3.10**
70.00–75.00	+3.10	0	**+3.10**
75.00–80.00	+3.10	−3	+3.10 − (3 × 5) = **−11.90**
80.00–81.50	−11.90	−1	−11.90 − (1 × 1.50) = **−13.40**

At an underlying price of 81.50, the position will show a loss of 13.40. We can also see that there are three breakeven prices for the position:

Between 62.00 and 65.00	$62.00 + 2.10/3 = \mathbf{62.70}$
Between 65.00 and 70.00	$65.00 + 6.90/2 = \mathbf{68.45}$
Between 75.00 and 80.00	$75.00 + 3.10/3 \approx \mathbf{76.03}$

All critical points for the position are shown in Figure 4-15.

Figure 4-15

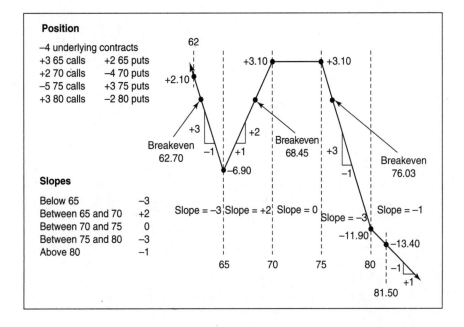

Position

–4 underlying contracts
+3 65 calls +2 65 puts
+2 70 calls –4 70 puts
–5 75 calls +3 75 puts
+3 80 calls –2 80 puts

Slopes

Below 65	–3
Between 65 and 70	+2
Between 70 and 75	0
Between 75 and 80	–3
Above 80	–1

5

Theoretical
Pricing Models

In Chapter 4, we considered the value of an option and the profit or loss resulting from an option strategy at the moment of expiration. From the expiration profit and loss (P&L) graphs, we can see clearly that the direction in which an underlying contract moves can be an important consideration in choosing an option strategy. A trader who believes that the underlying market will rise will be more inclined either to buy calls or sell puts. A trader who believes that the underlying market will fall will be more inclined either to buy puts or sell calls. In each case, the directional movement in the underlying market will increase the likelihood that the strategy will be profitable.

However, an option trader has an additional problem that we might call the "speed" of the market. If we ignore interest and dividend considerations, a trader who believes that a stock will rise in price within a specified period can be reasonably certain of making a profit if he is right. He can simply buy the stock, wait for it to reach his target price, and then sell the stock at a profit.

The situation is not quite so simple for an option trader. Suppose that a trader believes that a stock will rise in price from $100, its present price, to $115 within the next five months. Suppose also that a $110 call expiring in three months is available at a price of $2. If the stock rises to $115 by expiration, the purchase of the $110 call will result in a profit of $3 ($5 intrinsic value minus the $2 cost of the option). But is this profit a certainty? What will happen if the price of the stock remains below $110 for the next three months and only reaches $115 after the option expires? Then the option will expire worthless, and the trader will lose his $2 investment.

Perhaps the trader would do better to purchase a $110 call that expires in six months rather than three months. Now he can be certain that when the stock reaches $115, the call will be worth at least $5 in intrinsic value. But what if the price of the six-month option is $6? In this case, the trader still might show a loss. Even if the underlying stock reaches the target price of $115, there is no guarantee that the $110 call will ever be worth more than its $5 intrinsic value.

A trader in an underlying market is interested almost exclusively in the direction in which the market will move. Although an option trader is also sensitive to directional considerations, he must also give some thought to how fast the market is likely to move. If a trader in the underlying stock and an option trader in the same market take long market positions in their respective instruments and the market does in fact move higher, the stock trader is assured of a profit, while the option trader may show a loss. If the market fails to move sufficiently fast, the favorable directional move may not be enough to offset the option's loss in time value. A speculator will often buy options for their seemingly favorable risk-reward characteristics (limited risk, unlimited reward), but if he purchases options, not only must he be right about market direction, he must also be right about market speed. Only if he is right on both counts can he expect to make a profit. If predicting the correct market direction is difficult, correctly predicting direction and speed is probably beyond most traders' capabilities.

The concept of speed is crucial in trading options. Indeed, many option strategies depend only on the speed of the underlying market and not at all on its direction. If a trader is highly proficient at predicting directional moves in the underlying market, he is probably better advised to trade the underlying instrument. Only when a trader has some feel for the speed component can he hope to successfully enter the option market.

The Importance of Probability

One can never be certain about future market conditions, so almost all trading decisions are based on some estimate of probability. We often express our opinions about probability using words such as *likely*, *good chance*, *possible*, and *probable*. But in an option evaluation we need to be more specific. We need to define probability in way that will enable us to do the types of calculations required to make intelligent decisions in the marketplace. If we can do this, we will find that probability and the choice of strategy go hand in hand. If a trader believes that a strategy has a very high probability of profit and a very low probability of loss, he will be satisfied with a small potential profit because the profit is likely to be quite secure. On the other hand, if the probability of profit is very low, the trader will demand a large profit when market conditions develop favorably. Because of the importance of probability in the decision-making process, it will be worthwhile to consider some simple probability concepts.

Expected Value

Suppose that we are given the opportunity to roll a six-sided die, and each time we roll, we will be paid a dollar amount equal to the number that comes up. If we roll a one, we are paid \$1; if we roll a two, we are paid \$2; and so on up to six, in which case we are paid \$6. If we are given the opportunity to roll the die an infinite number of times, on average, how much do we expect to receive per roll?

We can calculate the answer using some simple arithmetic. There are six possible numbers, each with equal probability. If we add up the six possible outcomes $1 + 2 + 3 + 4 + 5 + 6 = 21$ and divide this by the six faces on the die, we get $21/6 = 3\frac{1}{2}$. That is, on average, we can expect to get back $3½ each time we roll the die. This is the average payback, or *expected value*. If we must pay for the privilege of rolling the die, what is a reasonable price? If we purchase the chance to roll the die for less than $3½, in the long run, we expect to show a profit. If we pay more than $3½, in the long run, we expect to show a loss. And if we pay exactly $3½, we expect to break even. Note the qualifying phrase *in the long run*. The expected value of $3½ is realistic only if we are allowed to roll the die many, many times. If we are allowed to roll only once, we cannot be certain of getting back $3½. Indeed, on any one roll, it is impossible to get back $3½ because no face of the die has exactly 3½ spots. Nevertheless, if we pay less than $3½ for even one roll of the die, the laws of probability are on our side because we have paid less than the expected value.

In a similar vein, consider a roulette bet. The roulette wheel has 38 slots, numbers 1 through 36 and 0 and 00.[1] Suppose that a casino allows a player to choose a number. If the player's number comes up, he receives $36; if any other number comes up, he receives nothing. What is the expected value for this proposition? There are 38 slots on the roulette wheel, each with equal probability, but only one slot will return $36 to the player. If we divide the one outcome where the player wins $36 by the 38 slots on the wheel, the result is $36/38 = \$0.9474$, or about 95 cents. A player who pays 95 cents for the privilege of picking a number at the roulette table can expect to approximately break even in the long run.

Of course, no casino will let a player buy such a bet for 95 cents. Under those conditions, the casino would make no profit. In the real world, a player who wants to purchase such a bet will have to pay more than the expected return, typically $1. The 5-cent difference between the $1 price of the bet and the 95-cent expected value represents the profit potential, or *edge*, to the casino. In the long run, for every dollar bet at the roulette table, the casino can expect to keep about 5 cents.

Given the preceding conditions, any player interested in making a profit would rather switch places with the casino. Then he would have a 5-cent edge on his side by selling bets worth 95 cents for $1. Alternatively, the player would like to find a casino where he could purchase the bet for less than its expected value of 95 cents, perhaps 88 cents. Then the player would have a 7-cent edge over the casino.

Theoretical Value

The *theoretical value* of a proposition is the price one would be willing to pay now to just break even in the long run. Thus far, the only factor we have considered in determining the value of a proposition is the expected value. We used this concept to calculate the 95-cent fair price for the roulette bet.

Suppose that in our roulette example the casino decides to change the conditions slightly. The player may now purchase the roulette bet for its expected value of 95 cents, and as before, if he loses, the casino will immediately collect

---

[1] We assume a roulette wheel with 38 slots, as is customary in the United States. In some parts of the world, a roulette wheel may have no slot numbered 00. This, of course, changes the probabilities.

his 95 cents. Under the new conditions, however, if the player wins, the casino will send him his $36 winnings in two months. Will both the player and the casino still break even on the proposition?

Where did the player get the 95 cents that he bet at the roulette wheel? In the immediate sense, he may have taken it out of his pocket. But a closer examination may reveal that he withdrew the money from his bank prior to visiting the casino. Because he won't receive his winnings for two months, he will have to take into consideration the two months of interest he would have earned had he left the 95 cents in the bank. The *theoretical value* of the bet is really the present value of its expected value, the 95 cents expected value discounted by interest. If interest rates are 12 percent annually, the theoretical value is

$$95 \text{ cents}/(1 + 0.12 \times 2/12) \approx 93 \text{ cents}$$

Even if the player purchases the bet for its expected return of 95 cents, he will still lose 2 cents because of the interest that he could have earned for two months if he had left his money in the bank. The casino, on the other hand, will take the 95 cents, put it in an interest-bearing account, and at the end of two months collect 2 cents in interest. Under the new conditions, if a player pays 93 cents for the roulette bet today and receives his winnings in two months, neither he nor the casino can expect to make any profit in the long run.

The two most common considerations in option evaluation are the expected return and interest. There may, however, be other considerations. Suppose that the player is a good client, and the casino decides to send him a 1-cent bonus a month from now. He can add this additional payment to the previous theoretical value of 93 cents to get a new theoretical value of 94 cents. This is similar to the dividend paid to owners of stock in a company. In fact, dividends can be an additional consideration in evaluating both stock and options on stock.

If a casino is selling roulette bets that have an expected value of 95 cents for a price of $1, does this guarantee that the casino will make a profit? It does if the casino can be certain of staying in business for the "long run" because over long periods of time the good and bad luck will tend to even out. Unfortunately, before the casino reaches the long run, it must survive the short run. It's possible that someone can walk up to the roulette wheel, make a series of bets, and have their number come up 20 times in succession. Clearly, this is very unlikely, but the laws of probability say that it could happen. If the player's good luck results in the casino going out of business, the casino will never reach the long run.

The goal of option evaluation is to determine, through the use of a theoretical pricing model, the theoretical value of an option. The trader can then make an intelligent decision whether the price of the option in the marketplace is either too low or too high and whether the theoretical edge is sufficient to justify making a trade. But determining the theoretical value is only half the problem. Because an option's theoretical value is based on the laws of probability, which are only reliable in the long run, the trader must also consider the question of risk. Even if a trader has correctly calculated an option's theoretical value, how will he control the short-term bad luck that goes with any probability calculation? We shall see that in the real world, an option's theoretical value is always open to question. For this reason, a trader's ability to manage risk is at least as important as his ability to calculate a theoretical value.

A Word on Models

What is a model? We can think of a model as a scaled-down or more easily managed representation of the real world. The model may be a physical one, such as a model airplane or architectural model, or it may be a mathematical one, such as a formula. In each case, we use the model to better understand the world around us. However, it is unwise, and sometimes dangerous, to assume that the model and the real world that it represents are identical in every way. We may have an excellent model, but it is unlikely to be an exact replica of the real world.

All models, if they are to be effective, require us to make certain prior assumptions about the real world. Mathematical models require the input of numbers that quantify these assumptions. If we feed incorrect data into a model, we can expect an incorrect representation of the real world. As every model user knows, "Garbage in, garbage out."

These general observations about models are no less true for option pricing models. An option model is only someone's idea of how an option might be evaluated under certain conditions. Because either the model itself or the data that we feed into the model might be incorrect, there is no guarantee that model-generated values will be accurate. Nor can we be sure that these values will bear any logical resemblance to actual prices in the marketplace.

A new option trader is like someone entering a dark room for the first time. Without any guidance, he may grope around, hoping that he eventually finds what he is looking for. The trader who is armed with a basic understanding of theoretical pricing models enters the same room with a candle. He can make out the general layout of the room, but the dimness of the candle prevents him from distinguishing every detail. Moreover, some of what he sees may be distorted by the flickering of the candle. In spite of these limitations, a trader is more likely to find what he is looking for with a small candle than with no illumination at all.[2]

The real problems with theoretical pricing models arise after the trader has acquired some sophistication. As he gains confidence, he may begin to increase the size of his trades. When this happens, his inability to make out every detail in the room, as well as the distortions caused by the flickering candle flame, take on increased importance. Now a misinterpretation of what he thinks he sees can lead to financial disaster because any error in judgment will be greatly magnified.

The sensible approach is to make use of a model, but with a full awareness of what it can and cannot do. Option traders will find that a theoretical pricing model is an invaluable tool to understanding the pricing of options. Because of the insights gained from a model, the great majority of successful option traders rely on some type of theoretical pricing model. However, an option trader, if he is to make the best use of a theoretical pricing model, must be aware of its

---

[2] One might also argue that a trader with a candle (i.e., theoretical pricing model) might drop the candle and burn down the entire building. Financial crises seem to occur when many traders drop their candles at the same time.

limitations as well as its strengths. Otherwise, he may be no better off than the trader groping in the dark.[3]

A Simple Approach

How might we adapt the concepts of expected value and theoretical value to the pricing of options? Consider an underlying contract that at expiration can take on one of five different prices: $80, $90, $100, $110, or $120. Assume, moreover, that each of the five prices is equally likely with 20 percent probability. The prices and probabilities are shown Figure 5-1.

What will be the expected value for this contract at expiration? Twenty percent of the time, the contract will be worth $80; 20 percent of the time, the contract will be worth $90; and so on, up to the 20 percent of the time, the contract is worth $120:

$$(20\% \times \$80) + (20\% \times \$90) + (20\% \times 100) + (20\% \times \$110)$$
$$+ (20\% \times \$120) = \$100$$

At expiration, the expected value for the contract is $100.

Now consider the expected value of a 100 call using the same underlying prices and probabilities. We can more easily see the value of the call by overlaying the parity graph for the call on our probability distribution. This has been done in Figure 5-2. If the underlying contract is at $80, $90, or $100, the call is worthless. If, however, the underlying contract is at $110 or $120, the option will be worth its intrinsic value of $10 and $20, respectively:

$$(20\% \times 0) + (20\% \times 0) + (20\% \times 0) + (20\% \times \$10) + (20\% \times \$20) = \$6$$

If we want to develop a theoretical pricing model using this approach, we might propose a series of possible prices and probabilities for the underlying contract at expiration. Then, given an exercise price, we can calculate the intrinsic value of the option at each underlying price, multiply this value by its associated probability, add up all these numbers, and thereby obtain an expected value for the option. The expected value for a call at expiration is

$$\sum_{i=1}^{n} p_i \max(S_i - X, 0)$$

where each S_i is a possible underlying price at expiration, and p_i is the probability associated with that price. The expected value for a put is

$$\sum_{i=1}^{n} p_i \max(X - S_i, 0)$$

---

[3] Some interesting discussion on the limitations of models: Fischer Black, "The Holes in Black Scholes," *Risk* 1(4):30–33, 1988; Stephen Figlewski, "What Does an Option Pricing Model Tell Us about Option Prices?" *Financial Analysts Journal*, September–October 1989, pp. 12–15; Fischer Black, "Living Up to the Model," *Risk* 3(3):11–13, 1990; and Emanuel Derman and Paul Wilmott, "The Financial Modelers' Manifesto" (January 2009), http://www.wilmott.com/blogs/paul/index.cfm/2009/1/8/Financial-Modelers-Manifesto.

Figure 5-1

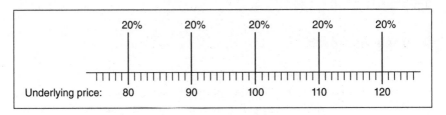

Figure 5-2

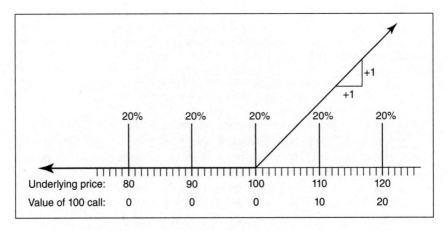

In the foregoing example, we used a simple scenario with only five possible price outcomes, each with identical probability. Obviously, this is not very realistic. What changes might we make to develop a model that more accurately reflects the real world? For one thing, we need to know the settlement procedure for the option. If the option is subject to stock-type settlement, we must pay the full price of the option. If the 100 call has an expected value of $6 at expiration, the theoretical value will be the present value of this amount. If interest rates are 12 percent annually (1 percent per month) and the option will expire in two months, the theoretical value of the option is

$$\frac{\$6.00}{1+(0.12\times2/12)} = \frac{\$6.00}{1.02} \approx \$5.88$$

What other factors might we consider? We assumed that all five price outcomes were equally likely. Is this a realistic assumption? Suppose that you were told that only two prices were possible at expiration, $110 and $250. If the current price of the underlying contract is close to $100, which do you think is more likely? Experience suggests that extreme price changes that are far away from today's price are less likely than small changes that remain close to today's price. For this reason, $110 is more likely than $250. Perhaps our probability distribution ought to reflect this by concentrating the probabilities around the current price of

Figure 5-3

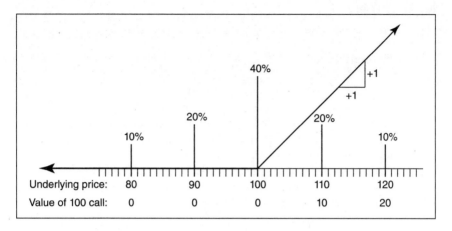

Underlying price:	80	90	100	110	120
Value of 100 call:	0	0	0	10	20

the underlying contract. One possible distribution is shown in Figure 5-3. Using these new probabilities, the expected value for the 100 call is now

$$(0\% \times 0) + (20\% \times 0) + (0\% \times 0) + (20\% \times \$10) + (10\% \times \$20) = \$4$$

If, as before, the option is subject to stock-type settlement, the theoretical value is

$$\frac{\$4.00}{1.02} \approx \$3.92$$

Note that the new probabilities did not change the expected value for the underlying contract. Because the probabilities are symmetrical around $100, the expected value for the underlying contract at expiration is still $100.

No matter how we assign probabilities, we will want to do so in such a way that the expected value for the underlying contract represents the most likely, or average, value at expiration. What is the most likely future value for the underlying contract? In fact, there is no way to know. But we might ask what the marketplace thinks the most likely value is. Recall what would happen if the theoretical forward price were different from the actual price of a forward contract in the marketplace. Everyone would execute an arbitrage by either buying or selling the forward contract and taking the opposite position in the cash market. In a sense, the marketplace must think that the forward price is the most likely future value for the underlying contract. If we assume that the underlying market is *arbitrage-free*, the expected value for the underlying contract must be equal to the forward price.

Suppose in our example that the underlying contract is a stock that is currently trading at $100 and that pays no dividend prior to expiration. The two-month forward price for the stock is

$$\$100 \times [1 + (0.12 \times 2/12)] = \$100 \times 1.02 = \$102$$

If $102 is the expected value for the stock, instead of assigning the probabilities symmetrically around $100, we may want to assign them symmetrically around $102. This distribution is shown in Figure 5-4. Now the expected value for the 100 call is

$$(10\% \times 0) + (20\% \times 0) + (40\% \times \$2) + (20\% \times \$12) + (10\% \times \$22) = \$5.40$$

and the theoretical value is

$$\frac{\$5.40}{1.02} \approx \$5.29$$

In the examples thus far, we have assumed a symmetrical probability distribution. But as long as the expected value is equal to the forward price, there is no requirement that the probabilities be assigned symmetrically. Figure 5-5 shows a distribution where the price outcomes are neither centered around the forward price nor are the probabilities symmetrical. Nonetheless, the expected value for the underlying contract is still equal to $102

$$(6\% \times 83) + (15\% \times 90) + (39\% \times \$99) + (33\% \times \$110) + (7\% \times \$123)$$
$$= 4.98 + 13.5 + 38.61 + 36.30 + 8.61 = \$102$$

Using these probabilities, the theoretical value of the 100 call is

$$\frac{(33\% \times \$10) + (7\% \times \$23)}{1.02} = \frac{3.30 + 1.61}{1.02} = \frac{4.91}{1.02} \approx \$4.81$$

The forward price of the underlying contract plays a central role in all option pricing models. For European options, the current price of the underlying contract is important only insofar as it can be turned into a forward price. Because of this, traders sometimes make the distinction between options that are at the money (the exercise price is equal to the current underlying price) and options which are *at the forward* (the exercise price is equal to the forward price at expiration). In many markets, at-the-forward options are the most actively traded, and such options are often used by traders as a benchmark for evaluating and trading other options.

Even if we assume an arbitrage-free market in the underlying contract, we still have a major hurdle to overcome. In our simplified model, we assumed that

Figure 5-4

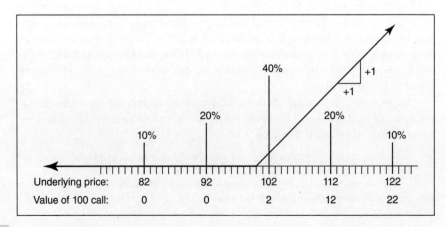

Figure 5-5

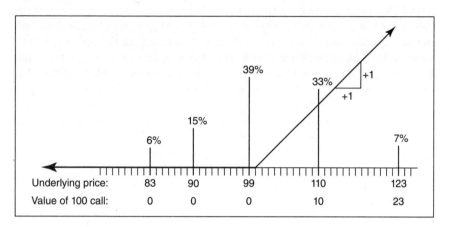

there were only five possible price outcomes. In the real world, however, there are an infinite number of possibilities. To enable our model to more closely approximate the real world, we would like to construct a probability distribution with every possible price outcome together with its associated probability. This may seem an insurmountable obstacle, but we will see in subsequent chapters how we might approximate such a probability distribution.

We can now summarize the necessary steps in developing a model:

1. Propose a series of possible prices at expiration for the underlying contract.

2. Assign a probability to each possible price with the restriction that the underlying market is arbitrage-free—the expected value for the underlying contract must be equal to the forward price.

3. From the prices and probabilities in steps 1 and 2, and from the chosen exercise price, calculate the expected value of the option.

4. Lastly, depending on the option's settlement procedure, calculate the present value of the expected value.

The Black-Scholes Model

One of the first attempts to describe traded options in detail was a pamphlet written by Charles Castelli and published in London in 1877, "The Theory of Options in Stocks and Shares."[4] This pamphlet included a description of some commonly used hedging and trading strategies such as the "call-of-more" and the "call-and-put." Today, these strategies are known as a *covered-write* and a *straddle*.

The origins of modern option pricing theory are most often ascribed to the year 1900, when French mathematician Louis Bachelier published *The Theory*

---

[4] A photocopy of the Castelli pamphlet, which is now in the public domain, is available at books.google.com.

of Speculation, the first attempt to use higher mathematics to price option contracts.[5] Although Bachelier's treatise was an interesting academic study, it resulted in little practical application because there were no organized option markets at that time. However, in 1973, concurrent with the opening of the Chicago Board Options Exchange, Fischer Black, at the time associated with the University of Chicago, and Myron Scholes, associated with the Massachusetts Institute of Technology, built on the work of Bachelier and other academics to introduce the first practical theoretical pricing model for options.[6] The *Black-Scholes model*,[7] with its relatively simple arithmetic and limited number of inputs, most of which were easily observable, proved an ideal tool for traders in the newly opened U.S. option market. Although other models have subsequently been introduced to overcome some of its original weaknesses, the Black-Scholes model remains the most widely used of all option pricing models.

In its original form, the Black-Scholes model was intended to evaluate European options (no early exercise permitted) on non-dividend-paying stocks. Shortly after its introduction, realizing that many stocks pay dividends, Black and Scholes added a dividend component. In 1976, Fischer Black made slight modifications to the model to allow for the evaluation of options on futures contracts.[8] In 1983, Mark Garman and Steven Kohlhagen of the University of California at Berkeley made additional modifications to allow for the evaluation of options on foreign currencies.[9] The futures version and the foreign-currency version are known formally as the *Black model* and the *Garman-Kohlhagen model*, respectively. However, the evaluation method in each variation, whether the original Black-Scholes model for stock options, the Black model for futures options, or the Garman-Kohlhagen model for foreign currency options, is so similar that they have all come to be known simply as the *Black-Scholes model*. The various forms of the model differ only in how they calculate the forward price of the underlying contract and the settlement procedure for the options. An option trader will simply choose the form appropriate to the options and underlying instrument in which he is interested.

Given its widespread use and its importance in the development of other pricing models, we will, for the moment, restrict ourselves to a discussion of the Black-Scholes model and its various forms. In later chapters we will consider the question of early exercise. We will also look at alternative methods for pricing options when we question some of the basic assumptions in the Black-Scholes model.

---

[5] See Louis Bachelier's *Theory of Speculation*, Mark Davis and Alison Etheridge, trans. (Princeton, NJ: Princeton University Press, 2006). A translation of Bachelier's treatise also appears in *The Random Character of Stock Market Prices*, Paul Cootner, ed. (Cambridge, MA: MIT Press, 1964).

[6] Fischer Black and Myron Scholes, "The Pricing of Options and Corporate Liabilities," *Journal of Political Economy* 81(3):637–654, 1973.

[7] Robert Merton, who, at the time, was, like Myron Scholes, associated with MIT, is also credited with some of the same work that led to the development of the original Black-Scholes model. His paper, "The Rational Theory of Option Pricing," appeared in the *Bell Journal of Economics and Management Science* 4(Spring):141–183, 1973. In recognition of Merton's contribution, the model is sometimes referred to as the *Black-Scholes-Merton model*. Scholes and Merton were awarded the Nobel Prize in Economic Sciences in 1997; Fischer Black, unfortunately, died in 1995.

[8] Fischer Black, "The Pricing of Commodity Contracts," *Journal of Financial Economics* 3:167–179, 1976.

[9] Mark B. Garman and Steven W. Kohlhagen, "Foreign Currency Option Values," *Journal of International Money and Finance* 2(3):239–253, 1983. We are speaking here of options on a physical foreign currency rather than options on a foreign-currency futures contract. The latter may be evaluated using the Black model for futures options.

The reasoning that led to the development of the Black-Scholes model is similar to the simple approach we took earlier in this chapter for evaluating options. Black and Scholes worked originally with call values, but put values can be derived in much the same way. Alternatively, we will see later that for European options there is a unique pricing relationship between an underlying contract and a call and put with the same exercise price and expiration date. This relationship will enable us to derive a put value from the companion call value or a call value from the companion put value.

To calculate an option's theoretical value using the Black-Scholes model, we need to know, at a minimum, five characteristics of the option and its underlying contract:

1. The option's exercise price

2. The time remaining to expiration

3. The current price of the underlying contract

4. The applicable interest rate over the life of the option

5. The volatility of the underlying contract

The last input, volatility, may be unfamiliar to a new trader. While we will put off a detailed discussion of this input to Chapter 6, from our previous discussion, we can reasonably infer that volatility is related to either the speed of the underlying market or the probabilities of different price outcomes.

If we know each of the required inputs, we can feed them into the theoretical pricing model and thereby generate a theoretical value (see Figure 5-6).

Black and Scholes also incorporated into their model the concept of a *riskless hedge*. For every option position, there is a theoretically equivalent position in the underlying contract such that, for small price changes in the underlying contract, the option position will gain or lose value at exactly the same rate as the underlying position. To take advantage of a theoretically mispriced option,

Figure 5-6

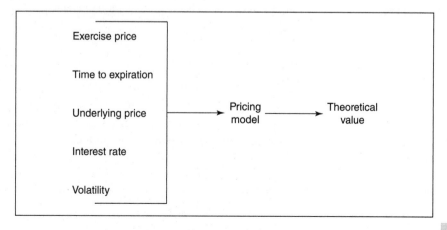

it is necessary to establish this riskless hedge by offsetting the option position with a theoretically equivalent underlying position. That is, whatever option position we take, we must take an opposing market position in the underlying contract. The correct proportion of underlying contracts needed to establish this riskless hedge is determined by the option's *hedge ratio*.

Why is it necessary to establish a riskless hedge? Recall that in our simplified approach, an option's theoretical value depended on the probability of various price outcomes for the underlying contract. As the price of the underlying contract changes, the probability of each outcome will also change. If the underlying price is currently $100 and we assign a 25 percent probability to $120, we might drop the probability for $120 to 10 percent if the price of the underlying contract falls to $90. By initially establishing a riskless hedge and then adjusting the hedge as market conditions change, we are taking into consideration these changing probabilities.

In this sense, an option can be thought of as a substitute for a position in the underlying contract. A call is a substitute for a long position; a put is a substitute for a short position. Whether the substitute position is better than an outright position in the underlying contract depends on the theoretical value of the option compared with its price in the marketplace. If a call can be purchased for less than its theoretical value or a put can be sold for more than its value, in the long run, it will be more profitable to take a long market position by purchasing calls or selling puts than by purchasing the underlying contract. In the same way, if a put can be purchased for less than its theoretical value or a call can be sold for more than its value, in the long run, it will be more profitable to take a short market position by purchasing puts or selling calls than by selling the underlying contract.

In later chapters we will discuss the concept of a riskless hedge in greater detail. For now, we simply summarize the four basic option positions, their corresponding market positions, and the appropriate hedges:

Option Position	Corresponding Market Position	Appropriate Hedge
Buy call(s)	Long	Sell underlying
Sell call(s)	Short	Buy underlying
Buy put(s)	Short	Buy underlying
Sell put(s)	Long	Sell underlying

For new traders, it may be helpful to point out that we are always doing the opposite with calls and the underlying (i.e., *buy* calls, *sell* the underlying; *sell* calls, *buy* the underlying) and doing the same with puts and the underlying (i.e., *buy* puts, *buy* the underlying; *sell* puts, *sell* the underlying). Especially with puts, more than a few new traders have initially done it backwards, buying puts and selling the underlying or selling puts and buying the underlying. This, of course, is no hedge at all.

Because the theoretical value obtained from a theoretical pricing model is no better than the inputs into the model, a few comments on each of the inputs will be worthwhile.

Exercise Price

There should never be any doubt about the exercise price of an option because it is fixed under the terms of the contract and does not vary over the life of the option.[10] A March 60 call cannot suddenly turn into a March 55 call. A September 100 put cannot turn into a September 110 put.

Time to Expiration

As with the exercise price, an option's expiration date is fixed and will not vary. A March 60 call will not suddenly turn into an April 60 call, nor will a September 100 put turn into an August 100 put. Of course, each day that passes brings us closer to expiration, so in this sense the time to expiration is constantly growing shorter. However, the expiration date, like the exercise price, is fixed by the exchange and will not change.

In financial models, one year is typically the standard unit of time. Therefore, time to expiration is entered into the Black-Scholes model as an annualized number. If we express time in terms of days, we must make the appropriate adjustment by dividing the number of days to expiration by 365. However, most option-evaluation computer programs already have this transformation incorporated into the software, so we need only enter the correct number of days remaining to expiration.

It may seem that we have a problem in deciding what number of days to enter into the model. We need the amount of time remaining to expiration for two purposes: (1) to determine the likelihood of price movement in the underlying contract and (2) to make interest calculations. For the former, we are only interested in days on which the price of the underlying contract can change. For exchange-traded contracts, this can only occur on business days. This might lead us to drop weekends and holidays from our calculations. On the other hand, for interest-rate purposes, we must include every day. If we borrow or lend money, we expect interest to accrue every day, no matter that some of those days are not business days.

However, this is not really a problem. In determining the likelihood of price movement in the underlying contract, we observe only business days because these are the only days on which price changes can occur. Then we scale these values to an annualized number before feeding it into the theoretical pricing model. The result is that we can feed into our model the actual number of days remaining to expiration, knowing that the model will interpret all inputs correctly.

Although traders typically express time to expiration in days, a trader may want to use a different measure. Especially as expiration approaches, a trader may prefer to use hours or even minutes. In theory, finer time increments should yield more accurate values. But there is a practical limitation to using very small increments of time. As time passes, the discrete increments of time we feed into a theoretical pricing model may not accurately represent the continuous passage

---

[10] An exchange may adjust the exercise price of a stock option as the result of a stock split or in the case of an extraordinary dividend. In practical terms, this is only an accounting change. The characteristics of the option contract remain essentially unchanged.

of time in the real world. Most traders have learned through experience that as expiration approaches, the use of a theoretical pricing model becomes less reliable because the inputs become less reliable. Indeed, very close to expiration, many traders stop using model-generated values altogether.

Underlying Price

Unlike the exercise price and time to expiration, the correct price of the underlying contract is not always obvious. At any one time, there is a bid price and an ask price (the *bid-ask spread*), and it may not be clear whether we ought to use one or the other of these prices or perhaps some price in between.

Consider an underlying market where the last trade price was 75.25 but that is currently displaying the following bid-ask spread:

$$75.20–75.40$$

If a trader is using a theoretical pricing model to evaluate options on this market, what price should he feed into the model? One possibility is 75.25, the last trade price. Another possibility might be 75.30, the midpoint of the bid-ask spread.

Even though we are focusing on the use of theoretical pricing models, we should emphasize that there is no law that says a trader must make any decisions based on or consistent with a theoretical pricing model. A trader can simply buy or sell options and hope that the trade turns out favorably. But a disciplined trader who uses a pricing model knows that he is required to hedge the option position by taking an opposing market position in the underlying contract. Therefore, the underlying price that he feeds into the theoretical pricing model ought to be the price at which he believes he can make the opposing trade. If the trader intends to purchase calls or sell puts, both of which are long market positions, he will hedge by selling the underlying contract. In this case, he will want to use something close to the bid price because that is the price at which he can probably sell the underlying. On the other hand, if the trader intends to sell calls or buy puts, both of which are short market positions, he will hedge by purchasing the underlying contract. Now he will want to use something close to the ask price because that is the price at which he can probably buy the underlying.

In practice, if the underlying market is very *liquid*, with a narrow bid-ask spread and many contracts available at each price, a trader who must make a quick decision may very well use a price close to the midpoint because that probably represents a reasonable estimate of where the underlying can be bought or sold. But in an *illiquid* market, with a very wide bid-ask spread and only a few contracts available at each price, the trader must give extra thought to the appropriate underlying price. In such a market, particularly if the prices are changing rapidly, it may be difficult to execute even a small order at the quoted prices.

Interest Rates

Because an option trade may result in either a cash credit or debit to a trader's account, the interest considerations resulting from this cash flow must also play a role in option evaluation. This is a function of interest rates over the life of the option.

Interest rates play two roles in the theoretical evaluation of options. First, they may affect the forward price of the underlying contract. If the underlying contract is subject to stock-type settlement, as we raise interest rates, we raise the forward price, increasing the value of calls and decreasing the value of puts. Second, interest rates may affect the present value of the option. If the option is subject to stock-type settlement, as we raise interest rates, we reduce the present value of the option. Although interest rates may affect both the forward price and the present value, in most cases, the same rate is applicable, and we need only input one interest rate into the model. If, however, different rates are applicable, as would be the case with foreign-currency options (the foreign-currency interest rate plays one role, and the domestic-currency interest rate plays a different role), the model will require the input of two interest rates. This is the case with the Garman-Kohlhagen version of the Black-Scholes model.

What interest rate should a trader use when evaluating options? Textbooks often suggest using the *risk-free rate*, the rate that applies to the most creditworthy borrower. In most markets, the government is considered the most secure borrower of funds, so the yield on a government security with a maturity equivalent to the life of the option is the general benchmark. For a 60-day option denominated in dollars, we might use the yield on a 60-day U.S. Treasury bill; for a 180-day option, we might use the yield on a 180-day U.S. Treasury bill.

In practice, no individual can borrow or lend at the same rate as the government, so it seems unrealistic to use the risk-free rate. To determine a more realistic rate, a trader might look to a freely traded market in interest-rate contracts. In this respect, traders often use either the *London Interbank Offered Rate* (LIBOR)[11] or the Eurocurrency markets to determine the applicable rate. For dollar-denominated options, Eurodollar futures traded at the Chicago Mercantile Exchange are often used to determine a benchmark interest rate.

The situation is further complicated by the fact that most traders do not borrow and lend at the same rate, so the correct interest rate will, in theory, depend on whether the trade will create a credit or a debit. In the former case, the trader will be interested in the borrowing rate; in the latter case, he will be interested in the lending rate. However, among the inputs into the model—the underlying price, time to expiration, interest rates, and volatility—interest rates tend to play the least important role. Using a rate that "makes sense" is usually a reasonable solution. Of course, for very large positions or for very long-term options, small changes in the interest rate can have a large impact. But for most traders, getting the interest rate exactly right is usually not a major consideration.

Dividends

We did not list dividends as a model input in Figure 5-5 because they are only a factor in the theoretical evaluation of stock options and then only if the stock is expected to pay a dividend over the life of the option. In order to evaluate a stock option, the model must accurately calculate the forward price for the stock.

---

[11] The *London Interbank Offered Rate* (LIBOR) is the rate paid by the London banks on dollar deposits. As such, it reflects the free-market interest rate for dollars. LIBOR is the underlying for Eurodollar futures traded at the Chicago Mercantile Exchange. The value of these contracts at maturity is determined by the average three-month LIBOR rate quoted by the largest London banks.

This requires us to estimate both the amount of the dividend and the date on which the dividend will be paid. In practice, rather than using the date of dividend payment, an option trader is likely to focus on the *ex-dividend date*, the date on which the stock is trading without the rights to the dividend. The exact dividend payment date is important in calculating the interest that can be earned on the dividend payment and thereby calculating a more accurate forward price. But for a trader ownership of the stock in order to receive the dividend is the primary consideration. A deeply in-the-money option may have many of the same characteristics as stock, but only ownership of the stock carries with it the rights to the dividend.

In the absence of other information, most traders assume that a company is likely to continue its past dividend policy. If a company has been paying a 75-cent dividend each quarter, it will probably continue to do so. However, until the company officially declares the dividend, this is not a certainty. A company may increase or reduce its dividend or omit it completely. If there is the possibility of a change in a company's dividend policy, a trader must consider its impact on option values. Additionally, if the ex-dividend date is expected just prior to expiration, a delay of several days will cause the ex-dividend date to fall after expiration. For purposes of option evaluation, this is the same as eliminating the dividend entirely. In such a situation, a trader will need to make a special effort to ascertain the exact ex-dividend date.

Volatility

Of all the inputs required for option evaluation, volatility is the most difficult for traders to understand. At the same time, volatility often plays the most important role in actual trading decisions. Changes in our assumptions about volatility can have a dramatic effect on an option's value. And the manner in which the marketplace assesses volatility can have an equally dramatic effect on an option's price. For these reasons, we will begin a detailed discussion of volatility in Chapter 6.

6

Volatility

What is volatility, and why is it so important in option evaluation? The option trader, like a trader in the underlying instrument, is interested in the direction of the market. But unlike a trader in the underlying, an option trader is also sensitive to the speed of the market. If the market for an underlying contract fails to move at a sufficient speed, options on that contract will have less value because of the reduced likelihood of the market going through an option's exercise price. In a sense, volatility is a measure of the speed of the market. Markets that move slowly are low-volatility markets; markets that move quickly are high-volatility markets.

One might guess intuitively that some markets are more volatile than others. During 2008, the price of crude oil began the year at $99 per barrel, reached a high of $144 per barrel in July, and finished the year at $45 per barrel. The price rose 58 percent and then dropped 69 percent. Yet few traders could imagine a major stock index such as the Standard and Poor's (S&P) 500 Index exhibiting similar fluctuations over a single year.

If we know whether a market will be relatively volatile or relatively quiet and can convey this information to a theoretical pricing model, any evaluation of options on that market will be more accurate than if we simply ignore volatility. Because option models are based on mathematical formulas, we will need some method of quantifying this volatility component so that we can feed it into the model in numerical form.

Random Walks and Normal Distributions

Consider for a moment the pinball maze pictured in Figure 6-1. When a ball is dropped into the maze at the top, it falls downward, pulled by gravity through a series of nails. When the ball encounters each nail, there is a 50 percent chance that the ball will move to the left and a 50 percent chance that it will move to the right. The ball then falls down a level where it encounters another nail. Finally, at the bottom of the maze, the ball falls into one of the troughs.

Figure 6-1 Random walk.

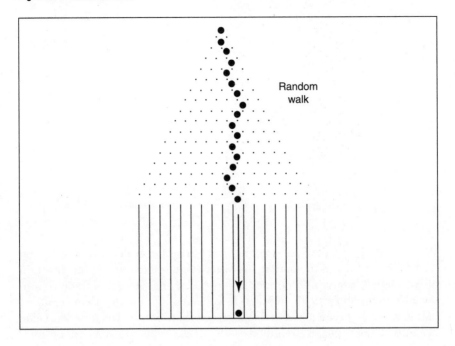

As the ball falls down through the maze, it follows a *random walk*. Once the ball enters the maze, nothing can be done to artificially alter its course, nor can one predict the path that the ball will follow through the maze.

As more balls are dropped into the maze, they might begin to form a distribution similar to that in Figure 6-2. Most of the balls tend to cluster near the center of the maze, with a decreasing number of balls ending up in troughs farther away from the center. If many balls are dropped into the maze, they will begin to form a bell-shaped or *normal distribution*.

If an infinite number of balls were dropped into the maze, the resulting distribution might be approximated by a *normal distribution curve* such as the one overlaid on the distribution in Figure 6-2. Such a curve is symmetrical (if we flip it from right to left, it looks the same), it has its peak in the center, and its tails always move down and away from the center.

Normal distribution curves are used to describe the likely outcomes of random events. For example, the curve in Figure 6-2 might also represent the results of flipping a coin 15 times. Each outcome, or trough, represents the number of heads that occur from each 15 flips. An outcome in trough 0 represents 0 heads and 15 tails; an outcome in trough 15 represents 15 heads and 0 tails. Of course, we would be surprised to flip a coin 15 times and get all heads or all tails. Assuming that the coin is perfectly balanced, some outcome in between, perhaps 8 heads and 7 tails, or 9 heads and 6 tails, seems more likely.

Suppose that we rearrange the nails in our maze so that each time a ball encounters a nail and moves either left or right, it must drop down two levels before it encounters another nail. If we drop enough balls into the maze, we may end up with a distribution similar to the curve in Figure 6-3. Because the

Figure 6-2 Normal distribution.

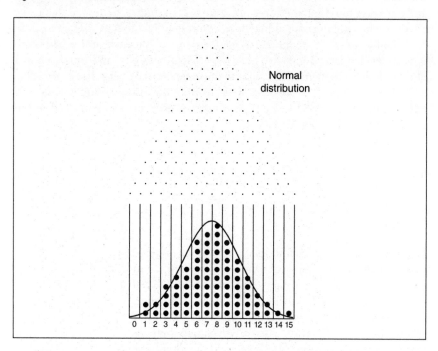

Normal distribution

0 1 2 3 4 5 6 7 8 9 10 11 12 13 14 15

Figure 6-3

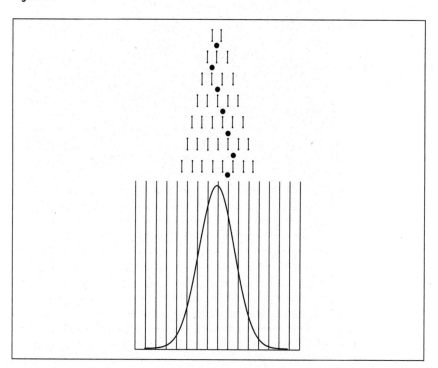

sideways movement of the balls is restricted, the curve will have a higher peak and narrower tails than the curve in Figure 6-2. In spite of its altered shape, the distribution is still normal, although one with slightly different characteristics.

Finally, we might again rearrange the nails so that each time a ball drops down a level, it must move two nails left or right before it can drop down to a new level. If we drop enough balls into the maze, we may get a distribution that resembles the curve in Figure 6-4. This distribution, although still normal, will have a much lower peak and spread out much more quickly than the distributions in either Figure 6-2 or Figure 6-3.[1]

Suppose that we now think of the ball's sideways movement as the up and down price movement of an underlying contract and the ball's downward movement as the passage of time. If the price movement of an underlying contract follows a random walk, the curves in Figures 6-2 through 6-4 might represent possible price distributions in a moderate-, low-, and high-volatility market, respectively.

Earlier in this chapter we suggested that the theoretical pricing of options begins by assigning probabilities to the various underlying prices. How should these probabilities be assigned? One possibility is to assume that, at expiration, the underlying prices are normally distributed. Given that there are many different normal distributions, how will our choice of distribution affect option evaluation?

Because all normal distributions are symmetrical, it may seem that the choice of distribution is irrelevant. Increased volatility may increase the likelihood of large upward movement, but this should be offset by the greater likelihood of large downward movement. However, there is an important distinction between

Figure 6-4

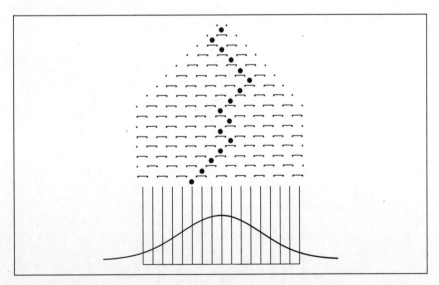

[1] The pinball maze, or *quincunx* (sometimes also called a *Galton board*), pictured in these examples is often used to demonstrate basic probability theory. Examples of a quincunx in action can be found at the following websites:

http://www.teacherlink.org/content/math/interactive/flash/quincunx/quincunx.html
http://www.mathsisfun.com/data/quincunx.html
http://www.jcu.edu/math/isep/Quincunx/Quincunx.html

Figure 6-5

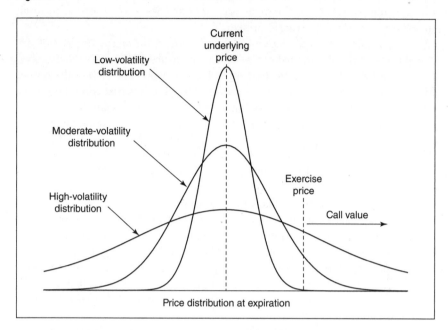

Low-volatility distribution

Current underlying price

Moderate-volatility distribution

High-volatility distribution

Exercise price

Call value

Price distribution at expiration

an option position and an underlying position. The expected value for an underlying contract depends on all possible price outcomes. The expected value for an option depends only on the outcomes that result in the option finishing in the money. Everything else is zero.

In Figure 6-5, we have three possible price distributions centered around the current price of an underlying contract. Suppose that we want to evaluate a call at a higher exercise price. The value of the call will depend on the amount of the distribution to the right of the exercise price. We can see that as we move from a low-volatility distribution, to a moderate-volatility distribution, to a high-volatility distribution, a greater portion of the possible price distribution lies to the right of the exercise price. Consequently, the option takes on an increasingly greater value.

We might also consider the value of a put at a lower exercise price. If we assume that movement is random, the same high-volatility distribution that will cause the call to take on greater value will also cause the put to take on greater value. In the case of the put, more of the distribution will lie to the left of the exercise price. Because our distributions are symmetrical, in a high-volatility market, all options, whether calls or puts, higher or lower exercise prices, take on greater value. For the same reason, in a low-volatility market, all options take on reduced values.

Mean and Standard Deviation

If we assume a normal distribution of prices, we will need a method of describing the appropriate normal distribution to the theoretical pricing model. Fortunately, all normal distributions can be fully described with two numbers—the *mean* and the *standard deviation*. If we know that a distribution is normal, and we also know the mean and standard deviation, then we know all the characteristics of the distribution.

Graphically, we can interpret the mean as the location of the peak of the distribution and the standard deviation as a measure of how fast the distribution spreads out. Distributions that spread out very quickly, such as the one in Figure 6-4, have a high standard deviation. Distributions that spread out very slowly, such as the one in Figure 6-3, have a low standard deviation.

Numerically, the mean is simply the average outcome, a concept familiar to most traders. To calculate the mean, we add up all the results and divide by the total number of occurrences. Calculation of the standard deviation is not quite so simple and will be discussed later. What is important at this point is the interpretation of these numbers, in particular, what a mean and standard deviation suggest in terms of likely price movement.

Let's go back to Figure 6-2 and consider the troughs numbered 0 to 15 at the bottom. We suggested that these numbers might represent the number of heads resulting from 15 flips of a coin. Alternatively, they might represent the number of times a ball goes to the right at each nail as it drops down through the maze. The first trough is assigned 0 because any ball that ends there must go left at every nail. The last trough is assigned 15 because any ball that ends there must go right at every nail.

Suppose that we are told that the mean and standard deviation in Figure 6-2 are 7.50 and 3.00, respectively.[2] What does this tell us about the distribution? The mean tells us the average outcome. If we add up all the outcomes and divide by the number of occurrences, the result will be 7.50. In terms of the troughs, the average result will fall halfway between troughs 7 and 8. (Of course, this is not an actual possibility. However, we noted in Chapter 5 that the average outcome does not have to be an actual possibility for any one outcome.)

The standard deviation determines not only how fast the distribution spreads out, but it also tells us something about the likelihood of a ball ending up in a specific trough or group of troughs. In particular, the standard deviation tells us the probability of a ball ending up in a trough that is a specified distance from the mean. For example, we may want to know the likelihood of a ball falling down through the maze and ending up in a trough lower than 5 or higher than 10. The answer to this question depends on the number of standard deviations the ball must move away from the mean. If we know this, we can determine the probability associated with that number of standard deviations.

The exact probability associated with any specific number of standard deviations can be found in most texts on statistics or probability. Alternatively, such probabilities can be easily calculated in most commonly used computer spreadsheet programs. For option traders, the following approximations will be useful:

±1 standard deviation takes in approximately 68.3 percent (about 2/3) of all occurrences.

---

[2] The reader who is familiar with the mean and standard deviation and who would like to check the arithmetic will find that the actual mean and standard deviation are 7.49 and 3.02. For simplicity, we have rounded these to 7.50 and 3.00.

±2 standard deviations takes in approximately 95.4 percent (about 19/20) of all occurrences.

±3 standard deviations takes in approximately 99.7 percent (about 369/370) of all occurrences.

Note that each number of standard deviations is preceded by a plus or minus sign. Because normal distributions are symmetrical, the likelihood of up movement and down movement is identical. The probability associated with each number of standard deviations is usually given as a decimal value, but a fractional approximation is often useful to traders, and this appears in parentheses.

Now let's try to answer our question about the likelihood of getting a ball in a trough lower than 5 or higher than 10. We can designate the divider between troughs 7 and 8 as the mean, 7½. If the standard deviation is 3, what troughs are within one standard deviation of the mean? One standard deviation from the mean is 7½ ± 3, or 4½ to 10½. Interpreting ½ as the divider between troughs, we can see that troughs 5 through 10 fall within 1 standard deviation of the mean. We know that one standard deviation takes in about two-thirds of all occurrences, so we can conclude that out of every three balls we drop into the maze, two should end up in troughs 5 through 10. Whatever is left over, one out of every three balls, will end up in one of the remaining troughs, 0 through 4 and 11 through 15. Hence, the answer to our original question about the likelihood of getting a ball in a trough lower than 5 or higher than 10 is about 1 chance in 3, or about 33 percent. (The exact answer is 100% − 68.3% = 31.7%.) This is shown in Figure 6-6.

Let's try another calculation, but this time we can think of the problem as a wager. Suppose that someone offers us 30 to 1 odds against dropping a ball into the maze and having it end up specifically in troughs 14 or 15. Is this bet worth making? One characteristic of standard deviations is that they are additive. In our example, if one standard deviation is 3, then two standard deviations are 6. Two standard deviations from the mean is therefore 7½ ± 6, or 1½ to 13½. We can see in Figure 6-6 that troughs 14 and 15 lie outside two standard deviations. Because the probability of getting a result within two standard deviations is approximately 19 out of 20, the probability of getting a result beyond two standard deviations is 1 chance in 20. Therefore, 30 to 1 odds may seem very favorable. Recall, however, that beyond two standard deviations also includes troughs 0 and 1. Because normal distributions are symmetrical, the chances of getting a ball specifically in troughs 14 or 15 must be half of 1 chance in 20, or about 1 chance in 40. At 30 to 1 odds, the bet must be a bad one because the odds do not sufficiently compensate us for the risk involved.

In Chapter 5, we suggested that a truly accurate theoretical pricing model would require us to assign probabilities to an infinite number of possible price outcomes for an underlying contract. Then, if we multiply each price outcome by its associated probability, we can use the results to calculate an option's theoretical value. The problem is that an infinite number of anything is not easy to work with. Fortunately, the characteristics of normal distributions are so well known that formulas have been developed that facilitate the computation of both the probabilities associated with every point along a normal distribution

Figure 6-6

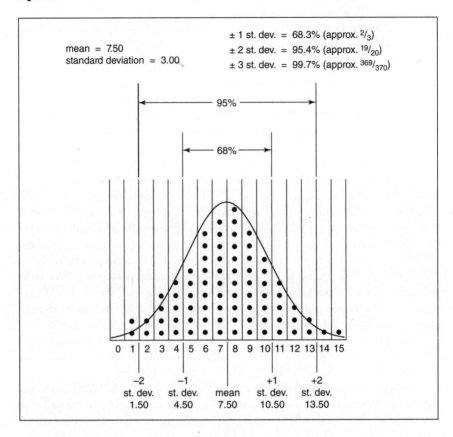

curve and the area under various portions of the curve. If we assume that prices of an underlying instrument are normally distributed, these formulas represent a unique set of tools to help us solve for an option's theoretical value.

Louis Bachelier was the first to make the assumption that the prices of an underlying contract are normally distributed. As we shall see, there are logical problems with this assumption. Consequently, over the years, the assumption has been modified to make it more consistent with real-world conditions. In its modified form, it is the basis for many theoretical pricing models, including the Black-Scholes model.

Forward Price as the Mean of a Distribution

If we decide to assign probabilities that are consistent with a normal distribution, how do we feed this distribution into a theoretical pricing model? Because all normal distributions can be described by a mean and a standard deviation, in some way we must feed these two numbers into our pricing model.

In Chapter 5, we suggested that any distribution ought to be centered around the most likely underlying price at expiration. Although we cannot know exactly what that price will be, if we assume that no arbitrage opportunity exists in the underlying contract, a logical guess is the forward price. If we make the assumption that the forward price represents the mean of a distribution, then in the long run, any trade made at the current underlying price will just break even. The various forms of the Black-Scholes model differ primarily in how they calculate the forward price. Depending on the type of underlying contract, whether a stock, a futures contract, or a foreign currency, the model takes the current underlying price, the time to expiration, interest rates, and, in the case of stocks, dividends to calculate the forward price. It then makes this the mean of the distribution.

Volatility as a Standard Deviation

In addition to the mean, to fully describe a normal distribution, we also need a standard deviation. When we input a volatility into a theoretical pricing model, we are actually feeding in a standard deviation. Volatility is just a trader's term for standard deviation. Because the Greek letter sigma (σ) is the traditional notation for standard deviation, in this text we will use the same notation for volatility.

At this point, it will help if we assign a working definition to volatility, although we will later modify this definition slightly. For the present, we will assume that the volatility we feed into a pricing model represents a one standard deviation price change, in percent, over a one-year period. For example, consider a contract with a one-year forward price of 100 and that we are told has a volatility of 20 percent. (We'll discuss later where this number might come from.) With a mean of 100 and a standard deviation of 20 percent, if we come back one year from now, there is a 68 percent probability that the contract will be trading between 80 and 120 ($100 \pm 20\%$), a 95 percent probability that the contract will be trading between 60 and 140 ($100 \pm 2 \times 20\%$), and a 99.7 percent probability that the contract will be trading between 40 and 160 ($100 \pm 3 \times 20\%$). These are the probabilities associated with one, two, and three standard deviations.

Instead of specifying the forward price, suppose that we are dealing with a stock that is currently trading at \$100 and that has the same 20 percent volatility. In order to determine the one-year probabilities, we must first determine the one-year forward price because this represents the mean of the distribution. If interest rates are 8 percent and the stock pays no dividends, the one-year forward price will be \$108. Now, a one standard deviation price change is 20% × \$108 = \$21.60. Thus, one year from now, we would expect the same stock to be trading between \$86.40 and \$129.60 (\$108 ± \$21.60) approximately 68 percent of the time, between \$64.80 and \$151.20 (\$108 ± 2 × \$21.60) approximately 95 percent of the time, and between \$43.20 and \$172.80 (\$108 ± 3 × \$21.60) approximately 99.7 percent of the time.

Returning to our contract with a forward price of 100, suppose that we come back at the end of one year and find that the contract, which we thought had a volatility of 20 percent, is trading at 35. Does this mean that the volatility of 20 percent was wrong? A price change of more than three standard deviations may be unlikely, but one should not confuse unlikely with impossible.

Flipping a perfectly balanced coin 15 times may result in 15 heads, even though the odds of this occurring are less than one chance in 32,000. If 20 percent is the right volatility, the probability that the price will fall from 100 to 35 in one year is less than one chance in 1,500. However, one chance in 1,500 is not impossible, and perhaps this was the one time in 1,500 when the price did indeed end up at 35. Of course, it is also possible that we had the wrong volatility. But we can't make that determination without looking at a large number of price changes for the contract so that we have a representative price distribution.

Scaling Volatility for Time

Like interest rates, volatility is always expressed as an annualized number. If someone says that interest rates are 6 percent, no one needs to ask whether that means 6 percent per day, 6 percent per week, or 6 percent per month. Everyone knows that it means 6 percent per year. The same is true of volatility.

We might logically ask what an annual volatility tells us about the likelihood of price changes over some shorter period of time. Although interest rates are proportional to time (we simply multiply the rate by the amount of time), volatility is proportional to the square root of time. To calculate a volatility, or standard deviation, over some period of time other than one year, we must multiply the annual volatility be the square root of time, where the time period t is expressed in years

$$\text{Volatility}_t = \text{volatility}_{annual} \times \sqrt{t}$$

Traders typically calculate volatility for an underlying contract by observing price changes at regular intervals. Let's begin by assuming that we plan to observe price changes at the end of every day. Because there are 365 days in a year, it might seem that prices can change 365 times per year. In this text, though, we are focusing primarily on exchange-traded contracts. Because most exchanges are closed on weekends and holidays, if we observe the price of an underlying contract at the end of every day, prices cannot really change 365 times per year. Depending on the exchange, there are probably somewhere between 250 and 260 trading days in a year.[3] Because we need the square root of the number of trading days, for convenience, many traders assume that there are 256 trading days in a year given that the square root of 256 is a whole number, 16. If we make this assumption, then

$$\text{Volatility}_{daily} = \text{volatility}_{annual} \times \sqrt{1/256} = \text{volatility}_{annual} \times 1/16 = \frac{\text{volatility}_{annual}}{16}$$

To approximate a daily standard deviation, we can divide the annual volatility by 16.

Returning to our contract trading at 100 with a volatility of 20 percent, what is a one standard deviation price change from one day to the next?

---

[3] As markets around the world become more integrated, and with the advent of electronic trading, it may become more difficult to determine exactly what fraction of a year one day represents. Depending on the contract and exchange, in some cases it may be sensible to look at prices every day, 365 days per year.

The answer is 20%/16 = 1¼%, so a one standard deviation daily price change is 1¼% × 100 = 1.25. We expect to see a price change of 1.25 or less approximately two trading days out of every three and a price change of 2.50 or less approximately 19 trading days out of every 20. Only one day in 20 would we expect to see a price change of more than 2.50.

We can do the same type of calculation for a weekly standard deviation. Now we must ask how many times per year prices can change if we look at prices once a week. There are no complete weeks when no trading takes place, so we must make our calculations using all 52 trading weeks in a year. Therefore,

$$\text{Volatility}_{weekly} = \text{volatility}_{annual} \times \sqrt{1/52} \approx \text{volatility}_{annual} \times 1/7.2 = \frac{\text{volatility}_{annual}}{7.2}$$

To approximate a weekly standard deviation, we can divide the annual volatility by 7.2. Dividing our annual volatility of 20 percent by the square root of 52, or approximately 7.2, we get 20%/7.2 » 2.78. For our contract trading at 100, we would expect to see a price change of 2.78 or less two weeks out of every three, a price change of 5.56 or less 19 weeks out of every 20, and only one week in 20 would we expect to see a price change of more than 5.56.

If we want to be as accurate as possible, when estimating a daily or weekly standard deviation, we ought to begin by calculating the one-day or one-week forward price. But for short periods of time, the forward price is so close to the current price that most traders assume for convenience that a one-day or one-week distribution is centered around the current price.

Suppose that a stock is trading at $45 per share and has an annual volatility of 37 percent. What is an approximate one and two standard deviation price range from one day to the next and from one week to the next? For one day, we can divide the annual volatility by 16 (the square root of 256, the number of trading days in a year)

$$\$45 \times \frac{37\%}{16} \approx \$1.04$$

A one and two standard deviation daily price range is approximately

$45 ± $1.04 ≈ $43.96 to $46.04   (one standard deviation)
$45 ± (2 × $1.04) ≈ $42.92 to $47.08   (two standard deviations)

For one week, we can divide the annual volatility by 7.2 (the square root of 52, the number of trading weeks in a year)

$$\$45 \times \frac{37\%}{7.2} = \$2.31$$

A one and two standard deviation weekly price range is approximately

$45 ± $2.31 ≈ $42.69 to $47.31   (one standard deviation)

$45 ± (2 × $2.31) ≈ $40.38 to $49.62   (two standard deviations)

When we scale volatility for time, the same probabilities still apply. Approximately 68 percent of the occurrences will fall within one standard deviation. Approximately 95 percent of the occurrences will fall within two standard deviations.

Volatility and Observed Price Changes

Why might a trader want to estimate daily or weekly price changes from an annual volatility? Volatility is the one input into a theoretical pricing model that cannot be directly observed. Yet many option strategies, if they are to be successful, require a reasonable assessment of volatility. Therefore, an option trader needs some method of determining whether his expectations about volatility are being realized in the marketplace. Unlike directional strategies, whose success or failure can be immediately observed from current prices, there is no such thing as a current volatility. A trader must usually determine for himself whether he is using a reasonable volatility input into the theoretical pricing model.

Previously, we estimated that for a $45 stock with an annual volatility of 37 percent, a one standard deviation price change is approximately $1.04. Suppose that over five days we observe the following daily settlement price changes:

+$0.98, −$0.65, −$0.70, +$0.25, −$0.85

Are these price changes consistent with a 37 percent volatility?

We expect to see a price change of more than $1.04 (one standard deviation) about one day in three. Over five days, we would expect to see at least one day, and perhaps two days, with a price change greater than one standard deviation. Yet, during this five-day period, we did not see a price change greater than $1.04 even once. What conclusions can be drawn from this? One thing seems clear: these five price changes do not appear to be consistent with a 37 percent volatility.

Before making any decisions, we ought to consider any unusual conditions that might be affecting the observed price changes. Perhaps this was a holiday week, and as such, it did not reflect normal market activity. If this is our conclusion, then 37 percent may still be a reasonable volatility estimate. On the other hand, if we can see no logical reason for the market being less volatile than predicted by a 37 percent volatility, then we may simply be using the wrong volatility. If we come to this conclusion, perhaps we ought to consider using a lower volatility that is more consistent with the observed price changes. If we continue to use a volatility that is not consistent with the actual price changes, then we have the wrong volatility. If we have the wrong volatility, we have the wrong probabilities. And if we have the wrong probabilities, we are generating incorrect theoretical values, thereby defeating the purpose of using a theoretical pricing model in the first place.

Admittedly, five days is a very small number of price changes, and it is unlikely that a trader will rely heavily on such a small sample. If we flip a coin five times and it comes up heads each time, we may not be able to draw any definitive conclusions. But if we flip the coin 50 times and it comes up heads every time, now we might conclude that there is something wrong with the coin. In the same way, most traders prefer to see larger price samplings, perhaps 20 days, or 50 days, or 100 days, before drawing any dramatic conclusions about volatility.

Exactly what volatility is associated with the five price changes in the foregoing example? Without doing some rather involved arithmetic, it is difficult to say.

(The answer is actually 27.8 percent.) However, if a trader has some idea of the price changes he expects, he can easily see that the changes over the five-day period are not consistent with a 37 percent volatility.[4]

We have used the phrase *price change* in conjunction with our volatility estimates. Exactly what do we mean by this? Do we mean the high/low during some period? Do we mean open-to-close price changes? Or is there another interpretation? Although various methods have been suggested to estimate volatility, the most common method for exchange-traded contracts has been to calculate volatility based on settlement-to-settlement price changes. Using this approach, when we say that a one standard deviation daily price change is $1.04, we mean $1.04 from one day's settlement price to the next day's settlement price. The high/low or open/close price range may have been either more or less than this amount, but it is the settlement-to-settlement price change on which we focus.[5]

A Note on Interest-Rate Products

For some interest-rate products, primarily Eurocurrency interest-rate futures, the listed contract price represents the interest rate associated with that contract, expressed as a whole number, subtracted from 100.[6] If the London Interbank Offered Rate (LIBOR), the interest paid on dollar deposits outside the United States, is 7.00 percent, the associated Eurodollar futures contract traded at the Chicago Mercantile Exchange will be trading at $100 - 7.00 = 93.00$. If Euro Interbank Offered Rate (Euribor), the interest paid on euro deposits outside the European Economic Union, is 4.50 percent, the associated Euribor futures contract traded at the London International Financial Futures Exchange will be trading at $100 - 4.50 = 95.50$. Volatility calculations for these contracts are done using the rate associated with the contract (the *rate volatility*) rather than the price of the contract (the *price volatility*).

If a Eurodollar futures contract is trading at 93.00 with a volatility of 26 percent, an approximate daily and weekly one standard deviation price change is

$$(100-93) \times \frac{26\%}{16} \approx 0.11 \quad \text{(daily standard deviation)}$$

$$(100-93) \times \frac{26\%}{7.2} \approx 0.25 \quad \text{(weekly standard deviation)}$$

---

[4] A price change greater than two standard deviations will occur about 1 time in 20. Because there are approximately 20 trading days in a month, as an additional benchmark, most traders expect to see a daily two standard deviation occurrence about once a month.

[5] Alternative methods of estimating volatility have also been proposed when trading is continuous or when there is no well-defined daily settlement price. See, for example, Michael Parkinson, "The Extreme Value Method of Estimating the Variance of the Rate of Return," *Journal of Business* 53(1):61–64, 1980; Mark B. Garman and Michael J. Klass, "On the Estimation of Security Price Volatilities from Historical Data," *Journal of Business* 53(1):67–78, 1980; and Stan Beckers, "Variance of Security Price Returns Based on High, Low, and Closing Prices," *Journal of Business* 56(1):97–112, 1983.

[6] This method of quoting Eurocurrency contracts is used so that moves in Eurocurrency contracts will tend to mimic moves in bond prices. If interest rates rise, both bond prices and Eurocurrency futures will fall; if interest rates fall, both bond prices and Eurocurrency futures will rise.

To be consistent, if we index Eurodollar futures prices from 100, we must also index exercise prices from 100. Therefore, a 93.00 exercise price in our pricing model is really a 7.00 percent (100 − 93.00) exercise price. This transformation also requires us to reverse the type of option, changing calls to puts and puts to calls. To see why, consider a 93.00 call. For this call to go into the money, the underlying contract must rise above 93.00. But this requires that interest rates fall below 7.00 percent. Therefore, a 93.00 call in listed terms is the same as a 7.00 percent put in interest-rate terms. A model that is correctly set up to evaluate options on Eurodollar or other types of indexed interest-rate contracts will make this transformation automatically. The price of the underlying contract and the exercise price are subtracted from 100, with listed calls treated as puts and listed puts treated as calls.

This type of transformation is not required for most bonds and notes. Depending on the coupon rate, the prices of these products may range freely without upper limit, often exceeding 100. Exchange-traded options on bond and note futures are therefore most often evaluated using a traditional pricing model. However, interest-rate products present other problems that may require specialized pricing models.

It is possible to take an instrument such as a bond and calculate the current yield based on its price in the marketplace. If we were to take a series of bond prices and from these calculate a series of yields, we could calculate the *yield volatility*, that is, the volatility based on the change in yield. We might then use this number to evaluate the theoretical value of an option on the bond, although to be consistent we would also have to specify the exercise price in terms of yield. Because it is possible to calculate the volatility of an interest-rate product using these two different methods, interest-rate traders usually make a distinction between yield volatility (the volatility calculated from the current yield on the instrument) and price volatility (the volatility calculated from the price of the instrument in the marketplace).

Lognormal Distributions

Thus far we have assumed that the prices of an underlying instrument are normally distributed. Is this a reasonable assumption? Beyond the question of the exact distribution of prices in the real world, the normal distribution assumption has one serious flaw. A normal distribution is symmetrical. For every possible upward move in the price of an underlying instrument, there must be the possibility of a downward move of equal magnitude. If we allow for the possibility of a $50 contract rising $75 to $125, we also must allow for the possibility of the contract dropping $75 to a price of −$25. But negative prices are clearly not possible for traditional stocks or commodities.

We have defined volatility in terms of the percent changes in the price of an underlying instrument. In this sense, an interest rate and volatility are similar in that they both represent a *rate of return*. The primary difference between interest and volatility is that interest accrues only at a positive rate, whereas volatility is a combination of positive and negative rates of return. If we invest money at a fixed interest rate, the value of the principal will always grow.

However, if we invest in an underlying instrument with a volatility other than zero, the instrument may go up or down in price, resulting in either a profit (a positive rate of return) or a loss (a negative rate of return).

A rate-of-return calculation must specify not only the rate that is being used but also the time intervals over which the returns are calculated. Suppose that we invest $1,000 for one year at an annual interest rate of 12 percent. How much will we have at the end of one year? The answer depends on how the 12 percent interest on our investment is paid out.

Rate of Payment	Value after One Year	Total Yield
12% once a year	$1,120.00	12.00%
6% twice a year	$1,123.60	12.36%
3% every three months	$1,125.51	12.55%
1% every month	$1,126.83	12.68%
12%/52 every week	$1,127.34	12.73%
12%/365 every day	$1,127.47	12.75%
12% compounded continuously	$1,127.50	12.75%

As interest is paid more frequently, even though it is paid at the same rate of 12 percent per year, the total yield on the investment increases. The yield is greatest when interest is paid continuously. In this case, it is just as if interest is paid at every possible moment in time.

Although less common, we can do the same type of calculation using a negative interest rate. For example, suppose that we make a bad investment of $1,000 and lose money at a rate of 12 percent annually (interest rate = −12%). How much will we have at the end of a year? The answer, again, depends on the frequency at which our losses accrue.

Rate of Payment	Value after One Year	Total Yield
−12% once a year	$880.00	−12.00%
−6% twice a year	$883.60	−11.64%
−3% every three months	$885.29	−11.47%
−1% every month	$886.38	−11.36%
−12%/52 every week	$886.80	−11.32%
−12%/365 every day	$886.90	−11.31%
−12% compounded continuously	$886.92	−11.31%

In the case of a negative interest rate, as losses are compounded more frequently, even though at the same rate of −12 percent per year, the smaller the total loss, and consequently, the smaller the negative yield.

In the same way that interest can be compounded at different intervals, volatility can also be compounded at different intervals. The Black-Scholes model is a *continuous-time* model. The model assumes that volatility is compounded continuously, just as if the price changes in the underlying contract, either up or down, are taking place continuously but at an annual rate corresponding to the volatility associated with the contract. When the percent price changes are normally distributed, the continuous compounding of these price changes will result in a *lognormal distribution* of prices at expiration. Such a distribution is shown in Figure 6-7. The entire distribution is skewed toward the upside because upside price changes (a positive rate of return) will be greater, in absolute terms, than downside price changes (a negative rate of return). In our interest-rate example, a continuously compounded rate of return of +12 percent yields a profit of $127.50 after one year, whereas a continuously compounded rate of return of −12 percent yields a loss of only $113.08. If the 12 percent is a volatility, then a one standard deviation upward price change at the end of one year is +$127.50, whereas a one standard deviation downward price change is −$113.08. Even though the rate of return is a constant 12 percent, the continuous compounding of 12 percent yields different upward and downward moves.

Note also the location of the mean of the distributions in Figure 6-7. The mean can be thought of as the "balance point" of the distribution. For a normal distribution, the peak of the distribution, or *mode*, and the mean have the same location, exactly in the middle of the distribution. But in a lognormal distribution the right tail, which is open-ended, is longer than the left tail, which is bounded by zero. Because there is more "weight" to the right of the peak, the mean of the lognormal distribution must be located to the right of the peak.

Figure 6-7

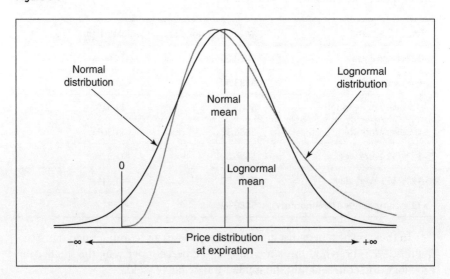

OPTION VOLATILITY AND PRICING

Continuous rates of return can be calculated using the exponential function,[7] denoted by either $\exp(x)$ or e^x. In the preceding examples,

$$\$1,000 \times e^{0.12} = \$1,127.50 \quad \text{and} \quad \$1,000 \times e^{-0.12} = \$886.92$$

No matter how large the negative interest rate, continuous compounding precludes the possibility of an investment falling below zero because it is impossible to lose more than 100 percent of an investment. Consequently, in a lognormal distribution, the value of the underlying instrument is bounded by zero on the downside. Clearly, this is a more realistic representation of the real world than a normal distribution.

We can see the effect of using a lognormal distribution rather than a normal distribution by considering the value of a 90 put and 110 call with a forward price of 100 for the underlying contract with six months to expiration and a volatility of 30 percent

Contract	Value if Price Distribution Is Normal	Value if Price Distribution Is Lognormal
90 put	4.37	4.00
110 call	4.37	4.74

Under a normal distribution assumption, both the call and put have exactly the same value because they are both 10 percent out of the money. But under the lognormal distribution assumption in the Black-Scholes model, the 110 call will always have a greater value than the 90 put. The value of the 110 call can potentially appreciate without limit because the price of the underlying contract has no limit on the upside. The 90 put, however, can only rise to a maximum value of 90 because the price of the underlying contract can never fall below zero.

Of course, the values in the preceding example are true only in theory. There is no law that prevents the 90 put from trading at a price greater than the 110 call. Indeed, such price relationships occur in many markets for a variety of reasons that we will discuss later. However, one possible explanation is that the marketplace disagrees with the assumptions on which the model is based. Perhaps the marketplace believes that a lognormal distribution is not an accurate representation of possible prices. And perhaps the marketplace is right!

Interpreting Volatility Data

When traders discuss volatility, even experienced traders may find that they are not always talking about the same thing. When a trader says that the volatility is 25 percent, this statement may take on a variety of meanings. We can avoid confusion in subsequent discussions if we define some of the different ways in

---

[7] It will be useful for an option trader to become familiar with the characteristics of the exponential function [e^x or $\exp(x)$] and its inverse, the logarithmic function [$\ln(x)$]. These can be found in any algebra or finance text.

which traders refer to volatility. We can begin by dividing volatility into two categories—*realized volatility,* which we associate with an underlying contract, and *implied volatility*, which we associate with options.

Realized Volatility

The realized volatility is the annualized standard deviation of percent price changes of an underlying contract over some period of time.[8] When we calculate realized volatility, we must specify both the interval at which we are measuring the price changes and the number of intervals to be used in the calculations. For example, we might talk about the 50-day volatility of an underlying contract. Or we might talk about the 52-week volatility of a contract. In the former case, we are calculating the volatility from the daily price changes over a 50-day period.[9] In the latter case, we are calculating the volatility from the weekly price changes over a 52-week period.

On a graph of realized volatility, each point represents the volatility over a specified period using price changes over a specified interval. If we graph the 50-day volatility of a contract, each point on the graph represents the annualized standard deviation of the daily price changes over the previous 50 days. If we graph the 52-week volatility, each point on the graph represents the annualized standard deviation of the weekly price changes over the previous 52 weeks.

Traders may also refer to realized volatility in the future (*future realized volatility*) and realized volatility in the past (*historical realized volatility*). The future realized volatility is what every trader would like to know—the volatility that best describes the future distribution of price changes for an underlying contract. In theory, it is the future realized volatility over the life of the option that we need to input into a theoretical pricing model. If a trader knows the future realized volatility, he knows the right "odds." When he feeds this number into a theoretical pricing model, he can generate accurate theoretical values because he has the right probabilities. Like the casino, he may lose in the short run because of bad luck, but in the long run, with the probabilities in his favor, the trader can be reasonably certain of making a profit.

Clearly, no one knows what the future holds. However, if a trader intends to use a theoretical pricing model, he must try to make an estimate of future realized volatility. In option evaluation, as in other disciplines, a good starting point is historical data. What typically has been the historical realized volatility of a contract? If, over the past 10 years, the volatility of a contract has never been less than 10 percent nor more than 30 percent, a guess for the future volatility of either 5 or 40 percent hardly makes sense. This does not mean that either of these extremes is impossible. But based on past performance, and in the absence of any extraordinary circumstances, a guess within the historical limits of 10 and 30 percent is probably more realistic than a guess outside these limits. Of course,

---

[8] In order to turn price changes into continuously compounded returns, volatility is most often calculated using logarithmic price changes—the natural logarithm of the current price divided by the previous price. In most cases, there is little practical difference between the percent price changes and logarithmic price changes.

[9] For exchange-traded contracts, volatility calculations using daily intervals typically include only business days because these are the only days on which prices can actually change. If there are five trading days per week, a 50-day volatility covers a period of approximately 10 weeks.

10 to 30 percent is still a very wide range. But at least the historical data offers a starting point. Additional information may help to further narrow the estimate.

As option traders have come to appreciate the importance of volatility as an input into a pricing model, volatility forecasting models have been developed in an attempt to more accurately predict future realized volatility. If a trader has access to a volatility *forecast* that he believes is reliable, he will want to use this forecast to make a better decision as to the future realized volatility. We will put off a discussion of possible forecasting methods until later chapters.

When we calculate volatility over a given period of time, we still have a choice of the time intervals over which to measure the price changes in the underlying contract. A trader might consider whether the choice of intervals, even if the intervals cover the same time period, might affect the results. For example, we might look at the 250-day volatility, the 52-week volatility, and the 12-month volatility of a contract. All volatilities cover approximately one year, but one is calculated from daily price changes, one from weekly price changes, and one from monthly price changes.

For most underlying contracts, the interval that is chosen does not seem to greatly affect the result. It is possible that a contract will make large daily moves yet finish the week unchanged. However, this is by far the exception. A contract that is volatile from day to day is likely to be equally volatile from week to week or month to month. Figure 6-8 shows the 250-day realized volatility of the S&P 500 Index from 2003 through 2012, with the volatility calculated from price changes at three different intervals: daily, weekly, and every four weeks. The graphs are not identical, but they do seem to have similar characteristics. There is no clear evidence that using one interval rather than another results in consistently higher or lower volatility.

Figure 6-8 S&P 500 Index 250-day historical volatility.

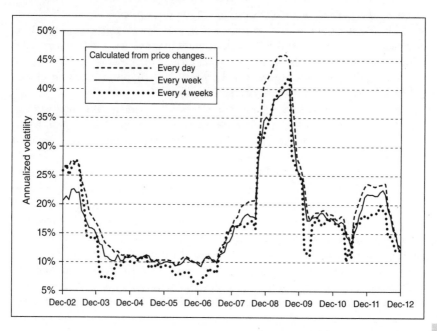

Implied Volatility

Unlike realized volatility, which is calculated from price changes in the underlying contract, implied volatility is derived from the price of an option in the marketplace. In a sense, the implied volatility represents the marketplace's consensus of what the future realized volatility of the underlying contract will be over the life of the option.

Consider a three-month 105 call on a stock that pays no dividend. If we are interested in purchasing this call, we might use a pricing model to determine the option's theoretical value. For simplicity, let's assume that the option is European (no early exercise) and that we will use the Black-Scholes model. In addition to the exercise price, time to expiration, and type, we also need the price of the stock, an interest rate, and a volatility. Suppose that the current stock price is 98.50, the three-month interest rate is 6.00 percent, and our best estimate of volatility over the next three months is 25 percent. When we feed this data into our model, we find that the option has a theoretical value of 2.94. However, when we check the price of the option in the marketplace, we find that the 105 call is trading very actively at a price of 3.60. How can we account for the fact that we think the option is worth 2.94, but the rest of the world seems to think that it's worth 3.60?

This is not an easy question to answer because there are many forces at work in the marketplace that cannot be easily identified or quantified. But one way we might try to answer the question is by making the assumption that everyone trading the option is using the same theoretical pricing model. If we make this assumption, the cause of the discrepancy must be a difference of opinion about one or more of the inputs into the model. Which inputs are the most likely cause?

It's unlikely to be either the time to expiration or the exercise price because these inputs are fixed in the option contract. What about the underlying price of 98.50? Perhaps we incorrectly estimated the stock price due to the width of the bid-ask spread. However, for most actively traded underlying contracts, it is unlikely that the spread will be wide enough to cause a discrepancy of 0.66 in the value of the option. In order to yield a value of 3.60 for the 105 call, we would actually have to raise the stock price to 100.16, and this is almost certainly well outside the bid-ask spread for the stock.

Perhaps our problem is the interest rate of 6.00 percent. But interest rates are usually the least important of the inputs into a theoretical pricing model. In fact, we would have to make a huge change in the interest-rate input, from 6.00 to 13.30 percent, to yield a theoretical value of 3.60.

This leaves us with one likely cause for the discrepancy—the volatility. In a sense, the marketplace seems be using a volatility that is different from 25 percent. To determine what volatility the marketplace is using, we can ask the following question: if we hold all other inputs constant (i.e., time to expiration, exercise price, underlying price, and interest rates), what volatility must we feed into our model to yield a theoretical value equal to the price of the option in the marketplace? In our example, we want to know what volatility will yield a value of 3.60 for the 105 call. Clearly, the volatility has to be higher than 25 percent, so we might begin to raise the volatility input into our model.

Figure 6-9

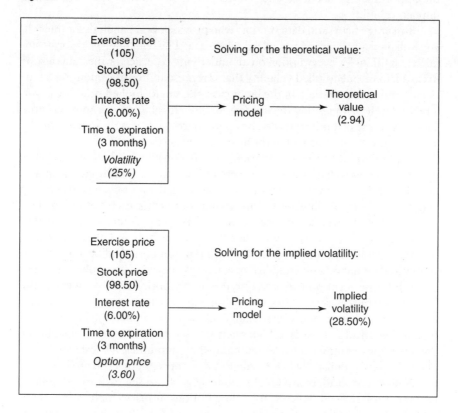

If we do, we find that at a volatility of 28.50 percent, the 105 call has a theoretical value of 3.60. The implied volatility of the 105 call—the volatility being implied to the underlying contract through the pricing of the option in the marketplace—is 28.50 percent.

When we solve for the implied volatility of an option, we are assuming that the theoretical value (the option's price), as well as all other inputs except volatility, are known. In effect, we are running the theoretical pricing model backwards to solve for the unknown volatility. In practice, this is easier said than done because most theoretical pricing models do not work in reverse. However, there are a number of relatively simple algorithms that can quickly solve for the implied volatility when all other inputs are known.

Implied volatility depends not only on the inputs into the theoretical pricing model but also on the theoretical pricing model being used. For some options, different models can yield significantly different implied volatilities. Problems can also arise when the inputs are not contemporaneous. If an option has not traded for some time and market conditions have changed, using an outdated option price will result in a misleading or inaccurate implied volatility. Suppose in our example that the price of 3.60 for the 105 call reflected the last trade, but that trade took place two hours ago when the underlying stock price was actually 99.25. At a stock price of 99.25, the implied volatility of the option, at a price of 3.60, is actually 26.95 percent. This underscores the importance of accurate and contemporaneous inputs when calculating implied volatilities.

Brokerage firms and data vendors who provide option analysis for their clients will typically include implied volatility data. The data may incorporate implied volatilities for every option on an underlying contract, or the data may be in the form of one implied volatility that is representative of options on a particular underlying market. In the latter case, the single implied volatility is usually the result of weighting the individual implied volatilities by some criteria, such as volume of options traded or open interest, or, as is most common, by assigning the greatest weight to the at-the-money options.

Implied volatility in the marketplace is constantly changing because option prices, as well as other market conditions, are constantly changing. It is as if the marketplace were continuously polling all the participants to come up with a consensus volatility for the underlying contract for each expiration. This is not a poll in the true sense because the traders do not confer with each other and then vote on the correct volatility. However, as bids and offers are made, the price at which an option is trading will represent an equilibrium between supply and demand. This equilibrium can be expressed as an implied volatility.

While the term *premium* really refers to an option's price, because the implied volatility is derived from an option's price, traders sometimes use premium and implied volatility interchangeably. If the current implied volatility is high by historical standards or high relative to the recent historical volatility of the underlying contract, a trader might say that premium levels are high; if implied volatility is unusually low, he might say that premium levels are low.

New option traders are taught, quite sensibly, to sell overpriced options and buy underpriced options. By selling options at prices higher than theoretical value or buying options at prices lower than theoretical value, a trader creates a positive theoretical edge. But how should a trader determine the degree to which an option is overpriced or underpriced? This sounds like an easy question to answer. Isn't the amount of the mispricing equal to the difference between the option's price and its value? The question arises because there is more than one way to measure this difference. Returning to our example of the 105 call, we might say that with a theoretical value of 2.94 and a price of 3.60, the 105 call is 0.66 overpriced. But in volatility terms the option is 3.50 volatility points overpriced because its theoretical value is based on a volatility of 25 percent (our volatility estimate), while its price is based on a volatility of 28.50 percent (the implied volatility). Given the unusual characteristics of options, it is often more useful for a trader to consider an option's price in terms of implied volatility rather than total points.

Implied volatility is often used by traders to compare the relative pricing of options. In our example, the 105 call is trading at 3.60 with an implied volatility of 28.50 percent. Suppose that a 100 call under the same conditions is trading at 5.40. In total points, the 100 call is clearly more expensive than the 105 call (5.40 versus 3.60). But if, at a price of 5.40, the 100 call has an implied volatility of 27.51 percent, most traders will conclude that in theoretical terms the 100 call is almost a full percentage point less expensive (27.51 percent versus 28.50 percent) than the 105 call. Traders, in fact, talk about implied volatility as if it were the price of an option. A trader who buys the 100 call at a price of 5.40 might say that she bought the call at 27.51 percent. A trader who sells the 105 call at a price of 3.60 might say that he sold the call at 28.50 percent. Of course, options are really bought and sold in the appropriate currency. But from an option trader's point of view the implied volatility is often a more useful expression of an option's price than its actual price in currency units.

Even if the implied volatility of the 100 call is 27.51 percent and the implied volatility of the 105 call is 28.50 percent, this does not necessarily mean that a trader ought to buy the 100 call and sell the 105 call. A trader also will need to consider what will happen if his estimate of volatility turns out to be incorrect. If the future realized volatility over the life of the options turns out to be 25 percent, both the 100 call and the 105 call are overpriced, and the sale of either option should, in theory, result in a profit. But what will happen if the trader's volatility estimate is wrong, and the future realized volatility turns out to be 32 percent? Now the sale of either option will result in a loss. The consequences of being wrong about volatility are an important consideration, and this is something we will look at more closely in subsequent chapters. However, in the absence of other considerations, the lower implied volatility of the 100 call suggests that it is likely to be the better value.

Although option traders may at times refer to any of the various interpretations of volatility, two of these stand out in importance—the future realized volatility and the implied volatility. The future realized volatility of an underlying contract determines the *value* of options on that contract. The implied volatility is a reflection of an option's *price*. These two numbers, value and price, are what all traders, not just option traders, are concerned with. If a contract has a high value and a low price, a trader will want to be a buyer. If a contract has a low value and a high price, a trader will want to be a seller. For an option trader, this usually means comparing the expected future realized volatility with the implied volatility. If implied volatility is low with respect to the expected future volatility, a trader will prefer to buy options; if implied volatility is high, a trader will prefer to sell options. Of course, future volatility is an unknown, so a trader will look at historical and, if available, forecast volatility to help in making an intelligent guess about the future. In the final analysis, though, it is the future realized volatility that determines an option's value.

A commonly used analogy to help new traders better understand the role of volatility is to think of volatility as being similar to the weather. Suppose that a trader living in Chicago gets up on a July morning and must decide what clothes to wear that day. Will he consider putting on a heavy winter coat? This is probably not a logical choice because he knows that *historically* it is not sufficiently cold in Chicago in July to warrant wearing a winter coat. Next, he might turn on the radio or television to listen to the weather *forecast*. The forecaster is predicting clear skies with very warm temperatures close to 90°F (32°C). Based on this information, the trader has decided that he will wear a short-sleeve shirt and does not need a sweater or jacket. And he certainly won't need an umbrella. However, just to be sure, he decides to look out the window to see what the people passing in the street are wearing. To his surprise, everyone is wearing a coat and carrying an umbrella. Through their choice of clothing, the people outside are *implying* different weather than the forecast. Given the conflicting information, what clothes should the trader wear? He must make some decision, but whom should he believe, the weather forecaster or the people in the street? There can be no certain answer because the trader will not know the *future* weather until the end of the day. Much will depend on the trader's knowledge of local conditions. Perhaps the trader lives in an area far removed from where the weather forecaster is located. Then he must give added weight to local conditions.

The decision on what clothes to wear, like every trading decision, depends on a great many factors. Not only must the decision be made on the basis of the best available information, but the decision must also be made with consideration for the possibility of error. What are the benefits of being right? What are the consequences of being wrong? If a trader fails to take an umbrella and it rains, this may be of little consequence if the bus picks him up right outside his residence and drops him off right outside his place of work. On the other hand, if he must walk several blocks in the rain, he might become sick and have to miss several days of work. The choices are never easy, and one can only hope to make the decision that will turn out best in the long run.

Changing our assumptions about volatility can often have a dramatic effect on the value of an option. Figure 6-10 shows the prices, theoretical values, and implied volatilities for several gold options on July 31, 2012. Figure 6-11 focuses specifically on how these values change as we increase volatility from 14 to 18 percent. Looking for the moment at call values, although all the options increase in value, the 1600 call, the at-the-money option, increases the most, rising from 41.65 to 51.60, a total of 9.95. At the same time, the 1800 call shows the greatest increase in percent terms. Its value more than triples from 0.78 to 3.05, a total increase of 291 percent. These are important principles to which we will return later but that are worth stating now:

1. In total points, a change in volatility will have a greater effect on an at-the-money option than on an equivalent in-the-money or out-of-the-money option.

2. In percent terms, a change in volatility will have a greater effect on an out-of-the-money option than on an equivalent in-the-money or at-the-money option.

These same principles apply to puts as well as calls. The 1600 put increases the most in total points, rising from 29.26 to 39.21, a total of 9.95. The 1400 put increases the most in percent terms, from 0.13 to 0.89, or 585 percent.

No matter how one measures change, in-the-money options tend to be the least sensitive to changes in volatility. As an option moves deeply into the money, it becomes more sensitive to changes in the underlying price and less sensitive to changes in volatility. Because it is often volatility characteristics that investors and traders are looking for when they go into an options market, it should not come as a surprise that most of the trading volume in option markets is concentrated in at-the-money and out-of-the-money options, the options that are most sensitive to changes in volatility.

Figure 6-10 Gold eight-week (40 trading days) historical volatility.

July 31, 2012
October gold futures = 1612.4
Time to October expiration = 8 weeks (56 days)
Interest rate = 0.50%*

Exercise Price	Settlement Price	Implied Volatility	Theoretical Value If Volatility Is ...		
			Volatility = 14%	Volatility = 18%	Volatility = 22%
October calls					
1400	215.2	22.36%	212.37	213.13	214.98
1500	122.5	19.01%	116.05	121.01	127.34
1600	50.8	17.68%	41.65	51.6	61.57
1700	16.1	18.42%	8.08	15.28	23.49
1800	5.3	20.46%	0.78	3.05	7
October puts					
1400	2.9	22.26%	0.13	0.89	2.74
1500	10.2	19.02%	3.74	8.7	15.02
1600	38.4	17.68%	29.26	39.21	49.18
1700	103.7	18.45%	95.61	102.82	111.03
1800	192.8	20.50%	188.23	190.51	194.46

*The prices in Figures 6-10 and 6-12 occurred during a period of unusually low interest rates.

In Figures 6-12 and 6-13, we can see that the same principles apply to longer-term options. The at-the-money options (the December 1600 call and put) change most in total points, whereas the out-of-the-money options (the December 1800 call and 1400 put) change most in percent terms. As we would expect, the December option values are greater than the October option values with the same exercise price. But look at the magnitude of the changes as we change volatility. For the same exercise price, in total points, the December (long-term) options always change more than the October (short-term) options. This leads to a third principle of option evaluation:

3. A change in volatility will have a greater effect on a long-term option than an equivalent short-term option.

The reader may have noticed several interesting points in the foregoing figures. First, although implied volatilities may vary across exercise prices, calls and puts with the same exercise price and that expire at the same time have very similar implied volatilities. Second, when we change volatility, calls and

Figure 6-11

July 31, 2012 October gold futures = 1612.4 Time to October expiration = 8 weeks (56 days) Interest rate = 0.50%				
Exercise Price	Volatility = 14%	Volatility = 18%	Net Change in Value	Percent Change in Value
October calls				
1400	212.37	213.13	0.76	<1%
1500	116.05	121.01	4.96	4.00%
1600	41.65	51.6	9.95	24.00%
1700	8.08	15.28	7.2	89.00%
1800	0.78	3.05	2.27	291.00%
October puts				
1400	0.13	0.89	0.76	585.00%
1500	3.74	8.7	4.96	133.00%
1600	29.26	39.21	9.95	34.00%
1700	95.61	102.82	7.21	8.00%
1800	188.23	190.51	2.28	1.00%

puts with the same exercise price and time to expiration change by approximately the same amount. These characteristics are the result of an important relationship[10] between calls and puts at the same exercise price, a relationship that we will examine in more detail in Chapter 15.

Finally, we might ask how much the volatility of gold can change over an eight-week period? Is a 4 percentage point change a real possibility? In fact, from Figure 6-14, the eight-week historical volatility for the 3½ years leading up to July 2012, we can see that such changes are not at all uncommon.

Given its importance, it is not surprising that serious option traders spend a considerable amount of time thinking about volatility. From the historical, forecast, and implied volatility, a trader must try to make an intelligent decision about future volatility. From this, he will try to choose option strategies that will be profitable when he is right but that will not result in a serious loss when he is wrong. Because of the difficulty in predicting volatility, a trader must always look for strategies that will leave the greatest margin for error. No trader will survive very long pursuing strategies based on a future volatility estimate of 20 percent if such a strategy results in a significant

---

[10] Some readers may already be familiar with this relationship—*put-call parity*.

Figure 6-12

July 31, 2012
December gold futures = 1614.6
Time to December expiration = 17 weeks (119 days)
Interest rate = 0.50%

Exercise Price	Settlement Price	Implied Volatility	Theoretical Value If Volatility Is ...		
			Volatility = 14%	Volatility = 18%	Volatility = 22%
December calls					
1400	226.3	22.00%	216.03	220.06	226.3
1500	142.7	20.17%	126.41	136.59	148.05
1600	78.8	19.51%	58.78	73.31	87.86
1700	40	19.93%	20.71	33.52	47.1
1800	20.4	21.07%	5.44	13.03	22.84
December puts					
1400	11.9	21.92%	1.78	5.81	12.04
1500	28.2	20.14%	12	22.18	33.64
1600	64.2	19.50%	44.2	58.74	73.25
1700	125.3	19.94%	105.98	118.79	132.36
1800	205.5	21.07%	190.54	198.13	207.94

loss when volatility actually turns out to be 18 or 22 percent. Given the shifts that occur in volatility, a 2 percentage point margin for error may be no margin for error at all.

We have not yet concluded our discussion of volatility. But before continuing, it will be useful to look at option characteristics, trading strategies, and risk considerations. We will then be in a better position to examine volatility in greater detail.

Figure 6-13

July 31, 2012 December gold futures = 1614.6 Time to December expiration = 17 weeks (119 days) Interest rate = 0.50%				
Exercise Price	Volatility = 14%	Volatility = 18%	Net Change in Value	Percent Change in Value
December calls				
1400	216.03	220.06	4.03	2%
1500	126.41	136.59	10.18	8%
1600	58.78	73.31	14.53	25%
1700	20.71	33.52	12.81	62%
1800	5.44	13.03	7.59	140%
December puts				
1400	1.78	5.81	4.03	226%
1500	12.00	22.18	10.18	85%
1600	44.20	58.74	14.54	33%
1700	105.98	118.79	12.81	12%
1800	190.54	198.13	7.59	4%

Figure 6-14 Gold eight-week (40 trading days) historical volatility.

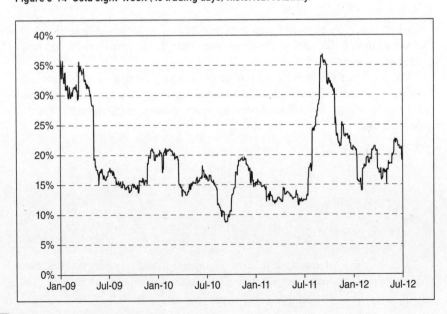

7

Risk Measurement I

Every trader who enters the marketplace must balance two opposing considerations—reward and risk. A trader hopes that his analysis of market conditions is correct and that this will lead to profitable trading strategies. But no sensible trader can afford to ignore the possibility of error. If he is wrong and market conditions change in a way that adversely affects his position, how badly might the trader be hurt? A trader who fails to consider the risks associated with his position is certain to have a short and unhappy career.

A trader who purchases stock or a futures contract is concerned almost exclusively with the direction in which the market moves. If the trader has a long position, he is at risk from a declining market; if he has a short position, he is at risk from a rising market. Unfortunately, the risks with which an option trader must deal are not so simple. A wide variety of forces can affect an option's value. If a trader uses a theoretical pricing model to evaluate options, any of the inputs into the model can represent a risk because there is always a chance that the inputs have been estimated incorrectly. Even if the inputs are correct under current market conditions, over time, conditions may change in a way that will adversely affect the value of his option position. Because of the many forces affecting an option's value, prices can change in ways that may surprise even experienced traders. Because decisions often must be made quickly, and sometimes without the aid of a computer, much of an option trader's education focuses on understanding the risks associated with an option position and how changing market conditions are likely to change the value of the position.

Let's begin by summarizing some basic risk characteristics of options, as shown in Figure 7-1. The general effect on option values of changes in the underlying price, volatility, and time to expiration are well defined regardless of the type of option. But the effect of changing interest rates may vary depending on the underlying contract and settlement procedure.

A change in interest rates can affect options in two ways. First, it may change the forward price of the underlying contract. Second, it may change the present value of the option. In stock option markets, rising interest rates will increase the forward price, causing call values to rise and put values to fall. At the same time, higher interest rates will reduce the present value of both

Figure 7-1 Effect of changing market conditions on option values.

If....	Call values will....	Put values will....
The price of the underlying contract rises	rise	fall
The price of the underlying contract falls	fall	rise
Volatility rises	rise	rise
Volatility falls	fall	fall
Time passes	fall*	fall*

*In some unusual cases it may be possible for the value of an option to rise as time passes, even if all other market conditions are unchanged. The circumstances which can cause this will be discussed later.

calls and puts. Put values clearly will fall because both results have the effect of reducing put values. For calls, though, the results have opposing effects. The higher forward price will cause the call to increase in value, but the higher interest rate will reduce the present value of the call. Because the price of a stock is always greater than the price of an option, the increase in the forward price will always have a greater effect than the reduced present value. Consequently, call options on stocks will rise in value as interest rates rise and fall as interest rates fall. Put options on stocks will do just the opposite, falling in value as interest rates rise and rising in value as interest rates fall.

The value of a stock option will also depend on whether a trader has a long or short stock position. If a trader's option position also includes a short stock position, he is effectively reducing the interest rate by the borrowing costs required to sell the stock short (see the section "Short Sales" in Chapter 2). This will reduce the forward price, thereby lowering the value of calls and raising the value of puts. As a consequence, the trader who is carrying a short stock position ought to be willing to sell calls at a lower price or buy puts at a higher price. If the trader either sells calls or buys puts, he will hedge by purchasing stock, which will offset his short stock position.

The fact that option values depend on whether the trader hedges with long stock or short stock presents a complication that most traders would prefer to avoid. This leads to a useful rule for stock option traders:

Whenever possible a trader should avoid a short stock position.

As a corollary, many active option traders prefer to carry some long stock as part of their position. Then, if the trader must sell stock to hedge a position, he will be able to sell the stock long rather than short. The trader need not worry about using a different interest rate because any long stock transaction is always subject to the long, or ordinary, interest rate. Nor will he have to worry about any regulatory restrictions on the short sale of stock.

Although stock options are always assumed to be subject to stock-type settlement, with immediate cash payment for the option, the settlement procedure for options on futures contracts may vary depending on the exchange. In the United States, options on futures are subject to stock-type settlement, while outside the United States, options on futures are usually subject to futures-type settlement. In the latter case, no money changes hands when either the option or the underlying futures contract is traded. Consequently, interest rates become irrelevant—neither the forward price nor the present value is affected. Options on futures that are subject to futures-type settlement are therefore insensitive to changes in interest rates. If, however, options on futures are subject to stock-type settlement, increasing interest rates will leave the forward price unchanged but will reduce the option's present value. As a result, both call and put values will decline. The effect, however, is usually small because the value of the option, unless it is very deeply in the money, is small relative to the value of the underlying contract. Futures options are therefore much less sensitive to changes in interest rates than options on stocks.

We also might consider the case of foreign-currency options.[1] Here the situation is more complex because the value of the option is affected by two interest rates—a domestic rate and a foreign rate. Going back to the forward pricing relationships in Chapter 2, where S is the spot exchange rate, we can see that the forward price for a foreign currency will fall if we increase the foreign rate (the denominator becomes larger) and rise if we reduce the foreign rate (the denominator becomes smaller)

$$F = S \times \frac{1 + r_d \times t}{1 + r_f \times t}$$

This means that call values will fall and put values will rise as we increase the foreign rate.

We can also see that the forward price for a currency will rise if we increase the domestic rate (the numerator becomes larger) and fall if we reduce the domestic rate (the numerator becomes smaller). But for options that are subject to stock-type settlement, an increase in the domestic rate will also reduce the present value of the option. As with stock options, the increase in the forward price will tend to dominate. Therefore, as we increase the domestic rate, call values will rise and put values will fall. The effects of changing interest rates are summarized in Figures 7-2 and 7-3.

If we are evaluating options on stock and the stock is expected to pay a dividend over the life of the option, a change in the dividend will also affect the value of the option because it will change the forward price of the stock. Increasing the dividend will reduce the forward price, causing call values to fall and put values to rise. Reducing the dividend will increase the forward price, causing call values to rise and put values to fall.

Even if we are familiar with the general effects of changing market conditions on option values, we still need to determine the magnitude of the risk. If market conditions change, will the change in option values be large or small, representing either a major or minor risk, or something in between? Fortunately, in addition to the theoretical value, pricing models generate a variety of other numbers that enable us to determine both the direction and magnitude of the change. These numbers, known variously as the *Greeks* (because they are commonly abbreviated with Greek letters), the *risk measures*, or (for the mathematically inclined)

---

[1] We are referring here to options on the actual foreign currency rather than options on foreign-currency futures. In the latter case, the characteristics are the same as for any other futures option.

Figure 7-2 Effect of changing interest rates on option values.

	If domestic rates rise	If domestic rates fall	If foreign rates rise	If foreign rates fall
stock option calls will	rise	fall	not applicable	not applicable
stock option puts will	fall	rise	not applicable	not applicable
futures option calls (stock-type settlement)	fall	fall	not applicable	not applicable
futures option puts (stock-type settlement)	fall	fall	not applicable	not applicable
futures option calls (futures-type settlement)	no effect	no effect	not applicable	not applicable
futures option puts (futures-type settlement)	no effect	no effect	not applicable	not applicable
foreign currency option calls	rise	fall	fall	rise
foreign currency option puts	fall	rise	rise	fall

Figure 7-3 Effect of changing dividends on stock option values.

	If the dividend is raised	If the dividend is cut
stock option calls will	fall	rise
stock option puts will	rise	fall

the *partial derivatives*, will not answer all our questions concerning changing market conditions, but they are an important starting point in analyzing the risks associated with both simple and complex option positions.

The Delta

The *delta* (Δ) is a measure of an option's risk with respect to the direction of movement in the underlying contract. A positive delta indicates a desire for upward movement; a negative delta indicates a desire for downward movement. The delta has several different interpretations, any of which may be useful to a trader depending on the types of strategies being executed.

Rate of Change

At expiration, an option is worth exactly its intrinsic value. Prior to expiration, however, the theoretical value of an option is a curve that will approach intrinsic value as the option goes very deeply into the money or very far out of the money. This is shown in Figure 7-4. As the underlying price rises, the slope of the graph approaches +1; as the underlying price falls, the slope of the graph approaches zero. The delta of the call at any given underlying price is the slope of the graph—the rate of change in the option's value with respect to movement in the underlying contract.

Assuming that all other market conditions remain unchanged, a call option can never gain or lose value more quickly than the underlying contract, nor can it move in the opposite direction of the underlying market. The delta of a call must therefore have an upper bound of 1.00 if the call is very deeply in the money and a lower bound of 0 if the call is very far out of the money. Most calls will have deltas somewhere between 0 and 1.00, changing value more slowly than changes in the price of the underlying contract. A call with a delta of 0.25 will change its value at 25 percent of the rate of change in the price of the underlying contract. If the underlying rises (falls) 1.00, the option can be expected to rise (fall) 0.25. A call with a delta of 0.75 will change its value at 75 percent of the rate of change in the price of the underlying contract. If the underlying rises (falls) 0.60, the option can be expected to gain (lose) 0.45 in value. A call with a delta close to 0.50 will rise or fall in value at just about half the rate of change in the price of the underlying contract.

Puts have characteristics similar to calls except that put values move in the opposite direction of the underlying market. In Figure 7-5, we can see that when the underlying price rises, puts lose value; when the underlying price falls, puts gain value. For this reason, puts always have negative deltas, ranging from 0 for far out-of-the-money puts to −1.00 for deeply in-the-money puts. As with call deltas, put deltas measure the rate of change in the put's value with respect to a change in the price of the underlying, but the negative sign indicates that the change will be in the opposite direction of the underlying contract.

Figure 7-4 Theoretical value of a call.

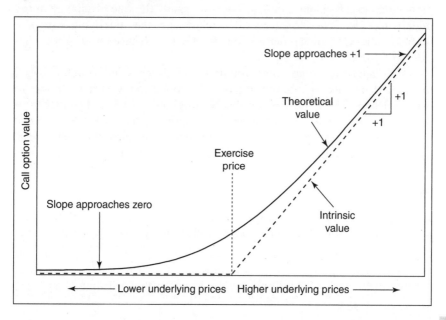

Figure 7-5 Theoretical value of a put.

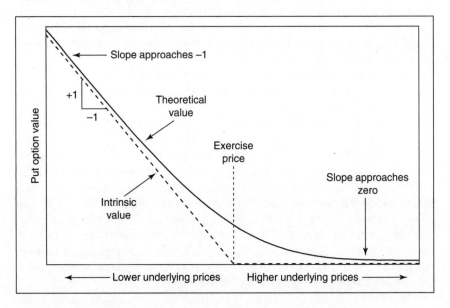

A put with a delta of −0.10 will change its value at 10 percent of the rate of change in the price of the underlying contract, but in the opposite direction. If the underlying moves up (down) 0.50, the put can be expected to lose (gain) 0.05 in value. A put with a delta of −0.50 will change its value at approximately half the rate of the underlying, but in the opposite direction.

An option position is often combined with a position in the underlying contract. To determine the total risk of a combined position, we will need to assign a delta value to the underlying contract. Logically, a position in the underlying contract will gain or lose value at exactly the rate of change in the underlying price. Therefore, regardless of whether the underlying is stock, a futures contract, or some other instrument, the underlying contract always has a delta of 1.00.

Although delta values range from 0 to 1.00 for calls and from 0 to −1.00 for puts, it has become common practice among many option traders to express delta values as a whole number by dropping the decimal point, a convention that we will follow in this text.[2] Using this format, the delta of a call will fall within the range of 0 to 100, and the delta of a put within the range of −100 to 0. An underlying contract will always have a delta of 100.

Hedge Ratio

In Chapter 5, we introduced the concept of a *riskless*, or *neutral*, hedge, a position that, within a small price range, will neither gain nor lose value as the

---

[2] This convention originated in the U.S. stock option market, where it became common for stock option traders to equate one delta with one share of stock. Because the underlying contract consisted of 100 shares, traders assigned a delta of 100 to the underlying contract. Many futures option traders also express the delta using this whole-number format.

price of the underlying contract moves up or down. We can determine the proper number of underlying contracts to option contracts required for such a hedge by dividing 100 (the delta of the underlying contract) by the option's delta. For a call option with a delta of 50, the proper hedge ratio is 100/50, or 2/1. For every two options purchased (sold), we need to sell (buy) one underlying contract to establish a neutral hedge. A call option with a delta of 40 requires the sale (purchase) of two underlying contracts for every five options purchased (sold) because 100/40 = 5/2.

The hedge ratio interpretation also applies to puts, except that when we buy puts, we need to buy the underlying contract, and when we sell puts, we need to sell the underlying contract. A put with a delta of –75 will require the purchase (sale) of three underlying contracts for each four puts purchased (sold) because 100/–75 = 4/–3.

A position is neutrally hedged, or *delta neutral*, if the total of all the deltas that make up the position add up to 0. If we buy two calls with a delta of 50 each and sell one underlying contract, the total delta position is

$$\begin{array}{r} +2 \times 50 \\ \underline{-1 \times 100} \\ 0 \end{array}$$

If we sell four puts with a delta of –75 each and sell three underlying contracts, the total delta position is

$$\begin{array}{r} +4 \times -75 \\ \underline{-3 \times 100} \\ 0 \end{array}$$

Both positions are delta neutral.[3]

A position that is delta neutral has no particular preference for either upward or downward movement in the price of the underlying contract. Although a trader may take whatever delta position he feels is appropriate, either bullish (delta positive) or bearish (delta negative), we will see in Chapter 8 that a trader who is trying to capture the theoretical value of an option must start with and maintain a delta-neutral position over the entire life of an option.

Theoretical or Equivalent Underlying Position

Many option traders come to the option market after trading in the underlying contract. Futures option traders often start their careers by trading futures; stock option traders often start by trading stock. If a trader has become accustomed to evaluating his risk in terms of the number of underlying contracts bought or sold (either futures contracts or shares of stock), he can use the delta to equate the directional risk of an option position with a position of similar size in the underlying market.

Because an underlying contract always has a delta of 100, in terms of directional risk, each 100 deltas in an option position is theoretically equivalent

---

[3] It is customary to indicate the purchase of a contract or contracts with a plus sign (a long contract position) and the sale of a contract or contracts with a negative sign (a short contract position).

to one underlying contract. A trader who owns an option with a delta of 50 is long, or controls, approximately half of an underlying contract. If he owns 10 such contracts, he is long 500 deltas or, in equivalent terms, five underlying contracts. If the underlying is a futures contract, the trader is theoretically long five such contracts. If the underlying is a stock contract consisting of 100 shares of stock, he is theoretically long 500 shares of stock. The trader has a similar theoretical position if he sells 20 puts with a delta of –25 each because –20 × –25 = +500.

It is important to emphasize the theoretical aspect of the delta interpretation as an equivalent to an underlying position. An option is not simply a surrogate for an underlying position. An actual underlying position is almost exclusively sensitive to directional moves in the underlying market. An option position, while sensitive to directional moves, is also sensitive to other changes in market conditions. An option trader who looks only at his delta position may be ignoring other factors that could have a far greater impact on his position. The delta represents an equivalent underlying position only under very narrowly defined market conditions.

Which interpretation—rate of change in the theoretical value, the hedge ratio, or the equivalent underlying position—should a trader use? That depends on how the trader intends to use the delta. A trader who has a delta position of +500 knows that he has a position that is similar to being long five underlying contracts (the equivalent-underlying-position interpretation). If he is a disciplined theoretical trader striving to maintain a delta-neutral position, he must sell five underlying contracts (the hedge-ratio interpretation). And finally, if he is bullish and maintains his current delta position of +500, the value of his position will change at approximately five times, or 500 percent, of the rate of change in the price of the underlying contract (the rate-of-change interpretation). If the price of the underlying contract rises by 2.00, the trader's position should gain approximately 10.00. If the price of the underlying contract falls by 1.25, the trader's position should lose approximately 6.25. Mathematically, all these interpretations are the same. A trader will choose a delta interpretation that is consistent with his approach to trading.

Probability

There is one other interpretation of the delta that is perhaps of less practical use, but is still worth mentioning. If we ignore the sign of the delta (positive for calls, negative for puts), the delta is approximately equal to the probability that the option will finish in the money. A call with a delta of 25 or a put with a delta of –25 has approximately a 25 percent chance of finishing in the money. A call with a delta of 75 or a put with a delta of –75 has approximately a 75 percent chance of finishing in the money. As an option's delta moves closer to 100, or –100 for puts, the option becomes more and more likely to finish in the money. As the delta moves closer to 0, the option becomes less and less likely to finish in the money. This also explains why at-the-money options tend to have deltas close to 50. If we assume that price changes are random, there is half a chance that the market will rise (the option goes into the money) and half a chance that the market will fall (the option goes out of the money).[4]

Of course, the delta is only an approximation of the probability because interest considerations and, in the case of stock options, dividends may distort this interpretation. Moreover, most option strategies depend not only on whether an option finishes in the money but also by how much. If a trader sells an option with a delta of 10 in the belief that the option will expire worthless nine times out of 10, he may indeed be correct. But, if on the tenth time he loses an amount greater than the total premium he took in the nine times the option expired worthless, the trade will result in a negative expected return. To trade options intelligently, we need to consider not only how often a strategy wins or loses but also how much it wins or loses. Every experienced trader is willing to accept several small losses if he can occasionally offset these with one big win that more than offsets the losses. In the same way, no experienced trader will want to pursue a strategy that leads to multiple small profits but occasionally results in a disastrous loss.[5]

The Gamma

Figure 7-6 shows call and put delta values using the whole-number format. Even though deltas range from 0 to 100 for calls and from −100 to 0 for puts, the graphs are not straight lines. As the underlying price rises or falls, the slope of the graph changes, approaching 0 at both extremes. If this were not true, the delta values of calls could fall below 0 or rise above 100, and the delta values of puts could fall below −100 or rise above 0. The slope appears to be greatest when the underlying price is close to the option's exercise price.

The *gamma* (Γ), sometimes referred to as the option's *curvature*, is the rate of change in the delta as the underlying price changes. The gamma is usually expressed in deltas gained or lost per one-point change in the underlying, with the delta increasing by the amount of the gamma when the underlying rises and falling by the amount of the gamma when the underlying falls. If an option has a gamma of 5, for each point rise (fall) in the price of the underlying, the option will gain (lose) 5 deltas.[6] If the option initially has a delta of 25 and the underlying moves up (down) one full point, the new delta of the option will be 30 (20). If the underlying moves up (down) another point, the new delta will be 35 (15).[7]

From Figure 7-6, we can see that the delta graphs of both calls and puts have essentially the same shape and that the graphs always have a positive slope.

---

[4] Because option values are based on the forward price of the underlying contract, it is actually the at-the-forward option that tends to have a delta closest to 50. This is one reason why options that are seemingly out of the money can have deltas greater than 50. With a stock at 100, one year to expiration, and an interest rate of 10 percent, the forward price for the stock is 110. Under these conditions, the 110 call will have a delta close to 50, while the 105 call will have a delta greater than 50.

[5] In fact, the delta is only an approximation of the probability that an option will finish in the money. We will see later that the Black-Scholes model generates a number that more precisely reflects this probability.

[6] In fact, the delta is only an approximation of the probability that an option will finish in the money. We will see later that the Black-Scholes model generates a number that more precisely reflects this probability.

[7] For simplicity, we assume here that the gamma is constant. In reality, the gamma, like all risk measures, will change as market conditions change.

Figure 7-6 Delta values.

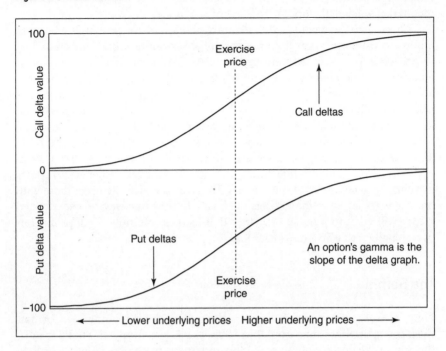

This suggests that calls and puts with the same exercise price and time to expiration have the same gamma values and that these values are always positive. This may seem strange to a new trader who, because of the delta, tends to associate positive numbers with calls and negative numbers with puts. But regardless of whether we are working with calls or puts, we always add the gamma to the old delta as the underlying price rises and subtract the gamma from the old delta as the underlying price falls. When a trader is long options, whether calls or puts, he has a long gamma position.

For example, consider both an at-the-money call with a delta of 50 and an at-the-money put with a delta of −50. How will the delta change as the underlying price changes if both options have gamma values of 5? If the underlying price rises one full point, we add the gamma of 5 to the call delta of 50 to get the new delta of 55. To get the new put delta if the underlying contract rises one point, we also *add* the gamma of 5 to the put delta of −50 to get the new delta of −45. This is intuitively logical—as the underlying price rises, at-the-money calls move into the money and at-the-money puts move out of the money. If the underlying contract falls one full point, in both cases we *subtract* the gamma, resulting in a call delta of 50 − 5 = 45 and a put delta of −50 − 5 = −55. Now the call is moving out of the money and the put is moving into the money.

Because all options individually have positive gamma values, we can create a positive gamma position by buying options, either calls or puts, and a negative gamma position by selling options. For a complex position consisting of many different options, we use the same interpretation of the gamma as we do for individual options, adding the gamma to the old delta as the underlying contract rises and subtracting the gamma as the market falls. A positive gamma position will gain deltas as the market rises (we are adding a positive number) and lose deltas as the market falls (we are subtracting a positive number). A negative gamma position will behave in just the opposite way, losing deltas as the market rises (we are adding a *negative* number) and gaining deltas as the market falls (we are subtracting a *negative* number). Moreover, the rate of change in the delta will be determined by the size of the gamma position. New traders are often advised to avoid large gamma positions, particularly negative ones, because of the speed with which the directional risk, as reflected by the delta, can change.

While the delta is a measure of how an option's value will change if the underlying price changes, it is important to remember that it represents an instantaneous measure. It is only valid for very small price changes. If the underlying makes a sizable move, any estimate of the option's new value using a constant delta will become less and less reliable. We can, however, improve this estimate if we also take into consideration the gamma.

Suppose that at price S_1 a call has a theoretical value C, a delta Δ, and a gamma Γ. If the price of the underlying changes from S_1 to S_2, what should be the new value of the option? One approach might be to simply multiply the change in price, $S_2 - S_1$, by the delta and add it to the original value C

$$C + [\Delta \times (S_1 - S_2)]$$

But this assumes that the delta is constant, which it is not. As the underlying price moves from S_1 to S_2, the delta of the option is also changing. When the underlying price reaches S_2, the new delta of the option will be

$$\Delta + (S_1 - S_2) \times \Gamma$$

Which delta should we use for our calculation, the original delta (Δ) or the new delta $[\Delta + (S_1 - S_2) \times \Gamma]$? Rather than use either of these delta values, we might logically use the average delta over the price range $S_1 - S_2$

$$\text{Average delta} = [\Delta + \Delta + (S_1 - S_2) \times \Gamma]/2 = \Delta + (S_1 - S_2) \times \Gamma/2$$

This is not a precise solution because the gamma also changes as the underlying price changes, but it will yield a better estimate than using a constant delta. Using the average delta, the new value of the option should be approximately[8]

$$C + (S_1 - S_2) \times [\Delta + (S_1 - S_2) \times \Gamma/2] = C + [(S_1 - S_2) \times \Delta] + [(S_1 - S_2)^2 \times \Gamma/2]$$

This approach applies equally well to puts, as long as we remember that a put will have a negative delta.

For example, suppose that at an underlying price of 97.50, a call option has a theoretical value of 3.65, a delta of 40, and a gamma of 2.5. If the underlying contract rises to 101.50, what should be the option's new value?

At the new underlying price of 101.50, the delta of the option is

$$40 + 4 \times 2.5 = 50$$

---

[8] When using the delta to estimate the change in an option's value, we need to remember that it is really a percent value, or a value between 0 and 1.00.

The average delta as the underlying price rises from 97.50 to 101.50 is

$$(40 + 50)/2 = 45$$

Using the average delta, the new option value is approximately

$$3.65 + (4.00 \times 0.45) = 5.45$$

The Theta

An option's value is made up of intrinsic value and time value. As time passes, the time-value portion gradually disappears until, at expiration, the option is worth exactly its intrinsic value. This can be seen in Figures 7-7 and 7-8.

The *theta* (Θ), or *time decay*, is the rate at which an option loses value as time passes, assuming that all other market conditions remain unchanged. It is usually expressed as value lost per one day's passage of time. An option with a theta of 0.05 will lose 0.05 in value for each day that passes with no movement in the underlying contract. If its theoretical value today is 4.00, one day later it will be worth 3.95. Two days later it will be worth 3.90.

Almost all options lose value as time passes. For this reason, it is common to express the theta as a negative number, a convention that we will follow in this text. An option with a theta of −0.05 will lose 0.05 for each day that passes with no changes in any other market conditions.

We will look at theta in greater detail in Chapter 9. For now, there is one important characteristic of theta that is worth mentioning: if an option is exactly at

Figure 7-7 Theoretical value of a call as time passes.

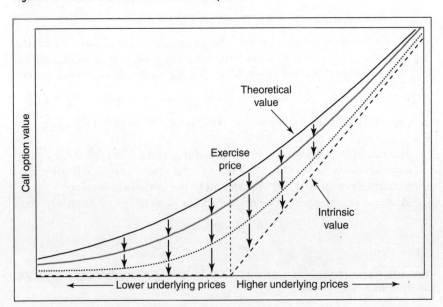

Figure 7-8 Theoretical value of a put as time passes.

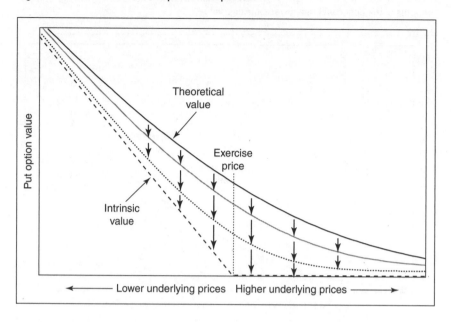

the money as time passes, the theta of the option increases. With three months remaining to expiration, an at-the-money option may have a theta of –0.03. However, with three weeks to expiration, the same option, if it is still at the money, may have a theta of –0.06. And with three days to expiration, the option may have a theta of –0.16. The theta becomes increasingly large as expiration approaches.

Is it ever possible for an option to have a positive theta such that if nothing changes, the option will be worth more tomorrow than it is today? In fact, this can happen because of the depressing effect of interest rates. Consider a 60 call on an underlying contract that is currently trading at 100. How much might this call be worth if we know that at expiration the underlying contract will still be at 100? At expiration, the option will be worth 40, its intrinsic value. However, if the option is subject to stock-type settlement, today it will only be worth the present value of 40, perhaps 39. If the underlying price remains at 100, as time passes, the value of the option must rise from 39 (its value today) to 40 (its intrinsic value at expiration). The option in effect has negative time value and therefore a positive theta. It will be worth slightly more as each day passes. This is shown in Figure 7-9.

Instances of negative time value and, consequently, positive theta are relatively rare. At a minimum, the option must be subject to stock-type settlement, it must be deeply in the money, and it must also be European with no possibility of early exercise. If the option were American, everyone would exercise it today in order to earn interest on the intrinsic value. We will discuss this situation in greater detail when we take a closer look at early exercise of American options.

Figure 7-9 If an option has negative time value, its theta will be positive; as time passes, the value of the option will rise toward intrinsic value.

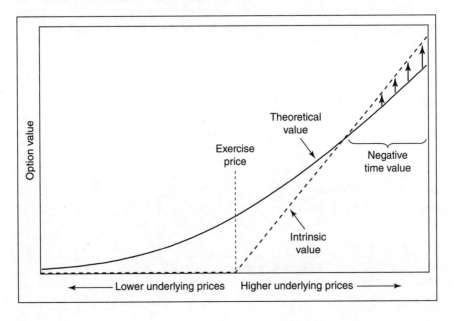

The Vega

Just as option values are sensitive to changes in the underlying price (delta) and to the passage of time (theta), they are also sensitive to changes in volatility. This is shown in Figures 7-10 and 7-11. Although the terms *delta*, *gamma*, and *theta* are used by all option traders, there is no one generally accepted term for the sensitivity of an option's theoretical value to a change in volatility. The most commonly used term in the trading community is *vega*, and this is the term that will be used in this text. But this is by no means universal. Because vega is not a Greek letter, a common alternative in academic literature, where Greek letters are preferred, is *kappa* (K).[9]

The vega of an option is usually expressed as the change in theoretical value for each one percentage point change in volatility. Because all options gain value with rising volatility, the vega for both calls and puts is positive. If an option has a vega of 0.15, for each percentage point increase (decrease) in volatility, the option will gain (lose) 0.15 in theoretical value. If the option has a theoretical value of 3.25 at a volatility of 20 percent, then it will have a theoretical value of 3.40 at a volatility of 21 percent and a theoretical value of 3.10 at a volatility of 19 percent.

---

[9] Traders tend to prefer the term vega because it starts with a v and is therefore a convenient reminder that it is associated with volatility. Vega is sometimes abbreviated with the Greek letter nu (ν) because in written form it is similar to a *v*.

Figure 7-10 Theoretical value of a call with changing volatility.

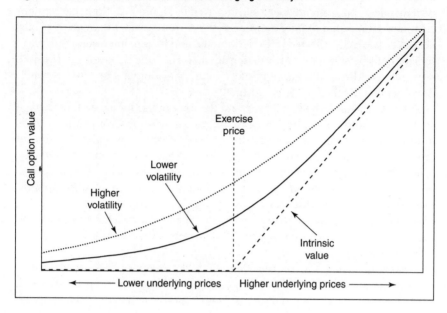

Figure 7-11 Theoretical value of a put with changing volatility.

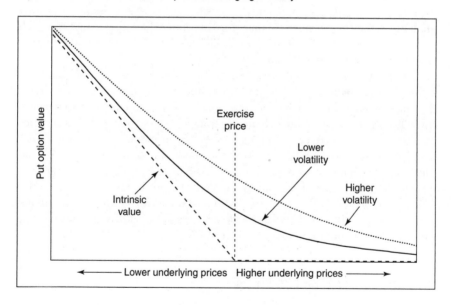

The Rho

The sensitivity of an option's theoretical value to a change in interest rates is given by its *rho* (**P**), usually expressed as the change in theoretical value for each one percentage point change in interest rates. Unlike the other sensitivities, one cannot generalize about the rho because its characteristics depend on the type of underlying instrument and the settlement procedure for the options. The general effects have already been summarized in Figure 7-2. Note that foreign-currency options that require delivery of the currency rather than delivery of a futures contract are affected by both domestic and foreign interest rates. Hence, such options have two interest-rate sensitivities, rho_1 (the domestic interest-rate sensitivity) and rho_2 (the foreign interest-rate sensitivity). The latter is sometimes denoted by the Greek letter phi (Φ).

If both the underlying contract and the options are subject to futures-type settlement, the rho must be 0 because no cash flow results from either a trade in the underlying contract or a trade in the options. When options on futures are subject to stock-type settlement, the rho associated with both calls and puts is negative. An increase in interest rates will decrease the value of such options because it raises the cost of carrying the options. In the case of stock options, calls will have positive rho values (an increase in interest rates will make calls a more desirable alternative to buying the stock) and puts will have negative rho values (an increase in interest rates will make puts a less desirable alternative to selling the stock).

Although changes in interest rates can affect an option's theoretical value, the interest rate is usually the least important of the inputs into a pricing model. For this reason, the rho is usually considered less critical than the delta, gamma, theta, or vega. Indeed, few individual traders worry about the rho. However, a firm or trader who has a very large option position should at least be aware of the interest-rate risk associated with the position. As with any risk, if it becomes too large, it may be necessary to take steps to reduce the risk. Because of its relatively minor importance, in most examples, we will disregard the rho in analyzing option strategies and managing risk.

We know that the delta of an underlying contract is always 100, but what is the gamma, theta, vega, and rho of an underlying contract? The gamma is the rate of change in the delta with respect to movement in the underlying contract. But the delta of an underlying contract is always 100 regardless of price changes. Therefore, the gamma must be 0. An underlying contract does not decay, so its theta must also be 0. Nor is the underlying contract subject to volatility considerations, so its vega must be 0. And finally, changes in interest rates do not affect the value of an underlying contract, so the rho must also be 0.[10] The only risk measure we associate with an underlying contract is the delta; everything else is 0. The signs of the risk measures for an underlying contract, for calls, and for puts are summarized in Figure 7-12.

Interpreting the Risk Measures

If a trader has a position consisting of only a small number of options, it is probably not necessary to do a detailed risk analysis. In all likelihood, the trader already has a fairly clear picture of the potential risks and rewards associated

---

[10] A trader might argue that if interest rates rise or fall, it may change the forward price, which can, in turn, affect option values. But, from an option trader's point of view, the value of an underlying contract is not directly affected by changes in interest rates.

Figure 7-12

If you are ...	Your delta position is	Your gamma position is	Your theta position is	Your vega position is	Your rho position is
Long the underlying contract	+	0	0	0	0
Short the underlying contract	+	0	0	0	0
Long calls	+	+	−	+	+ (on stock) − (on futures)*
Short calls	−	−	+	−	− (on stock) + (on futures)*
Long puts	−	+	−	+	− (on stock) − (on futures)*
Short puts	+	−	+	−	− (on stock) + (on futures)*

*This applies when options on futures are subject to stock-type settlement.
If options on futures are subject to futures-type settlement, the effective rho is zero.

with the position. However, if the position becomes more complex, with options at different expiration dates over a wide range of exercise prices, it may not be immediately apparent what risks the trader has taken on. A good starting point in analyzing the risk of a position is to consider the risk measures associated with the position.

Figure 7-13 shows a theoretical evaluation for a hypothetical series of options on stock, where the underlying contract is 100 shares. Figure 7-14 shows several different positions with the total delta, gamma, theta, vega, and rho for each position. We will assume that each position was initiated at the quoted prices.

First, note that all risk measures are additive. To determine the total risk measure for a position, we multiply each risk measure by the number of contracts (using a plus sign for a purchase and a minus sign for a sale), and add everything up.

Let's consider the risk of Position 1 in Figure 7-14. Before doing this, however, we might ask a more fundamental question: why might someone take such a position in the first place? Like every trader, an option trader wants to make trades that result in a profit. To have the best chance of achieving this goal, an option trader will try to create positions with a positive theoretical edge, either buying options at prices less than theoretical value and/or selling options at prices greater than theoretical value. Although this is not a guarantee that the position will show a profit, by creating a positive theoretical edge, the trader, like a casino, has the laws of probability working in his favor. Therefore, a trader should first consider whether a position has a positive theoretical edge.

In Position 1, we sold 10 June 95 calls at a price of 8.55, but the theoretical value of the options was 8.33, so the sale created a theoretical edge of

Figure 7-13

Stock price = 99.50	Time to June expiration = 91 days				
Volatility = 25%	Expected dividend = 0		Interest rate = 6.00%		

June Calls

Exercise Price	Call Price	Theoretical Value	Delta	Gamma	Theta	Vega	Rho
90	12.30	11.96	84	2.0	−0.029	0.122	0.178
95	8.55	8.33	71	2.8	−0.034	0.170	0.155
100	5.55	5.44	56	3.2	−0.035	0.196	0.124
105	3.15	3.32	40	3.1	−0.032	0.192	0.091
110	1.80	1.90	27	2.6	−0.027	0.163	0.062

June Puts

Exercise Price	Put Price	Theoretical Value	Delta	Gamma	Theta	Vega	Rho
90	1.45	1.12	−16	2.0	−0.014	0.122	−0.043
95	2.63	2.42	−29	2.8	−0.0.19	0.170	−0.078
100	4.55	4.45	−44	3.2	−0.019	0.196	−0.121
105	7.10	7.26	−60	3.1	−0.015	0.195	−0.167
110	10.70	10.77	−73	2.6	−0.009	0.163	−0.209

Figure 7-14

Position	Theoretical Edge	Delta	Gamma	Theta	Vega	Rho
1. −10 June 95 calls	10 x +.22	−10 x 71	−10 x 2.8	−10 x −.034	−10 x .170	−10 x .155
+7 underlying contracts	0	+7 x 100	0	0	0	0
	+2.20	−10	−28	+.34	−1.70	−1.55
2. +10 June 100 calls	10 x −.11	+10 x 56	+10 x 3.2	+10 x −.035	+10 x .196	+10 x .124
+10 June 100 puts	10 x −.10	+10 x −44	+10 x 3.2	+10 x −.019	+10 x .196	+10 x −.121
	−2.10	+120	+64	−.54	+3.92	+.30
3. +10 June 105 puts	10 x +.16	+10 x −60	+10 x 3.1	+10 x −.015	+10 x .192	+10 x −.167
−20 June 95 puts	20 x +.21	−20 x −29	−20 x 2.8	−20 x −.019	−20 x .170	−20 x −.078
	+5.80	−10	−25	+.23	−1.48	+.11
4. +10 June 100 calls	10 x −.11	+10 x 56	+10 x 3.2	+10 x −.035	+10 x .196	+10 x .124
−10 June 90 calls	10 x +.34	−10 x −84	−10 x 2.0	−10 x −.029	−10 x .122	−10 x .178
	+2.30	−280	−12	−.06	+.74	−.54
5. −10 June 100 puts	10 x +.10	−10 x −44	−10 x 3.2	−10 x −.019	−10 x .196	−10 x −.121
+20 June 105 puts	20 x +.16	+20 x −60	+20 x 3.1	+20 x −.015	+20 x .192	+20 x −.167
−10 June 110 puts	10 x −.07	−10 x −73	−10 x 2.6	−10 x −.009	−10 x .163	−10 x −.209
	+3.50	−30	+4	−.02	+.25	−.04

0.22 per option. What about the theoretical edge for the trade in the underlying? From an option trader's point of view, the theoretical value of an underlying contract is simply the price at which it was traded. Consequently, the theoretical edge for any underlying trade is always 0. The position has a total theoretical edge of +2.20.

The total delta of Position 1 is –10. Although this indicates a very slight preference for downward movement, for practical purposes, almost all traders would consider the position delta neutral.

The total gamma of the position is –28. We know that a positive or negative delta indicates a desire for upward or downward movement in the price of the underlying contract, but what does a positive or negative gamma indicate? Consider what will happen to our delta position if the underlying stock starts to rise. Just as with an individual option, for each point increase, we add the gamma to the old delta to get the new delta. But we are adding a negative number (–28). If the stock rises one full point to 100.50, the delta will be

$$-10 + (-28) = -38$$

If the stock rises another point to 101.50, the delta will be

$$-38 + (-28) = -66$$

As the market rises, the delta becomes a larger negative number. Because a negative delta indicates a desire for downward movement, the more the market rises, the more we would like it to decline.

Now consider what will happen to our delta position if the underlying stock starts to fall. For each point decline, we subtract the gamma from the delta. If the stock falls one point to 98.50, the new delta will be

$$-10 - (-28) = +18$$

If the stock falls another point to 97.50, the delta will be

$$+18 - (-28) = +46$$

As the market falls, the delta becomes a larger positive number. For the same reason we do not want the stock price to rise (we are creating a larger negative delta in a rising market), we also do not want the stock price to fall (we are creating a larger positive delta in a falling market). If we do not want the market to rise and we do not want the market to fall, there is only one favorable outcome remaining: we must want the market to sit still. In fact, a negative gamma position is a good indication that a trader either wants the underlying market to sit still or move only very slowly. A positive gamma position indicates a desire for very large and swift moves in the underlying market.

Whereas delta is a measure of directional risk, gamma can be thought of as a measure of *magnitude risk*. Do we want moves of smaller magnitude (a negative gamma) or larger magnitude (a positive gamma)? Alternatively, gamma also can be thought of as the speed at which we want the market to move. Do we want the underlying price to move slowly (a negative gamma) or quickly (a positive gamma)? Taken together, the delta and gamma tell us something about the direction and speed that will either help or hurt our position. In Position 1, we want a slow (negative gamma) downward (negative delta) move in the underlying price.

The worst situation would be a swift upward move. Then we would be on the wrong side of both the direction (delta) and speed (gamma) of the market.

How will we feel about our position if the stock remains close to 99.50? From the negative gamma, we know that we want the market to remain relatively quiet. If the market does what we want it to do, we ought to expect our position to show a profit. Where will this profit come from? The profit will come from the theta of +0.34. For each day that passes with no movement in the underlying price, the position should show a profit of approximately 0.34. This underscores an important principle of option risk analysis: gamma and theta are almost always of opposite sign.[11] A positive gamma will be accompanied by a negative theta, and vice versa. Moreover, the magnitudes of the risks will tend to correlate. A large gamma will be accompanied by a large theta, but of opposite sign. A small gamma will be accompanied by a small theta. An option trader cannot have it both ways. Either market movement will help the position (positive gamma) or the passage of time (positive theta) will—but not both.

The vega of Position 1 is −1.70. This indicates a desire for declining volatility. For each point decline in volatility, the value of our position, which was initially +2.20, will increase by 1.70; for each point increase, the value will fall by 1.70. This seems to correspond to our gamma risk. If we have a negative gamma, we want the market to remain relatively quiet. Isn't this the same as saying we want lower volatility? Most traders, however, make an important distinction between the gamma and vega. The gamma is a measure of whether we want higher or lower *realized* volatility (whether we want the underlying contract to be more volatile or less volatile). The vega is a measure of whether we want higher or lower *implied* volatility. Although the volatility of the underlying contract and changes in implied volatility are often correlated, this is not always the case. In some cases, the underlying contract can become more volatile while implied volatility is falling. In other cases, the underlying contract can become less volatile while implied volatility is rising. We will look at the conditions that can cause this in Chapter 11, where we look at some of the common volatility spreads.

Suppose that we raise the volatility of 25 percent in Figure 7-13 to a volatility of 26 percent. What should be our theoretical profit now? We know that for each point increase in volatility, we need to add the vega (−1.70) to the old value (+2.20) to get the new value. Our theoretical profit at 26 percent will be

$$+2.20 + (-1.70) = +0.50$$

If we raise the volatility another percentage point to 27 percent, our theoretical edge turns negative

$$+0.50 + (-1.70) = -1.20$$

We can see that the position has a *breakeven* volatility of approximately

$$25(\%) + (-2.20/-1.70)(\%) = 25(\%) + 1.29(\%) = 27.29(\%)$$

---

[11] Interest considerations may occasionally result in a position with a gamma and theta of the same sign. However, in such a case, the magnitudes of the numbers are likely to be very small.

Of course, a more common name for the breakeven volatility is implied volatility. Although traders most commonly associate implied volatility with individual options, we can also apply the concept to more complex positions. The implied volatility of a position is the volatility that must occur over the life of a position such that, in theory, the position will just break even. We can make a rough estimate of a position's implied volatility by dividing the total theoretical edge by the total vega and adding this number to the volatility used to evaluate the position.

The last risk measure for Position 1 is the rho of -1.55. For each percentage point decline in the interest rate, the position will show an additional profit of 1.55. For each percentage point increase in the interest rate, the position profit will be reduced by 1.55. It should not come as a surprise that rho is negative because the long stock position will inevitably dominate the cash flow, resulting in a debit. If the interest rate falls, it will cost less to carry this debit. If the interest rate rises, it will cost more.

The risks and rewards associated with each type of risk measure are summarized in Figure 7-15. The reader should take a few moments to look over the risk characteristics of the other positions in Figure 7-14. What combination of market conditions (e.g., changes in underlying price, time, implied volatility, and interest rate) will most help each position? What combination will most hurt each position?

Figure 7-15

If your delta position is …	You want the underlying price to…
Positive	Rise
Negative	Fall
If your gamma position is …	**You want the underlying contract to…**
Positive	Make big moves or move very quickly
Negative	Sit still or move very slowly
If your theta position is …	**The passage of time will…**
Positive	Increase the value of your position
Negative	Reduce the value of your position
If your vega position is …	**You want implied volatility to…**
Positive	Rise
Negative	Fall
If your rho position is …	**You want interest rates to…**
Positive	Rise
Negative	Fall

The alert reader may have noticed something odd about Position 2: it has a *negative theoretical edge*. This is not a misprint. It indicates that if the inputs into the model are correct, in the long run, the strategy will lose money. Of course, no trader will intentionally put on such a position, but in a market where conditions are constantly changing, a position that initially seemed sensible may under new conditions represent a losing strategy. When this occurs, a trader will make every effort to close out the position. The longer the trader holds the position, the more likely it is that it will result in a loss.[12]

One final observation for the prospective trader: all the numbers we have discussed in this chapter—the theoretical value, delta, gamma, theta, vega, and rho—are constantly changing, so the profitability and risks associated with different strategies are constantly changing. The importance of analyzing risk cannot be overemphasized. Most traders who fail at option trading do so because they fail to fully analyze and understand risk. But there is another type of trader, one who attempts to analyze every possible risk. When this happens, the trader finds it difficult to make any trading decisions at all; he is stricken with *paralysis through analysis*. A trader who is so concerned with risk that he is afraid to make a trade cannot profit, no matter how well he understands options. When a trader enters the marketplace, he has chosen to take on some risk. The delta, gamma, theta, vega, and rho enable him to identify risk; they do not eliminate risk. The intelligent trader uses these numbers to help decide beforehand which risks are acceptable and which risks are not.

---

[12] In theory, a trader will never create a position with a negative theoretical edge, at least as an initial trade. However, once a position has been established, in light of a larger overall position, a trader will sometimes intentionally execute a trade with a negative theoretical edge. A trader might be willing to give up a small amount of theoretical profit in order to make the remaining potential profit more secure. This, of course, is the whole objective behind hedging.

Dynamic Hedging

8

From our discussion thus far, it ought to be obvious why serious option traders use theoretical pricing models. First, a model tells us something about an option's value. We can compare this value with the price of the option in the marketplace and from this choose an appropriate strategy. Second, once we have taken a position, the model helps us quantify many of the risks that option trading entails. By understanding these risks, we will be better prepared to minimize our losses when market conditions move against us and maximize our profits when market conditions move in our favor.

In discussing the performance of a theoretical pricing model, it is important to remember that all models are probability based. Even if we assume that we have all the right inputs into the model and that the model itself is correct, there is no guarantee that we will show a profit on any one trade. More often than not, the actual results will deviate, sometimes significantly, from what is predicted by the theoretical pricing model. It is only over many trades that the results will even out so that, on average, we achieve a result close to that predicted by the theoretical pricing model.

However, option-pricing theory also suggests that for a single option trade there is a method by which we can reduce the variations in outcome so that the actual results will more closely approximate what is predicted by the theoretical pricing model. By treating the life of an option as a series of bets, rather than one bet, the model can be used to replicate long-term probability theory.

Consider the following situation:

> Stock price = $97.70
> Time to June expiration = 10 weeks
> Interest rate = 6.00 percent

Suppose that we are using a theoretical pricing model to evaluate June options on this stock. We already have three inputs into the model—underlying price, time to expiration, and the interest rate—but we still need three additional inputs—exercise price, type, and volatility. Given that we can choose from among the available exercise prices and that we can also choose the type of option (either call or put), we still lack the one unobservable input—volatility. In theory, we would like to know the future realized volatility of the underlying stock over the next 10 weeks. Clearly, we can never know the future, but let's imagine that we have a crystal ball that can predict the future. When we look into our crystal ball, we see that the volatility of the stock over the next 10 weeks will be 37.62 percent.

The June 100 call, being very close to at the money, is likely to be actively traded, so let's focus on that option. Feeding our inputs into the Black-Scholes model, we find that the June 100 call has a theoretical value of 5.89. When we check its price in the marketplace, we find that it is being offered at 5.00. How can we profit from this discrepancy?

Clearly, our first move will be to purchase the June 100 call because it is underpriced by 0.89. Can we now walk away from the position and come back at expiration to collect our money? In our previous discussion of theoretical pricing models, we noted that the purchase or sale of a theoretically mispriced option requires us to establish a neutral hedge by taking an opposing position in the underlying contract. When this is done correctly, for small changes in the price of the underlying contract, the increase or decrease in the value of the option position will exactly offset the decrease or increase in the value of the opposing position in the underlying contract. Such a hedge is unbiased, or neutral, with respect to directional moves in the underlying contract.

In order to establish the appropriate riskless hedge, we need to determine the delta of the June 100 call. Using our theoretical pricing model, we find that the option has a delta of 50. For each call we purchase, we must sell 0.50, or one-half, of an underlying contract. Because it is usually not possible to buy or sell fractional underlying contracts, let's assume that we buy 100 June 100 calls and sell 50 underlying contracts.[1] We now have the following delta-neutral position:

Position	Contract Delta	Delta Position
Long 100 June 100 calls	50	+5,000
Short 50 underlying contracts	100	−5,000

Suppose that one week later the price of the stock has moved up to 99.50. At this point, we can feed the new market conditions into our theoretical pricing model:

Stock price = 99.50
Interest rate = 6.00 percent
Time to June expiration = 9 weeks
Volatility = 37.62 percent

Note that we have made no change in the interest rate or volatility. Theoretical pricing models typically assume that these two inputs remain constant over the life of the option.[2] Based on the new inputs, we can calculate the new delta for the June 100 call, in this case 54.

---

[1] The underlying contract for most stock options is 100 shares of stock. The proper hedge is therefore equivalent to selling 5,000 shares of stock.
[2] Whether this is in fact a realistic assumption we will leave for a later discussion.

Position	Contract Delta	Delta Position
Long 100 June 100 calls	54	+5,400
Short 50 underlying contracts	100	−5,000

Our delta position is now +400. We can think of this as the end of one bet, with another bet about to begin.

Whenever we begin a new bet, we are required to return to a delta-neutral position. In our example, it will be necessary to reduce our position by 400 deltas. There are a number of ways to do this, but to keep our present calculations as simple as possible and to remain consistent with the theoretical pricing model, we will make the necessary trades in the underlying contract because an underlying contract always has a delta of 100. We can return to delta neutral by selling 4 underlying contracts. Our position is now

Position	Contract Delta	Delta Position
Long 100 June 100 calls	54	+5,400
Short 54 underlying contracts	100	−5,400

We are again delta neutral and about to begin a new bet. As before, our new bet depends only on the volatility of the underlying contract, not its direction.

The extra four underlying contracts that we sold were an *adjustment* to our position. In option trading, adjustments are trades that are made primarily to ensure that a position remains delta neutral. In our case, the sale of the four extra contracts has no effect on our theoretical edge because, from an option trader's point of view, an underlying contract has no theoretical value. The trade is made solely for the purpose of adjusting our hedge to remain delta neutral.

In Chapter 17, we will look at the use of options to protect a preexisting position. Such protective strategies usually employ a *static hedge*, whereby opposing market positions are taken in different contracts, with the entire position being carried to a fixed maturity date. To capture an option's mispricing, the theoretical pricing model requires us to employ a *dynamic hedging* strategy. We must periodically reevaluate the position to determine the delta of the position and then buy or sell an appropriate number of underlying contracts to return to delta neutral. This procedure must be followed over the entire life of the option.

Because volatility is assumed to compound continuously, theoretical pricing models assume that adjustments are also made continuously and that the hedge is being adjusted at every moment in time. Such continuous adjustments are not possible in the real world because a trader can only trade at discrete intervals. By making adjustments at regular intervals, we are conforming as closely as possible to the principles of the theoretical pricing model.

The entire dynamic hedging process for our hedge, with adjustments made at weekly intervals, is shown in Figure 8-1. At the end of each interval, the delta of the June 100 call was recalculated from the time remaining to expiration, the current price of the underlying contract, an interest rate of 6.00 percent, and a volatility of 37.65 percent. Note that we did not change the volatility,

Figure 8-1

Stock price = 97.70	Time to June expiration = 10 weeks Interest rate = 6.00% Volatility = 37.62%						
June 100 call:	Price = 5.00 (Implied volatility = 32.40%) Theoretical value = 5.89 Delta = 50						
Week	Share Price	Delta of 100 Call	Total Delta Position	Adjustment (Contracts)	Total Adjustments	Adjustment Cash Flow	Interest on Adjustments
0	97.70	50	0				
1	99.50	54	+400	Sell 4	Short 4	+398.00	+4.12
2	92.75	35	−1900	Buy 19	Long 15	−1762.25	−16.22
3	95.85	43	+800	Sell 8	Long 7	+766.80	+6.18
4	96.20	43	0	None	Long 7	0	0
5	102.45	62	+1900	Sell 19	Short 12	+1946.55	+11.20
6	93.30	28	−3400	Buy 34	Long 22	−3172.20	−14.60
7	91.15	17	−1100	Buy 11	Long 33	−1002.65	−3.46
8	95.20	27	+1000	Sell 10	Long 23	+952.00	+2.19
9	102.80	72	+4500	Sell 45	Short 22	+4626.00	+5.32
10	103.85			Buy 22		−2284.70	

even though other market conditions may have changed. Volatility, like interest rates, is assumed to be constant over the life of the option.[3]

What will we do with our position at the end of 10 weeks when the options expire? At that time, we plan to close out the position by

1. Letting any out-of-the-money options expire worthless

2. Selling any in-the-money options at parity (intrinsic value) or, equivalently, exercising them and offsetting them against the underlying contract

3. Liquidating any outstanding underlying contracts at the market price

Let's go through this procedure step by step and see what the complete results of our hedge are.

Original Hedge

At June expiration (week 10), with the underlying contract at 103.85, we can close out the June 100 calls by either selling them at 3.85 or exercising the calls

---

[3] In practice, as new information becomes available, traders are constantly changing their opinions about interest rates and volatility. Here we make the assumption of constant volatility and interest rates in order to be consistent with option pricing theory.

and selling the underlying contract. Either method will result in a credit of 3.85 to our account. Because we originally paid 5.00 for each option, we will show a loss on our option position of

$$100 \times (3.85 - 5.00) = 100 \times -1.15 = -115.00$$

As part of our original hedge, we also sold 50 underlying contracts at 97.70. At expiration, in order to close out the position, we were required to buy them back at 103.85, for a loss of 6.15 per contract. Our total loss on the underlying trade is therefore

$$50 \times (97.70 - 103.85) = 50 \times -6.15 = -307.50$$

Adding this to our option loss, the total loss on the original hedge is

$$-115.00 - 307.50 = -422.50$$

This certainly does not appear to have been successful. We expected to make money on the position, yet it appears that we have a sizable loss.

Adjustments

Fortunately, the original hedge was not our only transaction. In order to remain delta neutral over the 10-week life of the option, we were forced to buy and sell underlying contracts. At the end of week 1, we were long 400 deltas, so we were required to sell four underlying contracts at 99.50. At the end of week 2, we were short 1,900 deltas, so we were required to buy 19 underlying contracts at 92.75, and so on each week until the end of week 10. At expiration, with the underlying contract at 103.85, we bought in the 22 underlying contracts that we were short at the end of week 9.

In this example, each time the underlying price rose, our delta position became positive, so we were forced to sell underlying contracts, and each time the underlying price fell, our delta position became negative, so we were forced to buy underlying contracts. Because our adjustments depended only on our delta position, we were forced to do what every trader wants to do: buy low and sell high.

The result of making all the adjustments required to maintain a delta-neutral position was a profit of 467.55. (The reader may wish to confirm this by adding up the cash flow from all the trades in the adjustment column in Figure 8-1.) This profit more than offset the losses incurred from the original hedge.

Interest Lost on the Option Position

We originally bought 100 June options at a price of 5.00 each, for a total cash outlay of 500.00. At the assumed interest rate of 6.00 percent, the cost of financing the option purchase for the 10-week (70-day) life of the position was

$$-500.00 \times 6\% \times 70/365 = -5.75$$

Interest Earned on the Stock Position

To establish our initial hedge, we sold 50 underlying stock contracts at a price of 97.70 each, for a total credit of 4,885.00. Over the life of the hedge, we were able to earn total interest in the amount of

$$+4{,}885 \times 6\% \times 70/365 = +56.21$$

Interest on the Adjustments

Each week we were forced to buy or sell underlying contracts in order to remain delta neutral. As a result, there was either a cash debit on which we were required to pay interest or a cash credit on which we were able to earn interest. For example, at the end of week 1, we were forced to sell four underlying contracts at a price of 99.50 each, for a total credit of $4 \times 99.50 = 398.00$. The interest earned on this credit for the remaining nine weeks was

$$+398.00 \times 6\% \times 63/365 = +4.12$$

At the end of week 2, we were forced to buy 19 underlying contracts at a price of 92.75 each, for a total debit of $19 \times 92.75 = 1{,}762.25$. The interest cost on this debit over the remaining eight weeks was

$$-1{,}762.25 \times 6\% \times 56/365 = -16.22$$

Adding up the interest on all the adjustments, we get a total of –5.28.

Dividends

To keep our example relatively simple, we have assumed that the stock pays no dividend over the life of the option. If the stock were to pay a dividend, any long stock position resulting from either the original hedge or the adjustment process would receive the dividend. Any short stock position would be required to pay out the dividend. There also would be an interest consideration on the amount of the dividend, interest either earned or interest lost, between the date of the dividend payment and expiration. The dividend and the interest on the dividend would then become part of the total profit or loss.

What was the total cash flow resulting from the entire 10-week hedge? This amount, +90.24, is shown in Figure 8-2. Of course, this represents the cash flow at the end of 10 weeks. To obtain the initial or present value, we need to discount backwards over 10 weeks at an interest rate of 6.00 percent. This gives us a final value, or total profit and loss (P&L), of

$$\frac{90.24}{1+0.06 \times 70/365} = 89.21$$

How does this final value of 89.21 compare with our predicted profit or loss? We purchased 100 June options at a price of 5.00 each, but the options had a theoretical value of 5.89, so the theoretical profit was

$$100 \times (5.89 - 5.00) = +89.00$$

Figure 8-2

Dynamic Hedging Results		
Original hedge P&L:		−422.50
Option P&L	$100 \times (3.85 - 5.00) = -115.00$	
Stock P&L	$50 \times (97.70 - 103.85) = -307.50$	
Adjustment P&L:		+467.55
Carry (interest) on the options:		
	$100 \times -5.00 \times 6.00\% \times 70/365 = -5.75$	−5.75
Carry (interest) on the stock:		
	$50 \times +97.70 \times 6.00\% \times 70/365 = +56.21$	+56.21
Interest on the adjustments:		−5.27
Total cash flow:		+90.24
Discounted cash flow:	$90.24/(1 + 0.06 \times 70/365) = 89.21$	+89.21
Predicted P&L:	$100 \times (5.89 - 5.00) = 100 \times 0.89 = 89.00$	+89.00

In our example, the profit and loss were made up of five components. Two of these were positive (the adjustments and the interest earned on stock), while three were negative (the original hedge, the option carrying costs, and interest on the adjustments). Is this always the case? Because price movement in the underlying contract is assumed to be random, it is impossible to determine beforehand which components will be profitable and which will not. It would also be possible to construct an example where the original hedge was profitable and the adjustments were not. The important point is that if a trader's inputs are correct, in some combination, he can expect to show a profit or loss approximately equal to that predicted by the theoretical pricing model.

Of all the inputs, volatility is the only one that is not directly observable. Where did our volatility figure of 37.62 percent come from? Obviously, it is not possible to know the future volatility. In our example the 10 price changes in Figure 8-1 do in fact represent an annualized volatility of 37.62 percent. The complete calculations are given in Appendix B.

In the foregoing example, we assumed that the market was *frictionless*, that no external factors affected the total profit or loss. This assumption is basic to many financial models. In a frictionless market, we assume that

1. Traders can freely buy or sell the underlying contract without restriction.

2. Traders can borrow and lend as much money as desired at one constant interest rate.

3. Transaction costs are zero.

4. There are no tax consequences.

A trader will immediately realize that option markets are not frictionless because in the real world, each of these assumptions is violated to a greater or lesser degree. In our example, we were required to sell stock to initiate the original hedge. If we did not own the stock, we would need to *sell short* by first borrowing the stock and then making delivery. In some markets, short sales may be difficult to execute because of exchange or regulatory restrictions. Moreover, even if a short sale is possible, a trader typically will not receive full interest on the proceeds from the short sale.

Turning to options on futures, in some markets, there is a daily limit on the amount of allowable price movement for a futures contract. When this limit is reached, the market is *locked*, and no further trading can take place until the price of the futures contract comes off its limit. Clearly, in such markets, the underlying contract cannot always be freely bought or sold.

Concerning interest rates, different rates apply to different market participants. The rate that applies to an individual trader will not be the same rate that applies to a large financial institution. Moreover, even for the same trader, different rates can apply to different transactions. If a trader has a debit balance, it will cost him more to carry that debit; if he has a credit balance, he will not earn as much on that credit. There is a spread, and perhaps a fairly large one, between a trader's borrowing and lending rate. Fortunately, the interest-rate component is usually the least important of the inputs into a theoretical pricing model. Even though the applicable interest rate may vary from trader to trader, in general, it will cause only minor changes in the total profit or loss in relation to the profit or loss resulting from other inputs.

Transaction costs, on the other hand, can be a very real consideration. If these costs are high, the hedge in Figure 8-1 might not be a viable strategy; all the profits could be eaten up by brokerage and exchange fees. The desirability of a strategy will depend not only on the trader's initial transaction costs but also on the subsequent costs of making adjustments. The adjustment cost is a function of a trader's desire to remain delta neutral. A trader who wants to remain delta neutral at every moment will have to adjust more often, and more adjustments mean greater transaction costs.

If a trader initiates a hedge but adjusts less frequently or does not adjust at all, how will this affect the outcome? Because theoretical evaluation of options is based on the laws of probability, a trader who initiates a theoretically profitable hedge still has the odds on his side. Although he may lose on any one individual hedge, if given a chance to initiate the same hedge repeatedly at a positive theoretical edge, on average, he should profit by the amount predicted by the theoretical pricing model. The adjustment process is simply a way of smoothing out the winning and losing hedges by forcing the trader to make more bets, always at the same favorable odds. A trader who is disinclined to adjust is at greater risk of not realizing a profit on any one hedge. Adjustments do not in themselves alter the expected return; they simply reduce the short-term effects of good and bad luck.

Based on the foregoing discussion, a retail customer and a professional trader are likely to approach option trading in a somewhat different manner, even if both understand and use the values generated by a theoretical pricing model. A professional trader, particularly if he is an exchange member, has relatively low transaction costs. Because adjustments cost him very little in relation to the expected theoretical profit from a hedge, he will be inclined to make frequent adjustments. In contrast, a retail customer who establishes the same hedge will be less inclined to adjust or will adjust less frequently because any adjustments will reduce the profitability of the position. A retail customer who understands the laws of probability will realize that his position has the same favorable odds as the professional trader's position, but he should also realize that his position is more sensitive to the effects of short-term good and bad luck. Even though the retail customer may occasionally experience larger losses than the professional trader, he will also occasionally experience larger profits. In the long run, on average, both should end up with approximately the same profit.[4]

Taxes may also be a factor in evaluating an option strategy. When positions are initiated, when they are liquidated, how the positions overlap, and the relationship between different instruments (e.g., options, stock, futures, physical commodities, etc.) may have different tax consequences. Such consequences may affect the value of a diversified portfolio, and for this reason, portfolio managers must be sensitive to the tax ramifications of a strategy. Because each trader has unique tax considerations and this book is intended as a general guide to option evaluation and strategies, we will simply assume that each trader wishes to maximize his pretax profits and that he will worry about taxes afterward.

It may seem like a fortunate coincidence that the theoretical P&L in our example and the actual P&L are so close. In fact, the example in Figure 8-1 was carefully constructed to demonstrate why the dynamic hedging process is so important. In the real world, it is unlikely that the actual results from any one hedge will so closely match the theoretical results.

Figure 8-3 illustrates in graphic terms the dynamic hedging process. We determined the initial delta of the option (the dotted line) at the underlying price of 97.70 and then took an opposing delta position in the underlying contract (the dashed line). For very small moves in the underlying price, the profit from one position offset the loss from the other position. As the changes in the underlying price in either direction become greater, because of the option's curvature (its gamma), there is a mismatch between these two positions. With a falling underlying price, the rate at which the option position loses value begins to decline; with a rising underlying price, the rate at which the option position gains value begins to increase. In Figure 8-3a, we can see this mismatch, or unhedged amount, at an underlying price of 99.50.

With the underlying price at 99.50, we captured the value of this mismatch by adjusting the position to return to delta neutral. This is shown in Figure 8-3b. We recalculated the delta at the new underlying price and took a new opposing position in the underlying contract. When the underlying price fell to 92.75, there was again a mismatch equal to the unhedged amount.

---

[4] This, of course, ignores the very real advantage the professional trader often has from being able to buy at the bid price and sell at the ask price. A retail customer can never hope to match the profit resulting from this advantage, nor should he try to do so.

Figure 8-3

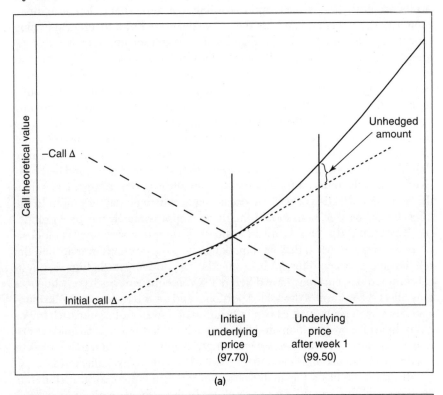

(a)

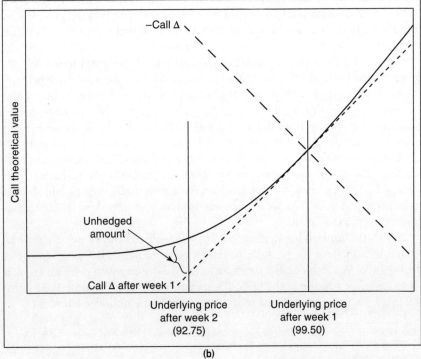

(b)

By rehedging the position each week, we were able to capture a series of profits resulting from the mismatch between the option's changing delta and the fixed delta of the underlying contract. Of course, while time was passing, there were also interest considerations. But most of the option's value was determined by the amount earned on the rehedging process. In theory, if we ignore interest, the sum of all these small profits (the unhedged amounts in Figure 8-3) should approximately equal the value of the option

$$\text{Option theoretical value} = \{\cdot\} + \{\cdot\} + \{\cdot\} + \cdots + \{\cdot\} + \{\cdot\} + \{\cdot\}$$

In our example, rehedging took place at discrete intervals, equivalent to making a finite number of bets, all with the same positive theoretical edge. If we want to exactly replicate the option's theoretical value, we need to make an infinite number of bets. This, in theory, can only be achieved by continuous rehedging of the position at every possible moment in time. If such a process were possible, and if all the assumptions on which the model is based were accurate, then the rehedging process would indeed replicate the exact value of the option.

Of course, continuous rehedging is not possible in the real world. Nor are all the model assumptions entirely accurate. Nonetheless, most traders have found through experience that using a dynamic hedging strategy, even if only at discrete intervals, is the best way to capture the difference between an option's price and its theoretical value.

Given that continuous rehedging is not possible, how often should a trader rehedge? The answer to this question will depend on each trader's cost structure and risk tolerance. We have already noted that a trader's transaction costs are likely to affect the frequency at which adjustments are made. Higher transaction costs will often lead to less frequent adjustments. If we ignore the question of transaction costs, there are two common approaches to rehedging: rehedge at regular intervals or rehedge whenever the delta becomes unbalanced by a predetermined amount.

The position in Figure 8-1 is an example of the first approach—rehedging at regular intervals. Here we made adjustments to the position at the end of each week. Of course, we might have made adjustments at the end of each day or even every hour if we were willing to recalculate the deltas so frequently. The more often rehedging takes place, the more likely it is that the final result will approximate the results predicted by the model. In our example, we used weekly intervals for no other reason than 10 lines seemed to fit nicely on the page.

Most traders do not insist on maintaining an exactly delta-neutral position. Within limits, they are willing to accept some directional risk. The more directional risk a trader is willing to accept, the less frequent the adjustments. And the less frequent the adjustments, the more likely the actual results will differ from the results predicted by the theoretical pricing model. For example, if a trader decides that he is willing to accept a directional risk up to 500 deltas, no rehedging would take place after week 1 (+400 deltas). If the trader is willing to accept a directional risk up to 1,000 deltas, no rehedging would take place at the end of week 1 (+400 deltas), week 3 (+800 deltas), and week 8 (+1,000 deltas). And if the trader is willing to accept a directional risk up to 1,500 deltas,[5] no rehedging would take place at the end of week 1 (+400 deltas), week 3 (+800 deltas), week 7 (−1,100 deltas), and week 8 (+1,000 deltas). In each case, because of the less frequent rehedging, the actual results are more likely to differ from the predicted results.

Note that after the hedge in Figure 8-1 was initiated, no subsequent trades were made in the option market. The trader's only concern was the realized volatility, or price fluctuations, in the underlying market. These price fluctuations determined the size and frequency of the adjustments, and in the final analysis, it was the adjustments that determined the profitability of the hedge. We might think of the hedge as a race between the loss in time value of the June 100 calls and the cash flow resulting from the adjustments, with the theoretical pricing model acting as the judge. Under the assumptions of the model, if options are purchased at less than theoretical value, the adjustments will win the race; if options are purchased at more than theoretical value, the loss in time value will win the race. The conditions of the race are determined by the inputs into the theoretical pricing model.

We assumed in our example that the future volatility was known to be 37.62 percent. What will be the outcome if volatility is something other than 37.62 percent? Suppose, for example, that volatility turns out to be higher than 37.62 percent. Higher volatility means greater price fluctuations, resulting in more and larger adjustments. In our example, more adjustments mean more profit. This is consistent with the principle that higher volatility increases the value of options.

What about the opposite, if volatility is less than 37.62 percent? Lower volatility means smaller price fluctuations, resulting in fewer and smaller adjustments. This will reduce the profit. If the volatility is low enough, the adjustment profit will just offset the other components, so the total profit from the hedge will be exactly zero. This *breakeven volatility* is identical to the option's implied volatility at the original trade price. Using the Black-Scholes model, we find that the implied volatility of the June 100 call at a price of 5.00 is 32.40 percent. At this volatility, the race between profits from the adjustments and the loss in the option's time value will end in an exact tie. Above a volatility of 32.40 percent, we expect the hedge, including adjustments and interest, to show a profit; below 32.40 percent, we expect the hedge to show a loss.

Because we needed to make adjustments to realize a profit, it may seem that every profitable hedge requires us to maintain the position until expiration. In practice, this may not be necessary. Suppose that immediately after we establish the hedge, the implied volatility in the option market increases from 32.40 percent, the implied volatility at which we bought the June 100 calls, to 37.62 percent, the realized volatility of the underlying contract we expect over the life of the option. What will happen to the price of the June 100 call? Its price will rise from 5.00 (an implied volatility of 32.40 percent) to 5.89 (an implied volatility of 37.62 percent). We can then sell our calls for an immediate profit of 0.89 per option. Of course, if we want to close out the hedge,

---

[5] These delta numbers were chosen only to illustrate the effect of rehedging based on a predetermined delta risk. Even a directional risk of 500 deltas might be more than many traders are willing to accept.

we must also buy back the 50 underlying contracts that we originally sold. What effect will the change in implied volatility have on the price of these contracts? Implied volatility is a characteristic associated with options, not with underlying contracts. Consequently, we expect the underlying contract to continue to trade at its original price of 97.70. By purchasing our 50 outstanding underlying contracts at a price of 97.70, we will realize an immediate total profit from the hedge of 89.00, exactly the amount predicted by the theoretical pricing model. If we can do all this, there is no reason to hold the position for the full 10 weeks.

How likely is an immediate reevaluation of implied volatility from 32.40 to 37.62 percent? Although swift changes in implied volatility occur occasionally, more often changes occur gradually over a period of time and are the result of equally gradual changes in the volatility of the underlying contract. As the volatility of the underlying contract changes, option demand rises and falls, and this demand is reflected in a corresponding rise or fall in the implied volatility. In our example, if the price of the underlying contract begins to fluctuate at a volatility greater than 32.40 percent, we can expect implied volatility to rise. If implied volatility ever reaches our target of 37.62 percent, we can simply sell our calls and buy our underlying contracts, thereby realizing our expected profit of 89.00 without having to hold the position for the full 10 weeks. But option prices are subject to a wide variety of market forces, not all of them theoretical. There is no guarantee that implied volatility will ever reevaluate upward to 37.62 percent. In this case, we will have to hold the position and continue to adjust for the full 10 weeks to realize our profit.

Every trader hopes that implied volatility will reevaluate as quickly as possible toward his volatility target. It not only enables him to realize his profits more quickly, but it eliminates the risk of holding a position for an extended period of time. The longer a position is held, the greater the possibility of error from the inputs into the model.

Not only might implied volatility not reevaluate favorably, it also might move against us, even if the actual volatility of the underlying contract moves in our favor. Suppose that after initiating our hedge, implied volatility immediately falls from 32.40 to 30.35 percent. The price of the June 100 call will fall from 5.00 to 4.65, and we will have an immediate loss of $100 \times -0.35 = -35.00$. Does this mean that we made a bad trade and should close out the position? If the volatility forecast of 37.65 percent turns out to be correct, the options will still be worth 5.89 by expiration. If we hold the position and adjust, we can eventually expect a profit of 89.00 points. Realizing this, we ought to maintain the position as we originally intended. Even though an adverse move in implied volatility is unpleasant, it is something with which all traders must learn to cope. Just as a speculator can rarely hope to pick the exact bottom or top at which to take a long or short position, an option trader can rarely hope to pick the exact bottom or top in implied volatility. He must try to establish positions when market conditions are favorable. But he must also realize that conditions might become even more favorable. If they do, his initial trade may show a temporary loss. This is something a trader learns to accept as a practical aspect of trading.

Let's look at one other dynamic hedging example, this time in the form of an overpriced put in the futures option market. Suppose that current market conditions are as follows:

Futures price = 61.85
Time to March expiration = 10 weeks
Interest rate = 8.00 percent

Again, let's assume that we know the true volatility of the underlying contract over the 10-week life of the option, in this case 21.48 percent. In this example, we will focus on the March 60 put, with a theoretical value of 1.46 but a price of 1.70, equivalent to an implied volatility of 23.92 percent.

Because the put is overpriced, we will begin by selling 100 March 60 puts, with a delta of −35 each, and simultaneously selling 35 underlying futures contracts. We will then follow a dynamic hedging procedure by recalculating the put delta at the end of each week and buying or selling futures to remain delta neutral. At expiration, we will close out the entire position. The entire dynamic hedging process is shown in Figure 8-4.

The cash flow in this example is slightly different from that in our stock option example. Although these are options on futures contracts and in many markets are subject to futures-type settlement, we will follow the U.S. convention and assume that the options are subject to stock-type settlement, requiring immediate and full cash payment. Futures, however, are always subject to futures-type settlement: there is no initial cash outlay, but a cash flow, in the form of variation, will result whenever the price of the futures contract changes. When this occurs, there will be a cash credit, on which interest can be earned, or a cash debit, on which interest must be paid.

Figure 8-4

Futures price = 61.85	Time to March expiration = 10 weeks					
	Interest rate = 8.00% Volatility = 21.48%					
March 60 put:	Price = 1.70 (Implied volatility = 23.92%)					
	Theoretical value = 1.46 Delta = −35					
Week	Share Price	Delta of 60 Put	Total Delta Position	Adjustment (Contracts)	Total Adjustments	Variation	Interest on Variation
---	---	---	---	---	---	---	---
0	61.85	−35	0				
1	60.83	−42	+700	Sell 7	Short 7	+35.70	+0.49
2	62.78	−28	−1400	Buy 14	Long 7	−81.90	−1.01
3	63.16	−24	−400	Buy 4	Long 11	−10.64	−0.11
4	61.68	−34	+1000	Sell 10	Long 1	+35.52	+0.33
5	59.86	−50	+1600	Sell 16	Short 15	+61.88	+0.47
6	62.88	−21	−2900	Buy 29	Long 14	−151.00	−0.93
7	61.50	−31	+1000	Sell 10	Long 4	+29.98	+0.13
8	62.60	−15	−1600	Buy 16	Long 20	−34.10	−0.10
9	60.18	−45	−3000	Sell 30	Short 10	+36.30	+0.06
10	58.61			Buy 10			

All P&L components for this example are shown in Figure 8-5. Three of these components are the same as in the stock option example: the P&L on the original hedge, the P&L resulting from the delta-neutral dynamic hedging process, and the carrying cost on the options. However, the interest on the initial stock position, as well as the interest on the adjustments, has been replaced by the interest on the variation credits and debits.

For example, as part of our original hedge, we sold 35 futures contracts at a price of 61.85. After week 1, the futures price declined to 60.83. As a result, we received a variation payment of

$$35 \times (61.85 - 60.83) = 35.70$$

We were able to earn 8.00 percent on this amount for the nine weeks (63 days) remaining to expiration

$$35.70 \times 8\% \times 63/365 = 0.49$$

At the end of week 1, in order to remain delta neutral, we were forced to sell seven futures contracts. This, together with our initial sale of 35 futures, left us short a total of 42 futures. After week 2, the futures price rose to 62.78. The result was a variation debit of

$$42 \times (60.83 - 62.78) = -81.90$$

In order to finance this debit for the eight weeks (56 days) remaining to expiration, we incurred an interest cost of

$$-81.90 \times 8\% \times 56/365 = -1.01$$

The total interest on all variation cash flows was −0.67.

Figure 8-5

Dynamic Hedging Results		
Original hedge P&L:		+144.40
Option P&L	$100 \times (1.70 - 1.39) = +31.00$	
Futures P&L	$35 \times (61.85 - 58.61) = +113.40$	
Adjustment P&L:		−122.01
Carry (interest) on the options:		
	$100 \times +1.70 \times 8.00\% \times 70/365 = +2.61$	+2.61
Interest on the variation:		−0.67
Total P&L:		+24.33
Discounted cash flow:	$24.33/(1 + 0.08 \times 70/365) = 23.96$	+23.96
Predicted P&L:	$100 \times (1.70 - 1.46) = 100 \times 0.24 = 24.00$	+24.00

The total cash flow of 24.33 and the present value of this amount, 23.96, are shown in Figure 8-5. The predicted theoretical profit was

$$100 \times (1.70 - 1.46) = 24.00$$

In both our stock option and futures option examples, we were able use the dynamic hedging process to capture the difference between the option's theoretical value and its price. In a sense, dynamic hedging enabled us to take the other side of the trade, but at the option's true theoretical value. When we bought calls in our stock option example, we sold the same calls at theoretical value through the dynamic hedging process. When we sold puts in our futures option example, we bought the same puts at theoretical value through the dynamic hedging process. From this, we can deduce an important principle of option evaluation:

In theory, we can replicate an option position through a dynamic hedging process. The cost of this replication is equal to the sum of all the cash flows resulting from the dynamic hedging process. The present value of this sum is equal to the option's theoretical value.

Risk Measurement II

9

Just as an option's theoretical value is sensitive to changes in market conditions, the sensitivities themselves also change as market conditions change. This underscores an important aspect of option trading: nothing remains constant. Depending on market conditions, the same position can exhibit a wide range of risk characteristics. Today's small risk can become tomorrow's big risk.

Although it is impractical to analyze every potential risk, intelligent trading of options still requires us to consider the risk of a position under a wide variety of market conditions. Every serious trader's education must include an understanding of the many different ways in which the risk of a position can change. Having some awareness of how the sensitivities change with changing market conditions is vital if we expect to intelligently manage the very real risks that option trading entails. In this chapter, we will take a closer look at how option risk measures change as market conditions change and how this affects the characteristics of a position.

Delta

We have already looked at the sensitivity of the delta to one possible change in market conditions. In Figure 7-6, we saw that delta changes as the price of the underlying contract changes and that this change is represented by the option's gamma. In addition to changes in the underlying price, the delta is also sensitive to changes in volatility and time.

Figure 9-1 shows what happens to the delta of a call as volatility changes. As volatility increases, the delta of an out-of-the-money call rises and the delta of an in-the-money call falls, with both deltas tending toward 50. This is logical because in a low-volatility market an out-of-the-money call is more likely to remain out of the money and therefore have a delta that is closer to 0, while an in-the-money call is more likely to remain in the money and therefore have a delta that is closer to 100. In a high-volatility market, we have the opposite effect. An out-of-the-money call has a greater likelihood of going into the money;

an in-the-money call has a greater likelihood of going out of the money. Consequently, the deltas of both options will move toward 50.

Note that the delta of an at-the-money option tends to remain close to 50 regardless of volatility. This is true in general, although changing interest rates or, in the case of stock options, changing dividends may alter the forward price. Because theoretical pricing models evaluate options in relation to the forward price, the delta of an at-the-money call may in fact be either more or less than 50. Even if the option is exactly at the forward (the exercise price and forward price are the same), a call will still have a delta that is slightly greater than 50 because of the lognormal distribution used to evaluate the option. This is evident in Figure 9-1, where the delta of an at-the-money call tends to increase slightly as volatility increases.

Because an option's delta changes as volatility changes, no trader can be certain that a position is really delta neutral. The delta depends on the volatility of the underlying contract, and this is something that will occur in the future over the life of the option. The volatility we use to calculate the delta is a guess. We might guess right, but we also might guess wrong. And if we guess wrong, our delta values will be wrong.

Rather than try to guess the future volatility, many traders use the *implied delta*, the delta that results from using the implied volatility. Using this approach, the delta will change as implied volatility changes, even if the underlying contract remains the same. Consider a trader who owns 40 call

Figure 9-1 Call delta values as volatility changes.

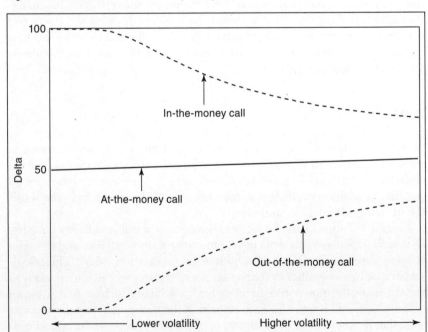

options with an implied volatility of 32 percent and a corresponding implied delta of 25 each. Because $40 \times 25 = 1,000$, to hedge the position delta neutral, the trader will sell 10 underlying contracts. If, however, implied volatility rises to 36 percent, the delta of the options will tend toward 50. If the new implied delta is 30, the trader's delta position is now $(40 \times 30) - (10 \times 100) = +200$. The trader's position changed from neutral to bullish even though no other market conditions changed.

Because the delta depends on the volatility, but volatility is an unknown factor, calculation of the delta can pose a major problem for a trader, especially for a large option position. Using the implied volatility to calculate the delta is only one possible approach.

Figure 9-2 shows what happens to call deltas as time passes. Note the similarities to Figure 9-1. Delta values move toward 50 if we increase either time to expiration or volatility and move away from 50 if we reduce either of these inputs. In many situations, time and volatility will have a similar effect on options. More time, like higher volatility, increases the likelihood of large price changes. Less time, like lower volatility, reduces the likelihood of large price changes. If a trader cannot immediately determine the effect on an option's value or sensitivity of changing time, he might instead consider the effect of changing volatility. Conversely, if he cannot determine the effect of changing volatility, he might consider the effect of changing time. Both effects are likely to be similar.

Figure 9-2 Call delta values as time passes.

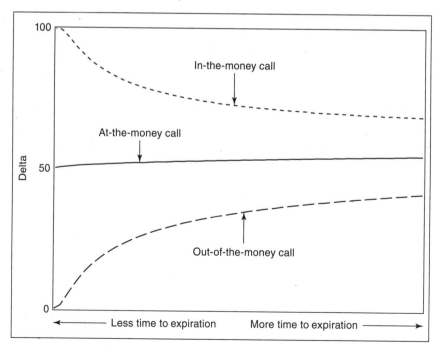

Figure 9-3 Put delta values as volatility changes.

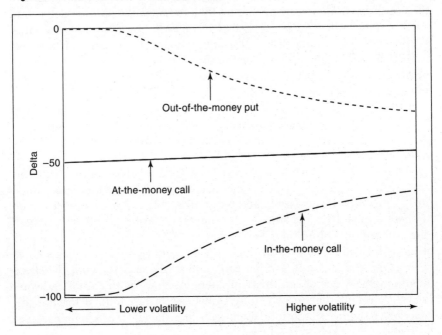

The effects of volatility and time on put deltas are the same as those on call deltas, except that put deltas tend toward 0 and −100 as volatility falls or time passes and toward −50 as volatility rises. This is shown in Figures 9-3 and 9-4.

Figure 9-4 Put delta values as time passes.

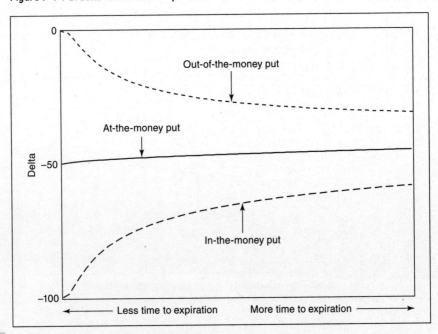

An alternative method of displaying the effects of changing time and volatility on delta values is shown in Figure 9-5. This is similar to Figure 7-6 except that we have varied time and volatility. As we lower time or reduce volatility, delta values for calls move very quickly toward either 0 for out-of-the-money options or 100 for in-the-money options.

Because delta values are affected by the passage of time, a position that is delta neutral today may not be delta neutral tomorrow, even if all other market conditions remain unchanged. Of course, with many months remaining to expiration, the passage of even several days may have little effect on the delta. If, however, expiration is quickly approaching, the passage of just one day, because it represents a large portion of the option's remaining life, can have a dramatic effect on the delta.

As option traders have become more aware of the importance of risk management, they have begun to pay closer attention to changes in the sensitivities themselves as market conditions change. In some cases, they have also begun to attach names (although not necessarily Greek letters) to these higher-order sensitivities. The sensitivity of the delta to a change in volatility is sometimes referred to as the option's *vanna*. The sensitivity of the delta to the passage of time is sometimes referred to as the option's *delta decay* or its *charm*.[1]

Which delta values are the most sensitive to changes in volatility (vanna) and time (charm)? We know that delta values will tend either toward 50 as

Figure 9-5 Call delta values as time passes or volatility declines.

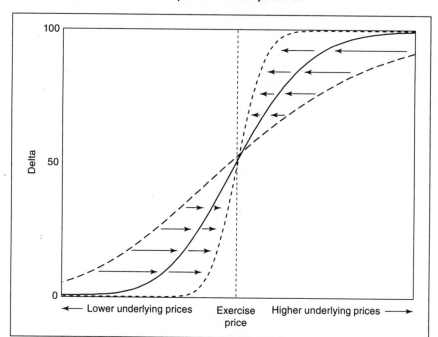

---

[1] In mathematics, the "sensitivity of a sensitivity" is a second-order sensitivity. The gamma, vanna, and charm are all second-order sensitivities (the sensitivity of the delta to a change in underlying price, volatility, and time to expiration, respectively).

we increase volatility or time, or away from 50 (toward 0 or 100) as we reduce volatility or time. Logically, delta values that are already close to 0, 50, or 100 are the least likely to change. At the same time, delta values that are approximately midway between these numbers are most likely to change. This is borne out by Figures 9-6 and 9-7, the vanna and charm for options with different deltas. Note that the shapes of the graphs are identical for calls and puts, with the vanna and charm approximately 0 around a delta of 50 or −50.[2] We can also see that vanna and charm are greatest for call delta values close to 20 and 80 and put delta values close to −20 and −80. Options with these deltas will move the most quickly toward 50 if we raise volatility or away from 50 if we lower volatility or reduce time to expiration.

The three vanna graphs also show that the vanna moves in the opposite direction of volatility, falling as we raise volatility and rising as we reduce volatility. The graphs of the charm exhibit similar characteristics with respect to the passage of time, falling with more time to expiration and rising with less time to expiration.

In Figures 9-6 and 9-7, we have ignored the effect of changing time on the vanna and the effect of changing volatility on the charm. From previous discussions, we might expect time and volatility to have the same effect on both these values. However, whereas vanna values are affected by changes in volatility, they are not significantly affected by changes in time to expiration. Whereas charm values are affected by time to expiration, they are not significantly affected by changes in volatility.

Figure 9-6 Vanna of an option.

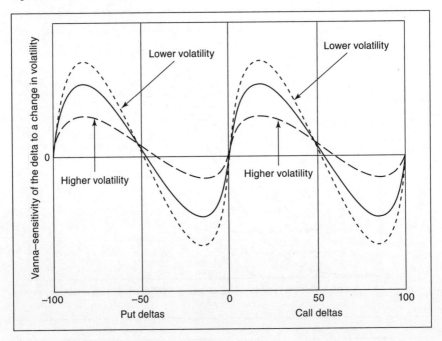

---

[2] The vanna is actually 0 for delta values slightly larger than 50 and smaller than −50. This is due to the non-symmetrical characteristic of the lognormal distribution.

Figure 9-7 Charm of an option.

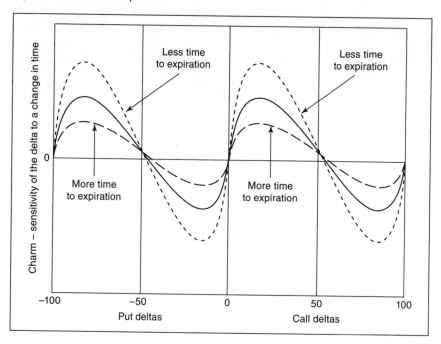

Theta

The theta of an option, the rate at which it decays, will vary depending not only on market conditions but also on whether an option is in the money, at the money, or out of the money. In Figure 9-8, we can see that the theta of an option is greatest when it is at the money. As the option moves either into or out of the money, its theta declines. Because the theta of an option is a function of its time value, and because very deeply in the money options and very far out of the money options have very little time value, it is logical that such options have a very low theta.

Note also that when all other conditions are the same, an at-the-money option at a higher underlying price has a greater theta value than an at-the-money option with lower underlying price. To understand why, consider two calls, one with an exercise price of 10 and one with an exercise price of 1,000, where both options are at the money and both calls have the same amount of time to expiration and the same implied volatility. Which option will be worth more? Clearly, the 1,000 call will be worth more because it represents the right to buy a more valuable asset.[3] Because both options are at the money and therefore consist solely of time value, the theta of the 1,000 call must be greater than the theta of the 10 call.

---

[3] In fact, the theoretical value and theta of two otherwise identical at-the-money options are proportional to their exercise prices. In this example, the 1,000 call will be worth exactly 100 times more than the 10 call, and its theta will be exactly 100 times greater.

Figure 9-8 Theta of an option as the underlying price changes.

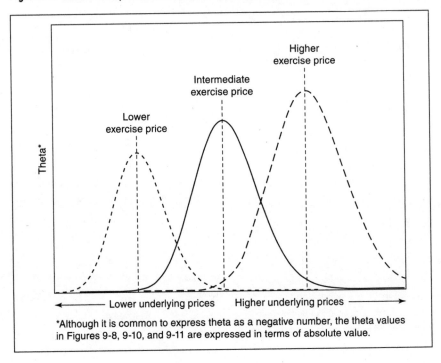

*Although it is common to express theta as a negative number, the theta values in Figures 9-8, 9-10, and 9-11 are expressed in terms of absolute value.

Figure 9-9 shows the theoretical value of an in-the-money, at-the-money, and out-of-the-money option as time passes. Early in the option's life, the rate of decay (the slope of the theoretical-value graph) is similar for each option. But late in the option's life, as expiration approaches, the rate of decay slows for in-the-money and out-of-the-money options, whereas it accelerates for an at-the-money option, approaching infinity at the moment of expiration. These characteristics, which apply to both calls and puts, are shown in Figure 9-10.[4]

The effect on the theta of changing volatility is shown in Figure 9-11. If we ignore interest, with a 0 volatility, the theta of any option will be 0. As we increase volatility, we increase the time premium, at the same time increasing the theta.

Note that the graph of the at-the-money option is essentially a straight line, with the theta being directly proportional to the volatility. For an at-the-money option, the theta at a volatility of 20 percent is exactly double the theta at a volatility of 10 percent. The same is not necessarily true for higher exercise prices (out-of-the-money calls and in-the-money puts) or lower exercise prices (in-the-money calls and out-of-the-money puts). The theta tends to decline as volatility declines but may become 0 well before the volatility is 0.

---

[4] The theta values for in-the-money and out-of-the-money options are actually slightly different. However, the values are so close that in Figure 9-10 we use one line to represent both options.

Figure 9-9 Theoretical value of an option as time passes.

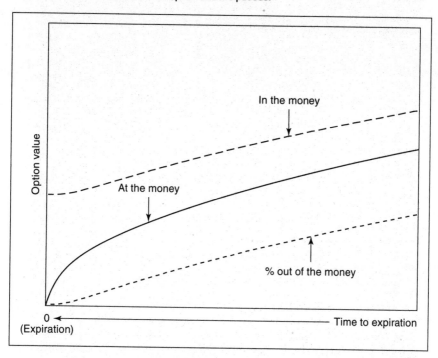

Figure 9-10 Theta of an option as time passes.

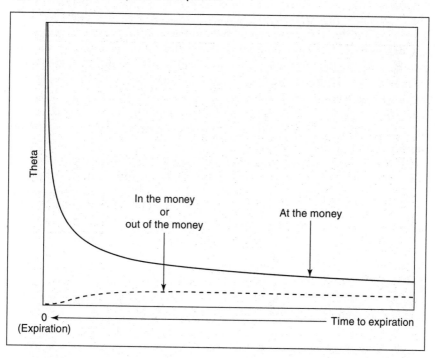

Figure 9-11 Theta of an option as volatility changes.

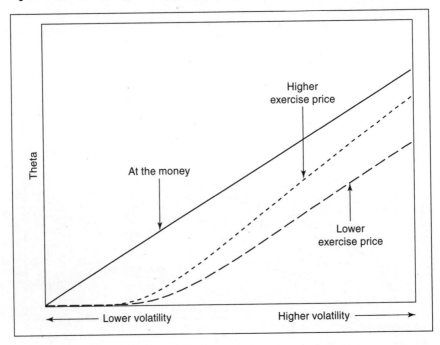

Figure 9-11 was constructed with the higher and lower exercise prices equally far away from the current underlying price. Note that the higher exercise price has a greater theta than the lower exercise price, with the difference increasing with increasing volatility. We touched on the explanation for this in Chapter 6. If a call and a put are both equally out of the money, under the assumptions of a lognormal distribution, the out-of-the-money call (the higher exercise price) will carry greater time premium than the out-of-the-money put (the lower exercise price). If there is no movement in the price of the underlying contract, the option with more time premium (the higher exercise price) must necessarily decay more quickly than the option with less time premium (the lower exercise price).

If we know the value of an option today, is there any way to estimate the option's theta? There is no convenient method for estimating the theta of in-the-money and out-of-the-money options, but for an at-the-money option, we know that theta is directly proportional to volatility (Figure 9-11). We also know from Chapter 6 that volatility is proportional to the square root of time

$$\text{volatility}_t = \text{volatility}_{\text{annual}} \times \sqrt{t}$$

The theta of an at-the-money option must therefore be proportional to the square root of time. If TV_t is an option's theoretical value at time t (in days to expiration), then the theoretical value one day later TV_{t-1} is

$$TV_{t-1} = TV_t \times \sqrt{(t-1)/t}$$

The theta is therefore

$$TV_t - TV_t \times \sqrt{(t-1)/t} = TV_t \times \left[1 - \sqrt{(t-1)/t}\right]$$

As time passes, the value of $1 - \sqrt{(t-1)/t}$ becomes increasingly large. Consequently, the theta of an at-the-money option will also become increasingly large (Figure 9-7).

For example, consider an at-the-money option with a theoretical value of 2.50 and 30 days remaining to expiration. The option's theta will be approximately

$$2.50 \times \left(1 - \sqrt{29/30}\right) = 2.50 \times (1 - 0.9832) \approx 0.042$$

One day later, with 29 days remaining to expiration, the theta will be

$$(2.50 - 0.042) \times \left(1 - \sqrt{28/29}\right) = 2.458 \times (1 - 0.9826) \approx 0.043$$

Vega

Figure 9-12 shows the vega of an option as we change the underlying price. Note that this figure is almost identical to Figure 9-8. As with the theta, the vega is greatest when an option is at the money, and an at-the-money option with

Figure 9-12 Vega of an option as the underlying price changes.

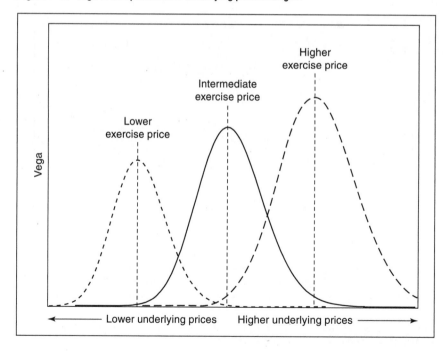

a higher exercise price has a greater vega than an at-the-money option with a lower exercise price. Moreover, the vega of an at-the-money option is proportional to its exercise price. Assuming that all other conditions are the same, an at-the-money option with an exercise price of 100 will have a vega that is twice that of an option with an exercise price of 50. Note that the term *vanna*, which previously referred to the sensitivity of delta to a change in volatility, can also refer to the sensitivity of the vega to a change in the underlying price. Both interpretations are mathematically identical.

Figure 9-13 shows the theoretical value of an in-the-money, at-the-money, and out-of-the-money option as we change volatility. Of particular note is the fact that the value of an at-the-money option is essentially a straight line. Because the vega is the slope of the graph, we can conclude that the vega of an at-the-money option is relatively constant with respect to changes in volatility. Whether volatility is 20 percent, 30 percent, or some higher value, the vega of an at-the-money option will be the same.

The effect on the vega of changing volatility is shown in Figure 9-14. While the vega of the at-the-money option is relatively constant, the vega values of in-the-money and out-of-the-money options tend to rise with higher volatility.[5] This is logical when we recall that as we raise volatility, the deltas of in-the-money and out-of-the-money options tend toward 50, causing the options to act more and more as if they are at the money. Because at-the-money options have the greatest vega (see Figure 9-12), we would expect the

Figure 9-13 Theoretical value of an option as volatility changes.

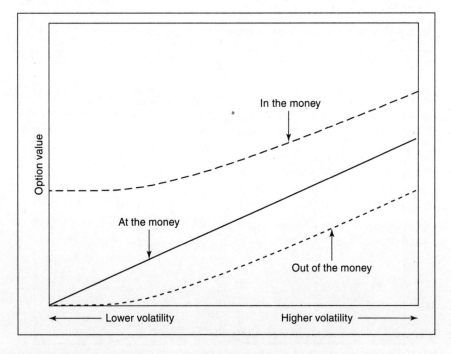

---

[5] In fact, we can see from Figure 9-14 that the vega of an at-the-money option declines very slightly as we raise volatility. This will be discussed in greater detail in Chapter 18.

Figure 9-14 Vega of an option as volatility changes.

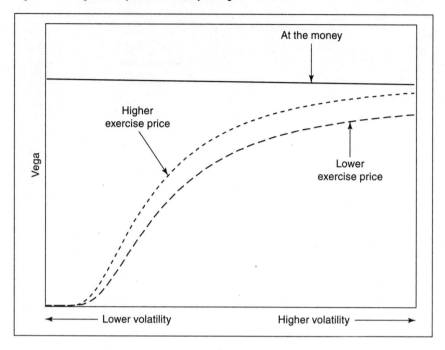

vega values to rise. The sensitivity of vega to a change in volatility is some-times referred to as either the *volga* or the *vomma* (both terms are a contraction of volatility and gamma—either *vol*atility *ga*mma or *vol*atility ga*mma*).

Figure 9-15 shows volga values for calls and puts with varying deltas. We have already noted that an at-the-money option with a delta of approximately 50 has a relatively constant vega and, consequently, a volga close to 0. How-ever, as an option moves either into the money or out of the money, the volga begins to increase, reaching its maximum for calls with deltas of approximately 10 and 90 and puts with deltas of approximately –10 and –90. Additionally, as we increase time, volga values for in-the-money and out-of-the-money options become more sensitive to the passage of time, with long-term options having greater volga values than short-term options.

In Figure 9-16, we can see how vega values change as time changes, rising as we increase time to expiration and falling as we reduce time. This characteristic, that long-term options are always more sensitive to changes in volatility than short-term options, was introduced in Chapter 6 (see Figures 6-11 and 6-12).

The sensitivity of the vega to changes in time to expiration, sometimes referred to as either *vega decay* or *DvegaDtime,* is shown in Figure 9-17. The vega of options with delta values between 10 and 90 tends to be the most sensitive to the passage of time. This sensitivity increases as we reduce time to expiration; as time passes, the vega of short-term options will change more quickly than the vega of long-term options.

Figure 9-15 Volga (vomma) of an option.

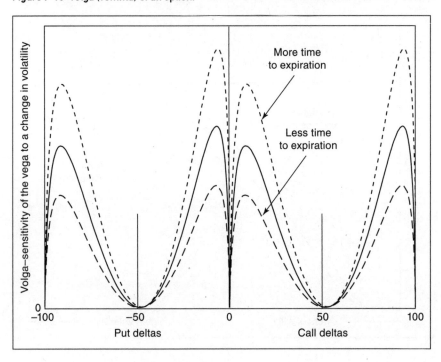

Figure 9-16 Vega of an option as time passes.

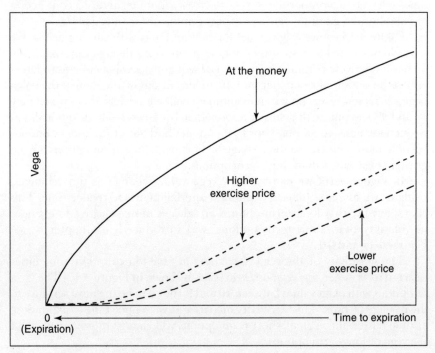

Figure 9-17 Vega decay of an option.

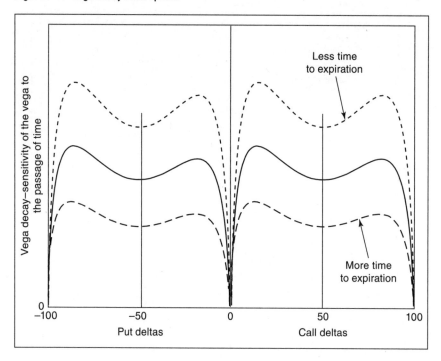

Gamma

The gamma measures the sensitivity of the delta to a change in the underlying price. But the gamma itself is sensitive to changes in market conditions.[6]

In Figure 9-18, we can see that the gamma is greatest when an option is at the money. This is similar to theta and vega, which are also greatest when an option is at the money, and leads to an important principle of option trading: *gamma, theta, and vega are greatest when an option is at the money.* Because of this, at-the-money options tend to be the most actively traded in most option markets. Such options have the characteristics that traders are looking for when they go into an option market.

Unlike the theta and vega of at-the-money options, which increase at higher exercise prices, the gamma of an at-the-money option declines at higher exercise prices. To understand why, recall that the gamma is the change in the delta per one-point change in the underlying price. But theoretical pricing models measure change in percentage terms. By this measure, a one-point price change with the underlying at 50 (a 2 percent change) is greater than

---

[6] Because the gamma is a second-order sensitivity—the sensitivity of the delta to a change in the underlying price—the sensitivity of gamma to a change in market conditions is a third-order sensitivity. For a discussion of some of the higher-order sensitivities, see Espen Gaarder Haug, *The Complete Guide to Option Pricing Formulas* (New York: McGraw-Hill, 2007); Espen Gaarder Haug, "Know Your Weapon, Part 1," *Wilmott Magazine*, May 2003: 49–57, also available at http://www.wilmott.com/pdfs/050527_haug.pdf; and Espen Gaarder Haug, "Know Your Weapon, Part 2," *Wilmott Magazine*, July–August 2003:50–56, also available at http://www .nuclearphynance.com/User percent20Files/2552/0307_haug.pdf.

Figure 9-18 Gamma of an option as the underlying price changes.

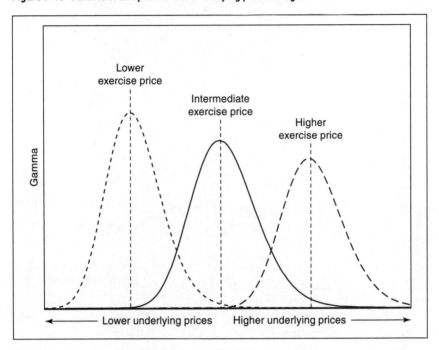

a one-point price change with the underlying at 100 (a 1 percent change). Although the theta and vega of at-the-money options are proportional to their exercise prices, the gamma is inversely proportional. The gamma of an option with an exercise price of 50 will be twice as large as the gamma of an option with an exercise price of 100.

Because at-the-money options have the greatest gamma, as the underlying price moves toward the exercise price, the gamma of an option will rise, and as the underlying price moves away from the exercise price, the gamma will fall. The sensitivity of the gamma to a change in the underlying price, sometimes referred to as the *speed*, is shown in Figure 9-19. The speed is greatest for out-of-the-money options with deltas close to 15 for calls and −15 for puts and for in-the-money options with deltas close to 85 for calls and −85 for puts. As we increase time to expiration or volatility, the speed of an option declines; as we reduce time to expiration or volatility, the speed rises. The gamma is least sensitive to changes in the underlying price for at-the-money options (a delta close to 50 for calls or −50 for puts) or for very deeply in-the-money or very far out-of-the-money options (deltas close to 0 and close to 100 for calls or −100 for puts).

The gamma will also be sensitive to changes in time to expiration and volatility. This is shown in Figure 9-20. We know that gamma is greatest when an option is at the money and declines as the option moves either into the money or out of the money. Of particular importance is the fact that the gamma of an at-the-money option rises as time passes or as we reduce volatility and falls as we increase volatility. To see why, consider a 100 call with the market at 97.50.

Figure 9-19 Speed of an option.

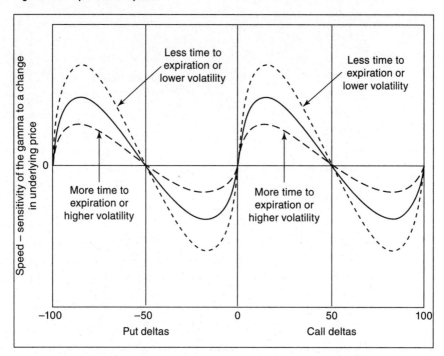

Because the option is currently out of the money, its delta is less than 50. We also know that as time passes or we reduce volatility, delta values move away from 50. If we are close to expiration or in a very low-volatility market, the delta of the option will be well below 50, perhaps 25. If the underlying market should then rise 5 points to 102.50, the delta of the option will be greater than 50, perhaps 75. With the underlying market rising from 97.50 to 102.50 and the delta rising from 25 to 75, the approximate gamma should be

$$\frac{75 - 25}{102.50 - 97.50} = \frac{50}{5} = 10$$

If, however, expiration is far in the future or we are in a high-volatility market, the delta of the 100 call will stay close to 50. With the underlying market at 97.50, the delta of the option may be 45. If the market then rises to 102.50, the delta may be only 55. The approximate gamma is then

$$\frac{55 - 45}{102.50 - 97.50} = \frac{10}{5} = 2$$

The effect is just the opposite for in-the-money and out-of-the-money options. The gamma will fall if we reduce volatility and rise if we increase volatility.[7] Because gamma and theta are closely related, if we were to graph

---

[7] This is a general rule. Sometimes an option that is only slightly in the money or out of the money will act like an at-the-money option. Whether an option's characteristics will resemble those of an at-the-money, in-the-money, or out-of-the-money option will depend on a variety of factors, including volatility and time to expiration.

Figure 9-20 Gamma of an option as time passes or volatility changes.

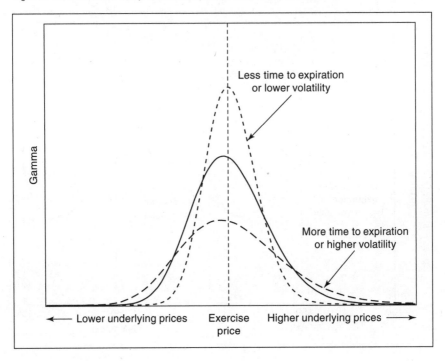

the gamma of an option as time passes, the result would be very similar to Figure 9-10, with the gamma instead of the theta along the y-axis.

The sensitivity of the gamma to the passage of time, sometimes referred to as its *color*, is shown in Figure 9-21. The color is greatest for at-the-money calls and puts, with gamma values becoming smaller as we increase time to expiration and larger as we reduce time (hence a negative color value). Calls with deltas close to 5 or 95 and puts with deltas close to −5 or −95 also have large color values. Here, however, an increase in time causes gamma values to rise, whereas the passage of time causes gamma values to fall (a positive color). Moreover, reducing time or volatility will increase color values, making an option's gamma more sensitive to changes in the passage of time. Increasing time or volatility will reduce color values, making an option's gamma less sensitive to the passage of time. Calls with deltas close to 15 or 85 and puts with deltas close to −15 and −85 tend to have color values close to 0. The gamma values of such options will be relatively insensitive to the passage of time.

The sensitivity of an option's gamma to a change in volatility, sometimes referred to as its *zomma*, is shown in Figure 9-22. Zomma characteristics are similar to color characteristics. The zomma is large for at-the-money calls and puts, with gamma values becoming smaller as volatility rises and larger as volatility falls (a negative zomma). Calls with deltas close to 5 or 95 and puts with deltas close to −5 or −95 also have large zomma values. Here, however, an

Figure 9-21 Color of an option.

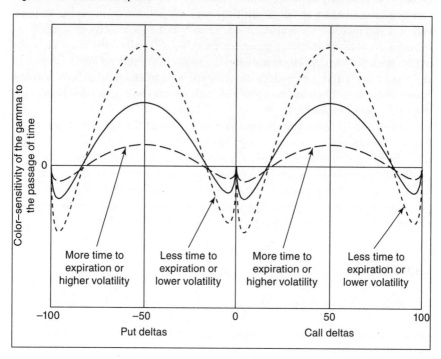

- More time to expiration or higher volatility
- Less time to expiration or lower volatility
- More time to expiration or higher volatility
- Less time to expiration or lower volatility

Color–sensitivity of the gamma to the passage of time

-100   -50   0   50   100
Put deltas   Call deltas

Figure 9-22 Zomma of an option.

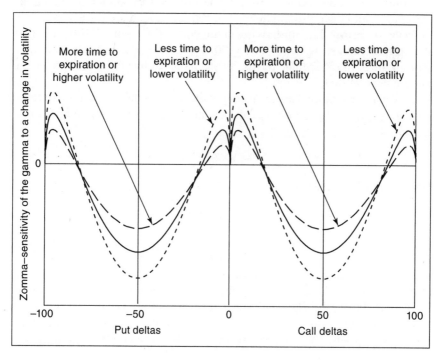

- More time to expiration or higher volatility
- Less time to expiration or lower volatility
- More time to expiration or higher volatility
- Less time to expiration or lower volatility

Zomma–sensitivity of the gamma to a change in volatility

-100   -50   0   50   100
Put deltas   Call deltas

increase in volatility causes gamma values to rise and a decline in volatility causes gamma values to fall (a positive zomma). Moreover, reducing time or volatility will increase the zomma, making an option's gamma more sensitive to changes in volatility. Increasing time or volatility will reduce the zomma, making an option's gamma less sensitive to changes in volatility. Calls with deltas close to 15 or 85 and puts with deltas close to −15 and −85 tend to have zomma values close to 0. The gamma values of such options will be relatively insensitive to changes in volatility.

Given the fact that the gamma is greatest for at-the-money options and that the gamma of an at-the-money option increases as time passes or volatility declines, experienced traders know that at-the-money options close to expiration in a low-volatility environment are among the riskiest options that one can trade. Although these *gamma options* initially have delta values close to 50, their deltas can change dramatically with only small moves in the price of the underlying contract, moving very quickly toward 0 or 100.

Lambda (Λ)

The delta tells us the point change in an option's value for a given point change in the price of the underlying contract. But we might also ask how an option's value changes in percentage terms for a given percentage change in the underlying price.

Consider a call option with a theoretical value of 4.00 and a delta of 20, with the underlying contract trading at a price of 100. If the underlying contract rises one point to 101, the new delta of the option (ignoring the gamma) should be approximately 4.20. But how much are these changes in percentage terms? The underlying changed by 1 percent (1/100), whereas the option changed by 5 percent (0.20/4.00). The option has a *lambda*, or *elasticity*, of 5. In percentage terms, it will change at five times the rate of the underlying contract.

We can see that the lambda is simply the option's delta (using the decimal format) multiplied by the ratio of the underlying price S to the option's theoretical value

$$\Lambda = \Delta \times (S/TV)$$

In our example, lambda is

$$0.20 \times 100/4.00 = \mathbf{5}$$

Traders sometimes refer to the lambda as the option's *leverage value*. Although lambda is not a widely used risk measure, it may still be worth looking at some basic lambda characteristics. These are shown in Figures 9-23 (call lambda values) and 9-24 (put lambda values). Logically, because the lambda is calculated from the delta, calls have positive lambda values and puts have negative lambda values. We can see that the lambda is greatest for out-of-the-money options—as the underlying price rises, call lambda values decline

Figure 9-23 Lambda of a call as time passes or volatility changes.

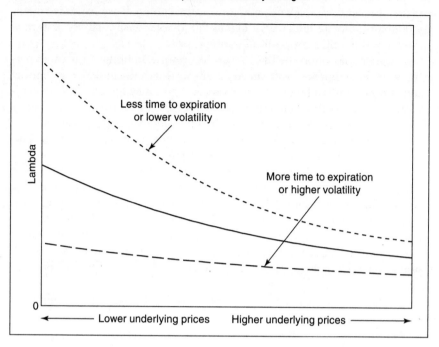

Figure 9-24 Lambda of a put as time passes or volatility changes.

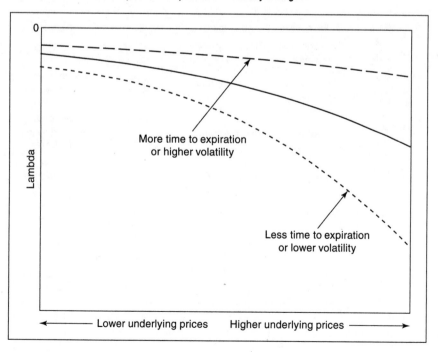

and put lambda values rise (they take on large negative values). Lambda values are also sensitive to changes in time and volatility. If we increase volatility, lambda values for both calls and puts fall. If we reduce volatility or as time passes, lambda values for both calls and puts rise.

A trader who wants the biggest possible return on his investment, in percentage terms, compared with an equal investment in the underlying contract can maximize his lambda by trading out-of-the-money options close to expiration in a low-volatility environment. Of course, this is true only in theory. There may be other considerations, such as the bid-ask spread and liquidity of the option market, that might make a large lambda position impractical compared with a similar position in the underlying market.

It may seem that we have gone into undue detail in our examination of the option risk measures. Although it is certainly true that not every risk is important in every situation, experienced traders have learned that it is almost impossible to overemphasize the importance of risk management in option trading. Because options are affected by so many different market forces, unless a trader is aware of and understands the many ways in which option values change, he cannot hope to successfully manage the very real risks that option trading entails.

A summary of the primary risk characteristics discussed in this chapter is given in Figures 9-25 and 9-26.

Figure 9-25 Traditional risk measures.

C = call theoretical value P = put theoretical value S = underlying price or spot price t = time to expiration σ = annual volatility r = domestic interest rate rf = foreign interest rate				
Risk Name	**Sensitivity of the**	**To a Change in**	**Math**	**Maximized**
Delta (Δ)	Theoretical value (in points)	Underlying price (in points)	$\partial C/\partial S \approx \partial P/\partial S + 1$	Deeply in the money
Lambda (Λ) [omega (Ω)] elasticity	Theoretical value (in percent)	Underlying price (in percent)	$\Delta c*(S/C)$ $\Delta p*(S/P)$	Out of the money Close to expiration Low volatility
Gamma (Γ) curvature	Delta	Underlying price	$\partial^2 C/\partial S^2 =$ $\partial^2 P/\partial S^2$ $\partial\Delta/\partial S$	At the money Close to expiration Low volatility
Theta (Θ) time decay	Theoretical value	Time to expiration	$\partial C/\partial t$ $\partial P/\partial t$	At the money Close to expiration Low volatility
Vega	Theoretical value	Volatility	$\partial C/\partial\sigma = \partial P/\partial\sigma$	At the money Long term
Rho (P)	Theoretical value	Interest rate	$\partial C/\partial r$ $\partial P/\partial r$	Deeply in the money Long term
Rhof or phi (Φ)	Theoretical value	Foreign interest rate or dividend yield	$\partial C/\partial rf$ $\partial P/\partial rf$	Deeply in the money Long term

Figure 9-26 Nontraditional higher-order risk measures.

Risk Name	Sensitivity of the	To a Change in	Math	Maximized
Vanna	Delta	Volatility	$\partial^2 C/\partial S \partial\sigma$	15-20, 80-85 delta
	Vega	Underlying price	$\partial^2 P/\partial S \partial\sigma$	Low volatility
Charm	Delta	Time	$\partial^2 C/\partial S \partial t$	15-20, 80-85 delta
delta decay	Theta	Underlying price	$\partial^2 P/\partial S \partial t$	Close to expiration
Speed	Gamma	Underlying price	$\partial^3 C/\partial S^3 = \partial^3 P/\partial S$ $\partial^2\Delta/\partial S^2 \ \partial\Gamma/\partial S$	15-20, 80-85 delta Low volatility Close to expiration
Color gamma decay	Gamma Charm	Time to expiration Underlying price	$\partial^3 C/\partial S^2 \partial t$ $\partial^3 P/\partial S^2 \partial t$ $\partial\Gamma/\partial t$	At the money Close to expiration Low volatility
Volga (vomma)	Vega	Volatility	$\partial^2 C/\partial\sigma^2 =$ $\partial^2 P/\partial\sigma^2$	10, 90 delta Long term Low volatility
Vega decay	Vega	Time	$\partial^2 C/\partial\sigma \partial t$ $\partial^2 P/\partial\sigma \partial t$	20, 80 delta Close to expiration
Zomma	Gamma Vanna	Volatility Underlying price	$\partial^3 C/\partial S^2 \partial\sigma =$ $\partial^3 P/\partial S^2 \partial\sigma$ $\partial\Gamma/\partial\sigma$	At the money Close to expiration Low volatility

10

Introduction to Spreading

In option markets, as in all markets, there are many different approaches to trading. At one time, *scalping* was a popular strategy among traders on the floors of futures exchanges. By observing the activity in a particular market, a scalper would try to determine an equilibrium price that reflected a balance between buyers and sellers. The scalper would then quote a bid-ask spread around this equilibrium price, attempting to buy at the bid price and sell at the offer price as often as possible without taking either a long or short position for any extended period of time. The scalper made no attempt to determine the theoretical value of the contract. Although the profit from each trade might be small, if a trader was able to trade often enough, he expected to show a reasonable profit. Scalping, however, requires a highly liquid market, and option markets are rarely sufficiently liquid to support this type of trading.

A different type of trading strategy involves speculating on the direction in which the underlying contract will move. The directional position can be taken in a variety of ways—in the cash market, in the futures market, or in the option market. Unfortunately, even when an underlying market moves in the expected direction, taking a directional position in an option market will not necessarily be profitable. Many different forces, including changes in volatility and the passage of time, can affect an option's price. If a trader's sole consideration is direction, he is usually better advised to take the position in the underlying market. If he does and he is right, he is assured of making a profit.

Most successful option traders are *spread* traders. Because option evaluation is based on the laws of probability and the laws of probability can be expected to even out only over long periods of time, option traders must often hold positions for extended periods. Over short periods of time, while the trader is waiting for an option position to move toward theoretical value, the position may be affected by a variety of changes in market conditions that threaten its potential profit. Indeed, over short periods of time, there is no guarantee that an option position will react in a manner consistent with a theoretical pricing model.

Spreading enables an option trader to take advantage of theoretically mispriced options while at the same time reducing the effects of short-term "bad luck."

What Is a Spread?

A *spread* is a strategy that involves taking opposing positions in different but related instruments. Most commonly, a spread will consist of positions that move in the opposite direction with respect to changes in market conditions. When market conditions change, one position is likely to gain value, while the other position is likely to lose value. Of course, if the values change at the same rate, the value of the spread will never change. A profitable spreading strategy is predicated on the assumption that the values of the positions will change at different rates.

Many common spreading strategies are based on arbitrage relationships, buying and selling the same or very closely related instruments in different markets to profit from a mispricing. The *cash-and-carry strategy* common in commodity markets is an example of this type of spread. Given the current cash price, interest rate, and storage and insurance costs, a commodity trader can calculate the value of a forward contract. If the actual market price of the forward contract is higher than the calculated value, the trader will create a spread by purchasing the commodity, selling the overpriced forward contract, and carrying the position to maturity.[1]

Consider a commodity trading at a price of $700. If interest rates are 6 percent annually and storage and insurance costs combined are $5 per month, what should be the value of a two-month forward contract?

$$\text{Forward price} = \text{cash price} + \text{interest} + \text{storage and insurance}$$
$$= \$700 + (\$700 \times 0.06 \times 2/12) + (2 \times \$5)$$
$$= \$717$$

If the actual price of the two-month forward contract is $725, the trader might buy the commodity for $700, sell the forward contract for $725, and carry the position to maturity. The total cash flow in terms of debits (–) and credits (+) will be

Cost of borrowing $700 for two months at 6.00 percent	–$7
Cost of buying the commodity	–$700
Cost of storing and insuring the commodity for two months	–$10
Amount received for the commodity at maturity	+$725

The total profit resulting from this strategy is

$$-\$7 - \$700 - \$10 + \$725 = +\$8$$

This is exactly the amount by which the forward contract was mispriced. The resulting profit will be unaffected by fluctuations in the price of either the

---

[1] The opposite type of arbitrage, selling the commodity and buying a forward contract, is not usually possible in commodity markets because commodities, unlike financial instruments, cannot be borrowed and sold short.

commodity itself or the forward contract because all cash flows were determined at the time the strategy was initiated. Whether the commodity rises to $800 or falls to $600, the profit is still $8.

Another type of spreading strategy involves buying and selling futures contracts of different maturities on the same underlying commodity. In the preceding example, we calculated the value of a two-month forward contract on a commodity at $717. We can do a similar calculation for a four-month forward contract. Here, however, the cost of borrowing will be compounded because we will need to borrow $700 for the first two-month period at 6 percent and then borrow $717 for the second two-month period, also at 6 percent.[2]

Cost of borrowing $700 for two months at 6.00 percent and then
borrowing $717 for another two months at 6.00 percent:
$-(700 \times 0.06/6) - (717 \times 0.06/6) = -7.00 - 7.17$ −$14.17
Cost of buying the commodity   −$700.00
Cost of storing and insuring the commodity for four months   −$20.00

The value of the four-month forward contract ought to be

$$\text{Four-month forward price} = \$700.00 + \$14.17 + \$20.00$$
$$= \$734.17$$

If there are two-month- and four-month exchange-traded futures contracts on this commodity, there should be a $17.17 difference, or spread, between the prices of the two contracts. If the spread between months is actually $20, a trader might buy the two-month contract and sell the four-month contract. The trader cannot tell whether either contract individually is overpriced or underpriced. But he knows that at a price of $20, the spread is $2.83 too expensive.

Assuming that the trader has accurately evaluated the spread, how will he make this $2.83 profit? One possibility is that the price of the futures spread will return to its expected value of $17.17. Having sold the spread (sell the four-month futures contract, buy the two-month futures contract), the trader can close out the position by purchasing the spread (buy the four-month futures contract, sell the two-month futures contract).

If the price of the spread does not return to its expected value, the trader can carry the entire position to maturity. Suppose that the spread was originally created by purchasing the two-month forward contract at a price of $717 and selling the four-month forward contract at a price of $737. If carried to maturity, the cash flow from the entire position will be as follows:

At the maturity of the two-month futures contract:
  Borrow $717 for two months at 6.00 percent   −$7.17
  Buy the commodity at the agreed-on two-month
  forward price   −$717.00
  Store and insure the commodity for the two months
  to maturity of the four-month futures contract   −$10.00

[2] For simplicity, we have assumed a constant interest rate. In fact, the cost of borrowing money for the second two-month period may be different from the cost of borrowing for the first two-month period. We have also ignored the cost of borrowing money to pay for storage and insurance. This will add a very small additional cost to the strategy.

At maturity of the four-month futures contract:
Deliver the commodity and receive the agreed-on
four-month forward price   +$737.00
Total profit   +$2.83

Of course, the trader could have achieved the same result by simply selling the four-month forward contract and buying the commodity. However, although a trader may have easy access to a futures exchange, he may find that his access to the physical commodity market is limited because such markets are typically dominated by large corporations. In such a case, he may find that it is both simpler and cheaper to execute the spread in the futures market.

Spreading strategies are often done to reduce one or more risks. In a cash-and-carry strategy, much of the directional risk is eliminated because the value of the long cash contract and the value of the short forward contract will tend to move in opposite directions. But a spreading strategy will not necessarily eliminate all risks. In our example, we assumed that we were able to borrow money at a fixed rate, thereby eliminating any interest-rate risk. We also assumed that storage and insurance costs were fixed when the strategy was initiated. If we are dealing only with futures contracts, changes in interest rates, as well as changes in storage and insurance costs, may affect the price relationship between futures months. If the changes are large enough, a seemingly profitable spreading strategy may in fact become unprofitable. In the preceding example, if interest rates and storage costs rise after the strategy has been initiated, the spread between the two-month and four-month futures contract will widen, resulting in a smaller profit to the trader or perhaps even a loss.

Our examples thus far were both *intramarket* commodity spreads, with all contract values based on the same underlying commodity. However, if a trader can identify a price relationship between two different commodities or two different financial instruments, he might consider an *intermarket* spread, buying in one market and selling in a different market. As with all spreads, the strategy is based on the assumption that there is an identifiable relationship between the prices of different contracts. When the price spread between the two contracts appears to violate this relationship, it represents an opportunity for the trader.

In the fixed-income markets, a common strategy involves buying or selling short-term interest-rate instruments and taking an opposing position in long-term interest-rate instruments. The value of the spread depends on changes in the yield curve—the relationship between short- and long-term interest rates.

Consider two futures contracts with the same time to maturity, a 10-year Treasury note future trading at price of $116\,^{14}/_{32}$ and a 30-year Treasury bond future trading at a price of $118\,^{27}/_{32}$.[3] The spread between the two is

$$118\,^{27}/_{32} - 116\,^{14}/_{32} = 2\,^{13}/_{32}$$

The prices of Treasury contracts move in the opposite direction of interest rates. If interest rates rise, Treasury prices will fall; if interest rates fall, Treasury

---

[3] Treasury note and bond prices are typically quoted in points and 32nds of par value.

prices will rise. If a trader believes that interest rates will rise but that long-term rates will rise more quickly than short-term rates, he might sell the 10-year/30-year spread.[4] If he is correct, the spread will narrow, perhaps at a later date trading at

$$115^{10}/_{32} - 113^{7}/_{32} = 2^{3}/_{32}$$

If the trader originally sold the spread at $2^{13}/_{32}$ and later buys the spread back at $2^{3}/_{32}$, he will show a profit of

$$2^{13}/_{32} - 2^{3}/_{32} = {}^{10}/_{32}$$

As a somewhat different intermarket spread, suppose that a trader observes the prices of two commodities, Commodity A and Commodity B, over an extended period and concludes that Commodity B tends to trade at a price that is three times greater than that of Commodity A. That is,

$$\text{Price of Commodity B} = 3 \times \text{price of Commodity A}$$

If the price of Commodity A is 50, the price of Commodity B ought to be 150. If the price of Commodity A is 200, the price of Commodity B ought to be 600. Although prices may occasionally deviate from this, they eventually seem to revert to this 3:1 relationship. Given this relationship, what will a trader do if the current prices of the commodities are

Price of Commodity A = 120
Price of Commodity B = 390

With prices of 120 and 390, Commodity B is trading at a multiple of 3.25 times Commodity A. Given the historical relationship, Commodity B seems to be trading at a price that is too high compared with Commodity A. Either Commodity B ought to be trading at 360 (3 × 120) or Commodity A ought to be trading at 130 (390/3).

If the trader believes that the prices are likely to return to their 3:1 historical relationship, he might purchase three contracts of Commodity A for 120 each and sell one contract of Commodity B at a price of 390

+3 Commodity A for 120	−360
−1 Commodity B at 390	+390
Total credit	+30

If at a later date the contract prices return to their 3:1 relationship, the trader can close out the position at no cost, leaving him with the expected profit of 30. This profit will be independent of the actual prices of the two commodities as long as the 3:1 relationship is maintained.

The strategy that we have just described involves buying and selling unequal numbers of contracts, sometimes referred to as a *ratio strategy*. It is common in markets where there is a perceived relationship between products with similar characteristics but that trade at different prices. In the precious metals

---

[4] Traders refer to this as the NOB spread (notes over bonds).

market, a trader might spread gold against silver, even though gold trades at a price many times that of silver. In the agricultural market, a trader might spread corn against soybeans, even though soybean prices are always greater than corn prices. In the stock index market, a trader might spread the Standard and Poor's (S&P) 500 Index against the Dow Jones Industrial Average Index. All these spreads differ from previous strategies in that they depend on an observed and perhaps less well-defined relationship than that between the cash price and the futures price or between the prices of different futures months. Because the relationship is less reliable, these types of spreads carry greater uncertainty and therefore greater risk. Nonetheless, if a trader believes that his analysis of a price relationship is accurate, the strategy may be worth pursuing.

Thus far, all our spreading examples have consisted of two sides, or *legs*. In the first example, one leg consisted of a physical commodity and one leg consisted of a forward contract. In the second example, the legs consisted of two different futures contracts. In the third example, the legs consisted of two different commodities. But spreading strategies may consist of many legs as long as a price relationship between the different legs can be identified.

In energy markets, a common spreading strategy consists of buying or selling crude oil futures and taking an opposing position in futures in products that are made from crude oil—gasoline and heating oil. The value of this *crack spread* depends on the cost of refining, or *cracking*, crude oil into its derivative products, as well as the demand for these products relative to the cost of crude oil. If the costs of refining rise or the demand for refined products rises, the value of the spread will widen. If costs fall or demand falls, the value of the spread will narrow.[5]

There are a number of ratios in which the crack spread can be traded, but one common ratio is the 3:2:1—3 gallons of crude oil to yield 2 gallons of gasoline and 1 gallon of heating oil. Because the value of the refined products is greater than that of crude oil, a trader is said to buy the spread when he buys the products and sells crude oil.

$$\text{Price of the 3:2:1 crack spread} = (2 \times \text{gasoline}) + (1 \times \text{heating oil}) - (3 \times \text{crude oil})$$

A trader who believes that the demand for refined products will fall can sell the crack spread. A trader who believes that demand will rise can buy the spread.

In some markets, it may be necessary to execute each leg of a spread separately because there may be no counterparty willing to execute the entire spread at one time. If the spread consists of multiple legs and the trader has only been able to execute one leg, he will be at risk until he completes the spread by executing the remaining legs. If the trader must execute the spread one leg at a time, he needs to consider the risk resulting from this piecemeal execution. Determining how best to execute a spread is usually a matter of experience. It is often true that some legs, owing to the liquidity in

---

[5] A similar type of three-sided spread is available in the soybean market. The *crush spread* consists of buying or selling soybean futures and taking an opposing futures position in the products that are made from soybeans—soybean oil and soybean meal.

the respective markets, will be more difficult to execute than other legs. As a consequence, most traders learn that it is usually best to execute the more difficult leg first. If a trader does this, he will find that execution risk is reduced because he will be able to more easily complete the spread. If, on the other hand, a trader executes the easier leg first, he may be left with a *naked* position if he is unable to execute the remaining legs in a timely manner or at a reasonable price.

Fortunately, in many markets, spreads are traded all at one time as if they are one contract. A quote for the spread will typically consist of one bid price and one offer price, no matter how complex the spread. Consider a spread that consists of buying Contract A and selling Contracts B and C with the following bid-ask quotes:

Contract	Bid	Ask
A	128	131
B	47	49
C	68	70

From the bid-ask quotes for each of the individual contracts, the current market for the spread is

Bid: $128 - 49 - 70 = 9$ (buy Contract A, sell Contracts B and C)
Ask: $131 - 47 - 68 = 16$ (sell Contract A, buy Contracts B and C)

If a trader wants to buy the spread, he can immediately trade all three contracts individually and pay a total of 16. If he wants to sell the spread, he can do so at a price of 9. But a trader may take the position that because he is trading multiple contracts, he ought to get some discount. A market maker in this spread will often take the view that because he has less risk when he executes all contracts at one time, he is willing to do so at a price more favorable to the trader. If the trader asks for a market for the entire spread, he will often find that the difference between the bid price and ask price is narrower than the sum of the bid-ask prices, perhaps 11 bid, 14 offer. Executing the entire spread as one transaction will clearly be better than executing the spread as three individual transactions.

Even if a spread is executed as one trade, many exchanges require that parties trading a spread still report the prices of the individual contracts. If this is the case, what prices should be reported if a trader buys the entire spread at a price of 14? In fact, the individual prices really don't matter. Whether the trader pays 129 for Contract A and sells Contracts B and C at 47 and 68 ($129 - 47 - 68 = 14$) or pays 131 for Contract A and sells Contracts B and C at 48 and 69 ($131 - 48 - 69 = 14$), the total price is still 14. Indeed, the parties could decide for whatever reason to trade Contract A at a price of 200 and Contracts B and C at prices of 86 and 100 ($200 - 86 - 100 = 14$). As far as the parties to the trade are concerned, all that matters is that the individual prices add up to the agreed-on spread price of 14.[6]

---

[6] In practice, when reporting the price of a spread, exchanges prefer that the parties to the trade use prices for the individual contracts that reflect current market conditions. Otherwise, it may appear that someone is engaging in unethical or illegal market activity. The exchange will not be happy if the parties report prices of 200, 86, and 100, even though these prices still add up to a total spread price of 14.

Option Spreads

At the beginning of this chapter, we defined a spread as consisting of opposing positions in related instruments. But what do we mean by a *position*? In the spread examples thus far, the positions were based on directional considerations. If the value of one position rises as a result of a directional move in the underlying market, the value of the opposing position is expected to decline, even though ultimately the price of the spread is expected to converge to some projected value. We can also create directional spreads in the option market by taking opposing but unequal delta positions in different contracts. As with our other spreads, the value of such a spread will depend on directional movement in the underlying contract.

While the prices of options are affected by directional moves in the underlying market, they can also be affected by other factors. In an option market, we might create a spread by taking a long gamma position in one option and a short gamma position in a different option, or by taking a long vega position and a short vega position, or even a long and short rho position. The value of each of these spreads will depend on factors other than directional moves in the underlying market. The gamma spread will be sensitive to the volatility of the underlying market. The vega spread will be sensitive to changes in implied volatility. And the rho spread will be sensitive to changes in interest rates.

The dynamic hedging examples in Chapter 8 are typical *gamma spreads*. We initiated the spreads by either purchasing or selling options and then offsetting the option's delta with an opposing delta position in the underlying contract. However, although an underlying contract has no gamma, an option does have a gamma. As a result, the entire position had either a positive or a negative gamma. From this we demonstrated that the value of the position depended not on the direction of movement in the underlying contract but on the volatility of the underlying contract.

Many option spreads are dynamic, requiring periodic adjustments. But a spread can also be *static*. Once initiated, the spread is carried to expiration without adjustments. This is usually done only when the risk characteristics of the spread are well defined and limited.

Perhaps in no other market are spreading strategies as widely employed as they are in option markets. There are a number of reasons for this:

1. *A trader might perceive a relative mispricing between contracts.* Just as a trader might calculate the value of a futures contract in relation to the price of a cash contract, an option trader might try to identify the value of one option contract in relation to another option. Although it may not be possible to determine the exact value of either contract, the trader might be able to estimate the relative value of the contracts. If prices in the marketplace deviate from this relative value, a trader will try to profit by either buying or selling the spread.

   In many markets, traders express a mispricing in terms of how much the price of a contract differs from its value. In option markets, the mispricing is often expressed in terms of volatility. Consider two options, one that has a theoretical value of 7.00 and is trading at a price of 8.00 and another that has a theoretical value of 6.00 and is trading at a price of 6.75. Which option represents a greater mispricing? Looking only at the option prices, the first option appears to be overpriced by 1.00, whereas the second option appears to be overpriced by only 0.75. But suppose that the volatility used to calculate the theoretical value is 23 percent. Because both options are overpriced, we know that their implied volatilities must be greater than 23 percent. If the implied volatility of the option trading at 8.00 is 26 percent, while the implied volatility of the option trading at 6.75 is 28 percent, an option trader is likely to conclude that in volatility terms, the second option is more overpriced.

Option Theoretical Value (Using a Volatility of 23%)	Option Price	Option Implied Volatility
7.00	8.00	26%
6.00	6.75	28%

2. *A trader may want to construct a position that reflects a particular view of market conditions.* Options can be combined in an almost infinite variety of ways such that a position will yield a profit when market conditions move favorably. At the same time, options can be combined in ways that will limit loss when conditions turn unfavorable. We looked at some examples of this in Chapter 4. Of course, even if a trader is able to construct a position that exactly reflects his view of market conditions, he will have to decide whether the prices at which the trades can be executed make the position worthwhile.

3. *Spreading strategies help to control risk.* This is particularly important for someone who is making decisions based on a theoretical pricing model. In Chapter 5, we stressed the fact that all commonly used pricing models are probability based and that outcomes predicated on the laws of probability are only reliable *in the long run*. In the short run, any one outcome can deviate from the expected outcome. If a trader wants to be successful in options, he must ensure that he remains in the game for the long run. If he is unlucky in the short run and must leave the game, the long-term probability theory does him no good. Spreading is the primary method by which traders limit the short-term effects of "bad luck."

In addition to reducing the effects of short-term bad luck, spreading strategies can also help protect a trader against incorrectly estimated inputs into the theoretical pricing model. Suppose that a trader estimates that over the life of an option, the volatility of an underlying contract will be 35 percent. Based on this, he determines that a certain call option, which is currently trading at a price of 4.00, has a theoretical value of 3.50. If the call has a delta of 25, the trader might try to capture this mispricing by selling four calls at a price of 4.00

each and buying one underlying contract and dynamically hedging the position over the life of the option. The total theoretical edge for the position is $4 \times 0.50 = 2.00$. Of course, if the trader can make 2.00 with a 4×1 spread, it may occur to him that he can make 20.00 if he increases the size of the spread to 40×10. Why stop now? The trader can make 200.00 if he increases the size to 400×100.

Even if the market is sufficiently liquid to absorb the increased size, is this a reasonable approach to trading? Should a trader simply find a theoretically profitable strategy and do it as many times as possible in order to maximize the potential profit? At some point, the intelligent trader will have to consider not only the potential profit of a strategy but also its risks. After all, the trader's volatility estimate of 35 percent is just that, an estimate. What will happen if volatility actually turns out to be some higher number, perhaps 40 percent, or 45 percent? If the calls that the trader sold at 4.00 are worth 4.50 at a volatility of 45 percent, and volatility actually turns out to be 45 percent, then the hoped-for profit of 200.00 (assuming a size of 400×100) will turn into a loss of 200.00.

A trader must always consider the effects of an incorrect estimate and then decide how much risk he is willing to take. If the trader in this example decides that he can survive if volatility goes no higher than 40 percent (a 5 percentage point margin for error), he might only be willing to do the spread 40×10. But, if there is some way to increase his breakeven volatility to 45 percent (a 10 percentage point margin for error), he might indeed be willing to do the spread 400×100. Option spreading strategies enable traders to profit under a wide variety of market conditions by giving them an increased margin for error in estimating the inputs into a theoretical pricing model. No trader will survive very long if his livelihood depends on estimating each input with 100 percent accuracy. But if he has constructed an intelligent spreading strategy that allows for a large margin of error, the experienced trader can survive even when his estimates of market conditions turn out to be incorrect.

To see how spreading strategies can be used to reduce risk, recall our example in Chapter 5 where a casino is selling a roulette bet with an expected value of 95 cents for $1.00. The casino knows that based on the laws of probability, it has a 5 percent theoretical edge. Suppose that a customer comes into the casino and proposes to bet $2,000 on one number at the roulette table. Should the casino allow the bet? The casino owner knows that the odds are on his side and that he will most likely get to keep the $2,000 bet, but there is always a chance that the player's number will come up. If it does, the casino will lose $70,000 (the $72,000 payoff less the $2,000 cost of the bet). If the casino is backed by millions of dollars, the loss of $70,000 will not severely interfere with the casino's continuing operations. If, however, the casino is only backed by $50,000, the loss of $70,000 will put the casino out of business. And if the casino goes out of business, it can no longer rely on its 5 percent edge because this is an expectation that is only reliable in the long run. And the long run has just been eliminated.

Now consider a slight variation where two customers come into the casino and propose to place bets of $1,000 each at the roulette table, but they also agree not to bet on the same number. Whichever number one player chooses, the other will choose a different number. As with the first scenario, where one player makes a single $2,000 bet, the casino's potential reward in this new scenario is also $2,000. If neither number comes up, the casino gets to keep the two $1,000 bets. But what is the risk to the casino now? In the worst case, the casino can only lose $34,000, the $36,000 payoff if one player wins less the cost of the two $1,000 bets. The two bets are mutually exclusive—if one player wins, the other must lose.

In return for the reduced risk, it might seem that the casino must give up some of its theoretical edge. We tend to assume that there is a tradeoff between risk and reward. But the edge to the casino in both cases is still the same 5 percent. Regardless of the amount wagered or the number of individual bets, the laws of probability specify that in the long run the casino gets to keep 5 percent of everything that is bet at the roulette table. In the short run, however, the risk to the casino is greatly reduced with two $1,000 bets because the bets have been *spread* around the table.

Casinos do not like to see an individual player wager a large amount of money on one outcome, whether at roulette or any other casino game. This is why casinos have betting limits. The laws of probability are still in the casino's favor, but if the bet is large enough and the bettor happens to win, the short-term bad luck can overwhelm the casino. From the casino's point of view, the ideal scenario is for 38 players to place 38 bets of $1,000 each on all 38 numbers at the roulette table. Now the casino has a perfect spread position. One player will collect $36,000, but with $38,000 on the table, the casino has a sure profit of $2,000.

Looking at the situation from the player's point of view, if the player knows that the odds are against him and he wants the greatest chance of showing a profit, his best course is to wager the maximum amount on one outcome and hope that in the short run he gets lucky. If he continues to make bets over a long period of time, the laws of probability eventually will catch up with him, and the casino will end up with the player's money.

An option trader prefers to spread for the same reason that the casino prefers the bets to be spread around the table: spreading maintains profit potential but reduces short-term risk. There is rarely a perfect spread position for an option trader, but an intelligent option trader learns to spread off the risk in as many different ways as possible to minimize the effects of short-term bad luck. An important part of any serious option trader's education consists of learning a wide variety of spreading strategies.

New traders are sometimes astonished at the size of the trades an experienced option trader is prepared to make. How can the trader afford to do this? His financial resources certainly play a role in the risk he is willing to accept. But equally important is his ability to spread off risk. An experienced trader may know many different ways to spread off the risk, using other options, futures contracts, cash contracts, or some combination of these. While he may not be able to completely eliminate his risk, he may be able to reduce it to such an extent that his risk is actually less than that of a much smaller trader who does not know how to spread or knows only a limited number of spreading strategies.

Volatility Spreads

In Chapter 8, we showed that it is possible, at least in theory, to capture an option's mispricing in the marketplace by employing a dynamic hedging strategy. The first step in this process involves hedging the option position, delta neutral, by taking an opposing market position in the underlying contract. But the underlying contract is not the only way in which we can hedge an option position. We might instead take our opposing delta position with other options.

Consider a call with a delta of 50 that appears to be underpriced in the marketplace. If we buy 10 calls, resulting in a delta position of +500, we might hedge the position in any of the following ways:

> Sell five underlying contracts.
> Buy puts with a total delta of −500.
> Sell calls, different from those that we purchased, with a total delta of −500.
> Do a combination of any of the preceding such that we create a total delta of −500.

There are clearly many different ways of hedging our 10 calls. Regardless of which method we choose, each spread will have certain features in common:

> Each spread will be approximately delta neutral.
> Each spread will be sensitive to changes in the price of the underlying instrument.
> Each spread will be sensitive to changes in implied volatility.
> Each spread will be sensitive to the passage of time.

Spreads with the foregoing characteristics fall under the general heading of *volatility spreads*. In this chapter, we will look at the most common types of volatility spreads, initially by examining their expiration values and then by considering their delta, gamma, theta, vega, and rho characteristics.

Straddle

A *straddle* consists of a call and a put where both options have the same exercise price and expiration date. In a straddle, both options are either purchased (a *long straddle*) or sold (a *short straddle*). Examples of long and short straddles, with their expiration profit-and-loss (P&L) graphs, are shown in Figures 11-1 and 11-2.

At expiration, the value of a straddle can be expressed as a simple parity graph. But what about its value prior to expiration? As with all option positions, some changes in market conditions will help the strategy and some changes will hurt. From Figure 11-1, we can see that a long straddle becomes more valuable when the underlying market moves away from the exercise price and less valuable as time passes if no movement occurs. At the same time, any increase in volatility will help, while any decline will hurt. These characteristics are indicated by the risk measures associated with the position:

> +Gamma (desire for movement in the underlying contract)
> –Theta (the value of the position declines as time passes)
> +Vega (the value of the position increases as implied volatility rises)

The characteristics of a short straddle are shown in Figure 11-2:

> –Gamma (movement in the underlying contract will hurt the position)
> +Theta (the value of the position increases as time passes)
> –Vega (the value of the position increases as implied volatility falls)

Figure 11-1 Long straddle as time passes or volatility declines.

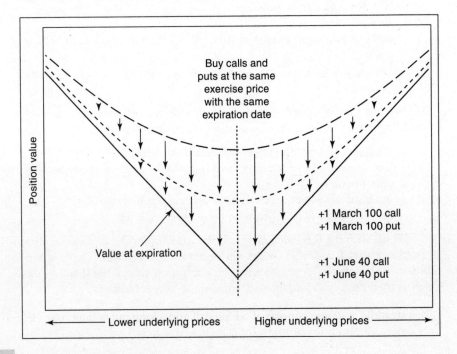

Buy calls and
puts at the same
exercise price
with the same
expiration date

Position value

+1 March 100 call
+1 March 100 put

+1 June 40 call
+1 June 40 put

Value at expiration

◄──── Lower underlying prices   Higher underlying prices ────►

Figure 11-2 Short straddle as time passes or volatility declines.

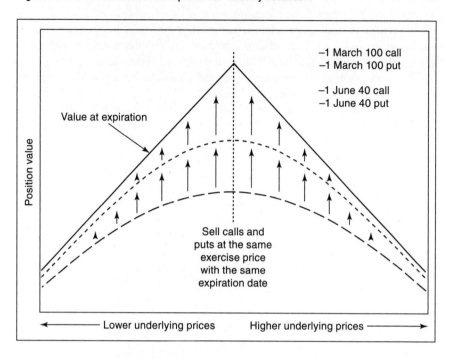

Straddles are most often executed one to one (one call for each put) using at-the-money options. When this is done, the spread will be approximately delta neutral because the delta values of the call and put will be close to 50 and −50. A straddle can also be done with options that are either in the money or out of the money. For example, with the underlying contract trading at 100, we might buy the September 95 straddle. If the September 95 calls, which are in the money, have a delta of 75 and the September 95 puts, which are out of the money, have a delta of −25, the total delta will be 75 − 25 = 50, resulting in a *bull straddle*. If we want the straddle to be delta neutral, we will need to adjust the number of contracts by purchasing three puts for every call:

> Buy 1 September 95 call (delta = 75).
> Buy 3 September 95 puts (delta = −25).

This spread still qualifies as a straddle because we are buying calls and puts at the same exercise price. But, more specifically, this is a *ratio straddle* because the number of long market contracts (the calls) and the number of short market contracts (the puts) are unequal.

Strangle

Like a straddle, a *strangle* consists of a long call and a long put (a long strangle) or a short call and a short put (a short strangle), where both options expire at the same time. But in a strangle the options have different exercise prices. Typical long and short strangles are shown in Figures 11-3 and 11-4.

As with a straddle, strangles are most often done one to one (one call for each put). In order to ensure that the position is delta neutral, exercise prices are usually chosen so that the call and put deltas are approximately equal.

If a strangle is identified only by its expiration month and exercise prices, there may be some confusion as to the specific options involved. A March 90/110 strangle might consist of a March 90 put and a March 110 call. But it might also consist of a March 90 call and a March 110 put. Both strategies are consistent with the definition of a strangle. To avoid confusion, a strangle is commonly assumed to consist of out-of-the-money options. If the underlying market is currently at 100 and a trader wants to purchase the March 90/110 strangle, everyone will assume that he wants to purchase a March 90 put and a March 110 call. Although both strangles have essentially the same P&L profile, in-the-money options tend to be less actively traded than their out-of-the-money counterparts. A strangle consisting of in-the-money options is sometimes referred to as a *guts*.

Note that the risk characteristics of a strangle are similar to those of a straddle:

> Long strangle: +gamma/–theta/+vega
> Long straddle: +gamma/–theta/+vega

A new option trader often finds long straddles and strangles attractive because strategies with limited risk and unlimited profit potential offer great appeal, especially when the profit is unlimited in both directions. However,

Figure 11-3 Long strangle as time passes or volatility declines.

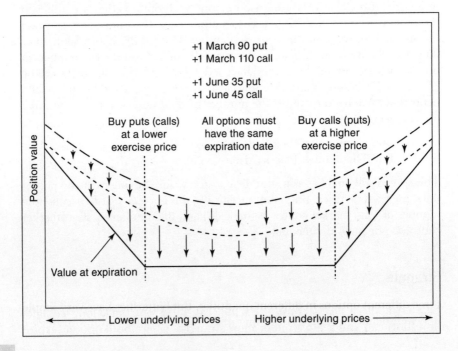

Figure 11-4 Short strangle as time passes or volatility declines.

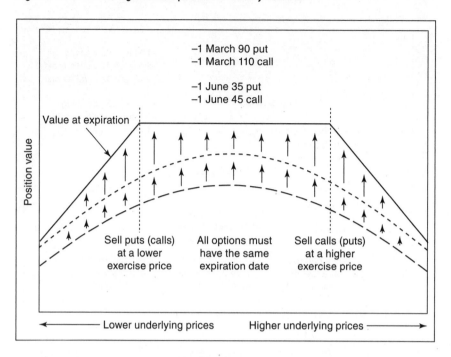

if the hoped-for movement fails to materialize, a trader will find that losing money, even a limited amount, can also be a painful experience. This is not an endorsement of either long or short straddles. Under the right conditions, either strategy may be sensible. But an intelligent trader needs to consider not only whether the risk and reward is limited or unlimited but also the likelihood of the various outcomes. This, of course, is one important reason for using a theoretical pricing model.

Butterfly

Thus far we have looked at spreads that involve buying or selling two different option contracts. However, we can also construct spreads consisting of three, four, or even more different options. A *butterfly* is a common three-sided spread consisting of options with equally spaced exercise prices, where all options are of the same type (either all calls or all puts) and expire at the same time. In a long butterfly, the outside exercise prices are purchased and the inside exercise price is sold, and vice versa for a short butterfly. Moreover, the ratio of a butterfly never varies. It is always 1 × 2 × 1, with two of each inside exercise price traded for each one of the outside exercise prices. Typical long and short butterflies are shown in Figures 11-5 and 11-6.

To a new trader, a butterfly may look quite complex since it involves three different options in different quantities. But butterflies have very simple and well-defined characteristics that make them popular trading strategies.

Figure 11-5 Long butterfly as time passes or volatility declines.

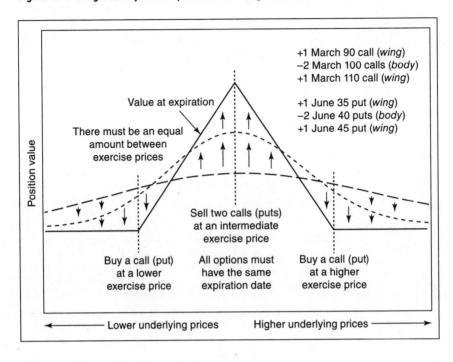

+1 March 90 call (*wing*)
−2 March 100 calls (*body*)
+1 March 110 call (*wing*)

+1 June 35 put (*wing*)
−2 June 40 puts (*body*)
+1 June 45 put (*wing*)

Value at expiration

There must be an equal amount between exercise prices

Sell two calls (puts) at an intermediate exercise price

Buy a call (put) at a lower exercise price

All options must have the same expiration date

Buy a call (put) at a higher exercise price

Position value

Lower underlying prices   Higher underlying prices

Figure 11-6 Short butterfly as time passes or volatility declines.

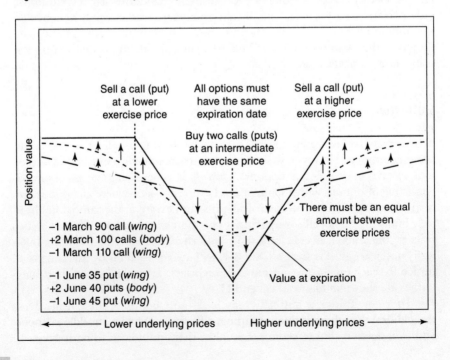

Sell a call (put) at a lower exercise price

All options must have the same expiration date

Sell a call (put) at a higher exercise price

Buy two calls (puts) at an intermediate exercise price

There must be an equal amount between exercise prices

−1 March 90 call (*wing*)
+2 March 100 calls (*body*)
−1 March 110 call (*wing*)

−1 June 35 put (*wing*)
+2 June 40 puts (*body*)
−1 June 45 put (*wing*)

Value at expiration

Position value

Lower underlying prices   Higher underlying prices

To understand these characteristics, let's consider the value of a long butterfly at expiration:

		Underlying Price at Expiration		
		80	100	120
+1 March 90 call	Position value	0	+10	+30
−2 March 100 calls	Position value	0	0	−40
+1 March 110 call	Position value	0	0	+10
Total		0	+10	0

If the underlying price is below 90 at expiration, all the calls will expire worthless, and the value of the position will be 0. If the underlying contract is above 120 at expiration, the combined value of the 90 and 110 calls will equal the value of the two 100 calls. Again, the value of the butterfly will be 0. Now suppose that the underlying contract is between 90 and 110 at expiration, specifically, right at the inside exercise price of 100. The 90 call will be worth 10.00, while the 100 and 110 calls will be worthless. The position will be worth exactly 10.00. If the underlying moves away from 100, the value of the butterfly will decline, but its value can never fall below 0. Summarizing, at expiration, a butterfly is worthless if the underlying contract is above or below the outside exercise prices (sometimes referred to as the *wings* of the butterfly). It has its maximum value at expiration when the underlying contract is right at the inside exercise price (sometimes referred to as the *body* of the butterfly). And the maximum value is always equal to the amount between exercise prices, in our example 10.00.

Because a butterfly at expiration always has a value between 0 and the amount between exercise prices, in our example, a trader should be willing to pay some amount between 0 and 10.00 for the position. The exact amount depends on the likelihood of the underlying contract finishing close to the inside price at expiration. If there is a high probability of this occurring, a trader might be willing to pay as much as 8.00 for the butterfly since it might very well expand to its full value of 10.00. If, however, there is a low probability of this occurring and, consequently, a high probability that the underlying contract will finish outside the extreme exercise prices, a trader may only be willing to pay 1.00 or 2.00 because he may very well lose his entire investment. This also explains why our example position is a *long* butterfly. Because the position can never be worth less than 0, a trader will always be required to pay some amount for the position. Otherwise, there would be a riskless profit opportunity. When a position requires an outlay of cash, a trader has bought, or is long, the position.

A butterfly will tend to be delta neutral when the inside exercise price is approximately at the money. Under these conditions, a long butterfly will tend to act like a short straddle, while a short butterfly will tend to act like a long straddle. With either a long butterfly or a short straddle, a trader wants the underlying market to sit still (−gamma, +theta) and implied volatility to fall (−vega). With either a short butterfly or a long straddle, a trader wants the underlying market to make a large move (+gamma, −theta) and implied volatility to rise (+vega). But there is one important difference. While a straddle is open-ended in terms of either profit potential or risk, a butterfly is strictly limited.

It can never be worth less than 0 nor more than the amount between exercise prices. This is important for a trader who might want to sell straddles but who is uncomfortable with the possibility of unlimited loss. Of course, there is always a risk-reward tradeoff. If a long butterfly has reduced risk when the trader is wrong, it will also have increased profit when the trader is right. For this reason, butterflies tend to be executed in much larger sizes than straddles. A trader may find that buying 300 butterflies (300 × 600 × 300) is actually less risky than selling 100 straddles. In option trading, size and risk do not always correlate. Some strategies done in large sizes can have a relatively small risk, while other strategies, even when done in small sizes, can have a relatively large risk. Risk depends not only on the size in which a strategy is executed but also on the characteristics of the strategy.

We know that a butterfly at expiration is worth its maximum when the underlying contract is right at the inside exercise price. If we assume that all options are European, with no possibility of early exercise, both a call and a put butterfly with the same exercise prices and the same expiration dates desire exactly the same outcome and therefore have identical characteristics. Both the March 90/100/110 call butterfly and the March 90/100/110 put butterfly will be worth a maximum of 10.00 with the underlying price exactly at 100 at expiration and a minimum of 0 with the underlying price below 90 or above 110. If both butterflies are not trading at the same price, there is a sure profit opportunity available by purchasing the cheaper and selling the more expensive.[1]

Condor

Just as a butterfly can be thought of as a straddle with limited risk or reward, a *condor* can be thought of as a strangle with limited risk or reward. A condor consists of four options, two inside exercise prices (the body of the condor) and two outside exercise prices (the wings of the condor).[2] The ratio of a condor is always 1 × 1 × 1 × 1. Although the amount between the two inside exercise prices can vary, there must be an equal amount between the two lowest exercise prices and the two highest exercise prices. As with a butterfly, all options must expire at the same time and be of the same type (either all calls or all puts). In a long condor, the two outside exercise prices are purchased and the two inside exercise prices are sold, and vice versa for a short condor. Typical long and short condors are shown in Figures 11-7 and 11-8.

The value of a condor at expiration can never be less than 0 nor more than the amount between the two higher or the two lower exercise prices. A trader who buys a condor will pay some amount between these values, expecting that the underlying contract will finish between the two intermediate exercise prices, where the condor will be worth its maximum. A trader who sells a condor will take in some amount, expecting that the underlying contract will finish outside the extreme exercise prices, where the condor will be worthless.

---

[1] This is not necessarily true for butterflies consisting of American options, where early exercise is a possibility. A sure profit would exist only if one could be certain of carrying the position to expiration.

[2] Butterflies and condors fall under the general category of strategies known as wingspreads.

Figure 11-7 Long condor as time passes or volatility declines.

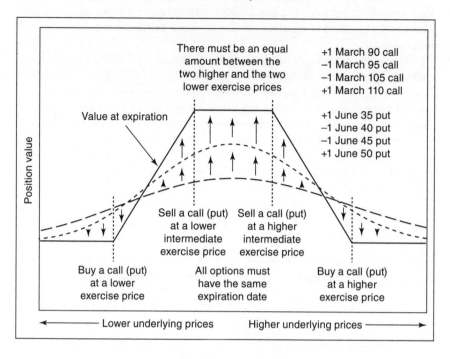

There must be an equal amount between the two higher and the two lower exercise prices

+1 March 90 call
−1 March 95 call
−1 March 105 call
+1 March 110 call

+1 June 35 put
−1 June 40 put
−1 June 45 put
+1 June 50 put

Value at expiration

Position value

Sell a call (put) at a lower intermediate exercise price

Sell a call (put) at a higher intermediate exercise price

Buy a call (put) at a lower exercise price

All options must have the same expiration date

Buy a call (put) at a higher exercise price

Lower underlying prices   Higher underlying prices

Figure 11-8 Short condor as time passes or volatility declines.

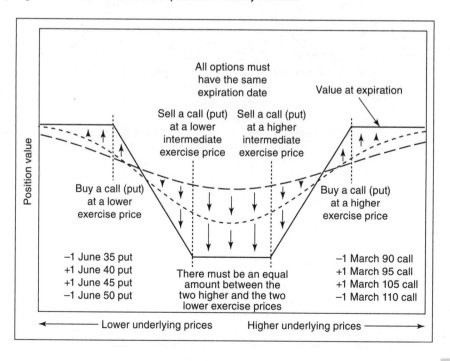

All options must have the same expiration date

Value at expiration

Position value

Sell a call (put) at a lower intermediate exercise price

Sell a call (put) at a higher intermediate exercise price

Buy a call (put) at a lower exercise price

Buy a call (put) at a higher exercise price

−1 June 35 put
+1 June 40 put
+1 June 45 put
−1 June 50 put

There must be an equal amount between the two higher and the two lower exercise prices

−1 March 90 call
+1 March 95 call
+1 March 105 call
−1 March 110 call

Lower underlying prices   Higher underlying prices

A condor will be approximately delta neutral when the underlying contract is midway between the two inside exercise prices. When all options are European, the value and characteristics of a call condor and put condor will be identical.

The four volatility spreads that we just described—straddles, strangles, butterflies, and condors—all have symmetrical P&L graphs. When executed delta neutral, as is most common, these strategies have no preference as to the direction of movement in the underlying market. Long straddles and strangles and short butterflies and condors prefer movement in the underlying market and an increase in implied volatility (+gamma, –theta , +vega). Short straddles and strangles and long butterflies and condors prefer no movement in the underlying market and a decline in implied volatility (–gamma, +theta, –vega). These characteristics are summarized in Figure 11-9.

Figure 11-9 Symmetrical strategies.

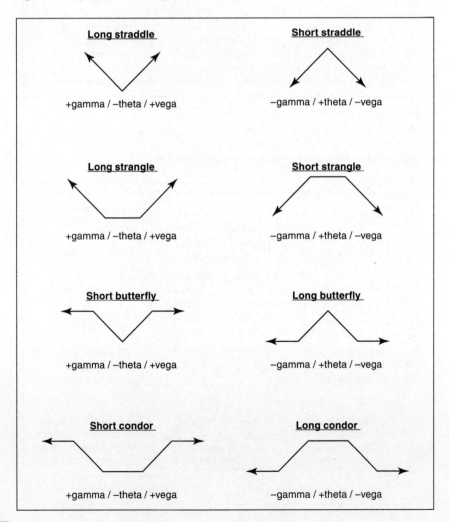

Ratio Spread

In a volatility spread, a trader need not be totally indifferent to the direction of movement in the underlying market. The trader may believe that movement in one direction is more likely than movement in the other direction. Given this, the trader may wish to construct a spread that either maximizes his profit or minimizes his loss when movement occurs in one direction rather than the other. In order to achieve this, a trader can construct a *ratio spread*—buying and selling unequal numbers of options where all options are the same type and expire at the same time. As with other volatility positions, the spread is typically delta neutral.

Consider the following delta-neutral position with the underlying contract trading at 100 (delta values are in parentheses):

Contract Position	Price per Contract
+3 October 105 call (25)	1.00
–1 October 95 call (75)	6.00

Now let's consider three possible prices for the underlying contract at expiration:

Underlying Price	95 Call P&L	105 Call P&L	Total P&L
80	+6.00 – 0 = +6.00	3 × (–1.00 + 0) = –3.00	**+3.00**
120	+6.00 – 25.00 = –19.00	3 × (–1.00 + 15.00) = +42.00	**+23.00**
100	+6.00 – 5.00 = +1.00	3 × (–1.00 + 0) = –3.00	**–2.00**

If the underlying contract makes a very big move in either direction, the position will show a profit. Of course, the profit will be much larger if the move is upward. If the underlying sits at 100 until expiration, the position will show a loss. This *call ratio spread*, where more calls are purchased than sold, wants movement in the underlying contract but clearly prefers upward movement, where the potential profit is unlimited. The P&L diagram for this type of strategy is shown in Figure 11-10.

The same type of position can be created using puts. A *put ratio spread*, where more puts are purchased than sold, also prefers movement in the underlying contract. But now there is a preference for downward movement because the profit potential on the downside will be unlimited. This is shown in Figure 11-11.

A ratio spread where more options are purchased than sold is sometimes referred to as *backspread*. Regardless of whether the spread consists of calls or puts, this type of spread always wants movement in the underlying market (+gamma, –theta) and/or an increase in implied volatility (+vega).

In a ratio spread where more options are purchased than sold, the spread will be worthless if the underlying contract makes a large enough downward move in the case of calls or a large enough upward move in the case of puts. For either spread to result in a profit, it must be executed initially for a credit, and this is a typical characteristic of these types of spreads. Indeed, under the assumptions of a traditional theoretical pricing model, a delta-neutral ratio spread where more options are purchased than sold should always result in a credit.

Figure 11-10 Call ratio spread (buy more than sell) as time passes or volatility declines.

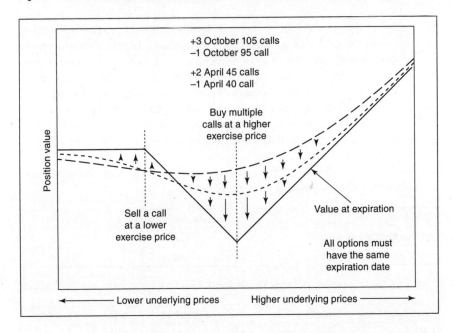

+3 October 105 calls
−1 October 95 call

+2 April 45 calls
−1 April 40 call

Buy multiple
calls at a higher
exercise price

Position value

Sell a call
at a lower
exercise price

Value at expiration

All options must
have the same
expiration date

◄─── Lower underlying prices   Higher underlying prices ───►

Ratio spreads are often used to limit the risk in one direction. If we sell more calls than we buy, the spread will act like a short straddle (−gamma, +theta, −vega) but with limited downside risk. If we sell more puts than we buy,

Figure 11-11 Put ratio spread (buy more than sell) as time passes or volatility declines.

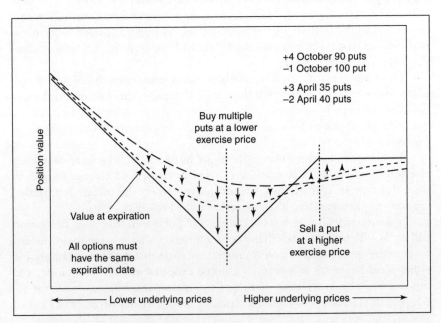

+4 October 90 puts
−1 October 100 put

+3 April 35 puts
−2 April 40 puts

Buy multiple
puts at a lower
exercise price

Position value

Value at expiration

All options must
have the same
expiration date

Sell a put
at a higher
exercise price

◄─── Lower underlying prices   Higher underlying prices ───►

Figure 11-12 Call ratio spread (sell more than buy) as time passes or volatility declines.

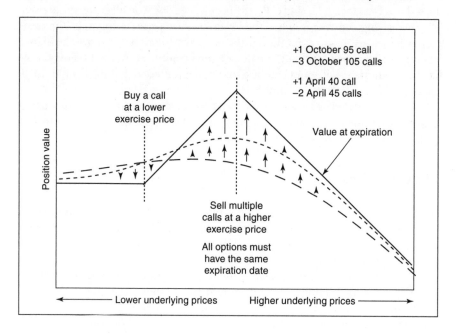

the spread will have limited upside risk. The P&L diagrams for these types of spreads are shown Figures 11-12 and 11-13.

Figure 11-13 Put ratio spread (sell more than buy) as time passes or volatility declines.

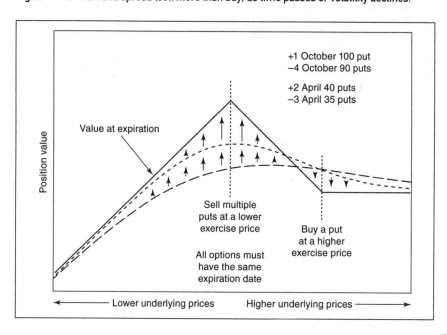

A ratio spread where more options are sold than purchased is sometimes referred to as *frontspread*.[3] Using calls, the position will be worthless at expiration if the underlying contract is below the lower exercise price. Using puts, the position will be worthless at expiration if the underlying contract is above the higher exercise price. The fact that the value of the position cannot fall below 0 limits the downside risk if more calls are sold than purchased and the upside risk if more puts are sold than purchased.

When executed as a single trade, ratio spreads are usually submitted using simple ratios, the most common being 2 to 1. However, other ratios—3 to 1, 4 to 1, or 3 to 2—are also relatively common.

Christmas Tree

Ratio spreads tend to mimic straddles, but with the risk or reward limited in one direction. We can also construct strategies that mimic strangles, but again with limited risk or reward in one direction. Such spreads are known as either *Christmas trees* or *ladders*.[4]

A call Christmas tree involves buying (selling) a call at a lower exercise price and selling (buying) one call each at two higher exercise prices. A put Christmas tree involves buying (selling) a put at a higher exercise price and selling (buying) one put each at two lower exercise prices. All options must be the same type and expire at the same time, with exercise prices most often chosen so that the entire position is delta neutral. When one option is bought and two options sold (a long Christmas tree), the position acts like a short strangle but with limited risk in one direction. When one option is sold and two options bought (a short Christmas tree), the position acts like a long strangle but with limited profit potential in one direction. P&L diagrams for typical Christmas trees are shown in Figures 11-14 through 11-17.

Although ratio spreads and Christmas trees have nonsymmetrical P&L graphs, their volatility characteristics tend to mimic straddles and strangles. A spread in which more options are purchased than sold will prefer movement in the underlying market and/or an increase in implied volatility (+gamma, –theta, +vega). A spread in which more options are sold than purchased will prefer no movement in the underlying market and/or a decline in implied volatility (–gamma, +theta, –vega). The characteristics of nonsymmetrical spreads are summarized in Figure 11-18.

Calendar Spread

If all options in a spread expire at the same time, the value of the spread at expiration depends solely on the underlying price. If, however, the spread consists of options that expire at different times, the spread's value depends not only on

---

[3] The terms backspread and frontspread date from the early days of option trading in the United States but are now used infrequently except by some older traders. Most traders simply refer to these strategies as ratio spreads, specifying whether more options are purchased or sold and the ratio of long to short options.
[4] The term *ladder* may also refer to a type of exotic option.

Figure 11-14 Long call Christmas tree as time passes or volatility declines.

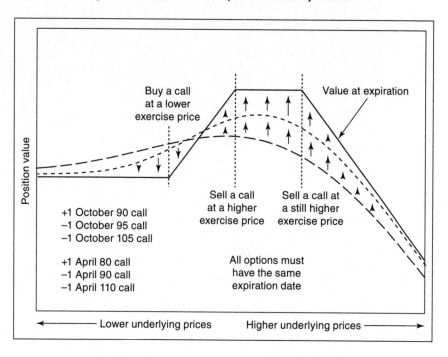

Buy a call
at a lower
exercise price

Value at expiration

Position value

+1 October 90 call
−1 October 95 call
−1 October 105 call

+1 April 80 call
−1 April 90 call
−1 April 110 call

Sell a call
at a higher
exercise price

Sell a call at
a still higher
exercise price

All options must
have the same
expiration date

◀—— Lower underlying prices   Higher underlying prices ——▶

Figure 11-15 Short call Christmas tree as time passes or volatility declines.

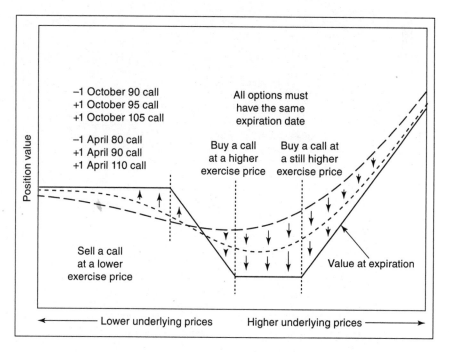

−1 October 90 call
+1 October 95 call
+1 October 105 call

−1 April 80 call
+1 April 90 call
+1 April 110 call

All options must
have the same
expiration date

Position value

Buy a call
at a higher
exercise price

Buy a call at
a still higher
exercise price

Sell a call
at a lower
exercise price

Value at expiration

◀—— Lower underlying prices   Higher underlying prices ——▶

Figure 11-16 Long put Christmas tree as time passes or volatility declines.

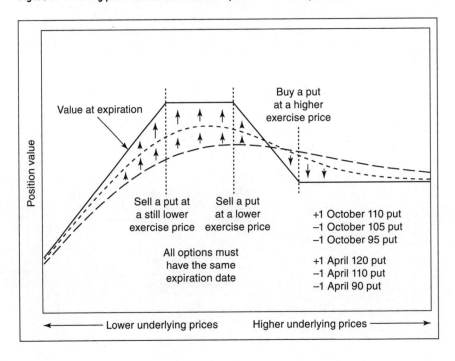

Value at expiration

Position value

Buy a put at a higher exercise price

Sell a put at a still lower exercise price

Sell a put at a lower exercise price

+1 October 110 put
−1 October 105 put
−1 October 95 put

+1 April 120 put
−1 April 110 put
−1 April 90 put

All options must have the same expiration date

◄——— Lower underlying prices   Higher underlying prices ———►

Figure 11-17 Short put Christmas tree as time passes or volatility declines.

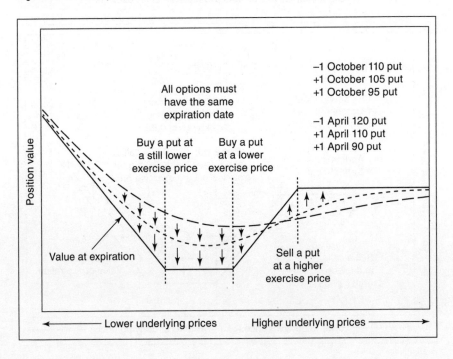

Position value

−1 October 110 put
+1 October 105 put
+1 October 95 put

−1 April 120 put
+1 April 110 put
+1 April 90 put

All options must have the same expiration date

Buy a put at a still lower exercise price

Buy a put at a lower exercise price

Value at expiration

Sell a put at a higher exercise price

◄——— Lower underlying prices   Higher underlying prices ———►

Figure 11-18 Nonsymmetrical strategies.

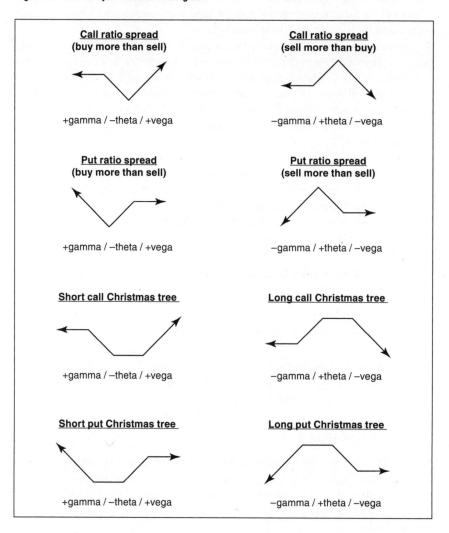

where the underlying market is when the short-term option expires but also on what will happen between that date and the date on which the long-term option expires. Calendar spreads, sometimes referred to as *time spreads* or *horizontal spreads*,[5] consist of option positions that expire in different months.

The most common type of calendar spread consists of opposing positions in two options of the same type (either both calls or both puts) where both options have the same exercise price. When the long-term option is purchased and the short-term option is sold, a trader is long the calendar spread; when the short-term option is purchased and the long-term option is sold, the trader is short the calendar spread. Because a long-term option will typically be worth

---

[5] In the early days of floor trading on option exchanges, expiration months were listed horizontally on the exchange display boards—hence the term *horizontal spread* for strategies consisting of options with different expiration months.

more than a short-term option, this is consistent with the practice of referring to any strategy that is executed at a debit as a long position and any spread that is executed for a credit as a short position.

Although calendar spreads are most commonly executed one to one (one contract purchased for each contract sold), a trader may ratio a calendar spread to reflect a bullish, bearish, or neutral market sentiment. For purposes of discussion, we will focus on one-to-one calendar spreads (one long-term option for each short-term option) that are approximately delta neutral. Because at-the-money options have delta values close to 50, the most common calendar spreads consist of long and short at-the-money options.[6]

The value of a calendar spread depends not only on movement in the underlying market but also on the marketplace's expectations about future market movement as reflected in the implied volatility. Because of this, a calendar spread has characteristics that differ from the other spreads we have discussed. If we assume that the options making up a calendar spread are approximately at the money, calendar spreads have two important characteristics:

1. A calendar spread will increase in value if time passes with no movement in the underlying contract.

2. A calendar spread will increase in value if implied volatility rises and decline in value if implied volatility falls.

Why should a calendar spread become more valuable as time passes? Consider the following spread, where the underlying contract, which is currently trading at 100, is the same for both options:

+1 June 100 call
−1 April 100 call

Suppose that there are four months remaining to June expiration and two months remaining to April expiration. If we assume a constant underlying price of 100 and a constant volatility of 20 percent, the value of the individual options as time passes, as well as the value of the spread, is shown in Figure 11-19.

The spread is initially worth 1.34, but as time passes, both options begin to decay. However the April option, with less time remaining to expiration, decays more rapidly than the June option. Over the first month, the April option loses 0.96, while the June option loses only 0.61. The spread has increased to 1.69.

Over the next month, with the underlying contract still at 100, the April option, because it is at the money, must give up its entire value of 2.30. The June option will also continue to decay, and at a slightly greater rate, losing 0.73. But the calendar spread has still increased to 3.26.

The increase in value of the calendar spread as time passes is the result of an important characteristic of theta that was noted in Chapter 8: as time to expiration grows shorter, the theta of an at-the-money option increases.

---

[6] To be more exact, at-the-forward options tend to have deltas closest to 50. For this reason, a trader might prefer a calendar spread that consists of at-the-forward options.

Figure 11-19 The value of a calendar spread as time passes.

Contract Month		Time to Expiration	
June	4 months	3 months	2 months
April	2 months	1 month	0
Option		Value	
June 100 call	4.60	3.99	3.26
April 100 call	3.26	2.30	0
Spread value	1.34	1.69	3.26

A short-term at-the-money option decays more rapidly than a long-term at-the-money option.

What will happen if the underlying contract does not sit still but instead makes a large upward or downward move? The value of a calendar spread depends on the long-term option retaining as much time value as possible while the short-term option decays. This will be true if both options remain at the money because an at-the-money option always has the greatest amount of time value. As an option moves either into the money or out of the money, its time value will disappear. A long-term option will always have greater time value than a short-term option. But, if the movement in the underlying contract is large enough and the option moves very deeply into the money or very far out of the money, even a long-term option will eventually lose almost all or its time value. This will cause the calendar spread to collapse, as shown in Figure 11-20.

Now let's consider the effect of changing volatility on a calendar spread. The value of the April/June 100 call calendar spread at different volatilities is shown in Figure 11-21.

As we raise or lower volatility, both options rise or fall in value, but the June option changes more quickly than the April option. We touched on this characteristic in Chapter 6, where we noted that a change in volatility will have a greater effect on a long-term option than on an equivalent short-term option. In other words, long-term options have greater vega values than short-term

Figure 11-20 The value of a calendar spread as the underlying price changes.

	Theoretical Value if the Underlying Price Is . . .				
Option	80	90	100	110	120
June 100 call	0.10	1.07	4.60	11.39	20.31
April 100 call	0.01	0.36	3.26	10.51	20.04
Spread value	0.09	0.71	1.34	0.88	0.27

Figure 11-21 The value of a calendar spread as volatility changes.

Option	Theoretical Value if Volatility Is . . .				
	10 percent	15 percent	20 percent	25 percent	30 percent
June 100 call	2.30	3.45	4.60	5.75	6.90
April 100 call	1.63	2.44	3.26	4.07	4.88
Spread value	0.67	1.01	1.34	1.68	2.02

options. This difference in sensitivity to a change in volatility causes the calendar spread to widen if we increase volatility and to narrow if we reduce volatility.

A trader who is long a calendar spread wants two apparently contradictory conditions in the marketplace. First, he wants the underlying contract to sit still in order to take advantage of the greater time decay for the short-term option. Second, he wants everyone to think that the market is going to move so that implied volatility will rise, causing the long-term option to rise in price more quickly than the short-term option. Can this happen? Can the market remain unchanged yet everyone think that it will move? In fact, it happens quite often because events that do not have an immediate effect on the underlying contract may be perceived to have a future effect on the underlying.

The most common example occurs when news is pending that is likely to affect the underlying contract but whose exact effect is unknown. Consider a company that announces that its CEO will make an important statement one week from today. If no one knows the content of the statement, there is unlikely to be any significant change in the company's stock price prior to the statement. But traders will assume that the statement, when it is made, will have an effect, perhaps a dramatic one, on the stock price. The possibility of future movement in the stock price will cause implied volatility to rise. This combination of conditions—the lack of movement in the underlying stock together with rising implied volatility—will cause calendar spreads to widen.

Of course, the assumption of future stock movement as a result of the CEO's statement is just that—an assumption. If the statement turns out to be irrelevant to the company's fortunes (the CEO wanted to announce that he and his wife just became grandparents), any presumption of future volatility is removed. The result will be a decline in implied volatility, causing calendar spreads to narrow.

The effect of implied volatility is what distinguishes time spreads from the other types of spreads we have discussed. Long straddles, long strangles, and short butterflies all want the volatility of the underlying contract as well as implied volatility to rise (+gamma, +vega). Short straddles, short strangles, and long butterflies all want the volatility of the underlying contract as well as implied volatility to fall (−gamma, −vega). But with calendar spreads underlying volatility and implied volatility have opposite effects. A quiet market or an increase in implied volatility will help a long calendar spread (−gamma, +vega), while a big move in the underlying market or a decline in implied volatility will

Figure 11-22 Long calendar spread as time passes.

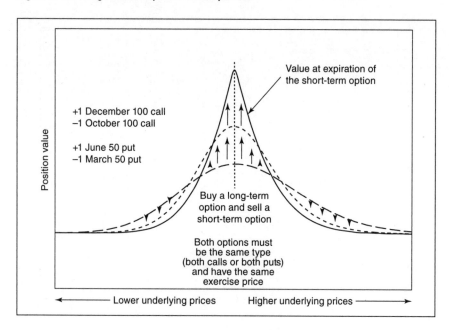

help a short calendar spread (+gamma, −vega). This opposite effect is what gives calendar spreads their unique characteristics.

Figures 11-22 and 11-23 show the value of long and short calendar spreads as time passes. Figures 11-24 and 11-25 show the value as volatility changes.

Figure 11-23 Short calendar spread as time passes.

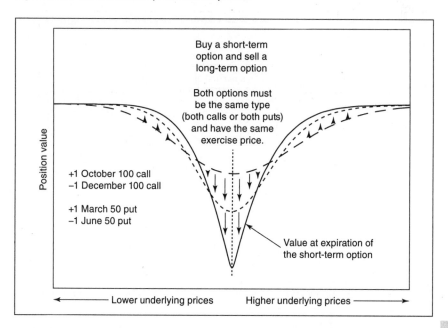

Figure 11-24 Long calendar spread as volatility declines.

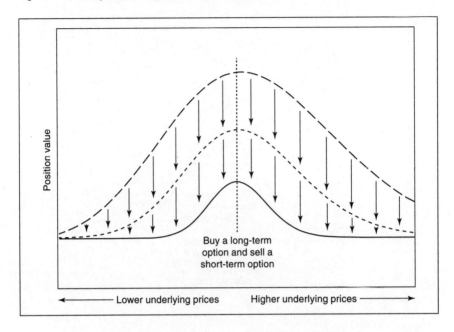

Buy a long-term
option and sell a
short-term option

Position value

← Lower underlying prices   Higher underlying prices →

Although the effects of time and volatility apply to calendar spreads in all markets, there may be other considerations, depending on the specific underlying market. In the foregoing examples, we assumed that the underlying contract for both the short- and long-term option was the same. In the stock option

Figure 11-25 Short calendar spread as volatility declines.

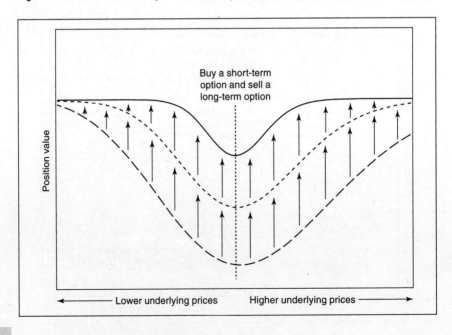

Buy a short-term
option and sell a
long-term option

Position value

← Lower underlying prices   Higher underlying prices →

market, this will always be true. The underlying contract for General Electric (GE) options, regardless of the expiration month, is always GE stock. And GE stock can only have a single price at any one time. But in a futures market the underlying for a futures option is a specific futures contract, and different option expirations can have different underlying futures contracts.

Consider a futures market where there are four futures months: March, June, September, and December. If serial months are available, an April/June calendar spread will have the same underlying contract, June futures. But a March/June calendar spread will have one underlying contract for March options, a March future, and a different underlying contract for June options, a June future. Although one might expect March futures and June futures to move together, there is no guarantee that they will. Particularly in commodity markets, short-term supply and demand considerations can cause futures contracts on the same commodity to move in different directions. In addition to volatility considerations, a trader who buys a June/March call calendar spread must also consider the possibility that March futures will rise relative to June futures.

In order to offset the risk of futures contracts moving against a calendar-spread position, it is common in commodity futures markets for a trader to offset a calendar spread with an opposing position in the futures market. In our example, if a trader buys the March/June call calendar spread, he can offset the position by purchasing March futures and selling June futures.

How many futures spreads should the trader execute? If he wants a position that is sensitive only to volatility, he ought to trade the number of futures spreads required to be delta neutral. If both calls are at the money, with deltas of approximately 50, a trader who buys 10 call calendar spreads (buy 10 June calls, sell 10 March calls) will be long 500 deltas in June and short 500 deltas in March. Therefore, he should buy 5 March futures contracts and sell 5 June futures contracts. The entire position will be (delta values are in parentheses)

+10 June calls (+500), − June futures (−500)
−10 March calls (−500), +5 March futures (+500)

This type of balancing is not necessary—indeed, not possible—in stock options because the underlying for all months is identical.

Time Butterfly

In futures markets, as opposed to option markets, a butterfly is a position in three futures months. A trader will buy (sell) one each of a short- and long-term futures contract and sell (buy) two intermediate-term futures contracts. A similar type of strategy can be done in option markets. A traditional option butterfly consists of options at three different exercise prices but with the same expiration date. A time butterfly (sometimes shortened to *time fly*) consists of options at the same exercise price but with three different expiration dates. All options must be the same type (either all calls or all puts), with approximately the same amount of time between expirations. The outside expiration months are usually referred to as the *wings* and the inside expiration month as the *body*. Some typical time butterflies might be

+1 May 100 call (wing)   −1 January 50 put (wing)
−2 June 100 calls (body)   +2 March 50 puts (body)
+1 July 100 call (wing)   −1 May 50 put (wing)

−1 March 70 call (wing)   +1 February 25 put (wing)
+2 June 70 calls (body)   −2 June 25 puts (body)
−1 September 70 call (wing)   +1 October 25 put (wing)

Note that a time butterfly consists of simultaneously buying or selling a long-term calendar spread and taking an opposing position in a short-term calendar spread, where each spread has one common expiration month. The example May/June/July 100 call time butterfly consists of buying the May 100 call and selling the June 100 call (selling the May/June calendar spread) and simultaneously selling the June 100 call and buying the July 100 call (buying the June/July calendar spread).

If all options remain at the money, as time passes, the value of a calendar spread will increase. The short-term spread must therefore be worth more than the long-term spread. Consequently, if we buy the short-term calendar spread and sell the long-term calendar spread (buying the body and selling the wings), in total, we will pay more than we receive. Because the entire position will result in a debit, we are *long* the time butterfly. If we do the opposite, selling the short-term calendar spread and buying the long-term spread (selling the body and buying the wings), we are *short* the time butterfly.[7] This can be somewhat confusing because in a traditional butterfly consisting of different exercise prices, the combination of buying the wings and selling the body results in a debit. But in a time butterfly consisting of different expiration months, buying the wings and selling the body results in a credit.

The value of a long time butterfly as time passes and as volatility falls is shown in Figures 11-26 and 11-27. The value of the spread will tend to collapse as the underlying contract moves away from the exercise price, implying that the spread has a negative gamma. Consequently, the spread must also have a positive theta. Finally, the value of the spread falls as volatility declines, implying that the spread has a positive vega. In sum, a long time butterfly has characteristics similar to those of a long calendar spread.

Effect of Changing Interest Rates and Dividends

Thus far we have considered only the effects of changes in underlying price, time, and volatility on the value of a volatility spread. What about changes in interest rates and, in the case of stocks, dividends?

---

[7] We are making the assumption here that the implied volatility of all expirations is the same. If the implied volatility differs across expiration months, a long time butterfly might in fact result in a credit.

Figure 11-26 Long time butterfly as time passes.

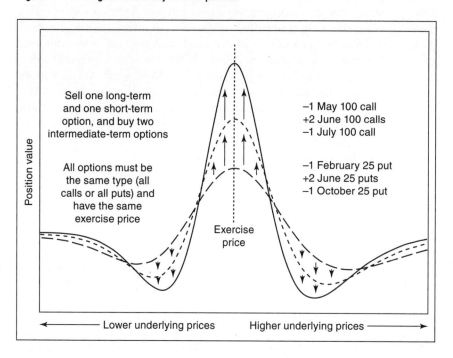

Sell one long-term
and one short-term
option, and buy two
intermediate-term options

All options must be
the same type (all
calls or all puts) and
have the same
exercise price

−1 May 100 call
+2 June 100 calls
−1 July 100 call

−1 February 25 put
+2 June 25 puts
−1 October 25 put

Exercise
price

Position value

◄─────── Lower underlying prices   Higher underlying prices ───────►

Figure 11-27 Long time butterfly as volatility declines.

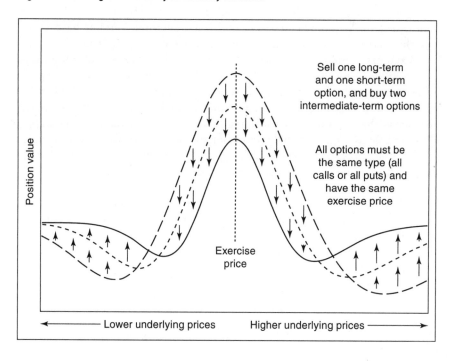

Sell one long-term
and one short-term
option, and buy two
intermediate-term options

All options must be
the same type (all
calls or all puts) and
have the same
exercise price

Exercise
price

Position value

◄─────── Lower underlying prices   Higher underlying prices ───────►

Because there is no carrying cost associated with the purchase or sale of a futures contract, interest rates have only a minor impact on futures options and, consequently, a relatively minor effect on the value of all futures option volatility spreads.[8] However, in a stock option market, a change in interest rates will cause the forward price of stocks to change. If all options in a spread expire at the same time, the change in forward price is likely to affect all options equally, causing only small changes in the value of the spread. However, if we have a stock option position involving two different expiration dates, we must consider two different forward prices. And these two forward prices may not be equally sensitive to a change in interest rates.

Consider the following situation:

Stock price = 100 interest rate = 8.00% dividend = 0

Suppose that a trader buys a call calendar spread:

+10 June 100 calls
−10 March 100 calls

If there are three months remaining to March expiration and six months remaining to June expiration, the forward prices for March stock and June stock are 102.00 and 104.00, respectively. If interest rates rise to 10 percent, the forward price for March will be 102.50 and the forward price for June will be 105. With more time remaining to June expiration, the June forward price is more sensitive to a change in interest rates. Assuming that the deltas of both options are approximately equal, the June option will be more affected by the increase in interest rates than the March option, and the calendar spread will expand. In the same way, if interest rates decline, the calendar spread will narrow because the June forward price will fall more quickly than the March forward price. A long call calendar spread in the stock option market must therefore have a positive rho, and a short call calendar spread must have a negative rho.

Changes in interest rates have the opposite effect on stock option puts. In our example, if interest rates rise from 8 to 10 percent, the June forward price will rise more than the March forward price. If we assume, again, that the deltas of both options are approximately equal, and recalling that puts have negative deltas, the June put will show a greater decline in value than the March put. The put calendar spread will therefore narrow. In the same way, if interest rates decline, the put calendar spread will expand. A long put calendar spread in the stock option market must therefore have a negative rho, and a short put calendar spread must have a positive rho.

The degree to which stock option calendar spreads are affected by changes in interest rates depends primarily on the amount of time between expirations. If there are six months between expirations (e.g., March/September), the effect will be much greater than if there is only one month between expirations (e.g., March/April).

---

[8] Interest rates can, of course, affect the relative value of different futures months. As noted, we can offset this risk by trading a futures spread along with the futures option calendar spread.

Changes in dividends can also affect the value of stock option calendar spreads because it may change the forward price of the stock. Dividends, however, have the opposite effect on stock options as changes in interest rates. An increase in the dividend lowers the forward price of stock, while a cut in the dividend raises the forward price. If all options expire at the same time, the change in the forward price for the stock will have an equal effect on all options, and the change in the value of a spread will be negligible. But in a calendar spread, if at least one dividend payment is expected between the expiration dates, an increase in dividends will cause a call calendar spread to narrow and put calendar spread to expand. A decrease in dividends will have the opposite effect, causing a call calendar spread to widen and a put calendar spread to narrow. Even though there is no Greek letter associated with dividend risk, we might say that a call calendar spread has negative dividend risk (its value falls as dividends rise) and a put calendar spread has positive dividend risk (its value rises as dividends rise). Examples of the effects of changing interest rates and dividends on stock option calendar spreads are shown in Figure 11-28.

In Figure 11-28, we can see that an increase in interest rates will reduce the value of a put calendar spread and an increase in dividends will reduce the value of a call calendar spread. Indeed, if we raise interest rates high enough, the put calendar spread can take on a negative value, with the long-term put having a lower value than the short-term put. The same will be true for a call calendar spread if we increase dividends enough. If a stock pays no dividends, the value of a call calendar spread should always have some value greater than 0. Even if volatility is very low, the spread should still be worth a minimum of the cost of carry on the stock between expiration months. This is only true, however, if a trader can carry a short stock position between expiration months. If a situation arises where no stock can be borrowed, the trader who owns a call calendar spread may be forced to exercise his long-term option, thereby losing the time value associated with the option. This is sometimes referred to as a *short squeeze*.

Figure 11-28 Effect of changing interest rates and changing dividends on stock option calendar spreads.

Stock price = 100 Volatility = 20% Dividend = 0 Time to March expiration = 3 months Time to June expiration = 6 months					
If the interest rate is...	0 percent	3 percent	6 percent	9 percent	12 percent
June 100 call	5.64	6.37	7.16	7.99	8.87
March 100 call	3.99	4.36	4.75	5.16	5.58
Call spread value	1.65	2.01	2.41	2.83	3.29
June 100 put	5.64	4.88	4.20	3.59	3.05
March 100 put	3.99	3.61	3.26	2.93	2.63
Put spread value	1.65	1.27	0.94	0.66	0.42

(continued)

Figure 11-28 (*continued*)

Stock price = 100 Volatility = 20% Interest rate = 6.00% Time to March expiration = 3 months Time to June expiration = 6 months					
If quarterly dividend is...	0	0.50	1.00	1.50	2.00
June 100 call	7.16	6.57	6.00	5.47	4.96
March 100 call	4.75	4.46	4.19	3.93	3.68
Call spread value	2.41	2.11	1.81	1.54	1.28
June 100 put	4.20	4.60	5.02	5.47	5.95
March 100 put	3.26	3.47	3.70	3.93	4.17
Put spread value	0.94	1.13	1.32	1.54	1.78

Diagonal Spreads

A *diagonal spread* is similar to a calendar spread except that the options have different exercise prices. Although many diagonal spreads are executed one to one (one long-term option for each short-term option), diagonal spreads can also be ratioed, with unequal numbers of long and short market contracts. With the large number of variations in diagonal spreads, it is almost impossible to generalize about their characteristics. Each diagonal spread must be analyzed separately to determine the risks and rewards associated with the spread.

There is, however, one type of diagonal spread about which we can generalize. If a diagonal spread is done one to one and both options are of the same type and have approximately the same delta, the diagonal spread will act very much like a conventional calendar spread. Examples of this type of diagonal spread are shown in Figure 11-29 (delta values are in parentheses).

Even though there are many different volatility spreads, traders tend to classify spreads in terms of their basic volatility characteristics. While some volatility spreads may prefer movement in one direction rather than the other, a

Figure 11-29 Diagonal spreads.

Time to June expiration = 4 months Time to April expiration = 2 months Underlying price = 100 Volatility = 30%	
+1 June 115 call	2.20 (23)
−1 April 110 call	1.60 (23)
+1 June 80 put	0.72 (−8)
−1 April 85 put	0.48 (−8)

trader who initiates a volatility spread is concerned primarily with the magnitude of movement in the underlying contract and only secondarily with the direction of movement. Therefore, all volatility spreads tend to be approximately delta neutral. If a trader has a large positive or negative delta such that directional considerations become more important than volatility considerations, the position can no longer be considered a volatility spread.

All spreads that are helped by movement in the underlying market have a positive gamma. All spreads that are hurt by movement in the underlying market have a negative gamma. A trader who has a positive gamma position is said to be *long premium* and is hoping for a volatile market with large moves in the underlying contract. A trader who has a negative gamma is said to be *short premium* and is hoping for a quiet market with only small moves in the underlying market.

Because the effect of market movement and the effect of time decay always work in opposite directions, any spread with a positive gamma will necessarily have a negative theta, and any spread with a negative gamma will necessarily have a positive theta. If market movement helps, the passage of time hurts, and if market movement hurts, the passage of time helps. An option trader cannot have it both ways.

Finally, spreads that are helped by rising volatility have a positive vega. Spreads that are helped by falling volatility have a negative vega. In theory, the vega refers to the sensitivity of a theoretical value to a change in the volatility of the underlying contract over the life of the option. In practice, however, traders associate the vega with the sensitivity of an option's price to a change in implied volatility. Spreads with a positive vega will be helped by any increase in implied volatility and hurt by any decline; spreads with a negative vega will be helped by any decline in implied volatility and hurt by any increase. The delta, gamma, theta, and vega characteristics of the primary types of volatility spreads are summarized in Figure 11-30.

Because volatility spreads tend to be delta neutral and the theta and gamma are always of opposite sign, we can place volatility spreads into one of four categories depending on the effect of movement in the underlying contract (positive or negative gamma) and the effect of changes in implied volatility (positive or negative vega):

Gamma	Vega	Conditions that Will Help the Position
+	+	More volatile underlying contract; rising implied volatility
–	–	Less volatile underlying contract; falling implied volatility
+	–	More volatile underlying contract; falling implied volatility
–	+	Less volatile underlying contract; rising implied volatility

Of course, within each of these categories, some spreads will have larger gamma or vega values and some spreads will have smaller values. Of these, straddles and strangles tend to have the largest gamma and vega values and therefore the greatest risk. They will result in the greatest profit when the trader is correct in his assessment of market conditions, but they will result in the

Figure 11-30 Summary of common volatility spreads.

Spread	Delta*	Gamma	Theta	Vega	Downside Risk/Reward	Upside Risk/Reward
Long straddle	0	+	–	+	Unlimited reward	Unlimited reward
Long strangle	0	+	–	+	Unlimited reward	Unlimited reward
Short butterfly	0	+	–	+	Limited reward	Limited reward
Short condor	0	+	–	+	Limited reward	Limited reward
Call ratio spread (buy more than sell)	0	+	–	+	Limited reward†	Unlimited reward†
Put ratio spread (buy more than sell)	0	+	–	+	Unlimited reward†	Limited reward†
Short straddle	0	–	+	–	Unlimited risk	Unlimited risk
Short strangle	0	–	+	–	Unlimited risk	Unlimited risk
Long butterfly	0	–	+	–	Limited risk	Limited risk
Long condor	0	–	+	–	Limited risk	Limited risk
Call ratio spread (sell more than buy)	0	–	+	–	Limited risk†	Unlimited risk†
Put ratio spread (sell more than buy)	0	–	+	–	Unlimited risk†	Limited risk†
Long calendar spread	0	–	+	+	Limited risk	Limited risk
Short calendar spread	0	+	–	–	Limited reward	Limited reward

*We assume that initially all spreads are approximately delta neutral.
†We refer here to the great majority of delta-neutral ratio spreads, which result in a credit when buying more than selling and which result in a debit when selling more than buying.

greatest loss when the trader is wrong. Butterflies and condors are at the other end of the spectrum. These spreads yield smaller profits when the trader is right but also result in smaller losses when the trader is wrong. Ratio spreads and Christmas trees fall somewhere in between.

Volatility spreads can be further distinguished by their limited or unlimited risk-reward characteristics, both on the upside and on the downside. These characteristics are also summarized in Figure 11-30.

Figure 11-31 is an evaluation table with the theoretical value, delta, gamma, theta, vega, and rho of several different options. Following this table are examples of volatility spreads of the types discussed in this chapter, along with their total delta, gamma, theta, vega, and rho. (Although the examples in Figure 11-31 assume that the underlying is stock, except for the rho, the characteristics of each type of spread will tend to be the same for options on futures.) The reader will see that each spread does indeed have the positive or negative sensitivities summarized in Figure 11-30. Note also that a volatility spread need not be exactly delta neutral. (Indeed, as we saw in Chapter 7, no trader can say with absolute certainty whether a position is really delta neutral.) In practice, a volatility spread should have a delta that is small enough that the directional considerations are less important than the volatility considerations. This is often a subjective judgment.

Also included in Figure 11-31 is the theoretical value of each spread. This is simply the cash flow that results if each spread is executed at theoretical value. Purchases of options result in a cash debit (indicated with a negative sign), and sales represent a cash credit (indicated with a positive sign). In common terminology, a trader is said to be long the spread if it results in a cash debit and short the spread if it results in a cash credit.

Note that no price is given for any of the option contracts in Figure 11-31, and therefore, no theoretical edge can be calculated for any of the spreads. The prices at which a spread is executed may be good or bad, resulting in a positive or negative theoretical edge. But, once the spread has been established, the market conditions that will help or hurt the spread are determined by its characteristics, not by the initial prices. Like all traders, an option trader must not let his previous trading activity affect his current judgment. A trader's primary concern should not be what happened yesterday but what can be done today to make the most of the current situation, whether attempting to maximize a potential profit or minimize a potential loss.

Choosing an Appropriate Strategy

With so many spreads available, how can we decide which type of spread is best? First and foremost, we will want to choose spreads that have a positive theoretical edge to ensure that if we are right about market conditions, we have a reasonable expectation of showing a profit. Ideally, we want to construct a spread by purchasing options that are underpriced (too cheap) and selling options that are overpriced (too expensive). If we can do this, the resulting spread, whatever its type, will always have a positive theoretical edge.

More often, however, our opinion about volatility will result in all options appearing either overpriced or underpriced. When this happens, it will be impossible to both buy and sell options at advantageous prices. Such a market can be easily identified by comparing our volatility estimate with the implied volatility in the option marketplace. If implied volatility is lower than the volatility estimate, options will be underpriced. If implied volatility is higher than our estimate, options will be overpriced. This leads to the following principle:

If implied volatility is low, such that options generally appear underpriced, look for spreads with a positive vega. If implied volatility is high, such that options generally appear overpriced, look for spreads with a negative vega.

The theoretical values and deltas in Figure 11-31 have been reproduced in Figures 11-32 and 11-33, but now prices have been included, reflecting implied volatilities that differ from the volatility input of 20 percent. The prices in Figure 11-32 reflect an implied volatility of 17 percent. In this case, only spreads with a positive vega will have a positive theoretical edge:

> Long straddles and strangles
> Short butterflies and condors
> Ratio spreads—long more than short (including short Christmas trees)
> Long calendar spreads

The prices in Figure 11-33 reflect an implied volatility of 23 percent. Now only spreads with a negative vega will have a positive theoretical edge:

> Short straddles and strangles
> Long butterflies and condors
> Ratio spreads—short more than long (including long Christmas trees)
> Short calendar spreads

Figure 11-31 Examples of common volatility spreads.

Stock price = 100 Time to April expiration = 2 months Volatility = 20% Interest rate = 6.00% Dividend = 0

	Calls						Puts					
Exercise Price	Theoretical Value	Delta	Gamma	Theta	Vega	Rho	Theoretical Value	Delta	Gamma	Theta	Vega	Rho
April 90	11.17	93	1.7	-0.023	0.06	0.136	.27	-7	1.7	-0.008	0.06	-0.013
April 95	6.98	79	3.6	-0.031	0.12	0.119	1.04	-21	3.6	-0.016	0.12	-0.037
April 100	3.76	56	4.8	-0.035	0.16	0.088	2.77	-44	4.8	-0.019	0.16	-0.077
April 105	1.71	33	4.4	-0.030	0.15	0.052	5.67	-67	4.4	-0.013	0.15	-0.121
April 110	0.65	16	3.0	-0.019	0.10	0.025	9.56*	-84	3.0	-0.001	0.10	-0.156

Stock price = 100 Time to June expiration = 4 months Volatility = 20% Interest rate = 6.00% Dividend = 0

	Calls						Puts					
Exercise Price	Theoretical Value	Delta	Gamma	Theta	Vega	Rho	Theoretical Value	Delta	Gamma	Theta	Vega	Rho
June 90	12.55	87	1.8	-0.022	0.12	0.249	.76	-13	1.8	-0.008	0.12	-0.045
June 95	8.71	75	2.8	-0.026	0.18	0.221	1.83	-25	2.8	-0.011	0.18	-0.089
June 100	5.62	59	3.4	-0.027	0.22	0.178	3.64	-41	3.4	-0.011	0.22	-0.148
June 105	3.36	42	3.4	-0.025	0.23	0.130	6.28	-58	3.4	-0.008	0.23	-0.213
June 110	1.85	28	2.9	-0.020	0.19	0.086	9.68*	-72	2.9	-0.002	0.19	-0.274

*The options in this table are assumed to be European, so some values may be less than intrinsic value.

It may seem that if one encounters a market where all options are either underpriced or overpriced, the sensible strategies are either long straddles and strangles or short straddles and strangles. Such strategies will enable a trader to take a position with a positive theoretical edge on both sides of the spread. Straddles and strangles are certainly possible strategies when all options are too cheap or too expensive. But we will see in Chapter 13 that straddles and strangles, while often having a large positive theoretical edge, can also be among the riskiest of all strategies. For this reason, a trader will often want to consider other spreads such as ratio spreads and butterflies, even if such spreads entail buying some overpriced options or selling some underpriced options.

An important assumption in traditional theoretical pricing models is that volatility is constant over the life of an option. The volatility input into the model is assumed to be the one volatility that best describes price fluctuations in the underlying instrument over the life of the option. When all options expire at the same time, it is this one volatility that will, in theory, determine whether a spread is profitable or unprofitable. But a trader may also believe that implied volatility will rise or fall over time.

Because calendar spreads are particularly sensitive to changes in implied volatility, rising or falling implied volatility will often affect the profitability of calendar spreads. Consequently, we can add this corollary to the other spread guidelines:

> *Long calendar spreads are likely to be profitable when implied volatility is low but is expected to rise; short calendar spreads are likely to be profitable when implied volatility is high but is expected to fall.*

These are only general guidelines, and an experienced trader may decide to violate them if he has reason to believe that the implied volatility will not correlate with the volatility of the underlying contract. A long calendar spread might still be desirable in a high-implied-volatility market, but the trader must make a prediction of how implied volatility might change with changes in realized volatility. If the market stagnates, with no movement in the underlying contract, but the trader feels that implied volatility will remain high, a long calendar spread is a sensible strategy. The short-term option will decay, while the long-term option will retain its value. In the same way, a short calendar spread might still be desirable in a low-implied-volatility market if the trader feels that the underlying contract is likely to make a large move with no commensurate increase in implied volatility.

Adjustments

A volatility spread may be delta neutral initially, but the delta of the position will change as market conditions change—as the price of the underlying contract rises or falls, as volatility changes, and as time passes. A spread that is delta neutral today is unlikely to be delta neutral tomorrow. The use of a theoretical pricing model requires a trader to continuously maintain a delta-neutral position throughout the life of the spread. Continuous adjustments are neither possible nor practical in the real world of trading, so when a trader initiates a spread, he ought to give some thought as to how he will adjust the position. There are essentially four possibilities:

1. *Adjust at regular intervals.* In theory, the adjustment process is assumed to be continuous because volatility is assumed to be a continuous measure of the speed of the market. In practice, however, volatility is measured over regular time intervals, so a reasonable approach is to adjust a position at similar regular intervals. If a trader's volatility estimate is based on daily price changes, the trader might adjust daily. If the estimate is based on weekly price changes, he might adjust weekly. By doing this, the trader is making the best attempt to emulate the assumptions built into the theoretical pricing model.

2. *Adjust when the position becomes a predetermined number of deltas long or short.* Very few traders insist on being delta neutral all the time. Most traders accept that this is not a realistic approach both because a continuous adjustment process is physically impossible and because no one can be certain that all the assumptions and inputs in a theoretical pricing model, from which the delta is calculated, are correct. Even if one could be certain that all delta calculations were accurate, a trader might still be willing to take on some directional risk. But a trader ought to know just how much directional risk he is willing to accept. If he wants to pursue delta-neutral strategies but believes that he can comfortably live with a position that is up to 500 deltas long or short, then he can adjust the position any time his delta position reaches this limit. Unlike the trader who adjusts at regular intervals, a trader who adjusts based on a fixed number of deltas cannot be sure how often he will need to adjust his position. In some cases, he may have to adjust very frequently; in other cases, he may go for long periods of time without adjusting.

   The number of deltas, either long or short, that a trader is willing to accept without adjusting depends on many factors—the typical size of the trader's positions, his capitalization, and his trading experience. A new independent trader may find that he is uncomfortable with a position that is only 200 deltas long or short. A large trading firm may consider a position that is several thousand deltas long or short as being approximately delta neutral.

3. *Adjust by feel.* This suggestion is not made facetiously. Some traders have good market feel. They can sense when the market is about to move in one direction or another. If a trader has this ability, there is no reason why he shouldn't make use of it. Suppose that the underlying market is at 50.00 and a trader is delta neutral with a gamma of −200. If the market falls to 48.00, the trader can estimate that he is approximately 400 deltas long. If 400 deltas is the limit of the risk he is willing to accept, he might decide to adjust at this point. If, however, he is also aware that 48.00 represents strong support for the market,

he might choose not to adjust under the assumption that the market is likely to rebound from the support level. If he is right, he will have avoided an unprofitable adjustment. Of course, if he is wrong and the market continues downward through the support level, he will regret not having adjusted. But if the trader is right more often than not, there is no reason why he shouldn't take advantage of this skill.

4. *Don't adjust at all.* This is really an extension of the second possibility, adjusting by the number of deltas. A trader who does not adjust at all is willing to accept a directional risk equal to the maximum number of deltas that the position can take on. If the trader sells five straddles, the position can take on a maximum delta of ±500. The appeal of this approach is that it eliminates all subsequent transaction costs. But, if the position takes on a large delta, the directional considerations may become more important than the volatility considerations. If the position was initiated because of an opinion about volatility, does it make sense for a trader to subsequently change to an opinion about direction? Usually not. If the trader does not want to adjust the position but he also does not want directional considerations to dominate, the only choice left is to close out the position. If the trader decides not to adjust, when he initiates the position, he must decide under what conditions he will be willing to hold the position and under what conditions he will close the position.

Submitting a Spread Order

We noted in Chapter 10 that a spread order can often be executed all at one time and at one single price. This is particularly common in option markets, where spreads are quoted with a single bid price and a single offer price regardless of the complexity of the spread. Suppose that a trader is interested in buying a straddle and receives a quote from a market maker of 6.25/6.75. If the trader wants to sell the straddle, he will have to do so at a price of 6.25 (the bid price); if he wants to buy the straddle, he will have to pay 6.75 (the ask price). If the trader decides that he is willing to pay 6.75, neither he nor the market maker really cares whether the trader pays 3.75 for the call and 3.00 for the put or 2.00 for the call and 4.75 for the put or some other combination of call and put prices. The only consideration is that the prices of the call and put taken together add up to 6.75.

A market maker will always endeavor to give one bid price and one ask price for an entire spread. If the spread is a common type, such as a straddle, strangle, butterfly, or calendar spread, a bid and ask can usually be given very quickly. But market makers are only human. If a spread is very complex, involving several different options in unusual ratios, it may take a market maker several minutes to calculate the value of the spread. Regardless of the complexity of a spread, however, the market maker will make an effort to give his best two-sided (bid and ask) market.

Spread orders are common in almost all option markets, whether electronic or open outcry. Depending on the trading platform, an electronic exchange will usually allow traders to submit bids or offers for the most common types of spreads—simple call or put spreads, straddles, strangles, and calendar spreads. More complex spreads—butterflies, Christmas trees, and spreads with unusual ratios—must either be executed piecemeal or submitted to a broker for execution on an open-outcry exchange where an exact description of the spread can be communicated directly to one or more market makers.

Option spread orders may often be submitted with specific instructions as to how the spread is to be executed. Most commonly, a spread will be submitted as either a market order (an order to be filled at the current market price) or a limit order (an order to be filled only at a specified price). But the spread may also be submitted as a *contingency order* with special execution instructions. The following contingency orders, all of which are defined in Appendix A, are often used in option markets:

> All or none
> Fill or kill
> Immediate or cancel
> Market if touched
> Market on close
> Not held
> One cancels the other
> Stop limit order
> Stop loss order

A broker executing a spread order is responsible for adhering to any special instructions that accompany the order. Unless a trader is fully knowledgeable about market conditions or has a great deal of confidence in the broker who will be executing the order, it may be wise to submit specific instructions with the order as to how it is to be executed. Additionally, when one considers all the information that must be communicated with a spread order (i.e., the quantity, the expiration months, the exercise prices, the type of option, and whether the order is a buy or sell), it is easy to see how incorrect information might inadvertently be transmitted with the order. For this reason, it is also wise to double-check all orders before submitting them for execution. Option trading can be difficult enough without the additional problems of miscommunication.

Figure 11-32

Stock price = 100	Time to April expiration = 2 months	Volatility = 20%	Interest rate = 6.00%	Dividend = 0		
		Calls			Puts	
Exercise Price	Theoretical Value	Price (Implied Volatility = 17%)	Delta	Theoretical Value	Price (Implied Volatility = 17%)	Delta
April 90	11.17	11.03	93	.27	0.13	−7
April 95	6.98	6.64	79	1.04	0.70	−21
April 100	3.76	3.28	56	2.77	2.29	−44
April 105	1.71	1.27	33	5.67	5.23	−67
April 110	.65	.38	16	9.56*	9.29	−84

Stock price = 100	Time to June expiration = 4 months	Volatility = 20%	Interest rate = 6.00%	Dividend = 0		
		Calls			Puts	
Exercise Price	Theoretical Value	Price (Implied Volatility = 17%)	Delta	Theoretical Value	Price (Implied Volatility = 17%)	Delta
June 90	12.55	12.22	87	0.76	0.44	−13
June 95	8.71	8.17	75	1.83	1.29	−25
June 100	5.62	4.95	59	3.64	2.97	−41
June 105	3.36	2.68	42	6.28	5.60	−58
June 110	1.85	1.30	28	9.68	9.12	−72

Figure 11-33

Stock price = 100	Time to April expiration = 2 months	Volatility = 20%	Interest rate = 6.00%	Dividend = 0		
		Calls			Puts	
Exercise Price	Theoretical Value	Price (Implied Volatility = 23%)	Delta	Theoretical Value	Price (Implied Volatility = 23%)	Delta
April 90	11.17	11.36	93	.27	0.47	−7
April 95	6.98	7.35	79	1.04	1.41	−21
April 100	3.76	4.24	56	2.77	3.25	−44
April 105	1.71	2.16	33	5.67	6.12	−67
April 110	.65	0.97	16	9.56	9.87	−84

Stock price = 100	Time to June expiration = 4 months	Volatility = 20%	Interest rate = 6.00%	Dividend = 0		
		Calls			Puts	
Exercise Price	Theoretical Value	Price (Implied Volatility = 23%)	Delta	Theoretical Value	Price (Implied Volatility = 23%)	Delta
June 90	12.55	12.94	87	.76	1.15	−13
June 95	8.71	9.27	75	1.83	2.39	−25
June 100	5.62	6.29	59	3.64	4.31	−41
June 105	3.36	4.04	42	6.28	6.96	−58
June 110	1.85	2.45	28	9.68	10.27	−72

Long Straddle: Buy calls and puts with the same expiration date and exercise price.

	Theoretical Value (Cash Flow)	Total Delta	Total Gamma	Total Theta	Total Vega	Total Rho
+10 April 100 calls	10 x −3.76	+10 x 56	+10 x 4.8	+10 x −.035	+10 x .16	+10 x .088
+10 April 100 puts	10 x −2.77	+10 x −44	+10 x 4.8	+10 x −.019	+10 x .16	+10 x −.077
	−65.30	+120	+96.0	−.540	+3.20	+.110
+10 June 95 calls	10 x −8.71	+10 x 75	+10 x 2.8	+10 x −.026	+10 x .18	+10 x .221
+30 June 95 puts	30 x −1.83	+30 x −25	+30 x 2.8	+30 x −.011	+30 x .18	+30 x −.089
	−142.00	0	+112.0	−.590	+7.20	−.460

(continued)

Figure 11-33 (*continued*)

Short Straddle: Sell calls and puts with the same expiration date and exercise price.

	Theoretical value (Cash Flow)	Total Delta	Total Gamma	Total Theta	Total Vega	Total Rho
−20 April 105 calls	20 x +1.71	−20 x 33	−20 x 4.4	−20 x −.030	−20 x .15	−20 x .052
−10 April 105 puts	10 x +5.67	−10 x −67	−10 x 4.4	−10 x −.013	−10 x .15	−10 x −.121
	+90.90	+10	−132.0	+.730	−4.50	−.170
−10 June 100 calls	10 x −5.62	−10 x 59	−10 x 3.4	−10 x −.027	−10 x .22	−10 x .178
−10 June 100 puts	10 x −3.64	−10 x −41	−10 x 3.4	−10 x −.011	−10 x .22	10 x −.148
	+92.60	−180	−68.0	+.380	−4.40	−.300

Long Strangle: Buy calls and puts with the same expiration date but different exercise prices.

	Theoretical Value (Cash Flow)	Total Delta	Total Gamma	Total Theta	Total Vega	Total Rho
+10 April 95 puts	10 x −0.65	+10 x −21	+10 x 3.6	+10 x −0.016	+10 x 0.12	+10 x −0.037
+10 April 110 calls	10 x −1.04	+10 x 16	+10 x 3.0	+10 x −0.019	+10 x 0.10	+10 x 0.025
	−16.90	−50	+66.0	−.350	+2.20	−0.120
+20 June 90 puts	20 x −0.76	+20 x −13	+20 x 1.8	+20 x −0.008	+20 x 0.12	+20 x −0.045
+10 June 110 calls	10 x −1.85	+10 x 28	+10 x 2.9	+10 x −0.020	+10 x 0.19	+10 x 0.086
	−33.70	−20	+65.0	−0.360	+4.30	−0.040

Short Strangle: Sell calls and puts with the same expiration date but different exercise prices.

	Theoretical Value (Cash Flow)	Total Delta	Total Gamma	Total Theta	Total Vega	Total Rho
−30 April 100 puts	30 x +2.77	−30 x −44	−30 x 4.8	−30 x −0.019	−30 x 0.16	−30 x −0.077
−40 April 105 calls	40 x +1.71	−40 x 33	−40 x 4.4	−40 x −0.030	−40 x 0.15	−40 x 0.052
	+151.50	0	−320.0	+1.770	−10.80	+.230
−10 June 100 calls	10 x +5.62	−10 x 59	−10 x 3.4	−10 x −0.027	−10 x 0.22	−10 x 0.178
−10 June 105 puts	10 x +6.28	−10 x −58	−10 x 3.4	−10 x −0.008	−10 x 0.23	−10 x −0.213
	+119.00	−10	−68.0	+0.350	−4.50	+0.350

Long Butterfly: Buy one option at a lower exercise price and one option at a higher exercise price, and sell two options at an intermediate exercise price, where all options have the same expiration date and are the same type (either all calls or all puts); there must be an equal amount between exercise prices.

	Theoretical Value (Cash Flow)	Total Delta	Total Gamma	Total Theta	Total Vega	Total Rho
+10 April 95 calls	10 x −6.98	+10 x 79	+10 x 3.6	+10 x −0.031	+10 x 0.12	+10 x 0.119
−20 April 100 calls	20 x +3.76	−20 x 56	−20 x 4.8	−20 x −0.035	−20 x 0.16	−20 x 0.088
+10 April 105 calls	10 x −1.71	+10 x 33	+10 x 4.4	+10 x −0.030	+10 x 0.15	+10 x 0.052
	−11.70	0	−16.0	+0.090	−0.50	−0.050
+10 June 90 puts	10 x −0.76	+10 x −13	+10 x 1.8	+10 x −0.008	+10 x 0.12	+10 x −0.045
−20 June 95 puts	20 x +1.83	−20 x −25	−20 x 2.8	−20 x −0.011	−20 x 0.18	−20 x −0.089
+10 June 100 puts	10 x −3.64	+10 x −41	+10 x 3.4	+10 x −0.011	+10 x 0.22	+10 x −0.148
	−7.40	−40	−4.0	+0.030	−0.20	−0.150

Short Butterfly: Sell one option at a lower exercise price and one option at a higher exercise price, and buy two options at an intermediate exercise price, where all options have the same expiration date and are the same type (either all calls or all puts); there must be an equal amount between exercise prices.

	Theoretical Value (Cash Flow)	Total Delta	Total Gamma	Total Theta	Total Vega	Total Rho
−10 April 100 puts	10 x +2.77	−10 x −44	−10 x 4.8	−10 x −0.019	−10 x 0.16	−10 x −0.077
+20 April 105 puts	20 x −5.67	+20 x −67	+20 x 4.4	+20 x −0.013	+20 x 0.15	+20 x −0.121
−10 April 110 puts	10 x +9.56	−10 x −84	−10 x 3.0	−10 x −0.001	−10 x 0.10	−10 x −0.156
	+9.90	−60	+10.0	−0.060	+0.40	−0.090
−10 June 90 calls	10 x +12.55	−10 x 87	−10 x 1.8	−10 x −0.022	−10 x 0.12	−10 x 0.249
+20 June 95 calls	20 x +8.71	+20 x 75	+20 x 2.8	+20 x −0.026	+20 x 0.18	+20 x 0.221
−10 June 100 calls	10 x −5.62	−10 x 59	−10 x 3.4	−10 x −0.027	−10 x 0.22	−10 x 0.178
	+7.50	+40	+4.0	−0.030	+0.20	+0.150

(*continued*)

Figure 11-33 (*continued*)

Long Condor: Buy two options at two outside exercise prices and sell two options at two inside exercise prices, where all options have the same expiration date and are the same type (either all calls or all puts); there must be an equal amount between the two higher and two lower exercise prices.

	Theoretical Value (Cash Flow)	Total Delta	Total Gamma	Total Theta	Total Vega	Total Rho
+10 April 90 calls	10 x −11.17	+10 x 93	+10 x 1.7	+10 x −0.023	+10 x 0.06	+10 x 0.136
−10 April 95 calls	10 x +6.98	−10 x 79	−10 x 3.6	−10 x −0.031	−10 x 0.16	−10 x 0.119
−10 April 105 calls	10 x +1.71	−10 x 33	−10 x 4.4	−10 x −0.030	−10 x 0.15	−10 x 0.052
+10 April 110 calls	10 x −0.65	+10 x 16	+10 x 3.0	+10 x −0.019	+10 x 0.10	+10 x 0.025
	−31.30	−30	−33.0	+0.190	−1.10	−0.100
+10 June 95 puts	10 x −1.83	+10 x −25	+10 x 2.8	+10 x −0.011	+10 x 0.18	+10 x −0.089
−10 June 100 puts	10 x +3.64	−10 x −41	−10 x 3.4	−10 x −0.011	−10 x 0.22	−10 x −0.148
−10 June 105 puts	10 x +6.28	−10 x −58	−10 x 3.4	−10 x −0.008	−10 x 0.23	−10 x −0.213
+10 June 110 puts	10 x −9.68	+10 x −72	+10 x 2.9	+10 x −0.002	+10 x 0.19	+10 x −0.274
	−15.90	+20	−11.0	+0.060	−0.80	−0.020

Short Condor: Sell two options at two outside exercise prices and buy two options at two inside exercise prices, where all options have the same expiration date and are the same type (either all calls or all puts); there must be an equal amount between the two higher and two lower exercise prices.

	Theoretical Value (Cash Flow)	Total Delta	Total Gamma	Total Theta	Total Vega	Total Rho
−10 April 90 puts	10 x +.27	−10 x −7	−10 x 1.7	−10 x −0.008	−10 x 0.06	−10 x −0.013
+10 April 95 puts	10 x −1.04	+10 x −21	+10 x 3.6	+10 x −0.016	+10 x 0.12	+10 x −0.037
+10 April 100 puts	10 x −2.77	+10 x −44	+10 x 4.8	+10 x −0.019	+10 x 0.16	+10 x −0.077
−10 April 105 puts	10 x +5.66	−10 x −67	−10 x 4.4	−10 x −0.013	−10 x 0.15	−10 x −0.121
	+21.30	+90	+23.0	−0.140	+0.70	+0.200
+10 June 90 calls	10 x −1.83	+10 x 87	+10 x 1.8	+10 x −0.008	+10 x 0.12	+10 x 0.249
−10 June 95 calls	10 x +3.64	−10 x 75	−10 x 2.8	−10 x −0.011	−10 x 0.18	−10 x 0.221
−10 June 105 calls	10 x +6.28	−10 x 42	−10 x 3.4	−10 x −0.008	−10 x 0.23	−10 x 0.130
+10 June 110 calls	10 x −9.68	+10 x 28	+10 x 2.9	+10 x −0.002	+10 x 0.19	+10 x 0.086
	+23.30	+20	+15.0	−0.090	+1.00	+0.160

Call Ratio Spread (long more than short): Buy more calls at a higher exercise price and sell fewer calls at a lower exercise price where all options have the same expiration date.

	Theoretical Value (Cash Flow)	Total Delta	Total Gamma	Total Theta	Total Vega	Total Rho
+20 April 110 calls	20 x −0.65	+20 x 16	+20 x 3.0	+20 x −0.019	+20 x 0.10	+20 x 0.025
−10 April 105 calls	10 x +1.71	−10 x 33	−10 x 4.4	−10 x −0.030	−10 x 0.15	−10 x 0.052
	+4.10	−10	+16.0	−0.080	+0.50	−0.020
+30 June 110 calls	30 x −1.85	+30 x 28	+30 x 2.9	+30 x −0.020	+30 x 0.19	+30 x 0.086
−10 June 90 calls	10 x +12.55	−10 x 87	−10 x 1.8	−10 x −0.022	−10 x 0.12	−10 x 0.249
	+70.00	−30	+69.0	−0.380	+4.50	+0.090

Call Ratio Spread (short more than long): Sell more calls at a higher exercise price and buy fewer calls at a lower exercise price where all options have the same expiration date.

	Theoretical Value (Cash Flow)	Total Delta	Total Gamma	Total Theta	Total Vega	Total Rho
+20 April 95 calls	20 x −6.98	+20 x 79	+20 x 3.6	+20 x −0.031	+20 x 0.12	+20 x 0.119
−30 April 100 calls	30 x +3.76	−30 x 56	−30 x 4.8	−30 x −0.035	−30 x 0.16	−30 x 0.088
	−26.80	−100	−72.0	+0.430	−2.40	−0.260
+10 June 100 calls	10 x −5.62	+10 x 59	+10 x 3.4	+10 x −0.027	+10 x 0.22	+10 x 0.178
−20 June 110 calls	20 x −1.85	−20 x 28	−20 x 2.9	−20 x −0.020	−20 x 0.19	−20 x 0.086
	−19.20	+30	−24.0	+0.130	−1.60	+0.060

(*continued*)

Figure 11-33 (*continued*)

Put Ratio Spread (long more than short): Buy more puts at a lower exercise price and sell fewer puts at a higher exercise price where all options have the same expiration date.

	Theoretical Value (Cash Flow)	Total Delta	Total Gamma	Total Theta	Total Vega	Total Rho
+40 April 95 puts	40 x −1.04	+40 x −21	+40 x 3.6	+40 x −0.016	+40 x 0.12	+40 x −0.037
−10 April 110 puts	10 x +9.56	−10 x −84	−10 x 3.0	−10 x −0.001	−10 x 0.10	−10 x −0.156
	+54.00	0	+114.0	−0.630	+3.80	+0.080
+50 June 95 puts	50 x −1.83	+50 x −25	+50 x 2.8	+50 x −0.011	+50 x 0.18	+50 x −0.089
−20 June 105 puts	20 x +6.28	−20 x −58	−20 x 3.4	−20 x −0.008	−20 x 0.23	−20 x −0.213
	+34.10	−90	+72.0	−0.390	+4.40	−0.190

Put Ratio Spread (short more than long): Sell more puts at a lower exercise price and buy fewer puts at a higher exercise price where all options have the same expiration date.

	Theoretical Value (Cash Flow)	Total Delta	Total Gamma	Total Theta	Total Vega	Total Rho
+10 April 105 puts	10 x −5.67	+10 x −67	+10 x 4.4	+10 x −0.013	+10 x 0.15	+10 x −0.121
−30 April 95 puts	30 x +1.04	−30 x −21	−30 x 3.6	−30 x −0.016	−30 x 0.12	−30 x −0.037
	−25.50	−40	−64.0	+0.350	−2.10	−0.100
+30 June 105 puts	30 x −6.28	+30 x −58	+30 x 3.4	+30 x −0.008	+30 x 0.23	+30 x −0.213
−40 June 100 puts	40 x +3.24	−40 x −41	−40 x 3.4	−40 x −0.011	−40 x 0.22	−40 x −0.148
	−42.80	−100	−34.0	+0.020	−1.90	−0.470

Long Call Christmas Tree: Buy a call at at a lower exercise price and sell one call each at two higher exercise prices, where all options have the same expiration date.

	Theoretical Value (Cash Flow)	Total Delta	Total Gamma	Total Theta	Total Vega	Total Rho
+10 April 100 calls	10 x −3.76	+10 x 56	+10 x 4.8	+10 x −0.035	+10 x 0.16	+10 x 0.088
−10 April 105 calls	10 x +1.71	−10 x 33	−10 x 4.4	−10 x −0.030	−10 x 0.15	−10 x 0.052
−10 April 110 calls	10 x +0.65	−10 x 16	−10 x 3.0	−10 x −0.019	−10 x 0.10	−10 x 0.025
	−14.00	+70	−26.0	+0.140	−0.90	+0.110
+10 June 90 calls	10 x −12.55	+10 x 87	+10 x 1.8	+10 x −0.022	+10 x 0.12	+10 x 0.249
−10 June 100 calls	10 x +5.62	−10 x 59	−10 x 3.4	−10 x −0.027	−10 x 0.22	−10 x 0.178
−10 June 110 calls	10 x +1.85	−10 x 28	−10 x 2.9	−10 x −0.020	−10 x 0.19	−10 x 0.086
	−50.80	0	−45.0	+0.250	−2.90	−0.150

Short Call Christmas Tree: Sell a call at at a lower exercise price and buy one call each at two higher exercise prices, where all options have the same expiration date.

	Theoretical Value (Cash Flow)	Total Delta	Total Gamma	Total Theta	Total Vega	Total Rho
−10 April 90 calls	10 x +11.17	−10 x 93	−10 x 1.7	−10 x −0.023	−10 x 0.06	−10 x 0.136
+10 April 100 calls	10 x −3.76	+10 x 56	+10 x 4.8	+10 x −0.035	+10 x 0.16	+10 x 0.088
+10 April 105 calls	10 x −1.71	+10 x 33	+10 x 4.4	+10 x −0.030	+10 x 0.15	+10 x 0.052
	+57.00	−40	+75.0	−0.420	+2.50	+0.040
−10 June 95 calls	10 x +8.71	−10 x 75	−10 x 2.8	−10 x −0.026	−10 x 0.18	−10 x 0.221
+10 June 105 calls	10 x −3.36	+10 x 42	+10 x 3.4	+10 x −0.025	+10 x 0.23	+10 x 0.130
+10 June 110 calls	10 x +1.85	+10 x 28	+10 x 2.9	+10 x −0.020	+10 x 0.19	+10 x 0.086
	+35.00	−50	+35.0	−0.190	+2.40	−0.050

(continued)

Figure 11-33 (*continued*)

<table>
<tr><td colspan="7">Long Put Christmas Tree: Sell one put each at two lower exercise prices and buy a put at higher exercise price, where all options have the same expiration date.</td></tr>
<tr><td></td><td>Theoretical Value (Cash Flow)</td><td>Total Delta</td><td>Total Gamma</td><td>Total Theta</td><td>Total Vega</td><td>Total Rho</td></tr>
<tr><td>−10 April 95 puts</td><td>10 x +1.04</td><td>−10 x −21</td><td>−10 x 3.6</td><td>−10 x −0.016</td><td>−10 x 0.12</td><td>−10 x −0.037</td></tr>
<tr><td>−10 April 100 puts</td><td>10 x +2.77</td><td>−10 x −44</td><td>−10 x 3.8</td><td>−10 x −0.019</td><td>−10 x 0.16</td><td>−10 x −0.077</td></tr>
<tr><td>+10 April 105 puts</td><td>10 x −5.67</td><td>+10 x −67</td><td>+10 x 4.4</td><td>+10 x −0.013</td><td>+10 x 0.15</td><td>+10 x −0.121</td></tr>
<tr><td></td><td>−18.60</td><td>−20</td><td>−30.0</td><td>+0.220</td><td>−1.30</td><td>−0.070</td></tr>
<tr><td>−10 June 90 puts</td><td>10 x +.76</td><td>−10 x −13</td><td>−10 x 1.8</td><td>−10 x −0.008</td><td>−10 x 0.12</td><td>−10 x −0.045</td></tr>
<tr><td>−10 June 105 puts</td><td>10 x +6.28</td><td>−10 x −58</td><td>−10 x 3.4</td><td>−10 x −0.008</td><td>−10 x 0.23</td><td>−10 x −0.213</td></tr>
<tr><td>+10 June 110 puts</td><td>10 x −9.68</td><td>+10 x −72</td><td>+10 x 2.9</td><td>+10 x −0.002</td><td>+10 x 0.19</td><td>+10 x −0.274</td></tr>
<tr><td></td><td>−26.40</td><td>−10</td><td>−23.0</td><td>+0.140</td><td>−1.60</td><td>−0.160</td></tr>
<tr><td colspan="7">Short Put Christmas Tree: buy one put each at two lower exercise prices and sell a put at a higher exercise price, where all options have the same expiration date.</td></tr>
<tr><td></td><td>Theoretical Value (Cash Flow)</td><td>Total Delta</td><td>Total Gamma</td><td>Total Theta</td><td>Total Vega</td><td>Total Rho</td></tr>
<tr><td>+10 April 95 puts</td><td>10 x −1.04</td><td>+10 x −21</td><td>+10 x 3.6</td><td>+10 x −0.016</td><td>+10 x 0.12</td><td>+10 x −0.037</td></tr>
<tr><td>+10 April 105 puts</td><td>10 x −5.67</td><td>+10 x −67</td><td>+10 x 4.4</td><td>+10 x −0.013</td><td>+10 x 0.15</td><td>+10 x −0.121</td></tr>
<tr><td>−10 April 110 puts</td><td>10 x +9.56</td><td>−10 x −84</td><td>−10 x 3.0</td><td>−10 x −0.001</td><td>−10 x 0.10</td><td>−10 x −0.156</td></tr>
<tr><td></td><td>+28.50</td><td>−40</td><td>+50.0</td><td>−0.280</td><td>+1.70</td><td>−0.020</td></tr>
<tr><td>+10 June 90 puts</td><td>10 x −.76</td><td>+10 x −13</td><td>+10 x 1.8</td><td>+10 x −0.008</td><td>+10 x 0.12</td><td>+10 x −0.045</td></tr>
<tr><td>+10 June 95 puts</td><td>10 x −1.83</td><td>+10 x −25</td><td>+10 x 2.8</td><td>+10 x −0.011</td><td>+10 x 0.18</td><td>+10 x −0.089</td></tr>
<tr><td>−10 June 100 puts</td><td>10 x +3.64</td><td>−10 x −41</td><td>−10 x 3.4</td><td>−10 x −0.011</td><td>−10 x 0.22</td><td>−10 x −0.148</td></tr>
<tr><td></td><td>+10.50</td><td>+30</td><td>+12.0</td><td>−0.080</td><td>+0.80</td><td>+0.140</td></tr>
<tr><td colspan="7">Long Calendar Spread: Buy a long-term option and sell a short-term option where both options have the same exercise price and are the same type (either both calls or both puts).</td></tr>
<tr><td></td><td>Theoretical Value (Cash Flow)</td><td>Total Delta</td><td>Total Gamma</td><td>Total Theta</td><td>Total Vega</td><td>Total Rho</td></tr>
<tr><td>+10 June 100 calls</td><td>10 x −5.62</td><td>+10 x 59</td><td>+10 x 3.4</td><td>+10 x −0.027</td><td>+10 x 0.22</td><td>+10 x 0.178</td></tr>
<tr><td>−10 April 100 calls</td><td>10 x +3.76</td><td>−10 x 56</td><td>−10 x 4.8</td><td>−10 x −0.035</td><td>−10 x 0.16</td><td>−10 x 0.088</td></tr>
<tr><td></td><td>−18.60</td><td>+30</td><td>−14.0</td><td>+0.080</td><td>+0.60</td><td>+0.900</td></tr>
<tr><td>+10 June 95 puts</td><td>10 x −1.83</td><td>+10 x −25</td><td>+10 x 2.8</td><td>+10 x −0.011</td><td>+10 x 0.18</td><td>+10 x −0.089</td></tr>
<tr><td>−10 April 95 puts</td><td>10 x +1.04</td><td>−10 x −21</td><td>−10 x 3.6</td><td>−10 x −0.016</td><td>−10 x 0.12</td><td>−10 x −0.037</td></tr>
<tr><td></td><td>−7.90</td><td>−40</td><td>−8.0</td><td>+0.050</td><td>+0.60</td><td>−0.520</td></tr>
<tr><td colspan="7">Short Calendar Spread: Buy a short-term option and sell a long-term option where both options have the same exercise price and are the same type (either both calls or both puts).</td></tr>
<tr><td></td><td>Theoretical Value (Cash Flow)</td><td>Total Delta</td><td>Total Gamma</td><td>Total Theta</td><td>Total Vega</td><td>Total Rho</td></tr>
<tr><td>+10 April 105 calls</td><td>10 x −1.71</td><td>+10 x 33</td><td>+10 x 4.4</td><td>+10 x −0.030</td><td>+10 x 0.15</td><td>+10 x 0.052</td></tr>
<tr><td>−10 June 105 calls</td><td>10 x +3.36</td><td>−10 x 42</td><td>−10 x 3.4</td><td>−10 x −0.025</td><td>−10 x 0.23</td><td>−10 x 0.130</td></tr>
<tr><td></td><td>+16.50</td><td>−90</td><td>+10.0</td><td>−0.050</td><td>−0.80</td><td>−0.780</td></tr>
<tr><td>+10 April 100 puts</td><td>10 x −2.77</td><td>+10 x −44</td><td>+10 x 4.8</td><td>+10 x −0.019</td><td>+10 x 0.16</td><td>+10 x −0.077</td></tr>
<tr><td>−10 June 100 puts</td><td>10 x −3.64</td><td>−10 x −41</td><td>−10 x 3.4</td><td>−10 x −0.011</td><td>−10 x 0.22</td><td>−10 x −0.148</td></tr>
<tr><td></td><td>+8.70</td><td>−30</td><td>+14.0</td><td>−0.080</td><td>−0.60</td><td>+0.710</td></tr>
</table>

12

Bull and Bear Spreads

Although delta-neutral volatility trading is the foundation of theoretical option pricing, there is no law that requires a trader to initiate and maintain a delta-neutral position. Many traders prefer to trade from a bullish or bearish perspective. The trader who wishes to take a directional position has the choice of doing so in either the underlying instrument itself, buying or selling a futures contract or stock, or by taking the position in the option market. If the trader takes a directional position in the option market, he must still be aware of the volatility implications. Otherwise, he may be no better off, and perhaps even worse, than if he had taken an outright position in the underlying contract.

Naked Positions

Because the purchase of calls or the sale of puts will create a positive delta position and the sale of calls or purchase of puts will create a negative delta position, we can always take a directional position in a market by taking an appropriate naked position in either calls or puts. If implied volatility is high, we can sell puts to create a bullish position or sell calls to create a bearish position. If implied volatility is low, we can buy calls to create a bullish position or buy puts to create a bearish position.

The problem with this approach is that there is very little margin for error. If we purchase options, we will lose money not only if the market moves in the wrong direction but also if the market fails to move fast enough to offset the option's time decay. If we sell options, time will work in our favor, but we face the prospect of unlimited risk if the market moves violently against us. An experienced trader will prefer a strategy that improves the risk-reward tradeoff by looking for positions with the greatest possible margin for error. This philosophy applies no less to directional strategies than to volatility strategies.

Bull and Bear Ratio Spreads

Consider a situation where we believe that implied volatility is too high. One possible strategy is a ratio spread where more options are sold than purchased. With the underlying market at 101, ten weeks remaining to June expiration, and a volatility of 30 percent, a June 100 call has a delta of 56 and a June 110 call has a delta of 28.[1] A delta-neutral spread might consist of

>Buy 1 June 100 call (56)
>Sell 2 June 110 calls (28)

Because the spread is delta neutral, it has no particular preference for upward or downward movement in the underlying market.

Now suppose that we believe that this ratio spread is a sensible strategy, but at the same time, we are also bullish on the market. There is no law that requires us to do this spread in a delta-neutral ratio. If we want the spread to reflect a bullish sentiment, we might adjust the ratio slightly

>Buy 2 June 100 calls (56)
>Sell 3 June 110 calls (28)

We have essentially the same ratio spread, but with a bullish bias. This is reflected in the total delta of +28.

There is, however, an important limitation if we use a ratio strategy to create a bullish or bearish position. In our example, we are initially bullish, but the position is still a ratio spread with a negative gamma. If the underlying market moves up too quickly, the spread can invert from a positive to a negative delta. If the market rises far enough, to 130 or 140, eventually all options will go deeply into the money, and the deltas of both the June 100 and June 110 calls will approach 100. We will be left with a delta position of −100. Even though we may be correct in our bullish sentiment, the volatility characteristics of the position will eventually outweigh any considerations of market direction. The delta values of both ratios, 1 × 2 and 2 × 3, with respect to changes in the underlying price, are shown in Figure 12-1.

The delta can also invert in a ratio spread in which more options are purchased than sold. Unlike a negative gamma position, where the inversion is caused by swift price movement in the underlying contract, this type of ratio spread can invert when volatility declines or time passes. Suppose that conditions are the same as in our preceding example, but we believe that implied volatility is too low. Now we might do the following delta-neutral strategy:

>Buy 2 June 110 calls (28)
>Sell 1 June 100 call (56)

However, if we are bullish on the market, we can, as in the preceding example, adjust the ratio to reflect this sentiment

>Buy 3 June 110 calls (28)
>Sell 1 June 100 call (56)

The delta position of +28 reflects this bullish bias.

---

[1] To generalize this and subsequent examples and to eliminate the differences between stock options and futures options, we will assume an interest rate of 0.

Figure 12-1 Delta of a ratio spread as the underlying price changes.

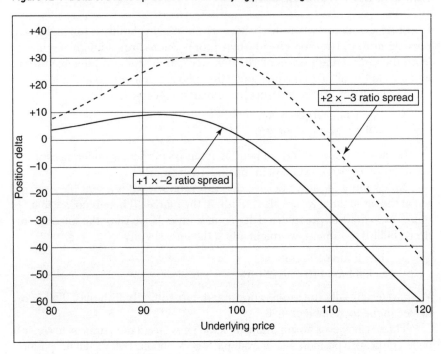

We know from Chapter 9 that as time passes or as volatility declines, all deltas move away from 50. If time passes with no movement in the underlying contract, the delta of the June 100 call will tend to rise, while the delta of the June 110 call will tend to decline. If, after a period of time, the delta of the June 100 call rises to 70 and the delta of the June 110 call falls to 15, the delta of the position will no longer be +28 but will instead be –25. Because this strategy is a volatility spread, the primary consideration, as before, is the volatility of the market. Only secondarily are we concerned with the direction of movement. If we overestimate volatility and the market moves more slowly than expected, the spread, which is initially delta positive, can instead become delta negative. The delta values of both positions with respect to the passage of time are shown in Figure 12-2.

Bull and Bear Butterflies and Calendar Spreads

Butterflies and calendar spreads can also be executed in a way that reflects a bullish or bearish bias. As with ratio spreads, though, their delta characteristics can invert as market conditions change.

With high implied volatility and the underlying contract at 100, we might create a delta-neutral position by buying the June 95/100/105 call butterfly (buy a 95 call, sell two 100 calls, buy a 105 call). We hope that the underlying will stay close to 100 so that at expiration the butterfly will widen to its maximum value of 5.00. If, however, we want to buy a butterfly but are also bullish

Figure 12-2 Delta of a ratio spread as time passes.

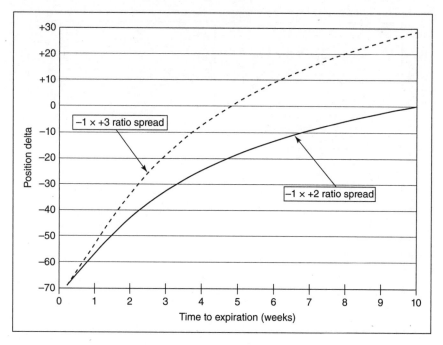

on the market, we can choose a butterfly in which the inside exercise price is above the current price of the underlying contract. If the underlying is currently at 100, we might choose to buy the June 105/110/115 call butterfly. Because this position wants the underlying contract to be at the inside exercise price of 110 at expiration and it is currently at 100, the position is a bullish butterfly. This will be reflected in the position having a positive delta.

Unfortunately, if the underlying market moves up too far, say, to 120, the butterfly will invert from a positive to a negative delta position. Now we want the market to fall back from 120 to 110. Whenever the underlying market is below 110, the position will be bullish; whenever the underlying market is above 110, the position will be bearish.

Conversely, if we are bearish, we can choose to buy a butterfly in which the inside exercise price is below the current price of the underlying market. But again, if the market moves down too quickly and goes through the inside exercise price, the position will invert from a negative to a positive delta. The delta position of a butterfly with respect to changes in the underlying price is shown in Figure 12-3.

We can also choose a bullish or bearish calendar spread. A long calendar spread always wants the short-term option to expire exactly at the money. A long calendar spread will be initially bullish if the exercise price is above the current price of the underlying contract.[2] With the underlying at 100, the June/

---

[2] In the futures market, the situation may be complicated by the fact that different futures months may be trading at different prices. Instead of choosing a traditional calendar spread, where both options have the same exercise price, the trader may have to choose a diagonal spread to ensure that the position is either bullish (delta positive) or bearish (delta negative).

Figure 12-3 Delta of a long butterfly as the underlying price changes.

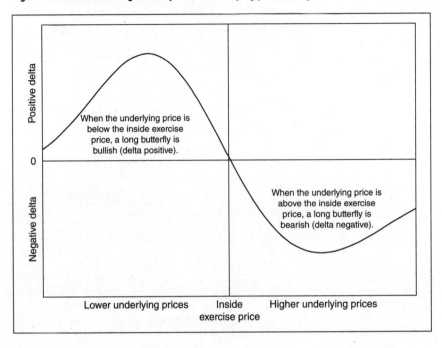

April 110 calendar spread (buy the June 110 option, sell the April 110 option of the same type) will be bullish because the trader will want the underlying price to rise to 110 by April expiration. The June/April 90 calendar spread (buy the June 90 option, sell the April 90 option of the same type) will be bearish because the trader will want the underlying price to fall to 90 by April expiration. But like a long butterfly, a long calendar spread has a negative gamma. If the underlying contract moves through the exercise price, the delta will invert. If the market moves from 100 to 120, the June/April 110 calendar spread, which was initially bullish, will become bearish. If the market moves from 100 to 80, the June/April 90 calendar spread, which was bearish initially, will become bullish. The delta values of long calendar spreads with respect to changes in the underlying price are shown in Figure 12-4.[3]

Vertical Spreads

Although we may take a bullish or bearish position by choosing an appropriate ratio spread, butterfly, or calendar spread, in each of these positions, volatility is still the primary concern. We can be right about market direction, but if we are wrong about volatility, the spread may not retain the directional characteristics that we originally intended.

---

[3] Figures 12-3 and 12-4 are very similar, and one might conclude that the characteristics of butterflies and calendar spreads are similar. But this is only true with respect to changes in the underlying price, as reflected in the delta. The spreads will react quite differently to the passage of time and changes in implied volatility.

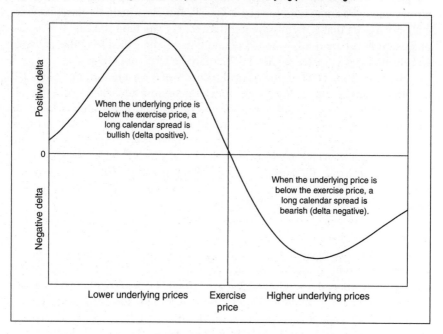

If we want to focus primarily on the direction of the underlying market, we might look for a spread in which the directional characteristics are the primary concern and the volatility characteristics are only of secondary importance. We would like to be certain that if the spread is initially bullish (delta positive), it will remain bullish under all possible market conditions, and if it is initially bearish (delta negative), it will remain bearish under all possible market conditions.

The most common class of spreads that meet these requirements are simple call and put spreads. One option is purchased and one option is sold, where both options are the same type (either both calls or both puts) and expire at the same time. The options are distinguished only by their different exercise prices. Such spreads may also be referred to as *credit* and *debit spreads* or *vertical spreads*.[4] Typical spreads of this type might be

> Buy 1 June 100 call
> Sell 1 June 105 call

or

> Buy 1 December 105 put
> Sell 1 December 95 put

Simple call and put spreads are initially either bullish or bearish, and they remain bullish or bearish no matter how market conditions change. Two options that have different exercise prices but that are otherwise identical cannot have identical deltas. In the first example, where the trader is long a June 100 call and short a June 105 call, the June 100 call will always have a delta greater than

---

[4] In the early days of trading on option exchanges, exercise prices were listed vertically on the exchange display boards—hence the term vertical spread for strategies consisting of options with difference exercise prices.

the June 105 call. If both options are deeply in the money or very far out of the money, the deltas may tend toward 100 or 0. But even then, the June 100 call will have a delta that is slightly greater than that of the June 105 call. In the second example, no matter how market conditions change, the December 105 put will always have a greater negative delta than the December 95 put.

At expiration, a call or put vertical spread will have a minimum value of 0 if both options are out of the money and a maximum value of the amount between exercise prices if both options are in the money. If the underlying contract is below 100 at expiration, the June 100/105 call spread will be worthless because both options will be worthless. If the underlying contract is above 105, the spread will be worth 5.00 because the June 100 call will be worth exactly five points more than the June 105 call. Similarly, the March 95/105 put spread will be worthless if the underlying market is above 105 at expiration, and it will be worth 10.00 if the market is below 95.

Because a vertical spread at expiration will always have a value between 0 and the amount between exercise prices, a trader can expect the price of such a spread to be somewhere within this range. A 100/105 call vertical spread will trade for some amount between 0 and 5.00; a 95/105 put vertical spread will trade for some amount between 0 and 10.00. The exact value will depend on the likelihood of the underlying market finishing below the lower exercise price, above the higher exercise price, or somewhere in between. If the market is currently at 80 and gives little indication of rising, the price of the 100/105 call vertical spread will be close to 0, while the price of the 95/105 put vertical spread will be close to 10.00. If the market is currently at 120 with little likelihood that it will fall, the price of the 100/105 call vertical spread will be close to 5.00, while the price of the 95/105 put vertical spread will be close to 0.

If we want to do a simple bull or bear vertical spread, we have essentially four choices. If we are bullish, we can choose a bull call spread or a bull put spread; if we are bearish, we can choose a bear call spread or a bear put spread. For example,

Bull call spread:	Buy a June 100 call
	Sell a June 105 call
Bull put spread:	Buy a June 100 put
	Sell a June 105 put
Bear call spread:	Sell a June 100 call
	Buy a June 105 call
Bear put spread:	Sell a June 100 put
	Buy a June 105 put

If we are bullish, we can buy a 100 call and sell a 105 call, or buy a 100 put and sell a 105 put (in both cases, buy the lower exercise price and sell the higher). If we are bearish, we can buy a 105 call and sell a 100 call, or buy a 105 put and sell and 100 put (in both cases, sell the lower exercise price and buy the higher). This may seem counterintuitive because one expects spreads that consist of puts to have characteristics that are the opposite of those that consist of calls. But regardless of whether a spread consists of calls or puts, *whenever a trader buys the lower exercise price and sells the higher exercise price, the position is bullish, and whenever a trader buys the higher exercise price and sells the lower exercise price, the position is bearish.*

We can see why this is true by considering either the deltas of the position or the potential profit and loss (P&L) for the position. Consider the two example bull spreads:

Bull call spread:	Buy a June 100 call
	Sell a June 105 call
Bull put spread:	Buy a June 100 put
	Sell a June 105 put

Both spreads must have a positive delta. The June 100 call has a greater positive delta than the June 105 call. The June 105 put has a greater negative delta than the June 100 put. Multiplying with a positive sign for a purchase and a negative sign for a sale and adding up the deltas give a total positive delta in each case.

In terms of potential profit or loss, the call spread will be done for a debit (the June 100 call will cost more than the June 105 call) and will expand to its maximum value of 5.00 if the underlying contract is above 105 at expiration. The put spread will be done for a debit (the June 100 put will cost less than the June 105 put) but will collapse to 0 if the underlying contract is above 105 at expiration. Each spread wants the underlying to rise above 105, so each spread must be bullish.

Not only will the total delta be very similar for call and put spreads that expire at the same time and that consist of the same exercise prices, but the profit or loss potential for each spread, whether a call spread or put spread, will be approximately the same.[5] The expiration P&L profiles for simple bull and bear spreads are shown in Figures 12-5 and 12-6.

Figure 12-5 Bull spread.

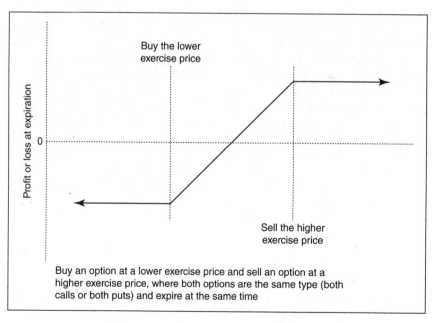

Buy the lower
exercise price

Profit or loss at expiration

0

Sell the higher
exercise price

Buy an option at a lower exercise price and sell an option at a
higher exercise price, where both options are the same type (both
calls or both puts) and expire at the same time

---

[5] We are assuming for the moment that all options are European, with no possibility of early exercise.

Figure 12-6 Bear spread.

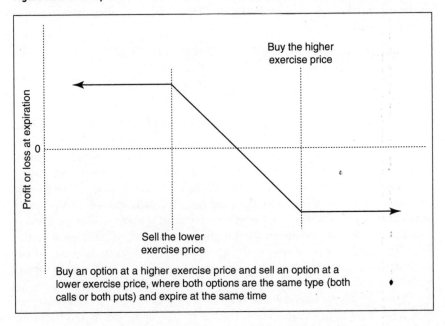

Given the many different exercise prices and expiration months available, how can we choose the bull or bear spread that best reflects our directional expectations and that gives us the best chance to profit from those expectations?

Because options have fixed expiration dates, a trader who wants to use options to take advantage of an expected market move must first determine his time horizon. Is the movement likely to occur in the next month? In the next three months? In the next nine months? If it is currently May and the trader foresees upward movement but believes that the movement is unlikely to occur within the next two months, it does not make much sense to take a position in June or July options. If his expectations are long term, he may have to take his position in September or even December options. Of course, as he moves farther out in time, market liquidity may become a problem. This is a factor that he will have to take into consideration.

Next, a trader will have to decide just how bullish or bearish he is. Is he very confident and therefore willing to take a very large directional position? Or is he less certain and willing to take only a limited position? Two factors determine the total directional characteristics of the position:

1. The delta of the selected spread

2. The size in which the spread is executed

A trader who wants to take a position that is 500 deltas long (equivalent to purchasing five underlying contracts) can choose a spread that is 50 deltas long and execute it 10 times. Or the trader can choose a different spread that is only

25 deltas long but execute it 20 times. Both strategies result in a position that is long 500 deltas.

In general, if all options expire at the same time and are close to at the money, the greater the amount between exercise prices, the greater will be the delta value of the spread. A 95/110 bull spread will be more bullish than a 95/105 bull spread, which will, in turn, be more bullish than a 95/100 bull spread.[6] Moreover, increasing the amount between exercise prices will also increase the spread's maximum potential profit or loss. This is shown in Figure 12-7.

Once a trader decides on the option expiration in which to take his directional position, he must decide which specific spread is best. That is, he must decide which exercise prices to use. Consider the following table of theoretical values and deltas:

Time to expiration = 8 weeks Volatility = 25 percent			
	95 call	100 call	105 call
Theoretical value	6.82	3.91	1.99
Delta	72	52	32

Suppose that we want to do a bull call spread with these options. One choice is to buy the 95 call and sell the 100 call. A second choice is to buy the 100 call and sell the 105 call. Which spread is best?

Figure 12-7 As the exercise prices become farther apart, the spread takes on greater bullish or bearish characteristics.

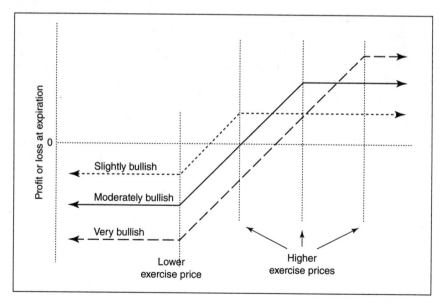

---

[6] This is not necessarily true for very deeply in-the-money spreads or very far out-of-the-money spreads. In such cases, the deltas of both options may be very close to 100 or 0, so separating the exercise prices will have little effect on the total delta of the spread.

The theoretical value and delta for each spread are

	95/100 Spread	100/105 Spread
Theoretical value	6.82 – 3.91 = **2.91**	3.91 – 1.99 = **1.92**
Delta	72 – 52 = **20**	52 – 32 = **20**

In theory, both spreads seem to be equally bullish because they are both long 20 deltas. But the 100/105 spread, with a value of 1.92, appears to be cheaper than the 95/100 spread, with a value of 2.91. From this we might conclude that the 100/105 spread represents the better value. But is the spread's value the only consideration? The value of a strategy is only important if we can compare it with the price of the strategy. But nowhere have we said anything about price.

From an option trader's point of view, the price of an option or strategy is determined by the implied volatility in the marketplace. In this example, our best estimate of volatility over the life of the options may be 25 percent, but what will be the prices of the options if the implied volatility is either higher or lower than 25 percent? Let's expand our table to include option values at volatilities of 20 and 30 percent (delta values are in parentheses).

Volatility	95 Call	95/100 Spread	100 Call	100/105 Spread	105 Call
20%	6.18	3.06	3.12	1.82	1.30
25%	6.82 (72)	2.91 (20)	3.91 (52)	1.92 (20)	1.99 (32)
30%	7.50	2.81	4.69	1.98	2.71

If implied volatility in the marketplace is 20 percent, the prices of the 95/100 spread and the 100/105 spread will be 3.06 and 1.82, respectively. If our best volatility estimate is 25 percent, we have a choice. We can pay 3.06 for a spread that we believe is worth 2.91 (the 95/100 spread), or we can pay 1.82 for a spread that we believe is worth 1.92 (the 100/105 spread). If creating a positive theoretical edge is our goal, the 100/105 spread, with a theoretical edge of .10, makes more sense than the 95/100 spread with its negative theoretical edge of –.15.

Now suppose that implied volatility in the marketplace is 30 percent. The prices of the 95/100 spread and the 100/105 spread are 2.81 and 1.98, respectively. Again we have a choice. We can pay 2.81 for a spread that is worth 2.91 (the 95/100 spread), or we can pay 1.98 for a spread that is worth 1.92 (the 100/105 spread). The 95/100 spread, with its positive theoretical edge of .10, is now the better choice.

Even though both spreads have the same delta values, under one volatility scenario, we seem to prefer the 95/100 spread, while under a different scenario, we seem to prefer the 100/105 spread. The reason becomes clear if we recall one of the basic characteristics of option evaluation introduced in Chapter 6:

If we consider three options—in the money, at the money, and out of the money— option that are identical except for their exercise prices, the at-the-money option is always the most sensitive in total points to a change in volatility.

If all options appear overpriced because we believe that implied volatility is too high, in total points, the at-the-money option will be the most overpriced. If all options appear underpriced because we believe that implied volatility is too low, in total points, the at-the-money option will be the most underpriced. This characteristic leads to a very simple rule for choosing bull and bear vertical spreads:

> *If implied volatility is low, the choice of spreads should focus on purchasing the at-the-money option. If implied volatility is high, the choice should focus on selling the at-the-money option.*

Now we can see why the 100/105 call spread is a better value if implied volatility is 20 percent, whereas the 95/100 spread is a better value if implied volatility is 30 percent. If implied volatility is low (20 percent), we prefer to buy the at-the-money (100) call. Having done this, we have only one choice if we want to create a bull spread—we must sell the out-of-the-money (105) call. On the other hand, if implied volatility is high (30 percent), we want to sell the at-the-money (100) call. Having done this, we again have only one choice if we want to create a bull spread—we must buy the in-the-money (95) call.

The same principle is equally true for bull and bear put spreads. We always want to focus on the at-the-money option, buying the at-the-money put when implied volatility is low and selling the at-the-money put when implied volatility is high. This is confirmed in the following table (delta values are in parentheses):

Volatility	95 Put	95/100 Spread	100 Put	100/105 Spread	105 Put
20%	1.18	1.94	3.12	3.18	6.30
25%	1.82 (−28)	2.09 (20)	3.91 (−48)	3.08 (20)	6.99 (−68)
30%	2.50	2.19	4.69	3.02	7.71

Suppose that we want to do a bear put spread when implied volatility is low. In this case, we want to buy the at-the-money (100) put. Having done this, we are forced to sell the out-of-the-money (95) put to create our bear spread (buy the higher exercise price, sell the lower). We will pay 1.94 for the spread, but the spread is worth 2.09. The result will be a delta position of −20 and a positive theoretical edge of .15.

Notice that in every case, whether in a low-volatility or high-volatility environment, the spread that includes the in-the-money option always has a higher price than the spread that includes the out-of-the-money option. To understand why, consider the result of choosing between a 95/100 and a 100/105 bull call spread under three different scenarios. In scenario 1, the market rises and is at 110 at expiration. If this happens, both spreads will show a profit because they will both widen to their maximum value of 5.00. In scenario 2, the market drops and is at 90 at expiration. Now both spreads will show a loss because they will both collapse to 0. Finally, consider the case where the underlying market fails to rise but also does not fall. It simply remains at 100 until expiration. If this happens, the 100/105 spread will collapse to 0, while the

95/100 spread will widen to its maximum value of 5.00. The 95/100 spread is always more valuable than the 100/105 spread because it profits in more cases. The 100/105 spread needs the market to rise to show a profit. The 95/100 spread does not need the market to rise; it just needs for the market not to fall. Because the 100/105 spread requires movement, it has a positive gamma and, consequently, a negative theta. It will decline in value as time passes. The 95/100 spread will profit even if the market sits still. It has a positive theta and, consequently, a negative gamma.

Note also the results if the market does move. If the market rises to 110, both spreads will show a profit, but the 100/105 spread will show a greater profit because it was purchased at a lower price. If the market falls to 90, both spreads will show a loss, but the 100/105 spread, because of its lower price, will show a smaller loss. If there is a greater likelihood that the market will move, we will always prefer the 100/105 spread. We will maximize our profits when we are right, and we will minimize our losses when we are wrong. The likelihood of movement will depend on our estimate of volatility. If our estimate is higher than the implied volatility, we are saying that there is a greater likelihood of movement, so we prefer the 100/105 spread. If our estimate of volatility is lower than the implied volatility, we are saying that there is a lower likelihood of movement, so we prefer the 95/100 spread.

Even though we have focused on the at-the-money option, a trader is not required to execute a bull or bear spread by first buying or selling the at-the-money option. Such spreads always involve two options, and a trader can choose to either execute the complete spread in one transaction or leg into the spread by trading one option at a time. In the latter case, a trader may decide to trade the in-the-money or out-of-the-money option first and trade the at-the-money option at a later time. This is a decision that a trader must make based on practical considerations. But regardless of how the spread is executed, the trader should focus on the at-the-money option, either buying it when implied volatility is low or selling it when implied volatility is high.

In practice, it is unlikely that one option will be exactly at the money. If there is no exactly at-the-money option, a trader can focus on an option that is closer to at the money. If the underlying market is at 103, with 95, 100, 105, and 110 calls available, it is logical to focus on the 105 call because it is closest to at the money. If implied volatility is low, a trader will want to buy the 105 call; if implied volatility is high, a trader will want to sell the 105 call. He can then trade a different option in order to create a bull or bear vertical spread.

Nor does a trader have to include the option that is closest to the money as part of his spread. A trader who has a strong directional opinion can choose a spread where both options are very far out of the money or very deeply in the money. The delta values of such spreads will be very low, but the trader can create a highly leveraged position by executing each spread many times. For example, with the underlying market at 100, a trader who is strongly bullish might buy the 115/120 call spread (assuming that such exercise prices are available). The cost of this spread will be very low because there is a high probability that the spread will expire worthless. But the trader will also be able to execute the spread many times because of its low cost. If he is right and the market does rise above 120, the spread will widen to its maximum value of 5.00, resulting in a very large profit. Regardless of the exercise prices chosen, if implied volatility is low, the trader should buy an option that is closer to the money, and if implied volatility is high, the trader should sell an option that is closer to the money.

Our choice of bull or bear strategies has focused thus far on the at-the-money option, typically the option whose delta is closest to 50. This does indeed tend to be the case for options on futures. In other markets, though, the at-the-money option may not be the option with a delta closest to 50 because, as discussed in Chapter 5, the theoretical value of an option depends not on the current price of the underlying contract but on the forward price. For this reason, the choice of bull or bear spreads should really focus on the *at-the-forward* option. Especially in the stock option market, if interest rates are high and there is a significant amount of time to expiration, the at-the-forward option may have an exercise price that is considerably higher than the current stock price. Having noted this distinction, for practical purposes, a trader will not go too far wrong if he focuses on the at-the-money option, buying it when implied volatility is low and selling it when implied volatility is high.

Before concluding our discussion of bull and bear spreads, it will be useful to look at graphs of the theoretical value, delta, gamma, vega, and theta for a typical bull vertical spread, as shown in Figures 12-8 through 12-13. The reader should take some time to look at these graphs not only because they highlight some of the important characteristics of this very common class of spreads but also because they serve as examples of some of the more important characteristics of risk measurement discussed in Chapter 9. This will be especially helpful when we take a closer look at risk analysis in later chapters.

Figure 12-8 Value of a bull spread as time passes or volatility declines.

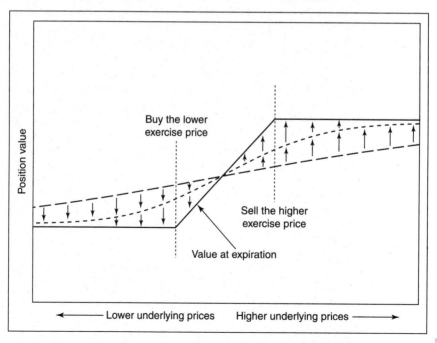

Figure 12-9 Delta of a bull spread as time passes or volatility declines.

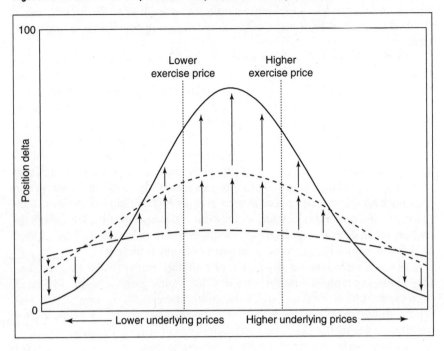

Figure 12-10 Gamma of a bull spread as time passes or volatility declines.

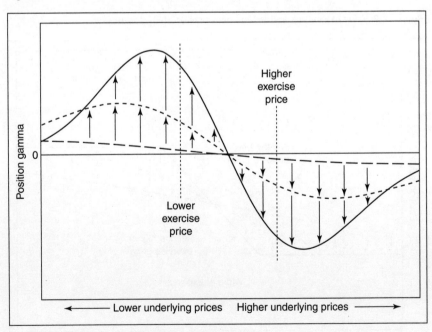

Figure 12-11 Vega of a bull spread as time passes or volatility declines.

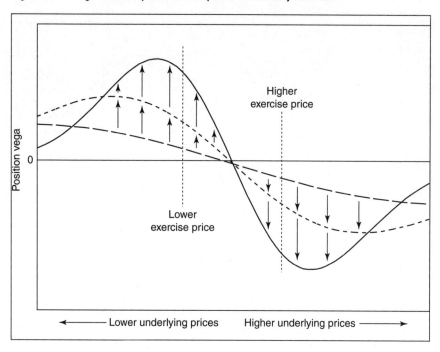

Figure 12-12 Theta of a bull spread as volatility declines.

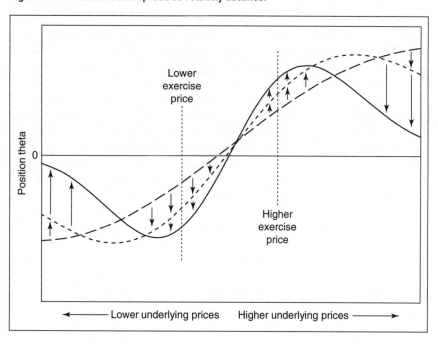

Figure 12-13 Theta of a bull spread as time passes.

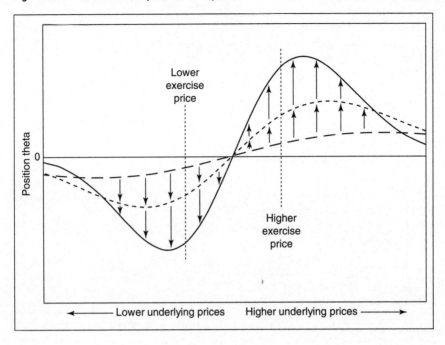

For the graphs of theoretical value, delta, gamma, and vega (Figures 12-8 through 12-11), the effect of time passing or volatility declining is similar. For the theta, however, there are slight differences, so separate theta graphs for declining volatility (Figure 12-12) and the passage of time (Figure 12-13) are shown. Note also that the maximum gamma, vega, and theta for vertical spreads tend to occur when the underlying price is either just below the lowest exercise price or just above the highest exercise price.

Finally, we might ask why a trader with a directional opinion might prefer a vertical spread to an outright long or short position in the underlying instrument. For one thing, a vertical spread is much less risky than an outright position. A trader who wants to take a position that is 500 deltas long can either buy 5 underlying contracts or buy 25 vertical call spreads with a delta of 20 each. The 25 vertical spreads may sound riskier than 5 underlying contracts, until we remember that a vertical spread has limited risk, whereas the position in the underlying has open-ended risk. Of course, greater risk also means greater reward. A trader with a long or short position in the underlying market can reap huge rewards if the market makes a large move in his favor. By contrast, the vertical spreader's profits are limited, but he will also be much less bloodied if the market makes an unexpected move in the wrong direction.

Ignoring interest considerations, the only way to profit from trading the underlying contract is to be right about direction. If we buy the underlying contract, the market must rise. If we sell the underlying, the market must fall. But, with options, one need not necessarily be right about market direction.

Options also offer the additional dimension of volatility. Depending on the exercise prices that have been chosen, if the trader has correctly estimated volatility, a bull spread can be profitable if the market fails to rise or in some cases even if it declines. A bear spread can be profitable even if the market fails to fall. This flexibility is just one of the factors that has lead to the dramatic growth in option markets.

13

Risk Considerations

When choosing a strategy, a trader must always try to find a reasonable balance between two opposing considerations—reward and risk. Ideally, a trader would like the greatest possible profit at the smallest possible risk. In the real world, however, high profit usually goes hand in hand with high risk, while low risk goes hand in hand with low profit. How should a trader balance these two considerations? Certainly, a strategy should have an expected profit that makes it worth executing. At the same time, the risk associated with the strategy must be kept within reasonable bounds. And whatever the risk, it should never be greater than what is commensurate with the potential reward.

In option trading, the reward is typically expressed in terms of *theoretical edge*—the average profit resulting from a strategy, assuming that the trader's assessment of market conditions is correct. Unfortunately, although the theoretical edge can be expressed as one number, the risk associated with an option position cannot be expressed in the same way. We know that options are subject to many different risks. If we want to intelligently analyze a strategy, we may be required to consider a variety of risks. A strategy may be reasonable with respect to some risks but unacceptable with respect to others.

Before proceeding further in our discussion, let's summarize the basic risks associated with an option position:

Delta (Directional) Risk. The risk that the underlying market will move in one direction rather than another. When we create a position that is delta neutral, we are trying to ensure that initially the position has no bias as to the direction in which the underlying instrument will move. A delta-neutral position does not necessarily eliminate all directional risk, but the position is typically immune to directional risks within a limited range.

Gamma (Curvature) Risk. The risk of a large move in the underlying contract, regardless of direction. The gamma position is a measure of how sensitive a position is to such moves. A positive gamma position does not really have gamma risk because such a position will, in theory, increase in value with movement in the underlying contract. A negative gamma position, however, can quickly lose its theoretical edge with a large move in the underlying contract. The effect of such a move must always be a consideration when analyzing the relative merits of different positions.

Theta (Time Decay) Risk.   This is the opposite side of gamma risk. Positions with positive gamma become more valuable with large moves in the underlying. But if movement helps, the passage of time hurts. A positive gamma always goes hand in hand with a negative theta; a negative gamma always goes hand in hand with a positive theta. A trader with a negative theta must consider the risk in terms of how much time can pass before the spread's theoretical edge disappears. The position wants movement, but if the movement fails to occur over the next day, next week, or next month, will the spread, in theory, still be profitable?

Vega (Volatility) Risk.   The risk that the volatility that we input into the theoretical pricing model will be incorrect. If we use the wrong volatility, we have the wrong probability distribution for the underlying contract. Because some positions have a positive vega and are hurt by declining volatility and some positions have a negative vega and are hurt by rising volatility, vega represents a risk to every position. A trader must always consider how much the volatility can move against him before the potential profit from a position disappears. Most traders prefer to interpret vega as the sensitivity of a position to a change in implied volatility. If implied volatility rises or falls, how will that change the prices of options that make up a position? If the changes hurt the position, will the trader be able to maintain the position in the face of adverse market conditions?

Rho (Interest-Rate) Risk.   The risk that the interest rate will change over the life of the option. A position with a positive rho will be helped by rising interest rates and hurt by declining rates; a position with a negative rho has just the opposite characteristics.[1] Except for special situations, the interest rate is the least important of the inputs into a theoretical pricing model. Consequently, rho is usually considered the least important of the risk measures.

Let's look at the relative importance of the various risks by considering several different option strategies.

Volatility Risk

For an option trader, volatility risk comes in two forms—the risk that he has incorrectly estimated the realized volatility of the underlying contract over the life of a strategy and the risk that implied volatility in the option market will change. Any spread that has a nonzero gamma or vega has volatility risk.

Consider the prices and values in the theoretical evaluation table in Figure 13-1.[2] What types of volatility strategies might be profitable under these conditions? Whether we compare option prices with their theoretical values or the

---

[1] We are considering only the interest-rate risk as it applies to the evaluation of options. Changes in interest rates can also affect the evaluation of an underlying contract, such as a bond, or even the shares in a company. But that is a separate matter.

[2] In order to focus only on volatility, we have assumed an interest rate of 0.

Figure 13-1

Underlying price = 48.40   Time to May expiration = 56 days   Volatility = 18%   Interest rate = 0%

Exercise Price	Calls							Puts						
	Price	Theoretical Value	Delta	Gamma	Theta	Vega	Implied Volatility	Price	Theoretical Value	Delta	Gamma	Theta	Vega	Implied Volatility
44	4.59	4.53	92	4.5	−0.0046	0.029	19.83%	0.20	0.13	−8	4.5	−0.0046	0.029	20.12%
46	2.99	2.86	78	8.8	−0.0091	0.057	20.25%	0.58	0.46	−22	8.8	−0.0091	0.057	20.09%
48	1.75	1.56	56	11.6	−0.0121	0.075	20.48%	1.35	1.16	−44	11.6	−0.0121	0.075	20.48%
50	0.93	0.73	33	10.7	−0.0111	0.069	20.88%	2.53	2.33	−67	10.7	−0.0111	0.069	20.88%
52	0.47	0.28	16	7.2	−0.0075	0.047	21.63%	4.06	3.88	−84	7.2	−0.0075	0.047	21.45%
54	0.23	0.09	6	3.7	−0.0038	0.024	22.46%	5.84	5.69	−94	3.7	−0.0038	0.024	22.73%

Time to July expiration = 112 days   Volatility = 18%   Interest rate = 0%

Exercise Price	Calls							Puts						
	Price	Theoretical Value	Delta	Gamma	Theta	Vega	Implied Volatility	Price	Theoretical Value	Delta	Gamma	Theta	Vega	Implied Volatility
44	4.96	4.82	84	5.0	−0.0052	0.064	20.12%	0.56	0.42	−16	5.0	−0.0052	0.064	20.12%
46	3.52	3.32	71	7.1	−0.0074	0.091	20.21%	1.13	0.92	−29	7.1	−0.0074	0.091	20.31%
48	2.38	2.12	55	8.2	−0.0085	0.106	20.42%	1.98	1.72	−45	8.2	−0.0085	0.106	20.42%
50	1.55	1.24	39	8.0	−0.0083	0.103	20.80%	3.14	2.86	−61	8.0	−0.0083	0.103	20.71%
52	0.97	0.69	25	6.6	−0.0069	0.085	21.14%	4.58	4.29	−75	6.6	−0.0069	0.085	21.25%
54	0.60	0.35	15	4.8	−0.0050	0.062	21.64%	6.21	5.95	−85	4.8	−0.0050	0.062	21.78%

implied volatilities of the options with the volatility input of 18 percent, we will reach the same conclusion: all options are overpriced. Recalling the general guidelines in Chapter 11, under these conditions, a trader will want to consider spreads with a negative vega:

> Short straddles and strangles
> Call or put ratio spreads—sell more than buy
> Long butterflies
> Short calendar spreads

Which of these categories is likely to represent the best spreading opportunity? And within each category, which specific spread might represent the best risk-reward tradeoff?

For the moment, let's focus on May options. Having eliminated the possibility of calendar spreads, any spread we choose will necessarily have a negative gamma and negative vega. But with 12 different May options available (6 calls and 6 puts), it's possible to construct a number of spreads that fall into this category. How can we make an intelligent decision about which spread might be best?

Initially, let's consider the three strategies shown in Figure 13-2: a short straddle that has been done in a 4:3 ratio to make it closer to delta neutral (Spread 1), a ratio call spread (Spread 2), and a long put butterfly (Spread 3). Each spread is approximately delta neutral and, as we would expect, has a positive theoretical edge. How can we evaluate the relative merits of each spread?

Initially, it may appear that Spread 1 is best because it has the greatest theoretical edge. If the volatility estimate of 18 percent turns out to be correct, Spread 1 will show a profit of 6.65, Spread 2 a profit of 1.80, and Spread 3 a profit of only .60.

But is theoretical edge our only concern? If this is true, we can simply do each spread in larger and larger size to make the theoretical edge as big as we want. Instead of doing Spread 2 in our original size of 10 × 20, we can increase the size fivefold to 50 × 100. This will also increase the theoretical edge fivefold to 9.00. This ostensibly makes Spread 2 a better strategy than Spreads 1 and 3. Clearly, theoretical edge cannot be the only consideration.

Figure13-2

		Theoretical Edge	Delta
Spread 1:	−15 May 48 calls	15 x +0.19	−15 x +56
	−20 May 48 puts	20 x +0.19	−20 x −44
		+6.65	+40
Spread 2:	+10 May 50 calls	10 x −0.20	+10 x +34
	−20 May 52 calls	20 x +0.19	−20 x +16
		+1.80	+20
Spread 3:	+10 May 46 puts	10 x −0.12	+10 x −22
	−20 May 48 puts	20 x +0.19	−20 x −44
	+10 May 50 puts	10 x −0.20	+10 x −67
		+0.60	−10

Theoretical edge is only an indication of what we expect to earn if we are right about market conditions. Because there is no guarantee that we will be right, we must give at least as much consideration to the question of risk. If we are wrong about market conditions, how badly might we be hurt?

In order to focus on the risk considerations, let's change the size of Spreads 2 and 3 so that their theoretical edge is approximately equal to that of Spread 1. We can achieve this by increasing the size of Spread 2 to 35 × 70 and increasing the size of Spread 3 to 100 × 200 × 100. The spreads in their new sizes with their total theoretical edge and risk sensitivities are shown in Figure 13-3. With all three spreads having a similar theoretical edge, we can now focus on the risks associated with each spread.

As with all volatility positions, one consideration is the possibility of a large price move in the underlying contract. Because each strategy has a negative gamma, any large move will hurt the position. But will each spread be hurt to the same degree? Because Spread 2 has the smallest negative gamma (−165.5), we might conclude that it has the smallest risk with respect to a large move. But this is true only under current market conditions. As market conditions change, all risk measures, including the gamma, will almost certainly change. If the underlying contract makes a very large move such that current market conditions no longer apply, it may not be clear what will happen to the risks associated with each spread.

It will be easier to analyze the relative risks of the spreads if we construct a graph of the theoretical profit or loss with respect to movement in the underlying contract. This has been done in Figure 13-4. We can see that each spread does indeed lose value as the underlying price moves either up or down.[3] However, we can also see that if there is a very large move, the spread characteristics begin to diverge. On both the upside and downside, the losses from Spread 1, the short straddle, continue to increase, resulting in potentially unlimited risk in either direction. Spread 2, the ratio spread, has unlimited upside risk. On the downside, though, it flattens out and eventually results in a very small profit. Spread 3, the long butterfly, flattens out on both the upside and downside, so its risk is limited regardless of direction.

Figure 13-3

		Theoretical Edge	Delta	Gamma	Theta	Vega
Spread 1:	−15 May 48 calls	15 x +0.19	−15 x +56	−15 x 11.6	−15 x −0.0121	−15 x 0.075
	−20 May 48 puts	20 x +0.19	−20 x −44	−20 x 11.6	−20 x −0.0121	−20 x 0.075
		+6.65	+40	−406.0	+0.4235	−2.625
Spread 2:	+35 May 50 calls	35 x −.20	+35 x +34	+35 x 10.7	+35 x −0.0111	+35 x 0.069
	−70 May 52 calls	70 x +0.19	−70 x +16	−75 x 7.2	−70 x −0.0075	−70 x 0.047
		+6.30	+70	−165.5	+0.1365	−0.875
Spread 3:	+100 May 46 puts	100 x −0.12	+100 x −22	+100 x 8.8	+100 x −0.0091	+100 x 0.057
	−200 May 48 puts	200 x +0.19	−200 x −44	−200 x 11.6	−200 x −0.0121	−200 x 0.075
	+100 May 50 puts	100 x −0.20	+100 x −67	+100 x 10.7	+100 x −0.0111	+100 x 0.069
		+6.00	−100	−370.0	+0.4000	−2.400

[3] Spreads 1 and 2, with their slightly positive delta, initially show a small gain as the market rises. Spread 3, with its slight negative delta, initially shows a small gain as the market falls.

Figure 13-4

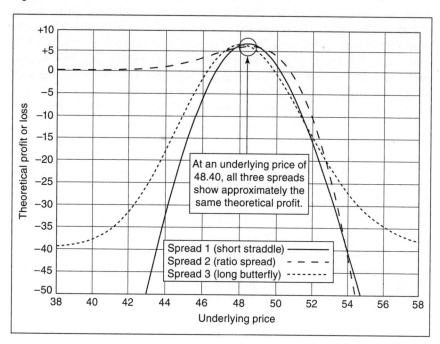

At an underlying price of 48.40, all three spreads show approximately the same theoretical profit.

Spread 1 (short straddle) ————
Spread 2 (ratio spread) — — — —
Spread 3 (long butterfly) ·········

Which spread is best? That depends on what the trader is worried about. If the trader is oblivious to the risk, it won't matter which spread he chooses. On average, each position will show a profit of approximately 6.00. If, however, the trader is more worried about a large downward move in the market, then perhaps Spread 2 is best. And if the trader is unwilling to accept the risk of unlimited loss in either direction, then perhaps Spread 3 is best.

In addition to the possibility of a large move, all three positions are exposed to the risk of an incorrect volatility estimate. Because each spread has a negative vega, there will be no problem if, over the life of the option, volatility turns out to be lower than 18 percent. In such a case, the spreads will show a profit greater than originally expected. On the other hand, if volatility turns out to be greater than 18 percent, this could present a problem. What will happen if volatility turns out to be 20 or 25 percent or some higher number? Each spread will be hurt because of the negative vega, but will they be hurt to the same degree?

Because Spread 2 has the smallest vega (–.875), we might initially conclude that it has the smallest volatility risk. But the vega, like the gamma, changes as market conditions change. If we raise volatility, the vega of Spread 1, the short straddle, will remain essentially unchanged because the vega of an at-the-money option is constant with respect to changes in volatility. But the vega of Spread 3, the long butterfly, will decline because the vega of in-the-money and out-of-the-money options (the May 46 and May 50 puts) will tend to increase as volatility rises. With Spread 2, the vega of both options, the May 50 call and the May 52 call, will begin to increase, so it's not immediately clear what will happen if we increase volatility.

We can analyze the volatility characteristics of each spread by constructing a graph of each spread's value with respect to changing volatility. This is shown in Figure 13-5. With a large change in volatility, the values of the three positions begin to diverge. If volatility rises, the spreads begin to lose value until, at some point, the potential profit becomes a loss. In terms of volatility risk, we might logically ask, how high can volatility rise before we begin to lose money? That is, we might want to determine the breakeven volatility, or *implied volatility*, for each spread. This is simply an extension of the general definition of implied volatility: the volatility over the life of an option, or options, at which the position will, in theory, show neither a profit nor a loss. In Figure 13-5, we can see that the breakeven volatility for Spread 1 (the short straddle) is approximately 21 percent, for Spread 2 (the ratio spread) approximately 23 percent, and for Spread 3 (the long butterfly) approximately 21.5 percent. This seems to confirm that Spread 2, the ratio spread, is the least risky with respect to volatility.

However, if volatility turns out to be higher than expected, why should it stop at 23 percent? What will happen if volatility turns out to be much higher, perhaps 30 percent or even 40 percent? Eventually, Spread 2, the ratio spread, which initially seemed to carry the least volatility risk, will begin to lose value at almost the same rate as Spread 1, the short straddle. On the other hand, at higher volatilities, the graph of Spread 3, the long butterfly, begins to flatten out, suggesting that there is a limit to how much it can lose. Of course, we know this because a butterfly has both limited profit potential and limited risk.

Although we might worry that volatility will increase to some value greater than 18 percent, we might also consider what will happen if volatility turns out to be less than 18 percent. For the same reason that rising volatility will hurt,

Figure 13-5

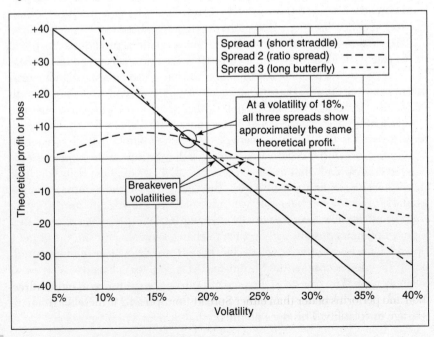

falling volatility should help. In Figure 13-5, we can see that as volatility falls below 18 percent, the profit resulting from each spread does indeed increase. However, as volatility falls well below 18 percent, the profit from Spread 2 begins to decline, eventually falling to almost 0. On the other hand, the profit from Spread 3 begins to accelerate.

The shapes of the graphs in Figure 13-5 are a result of each position's *volga*—the sensitivity of the vega to a change in volatility. (For a discussion of the volga, see Chapter 9, specifically Figure 9-15.) Spread 1 has a volga close to 0; its vega remains constant regardless of changes in volatility. Spread 2 has a negative volga. As volatility rises, the vega becomes more negative; as volatility falls, the vega becomes less negative. This means that as volatility rises or falls, changes in volatility work against the position, accelerating the rate of loss as volatility rises and reducing the rate of profit as volatility falls. In contrast, Spread 3 has positive volga. Changes in volatility work in favor of the position, reducing the rate of loss as volatility rises and increasing the rate of profit as volatility falls.

Although Figure 13-5 can be interpreted as the risk of using an incorrect volatility over the life of the options, it can also be interpreted as the risk of a sudden change in implied volatility. In terms of implied volatility risk, Spread 3 probably represents the best value. If implied volatility begins to rise, Spread 3 will initially lose money more quickly than Spread 2, but if implied volatility rises dramatically, Spread 3 will begin to outperform both Spreads 1 and 2 because the rate of loss will decline. And if implied volatility falls, Spread 3 will outperform both Spreads 1 and 2, increasing in value more quickly at lower volatilities.

Why are risk considerations so important? Every trader knows that there are times when a strategy will result in a profit and times when it will result in a loss. No one wins all the time. In the long run, however, a good trader's profits will more than offset his losses. For example, suppose that a trader chooses a strategy that will show a profit of $7,000 half the time and will show a loss of $5,000 the other half of the time. In the long run, the trader will show an average profit of $1,000. Suppose, though, that the first time that the trader executes the strategy, she loses $5,000, and the trader only has $3,000? Now the trader will not be able to stay in business for all those times when he is fortunate enough to show a profit of $7,000. Every trader knows that it is only over long periods of time that good luck and bad luck even out. Hence no trader will initiate a strategy where short-term bad luck might end his trading career.

Financial officers at large firms know that it is much easier to manage a steady cash flow than one that swings wildly. In a sense, every trader is his own financial officer. He must sensibly manage his finances so that he can avoid being ruined by the periods of back luck that will inevitably occur, no matter how skillfully he trades.

Practical Considerations

Considering only the gamma and vega risk, Spread 3 probably has the best risk characteristics. It has limited risk if there is a large move in either direction and performs better than either Spread 1 or Spread 2 if there is a dramatic change in volatility. This does not mean that Spread 3 performs better under all conditions. If the underlying market makes any downward move or there is a small to moderate upward move, Spread 2 outperforms Spreads 1 and 3. Spread 2 also has an advantage if there is a moderate increase in volatility.

Even if we assume that Spread 3, the long butterfly, offers the best theoretical risk-reward tradeoff, it may have some practical drawbacks. Butterflies are actively traded in many markets, but Spread 3 is a three-sided spread, as opposed to Spreads 1 and 2, which are two-sided spreads. A three-sided spread may be more difficult to execute in the marketplace and also may cost more in terms of the bid-ask spread. If a trader wants to execute the complete spread at one time, he may not be able to do so at his target prices. And if he tries to execute one leg at a time, he will be at risk from adverse changes in the market until the other legs can be executed.

Additionally, there is the question of market liquidity. In order to obtain a theoretical edge commensurate with Spreads 1 and 2, it was necessary to increase the size of the butterfly to 100 × 200 × 100. If there is insufficient liquidity in the May 46, 48, and 50 puts to support this size, it may not be possible to execute the butterfly in the size required to meet the trader's profit objective. Alternatively, it may be possible to execute part of the spread at favorable prices, but as the size increases, the prices may become less satisfactory. Moreover, for a retail customer, the increased size may entail greater transaction costs.

If trading considerations make Spread 3 impractical, a trader may have to choose between Spreads 1 (short straddle) and 2 (ratio spread). If this happens, Spread 2 is the clear winner. It allows for a much greater margin for error in both underlying price change (gamma risk) and volatility (vega risk). A trader who is given a choice between these two spreads will strongly prefer Spread 2.

In the real world, the choice of spreads is not always clear. One spread may be superior with respect to one type of risk, while a different spread may be superior with respect to a different risk. The ease with which a spread can be executed, as well as the cost of execution, will also play a role.

Let's consider three new spreads—Spread 4 (a short put calendar spread), Spread 5 (a diagonal call spread), and Spread 6 (a put diagonal ratio spread). In order to again focus on risk, the size of each spread has been adjusted so that the theoretical edge of all three spreads is similar. The total theoretical edge and risk sensitivities of each spread (all taken from the theoretical evaluation table in Figure 13-1) are shown in Figure 13-6.

Figure 13-6

	Theoretical Edge	Delta	Gamma	Theta	Vega
Spread 4: +85 May 48 puts	85 x −0.19	+85 x −44	+85 x 11.6	+85 x −0.0121	+85 x 0.075
−85 July 48 puts	85 x +0.26	−85 x −45	−85 x 8.2	−85 x −0.0085	−85 x 0.106
	+5.95	+85	+289.0	−0.3060	−2.635
Spread 5: +100 May 52 calls	100 x −0.19	+100 x +16	+100 x 7.2	+100 x −0.0075	+100 x 0.047
−100 July 54 calls	100 x +0.25	−100 x +15	−100 x 4.8	−100 x −0.0050	−100 x 0.062
	+6.00	+100	+240.0	−0.2500	−1.500
Spread 6: +30 May 48 puts	30 x −0.19	+30 x −44	+30 x 11.6	+30 x −0.0121	+30 x 0.075
−80 July 44 puts	80 x +0.14	−80 x +16	−80 x 5.0	−80 x −0.0052	−80 x 0.064
	+5.50	−40	−52.0	+0.0530	−2.870

Because each spread has a negative vega, we will again want to consider the risk that volatility will turn out to be greater than our estimate of 18 percent. The sensitivity of each spread to increasing volatility is shown in Figure 13-7. We can see that Spread 4 has an implied volatility of approximately 20.5 percent, Spread 5 approximately 22 percent, and Spread 6 approximately 20 percent. If rising volatility is our primary concern, Spread 5, the diagonal call spread, seems to entail the lowest risk. However, although Spread 5 loses the least in a rising-volatility market, it also shows a smaller profit in a falling-volatility market. This may seem like a reasonable tradeoff, except that with Spread 5, the positive effects of falling volatility begin to decline very quickly. This is due to the negative volga associated with the position. As volatility falls, the vega becomes less negative until, at a volatility of approximately 10 percent, the vega falls to 0. Spread 6, the put diagonal ratio spread, has an even larger negative volga; its vega turns positive if volatility falls below 11 percent. In contrast to both Spreads 5 and 6, Spread 4, the short calendar spread, has a volga of 0. Its vega remains constant regardless of whether volatility rises or falls. It offers an equal tradeoff between losses when volatility rises and profits when volatility falls.

What about the gamma risk of each spread? Here we have a situation where not all the spreads have a gamma with the same sign. Spread 6, the diagonal ratio spread, has a negative gamma, so it should be hurt by a large move in the underlying. Spreads 4 and 5, however, have a positive gamma and should profit from a large move. The graphs of the positions with respect to changes in the underlying price are shown in Figure 13-8.

We can see in Figure 13-8 that although Spread 6, the diagonal ratio spread, will be hurt by a move in the price of the underlying contract, the degree

Figure 13-7

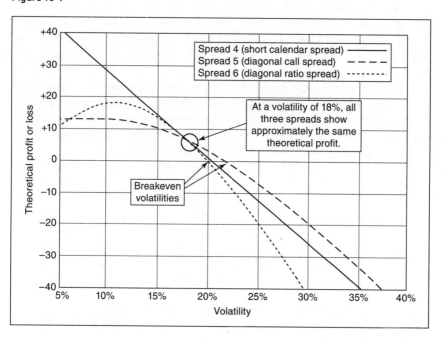

Figure 13-8

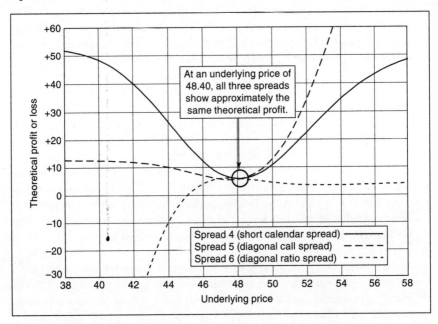

At an underlying price of 48.40, all three spreads show approximately the same theoretical profit.

Spread 4 (short calendar spread) ————
Spread 5 (diagonal call spread) — — — —
Spread 6 (diagonal ratio spread) - - - - - -

to which the move will hurt depends on the direction. With an upward move, the potential profit will decline. But even with a very large upward move, the spread will always retain some profit. On the downside, however, the spread's profit rapidly disappears, turning into a potentially unlimited loss if the downward move is large enough.

Spread 4, the short put calendar spread, and Spread 5, the diagonal call spread, both have positive gamma and will profit from a large move. Unlike Spread 4, though, which shows approximately equal profit in either direction, Spread 5 shows a greater profit in an upward move and a smaller profit in a downward move.[4]

There is, of course, a tradeoff between gamma and theta. If movement in the underlying price will increase the value of Spreads 4 and 5 (positive gamma), the passage of time with no movement will reduce the value (negative theta). It may be worthwhile to look at how much time can pass before each spread loses its theoretical edge. This is shown in Figure 13-9.

In Figure 13-9, Spread 4 exhibits the typical decay profile for a short calendar spread that is approximately at the money. As time passes, the position loses value at an increasingly greater rate. Spread 5, the diagonal call spread, also loses value as time passes. But after five weeks the decay turns positive, so that if nothing happens in the underlying market the position will eventually show a small profit. Spread 6, the diagonal ratio spread, initially shows a small increase in value as time passes. Eventually, though, this position is also subject to decay. After seven weeks, its potential profit disappears completely.

---

[4] It may appear from Figure 13-8 that Spread 5 has unlimited upside profit potential. In reality, the profit is limited by the fact that the spread between the value of the May 52 call and the July 54 call can never be greater than 2.00. This will occur if both options go very deeply into the money.

Figure 13-9

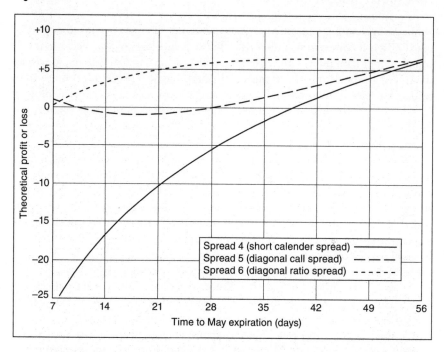

As must be obvious by now, the choice of spreads is never simple. As with all trading decisions, it is a question of risk and reward. Although there are many risks with which an option trader must deal, he will often have to ask himself which risk represents the greatest threat. Sometimes, in order to avoid one type of risk, he will be forced to accept a different risk. Even if the trader is willing to accept some risk in a certain area, he may decide that he will only do so to a limited degree. Then he may have to accept increased risks in other areas.

If given the choice between several different strategies, a trader can use a computer to determine the risk characteristics of the strategies under different market conditions. Unfortunately, it may not always be possible to analyze the choices in such detail. A trader may not have immediate access to the necessary computer support, or market conditions may be changing so rapidly that if he fails to make an immediate decision, opportunity may quickly pass him by. In such cases, the trader will often have to rely on his instincts in choosing a strategy. Although there is no substitute for experience, most traders quickly learn an important rule: *straddles and strangles are the riskiest of all spreads.* This is true whether one buys or sells these strategies. New traders sometimes assume that the purchase of straddles and strangles is not especially risky because the risk is limited. However, it can be just as painful to lose money day after day when one buys a straddle or strangle and the market fails to move as it is to lose the same amount of money all at once when one sells a straddle and the market makes a violent move. Of course, a trader who is right about volatility can reap large rewards from straddles and strangles. But an experienced trader knows that such strategies offer the least margin for error and will therefore prefer strategies with more desirable risk characteristics.

How Much Margin for Error?

What is a reasonable margin for error in assessing the risk of a position, particularly when it comes to volatility risk? There is no clear answer because it will usually depend on the volatility characteristics of a particular market, as well as the trader's experience in that market. In some cases, 5 percentage points may be an extremely large margin for error, and the trader will feel very confident with any strategy passing such a test. In other cases, 5 percentage points may be almost no margin for error at all, and the trader will find that the strategy is a constant source of worry.

Rather than focusing on margin for error, a better approach might be to focus on the correct size in which to do a spread given a known margin for error. Practical trading considerations aside, a trader should always choose the spread with the best risk-reward characteristics. But sometimes even the best spread will have only a small margin for error and consequently will entail significant risk. In such a case, a trader, if he wants to make a trade, ought to do so in small size. If, however, a trader can execute a spread with a very large margin for error, he ought to be willing to do the spread in a much larger size.

Consider a trader whose best estimate of volatility in a certain market is 25 percent. If implied volatility is lower than 25 percent, the trader will look for positions with a positive vega. If the best positive-vega strategy the trader can find is a 2×1 ratio spread with an implied volatility of 23 percent (only a 2-percentage-point margin for error), he will almost certainly keep the size of his strategy small, perhaps executing the spread only 10 times (20×10). If, however, the same spread has an implied volatility of 18 percent (a 7-percentage-point margin for error) and the trader believes that such a low volatility is extremely rare, he may have the confidence to execute the spread in a much larger size, perhaps 100×50.[5] The size of a trader's positions should depend on the riskiness of the positions, and this, in turn, depends on how much can go wrong before the strategy turns against the trader.

Dividends and Interest

In addition to the delta, gamma, theta, and vega risks that apply to all traders, stock option traders may also have to consider the risk of changes in interest rates and dividends.[6] When all options expire at the same time, the risk associated with changes in interest rates and dividends tends to be relatively small. Straddles, strangles, ratio spreads, and butterflies may change slightly because a change in interest rates or dividends will raise or lower the forward price. But all options are evaluated using one and the same forward price. For calendar spreads, however, where the options are evaluated using two different forward prices, long-term and short-term options can react differently to changes in these inputs.

---

[5] Size, of course, is relative. To a well-capitalized, experienced trader, even 100×50 may be a small trade.

[6] Depending on the settlement procedure, changes in interest rates can also affect futures options. But the effect, as discussed in Chapter 7, is usually quite small. Changes in interest rates can also affect futures options because they may change the price of the underlying futures contract. But this can be assessed as the risk of a change in the underlying price, not a change in interest rates.

Consider the evaluation table for stock options shown in Figure 13-10. With implied volatilities below the forecast of 29 percent, it makes sense to look for spreads with positive vegas. Suppose that we focus on the four spreads shown in Figure 13-11. Spreads 7 and 8 are long calendar spreads, while Spreads 9 and 10 are diagonal spreads. What are the relative merits of each spread?

Because all four spreads fall into the long calendar spread category, they all have the typical negative-gamma and positive-vega characteristics associated with such spreads. This is shown in Figures 13-12 and 13-13. Movement in the price of the underlying contract or falling volatility will reduce the value of the spread. Rising volatility will increase the value of the spread. (Spreads 7 and 8 have essentially identical volatility characteristics and are almost indistinguishable from each other in Figure 13-13.) Initially, the choice of spreads will depend on the risk of movement in the underlying contract as well as the risk of changes in implied volatility.

Because we are dealing with stock options, there are two additional risks—the risk of changing interest rates and the risk of changing dividends, assuming that at least one dividend payment falls between expirations. We know from Chapter 7 that stock option calls and puts react in just the opposite way to changes in interest rates and dividends. Rising interest rates or falling dividends cause calls to rise in value and puts to fall; falling interest rates and rising dividends cause calls to fall in value and puts to rise. Moreover, the impact of a change in either of these inputs will be greater for long-term options than for short-term options. We can measure the risk of changing interest rates by determining the total rho value for each spread. Even though there is no Greek for the dividend sensitivity, we can still use a computer to determine the dividend risk associated with each spread. The sensitivities for the individual options, as well as the total spread sensitivities, to changing interest rates and dividends are shown in Figure 13-14.

The call spreads (Spreads 7 and 9) have a positive rho and negative dividend sensitivity. The put spreads (Spreads 8 and 10) have a negative rho and positive dividend sensitivity. The value of each spread with respect to changes in these inputs is shown in Figures 13-15 and 13-16.

The interest-rate and dividend risk associated with volatility spreads is usually small compared with the volatility (gamma and vega) risk. Nonetheless, a trader ought to be aware of these risks, especially when a position is large and there is significant risk of a change in either interest rates or dividends.

What Is a Good Spread?

Option traders, being human, would rather talk about their successes than their disasters. If one were to eavesdrop on conversations among traders, it would probably seem that no one ever made a losing trade. Disasters, when they do occur, only happen to other traders. The fact is that every successful option trader has had his share of disasters. What separates successful traders from the unsuccessful ones is the ability to survive such occurrences.

Consider the trader who initiates a spread with a good theoretical edge and a large margin for error in almost every risk category. If the trader still

Figure 13-10

Stock price = 99.25		Expected dividend = 0.50 in 4 weeks and every 13 weeks thereafter				

Time to March expiration = 8 weeks   Volatility = 29%   Interest rate = 6%

Calls

Exercise Price	Price	Theoretical Value	Delta	Gamma	Theta	Vega	Implied Volatility
85	14.90	10.91	93	1.2	-0.0264	0.053	28.82%
90	10.51	10.65	83	2.3	-0.0371	0.098	27.53%
95	6.74	7.06	68	3.2	-0.0457	0.138	26.64%
100	3.85	4.32	51	3.6	-0.0477	0.154	25.98%
105	1.95	2.42	34	3.3	-0.0421	0.142	25.62%
110	0.88	1.25	21	2.6	-0.0319	0.111	25.47%

Puts

Price	Theoretical Value	Delta	Gamma	Theta	Vega	Implied Volatility
0.37	0.38	-7	1.2	-0.0125	0.053	28.84%
0.94	1.07	-17	2.3	-0.0224	0.098	27.61%
2.11	2.44	-32	3.2	-0.0316	0.138	26.59%
4.18	4.65	-49	3.6	-0.0314	0.154	25.97%
7.23	7.71	-66	3.3	-0.0250	0.142	25.58%
11.12	11.49	-79	2.6	-0.0140	0.111	25.47%

Time to June expiration = 21 weeks   Volatility = 29%   Interest rate = 6%

Calls

Exercise Price	Price	Theoretical Value	Delta	Gamma	Theta	Vega	Implied Volatility
85	16.70	16.90	84	1.3	-0.0256	0.149	27.64%
90	12.85	13.25	76	1.7	-0.0293	0.195	26.92%
95	9.52	10.11	66	2.0	-0.0316	0.229	26.41%
100	6.78	7.51	55	2.2	-0.0320	0.247	26.04%
105	4.64	5.44	45	2.2	-0.0306	0.246	25.76%
110	3.06	3.84	35	2.0	-0.0278	0.231	25.58%

Puts

Price	Theoretical Value	Delta	Gamma	Theta	Vega	Implied Volatility
1.40	1.61	-16	1.3	-0.0120	0.149	27.58%
2.44	2.84	-24	1.7	-0.0149	0.195	26.93%
3.99	4.58	-34	2.0	-0.0164	0.229	26.41%
6.13	6.86	-45	2.2	-0.0085	0.247	26.04%
8.87	9.67	-55	2.2	-0.0138	0.246	25.76%
12.18	12.95	-65	2.0	-0.0101	0.231	25.61%

Figure 13-11

		Theoretical Edge	Delta	Gamma	Theta	Vega
Spread 7:	+20 June 100 calls	20 x +0.73	+20 x +55	+20 x 2.2	+20 x −0.0320	+20 x 0.247
	−20 March 100 calls	20 x −0.47	−20 x +51	−20 x 3.6	−20 x −0.0477	−20 x 0.154
		+5.40	+80	−28.0	+0.3140	+1.860
Spread 8:	+20 June 95 puts	20 x +0.59	+20 x −34	+20 x 2.0	+20 x −0.0164	+20 x 0.229
	−20 March 95 puts	20 x −0.33	−20 x −32	−20 x 3.2	−20 x −0.0316	−20 x 0.138
		+5.20	−40	−20.0	+0.3030	+1.820
Spread 9:	+17 June 110 calls	17 x +0.78	+17 x +35	+17 x 2.0	+17 x −0.0278	+17 x 0.231
	−17 March 105 calls	17 x −0.47	−17 x +34	−17 x 3.3	−17 x −0.0421	−17 x 0.142
		+5.27	+17	−22.1	+0.2431	+1.513
Spread 10:	+65 June 85 puts	65 x +0.21	+65 x −16	+65 x 1.3	+65 x −0.0120	+65 x 0.149
	−65 March 90 puts	65 x −0.13	−65 x −17	−65 x 2.3	−65 x −0.0224	−65 x 0.098
		+5.20	+65	−65.0	+0.6760	+3.315

ends up losing money on the spread, does this mean that the trader has made a poor choice of spreads? Maybe a similar spread, but one with less margin for error, would have resulted in an even greater loss, perhaps a loss from which the trader could not recover.

It is impossible to take into consideration every possible risk. A spread that passed every risk test would probably have so little theoretical edge that it would not be worth doing. But the trader who allows himself a reasonable margin for error will find that even his losses will not lead to financial ruin. A good spread is not necessarily the one that shows the greatest profit when things go well; it

Figure 13-12

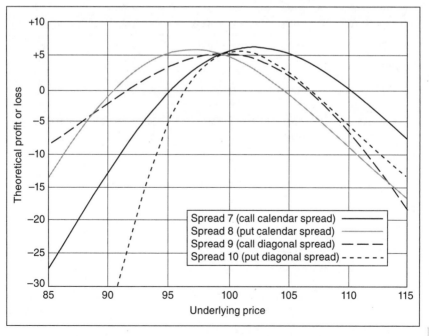

Figure 13-13

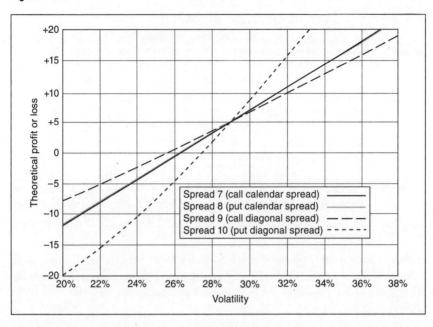

Figure 13-14 Interest-rate and dividend sensitivity.

March Options				
Exercise Price	Call Rho*	Put Rho*	Call Dividend Sensitivity‡	Put Dividend Sensitivity‡
85	0.118	−0.012	−0.924	0.072
90	0.109	−0.027	−0.826	0.169
95	0.093	−0.052	−0.681	0.315
100	0.071	−0.081	−0.509	0.487
105	0.048	−0.111	−0.342	0.653
110	0.030	−0.138	−0.208	0.788
June Options				
Exercise Price	Call Rho*	Put Rho*	Call Dividend Sensitivity‡	Put Dividend Sensitivity‡
85	0.266	−0.068	−1.668	0.308
90	0.247	−0.107	−1.498	0.478
95	0.220	−0.154	−1.300	0.676
100	0.188	−0.205	−1.089	0.887
105	0.154	−0.258	−0.880	1.096
110	0.122	−0.310	−0.688	1.288

*The interest-rate sensitivity is given as the point change in option value for each one-percentage-point (1.00%) change in interest rates.
‡The dividend sensitivity is given as the point change in option value for each point change in the dividend.

(continued)

Figure 13-14 (*continued*)

		Total Rho	Total Dividend Sensitivity
Spread 7:	+20 June 100 calls	+20 x +0.188	+20 x −1.089
	−20 March 100 calls	−20 x +0.071	−20 x −0.509
		+2.340	−11.600
Spread 8:	+20 June 95 puts	+20 x −0.154	+20 x +0.676
	−20 March 95 puts	−20 x −0.052	−20 x +0.315
		−2.040	+7.220
Spread 9:	+17 June 110 calls	+17 x +0.122	+17 x −0.688
	−17 March 105 calls	−17 x +0.048	−17 x −0.342
		+1.258	−5.882
Spread 10:	+65 June 85 puts	+65 x −0.068	+65 x +0.308
	−65 March 90 puts	−65 x −0.027	−65 x +0.169
		−2.665	+9.035

may be the one that shows the least loss when things go badly. Winning trades always take care of themselves. Losing trades that do not give back all the profits from the winning ones are just as important.

Efficiency

One method that traders sometimes use to compare the relative riskiness of potential strategies focuses on the risk-reward ratio, or *efficiency*, of the strategies. Suppose that a trader is considering two possible spreads, both with a positive gamma and a negative theta. The reward is represented by the

Figure 13-15 Interest-rate sensitivity.

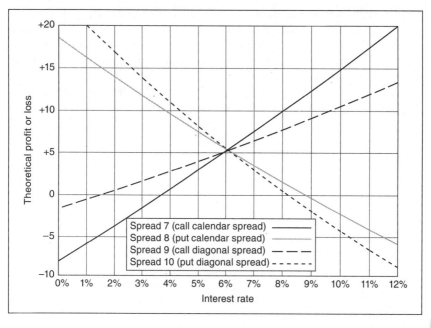

Figure 13-16 Dividend sensitivity.

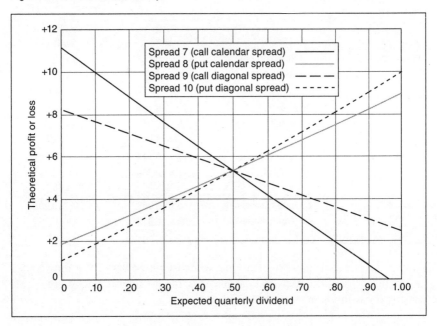

gamma, the potential profit when the underlying market moves. The risk is the theta, the money that will be lost through the passage of time if the underlying market fails to make sufficiently large moves. The trader would like the reward (the gamma) to be as large as possible compared with the risk (the theta). We might express this relationship as a ratio

$$\text{gamma/theta}$$

The larger the absolute value of this ratio, the more efficient the position.

In the same way, a trader who has a negative gamma and a positive theta wants the risk (the gamma) to be as small as possible compared with the reward (the theta). He therefore wants the absolute value of the gamma/theta ratio to be as large as possible.

For example, we might go back and calculate the efficiency of Spreads 1 through 3 in Figure 13-3. The efficiencies are

	Gamma/Theta	Efficiency
Spread 1	−406.0/0.4235	959
Spread 2	−165.5/0.1365	1,212
Spread 3	−370.0/0.4000	925

Because each spread has a negative gamma and positive theta, we want the efficiency to be as small as possible. We can see that Spread 3 is best, which is consistent with our previous analysis of each spread.

Assuming that all strategies have approximately the same theoretical edge, the efficiency can be a reasonable method of quickly comparing strategies where all options expire at the same time. In such cases, the gamma and theta are the primary risks to the position. If a strategy consists of options that expire at different times, the efficiency is only one consideration, and the sensitivity of the positions to changes in implied volatility (the vega) may also become important, as they were in our other spread examples. In such cases, a more detailed risk analysis will be necessary.

Adjustments

In Chapter 11, we considered the question of when a trader should adjust a position to remain delta neutral. In addition to deciding when to adjust, the trader also must consider how best to adjust because there are many different ways to adjust the total delta position. An adjustment to a trader's delta position may reduce his directional risk, but if he simultaneously increases his gamma, theta, or vega risk, he may inadvertently be exchanging one type of risk for another.

A delta adjustment made with the underlying contract is essentially a risk-neutral adjustment. The gamma, theta, and vega of an underlying contract are 0, so an adjustment made with the underlying contract will not change any of these risks. If a trader wants to adjust his delta position but wants to leave the other characteristics of the position unaffected, he can do so by purchasing or selling an appropriate number of underlying contracts.

An adjustment made with options will also reduce the delta risk, but at the same time, it will change the other risk characteristics. Because every option has not only a delta but also a gamma, theta, and vega, when an option is added to or subtracted from a position, it necessarily changes the total delta, gamma, theta, and vega of the position. This is something that new traders sometimes forget.

Consider a stock option market where the underlying contract is trading at 99.25 and all options appear to be overpriced. Suppose that a trader decides to sell the 95/105 strangle (sell the 95 put, sell the 105 call), with put and call deltas of −32 and 34, respectively. If the trader sells 20 strangles, the position is initially slightly delta negative because

$$(-20 \times +34) + (-20 \times -32) = -40$$

Suppose that a week passes and the underlying market has fallen to 97.00, with new delta values for the 95 put and 105 call of −39 and +25. Assuming that no adjustments have been made, the trader's delta position is now

$$(-20 \times -39) + (-20 \times +25) = +280$$

If the trader wants to hold the position but also wants to remain approximately delta neutral, he has three basic choices:

1. Sell underlying contracts.

2. Sell calls.

3. Buy puts.

Which method is best?

All other considerations being equal, whenever a trader makes an adjustment, she should do so with the intention of improving the risk-reward characteristics of the position. If the trader decides to adjust his delta position by purchasing puts, he also reduces his other risks because the gamma, theta, and vega associated with the put purchase are opposite in sign to the gamma, theta, and vega associated with the existing short strangle position.

Unfortunately, all other considerations may not be equal. Because implied volatility can remain high or low for long periods of time, it is quite likely that if all options were overpriced when the trader initiated his position, they will still be overpriced when he goes back into the market to make his adjustment. Even though the purchase of puts to become delta neutral will also reduce his other risks, such an adjustment will have the effect of reducing the theoretical edge. On the other hand, if all options are overpriced and the trader decides to sell additional calls to reduce the delta, the sale of the overpriced calls will have the effect of increasing the theoretical edge. If the trader decides that adding to his theoretical edge is of primary importance, he may decide to sell 11 additional 105 calls, leaving him approximately delta neutral because

$$(-20 \times -39) + (-31 \times +25) = -5$$

Now suppose that another week passes and the market has rebounded to 101.00, with new delta values for the 95 put and 105 call of −24 and +37. The position delta is now

$$(-20 \times -24) + (-31 \times +37) = -667$$

Again, if the trader wants to adjust, he has three basic choices—buy underlying contracts, buy calls, or sell puts. Assuming that all options are still overpriced and that the trader wants to continue to increase his theoretical edge, he may decide to sell an additional 28 of the 95 puts. The new total delta position is

$$(-48 \times -24) + (-31 \times +37) = +5$$

It should be clear what will result from these adjustments. If all options remain overpriced and the trader focuses solely on increasing his theoretical edge, he will continue to make whatever adjustments are necessary by selling overpriced options. This method of adjusting may indeed result in the greatest profit to the trader, but the strangle, which the trader was initially prepared to sell 20 times, now has increased in size to 48 × 31. If the market now makes a violent move in either direction, the adverse consequences will be greatly magnified. The new trader, overly concerned with always increasing his theoretical edge, often finds himself in just such a position. If the market makes a very swift move, the trader may not survive. For this reason, a new trader is usually well advised to avoid making adjustments that increase the size of a position.

No trader can afford to ignore the effect that adjustments will have on the total risk to a position. If he has a positive gamma or vega position, buying any additional options will increase his gamma or vega risk; if he has a negative gamma or vega position, selling any additional options will likewise increase his gamma or vega risk. A trader cannot afford to sell overpriced options or buy underpriced options ad infinitum. At some point, the size of the spread will simply become too large, and any additional theoretical edge will have to take a back seat to risk considerations. When this happens, there are only two choices:

1. Decrease the size of the spread.
2. Adjust in the underlying market.

A disciplined trader knows that sometimes, because of risk considerations, the best course is to reduce the size of the spread, even if it means giving up some theoretical edge. When open-outcry markets were flourishing, this could be particularly hard on a trader's ego if the trader had to personally go back into the market and either buy back options, that he originally sold, at a lower price or sell out options, that he originally purchased, at a higher price. However, if a trader is unwilling to swallow his pride from time to time, his trading career is likely to be a short one.

If a trader finds that any delta adjustment in the option market that reduces his risk will also reduce his theoretical edge and he is unwilling to give up any theoretical edge, his only recourse is to make adjustments in the underlying market. An underlying contract has no gamma, theta, or vega, so the risks of the position will remain essentially the same.

A Question of Style

Because most option pricing models assume that movement in the underlying contract is random, an option trader who trades purely from the theoretical values generated by a model should not have any prior opinion about market direction. In practice, however, many option traders begin their trading careers by taking positions in the underlying market, where direction is the primary consideration. Many traders therefore develop a style of trading based on presumed directional moves in the underlying market. A trader might, for example, be a trend follower, adhering to the philosophy that "the trend is your friend." Or he might be a contrarian, preferring to "buy weakness, sell strength."

Traders often try to incorporate their personal trading styles into their option strategies. One way to do this is to consider beforehand the adjustments that will be required for a certain strategy if the underlying market begins to move. A trader who sells straddles knows that such spreads have negative gamma. As the market moves higher, his delta position is becoming negative, and as the market moves lower, his delta position is becoming positive. If this trader likes to trade against the trend, he will avoid adjustments as much as possible because his position is automatically trading against the trend. Whichever way the market moves, the position always wants a retracement of this movement. On the other hand, a trader who sells the same straddles but prefers to trade with the trend will adjust at every opportunity. In order to remain delta neutral, he will be forced to buy underlying contracts as the market rises and sell underlying contracts as the market falls.

The opposite is true for a trader who buys straddles. He has a positive-gamma position. As the market rises, his delta position is becoming positive, and as the market falls, his delta position is becoming negative. If this trader likes to trade with the trend, he will adjust as little as possible in the belief that the market is likely to continue in the same direction. If, however, he prefers to trade against the trend, he will adjust as often as possible. Every adjustment will represent a profit opportunity if the market does in fact reverse its direction.

A trader with a negative gamma is always adjusting with the trend of the underlying market. A trader with a positive gamma is always adjusting against the trend of the underlying market. If a trader prefers to trade with the trend or against the trend, he should choose a strategy and an adjustment process that are appropriate to his preference. A trader who prefers to trade with the trend can choose a strategy with a positive gamma together with less frequent adjustments or a strategy with a negative gamma with more frequent adjustments. A trader who prefers to trade against the trend can choose a strategy with a negative gamma together with less frequent adjustments or a strategy with a positive gamma with more frequent adjustments. The purely theoretical trader will not have to worry about this because for him there is no such thing as a trend. However, for many traders, old habits, such as trading with or against the trend, are hard to break.

Liquidity

Every open option position entails risk. Even if the risk is limited to the current value of the options, by leaving the position open, the trader is risking the loss of that value. If the trader wants to eliminate the risk, he will have to take some action that will, in effect, close out the position. Sometimes this can be done through early exercise or by taking advantage of an opposing position to create an arbitrage. More often, however, in order to close out an open position, a trader must go into the marketplace and buy in any short options and sell out any long options.

An important consideration in deciding whether to enter into a trade is often the ease with which the trader can reverse the trade. Liquid option markets, where there are many buyers and sellers, are much less risky than illiquid markets, where there are few buyers and sellers. In the same way, a spread that consists of very liquid options is much less risky than a spread that consists of one or more illiquid options. If a trader is considering entering into a spread where the options are illiquid, he ought to ask himself whether he is willing to live with that position until expiration. If the market is very illiquid, this may be the only time that he will be able to get out of the position at anything resembling a fair price. If the spread consists of long-term options, the trader may find himself married to the position for better or worse, in sickness and in health, for what may seem like an eternity. If he is unwilling to commit his capital for such a lengthy period, perhaps he should avoid the position. Because there is greater risk associated with a long-term investment than with a short-term investment, a trader who does decide to take a position in long-term options ought to expect greater potential profit in the form of larger theoretical edge.[7]

New traders are often advised to begin trading in liquid markets. If a new trader makes an error resulting in a losing trade, in a liquid market, he will be able to keep his loss to a minimum because he will be able to exit the trade with relative ease. On the other hand, an experienced trader, especially a market maker, will often prefer to deal in less liquid markets. There may be less trading activity in such markets, but the bid-ask spread is much wider, resulting in greater theoretical edge each time a trade is made. Of course, any mistake can be a problem with which the trader will have to live for a long time. However, an experienced trader is expected to keep his mistakes to a minimum.

The most liquid options in any market are usually those that are short term and that are either at or slightly out of the money. Such options always have the narrowest bid-ask spread, and there are usually many traders willing to buy or sell these contracts. As a trader moves to longer-term options or to options that are more deeply in the money, he finds that the bid-ask spread begins to widen, and fewer and fewer traders are interested in these contracts. Although there is constant activity in at-the-money short-term options, deeply in-the-money long-term options may not trade for weeks at a time.

In addition to the liquidity of an option market, a trader should also give some thought to the liquidity of the underlying market. In an illiquid option market, a trader may find it difficult to adjust the position using options. If, however, the underlying market is liquid, he will at least be able to make his adjustment in that market with relative ease. The most dangerous markets in which to trade are those where both the options and the underlying contract are inactively traded. Only the most experienced and knowledgeable traders should enter such markets.

Figure 13-17 shows end-of-day bid-ask spreads and volume figures for Standard and Poor's (S&P) 500 Index options traded at the Chicago Board Options Exchange on March 1, 2010.[8] In general, the volumes are lower and bid-ask spreads are wider for back-month options or options that are deeply in the money compared with front-month options or options that are at the money or out of the money.

---

[7] This is the same reason that long-term interest rates tend to be higher than short-term rates. If one is willing to commit capital for a longer period, the potential reward should also be greater.

[8] Figure 13-17 represents only a partial listing of S&P 500 Index options. More exercise prices and expiration months were available than could conveniently be displayed here.

Figure 13-17 SPX Index options: Bid-ask spreads and trading volumes for March 1, 2010.

SPX index options: Bid-ask spread and trading volumes for March 1, 2010

SPX Index = 1115.71

Exercise Price	March Options				December Options			
	Call Bid-Ask	Call Volume	Put Bid-Ask	Put Volume	Call Bid-Ask	Call Volume	Put Bid-Ask	Put Volume
600	513.40 – 515.70	0	–0.05	0	508.50 – 510.90	0	0.05 – 0.55	0
650	463.40 – 465.70	0	–0.05	0	458.80 – 461.10	0	0.25 – 0.80	0
700	413.40 – 415.80	0	–0.05	0	409.20 – 411.50	0	0.90 – 1.15	0
750	363.40 – 365.80	0	–0.05	30	359.80 – 362.20	0	1.40 – 1.85	0
800	313.50 – 315.80	0	0.05 – 0.10	1,325	310.80 – 313.10	0	2.25 – 2.65	323
850	263.50 – 265.90	0	0.10 – 0.15	5,048	262.40 – 264.70	0	3.60 – 4.40	52
900	213.70 – 216.00	0	0.25 – 0.35	2,839	214.90 – 217.20	0	6.30 – 6.90	525
950	164.00 – 166.30	0	0.55 – 0.60	7,153	168.80 – 171.10	0	10.00 – 11.10	6
1,000	114.60 – 116.90	0	1.00 – .1.30	24,867	125.00 – 127.20	24	15.90 – 16.70	2,113
1,050	66.50 – 66.80	4	2.90 – 3.00	19,178	84.90 – 87.20	15	26.30 – 27.40	742
1,100	24.00 – 25.50	21	10.50 – 11.50	39,557	50.60 – 52.90	3,881	40.90 – 43.00	7,722
1,150	2.80 – 3.00	12,350	37.00 – 39.30	719	24.70 – 26.90	173	64.80 – 67.10	0
1,200	0.20 – 0.30	22,595	85.00 – 86.70	0	9.70 – 10.50	3,260	99.00 – 101.30	25
1,250	0.05 – 0.10	9,258	134.20 – 136.50	0	2.75 – 3.00	0	141.80 – 144.10	25
1,300	–0.05	8,895	184.20 – 186.50	0	0.35 – 0.90	0	189.50 – 191.80	0
1,350	–0.05	0	234.20 – 236.50	0	–0.50	0	238.90 – 241.30	0
1,400	–0.05	0	284.20 – 286.50	0	–0.40	0	288.80 – 291.10	0

(continued)

Figure 13-17 (continued)

SPX index options: Bid-ask spread and trading volumes for March 1, 2010				SPX Index = 1115.71			
	March Options				December Options		
Exercise Price	Call Bid-Ask	Call Volume	Put Bid-Ask	Put Volume	Call Bid-Ask	Call Volume	Put Bid-Ask	Put Volume
600	503.10 – 506.70	0	1.20 – 1.55	0	499.00 – 503.10	0	2.50 – 3.30	0
650	454.20 – 457.50	0	2.10 – 2.35	0	450.50 – 454.80	0	4.00 – 4.90	0
700	405.50 – 408.80	0	2.70 – 3.60	1	402.80 – 407.20	0	6.10 – 7.20	0
750	357.30 – 360.70	0	4.40 – 5.40	0	356.00 – 360.30	0	8.80 – 10.60	0
800	309.90 – 313.30	0	6.90 – 8.00	0	310.10 – 314.40	0	12.70 – 14.50	1,818
850	263.60 – 266.90	0	10.10 – 11.90	27	265.70 – 270.00	0	17.90 – 19.70	10
900	218.50 – 221.80	0	15.00 – 16.70	45	222.40 – 226.70	0	25.00 – 27.60	265
950	175.20 – 178.70	0	21.10 – 24.20	500	181.40 – 185.90	0	33.80 – 34.80	650
1,000	134.90 – 138.20	0	30.50 – 33.70	5,976	143.30 – 147.40	200	43.90 – 48.30	4,082
1,050	98.10 – 101.40	4	45.00 – 46.80	902	108.20 – 112.40	13	59.10 – 63.20	171
1,100	65.90 – 69.30	1,300	61.40 – 64.60	5,541	78.00 – 81.70	336	79.80 – 82.20	961
1,150	40.00 – 43.30	875	85.40 – 88.60	0	51.80 – 55.80	0	101.80 – 106.20	0
1,200	21.20 – 23.80	4,040	116.40 – 119.70	7	31.60 – 34.00	3,870	131.80 – 136.20	0
1,250	9.90 – 11.70	1,225	154.30 – 157.60	0	18.50 – 20.30	806	167.00 – 171.60	0
1,300	3.90 – 4.80	0	197.70 – 201.10	0	10.00 – 10.60	2	207.80 – 212.10	0
1,350	1.15 – 1.90	0	244.80 – 248.10	0	4.20 – 5.20	0	252.00 – 256.60	0
1,400	0.15 – 0.70	0	293.60 – 296.90	0	1.70 – 2.25	10,000	299.40 – 303.70	0

14

Synthetics

One important characteristic of options is that they can be combined with other options, or with underlying contracts, to create positions with characteristics which are almost identical to some other contract or combination of contracts. This type of replication enables us to do most option strategies in a variety of ways, and leads to many useful relationships between options and the underlying contract.

Synthetic Underlying

Consider the following position where all options are European (no early exercise permitted):

> long a June 100 call
> short a June 100 put

What will happen to this position at expiration? It may seem that one cannot answer the question without knowing where the underlying contract will be at expiration. Surprisingly, the price of the underlying contract does not affect the outcome. If the underlying contract is above 100, the put will expire worthless, but the trader will exercise the 100 call, thereby buying the underlying contract at 100. Conversely, if the underlying contract is below 100, the call will expire worthless, but the trader will be assigned on the 100 put, also buying the underlying contract at 100.

Ignoring for the moment the unique case when the underlying price is exactly 100, at June expiration the above position will always result in the trader buying the underlying contract at the exercise price of 100, either by choice (the underlying contract is above 100 and he exercises the 100 call) or by force (the underlying contract is below 100 and he is assigned on the 100 put). This position, a *synthetic long underlying*, has the same characteristics as a long underlying contract, but won't actually become an underlying contract until expiration.[1]

If the trader takes the opposite position, selling a June 100 call and buying a June 100 put, he has a synthetic short underlying position. At June expiration he will always sell the underlying contract at the exercise price of 100, either by choice (the underlying contract is below 100 and he exercises the 100 put) or by force (the underlying contract is above 100 and he is assigned on the 100 call).

We can express the foregoing relationships as follows:

$$\text{synthetic long underlying} \approx \text{long call} + \text{short put}$$

$$\text{synthetic short underlying} \approx \text{short call} + \text{long put}$$

where all options expire at the same time and have the same exercise price.

In our examples we created a synthetic position using the 100 exercise price. But we can create a synthetic using any available exercise price. A long June 110 call together with a short June 110 put is still a synthetic long underlying contract. The difference is that at June expiration the underlying contract will be purchased at 110. A short June 95 call together with a long June 95 put is a synthetic short underlying contract. At June expiration the underlying contract will be sold at 95.

We can also see why a call and put with the same exercise price and expiration date make up a synthetic underlying by constructing parity graphs of the options. This is shown in Figures 14-1a and 14-1b.

While not exactly identical (hence the use of an equivalent sign rather than an equal sign) a synthetic position acts very much like its real equivalent.

Figure 14-1a

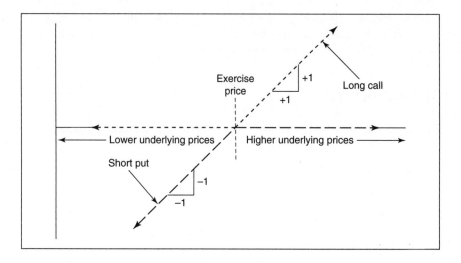

---

[1] Because the position will not turn into an underlying contract until expiration, it is sometimes referred to as a *synthetic forward contract*, which is perhaps a more accurate theoretical description. We will see later that pricing of this combination depends on the value of a forward contract.

Figure 14-1b

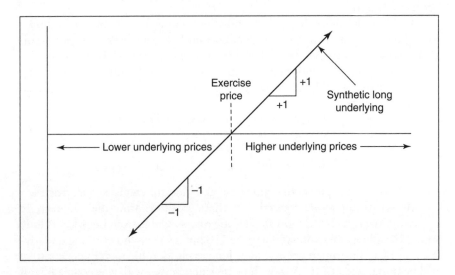

For each point the underlying instrument rises, a synthetic long position will gain approximately one point in value and a synthetic short position will lose approximately one point in value. This leads us to conclude, correctly, that the delta of a synthetic underlying position must be approximately 100. If the delta of the June 100 call is 75, the delta of the June 100 put will be approximately −25. If the delta of the June 100 put is −60, the delta of the June 100 call will be approximately 40. The absolute value of a call and put delta will always add up to approximately 100. We will see later that the settlement procedure and interest rates, as well as the possibility of early exercise, can cause the delta of a synthetic underlying position to be slightly more or less than 100. But for most practical purposes this is a reasonable estimate.

Synthetic Options

By rearranging the components of a synthetic underlying position we can create four additional synthetic contracts:

synthetic long call ≈ long an underlying contract + long put

synthetic short call ≈ short an underlying contract + short put

synthetic long put ≈ short an underlying contract + long call

synthetic short put ≈ long an underlying contract + short call

Again, all options must expire at the same time and have the same exercise price. Each synthetic position has a delta approximately equal to its real equivalent and will therefore gain or lose value at approximately the same rate as its real equivalent. The parity graphs for a synthetic long call are shown

Figure 14-2a

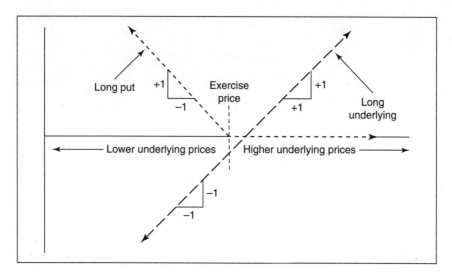

in Figures 14-2a and 14-2b. The graphs for a synthetic long put are shown in Figures 14-3a and 14-3b.

A new trader may initially find it difficult to remember which combination is equivalent to which synthetic option. This suggestion may help: *If we trade a single option and hedge it with an underlying contract, we have the same position, synthetically in the companion option* (the companion option being the opposite type, either a call or put, at the same exercise price).

Figure 14-2b

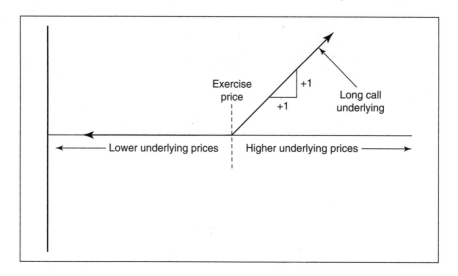

Figure 14-3a

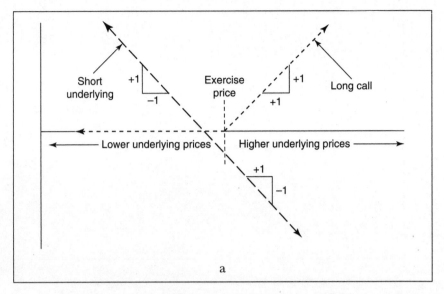

a

If we *buy* a call and hedge it by selling the underlying contract, we have synthetically *bought* a put.

If we *sell* a call and hedge it by buying an underlying contract, we have synthetically *sold* a put.

If we *buy* a put and hedge it by buying the underlying contract, we have synthetically *bought* a call.

If we *sell* a put and hedge it by selling an underlying contract, we have synthetically *sold* a call.

Figure 14-3b

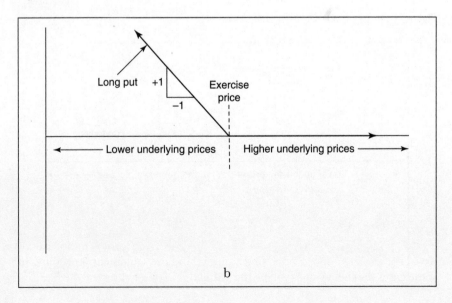

b

Thus far we have made no mention of the prices at which any of the contracts are traded. The prices will of course be important when deciding whether to create a synthetic position, and we will eventually address this question. But for the present we are considering only the characteristics of a synthetic position, and these are independent of the prices at which the contracts are traded. In Figures 14-2a and 14-3a the underlying position was taken at a price different than the exercise price. What gives the position its characteristics is not the prices of the contracts, but the slopes of the contracts. And the combined slopes are equivalent to a long call (Figure 14-2b) and a long put (Figure 14-3b).

Summarizing, there are six basic synthetic contracts—long and short an underlying contract, long and short a call, and long and short a put. If all options expire in June, using the 100 exercise price we have:

synthetic long underlying = long June 100 call + short June 100 put
synthetic short underlying = short June 100 call + long June 100 put

synthetic long June 100 call = long underlying + long June 100 put
synthetic short June 100 call = short underlying + short June 100 put

synthetic long June 100 put = short underlying + long June 100 call
synthetic short June 100 put = long underlying + short June 100 call

We know from the synthetic relationship that the absolute value of the deltas of calls and puts with the same exercise price and expiration date add up to approximately 100. We can also use synthetics to identify other important risk relationships.

We know that the gamma and vega of an underlying contract is zero. Since a long call and short put with the same exercise price and expiration date can be combined to create a long underlying contract, the gamma and vega of these combinations must also add up to zero. This means that the gamma and vega of a companion call and put must be identical. If the June call has a gamma of 5, so must the June 100 put. If the June 105 put has a vega of .20, so must the June 105 call. (To confirm this, it may be useful to go back and compare the companion delta, gamma, and vega values in Figures 7-13, 13-1, and 13-10.)

Because the gamma and vega of companion calls and puts is identical, option traders who focus on volatility make no distinction between calls and puts with the same exercise price and expiration date. Both have the same gamma and vega, and therefore the same volatility characteristics. If a trader owns a call and would prefer instead to own a put he need only sell the underlying contract. If he owns a put and would prefer to own a call, he need only buy the underlying contract. The volatility risk of a position depends not on whether the contracts are calls or puts, but on the exercise prices and expiration dates which make up the position.

Why isn't the theta, like the gamma and vega, of companion options identical? Depending on the underlying contract and the settlement procedure, in some cases the theta values will be the same. But in other cases the theta values in a synthetic will not add up to zero because of the cost of carry associated with either the underlying contract or the option contracts.

As an example, if we purchase stock and the stock price remains unchanged are we making money or losing money? It may seem that the position is just breaking even. But if we consider the cost of borrowing cash in order to buy the stock, then the position is losing money because of the interest cost. This will be reflected in the synthetic equivalent having a nonzero theta.

Unlike stock, there is no cost of carry associated with a futures contract. But if options on futures are subject to stock-type settlement there will be a cost of carry associated with the options. If companion options are trading at different prices there will be a different cost of carry, and this will result in the synthetic underlying position having a nonzero theta.

Finally, if we are dealing with options on futures, and the options are subject to futures-type settlement, there is no cost of carry associated with either the underlying contract or the options. In this case the companion calls and puts will indeed have the same theta.

Synthetics can explain some relationships that were previously discussed. In our discussion of vertical spreads we noted that a bull spread consists of buying the lower exercise price and selling the higher exercise price, regardless of whether the spread consisted of all calls or all puts. Using synthetics we can see why this is true:

Bull call spread	Synthetic equivalent
+1 June 100 call	+1 June 100 put / +1 underlying
−1 June 105 call	−1 June 105 put / −1 underlying

In the synthetic equivalent the long and short underlying contracts cancel out leaving a bull put spread

+1 June 100 put
−1 June 105 put

The call spread and put spread have similar characteristics, but they differ in terms of cash flow. The call spread is done for a debit, while the put spread is done for a credit. Since the spread has a maximum value of 5.00, in the absence of interest considerations, the value of the two spreads at expiration must add up to 5.00. If the call spread is trading for 3.00, the put spread must be trading for 2.00. If interest rates are nonzero, and the options are subject to stock-type settlement, their values today must add up to the present value of 5.00.

Using Synthetics in a Spreading Strategy

Since a synthetic has essentially the same characteristics as its real equivalent, any strategy can be done using a synthetic. This means that there can often be several different ways to create the same strategy.

Consider the following position:

+ 2 June 100 calls
−1 underlying contract

This combination doesn't seem to fit any previously discussed strategy. But suppose we write the June 100 calls separately:

> +1 June 100 call
> +1 June 100 call
> −1 underlying contract

We know that a long call and short underlying contract is a synthetic long put. Therefore, the position is really

> +1 June 100 call
> +1 June 100 put

which is easily recognizable as a long straddle.

Similarly, suppose we have

> +2 June 100 puts
> +1 underlying contract

We can write the June 100 puts separately

> +1 June 100 put
> +1 June 100 put
> +1 underlying contract

A long put and a long underlying contract is a synthetic long call. The entire position is again a long straddle:

> +1 June 100 put
> +1 June 100 call

From the foregoing examples, we can see that there are three ways to create a long straddle:

1. buy the call and buy the put
2. buy the call, and buy the put synthetically
3. buy the put, and buy the call synthetically

The latter two methods are *synthetic long straddles*. The best way to buy a straddle will depend on the prices of the synthetics compared to their real equivalents. We shall address the question of pricing synthetics in the next chapter.

Iron Butterflies and Iron Condors

Consider these two positions:

1. +1 June 95 put / +1 June 105 call
2. −1 June 100 call / −1 June 100 put

The first strategy is a long strangle; the second strategy is a short straddle. What will happen if we combine the two strategies? We can answer the question by rewriting the position using only calls or only puts. If we choose to express all contracts as calls we can rewrite each put as a synthetic:

Original position	Synthetic put equivalent
+1 June 95 put	+1 June 95 call / −1 underlying contract
−1 June 100 call	
−1 June 100 put	−1 June 100 call / +1 underlying contract
+1 June 105 call	

Replacing the puts with their synthetic equivalents, and canceling out the long and short underlying contracts, we are left with a long butterfly

+1 June 95 call
−2 June 100 calls
+1 June 105 call

If, instead of calls, we express all contracts as puts we will also end up with a long butterfly. This confirms the fact that a call and put butterfly are essentially the same. One is simply a synthetic version of the other.

An *iron butterfly* is a position which combines a strangle and straddle, with the straddle centered exactly in the middle of the strangle. It has the same characteristics as a traditional butterfly. But unlike a long butterfly (buy the outside exercise prices / sell the inside exercise price) which is done for a debit (hence the term long), the equivalent iron butterfly (buy the strangle / sell the straddle) is done for a credit. The straddle which we are selling is always more valuable than the strangle which we are buying. If we receive money when we put on the position then we are *short* the iron butterfly. Buying a traditional butterfly is equivalent to selling an iron butterfly.

What is an iron butterfly worth? We know that a long butterfly will have a value at expiration between zero and the amount between exercise prices. If we buy the June 95 / 100 / 105 butterfly we will pay some amount between zero and 5.00. We hope the underlying contract will finish at 100, in which case the butterfly will be worth its maximum of 5.00. If we sell the June 95 / 100 / 105 iron butterfly we will take in some amount between zero and 5.00. We also hope that the underlying will finish at 100, in which case all the options will be worthless and we will profit by the amount of the original sale.

At expiration the value of a butterfly and an iron butterfly must add up to the amount between exercise prices. Taking interest into consideration, the values today must add up to the present value of this amount. If we assume that interest rates are zero, and the June 95 / 100 / 105 butterfly is trading from 1.75, the June 95 / 100 / 105 iron butterfly should be trading for 3.25. Whether we buy the butterfly for 1.75, or sell the iron butterfly for 3.25, we want the same thing to happen, the market to remain close to the inside exercise price of 100. Both spreads will have the same profit or loss potential.

We can also create a condor synthetically by combining long and short strangles.

1. +1 June 90 put / +1 June 110 call
2. −1 June 95 put / −1 June 105 call

The first position is a long June 90 / 110 strangle; the second is a short June 95 / 105 strangle. If we express the entire position in terms of calls we can rewrite each put as a synthetic:

Original position	Synthetic put equivalent
+1 June 90 put	+1 June 90 call / −1 underlying contract
−1 June 95 put	−1 June 95 call / +1 underlying contract
−1 June 105 call	
+1 June 110 call	

Replacing the puts with their synthetic equivalents, and canceling out the long and short underlying contracts, we are left with a long condor

    +1 June 90 call
    −1 June 95 call
    −1 June 105 call
    +1 June 110 call

If we instead express all contracts as puts we will also end up with a long condor. This confirms that a call and put condor are essentially the same. One is simply a synthetic version of the other.

An *iron condor* is a position which combines a long strangle with a short strangle, with one strangle centered in the middle of the other strangle. While a long condor (buy the outside exercise prices / sell the inside exercise price) is done for a debit, the iron condor equivalent (sell the outside strangle / buy the inside strangle) is done for a credit. The inside strangle which we are selling is always more valuable than the outside strangle which we are buying. If we receive money when we put on the position then we are *short* the iron condor. Buying a traditional condor is equivalent to selling an iron condor.

At expiration the value of a condor and an iron condor must add up to the amount between the inside and outside exercise prices, in our example 5.00. Taking interest into consideration, the values must add up to the present value of this amount. If we assume that interest rates are zero, and the June 90 / 95 / 105 / 110 condor is trading for 3.75, the June 90 / 95 / 105 / 110 iron condor should be trading for 1.25. Whether we buy the condor for 3.75, or sell the iron butterfly for 1.25, we want the same thing to happen, the market to remain within the exercise prices of the inside strangle. Both spreads will have the same profit or loss potential.

The characteristics of some volatility spreads can often be more easily recognized when written in synthetic form. For example, in Chapter 11 we looked at spreads commonly known as Christmas trees. A typical long Christmas tree might be

    +1 June 95 call / −1 June 100 call / −1 June 105 call

The characteristics of this position may not have been immediately apparent. But suppose we use synthetics to rewrite the June 95 and 100 calls as puts

Original position	synthetic
(long call Christmas Tree)	equivalent

+1 June 95 call   +1 June 95 put / −1 underlying contract
−1 June 100 call   −1 June 100 put / +1 underlying contract
−1 June 105 call

Replacing the June 95 and 100 calls with their synthetic equivalents, and canceling out the long and short underlying contracts, we are left with

+1 June 95 put
−1 June 100 put
−1 June 105 call

If we focus first on the June 100 put and June 105 call, the position consists of a short strangle (the June 100 / 105 strangle) combined with a long put at a lower exercise price (the June 95 put). If we focus on the June 95 put and the June 100 put, the position consists of a bull put spread (the June 100 / 105 put spread) combined with a short call at a higher exercise price (the June 105 call). In both cases, we have a position with limited downside risk and unlimited upside risk.

Option Arbitrage

Suppose that we want to take a short position in an underlying contract that is currently trading at 102.00. We can simply sell the underlying contract at 102.00. However, we have an additional choice—we can take a short position synthetically by selling a call and buying a put with the same expiration date and exercise price. Which of these strategies is best? Suppose that we sell the December 100 call for 5.00 and buy the December 100 put for 3.00, for a total credit of 2.00. If the options are European, with no possibility of early exercise, at expiration, we will always sell the underlying contract at 100.00, either by exercising the put or by being assigned on the call. Because we have a credit of 2.00 from the option trades, we are in effect selling the underlying contract at its current price of 102.00. If there are no interest or dividend considerations, the profit or loss resulting from our synthetic position will be identical to the profit or loss resulting from the sale of the underlying contract at 102.00. Indeed, regardless of the individual prices of the December 100 call and put, as long as the price of the December 100 call is exactly 2.00 greater than the price of the December 100 put, the profit or loss will be the same for both positions. This is shown in Figure 15-1.

Now let's assume that we already have a synthetic short position:

>   −1 December 100 call
>   +1 December 100 put

If we want to get out of the position, what can we do? We can, of course, close out our synthetic by buying back the December 100 call and selling out the December 100 put. However, we can also offset the synthetic short position by buying the underlying contract.

>   −1 December 100 call
>   +1 December 100 put
>   +1 underlying contract

Figure 15-1

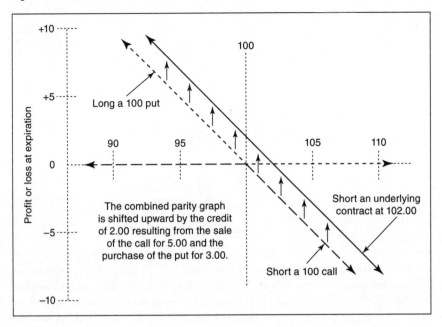

This position, usually referred to as a *conversion*,[1] is the most common type of option arbitrage. In a classic arbitrage strategy, a trader will try to buy and sell the same or very closely related contracts in different markets to profit from a mispricing. In a conversion, the trader is buying the underlying contract in the underlying market and selling the underlying contract, synthetically, in the option market. Taken together, the trades make up an arbitrage.

A trader can also take the opposite position, executing a *reverse conversion* (or *reversal*), by selling the underlying contract and buying it synthetically:

+1 December 100 call
−1 December 100 put
−1 underlying contract

Summarizing,

Conversion = long underlying + synthetic short underlying
= long underlying + short call + long put
Reversal = short underlying + synthetic long underlying
= short underlying + long call + short put

where the call and put always have the same exercise price and expiration date.

Whether a trader will want to take either of these positions depends on the prices of the contracts. If the synthetic portion (the long call and short put)

---

[1] Some traders refer to a conversion as a *forward conversion* because the synthetic portion of the strategy is really a synthetic forward contract. It will not turn into an underlying contract until expiration

is too expensive compared with the underlying contract, a trader will want to do a conversion. If the synthetic portion is too cheap, a trader will want to do a reverse conversion. How can we determine whether the synthetic is mispriced?

Let's begin by assuming that the underlying contract is stock. In a December 100 conversion, we will

> Sell a December 100 call
> Buy a December 100 put
> Buy stock

If we do all these trades and carry the position to expiration, what are the resulting credits and debits?

First, the credits. When we sell the call, we will receive the call price C. We can invest this amount over the life of the option and earn interest $C \times r \times t$. Because we own the stock, we will receive any dividends D that are paid prior to the December expiration. Finally, at expiration, we will either exercise the put or be assigned on the call. In either case, we will sell the stock and receive the exercise price X. The total credits are

> Call price C
> Interest earned on the call $C \times r \times t$
> Dividends, if any, D
> Exercise price X

Next, the debits. We will have to pay the put price P and the stock price S. In both cases, we will have to borrow the money, so there is the additional interest cost $P \times r \times t$ and $S \times r \times t$. The total debits are

> Put price P
> Interest cost to buy the put $P \times r \times t$
> Stock price S
> Interest cost to buy the stock $S \times r \times t$

In an arbitrage-free market, all credits and debits must be equal:

$$C + C \times r \times t + D + X = P + P \times r \times t + S + S \times r \times t$$

Traders sometimes refer to the synthetic portion of a conversion or reversal as a *combo*, either a long call and short put or a short call and long put. We can determine whether there is a relative mispricing and, consequently, an arbitrage opportunity by solving for the combo value $C - P$ in terms of all other components.

First, we group the call and put components on the left side and everything else on the right side

$$C + C \times r \times t - P + P \times r \times t = S + S \times r \times t - D - X$$

Next, we separate the interest-rate component

$$C \times (1 + r \times t) - P \times (1 + r \times t) = S \times (1 + r \times t) - D - X$$

and then isolate $C - P$

$$(C - P) \times (1 + r \times t) = S \times (1 + r \times t) - D - X$$

At this point, we might recognize part of the expression on the right: $S \times (1 + r \times t) - D$. This is the forward price for the stock. To simplify our notation, we can replace $S \times (1 + r \times t) - D$ with F

$$(C - P) \times (1 + r \times t) = F - X$$

Finally, we divide both sides by the interest component $1 + r \times t$

$$C - P = \frac{F - X}{1 + r \times t}$$

Simply stated, the difference between the call price and put price for European options with the same exercise price and expiration date must be equal to the present value of the difference between the forward price and exercise price. This relationship, one of the most important in option pricing, goes by various names. In textbooks, it is commonly referred to as *put-call parity*. Traders may also refer to it as the *combo value*, the *synthetic relationship*, or the *conversion market*.

The exact calculation of put-call parity depends on the underlying market and the settlement procedures for the options market. Let's look at several different cases.

Options on Futures

The simplest calculation occurs when the underlying is a futures contract and the options are subject to futures-type settlement. In this case, the effective interest rate is 0 because no money changes hands when either the underlying futures contract or the options are traded. Moreover, futures contracts pay no dividends, so we can express put-call parity in its simplest form as

$$C - P = F - X$$

With a December 100 call trading at 5.25 and a December 100 put trading at 1.50, what should be the price of the underlying December futures contract?

December 100 call	5.25
December 100 put	1.50
December futures contract	??

Because

$$C - P = 5.25 - 1.50 = 3.75$$

$F - X$ also must equal 3.75. The futures price must be 103.75.

What will happen in our example if the underlying futures contract is not trading at 103.75 but instead is trading at 104.00. We can see that

$$5.25 - 1.50 \neq 104.00 - 100$$

and

$$3.75 \neq 4.00$$

Everyone will want to execute a reverse conversion by buying the less expensive synthetic (buy the call, sell the put) and selling the more expensive underlying (the futures contract). Ignoring transaction costs, if all trades actually can be done at these prices, the strategy will result in an arbitrage profit of .25, the amount of the mispricing.

What will be the result of everyone attempting to do a reverse conversion? Because everyone wants to buy the call, there will be upward pressure on the call price. If the call price rises to 5.50 while all other prices remain unchanged, put-call parity is maintained because

$$5.50 - 1.50 = 104.00 - 100$$

Alternatively, as part of the reverse conversion, everyone wants to sell the put. This will put downward pressure on the put price. If the put price falls to 1.25, put-call parity is again maintained because

$$5.25 - 1.25 = 104.00 - 100$$

Finally, everyone wants to sell the futures contract, putting downward pressure on the futures price. If the futures contract falls to 103.75, put-call parity is again maintained because

$$5.25 - 1.50 = 103.75 - 100$$

Whether the call price rises, the put price falls, the futures price falls, or some combination of all three, the final result must be

$$C - P = F - X$$

This application of put-call parity, where all contracts are subject to futures-type settlement, is typically used for options traded on futures exchanges outside North America. When an exchange settles option prices at the end of the trading day, there may be inconsistencies having to do with the volatility value of an option. But the exchange will always try to assign settlement prices that are consistent with put-call parity. A table of settlement prices for Euro-bund options traded on Eurex is shown in Figure 15-2.[2] Note that in every case, put-call parity is maintained.

Put-call parity calculations become slightly more complicated when options on futures are subject to stock-type settlement, as they are on most futures exchanges in North America. Now we must discount by the interest-rate component

$$C - P = \frac{F - X}{1 + r \times t}$$

---

[2] The options in Figure 15-2 are in fact American and therefore entail the possibility of early exercise. However, when options on futures are subject to futures-type settlement, as they are on Eurex, we will see in Chapter 16 that there is effectively no difference between a European and an American option.

Figure 15-2 Settlement prices for Euro-bund options on May 25, 2010

Settlement prices for Euro-bund options on 25 May 2010.
The settlement prices reflect put-call parity in its simplest form. In every case:

call price – put price = futures price – exercise price

	June Futures = 129.38				September Futures = 128.90			
exercise price	June calls	June puts	July* calls	July* puts	Aug.* calls	Aug.* puts	Sep. calls	Sep. puts
126.00	3.39	.01	3.16	.26	3.45	.55	3.76	.86
126.50	2.89	.01	2.75	.35	3.07	.67	3.42	1.02
127.00	2.41	.03	2.37	.47	2.73	.83	3.09	1.19
127.50	1.93	.05	2.02	.62	2.40	1.00	2.78	1.38
128.00	1.48	.10	1.70	.80	2.10	1.20	2.50	1.60
128.50	1.06	.18	1.41	1.01	1.83	1.43	2.23	1.83
129.00	.71	.33	1.16	1.26	1.59	1.69	1.99	2.09
129.50	.43	.55	.94	1.54	1.37	1.97	1.76	2.36
130.00	.23	.85	.76	1.86	1.17	2.27	1.56	2.66
130.50	.12	1.24	.60	2.20	1.00	2.60	1.37	2.97
131.00	.05	1.67	.48	2.58	.85	2.95	1.21	3.31
131.50	.02	2.14	.37	2.97	.72	3.32	1.06	3.66
132.00	.01	2.63	.29	3.39	.61	3.71	.92	4.02

*July and August are serial months with no corresponding July or August futures. The underlying contract for July, August, and September options is the September futures contract.

With six months remaining to expiration and an annual interest rate of 6.00 percent, a December 100 call is trading for 4.90. What should be the price of the December 100 put if the underlying December futures contract is trading at 97.25? We know that

$$C - P = \frac{97.25 - 100}{1 + 0.06 \times 6/12} \approx -2.67$$

The difference between the call price and put price must be 2.67, with the negative sign indicating that the put price is greater than the call price

$$C - P = -2.67$$
$$P = C - (-2.67) = 4.90 + 2.67 = 7.57$$

The put must be trading for 7.57.

Locked Futures Markets

Many futures traders prefer not to become involved in options markets because of the apparent complexity of options. There is, however, one situation in which a futures trader ought to become familiar with basic option characteristics.

If a futures trader wants to make a trade but is prevented from doing so because the futures market has reached its daily limit, he may be able to trade futures synthetically by using options. The price at which the synthetic futures contact is trading can be determined through put-call parity.

Consider a futures market that has a daily up or down limit of 5.00. The futures contract closed the previous day at 126.75 but is now up limit at 131.75. No further futures trading can take place unless someone is willing to sell at a price of 131.75 or less. If, however, the options market is still open, a trader can buy or sell futures synthetically, even if this price is beyond the daily limit. He can either buy a call and sell a put (buying the futures contract) or sell a call and buy a put (selling the futures contract) with the same exercise price and expiration date. The price of the call and put, together with the exercise price, will determine the price at which the synthetic futures contract is trading.

Below is a hypothetical table of call and put prices together with the resulting synthetic futures price. For simplicity, we assume that there are no interest considerations. Because $C - P = F - X$, we can calculate the equivalent futures price $F = C - P + X$.

Exercise Price	Call Price	Put Price	Equivalent Synthetic Futures Price $(C - P + X)$
120	13.60	.35	133.25
125	9.35	1.05	133.30
130	5.75	2.55	133.20
135	3.15	4.95	133.20
140	1.55	8.30	133.25
145	0.70	12.40	133.30

There is some variation in the equivalent synthetic prices, possibly because the prices do not reflect the bid-ask spread or perhaps because the option prices have not been quoted contemporaneously. However, one can see that if the futures contract were still open for trading, its price would probably be somewhere in the range of 133.20 to 133.30. If a futures trader wants to buy or sell futures synthetically in the option market, he can expect to trade at a price within this range.

Options on Stock

Calculating put-call parity for stock options entails an additional step because we must first calculate the forward price for the stock. With six months remaining to expiration and an annual interest rate of 4.00 percent, a December 65 call is trading for 8.00. If the underlying stock is trading at 68.50 and total dividends of .45 are expected prior to expiration, what should be the price of the 65 put?

We begin with the forward price

$$F = 68.50 \times (1 + 0.04 \times 6/12) - 0.45 = 69.42$$

Then

$$C - P = \frac{69.42 - 65}{1 + 0.04 \times 6/12} \approx 4.33$$

The put price must be

$$8.00 - 4.33 = 3.67$$

An Approximation for Stock Options

When exchanges first began trading options, all activity took place in an open-outcry environment. Traders often had to make pricing decisions quickly and without the aid of computers. As a result, they often sought shortcuts by which they could more easily approximate prices. Even if the shortcut resulted in small errors, the value of being able to make faster decisions more than offset the small loss in accuracy.

Let's go back to basic put-call parity for stock options and replace the forward price F with the actual forward price for the stock

$$C - P = \frac{F - X}{1 + r \times t} \approx \frac{[S \times (1 + r \times t) - D] - X}{1 + r \times t}$$

How might we simplify this calculation?

Note that we are multiplying the stock price by the interest-rate component and then dividing the stock price, the dividend, and the exercise price by the same interest-rate component. We end up with the stock price itself less the discounted values of the dividend and exercise price

$$C - P = S - \frac{D}{(1 + r \times t)} - \frac{X}{(1 + r \times t)}$$

Dividends are typically small compared with the stock price and exercise price, so a reasonable approximation for the discounted value of the dividend is simply the dividend D itself. We might approximate the discounted value of the exercise price and eliminate the need to do any division by subtracting the interest on the exercise price from the exercise price itself

$$\frac{D}{1 + r \times t} \approx D$$

$$\frac{X}{1 + r \times t} \approx X - X \times r \times t$$

Substituting our approximations into the put-call parity equation, we have

$$C - P \approx S - (X - X \times r \times t) - D = S - X + X \times r \times t - D$$

The difference between the call price and put price is approximately equal to the stock price minus the exercise price plus interest on the exercise price minus expected dividends.

How good an approximation is this? Clearly, if interest rates are very high, the dividend is very large, or we are dealing with long-term options, the errors will begin to increase. But for short-term options our approximation often represents a reasonable tradeoff between speed and accuracy.

Let's go back to our previous stock option example:

Stock price = 68.50
Time to expiration = 6 months
Interest rate = 4.00 percent
Expected dividends = .45

We calculated the value of the 65 combo $(C - P)$ as 4.33. How will our approximation compare?

$$C - P \approx S - X + X \times r \times t - D$$
$$= 68.50 - 65 + 65 \times .04 \times 6/12 - .45$$
$$= 4.35$$

Our approximation differs by .02 from the true value. Depending on market conditions, this might be an acceptable margin of error in return for being able to make a faster trading decision.

All experienced traders are familiar with put-call parity, so any price imbalances are likely to be very short-lived. If the combo is overpriced compared with the underlying, all traders will want to execute a conversion (i.e., buy the underlying, sell the call, buy the put). If the combo is underpriced, all traders will want to execute a reversal (i.e., sell the underlying, buy the call, sell the put). Such activity, where everyone is attempting to do the same thing, will quickly force prices back into equilibrium. Indeed, price imbalances in the synthetic relationship are usually small and rarely last for more than a few seconds. When imbalances do occur, an option trader is usually willing to execute conversions or reversals in very large size because of the low risk associated with such strategies.

Put-call parity specifies the price relationship between three contracts—a call, a put, and an underlying contract. If the price of any two contracts is known, it should be possible to calculate the price of the third contract. If the prices in the marketplace do not seem to be consistent with this relationship, what might a trader infer?

Consider this stock option situation:

90 call = 7.20
90 put = 1.40
Time to expiration = 3 months
Interest rate = 8.00 percent
Expected dividends = .47

What should be the price of the underlying stock?
Using our stock option approximation for put-call parity, we know that

$$C - P \approx S - X + X \times r \times t - D$$

Therefore,

$$S \approx C - P + X - X \times r \times t + D$$
$$S \approx 7.20 - 1.40 + 90 - 90 \times 0.08 \times 3/12 + 0.47 = 94.47$$

Suppose, however, that the stock is actually trading at 94.30. Does this mean that there is an arbitrage opportunity?

The stock price calculation depended on assumptions about interest and dividends. Are we sure that those assumptions are correct? One possibility is that the interest rate we are using, 8 percent, is too low. If we assume that the contract prices and dividends are correct, we can calculate the *implied interest rate*

$$r = \frac{(C - P - S + X + D)/X}{t}$$

$$= \frac{(7.20 - 1.40 - 94.30 + 90 + 0.47)/90}{3/12}$$

$$= 0.0875 \ (8.75\%)$$

Another possibility is that the dividend we are using, .47, is too high. If we assume that the contract prices and interest are correct, we can calculate the *implied dividend*

$$D = S - C + P - X + X \times r \times t$$
$$= 94.30 - 7.20 + 1.40 - 90 + 90 \times .08 \times 3/12$$
$$= .30$$

The marketplace seems to be expecting a dividend of only .30. If our original calculation was based on an estimate of the expected divided, we ought to consider the possibility that the company will cut the dividend prior to expiration.

Arbitrage Risk

New traders who are learning to trade options professionally are often encouraged to focus on conversions and reversals because, they are told, these strategies, once executed, are essentially riskless. A word of warning: *very few strategies are truly riskless.* Some strategies entail greater risk, while others entail lesser risk. Rarely, however, does a strategy entail no risk. The risks of doing conversions or reversals may not be immediately apparent, but they exist nonetheless.

Execution Risk

Because no one wants to give away money, a trader is unlikely to be offered a profitable conversion or reversal all at one time. Consequently, a trader who focuses on these strategies will have to begin by executing one or two legs and then hope to execute the final leg(s) at a later time. He may, for example, initially purchase puts together with underlying contracts and hope to later complete the conversion by selling calls. However, if call prices begin to fall, he may never be able to profitably complete the conversion. Even a professional trader on an exchange, who would seem to be in a good position to know the prices of all three contracts, can be mistaken. He may create a long synthetic underlying position by purchasing a call and selling a put at what he believes are favorable prices. However, when he tries to sell the underlying contract to complete the reversal, he may find that the price is lower than he expected. Whenever a strategy is executed one leg at a time, there is always the risk of an adverse change in prices before the strategy can be completed.

Pin Risk

When we introduced the concept of a synthetic position, we assumed that at expiration, the underlying market would be either above the exercise price, in which case the call would be exercised, or below the exercise price, in which case the put would be exercised. But what will happen if the underlying market is exactly equal to, or *pinned* to, the exercise price at the moment of expiration?

Suppose that a trader has executed a June 100 conversion: he is short a June 100 call, long a June 100 put, and long the underlying contract. If the underlying contract is above or below 100 at expiration, there is no problem. Either he will be assigned on the call or he will exercise the put. In either case, the long underlying position will be offset, and he will have no market position on the day following expiration.

But suppose that at the moment of expiration, the underlying market is right at 100. The trader would like to be rid of his underlying position. If he is not assigned on the call, he can exercise his put; if he is assigned on the call, he can let the put expire. In order to make a decision, he must know whether the call will be exercised. But he won't know this until the day after expiration, when he either does or does not receive an assignment notice. If he finds out that he was not assigned on the call, it will be too late to exercise the put because it will have expired.

It may seem that an option that is exactly at the money at expiration will never be exercised because, in theory, it has no value. In fact, many at-the-money options are exercised. Even though the option has no theoretical value, it does have some practical value. For example, suppose that the owner of a call that is exactly at the money at expiration wants to take a long position in the underlying contract. He has two choices. He can either exercise the call or buy the underlying contract. Because an exchange-traded option typically includes the right of exercise in the original transaction cost, it is almost always cheaper to exercise the call. Even if there is a small transaction cost to exercise, an option, it will almost always be less than the cost of trading the underlying contract. Anyone owning an at-the-money option and choosing to take a long or short position at expiration will find that it is cheaper to exercise the option than to buy or sell the underlying contract.

Clearly, a trader who is short an at-the-money option at expiration has a problem. What can he do? One possibility is to make an educated guess as to whether the at-the-money option will be exercised. If the market appears to be strong on the last trading day, the trader might assume that it will continue higher following expiration. If the holder of the call sees the situation similarly, it is logical to assume that the call will be exercised. Hence the trader will choose not to exercise his put. Unfortunately, if the trader is wrong and he does not get assigned on the call, he will find himself with a long underlying position that he would rather not have. Conversely, if the market appears to be weak on the last trading day, the trader might make the assumption that he will not be assigned on the call. He will therefore choose to exercise the put. But, again, if he is wrong and does get an assignment notice, he will find himself with an unwanted short underlying position on the day following expiration.

The risk of a wrong guess can be further compounded by the fact that conversions and reversals, because of their low risk, are often done in large size. If the trader guesses wrong, he may find that on the day after expiration, he is naked long or short not one or two but many underlying contracts.

There can be no certain solution to the problem of pin risk. With many, perhaps thousands, of open contracts outstanding, some at-the-money options will be exercised and some won't. If the trader lets the position go to expiration and relies on luck, he is at the mercy of the fates, and this is a position that an intelligent option trader prefers to avoid. The practical solution is to avoid carrying a short at-the-money option position to expiration when there is a real possibility of expiration right at the exercise price. If the trader has a large number of June 100 conversions or reversals and expiration is approaching with the underlying market close to 100, the sensible course is to reduce the pin risk by reducing the size of the position. If the trader doesn't reduce the size, he may find that he is under increasing pressure to get out of a large number of risky contracts as expiration approaches.

Sometimes even a careful trader will find that he still has some outstanding at-the-money conversions or reversals as expiration approaches. If he is very concerned with the potential pin risk, he might simply liquidate the position at the prevailing market prices. Unfortunately, this is likely to result in a loss because the trader will be forced to trade each contract at an unfavorable price, either buying at the offer or selling at the bid. Fortunately, it is often possible to trade out of such a position all at once at a fair price.

Because conversions and reversals are common strategies, a trader who has an at-the-money conversion and is worried about pin risk can be fairly certain that there are also traders in the market who have at-the-money reversals and are worried about the same pin risk. If the trader with the conversion could find a trader with a reversal and cross positions with him, both traders would eliminate the pin risk associated with their positions. This is why on option exchanges one often finds traders looking for other traders who want to trade conversions or reversals at even money. This simply means that a trader wants to trade out of his position at a price that is fair to everyone involved so that everyone can avoid the problem of pin risk. Whatever profit a trader expected to make from the conversion or reversal presumably resulted from the opening trade, not from the closing trade.

Pin risk only occurs in option markets where exercise results in a long or short position in the underlying contract. In some markets, such as stock indexes, options are settled at expiration in cash rather than with the delivery of an underlying contract. When the option expires, there is a cash payment equal to the difference between the exercise price and underlying price, but no underlying position results. Consequently, there is no pin risk associated with this type of settlement.

Settlement Risk

Let's go back to our December 100 conversion example. But now let's assume that the underlying is a December futures contract

  −1 December 100 call
  +1 December 100 put
  +1 December futures contract

If the December futures contract is trading at 102.00, there are three months remaining to December expiration, interest rates are 8.00 percent, and all options are subject to stock-type (cash) settlement, the value of the December 100 synthetic combination (the difference between the December 100 call and the December 100 put) should be

$$\frac{102-100}{1+8\% \times 3/12} = 1.96$$

Suppose that a trader is able to sell a December 100 call for 5.00, buy a December 100 put for 3.00, and sell a December futures contract for 102.00. At expiration, the trader should realize a profit of .04 because he has done the December 100 conversion at .04 better than its value.

Shortly after the trader executes the conversion, the underlying December futures contract falls to 98.00. What will be the cash flow? The synthetic position will show a profit of approximately 4.00; the short call and long put together, because they make up a short underlying position, will appreciate by 4.00. But because the options are settled like stock, the profit on the synthetic position will be unrealized—there will be no cash credited to the trader's account. On the other hand, the trader is also long a December futures contract, and this contract, because it is subject to futures-type settlement, will result in an immediate debit of 4.00 when the market drops to 98.00. To cover this debit, the trader must either borrow the money or take the money out of an interest-bearing account. In either case, there will be a loss in interest, and this interest loss will not be offset by the unrealized profit from the option position. If the loss in interest is great enough, it may more than offset the profit of .04 that the trader originally expected from the position. In the most extreme case, where the trader does not have access to the funds required to cover the variation on the futures position, he may be forced to liquidate the position. Needless to say, forced liquidations are never profitable.

Of course, this works both ways. A rise in the price of the underlying futures contract to 106.00 will result in a loss of 4.00 on the synthetic option position; the short call and long put together will decline by 4.00. But this loss is unrealized—no money will actually be debited from the trader's account.[3] On the other hand, the rise in the futures contract will result in an immediate cash credit on which the trader can earn interest. This interest will increase the potential profit beyond the expected amount of .04.

---

[3] There may be a margin requirement associated with changes in the option prices. But, as discussed in Chapter 1, margin deposits, in theory, belong to the trader and therefore entail no loss of interest.

Option traders tend to assume that conversions and reversals are delta-neutral strategies. But this is not always true. An exactly delta-neutral position has no preference as to the direction of movement in the underlying contract. In our example, we can see that the trader prefers upward movement because he can earn interest on the variation credited to his account. With the underlying futures contract at 102, the deltas in our example might be

Contract Position	Delta Position
Short December 100 call	−57
Long December 100 put	−41
Long December futures contact	+100
Total	+2

The two extra deltas reflect the fact that the trader prefers the market to rise rather than fall so that cash will flow into his account from the futures position. The interest from this cash flow can result in an unexpected profit. A decline in the futures price will have the opposite effect and can result in an unexpected loss.

Under normal circumstances, few traders will concern themselves with the risk of being two deltas long or short. But conversions and reversals, because they are low-risk strategies, are often done in very large size. A trader who executes 300 of our sample conversions has a delta risk of 300 × +2 = +600. This is the same as being long an extra six futures contracts. The risk comes from the interest that can be earned on any cash credit or that must be paid on any cash debit resulting from movement in the underlying futures contract.

The amount by which the delta of a synthetic futures position will differ from 100 depends on the interest risk associated with the position. This, in turn, depends on two factors—the general level of interest rates and the amount of time remaining to expiration. The higher the interest rate and the more time remaining to expiration, the greater the risk. The lower the interest rate and the less time remaining to expiration, the less the risk. A 10 percent interest rate with nine months remaining to expiration represents a much greater risk than a 4 percent interest rate with one month remaining to expiration. In the former case, the deltas of a synthetic position may add up to 93, while in the latter case the deltas may add up to 99. In general, the total delta for a synthetic futures contract, where the options are subject to stock-type settlement, is

$$\frac{100}{1 + r \times t}$$

where r is the interest rate and t is the time to maturity of the options.

This type of *settlement risk* occurs only when the options and the underlying contract are subject to different settlement procedures.[4] There is no settlement

---

[4] A similar type of settlement risk occurs when a futures contract is used to hedge a physical commodity or security position. When the value of the physical commodity or security rises or falls, any profit or loss is unrealized. But the profit or loss on the futures position is immediately realized in the form of variation. The correct hedge is therefore not one to one but is determined by the interest on the variation from the futures position. Hedgers sometime refer to this risk as *tailing*.

risk when both contracts are subject to the same settlement procedure. If all contracts are subject to stock-type settlement, as they are in a typical stock option market, no cash flow results from fluctuations in the prices of the contracts prior to expiration. If all contracts are subject to futures-type settlement, as they are on most futures exchanges outside the United States, any cash flow resulting from changes in the price of the underlying futures contract will exactly offset the cash flow resulting from changes in prices of the option contracts.

Interest and Dividend Risk

Let's again go back to our December 100 conversion, but now let's assume that the underlying contract is stock.

> −1 December 100 call
> +1 December 100 put
> +1 stock contract

What are the risks of holding this position?

The stock price will always be greater than the option prices, so the entire position will be done for a debit approximately equal to the option's exercise price. Because the trader will have to borrow this amount, there will be an interest cost associated with the position. If interest rates rise over the life of the position, the interest costs will also rise, increasing the cost of holding the position and, consequently, reducing the potential profit. If interest rates fall, the potential profit will increase because the costs of carrying the position will decline.[5]

The opposite is true of a reverse conversion:

> +1 December 100 call
> −1 December 100 put
> −1 stock contract

Because the trader will receive cash from the sale of the stock, the position will earn interest over time. If interest rates rise, the interest earnings will also rise, increasing the value of the position. If interest rates fall, the interest earnings will fall, reducing the value of the position.

Clearly, conversions and reverse conversions are sensitive to changes in interest rates. This is reflected in their rho values. In the stock option market, a conversion has a negative rho, indicating a desire for interest rates to fall. A reverse conversion has a positive rho, indicating a desire for interest rates to rise. This is logical when we recall that in the stock option market calls have positive rho values and puts have negative rho values. In a conversion or reverse conversion, the signs of the call and the put rho positions will be the same, either both positive or both negative, because we are buying one option and selling the other.

---

[5] In theory, a trader can borrow money at a fixed rate, eliminating any interest-rate risk. In practice, however, traders usually finance their trading activities through their broker or clearing firm at a variable rate. The cost of borrowing or lending changes daily as interest rates rise or fall.

The fact that a conversion or reverse conversion includes a stock position also means that there is the risk of rising or falling dividends. In a conversion, we are long stock, so any increase in dividends will increase the value of the position, and any cut in dividends will reduce the value. In a reverse conversion, the opposite is true.

Even though there is no Greek letter used to represent dividend risk, we might say that a conversion has *positive dividend risk* and a reverse conversion has *negative dividend risk*. The former will be helped by any increase in dividends, while the latter will be hurt.

We can see the effect of changing interest and dividends by recalling our earlier example:

Stock price = 68.50
Time to expiration = 6 months
Interest rate = 4.00 percent
Expected dividend = .45

We calculated the approximate value of the combo $(C - P)$ as 4.35

$$C - P \approx S - X + X \times r \times t - D$$
$$= 68.50 - 65 + 65 \times .04 \times 6/12 - .45$$
$$= 4.35$$

If interest rates rise to 5.00 percent, the value will now be

$$68.50 - 65 + 65 \times .05 \times 6/12 - .45 \approx 4.68$$

If, on the other hand, the dividend is increased to .65, the value will be

$$68.50 - 65 + 65 \times .04 \times 6/12 - .35 = 4.15$$

A conversion or reversal entails risk because these strategies combine a synthetic underlying position, which is composed of options, with an actual position in the underlying contract. The risk arises because a synthetic position and the actual position, while very similar, can still have different characteristics, either in terms of settlement procedure, as in the futures option market, or in terms of interest or dividends, as in the stock option market. Is there any way to eliminate this risk?

One way to eliminate this risk is to eliminate the position in the underlying contract. Consider a conversion:

Short a call
Long a put
Long an underlying contract

If we want to maintain this position but would also like to eliminate the risk of holding an underlying position, we might replace the long underlying position with something that acts like an underlying contract but that isn't an underlying contract. One possibility is to replace the long underlying position with a deeply in-the-money call:

> Short a call
> Long a put
> Long a deeply in-the-money call

If the deeply in-the-money call has a delta of 100 and therefore acts like a long underlying contract, the position will have the same characteristics as the conversion.

In the same way, instead of buying a deeply in-the-money call, we can sell a deeply in-the-money put:

> Short a call
> Long a put
> Short a deeply in-the-money put

This type of position, where the underlying instrument in a conversion or reversal is replaced with a deeply in-the-money option, is known as a *three-way*. Although it eliminates some risks, a three-way is not without its own problems. If a trader sells a deeply in-the-money option to complete a three-way, he still has the risk of the market going through the exercise price. Indeed, as the underlying market moves closer and closer to the exercise price of the deeply in-the-money option, that option will act less and less like an underlying contract, and the entire position will act less and less like a true conversion or reversal.

Boxes

What else acts like an underlying contract but isn't an underlying contract? Another possibility is to replace the underlying position with a synthetic position, but a synthetic with a different exercise price. For example, suppose that we have a June 100 conversion:

> −1 June 100 call
> +1 June 100 put
> +1 underlying contract

At the same time, we also execute a June 90 reversal. The combined position is

+1 June 90 call	−1 June 100 call
−1 June 90 put	+1 June 100 put
−1 underlying contract	+1 underlying contract

The long and short underlying contracts cancel out, leaving

+1 June 90 call	−1 June 100 call
−1 June 90 put	+1 June 100 put

We have a synthetic long underlying position at the 90 exercise price and a synthetic short underlying position at the 100 exercise price. This position, known as a *box*, is similar to a conversion or reversal except that we have eliminated the risk associated with holding a position in the underlying contract. A trader is long the box when he is synthetically long at the lower exercise price and synthetically short at the higher exercise price. He is short the box when he is synthetically short at the lower exercise price and synthetically long at the higher exercise price. The example position is long a June 90/100 box.

Like a conversion or reversal, a box is an arbitrage—we are buying and selling the same contract but in different markets. In our example, we are buying the underlying contract in the 90 exercise price market and selling the same underlying contract in the 100 exercise price market.

How much is a box worth? Ignoring pin risk, at expiration, a trader who has a box will simultaneously buy the underlying contract at one exercise price and sell the underlying contract at the other exercise price. The value of the box at expiration will be exactly the amount between exercise prices. In our example, at expiration, the 90/100 box will be worth exactly 10.00 because the trader will simultaneously buy the underlying contract at 90 (exercise the 90 call or be assigned on the 90 put) and sell the underlying contract at 100 (exercise the 100 put or be assigned on the 100 call). If the box is worth 10.00 at expiration, how much is it worth today? If the options are subject to futures-type settlement, the value today is the same as the value at expiration. If, however, the options are subject to stock-type settlement, the value of the box today will be the present value of the amount between exercise prices. If our 90/100 box expires in three months with interest rates at 8 percent, the value today is

$$\frac{10.00}{1+3/12\times8\%} \approx 9.80$$

Because a box eliminates the risk associated with carrying a position in the underlying contract, boxes are even less risky than conversions and reversals, which are themselves low-risk strategies. When all options are European (there is no risk of early exercise) and the options are settled in cash rather than through delivery of the underlying contract (there is no pin risk), the purchase or sale of a box is identical to lending or borrowing funds over the life of the options. In our example, a trader who sells the 90/100 box for 9.80 has essentially borrowed funds from the buyer of the box for three months at an interest rate of 8 percent. Selling the box at a lower price is equivalent to borrowing funds at a higher interest rate. If the trader sells the three-month box at a price of 9.70, he has, in effect, agreed to borrow at an annual interest rate of 12 percent.

When no other method is available, a trading firm may be able to raise needed short-term cash by selling boxes. Because the firm will probably have to sell the boxes at a price lower than the theoretical value, this will increase the firm's borrowing costs. Moreover, there will still margin requirements and transaction costs associated with this strategy, increasing the borrowing costs further.

We originally introduced a box as a conversion at one exercise price and a reversal at a different exercise price. With the long and short underlying positions canceling out, we are left with two synthetic underlying positions:

+1 June 90 call   −1 June 100 call
−1 June 90 put   +1 June 100 put

The left side of the box is a synthetic long position at 90, and the right side is a synthetic short position at 100. Instead of dividing the box into a right side and a left side, suppose that we divide it into upper portion and a lower portion:

$$+1 \text{ June 90 call}/-1 \text{ June 100 call}$$
$$-1 \text{ June 90 put}/+1 \text{ June 100 put}$$

The strategy on the top is a bull vertical call spread (i.e., long June 90 call, short June 100 call), whereas the strategy on the bottom is a bear vertical put spread (i.e., long June 100 put, short June 90 put). Because a box is a combination of two vertical spreads, the combined prices of the vertical spreads must equal the value of the box.

With three months remaining to expiration and interest rates at 8 percent, the value of our June 90/100 box is 9.80. Suppose that a trader knows that the June 90/100 call spread is trading for 6.00. The trader can estimate the fair market price for the June 90/100 put spread because he knows that the 90/100 box is worth 9.80 and that the value of a call and put spread must add up to the value of the box. The price of the put spread must therefore be

$$9.80 - 6.00 = 3.80$$

If the trader believes that he can either buy or sell the call spread for 6.00 and he is asked for a market in the put spread, he will make his market around an assumed value of 3.80. He might, for example, make a market of 3.70 bid/3.90 ask. If he is able to buy the put spread for 3.70, he can then try to buy the call spread for 6.00. If he is successful, he will have paid a total of 9.70 for a box with a theoretical value of 9.80. Conversely, if he is able to sell the put spread for 3.90, he can then try to sell the call vertical for 6.00. If he is successful, he will have sold a box with a theoretical value of 9.80 for a price of 9.90.

Rolls

In a box, the risk of holding the underlying contract is offset by combining a conversion and reversal in the same month but at different exercise prices:

+1 June 90 call	−1 June 100 call
−1 June 90 put	+1 June 100 put
−1 underlying contract	+1 underlying contract

Suppose that we instead combine a conversion and reversal, not at different exercise prices, but in different expiration months:

+1 June 90 call	−1 August 90 call
−1 June 90 put	+1 August 90 put
−1 underlying contract	+1 underlying contract

If the long and short underlying positions cancel out, we are left with a *roll*:

+1 June 90 call	−1 August 90 call
−1 June 90 put	+1 August 90 put

We have a synthetic long underlying position in June and a synthetic short underlying position in August, where both positions have the same exercise price.

Although it is always possible to combine a conversion in one month with a reversal in a different month, in a roll, the underlying positions must cancel out.

For example, in a futures option market, the underlying for June may be a June futures contract and the underlying for August may be an August futures contract. Because they are different contracts, the long and short underlying positions will not offset each other. Hence the position is not a true roll.

Rolls are done most commonly in a stock option market, where the underlying contract for all expiration months is the same underlying stock. The long stock position in one expiration month will always offset the short stock position in the other expiration month.

What should be the value of a roll in the stock option market? The value of the roll must be the difference in the values of the combos

$$(C_l - P_l) - (C_s - P_s)$$

where C_l and P_l are the long-term call and put, and C_s and P_s are the short-term call and put.

For the moment, let's assume that the stock pays no dividends. We know the value of a combo

$$C - P = \frac{S - X}{1 + r \times t}$$

The value of the roll should therefore be

$$\left[S - \frac{X}{(1 + r_l \times t_l)} \right] - \left[S - \frac{X}{(1 + r_s \times t_s)} \right] = \frac{X}{(1 + r_s \times t_s)} - \frac{X}{(1 + r_l \times t_l)}$$

Excluding dividends, the value of the roll is the difference between the discounted values of the exercise price. Note that the value of the roll depends on two different interest rates—r_s, the interest to short-term expiration, and r_l, the interest to long-term expiration. These rates are usually very similar, which means that the preceding expression is almost always a positive number because the discounting on the short-term exercise price is less than the discounting on the long-term exercise price.

If the stock pays a dividend D between expirations, the value of the roll should also include this amount. Ignoring interest on dividends, the roll value is

$$\frac{X}{(1 + r_s \times t_s)} - \frac{X}{(1 + r_l \times t_l)} - D$$

Consider our June/August 90 roll, with two months to June expiration and four months to August expiration. If we assume a constant interest rate of 6 percent, and the stock is expected to pay a dividend of .40 between expirations, the value of the 90 roll is

$$\frac{90}{1 + 0.06 \times 2/12} - \frac{90}{1 + 0.06 \times 4/12} - 0.40 = 89.11 - 88.24 - 0.40 = 0.47$$

A trader who needs to make calculations without computer supportmight, as with conversions and reversals, might be willing to give up some accuracy in return for greater speed. How might a trader simplify the calculation of a roll?

A trader who is short a roll (i.e., long the short-term synthetic and short the long-term synthetic) will buy stock at the short-term expiration and sell stock at the long-term expiration, with both transactions taking place at the same exercise price. Additionally, because the trader will own the stock over the life of the roll, he will receive any dividends paid out over this period. The value of the roll should be approximately the cost of carrying the exercise price from one expiration to the other less any dividends that accrue

$$X \times r \times t - D$$

where t is the time between expirations. In our example, we have

$$90 \times .06 \times 2/12 - .40 = .90 - .40 = .50$$

Depending on the trading environment and the trader's ultimate goal, this error of .03 may or may not be acceptable.

Instead of writing a roll as a combination of synthetic long and short underlying positions, we can also write the roll as a combination of calendar spreads:

−1 June 90 call/+1 August 90 call
+1 June 90 put/−1 August 90 put

The strategy on the top is a long call calendar spread; the strategy on the bottom is a short put calendar spread. If we buy the call calendar spread and sell the put calendar spread, we have a roll. The value of the roll should therefore be equal to the difference between the two calendar spreads.[6]

Because the interest component is almost always greater than dividends, a long roll (i.e., buy the long-term synthetic, sell the short-term synthetic) will typically trade for a positive value, requiring an outlay of cash. Consequently, the call calendar spread will be more valuable than the put calendar spread. However, if dividends are greater than interest, a roll can have a negative value.[7] Then the normal relationship will be inverted: the put calendar spread will be more valuable than the call calendar spread.

In our earlier example, we calculated the value of the June/August 90 roll as .47. Suppose that the June/August 90 call calendar spread is trading for 2.25. What should be the value of the June/August 90 put calendar spread? We know that the difference between the spreads must be .47. The value of the put spread ought to be

$$2.25 - .47 = 1.78$$

In the same way, if the put spread is trading for 1.50, the call spread ought to be trading for

$$1.50 + .47 = 1.97$$

---

[6] Note that the value of a box is equal to the *sum* of two spreads, a bull spread and a bear spread, while the value of a roll is equal to the *difference* between two spreads, a call calendar spread and a put calendar spread.
[7] Traders need to be careful about what they mean by *buying* and *selling*. Usually, buying means paying some amount (a cash debit), while selling means receiving some amount (a cash credit). With some strategies, however, it may not be clear whether the trader is paying or receiving. Rolls are an example of this.

Because dividends are discrete amounts that apply equally to all rolls with the same expiration dates, the values of rolls with the same expiration date but different exercise prices should differ by approximately the interest on exercise prices. In our example, the value of the June/August 90 roll was .47. The value of the June/August 80 roll should differ from the value of the 90 roll by the interest on the difference between 80 and 90

$$0.47 - (90 - 80) \times .06 \times 2/12 = .47 - .10 = 0.37$$

Whiles a trader may execute a roll with the intention of eliminating the risk of holding the underlying contract, this risk is only eliminated up to the short-term expiration. At that time, the trader will either buy or sell the underlying stock at the exercise price. The position is therefore sensitive to changes in interest rates and dividends. Rolls fluctuate in value as interest rates rise or fall and as dividends are raised or lowered. The more time between expirations, the more sensitive a roll will be to these changes.

Time Boxes

A box or roll consists of long and short synthetic positions, either in the same month but at different exercise prices (a box) or in different months but at the same exercise price (a roll). We can also combine these strategies by taking synthetic positions at different exercise prices and in different months:

+1 June 90 call	−1 August 100 call
−1 June 90 put	+1 August 100 put

This position is usually referred to as either a *time box* or *diagonal roll*.

We can calculate the value of a time box in the same way we calculated the value of a roll—by taking the difference between the discounted exercise prices less expected dividends

$$\frac{X_s}{(1 + r_s \times t_s)} - \frac{X_l}{(1 + r_l \times t_l)} - D$$

where the subscripts s and l refer to short-term options and long-term options.

What should be the value of the June 90/August 100 time box if there are two months to June expiration and four months to August expiration, interest rates are a constant 6 percent, and the stock is expected to pay a dividend of .40 over this period?

$$\frac{X_s}{(1 + r_s \times t_s)} - \frac{X_l}{(1 + r_l \times t_l)} - D = \frac{90}{1.01} - \frac{100}{1.02} - 0.40 = -9.33$$

The negative sign indicates that if a trader wants to put on this position, he will have to pay 9.33. This is logical because the position consists of buying the lower-exercise-price synthetic (i.e., buy the underlying at 90 at June expiration) and selling the higher-exercise-price synthetic (i.e., sell the underlying at 100 at August expiration).

In the same way that boxes are made up of bull and bear spreads and rolls are made up of calendar spreads, time boxes are made up of diagonal spreads. We can write our time box as two diagonal spreads:

+1 June 90 call/−1 August 100 call
−1 June 90 put/+1 August 100 put

Are we paying or receiving money for each of these spreads? We are clearly paying for the put spread because the August 100 put will always be more valuable than the June 90 put. But it's not clear what the cash flow is for the call spread. The lower exercise price seems to imply that the June call will be more valuable, but the greater amount of time might in fact make the August call more valuable. The values of the call options will depend on both the underlying price and volatility. In some cases, we may pay for the call spread; in other cases, we may be paid. Regardless of the prices of the individual spreads, though, the total debit must be 9.33. If the call spread is trading for 3.50, the put spread ought to be trading for $9.33 - 3.50 = 5.83$. If the put spread is trading for 7.75, the call spread ought to be trading for $9.33 - 7.75 = 1.58$.

Because a time box is a combination of a box and a roll, if we can value a box and a roll, we ought to be able to value a time box. Suppose that we buy the June 90/100 box

+1 June 90 call   −1 June 100 call
−1 June 90 put   +1 June 100 put

and at the same time sell the June/August 100 roll

+1 June 100 call   −1 August 100 call
−1 June 100 put   +1 August 100 put

The long and short June 100 synthetics cancel out, leaving the June 90/August 100 time box:

+1 June 90 call   −1 August 100 call
−1 June 90 put   +1 August 100 put

The time box must therefore be a combination of buying the June 90/100 box and selling the June/August 100 roll.

Similarly, suppose that we buy the August 90/100 box

+1 August 90 call   −1 August 100 call
−1 August 90 put   +1 August 100 put

and at the same time sell the June/August 90 roll

+1 June 90 call   −1 August 90 call
−1 June 90 put   +1 August 90 put

The long and short August 90 synthetics cancel out, again leaving the June 90/August 100 time box:

+1 June 90 call   −1 August 100 call
−1 June 90 put   +1 August 100 put

In this case, the time box is a combination of buying the August 90/100 box and selling the June/August 90 roll.

From the foregoing examples, we can see that if we buy a long-term box and sell a lower-exercise-price roll or buy a short-term box and sell a higher-exercise-price roll, both combinations result in the same time box. We can confirm this by calculating the value of the June and August 90/100 boxes as well as the June/August 90 and 100 rolls

$$\text{June } 90/100 \text{ box} = \frac{10}{1+0.06\times 2/12} = 9.90$$

$$\text{August } 90/100 \text{ box} = \frac{10}{1+0.06\times 4/12} = 9.80$$

$$\text{June/August } 90 \text{ roll} = \frac{90}{1+0.06\times 2/12} - \frac{90}{1+0.06\times 4/12} - 0.40 = 0.47$$

$$\text{June/August } 100 \text{ roll} = \frac{100}{1+0.06\times 2/12} - \frac{100}{1+0.06\times 4/12} - 0.40 = 0.57$$

If we buy the June 90/100 box and sell the June/August 100 roll, the total value is

$$-9.90 + .57 = -9.33$$

If we buy the August 90/100 box and sell the June/August 90 roll, the total value is

$$-9.80 + .47 = -9.33$$

The total in both cases is equal to the value of the time box.

Using Synthetics in Volatility Spreads

Any mispriced arbitrage relationship will be quickly recognized by almost all traders. Consequently, there are few opportunities to profit from a mispriced conversion or reversal. When a mispricing does arise, it is likely to be small and very short-lived. Only a professional trader, who has low transaction costs and immediate access to markets, is likely to be able to profit from such a situation. But even if a trader does not intend to execute an arbitrage, he may be able to use a knowledge of arbitrage pricing relationships to execute a strategy at more favorable prices.

In Chapter 14, we noted that because there is a synthetic equivalent for every contract, there are three ways to buy a straddle:

1. Buy a call, buy a put.

2. Buy a call, buy a put synthetically (buy two calls, sell an underlying contract)

3. Buy a call synthetically, but a put (buy two puts, buy an underlying contract)

Suppose that we have the following prices for a call, a put, and an underlying stock:

	Bid	Offer
Stock	51.45	51.50
50 call	4.10	4.20
50 put	2.35	2.40

If there are three months remaining to expiration, interest rates are 4.00 percent, and we expect the stock to pay a dividend of .25 prior to expiration, what is the best way to buy the 50 straddle?

Assuming that we must sell at the bid price and buy at the offer price, if we buy the straddle outright, we will pay a total of 4.20 + 2.40 = 6.60. Suppose, however, that we buy the put synthetically (i.e., buy the call, sell the underlying). How much are we actually paying for the put?

Recall the approximation for put-call parity for stock options

$$\text{Call price} - \text{put price} = \text{stock price} - \text{exercise price}$$
$$+ \text{ interest on exercise price} - \text{expected dividends}$$

If we buy the put synthetically, we will have to pay 4.20 for the call and sell the stock at 51.45. Therefore,

$$4.20 - ?? = 51.45 - 50 + 50 \times .04 \times 3/12 - .25 = 1.70$$

The cost of buying the put synthetically must be 2.50. This is higher than the actual price of 2.40, so this is a worse choice than buying the straddle outright.

What about buying the call synthetically (i.e., buy the put, buy the underlying)? We will pay 2.40 for the put and 51.50 for the stock. This gives us

$$?? - 2.40 = 51.50 - 50 + 50 \times .04 \times 3/12 - .25 = 1.75$$

The synthetic call price is 4.15. This is in fact better than the actual call price of 4.20. If we buy the straddle synthetically, buying two calls and buying stock, we are paying a total of 4.15 + 2.40 = 6.55, or .05 better than buying the straddle outright.

How important is a savings of .05? That probably depends on several factors—the size in which the spread will be done, the liquidity of the market, and execution costs and brokerage fees. A professional trader, who has very low transaction costs and tends to trade in large volumes, ought to be very happy to save .05. On the other hand, a retail customer may find that the outright straddle, because it involves only two contracts rather than three, entails lower transaction costs and can be executed more easily in the marketplace. It might be a better practical choice, even if it means giving up a potential savings of .05.

It might seem that when we are able to trade a contract synthetically at a better price than the actual price, there must an arbitrage opportunity available.

But in our example no arbitrage opportunity exists. If we do a conversion (i.e., sell call, buy put, buy stock), the put-call parity calculation is

$$4.10 - 2.40 = 51.50 - 50 + 50 \times .04 \times 3/12 - .25$$
$$1.70 = 1.75$$

We will be selling stock, synthetically, at 1.70 and buying at 1.75.

If we instead do a reverse conversion (i.e., buy call, sell put, sell stock), the calculation is

$$4.20 - 2.35 = 51.45 - 50 + 50 \times .04 \times 3/12 - .25$$
$$1.85 = 1.70$$

Now we are buying stock, synthetically, at 1.85 and selling at 1.70. Because we must buy at the bid and sell at the offer, no arbitrage is available in either case. Our goal, however, was a volatility spread, not an arbitrage. And the bid-ask spreads were such that we were able to buy the straddle synthetically at a savings of .05.

Let's expand the number of options and consider a different example:

	Bid	Offer
45 call	7.40	7.55
45 put	0.70	0.75
50 call	4.10	4.20
50 put	2.35	2.40
55 call	1.95	2.00
55 put	5.10	5.25

If, as before, there are three months remaining to expiration and interest rates are 4 percent, what is the best way to buy the 45/50/55 butterfly?

We might begin by comparing the prices of the call and put butterflies. We know that these are equivalent strategies and ought to have the same prices.

Call butterfly:
Buy one 45 call   −7.55
Sell two 50 calls   +8.20
Buy one 55 call   <u>−2.00</u>
    −1.35
Put butterfly:
Buy one 45 put   −0.75
Sell two 50 puts   +4.70
Buy one 55 put   <u>−5.25</u>
    −1.30

Buying the put butterfly is slightly better than buying the call butterfly.

In addition to buying the call or put butterfly, we have a third choice—we can sell an iron butterfly. In Chapter 14, we noted that selling an iron butterfly (i.e., buy a strangle and sell a straddle) is equivalent to buying a butterfly. Moreover, the value of the iron butterfly and the value of an actual butterfly must add up to the present value of the amount between exercise prices. In our example, the values must add up to

$$5.00/(1 + .04 \times 3/12) = 4.95$$

Therefore, paying 1.30 for the put butterfly is the same as selling the iron butterfly for 4.95 − 1.30 = 3.65. At what price can we sell the iron butterfly?

Iron butterfly:

Buy one 45 put	−0.75
Buy one 55 call	−2.00
Sell one 50 put	+2.35
Sell one 50 call	+4.10
	+3.70

If buying the put butterfly for 1.30 is equivalent to selling the iron butterfly for 3.65, then selling the iron butterfly at a price of 3.70 must be .05 better. This, in theory, seems to be the best way to buy the 45/50/55 butterfly.

Even though selling the iron butterfly is best in theory, other factors, such as ease of execution and transaction costs, may play a role. Everything else being equal, though, selling the iron butterfly for 3.70 is the best way to execute our butterfly strategy.

The relationship between the prices of call butterflies, put butterflies, and iron butterflies is based on synthetic relationships—the ability to express any contract as a synthetic equivalent. The reader may wish to confirm that no arbitrage opportunities exist, either in the form of conversions, reverse conversions, or boxes. Our goal, however, was not to take advantage of an arbitrage opportunity but rather to find the best price at which to buy a butterfly. Our knowledge of synthetic pricing relationships enabled us to do this.

Figure 15-3 is a summary of basic arbitrage pricing relationships. Whenever a trader is considering a strategy, he ought to always ask whether he can do better by executing some part of his strategy synthetically. Usually this will not be possible because synthetic relationships tend to be very efficient. Occasionally, though, the trader will find that the synthetic position is slightly more favorable. And over a career of trading, even small savings can add up.

Figure 15-3 Summary of arbitrage relationships for European options.

Note: Calculations exclude interest on dividends.

C=call price P=put price F=underlying futures price S=underlying stock price X=exercise price
r=annual interest rate t=time to expiration in years D=expected dividends

	simple interest	continuous interest	approximation
put-call parity:	$C - P = (F-X)/(1+rt)$	$C - P = (F-X)e^{-rt}$	
	$C - P = S - X/(1+rt) - D$	$C - P = S - Xe^{-rt} - D$	$C - P \approx S - X + Xrt - D$
box value: X_l = lower exercise price X_h = higher exercise price	$(X_h - X_l)/(1+rt)$	$(X_h - X_l)e^{-rt}$	$(X_h - X_l) - (X_h - X_l)rt$
	long box = long (bull) call spread + long (bear) put spread		

roll value for stock options:
t_l = time to expiration
    for long-term option
t_s = time to expiration
    for short-term option
D = expected dividends
    between expirations
	$X/(1+r_s t_s) - X/(1+r_l t_l) - D$	$Xe^{-r_s t_s} - Xe^{-r_l t_l} - D$	$X(t_l - t_s)r - D$

	long roll = long call calendar spread + short put calendar spread		
time box (diagonal roll) for stock options:	$X_s/(1+r_s t_s) - X_l/(1+r_l t_l) - D$	$X_s e^{-r_s t_s} - X_l e^{-r_l t_l} - D$	
time box value = long-term box − lower exercise price roll = short-term box − higher exercise price roll			

16

Early Exercise of American Options

Thus far we have assumed that all option strategies involve holding a position to expiration. Because many exchange-traded options are American, carrying with them the right of early exercise, it will be worthwhile to consider some of the characteristics of American options. Specifically, we will want to answer three questions:

1. Under what circumstances might a trader consider exercising an American option prior to expiration?

2. If early exercise is deemed desirable, is there an optimal time to do so?

3. How much more should a trader be willing to pay for an American option over an equivalent European option?

In order for early exercise to be desirable, there must be some advantage to holding a position in the underlying contract rather than a position in the option contract. This advantage can come in the form of dividends that the owner of stock will receive or in the form of a positive cash flow on which interest can be earned. If there are no dividend or interest considerations, there is no value to early exercise. In that case,

value of an American option = value of a European option

This is generally true for options on futures traded on exchanges outside the United States, where the options are subject to futures-type settlement. Futures contracts do not pay dividends, and no cash flow takes place when either the underlying futures contract or options on that contract are traded. Even though the options may be American, there is effectively no early exercise value associated with such options.

Arbitrage Boundaries

When evaluating a contract, a trader might try to determine an *arbitrage boundary* for that contract—the lowest price (the lower arbitrage boundary) or highest price (the upper arbitrage boundary) at which the contract can trade without there being some arbitrage opportunity. Identifying the arbitrage boundaries for European and American options can help us understand the early exercise criteria for American options.

Consider these prices:

Contract	Price
June 90 call	9.90
Underlying contract	100.00

If the June 90 call is American, everyone will want to buy the call for 9.90, sell the underlying contract for 100.00, and immediately exercise the option. The resulting cash flow will be

Buy the June 90 call	−9.90
Sell the underlying contract	+100.00
Exercise the call	−90.00
Total profit and loss (P&L)	+.10

There is an arbitrage profit of 0.10.

Now consider these prices:

Contract	Price
June 70 put	4.80
Underlying contract	65.00

If the June 70 put is American, everyone will want to buy the put for 4.80, buy the underlying contract for 65.00, and immediately exercise the option. The resulting cash flow will be

Buy the June 70 put	−4.80
Buy the underlying contract	−65.00
Exercise the put	+70.00
Total P&L	+0.20

There is an arbitrage profit of 0.20.

We can conclude from these examples that an American option should never trade for less than intrinsic value. If it does, everyone will buy the option, hedge the position with the underlying contract, and exercise the option, all of which will result in an immediate arbitrage profit. We can express the lower arbitrage boundary for an American option as

For a call:	At least the maximum of $[0, S - X]$
For a put:	At least the maximum of $[0, X - S]$

where X is the exercise price, and S is the price of the underlying contract.

We have included the qualifier *at least* for both calls and puts because, as we will see, the lower arbitrage boundary for an American option may in fact be greater than intrinsic value. For the present, we will simply say that it cannot be less than intrinsic value.

To determine the lower arbitrage boundary for a European option, we can use put-call parity

$$C - P = \frac{F - X}{1 + r \times t}$$

The lowest possible price for a put is 0, so the lower arbitrage boundary for a European call must be

$$C \geq \frac{F - X}{1 + r \times t}$$

where F is either the price of an underlying futures contract or the forward price for an underlying stock.

For a futures option, the lower arbitrage boundary for a call is the present value of the intrinsic value. This means that if European options on futures are subject to stock-type settlement, the lower arbitrage boundary will always be less than intrinsic value because the present value must be less than intrinsic value.

For example,

  Futures price = 1,167.00
  Time to expiration = 6 months
  Interest rate = 4.00 percent

If options are subject to stock-type settlement, the lower arbitrage boundary for the 1,100 call is

$$\frac{1,167.00 - 1,100}{1 + 0.04 \times 6/12} = 65.69$$

Even though the intrinsic value is 67.00, the lower arbitrage boundary is 65.69.

For stock options, if we replace F with the forward price for the stock and we ignore interest on dividends, the lower arbitrage boundary for a European call is

$$C \geq S - \frac{X}{(1 + r \times t)} - D$$

A stock option call cannot trade for less than the stock price minus the discounted value of the exercise price less dividends. This means that the lower arbitrage boundary for an out-of-the-money stock option call can be greater than 0. For example,

  Stock price   = 49.50
  Time to expiration = 6 months
  Interest rate   = 4.00 percent
  Dividend   = 0

A 50 call, even though it is out of the money, has a lower arbitrage boundary of

$$\frac{49.50 - 50}{1 + 0.04 \times 6/12} = 0.48$$

If the call is trading for less than 0.48, say, 0.40, we can buy the call, sell the stock, and exercise the call at expiration. The cash flows will be

Buy the 50 call	−0.40
Pay interest on the call price (0.40 × 0.04 × 6/12)	−0.01
Sell stock	+49.50
Collect interest on the stock price (49.50 × 0.04 × 6/12)	+0.99
Exercise the call at expiration	−50.00
Total P&L	+0.08

This is exactly the difference between the call price of 0.40 and the lower arbitrage boundary of 0.48.

In this example, we can be certain of an arbitrage profit of at least 0.08 because we know that we can close out the position at expiration by exercising the call, thereby purchasing the stock back at a price no higher than 50. Suppose, however, that the stock price at expiration is less than 50. Instead of exercising the call, we can purchase the stock at its market price. This will result in an even greater profit than 0.08. The lower arbitrage boundary tells us the price below which there is an arbitrage opportunity and at the same time determines the *minimum* amount that can be made. The maximum amount can be even greater if at expiration the stock is trading at a price below the exercise price.

What is the lower arbitrage boundary for the 50 call if it is an American option? We might assume that it must be 0 because the option is out of the money, and no one would ever exercise an out-of-the-money option. But early exercise is a right, not an obligation. We can convert an American option into a European option simply by choosing not to exercise it early. The lower arbitrage boundary for an American option is therefore at least intrinsic value. If the lower arbitrage boundary for an equivalent European option is greater than intrinsic value, as it is in this example, then this number also serves as the lower arbitrage boundary for the American option:

$$\text{American call} \geq \text{maximum } [0,\ S-X,\ (F-X)/(1+r\times t)]$$

In this example, the lower arbitrage boundary for the 50 call is 0.48 regardless of whether the option is European or American.

Let's change our example slightly:

Stock price = 49.50
Time to expiration = 6 months
Interest rate = 4.00 percent
Dividend = 0.65 payable every three months (total dividend of 1.30)

What is the lower arbitrage boundary for a European 45 call?

$$\frac{49.50-45}{1+0.04\times 6/12}-1.30 = 4.08$$

If the call is American, its intrinsic value (49.50 − 45 = 4.50) is greater than the European value of 4.08. Therefore, the lower arbitrage boundary for an American 45 call is 4.50.

By reversing F and X, we can use put-call parity to determine the lower arbitrage boundary for a European put

$$P \geq \frac{X - F}{1 + r \times t}$$

As with a futures option call, the lower arbitrage boundary for a European put is the present value of the intrinsic value.

For stock options, we can replace F with the stock forward price, giving us the lower arbitrage boundary for a put

$$P \geq \frac{X}{1 + r \times t} - S + D$$

A stock option put cannot trade for less than the discounted value of the exercise price minus the stock price plus dividends.

Stock price = 49.50
Time to expiration = 6 months
Interest rate = 4.00 percent
Dividend = 0

The lower arbitrage boundary for a European 50 put must be 0 because

$$\frac{50}{1 + 0.04 \times 6/12} - 49.50 = -.48$$

If, however, the option is American, the lower arbitrage boundary will be the option's intrinsic value of 0.50.

Because we can always turn an American put into a European put simply by choosing not to exercise it, the lower arbitrage boundary for an American put is

American put $\geq$ maximum $[0, X - S, (X - F)/(1 + r \times t)]$

Because the lower arbitrage boundary for European options is a function of time, interest rates, and, in the case of stock, dividends, as time passes, the boundary is constantly changing. For futures options that are subject to stock-type settlement, the boundary is always rising because the present value is always rising toward intrinsic value. For stock options, however, the boundary may rise or fall depending on whether the forward price is greater than or less than the cash price. If the forward price is greater than the cash price (interest is greater than dividends), the lower arbitrage boundary will rise for calls and fall for puts. If the forward price is less than the cash price (interest is less than dividends), the boundary will fall for calls and rise for puts. A graphic representation of these changes is shown in Figures 16-1 through 16-4.

If the lower arbitrage boundary for a European option is less than intrinsic value, a European option can, in some cases, be worth less than intrinsic value. When this occurs, as time passes, the value of the option will rise toward intrinsic value. As a consequence, the option will have a positive theta. This was discussed in Chapter 7 and shown graphically in Figure 7-9.

Figure 16-1 Lower arbitrage boundary for a European call on futures (stock-type settlement).

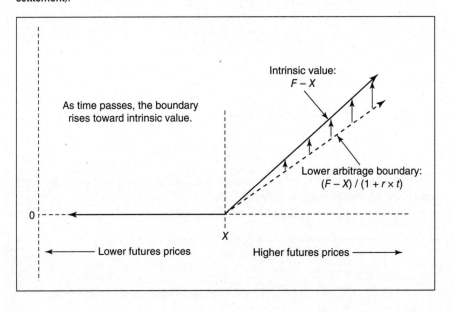

Figure 16-2 Lower arbitrage boundary for a European put on futures (stock-type settlement).

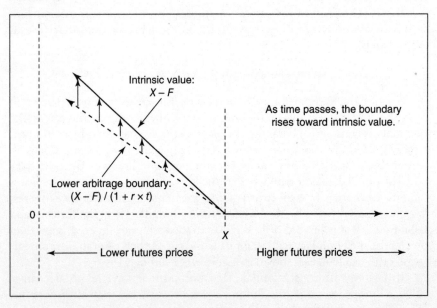

Figure 16-3 Lower arbitrage boundary for a European call on stock.

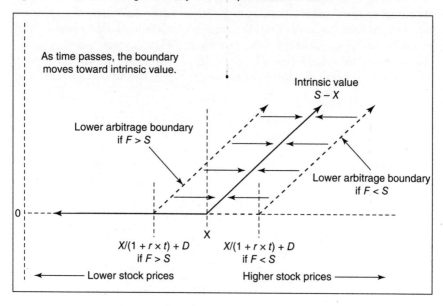

As time passes, the boundary moves toward intrinsic value.

Intrinsic value
S − X

Lower arbitrage boundary if F > S

Lower arbitrage boundary if F < S

0

$X/(1 + r \times t) + D$
if F > S

$X/(1 + r \times t) + D$
if F < S

X

← Lower stock prices

Higher stock prices →

Figure 16-4 Lower arbitrage boundary for a European put on stock.

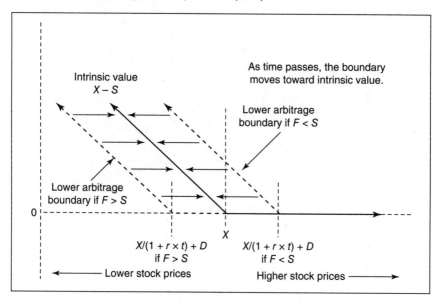

As time passes, the boundary moves toward intrinsic value.

Intrinsic value
X − S

Lower arbitrage boundary if F < S

Lower arbitrage boundary if F > S

0

$X/(1 + r \times t) + D$
if F > S

$X/(1 + r \times t) + D$
if F < S

X

← Lower stock prices

Higher stock prices →

Although traders are primarily interested in the lower exercise boundary for an option, for completeness, we might also want to determine the upper arbitrage boundary for an option. Because the underlying contract cannot fall below 0, the upper arbitrage boundary for an American put, whether on futures or stock, must be the exercise price. For a European put, which is subject to stock-type settlement, the upper boundary is the present value of the exercise price

$$\text{American put} \leq X$$
$$\text{European put} \leq X/(1 + r \times t)$$

To determine the upper arbitrage boundary for a call, we can use put-call parity

$$C - P = \frac{F - X}{1 + r \times t}$$

We know that the maximum value for a European put is $X/(1 + r \times t)$. Therefore, the maximum value for a European call is

$$C \leq \frac{F - X}{1 + r \times t} + \frac{X}{1 + r \times t} = \frac{F}{1 + r \times t}$$

A European call on a futures contract has a maximum value equal to the futures price discounted by interest. If options are subject to futures-type settlement, the maximum value is simply the price of the underlying futures contract.

For a European call on stock, we can replace F with the forward price for stock $S \times (1 + r \times t) - D$

$$C \leq \frac{S \times (1 + r \times t) - D - X}{1 + r \times t} + \frac{X}{1 + r \times t}$$

Ignoring interest on dividends gives us

$$C \leq \frac{S - D - X}{1 + r \times t} + \frac{X}{1 + r \times t} = S - D$$

A European call on stock has a maximum value equal to the stock price less dividends. An American call has a maximum value equal to the stock price. A summary of arbitrage boundaries is shown in Figure 16-5.

Early Exercise of Call Options on Stock

Under what conditions might we choose to exercise an American call option on stock prior to expiration? To answer this question, let's think about the components that make up the value of a call.

Clearly, if we are considering exercising an option, it must be in the money. Therefore, one component must be *intrinsic value*. A call also offers some protective value over a stock position because the call's loss is limited by the exercise price. The likelihood that the stock will fall below the exercise price depends on the volatility, so we might refer to this protective value as *volatility value*. As volatility rises, we are willing to pay more for the call. The call also includes some

Figure 16-5 Summary of arbitrage boundaries.

Lower Arbitrage Boundary		American	European
Options on futures (stock-type settlement)	Call	max[0, F − X]	max[0, (F − X)/(1 + r × t)]
	Put	max[0, X − F]	max[0, (X − F)/(1 + r × t)]
Options on stock	Call	max[0, S − X, S − X/(1 + r × t) − D]	max[0, S − X/(1 + r × t) − D]
	Put	max[0, X − S, X/(1 + r × t) − S + D]	max[0, X/(1 + r × t) − S + D]
Upper Arbitrage Boundary		**American**	**European**
Options on futures (stock-type settlement)	Call	F	F/(1 + r × t)
	Put	X	X/(1 + r × t)
Options on stock	Call	S	S − D
	Put	X	X/(1 + r × t)

interest-rate value. As interest rates rise, the call becomes a more desirable substitute for holding a stock position. Finally, there is *dividend value.* But unlike volatility value and interest value, both of which increase the value of the call, the dividend reduces the value of the call. Therefore,

Call value = intrinsic value + volatility value + interest value − dividend value

Suppose that we are able determine the value of each of these components and find that the dividend value is greater than the combined volatility value and interest value

Dividend value > volatility value + interest value

In this case, the value of the call will be less than intrinsic value. And, indeed, European options can, in some cases, trade for less than intrinsic value. But, if the call is American, it becomes an early exercise candidate because we can collect the intrinsic value now by simultaneously exercising the call and selling the stock.

How can we estimate the value of the volatility, interest-rate, and dividend components? The dividend component is simply the total dividend the stock is expected to pay over the life of the option. The interest value must be the interest that we would have to pay if we were to sell the call and buy the stock and carry this position to expiration. If the call is deeply in the money, its value will be very close to intrinsic value, and the total cash flow will be approximately equal to the exercise price

Intrinsic value = stock price − exercise price

We might reach the same conclusion by observing that if we exercise the call, we will have to pay the exercise price. The interest value must be the approximate cost of carrying the exercise price to expiration.

The volatility component is somewhat more difficult to determine. But we know that the volatility value depends on the likelihood of the stock price falling below the exercise price. The value of the companion put (the put with the same exercise price and expiration date as the call) must be a good estimate of this value. We know from put-call parity that the vegas of calls and puts with the same exercise price and expiration date are the same—they have the same sensitivity to changes in volatility. Therefore, their volatility values ought to be the same.[1]

For example, consider the following:

Stock price = 100
Time to expiration = 1 month
Interest rate = 6.00 percent
Dividend = 0.75, payable in 15 days

Is the 90 call an early exercise candidate if the price of the 90 put is 0.20?

We know the dividend value (0.75) and the volatility value (0.20), so the only component we need to calculate is the cost of carrying the exercise price to expiration

$$90 \times .06 \times 1/12 = .45$$

The early exercise criteria are satisfied because

Dividend value > volatility value + interest value
$$0.75 > 0.20 + 0.45 = 0.65$$

In Figure 16-6 we can see why the 90 call has become an early exercise candidate—its European value has fallen below intrinsic value.[2] If given the choice between exercising now or carrying the option position to expiration, we will come out ahead by 0.10 if we exercise now.

But are those our only two choices—exercise now or not at all? An American option can be exercised at any time prior to expiration. Instead of exercising today, what about exercising the option tomorrow? Or the day after that?

Suppose that we exercise today instead of exercising tomorrow. What will we gain, and what will we lose? We will lose one day's worth of volatility value. We will also lose one day's worth of interest on the exercise price. In return, we get ... nothing. We are exercising to get the dividend. But the dividend will not be paid for 15 days. Because we always give up some volatility value and some interest value when we exercise an American call option on stock prior to expiration, the only time we will consider exercising the option early is the day before the stock pays the dividend. On no other day will early exercise be optimal.

---

[1] Although the companion put also has some interest and dividend value, these components will tend to be small. Changing interest rates or dividends will cause the forward price to change, which is similar to changing the underlying price. But the put, with its small delta, will be relatively insensitive to these changes. Consequently, the out-of-the-money put has only a small interest-rate and dividend value. There is no sensitivity measure for dividends, but we can confirm that the put is relatively insensitive to changes in interest rates by noting that an out-of-the-money option has a small rho value compared with an in-the-money option.

[2] Figure 16-6 is clearly not drawn to scale. The point at which the European lower arbitrage boundary graph bends appears to be halfway between 90 and 100. The actual point is $X/(1 + r \times t) + D = 90/(1 + 0.06/12) + 0.75 = 90.30$.

Figure 16-6

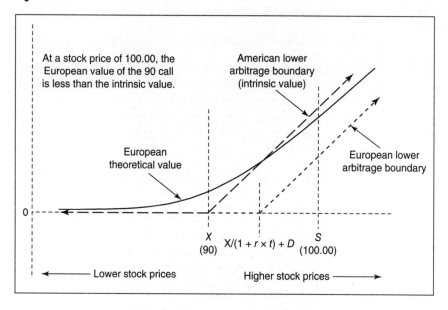

At a stock price of 100.00, the European value of the 90 call is less than the intrinsic value.

American lower arbitrage boundary (intrinsic value)

European theoretical value

European lower arbitrage boundary

0

X (90) $X/(1 + r \times t) + D$ S (100.00)

◄────── Lower stock prices   Higher stock prices ──────►

For an American call option on stock to be an early exercise candidate, the early exercise criteria must hold true over the entire life of the option

Dividend value > volatility value + interest value

But, for an option to be an *immediate* early exercise candidate, this condition must also hold true over the next day. For a call option on stock, the only day on which a trader need consider early exercise is the day before the stock pays a dividend. Indeed, if a stock pays no dividend over the life of the option, there is never any reason to exercise the call prior to expiration.

Early Exercise of Put Options on Stock

Under what conditions might we choose to exercise an American put option on stock prior to expiration? Just as we separated the value of a stock option call into its components, we can do the same with a stock option put. Again, we begin with the intrinsic value. To this, we can add the volatility value—the protective value afforded by the put in the event that the stock price rises above the exercise price. There will also be interest value—if we exercise the put, we will collect interest on the exercise price. Finally, there will be some dividend value.

Put value = intrinsic value + volatility value − interest value + dividend value

Note that volatility value and dividend value increase the value of the put, while the interest value reduces the put's value. Suppose that we are able to determine the value of each of these components and find that the interest value is greater than the combined volatility value and dividend value

$$\text{Interest value} > \text{volatility value} + \text{dividend value}$$

If this is true, the value of the option will be less than intrinsic value. But, if the option is American, it becomes an early exercise candidate because we can collect the intrinsic value right now by exercising the put.

We can estimate the value of these components in the same way we estimated them for a call. The interest value is the amount of interest we will earn on the exercise price to expiration if we exercise the put. The dividend value is the total dividend the stock is expected to pay over the life of the option. The volatility value is approximately the price of the companion out-of-the-money call.

Consider this situation:

Stock price = 100
Time to expiration = 2 months
Interest rate = 6.00 percent
Dividend = 0.40

Is the 120 put an early exercise candidate if the price of the 120 call is 0.55?

We know the volatility value (0.55) and dividend value (0.40). The interest on the exercise price to expiration is

$$120 \times .06 \times 1/6 = 1.20$$

The early exercise criteria are satisfied because

$$\text{Interest value} > \text{volatility value} + \text{dividend value}$$
$$1.20 > .55 + .40 = .95$$

We can see in Figure 16-7 that at a stock price of 100, the value of the European 120 put falls below intrinsic value, making the put an early exercise candidate. If given the choice between exercising now or carrying the option position to expiration, we will come out ahead by 0.25 if we exercise now.[3]

As with a call, for a put to be an immediate early exercise candidate, the early exercise criteria must hold true not only over the entire life of the option but also over the next day. We will exercise today only if we expect to gain more over the next day through early exercise than we lose. Will this be true for our 120 put?

Suppose that the dividend of 0.40 will be paid tomorrow. If we exercise today instead of tomorrow, we will gain one day's worth of interest

$$120 \times 0.06/365 = 0.02$$

In return, we are giving up one day's worth of volatility value as well as the value of the dividend. Even if we assume that the volatility value is negligible,

---

[3] Figure 16-7, like Figure 16-6, is not drawn to scale. The point at which the European lower arbitrage boundary graph bends is $X/(1 + r \times t) + D = 120/(1 + 0.06/6) + 0.40 = 119.21$.

Figure 16-7

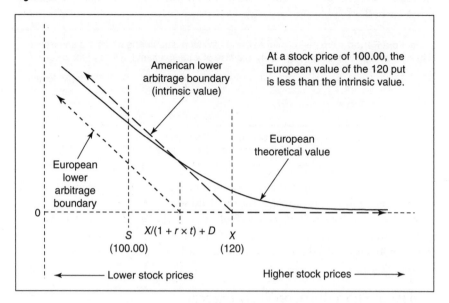

At a stock price of 100.00, the European value of the 120 put is less than the intrinsic value.

American lower arbitrage boundary (intrinsic value)

European theoretical value

European lower arbitrage boundary

0

S $X/(1 + r \times t) + D$ X
(100.00)   (120)

◄——————— Lower stock prices   Higher stock prices ——————►

the dividend of 0.40 that we will lose is far greater than the interest of 0.02 that we will earn. Clearly, we should wait one day before exercising the option, foregoing one day's worth of interest but retaining the value of the dividend.

Suppose that the dividend will be paid two days from now. If we exercise today instead of waiting until the dividend is paid, we will earn two days' worth of interest, 0.04, but we will still lose the dividend of 0.40. Waiting two days to exercise is still a better strategy.

When should we exercise a put early? Because a trader will not want to give up the value of the dividend, the most common day on which to exercise a stock option put early is the day on which the stock pays the dividend. But unlike stock option calls, where the *only* day on which the option ought to be exercised early is the day before the stock pays the dividend, a stock option put might be exercised any time prior to expiration. Early exercise will be optimal if the interest that can be earned is greater than the combined volatility and dividend value.

Ignoring the volatility value, we can see that no trader will exercise a put early if the total interest that can be earned is less than the dividend. In our example, where we expect to earn 0.02 in interest per day, early exercise can never be optimal if the dividend will be paid within the next 20 days because

$$0.40/.02 = 20$$

With fewer than 20 days to the dividend payment, we can never earn enough interest to offset the loss of the dividend. For put options, this *blackout period* can be easily calculated by dividing the dividend by the daily interest that can be earned on the exercise price. During this period, no knowledgeable trader will exercise a put because the loss of the dividend will be greater than the total interest earned.

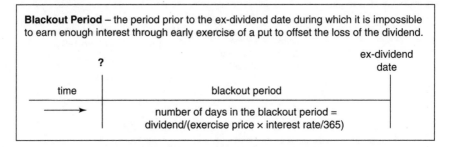

Blackout Period – the period prior to the ex-dividend date during which it is impossible to earn enough interest through early exercise of a put to offset the loss of the dividend.

This does not mean that a put should never be exercised prior to the dividend payment. In our example, if the dividend will be paid in 30 days and we exercise now, we will earn 30 days' worth of interest, that is, $30 \times 0.02 = 0.60$. This is greater than the 0.40 value of the dividend. As long as the volatility value over the next 30 days is less than 0.20, immediate early exercise is a sensible choice.

Impact of Short Stock on Early Exercise

Interest rates are an important factor in deciding whether to exercise a stock option early. If we reduce interest rates, calls are more likely to be exercised early (early exercise results in a smaller interest loss), and puts are less likely to be exercised early (early exercise results in smaller interest earnings). Because a short stock position entails a lower interest rate (the rate is reduced by the borrowing costs), a trader who has a short stock position is more likely to exercise a call option early. At the same time, a trader who does not already own stock will be less likely to exercise a put option early. This is consistent with the general rule that we proposed in Chapter 7:

Whenever possible, a trader should avoid a short stock position.

If a trader is carrying a short stock position, exercise of a call will reduce or eliminate this position. If a trader is carrying no stock position, exercise of a put will result in a short stock position. In the former case, a call is more likely to be exercised early; in the latter case, a put is less likely to be exercised early.

Early Exercise of Options on Futures

What happens when we exercise a futures option? Exercise of a call option enables us to buy the underlying futures contract at the exercise price. Exercise of a put option enables us to sell the underlying futures contract at the exercise price. Because the futures contract is subject to futures-type settlement, there will be a variation credit equal to the option's intrinsic value, the difference between the exercise price and the price of the futures contract. If the option is subject to futures-type settlement, exercise will cause the option to disappear, and we will be debited by an amount equal to the option's value. Assuming that the price of the option is equal to its intrinsic value, the credit and debit will cancel out, resulting in no cash flow. Because there is no cash flow, there can be no advantage to early exercise. If, however, the option is subject to stock-type settlement, as is the practice on futures exchanges in the United States, there is no cash flow when the option position disappears. The only cash flow is the variation credit on the futures position, a credit on which we can earn interest.

For a futures option to be an early exercise candidate, the option must be subject to stock-type settlement, and the interest that can be earned on the intrinsic value must be greater than the volatility value that we are giving up

$$\text{Interest value} > \text{volatility value}$$

The interest on the option's intrinsic value is either

$$(F - X) \times r \times t$$

for calls or

$$(X - F) \times r \times t$$

for puts.

As with stock options, we can estimate the volatility value of an option by looking at the price of the companion out-of-the-money option. Suppose that we have the following:

> Futures price = 100
> Time to expiration = 3 months
> Interest rate = 8.00 percent

Is the 80 call an early exercise candidate if the price of the 80 put is 0.15? The interest we can earn through early exercise is

$$(100 - 80) \times 0.08 \times 3/12 = 0.40$$

Because this is greater than the volatility value of .15, the option is an early exercise candidate. If given the choice between exercising now and holding the position to expiration, we will come out ahead by 0.25 if we exercise now. For the option to be an immediate early exercise candidate, it must also meet the early exercise criteria over the next day. One day's worth of interest must be greater than one day's worth of volatility value.

We can easily calculate one day's worth of interest

$$(100 - 80) \times .08/365 = 0.0044$$

How can we calculate one day's worth of volatility value? We know that the price of the companion option, in this case, the 80 put, is almost all volatility value. As each day passes, the value of the option will fall by one day's worth of volatility value. This daily loss in value is simply the option's theta. By determining the theta of the companion out-of-the-money option, we can estimate one day's worth of volatility value. Unlike the other calculations, this will require the use of a theoretical pricing model.

Using the Black-Scholes model, we find that the implied volatility of the 80 put is 24.68 percent. At this implied volatility, the option's theta is –0.0046, slightly greater (in absolute value) than the daily interest. If we exercise the 80 call today instead of tomorrow, we will gain 0.0044 in interest, but we will lose 0.0046 in volatility value. Because we will lose more than we gain, the option is not an immediate early exercise candidate.

When should we exercise the 80 call? Assuming that the early exercise criteria are met over the entire life of the option, we will want to exercise when the daily volatility value is less than the daily interest. In our example, we will want to exercise when the option's theta is less than .0044. Using the Black-Scholes model, we can estimate that this will occur in four days, at which time the theta of the 80 put will be –0.0043.[4]

Not exercising an option to retain the theta value may seem counter-intuitive. If we do not exercise the 80 call and the price of the futures contract does not move, we not only lose one day's worth of interest, but we also lose one day's worth of theta. But this is true only if the price of the futures contract does not move. If the futures contract does move, the fact that we have a positive gamma position will work in our favor. If the movement is large enough, we will prefer to hold the option position rather than a futures position. In an extreme case, if the futures contract were to fall below 80, we would clearly prefer the option position because of the protective value offered by the 80 call. How likely is it that we will get sufficient movement in the futures price over the next day to justify holding the 80 call rather than exercising it? This is one day's worth of volatility value—the theta of the 80 put.

For an American option that might be an early exercise candidate, we have considered two choices—hold the option or exercise the option. There is also a third choice—sell the option and replace it with a position in the underlying contract. The result is equivalent to exercising the option because both strategies result in the option position being replaced by an underlying position.

When does selling an option rather than exercising make sense? When we decide to exercise an American option prior to expiration, we have, in effect, concluded that the value of the option is equal to its intrinsic value. If the price of the option in the marketplace is exactly intrinsic value, there is no difference between exercising the option or selling the option and replacing it with an underlying position. If, however, the option is trading at a price greater than intrinsic value, and transaction costs are not a factor, the best choice will always be to sell the option and replace it with a position in the underlying contract. As a practical matter, however, selling an option that is an early exercise candidate will usually not be a viable alternative. If the option is deeply enough in the money to justify early exercise, the market for the option will be relatively illiquid. Under these conditions, the bid-ask spread is likely to be so wide that any sale will almost certainly have to be done at a price that is no greater than intrinsic value.

---

[4] The term *fugit* is sometimes used to refer to the number of days remaining until an option becomes an immediate early exercise candidate.

Protective Value and Early Exercise

When we exercise an option prior to expiration, we are giving up the protective value afforded by the option's exercise price. If the price of the underlying contract were to fall through the exercise price in the case of a call or rise through the exercise price in the case of a put, we would always prefer the option position to an underlying position. To better understand the consequences of giving up this protective value, let's go back to an earlier stock option example, but with the dividend payable tomorrow:

Stock price = 100
Time to expiration = 1 month
Interest rate = 6.00 percent
Dividend = 0.75, payable tomorrow

If the 90 put is trading at 0.20, we know that the 90 call is an immediate early exercise candidate because

Dividend value > volatility value + interest value
.75 > 0.20 + .45 = .65

If we exercise the 90 call, the result is that we will have no option position, but we will have a long position in the underlying stock. This is the same position that would result had we sold the option and bought the stock. However, if we sell a call and buy the underlying, this is synthetically equivalent to selling a put. In a sense, exercising the 90 call is the same as selling the 90 put. What will cause us to regret selling the 90 put? Whether we sell the 90 put or exercise the 90 call early, in both cases, we will regret our choice if the stock price is below 90 at expiration.

If exercising the 90 call is the same as selling the 90 put, we might ask, if we exercise the 90 call, at what price are we selling the 90 put? Because

.75 > 0.20 + 0.45 = 0.65

we can see that we will gain .10 by exercising the 90 call. This must mean that we have sold the 90 put at a price that is .10 better than its market price of 0.20. Therefore, exercising the 90 call is equivalent to selling the 90 put at a price of 0.30.

How can a trader who believes that early exercise is indicated protect himself from the possibility of the underlying contract going through the exercise price? The solution is simple: at the same time the trader exercises an option, he can purchase the companion out-of-the-money option. In our example, if the trader exercises the 90 call and simultaneously buys the 90 put at a price of 0.20, he will have the same protection afforded by the 90 call, but at a cost that is 0.10 lower. Whether the trader actually chooses to purchase the 90 put is a decision that he will have to make based on his assessment of market conditions. If the trader believes that implied volatility is low, a price of 0.20 will seem cheap, and he ought to be happy to purchase the 90 put. If implied volatility is high, a price of 0.20 will seem expensive, and the trader will look for some other way of controlling his downside risk.

Pricing of American Options

Our discussion thus far has focused on why and when an American option might be exercised prior to expiration. But we also want to consider the question of pricing. How much is an American option worth? Unless interest rates are 0 and there are no dividend considerations, an American option should always be worth more than an equivalent European option. But how much more?

The Black-Scholes model makes no attempt to evaluate American options because it is a European pricing model. When the Chicago Board Options Exchange opened in 1973, the first listed stock options were American. In spite of this, traders continued to use the Black-Scholes model for several years because no model of equal simplicity existed for American options. Traders tried to approximate American values by making adjustments to Black-Scholes–generated values.

For example, when a stock is expected to pay a dividend, an American call value can be approximated by comparing the Black-Scholes value of the call option under two circumstances:

1. The call expires the day before the stock goes ex-dividend.

2. The call expires on its customary date, but the underlying stock price used to evaluate the call is the current price less the expected dividend.

Whichever value is greater is the *pseudo-American* call value.

In the case of options on futures or put options on stock, traders used Black-Scholes–generated values but raised any option with a theoretical value less than parity to exactly parity. Unfortunately, neither of these methods resulted in a truly accurate value for an American option.

The first widely used model to evaluate American options was introduced in 1979 by John Cox of the Massachusetts Institute of Technology, Stephen Ross of Yale University, and Mark Rubinstein of the University of California at Berkeley.[5] Unlike the Black-Scholes model, which is closed form and therefore returns a single option value, the *Cox-Ross-Rubinstein*, or *binomial, model* is an algorithm or loop. The more times the model passes through the loop, the closer it comes to the true value of an American option. The Cox-Ross-Rubinstein model is relatively easy to understand, both intuitively and mathematically, and is the most common method by which students are introduced to option pricing theory. (We will take a closer look at binomial option pricing in Chapter 19.) However, in terms of computation, the model may require numerous passes through the loop to generate an acceptable value. In an effort to reduce the computational time required by the Cox-Ross-Rubinstein model, in 1987, Giovanni Barone-Adesi of the University of Alberta and Robert Whaley of Duke University introduced an alternative model for pricing American options.[6] Although the *Barone-Adesi-Whaley*, or *quadratic, model* is more

---

[5] John C. Cox, Stephen A. Ross, and Mark Rubinstein, "Option Pricing: A Simplified Approach," *Journal of Financial Economics* 7:229–263, 1979.
[6] Giovanni Baron-Adesi and Robert Whaley, "Efficient Analytic Approximation of American Option Values," *Journal of Finance* 42(2):301–320, 1987.

complex mathematically, it converges to an acceptable value for American options much more quickly than the Cox-Ross-Rubinstein model. The Barone-Adesi-Whaley model has the limitation of treating all cash flows as if they were interest payments that accumulate at a constant rate. Dividends, however, are paid all in one lump sum, and for this reason, the Cox-Ross-Rubinstein model is more often used to evaluate options on dividend-paying stocks.

In addition to generating values for American options, both the Cox-Ross-Rubinstein and Barone-Adesi-Whaley models specify when early exercise of an American option is optimal. Although we were somewhat subjective on this point in our earlier discussion, using a true American pricing model, an option is optimally exercised early when its theoretical value is exactly to parity and its delta is exactly 100.

The extent to which American and European option values differ depends on many factors, including time to expiration, volatility, interest rates, and, in the case of stock options, the amount of the dividend. The likelihood of early exercise will increase, and with it the difference between American and European values, as the option goes more deeply into the money. We can see this in Figure 16-8, the value of a 90 call on stock where

> Time to expiration = 7 weeks
> Interest rate = 6.00 percent
> Dividend = 1.00, payable in 4 weeks
> Volatility = 25 percent

As the underlying stock price rises from 90 to 110, the call moves from out of the money, with a very small likelihood of early exercise, to in the money, with

Figure 16-8 Theoretical value of a 90 call.

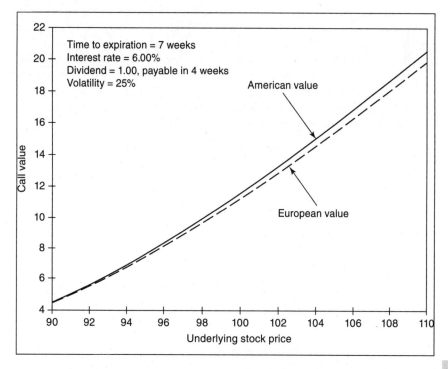

Figure 16-9 Difference between the theoretical value of an American and European 90 call (American value less European value).

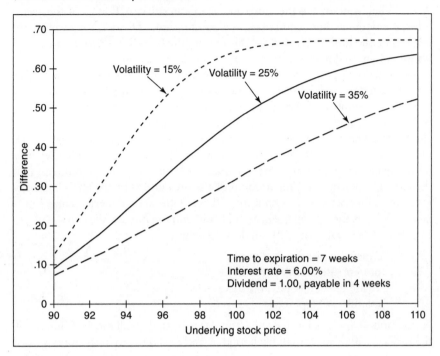

a very high likelihood. Figure 16-9 shows the net difference in values not only at a volatility of 25 percent but also at volatilities of 15 and 35 percent. At a higher volatility, the difference in values is smaller because the American call is less likely to be exercised early. At a lower volatility, the difference is greater because the call is more likely to be exercised early. In all cases, as the option goes more deeply into the money, the difference approaches 0.67, the amount of the dividend less the interest cost of purchasing the stock at 90 the day before the dividend is paid and carrying the position to expiration

$$1.00 - (90 \times 0.06 \times 22/365) \approx 0.67$$

Now consider the value of a 110 put under the same conditions. As with a call, the more deeply the put goes into the money, the greater the difference between the American value and the European value. This can be seen in Figure 16-10. The net difference under three volatility assumptions is shown in Figure 16-11. At a higher volatility, the difference in values is smaller because the American put is less likely to be exercised early. At a lower volatility, the difference is greater because the put is more likely to be exercised early. In all cases, as the option goes more deeply into the money, the difference approaches 0.38, the amount of interest that can be earned on the exercise price for the three weeks remaining to expiration following payment of the dividend

$$110 \times 0.06 \times 21/365 \approx 0.38$$

Figure 16-10 Theoretical value of a 110 put.

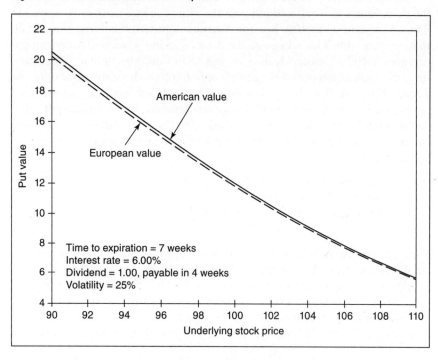

Figure 16-11 Difference between the theoretical value of an American and European 110 put (American value less European value).

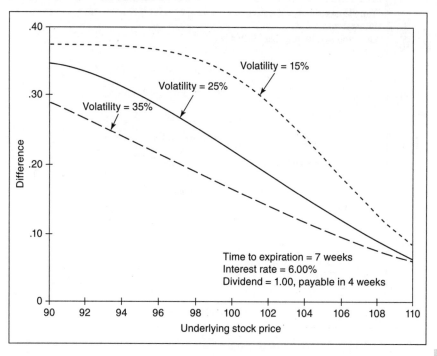

In our discussion of synthetics, we noted that for European stock options, the delta values of a call and put with the same exercise price and expiration date always add up to 100. But, for American options, the deltas can add up to more than 100. This is because the delta of an in-the-money American option goes to 100 more quickly than an equivalent European option. At the same time, the companion out-of-the-money option still retains some delta value. As a result, if we calculate the delta of the synthetic underlying (long call and short put) by adding the American call delta and subtracting the American put delta, we find that the deltas add up to more than 100. Figure 16-12 shows the American delta values for the 100 synthetic under the same conditions as in our preceding example:

Time to expiration = 7 weeks
Interest rate = 6.00 percent
Dividend = 1.00, payable in 4 weeks
Volatility = 25 percent

Higher volatility tends to reduce the differences between American and European options, so the delta of the synthetic will remain closer to 100.

Because delta values are affected by the likelihood of early exercise, arbitrage strategies such as conversions and reversals, boxes, and rolls, which may be delta neutral if all options are European, may not be delta neutral if the options are American. Although these strategies may deviate from delta neutral

Figure 16-12 Delta of the 100 synthetic (100 call delta − 100 put delta) if all options are American.

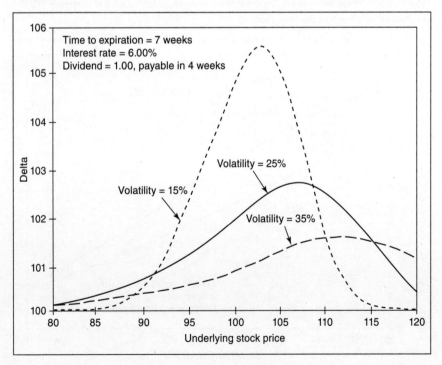

only by a small amount, the fact that they are often done in large sizes can result in additional risk that a trader should not ignore.

An American pricing model is necessary to evaluate individual American options, but it may still be possible to estimate the value of some strategies without the use of a pricing model. For example, suppose we know the following:

Time to expiration = 24 days
Interest rate = 6.00 percent
Dividend = 0.60, payable in 9 days

What should be the value of a 100/110 box if all options are American? To answer this question, we can first evaluate an equivalent European box. Then we can adjust the box value depending on which options might be exercised early.

The value of the European box is simply the present value of the amount between exercise prices

$$\frac{110-100}{1+0.06 \times 24/265} \approx 9.96$$

Now we can consider the various possibilities for early exercise:

Case 1: Both the 100 and 110 put are exercised early. The puts will be exercised the day the dividend is paid. The box value will increase by the interest earned on 10.00 for 15 days

$$9.96 + (10 \times 0.06 \times 15/365) = 9.96 + 0.025 = 9.985$$

Case 2: Both the 100 and 110 call are exercised early. The calls will be exercised the day before the dividend is paid. The box value will increase by the interest earned on 10.00 for 16 days

$$9.96 + (10 \times 0.06 \times 16/365) = 9.96 + 0.026 = 9.986$$

Case 3: Only the 110 put is exercised early. The box value will increase by the interest earned on 110 for 15 days

$$9.96 + (110 \times 0.06 \times 15/365) = 9.96 + 0.271 = 10.231$$

Case 4: Only the 100 call is exercised early. The box value will increase by the amount of the dividend less the interest cost on 100 for 16 days

$$9.96 + 0.60 - (100 \times 0.06 \times 16/365) = 9.96 + 0.60 - 0.263 = 10.297$$

Case 5: Both the 100 call and 110 put are exercised early. The box value will increase by the amount of the dividend plus the interest earned on 110 for 15 days less the interest cost on 100 for 16 days

$$9.96 + 0.60 + (110 \times 0.06 \times 15/365) - (100 \times 0.06 \times 16/365)$$
$$= 9.96 + 0.60 + 0.271 - 0.263 = 10.568$$

At very low stock prices, where both puts are early exercise candidates, and at very high stock prices, where both calls are early exercise candidates, the box will have a value close to 9.99. If one option, either the 100 call or 110 put, is an early exercise candidate, the value of the box will be somewhere between 10.23 and 10.30. Finally, the box will have its maximum value of approximately 10.57 if both the 100 call and the 110 put are early exercise candidates. This will occur if both options are in the money, most likely with the stock price close to 105. Volatility must also be low because in a high-volatility market, no one will want to give up an option's volatility value by exercising early. The value of the 100/110 box at different stock prices and under three different volatility assumptions is shown in Figure 16-13.

The difference between European and American values is usually greatest for options on dividend-paying stocks. But even futures options, if the options are subject to stock-type settlement, have some additional early exercise value. We can see this in Figure 16-14, the value of a 90 call on a futures contract, where

Time to expiration = 3 months
Interest rate = 8.00 percent
Volatility = 25 percent

The difference between the European and American option values is shown in Figure 16-15. Unlike a stock option, where there is a maximum difference, the difference for options on futures continues to increase as the option goes further into the money. This is because the early exercise value depends on the interest that can be earned on the option's intrinsic value. And the more deeply in the

Figure 16-13 Value of a 100/110 box if all options are American.

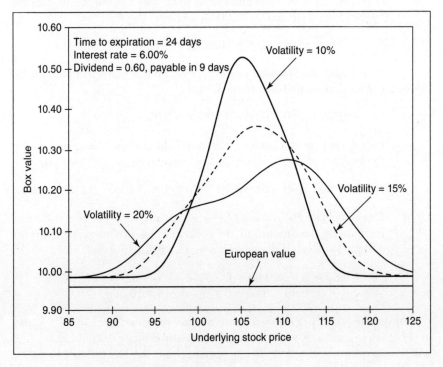

Figure 16-14 Theoretical value of a 90 call on a futures contract where the option is subject to stock-type settlement.

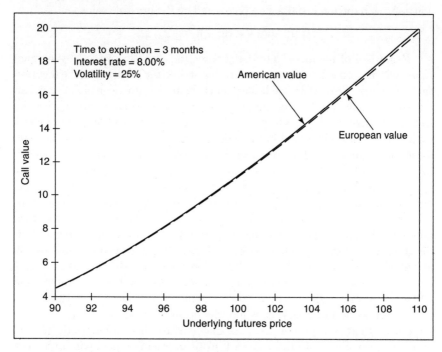

Figure 16-15 Difference between the theoretical value of an American and European 90 call on a futures contract where the options are subject to stock-type settlement (American value – European value).

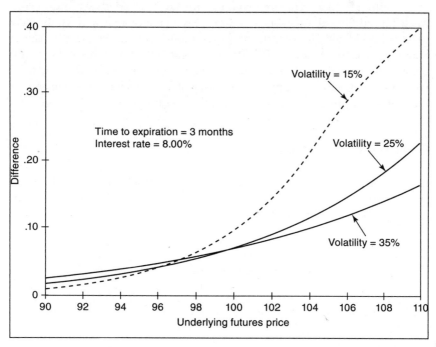

money, the greater the intrinsic value. In our example, with the underlying futures contract trading at 110, the additional early exercise value for the 90 call will approach the interest that can be earned on the intrinsic value

$$(110 - 90) \times 0.08 \times 3/12 = 0.40$$

Regardless of the model a trader chooses, the accuracy of model-generated values will depend at least as much on the inputs into the model as on the theoretical accuracy of the model itself. If a trader evaluates an American option using an incorrect volatility, an incorrect interest rate, or an incorrect underlying price, the fact that he derives his values from an American rather than a European model is likely to make little difference. Both models will generate incorrect values because the inputs are incorrect. The American model may produce less error, but that will be small consolation if the incorrect inputs lead to a large trading loss.

The importance of early exercise is greatest when there is a significant difference between the cost of carrying an option position and the cost of carrying a position in the underlying contract. This difference can be relatively large in the stock option market, where the cash outlay required to buy stock is much greater than the cash outlay required to buy options. Moreover, dividend considerations will also affect the cost of carrying a stock position compared with the cost of carrying an option position. A trader in a stock option market will usually find that the additional accuracy afforded by an American model will indeed be worthwhile.

In futures options markets, where the options are subject to futures-type settlement, there is no cost of carry associated with either options or the underlying futures contract. In this case, a European pricing model will suffice because there is no difference between European and American option values. Even if options on futures are subject to stock-type settlement, there is a relatively small cost associated with carrying an option position because the price of the option is small compared with the price of the underlying futures contract. The additional value for early exercise is therefore small and is only likely to be a consideration for very deeply in-the-money options. Practical considerations, such as the accuracy of the trader's volatility estimate, his ability to anticipate directional trends in the underlying market, and his ability to control risk through effective spreading strategies, will far outweigh any small advantage gained by using an American rather than a European model.[7]

Early Exercise Strategies

Early exercise of an option is a right rather than an obligation, and there are strategies that depend on someone making an error and not exercising an option early when it ought to be exercised. For example, consider this situation:

Stock price = 98.75
Time to expiration = 5 days
Dividend = 1.00, payable tomorrow

---

[7] Early exercise considerations may also be important in a foreign-exchange market if the interest rates associated with the domestic currency (the currency in which the option is settled) and foreign currency (the currency to be delivered in the event of exercise) are significantly different.

Suppose that there is a 90 call that is American and ought to be exercised today in order not to lose the dividend of 1.00. If this is true, the option ought to be worth approximately parity, or 8.75. Suppose that a trader is able to sell a 90 call for 8.75 and at the same time buy 100 shares of stock for 98.75. Because the 90 call ought to be exercised today, the trader probably will be assigned, requiring him to sell the stock at 90. If this occurs, excluding transaction costs, the trader will break even:

Sell the 90 call	+8.75
Buy stock	−98.75
On assignment, sell stock at 90	+90.00
	0

But suppose that the trader is not assigned on the 90 call. If the stock opens unchanged, its new price will be 97.75 (the stock price of 98.75 less the dividend of 1.00). Because the call is trading at parity, it will open at approximately 7.75. The trader will show a loss of 1.00 on the stock and a profit of 1.00 on the 90 call. But the trader, because he owns the stock, will also receive the dividend. Excluding transaction costs, the profit for the entire position will be equal to the dividend of 1.00.

In a *dividend play*, as the ex-dividend day approaches, a trader will try to sell deeply in-the-money calls and simultaneously buy an equal amount of stock. If the trader is assigned on the calls, as he should be, he will essentially break even. But, if he is not assigned, he will show a profit approximately equal to the amount of the dividend. What is the likelihood of the trader being assigned? Because assignment for most exchange-traded options is random, one determinant is the amount of open interest in the call that was sold. The more outstanding call options, the lower the likelihood of assignment. A second determinant is the relative sophistication of the market—whether most market participants are familiar with the criteria for early exercise. Dividend plays were much more common in the early days of option trading when the market was less sophisticated and many options that should have been exercised were not. As markets have become more efficient, only a professional trader with very low transaction costs will try to take advantage of such a possibility. Even then, he may find that he is assigned on the great majority of calls he has sold.

A trader also might attempt to execute an *interest play* by selling stock and simultaneously selling deeply in-the-money American puts that ought to be exercised early. If the puts are not exercised, the trader will profit by the amount of the interest he can earn on the exercise price (the proceeds of the stock sale and the put sale combined). This profit will continue to accrue as long as the puts remain unexercised. If the puts are exercised, the trader does no worse than break even. Again, only a professional trader, with low transaction costs, is likely to attempt such a strategy.

If options are subject to stock-type settlement, an interest play can also be done in a futures option market by either purchasing a futures contract and simultaneously selling a deeply in-the-money call or selling a futures contract and simultaneously selling a deeply in-the-money put. If the option is deeply enough in the money, it ought to be exercised early. But, if the option remains unexercised, the trader will continue to earn interest on the proceeds from the option sale. Because the amount on which the trader will earn interest is approximately the intrinsic value (the difference between the exercise price and futures price), this will not be as profitable as a similar strategy in the stock option market where the trader will earn interest on the exercise price. Still, if the transaction costs are low enough, it may be worthwhile.

Instead of entering into an early exercise strategy by selling options and trading the underlying contract, a trader may also be able to execute the strategy by trading deeply in-the-money call or put spreads. In our dividend-play example, the trader sold 90 calls and bought stock. Suppose that both the 85 call and the 90 call ought to be exercised to avoid losing the dividend. If this is true, the 85/90 call spread ought to be worth 5.00, exactly the difference between exercise prices. One might assume that if requested, a market maker will quote a bid price for this spread below 5.00, perhaps 4.90, and an ask price for the spread above 5.00, perhaps 5.10. In fact, a market maker might quote an identical bid and ask price of 5.00. This may seem illogical, quoting the same bid and ask price, but consider what will happen if the market maker is able to either buy or sell the spread at a price of 5.00.

If the market maker buys the spread (i.e., buy the 85 call, sell the 90 call), he will immediately exercise the 85 call, thereby purchasing stock. He has effectively entered into the same dividend play that we originally described (i.e., short call, long stock). If he is not assigned on the 90 call, he will again profit by the amount of the dividend. If, instead, the market maker sells the spread (i.e., sell the 85 call, buy the 90 call), he will immediately exercise the 90 call. Now he has executed the dividend play by purchasing stock and selling the 85 call. If he is not assigned on the 85 call, he will again profit by the amount of the dividend. The market maker is willing to give up the edge on the bid-ask spread in return for the potential profit that will result if the short options go unexercised.

Early Exercise Risk

How concerned should a trader be that an option that he has sold will be exercised early? "What will happen if I am suddenly assigned?" Early assignment can sometimes result in a loss. But there are many factors that can cause a trader to lose money; early exercise is only one such factor. A trader should be prepared to deal with the possibility of early exercise, just as he should be prepared to deal with the possibility of movement in the price of the underlying contract or the possibility of changes in implied volatility. Margin requirements established by the clearinghouses often require a trader to keep sufficient funds in his account to cover the possibility of early assignment. But this is not always true. If the trader is short deeply in-the-money options, an early assignment notice may cause a cash squeeze. If this happens, he will need sufficient capital to cover the situation. Otherwise, he may be forced to liquidate some or all of the remaining position. And forced liquidations are invariably losing propositions.

In spite of the risk of early assignment, it should rarely come as a surprise. A trader need only ask himself, "If I owned this option, would I logically exercise it now?" If the answer is yes then the trader ought to be prepared for assignment. If the answer is no and the trader is still assigned, it is probably good for the trader. It means that someone has mistakenly abandoned the option's interest or volatility value. When that happens, the trader who is assigned will find that he is the recipient of an unexpected gift.

17

Hedging with Options

Futures and options were originally introduced as insurance contracts, enabling market participants to transfer the risk of holding a position in the underlying instrument from one party to another. But unlike a futures contract, which essentially transfers all the risk, an option transfers only part of the risk. In this respect, an option acts much more like a traditional insurance policy than does a futures contract.

Even though options were originally intended to function as insurance policies, option markets have evolved to the point where, in most markets, hedgers (those wanting to protect an existing position) make up only a small portion of market participants. Other traders, including arbitrageurs, speculators, and spreaders, typically outnumber true hedgers. Nevertheless, hedgers still represent an important force in the marketplace, and any active market participant ought to be aware of the strategies a hedger might use to protect a position.

Many hedgers come to the marketplace as either *natural longs* or *natural shorts*. Through the course of normal business activity, they will profit from either a rise or fall in the price of some underlying instrument. The producer of a commodity is a natural long; if the price of the commodity rises, the producer will receive more when he sells in the marketplace. The user of a commodity is a natural short; if the price of the commodity falls, the user will have to pay less for it when he buys in the marketplace. In the same way, lenders and borrowers are natural longs and shorts in terms of interest rates. A rise in interest rates will help lenders and hurt borrowers. A decline in interest rates will have the opposite effect.

Other potential hedgers come to the marketplace because they have voluntarily chosen to take a long or short position and now wish to lay off part or all of the risk of that position. A speculator in a commodity may have taken a long or short position but wishes to temporarily reduce the risk associated with an outright long or short position. A fund manager may hold a portfolio of stocks but believes that the value of the portfolio may decline in the short term. If so, it may be less expensive to temporarily hedge the stocks with options or futures than to sell the stocks and buy them back at a later date.

As with insurance, there is a cost to hedging. The cost may be immediately apparent in the form of a cash outlay. But the cost may also be more subtle, either in terms of lost profit opportunity or in terms of additional risk under some circumstances. Every hedging decision is a tradeoff: what is the hedger willing to give up under one set of market conditions in return for protection under a different set of market conditions. A hedger with a long position who wants to protect his downside will almost certainly have to give up something on the upside; a hedger with a short position who wants to protect his upside will have to give up something on the downside.

Protective Calls and Puts

The simplest way to hedge an underlying position using options is to purchase either a put to protect a long position or a call to protect a short position. In each case, if the market moves adversely, the hedger is insulated from any loss beyond the exercise price. The difference between the exercise price and the current price of the underlying is similar to the deductible portion of an insurance policy. The price of the option is similar to the premium that one has to pay for the insurance policy.

Consider an American firm that expects to take delivery of €1 million worth of German goods in six months. If the contract requires payment in euros at the time of delivery, the American firm has acquired a short position in euros against U.S. dollars. If over the next six months the euro rises against the dollar, the goods will cost more in dollars; if the euro falls, the goods will cost less. If the euro is currently trading at 1.35 ($1.35 per euro) and remains there for the next six months, the cost to the American firm will be $1,350,000. If, however, at delivery the euro has risen to 1.45 ($1.45 per euro), the cost to the American firm will be $1,450,000.

The American firm can offset the risk it has acquired by purchasing a call option on euros, for example, a 1.40 call. For a complete hedge, the underlying contract will be €1 million, and the option will have an expiration date corresponding to the date on which payment is required. If the value of the euro begins to rise against the U.S. dollar, the firm will have to pay a higher price than expected when it takes delivery of the goods in six months. But the price it will have to pay for euros can never be greater than 1.40. If the price is greater than 1.40 at expiration, the firm will simply exercise its call, effectively purchasing euros at 1.40. If the price of euros is less than 1.40 at expiration, the firm will let the option expire worthless because it will be cheaper to purchase euros in the open market.

When used to hedge interest-rate risk, protective options are sometimes referred to as *caps* and *floors*. A firm that borrows funds at a variable interest rate has a short interest-rate position—falling interest rates will reduce its cost of borrowing, while rising interest rates will increase its costs. To *cap* the upside risk, the firm can purchase an interest-rate call, thereby establishing a maximum amount it will have to pay for borrowed funds. No matter how high interest rates rise, the borrower will never have to pay more than the cap's exercise price.

An institution that lends funds at a variable interest rate has a long interest-rate position—rising interest rates will increase its returns, while falling interest rates will reduce its returns. To set a *floor* on its downside risk, the institution can purchase an interest-rate put, thereby establishing a minimum amount it will receive for loaned funds. No matter how low interest rates fall, the lender will never receive less than the floor's exercise price.

A hedger who chooses to purchase a call to protect a short position or a put to protect a long position has risk limited by the exercise price of the option. At the same time, the hedger still maintains open-ended profit potential. If the underlying market moves in the hedger's favor, he can let the option expire and take advantage of the position in the open market. If, in our example, the euro falls to 1.25 at the time of delivery, the firm will simply let the 1.40 call expire unexercised. At the same time, the firm will purchase €1 million for $1,250,000, resulting in a windfall of $100,000.

There is a cost involved in buying insurance in the form of a protective call or put, namely, the price of the option. The cost of the insurance is commensurate with the amount of protection afforded by the option. If the price of a six-month 1.40 call is 0.02, the firm will pay an extra $20,000 (0.02 × 1 million) no matter what happens. A call option with a higher exercise price will cost less, but it also offers less protection in the form of an additional deductible amount. If the firm chooses to purchase a 1.45 call trading at .01, the cost for this insurance will only be $10,000 (0.01 × 1 million), but the firm will have to bear any loss up to a euro price of 1.45. Only above 1.45 is the firm fully protected. In the same way, a lower-exercise-price call will offer additional protection but at a higher price. A 1.35 call will protect the firm against any rise above 1.35, but if the price of the call is 0.04, the purchase of this protection will add an additional $40,000 (0.04 × 1 million) to the final cost.

The cost of purchasing a protective option and the insurance afforded by the strategy are shown in Figures 17-1 (protective put) and 17-2 (protective call).

Figure 17-1 Long an underlying position and long a protective put.

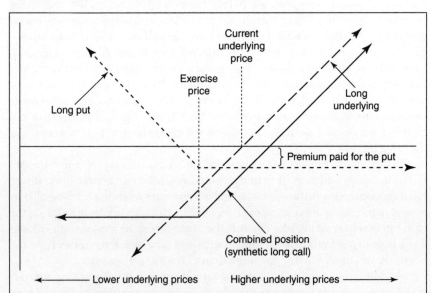

Figure 17-2 Short an underlying position and long a protective call.

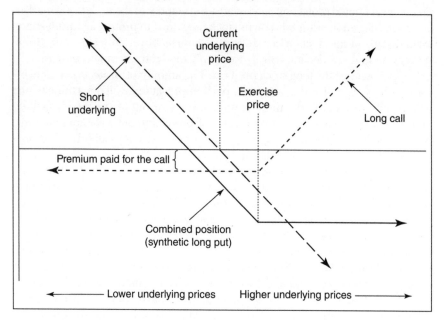

Because each strategy combines an underlying position with a long option position, it follows from Chapter 14 that the resulting protected position is a synthetic long option

$$\text{Short underlying} + \text{long call} \approx \text{synthetic long put}$$
$$\text{Long underlying} + \text{long put} \approx \text{synthetic long call}$$

A hedger who buys a put to protect a long underlying position has effectively created a long call position at the same exercise price. A hedger who buys a call to protect a short underlying position has effectively created long put position. In our example, if the firm purchases a 1.40 call to protect a short euro position, the combined position (i.e., short underlying, long call) is equivalent to owning a 1.40 put.

Which protective option should a hedger buy? This depends on the amount of risk the hedger is willing to bear, something that each hedger must determine individually. One thing is certain: there will always be a cost associated with the purchase of a protective option. If the insurance afforded by the option enables the hedger to protect his financial position, the cost may be worthwhile.

Covered Writes

If a hedger is averse to paying for protective options, which offer limited and well-defined risk, the hedger may instead consider selling, or writing, an option against an underlying position. This *covered write* (sometimes referred to as an *overwrite*) does not offer the limited risk afforded by the purchase of a protective option but does have the obvious advantage of creating an immediate cash credit. This credit offers limited protection against an adverse move in the underlying market.

Consider an investor who owns stock but wants to protect against a short-term decline in the stock price. He can, of course, buy a protective put. But if he believes that any decline is likely to be only moderate, he might instead sell a call option against the long stock position. The amount of protection the investor is seeking, as well as the potential upside appreciation, will determine which call he sells, whether in the money, at the money, or out of the money. Selling an in-the-money call offers a high degree of protection but will eliminate most of the upside profit potential. Selling an out-of-the-money call offers less protection but leaves room for additional upside profit.

Suppose that an investor owns a stock that is currently trading at 100. If he sells a 95 call at a price of 6.50, the sale of the call will offer a high degree of protection against a decline in the price of the stock. As long as the stock declines by no more than 6.50 to 93.50, the investor will do no worse than break even. Unfortunately, if the stock begins to rise, there will be no opportunity to participate in the rising stock price because the stock will be called away when the investor is assigned on the 95 call. Still, even if the stock rises, the investor will at least profit by the time premium of 1.50 that he received from the sale of the 95 call.

On the other hand, if the investor wants to participate in upside movement in the stock and is also willing to accept less protection on the downside, he might sell a 105 call. If the 105 call is trading at a price of 2.00, the sale of this option will only protect the investor down to a stock price of 98. But, if the stock price rises, the investor will participate up to a price of 105. Above 105, he can expect the stock to be called away, eliminating any further profit.

Which option should the investor sell? This is a subjective decision based on how much risk the investor is willing to accept, as well as the amount of upside appreciation in which he wants to participate. Many covered writes involve selling at-the-money options. Such options offer less protection than in-the-money calls and less profit potential than out-of-the-money options. But an at-the-money option has the greatest amount of time premium. If the market remains close to its current price, a position that is hedged by selling at-the-money options will show the greatest amount of appreciation.

The characteristics of a covered write and the protection afforded by the strategy are shown in Figures 17-3 (covered call) and 17-4 (covered put). Because each strategy combines an underlying position with a short option position, it follows from Chapter 14 that the resulting protected position is a synthetic short option:

Long underlying + short call ≈ synthetic short put
Short underlying + short put ≈ synthetic short call

A hedger who sells a call against a long underlying position has effectively created a short put position at the same exercise price. A hedger who sells a put to protect a short underlying position has effectively created short call put position. In our example, if the hedger sells a 105 call to protect a long stock position, the combined position (i.e., long underlying, short call) is equivalent to selling a 105 put.

Figure 17-3 Long an underlying position and short a covered call.

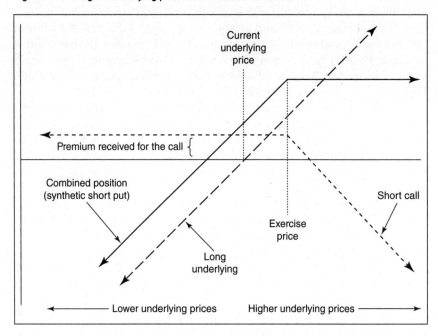

Current
underlying
price

Premium received for the call {

Combined position
(synthetic short put)

Short call

Exercise
price

Long
underlying

◄——— Lower underlying prices   Higher underlying prices ———►

Selling a covered call against a long stock position is one of the most pop-ular hedging strategies in equity option markets. When executed all at one time—buying stock and simultaneously selling a call on the stock—the strategy is referred to as a *buy/write*. The December 105 buy/write consists of buying

Figure 17-4 Short an underlying position and short a covered put.

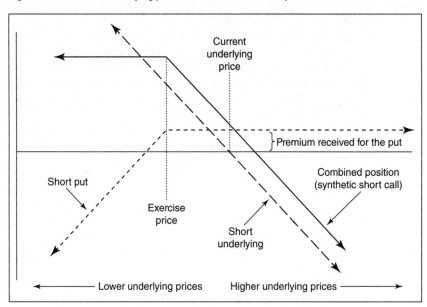

Current
underlying
price

Premium received for the put

Short put

Combined position
(synthetic short call)

Exercise
price

Short
underlying

◄——— Lower underlying prices   Higher underlying prices ———►

one stock contract (usually 100 shares) and simultaneously selling a December 105 call. As with any spread, it can be quoted as a single price (the stock price – the call price) and executed with a single counterparty. With a stock trading at 100 and the December 105 call trading at 2.00, the December 105 buy/write is trading at 98.00. The price quoted by a market maker might be 97.90 – 98.10. In total, the market maker is willing to buy the stock and sell the call for 97.90. He is willing to sell the stock and buy the call for 98.10.

Buy/writes are such common strategies that some exchanges publish indexes reflecting the performance of the strategy, usually against a major stock index. The Chicago Board Options Exchange BuyWrite Index (BXM) reflects the performance of a strategy consisting of buying a Standard and Poor's (S&P) 500 Index (SPX) portfolio and each month selling a slightly out-of-the-money one-month S&P 500 Index call option.[1]

A covered write can also be used to set a target price for either buying or selling an underlying instrument. An investor who owns a stock may decide that if the stock reaches a certain price, he will be willing to sell. By selling a call with an exercise price equal to the target price, the investor has effectively locked in the sale if the stock reaches the exercise price. If the stock does not reach the exercise price, the investor still gets to keep the premium received from the sale of the call.

Similarly, an investor who is willing to buy stock if the price declines by some given amount can sell a put with an exercise price equal to the target purchase price. If the stock falls below the exercise price, the investor will be assigned on the put, forcing him to purchase the stock. But that was his original intention. If the stock fails to fall below the exercise price, the investor gets to keep the premium received from the sale of the put. This strategy of selling puts to trigger the purchase of stock is often used by companies that want to initiate a buy-back program for their stock. By selling puts with exercise prices equal to the target buy-back price, the company either buys back its own stock or profits by the amount of the put premium.

The primary difference between selling a call to set a sale price and selling a put to set a purchase price is the way in which the trade is secured. The sale of a call is secured with ownership of the stock. But the sale of the put must be secured with enough cash to support the purchase of the stock should the put be exercised. The sale of a *cash-secured put* requires the investor to keep on deposit cash equal to the exercise price of the put. If the put is European with no possibility of early exercise, the investor can keep on deposit cash equal to the present value of the exercise price

$$\frac{X}{1 + r \times t}$$

The purchase of a protective option and the sale of a covered option are the two most common hedging strategies involving options. If given a choice between these strategies, which one should a hedger choose? In theory, the hedger ought to base his decision on the same criteria used by a trader: price versus value. If option

---

[1] A complete description of the CBOE Buy/Write Index, as well as its historical performance, can be found at http://www.cboe.com/micro/bxm/.

prices seem low, the purchase of a protective option makes sense. If option prices seem high, the sale of a covered option makes sense. From a trader's point of view, *low* or *high* is typically expressed in terms of implied volatility. By comparing implied volatility with the expected volatility over the life of the option, a hedger ought to be able to make a sensible determination as to whether he wants to buy or sell options. Of course, he is still left with the question of which exercise price to choose. This will depend on the amount of adverse or favorable movement the hedger foresees, as well as the risk he is willing to accept if he is wrong.

While theoretical considerations often play a role in a hedger's decision, these may be less important than practical considerations. If a hedger knows that a move in the underlying contract beyond a certain price will represent a threat to his business, then the purchase of a protective option at that exercise may be the most sensible strategy regardless of whether the option is theoretically overpriced.[2]

Many hedgers seem to have an aversion to buying protective options. "Why should I pay for an option when I will probably lose the premium?" This is, indeed, true. Most protective options do expire out of the money. The reasoning, however, seems illogical when one considers that most people willingly purchase insurance to protect their personal property. And the great majority of insurance policies expire without claims ever being made against them: houses do not burn down; people do not die; and cars are not stolen. This is the reason insurance companies make a profit. But most people do not buy insurance to make a profit. They do so for the peace of mind that the insurance policy affords. The same philosophy ought to apply to the purchase of options. If a hedger needs well-defined protection, the purchase of an option may be the best choice regardless of the fact that the option will most often expire worthless.

Collars

A hedger may want the limited risk afforded by the purchase of a protective option but may also be reluctant to pay the premium associated with such a strategy. What can he do? A *collar* involves simultaneously purchasing a protective option and selling a covered option against a position in an underlying contract.[3] Collars are popular hedging tools because they offer known protection at a low cost. At the same time, they still allow a hedger to participate, at least partially, in favorable market movement. With an underlying stock trading at 100, a hedger with a long position might choose to buy a 95 put and at the same time sell a 105 call. The hedger is insulated from any fall in price below 95 because he can then exercise his put. At the same time, he can participate in any upward move up to 105.

The terms *long* and *short*, when applied to collars, typically refer to the underlying position. A long underlying position together with a protective put

---

[2] Of course, if options seem wildly overpriced, a hedger may be reluctant to buy a protective option. But this is an unlikely scenario. If option prices are high, there is usually a valid reason.

[3] The collar strategy goes by a wide variety of names, including *fence, tunnel, cylinder, range forward,* or *split-strike conversion.*

and covered call is a long collar. A short underlying position together with a protective call and covered put is a short collar. The characteristics of a collar are shown in Figures 17-5 and 17-6. Because every contract can be expressed as a synthetic equivalent, we can see that a long collar (Figure 17-5) is simply a bull vertical spread, while a short collar (Figure 17-6) is simply a bear vertical spread. Both strategies have limited risk and limited reward.

Because a collar is a vertical spread, it will have the risk characteristics described in Chapter 12. A long collar will always have a positive delta; a short collar will always have a negative delta. The gamma, theta, and vega will be determined by the choice of exercise prices. If the underlying price is closer to the protective option, the position will usually have a positive gamma, negative theta, and positive vega. If the underlying price is closer to the covered option, the position will usually have a negative gamma, positive theta, and negative vega. Unless one option is much further out of the money than the other, these risk measures are likely to be similar, resulting in only a small gamma, theta, and vega position. A hedger might also choose exercise prices such that the collar will be approximately neutral with respect to the gamma, theta, or vega.

Collars are also popular because the sale of the covered option may off-set some or all of the cost of the protective option. When the price of the protective option is greater than the price of the covered option, as it is in Figure 17-5, the midsection of the combined position will fall below the profit and loss (P&L) graph for the underlying position. When the price of the protective

Figure 17-5 Long collar (long an underlying contract, long a protective put, short a covered call).

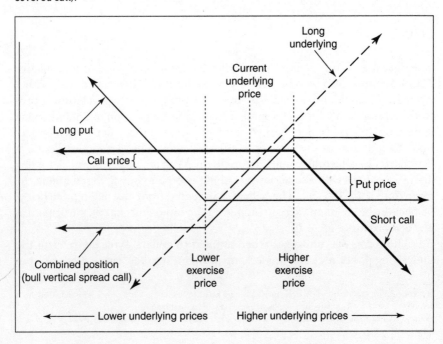

Figure 17-6 Short collar (short an underlying contract, long a protective call, short a covered put).

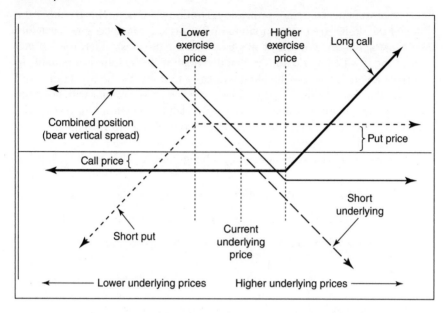

option is less than the price of the covered option, as it is in Figure 17-6, the midsection of the combined position will be above the P&L graph for the un-derlying position. If the price of the protective option and the covered option are the same, the strategy becomes a *zero-cost collar*. A summary of basic hedging strategies is given in Figure 17-7.

Figure 17-7 Summary of basic hedging strategies.

position	hedging strategy	advantages	disadvantages
long underlying	sell a future or forward	no downside risk	no upside profit potential
	buy a protective put	limited downside risk; unlimited upside profit potential	cost of the option
	sell a covered call	partial downside protection equal to the price of the call	unlimited downside risk; limited upside profit potential
	long collar (long a protective put/ short a covered call)	limited downside risk	limited upside profit potential
short underlying	buy a future or forward	no upside risk	no downside profit potential
	buy a protective call	limited upside risk; unlimited downside profit potential	cost of the option
	sell a covered put	partial upside protection equal to the cost of the put	unlimited upside risk; limited downside profit potential
	short collar (long a protective call/ short a covered put)	limited upside risk	limited downside profit potential

Complex Hedging Strategies

Because most hedgers are not professional option traders and have neither the time nor the desire to carefully analyze option prices, simple hedging strategies involving the purchase or sale of single options are the most widely used. However, if one is willing to do a more detailed analysis of options, it is possible to construct a wide variety of hedging strategies that involve both volatility and directional considerations. To do this, a hedger must be familiar with volatility and its impact on option values, as well as the delta as a measure of directional risk. The hedger can then combine his knowledge of options with the practical considerations of hedging.

As a first step in choosing a strategy, a hedger might consider the following:

1. Does the hedge need to offer protection against a worst-case scenario?

2. How much of the current directional risk should the hedge eliminate?

3. What additional risks is the hedger willing to accept?

A hedger who needs disaster insurance to protect against a worst-case scenario only has a choice of which option(s) to buy. Even so, he still needs to decide which exercise price to purchase and how many options. With a long position in an underlying contract currently trading at 100, a hedger decides to buy a put because he needs to limit the downside risk to some known and fixed amount. Which put should he buy?

If the hedger has determined that options are generally overpriced (i.e., implied volatility seems high), any option purchase will clearly be to the hedger's disadvantage. If his sole purpose is to hedge his downside risk without regard to upside profit potential, he ought to avoid options and hedge his position in the futures or forward market. If, however, he still wants upside profit potential, he must ask himself how much of a long position he wants to retain. If he is willing to retain 50 percent of his current long position, he ought to purchase puts with a total delta of −50. He can do this by purchasing one at-the-money put with a delta of −50 or several out-of-the-money puts whose deltas add up to −50. In a high-implied-volatility market, however, it is usually best to buy as few options as possible and sell as many options as possible. (This is analogous to constructing a ratio spread.) Hence, purchasing one put with a delta of −50 will be less costly, theoretically, than purchasing several puts with a total delta of −50. If the hedger wants to eliminate even more of the directional risk, say, 75 percent, under these circumstances, he will be better off purchasing one put with a delta of −75.

All other factors being equal, in a high-implied-volatility market, a hedger should buy as few options as possible and/or sell as many options as possible. Conversely, in a low-implied-volatility market, a hedger should buy as many options as possible and/or sell as few options as possible.

This means that if all options are overpriced (i.e., implied volatility seems high) and the hedger decides that he is willing to accept the unlimited downside risk that goes with the sale of a covered call, in theory, he ought to sell as many calls as possible to reach his hedging objectives. If he is trying to hedge 50 percent of his long underlying position, he can do a *ratio write* by selling several out-of-the-money calls with a total delta of 50 rather than selling a single at-the-money call with a delta of 50.

There is an obvious disadvantage if one sells multiple calls against a single long underlying position. Now the hedger not only has the unlimited downside risk that goes with a covered call position, but he also has unlimited upside risk because he has sold more calls than he can cover with the underlying. If the market moves up enough, he will be assigned on all the calls. Most hedgers want to restrict their unlimited risk to one direction, usually the direction of their natural position. A hedger with a long underlying position may be willing to accept unlimited downside risk, but he is probably unwilling to accept unlimited upside risk. A hedger with a short underlying position may be willing to accept unlimited upside risk, but he is probably unwilling to accept unlimited downside risk. A hedger who constructs a position with unlimited risk in either direction is presumably taking a volatility position. There is nothing wrong with this because volatility trading can be highly profitable. But a true hedger ought not lose sight of what his ultimate goal is—to protect an existing position and to keep the cost of this protection as low as possible.

A hedger can also protect a position by constructing one-to-one volatility spreads with deltas that yield the desired amount of protection. A hedger who wants to protect 50 percent of a short underlying position can buy or sell calendar spreads or butterflies with a total delta of +50. Such spreads offer partial protection within a range. The entire position still has unlimited upside risk but also retains unlimited downside profit potential. Such volatility spreads also give the hedger the choice of buying or selling volatility. If implied volatility is generally low, with the underlying market currently at 100, the hedger might protect a short underlying position by purchasing a 110 call calendar spread (i.e., purchase a long-term 110 call, sell a short-term 110 call). This spread has a positive delta and is also theoretically attractive because the low implied volatility makes a long calendar spread relatively inexpensive. If the 110 call calendar spread has a delta of +25, to hedge 50 percent of his directional risk, the hedger can buy two spreads for each short underlying position. Conversely, if implied volatility is high, the hedger can consider selling calendar spreads. Now he will have to choose a lower exercise price to achieve a positive delta. If he sells the 90 call calendar spread (i.e., purchase a short-term 90 call, sell a long-term 90 call), he will have a position with a positive delta and a positive theoretical edge. If he wants to protect 75 percent of his position and the spread has a delta of +25, he can sell the spread three times for each underlying position. (See Chapter 11 for characteristics of calendar spreads and butterflies.)

A hedger can also buy or sell vertical spreads to achieve a desired amount of protection. Depending on whether options are generally underpriced or overpriced (i.e., implied volatility is excessively low or high), the hedger will work around the at-the-money option. With the underlying market currently at 100, the hedger who wants to protect a long position can execute a bear vertical spread (i.e., sell the lower exercise price, buy the higher exercise price).

If implied volatility is high, he will prefer to sell an at-the-money option and buy an option at a higher exercise price. If implied volatility is low, he will prefer to buy an in-the-money option and sell an option at a lower exercise price. Each spread will have a negative delta but will also have a positive theoretical edge because the at-the-money option is the most sensitive to changes in volatility. (See Chapter 12 for characteristics of vertical spreads.)

As is obvious, using options to hedge a position can be just as complex as using options to construct trading strategies. Many factors go into the decision-making process. When a potential hedger is confronted for the first time with the multitude of possible strategies, he can understandably feel overwhelmed, to the point where he decides to abandon options completely. Perhaps a better approach is to consider a limited number of strategies (perhaps four or five) that make sense and compare the various risk-reward characteristics of the strategies. Given the hedger's general market outlook and his willingness or unwillingness to accept certain risks, it should then be possible to make an informed decision.

Hedging to Reduce Volatility

In addition to protecting a position against an adverse move in the underlying contract, hedging strategies have an additional important advantage—they tend to reduce the volatility of a position. To understand why this may be important, consider a portfolio manager who generates the following annual returns over a period of five years:

$$+19\% \quad -14\% \quad +27\% \quad -9\% \quad +22\%$$

His average annual return is

$$(19\% - 14\% + 27\% - 9\% + 22\%)/5 = +9\%$$

Now consider a second portfolio manager who generates these annual returns:

$$+25\% \quad -20\% \quad -23\% \quad +44 \quad +24$$

His average annual return is

$$(25\% - 20\% - 23\% + 44\% + 24\%)/5 = +10\%$$

Finally, a third portfolio manager generates these returns:

$$+35\% \quad +15 \quad -35 \quad +65\% \quad -20\%$$

His average annual return is

$$(35\% + 15\% - 35\% + 65\% - 20\%)/5 = +12\%$$

Portfolio Manager 3 trumpets his average annual return of 12 percent compared with Portfolio Managers 1 and 2, with returns of only 9 and 10 percent. Clearly, we ought to invest our money with Portfolio Manager 3. Or should we?

Perhaps we should consider not only what is happening each year but also how each portfolio performs over the entire five-year period. We can do this by taking the product of all the annual changes for each portfolio:

Portfolio 1: $1.19 \times 0.86 \times 1.27 \times 0.91 \times 1.22 = 1.4429$ (up 44.29%)
Portfolio 2: $1.25 \times 0.80 \times 0.77 \times 1.44 \times 1.24 = 1.3749$ (up 37.49%)
Portfolio 3: $1.35 \times 1.15 \times 0.65 \times 1.65 \times 0.80 = 1.3320$ (up 33.20%)

Even though Portfolio Manager 3 had the best average annual return, his portfolio fared the worst. Portfolio Manager 1, with the lowest annual return, fared the best, making 11 percent more over the five-year period than Portfolio Manager 3.

The explanation for this seemingly unexpected result has to do with the volatility, or standard deviation, of the returns. The returns for Portfolio Manager 3 fluctuated wildly from a high of +65 percent to a low of –35 percent. The returns for Portfolio Manger 1 fluctuated much less, between +27 percent and –14 percent. The greater volatility seemed to reduce the total return.

The results for each portfolio manager are summarized in Figure 17-8. We have also added a very boring Portfolio Manager 4, who plods along with a return of exactly 8 percent each year for the five-year period. In spite of having the lowest average return, his portfolio performed the best, gaining 46.93 percent over the entire period.

Our example does not mean that high volatility is unacceptable. A portfolio manager with highly volatile returns may still be preferable if his average return is also commensurably higher. This tradeoff between returns and volatility is often expressed by the *Sharpe ratio*, originally suggested by William Sharpe in 1966[4]

Average return/standard deviation of returns

The greater the Sharpe ratio, the more favorable the tradeoff between risk (volatility) and reward (returns). The standard deviation and the Sharpe ratio for all four portfolio managers are also given in Figure 17-8.

Figure 17-8 The greater the volatility, the lower the total return.

	year 1 returns	year 2 returns	year 3 returns	year 4 returns	year 5 returns	average annual return	total 5-year return	standard deviation	Sharpe ratio
Portfolio Manager 1:	+19%	–14%	+27%	–9%	+22%	+9%	+44.29%	+17.01%	.5291
Portfolio Manager 2:	+25%	–20%	–23%	+44%	+24%	+10%	+37.49%	+26.71%	.3744
Portfolio Manager 3:	+35%	+15%	–35%	+65%	–20%	+12%	+33.20%	+36.28%	.3308
Portfolio Manager 4:	+8%	+8%	+8%	+8%	+8%	+8%	+46.93%	0	----

---

[4] The returns used to calculate the Sharpe ratio are sometimes expressed as the returns in excess of some benchmark, such as a risk-free Treasury instrument.

Portfolio Insurance

Imagine that we hold a long position in an underlying asset such as stock and that we would like to protect our position against a possible decline in price over some period of time. One possible strategy is to purchase a protective put. Unfortunately, when we go into the market to purchase the put, we find that no market exists for options on our stock. What can we do?

If we were really able to purchase a put, our position would be

$$\text{Long stock} + \text{long put}$$

But we know that a long underlying position together with a long put is equivalent to a long call. What we really want is a long call position with the same exercise price and expiration date as the put that we wanted but were unable to buy.

What would be the characteristics of this call? We can determine this by using a theoretical pricing model. To do this, we need the basic inputs into the theoretical pricing model:

> Exercise price
> Time to expiration
> Underlying stock price
> Interest rate
> Volatility

Because we are not dependent on listed exercise prices and expiration dates (because none exist), the exercise price and expiration date can be of our own choosing. We can determine the stock price and interest rate from current market conditions. Only the volatility cannot be directly observed in the marketplace. But, if we have a database of historical price changes for the stock, we may be able to make a reasonable estimate of the stock's volatility.

Suppose that we feed all the inputs into a theoretical pricing model and determine that our intended call has a delta of 75. To replicate the call position, we need to own 75 percent of the underlying contract. We can achieve this by selling off 25 percent of our holdings in the stock. If we originally owned 1,000 shares, we need to sell 250 shares, leaving us with a long position of 750 shares.

Now suppose that at some later date we look at the new market conditions, recalculate the delta of the call, and find that it is now 60. To achieve the desired delta position, we must now sell off an additional 15 percent of our original holdings, or 150 shares. We are now long 600 shares of stock.

Suppose that we continue this process of periodically calculating the delta from current market conditions and buying or selling some percentage of our original holding in the underlying stock to achieve a position with the same delta as the presumed call option. Finally, suppose that at the target expiration date we buy back a sufficient amount of the stock so that we have 100 percent of our original holding. What should be the result of this entire process?

We are essentially going through the dynamic hedging process described in Chapter 8. Whereas in Chapter 8 we used dynamic hedging to capture the difference between an option's price in the marketplace and its theoretical value, in our current example, we cannot profit from a mispriced option because no option exists. But we can replicate the characteristics of the option to achieve a desired option position.

In Chapter 8 we presented a stock option example and a futures option example. In the stock option example, we bought a call at a price that was less than its theoretical value and then sold the call, through the dynamic hedging process, at a price that was equal to its theoretical value. In the futures option example, we sold a put at a price that was greater than its theoretical value and then bought the put, through the dynamic hedging process, at a price that was equal to its theoretical value. In both examples, we ended up with a profit equal to the difference between the option's price and its theoretical value.

Portfolio insurance, or *option replication*, is a method by which the dynamic hedging process is used to create a position with the same characteristics as an option. In theory, the method should achieve the same results as buying a protective option but without actually purchasing the option. Portfolio insurance can be used by a fund manager to insure the value of the securities in a portfolio against a drop in value. If a manager has a portfolio of securities currently valued at $100 million and wants to insure the value of the portfolio against a drop in value below $90 million, he can either buy a $90 million put or replicate the characteristics of a $90 million call. If he is unable to find someone willing to sell him a $90 million put, he can evaluate the characteristics of the $90 million call and continuously buy or sell a portion of his portfolio required to replicate the call position. In effect, he has created his own put.

Portfolio insurance strategies were widely used by fund managers prior to the stock market crash of 1987, especially by managers with a portfolio that tended to track a major index. If the portfolio manager wanted to buy protective puts but also believed that the prices of puts were inflated, he could create the puts himself at the "correct" theoretical value through the dynamic hedging process. Instead of buying or selling a portion of the portfolio, which could be expensive in terms of transaction costs, the portfolio manager could mimic the delta adjustments by buying or selling index futures to increase or reduce the total value of the portfolio. In return for a fee, firms that marketed portfolio insurance strategies assumed the responsibility of determining the characteristics of the option that the portfolio manager wanted to purchase by estimating the correct volatility and choosing the most appropriate option pricing model.[5] Some portfolio insurance firms generated additional fees by acting as a broker and executing the necessary adjustments in the index futures market.

Unfortunately, following the crash of 1987, practitioners came to realize that portfolio insurance would only achieve the desired results if the inputs into

---

[5] The firm most closely associated with portfolio insurance prior to the crash of 1987 was Los Angeles–based Leland, O'Brien, Rubinstein (with principals Hayne Leland, John O'Brien, and Mark Rubinstein).

the model were correct and the model itself was based on realistic assumptions.[6] No one foresaw the dramatic increase in volatility resulting from the crash, so the volatility input that was being used was clearly incorrect. At the same time, many of the model assumptions about dynamic hedging seemed to be violated in the real world. The upshot was that the cost of replicating an option through the dynamic hedging process became much more expensive than anyone had anticipated. As a result, portfolio insurance strategies fell out of favor with most fund managers.

---

[6] Some studies have suggested that the dynamic hedging required to implement portfolio insurance exacerbated the stock market crash of October 19, 1987. Because of the dramatic drop in the stock market, portfolio insurers were required to sell ever larger numbers of index futures contracts, creating a cascading effect in the market.

18

The Black-Scholes Model

Because of its importance as a foundation of option pricing theory, as well as its widespread use by traders, it will be worthwhile to take a closer look at the Black-Scholes model.[1] The discussion in this chapter is not meant to be a rigorous or detailed derivation of the model, which is better suited to a university textbook or to a class in financial engineering. Rather, we hope to present a more intuitive discussion of the workings of the model, as well as some observations on the values generated by the model.

Initially, rather than calculating the theoretical value of an option, Black and Scholes tried to answer this question: if the stock price moves randomly over time, but in a manner that is consistent with a constant interest rate and volatility, what must be the option price after each moment in time such that an option position that is correctly hedged will just break even? The answer to this question resulted in rather intimidating-looking equation

$$rS\frac{\partial C}{\partial S} + \frac{1}{2}\sigma^2 S^2 \frac{\partial^2 C}{\partial S^2} + \frac{\partial C}{\partial t} = rC$$

Although this equation might look mysterious to many readers, it is just a mathematician's way of expressing how changes in one set of variables—stock price S and time t—affect the value of something else, a call C. To determine the exact effect caused by changes in the variables, one must solve the equation.

Note that we did not refer to the volatility σ and interest rate r as variables. In the Black-Scholes equation, only the stock price and time are changing. As inputs into the model, the volatility and interest rate will affect the value of the

---

[1] The Black-Scholes model is sometimes referred to as the *Black-Scholes-Merton model* because Robert Merton, originally associated with the Massachusetts Institute of Technology, contributed significantly to the theory of option pricing. Merton and Scholes were jointly awarded the Nobel Prize in Economics in 1997 for their work on option pricing. Fischer Black, sadly, died in 1995.

option. But once they have been chosen, they are assumed to remain constant over the life of the option. This is consistent with the dynamic hedging examples in Chapter 8. Over the life of an option, we assumed that only the underlying price and time were changing. Everything else remained constant.

We have already encountered several of the components of the Black-Scholes equation in slightly different form. The terms

$$\frac{\partial C}{\partial S}, \quad \frac{\partial^2 C}{\partial S^2}, \quad \text{and} \quad \frac{\partial C}{\partial t}$$

are the more formal mathematical notation for the option's delta (Δ), gamma (Γ), and theta (Θ). The Black-Scholes equation states that changes in an option's value depend on the sensitivity of the option to changes in the stock price (the delta), the sensitivity of the option's delta to changes in the stock price (the gamma), and the sensitivity of the option to the passage of time (the theta).

Of course, the equation also includes volatility and interest-rate components. The interest-rate component plays two roles. First, because the Black-Scholes model values options from the forward price, the interest rate takes us from the spot price to the forward price (assuming that the stock pays no dividend). This spot-to-forward relationship appears in the equation as

$$rS$$

Second, the Black-Scholes equation initially gives us the expected value of the option as time passes. If we want to determine the option's theoretical value, we must discount the expected value backwards to get its present value. This expected-value-to-present-value relationship appears in the equation as

$$rC$$

Finally, there is a volatility component. The rate at which the delta changes depends not only on the gamma but on the speed at which the stock price is changing. The speed is expressed as a volatility or standard deviation σ. The volatility component and its effect on the gamma appear in the Black-Scholes equation as

$$\frac{1}{2}\sigma^2 S^2 \frac{\partial^2 C}{\partial S^2} = \frac{1}{2}\sigma^2 S^2\,\Gamma$$

We will not go into the formal derivation of the Black-Scholes equation in this text because it can be mathematically complex. But we might note that there is some similarity between the Black-Scholes equation and the method used in Chapter 7 to estimate the change in an option's value as the underlying price changes from S_1 to S_2. To approximate this change, we used the average delta over the price range

$$(S_1 - S_2) \times \Delta + (S_1 - S_2)^2 \times \Gamma/2 = (S_1 - S_2) \times \Delta + \tfrac{1}{2}(S_1 - S_2)^2 \times \Gamma$$

Recalling that

$$\frac{\partial C}{\partial S} \quad \text{and} \quad \frac{\partial^2 C}{\partial S^2}$$

represent the delta and gamma, we can see that there is a similarity between this relationship and the first two terms of the Black-Scholes equation.

$$(S_1 - S_2) \times \Delta + \tfrac{1}{2}(S_1 - S_2)^2 \times \Gamma$$

$$rS\frac{\partial C}{\partial S} + \frac{1}{2}\sigma^2 S^2 \frac{\partial^2 C}{\partial S^2}$$

The primary differences are the interest-rate component attached to S (the stock price must move from spot to forward) and the volatility component attached to the gamma. Although we assumed a discrete price change from S_1 to S_2, the Black-Scholes equation assumes an infinitesimally small, or instantaneous, price change.

This is, admittedly, a very simplistic attempt to explain the roles played by the various components in the Black-Scholes equation. However, even for someone who fully understands the model, being able to write out the equation does not necessarily yield a value. The real goal is to solve the equation so that it is possible to calculate the exact value of an option.

The solution to the Black-Scholes equation yields the well-known *Black-Scholes model*: if

> C = theoretical value of a European call
> S = the price of a non-dividend-paying stock
> X = exercise price
> t = time to expiration, in years
> σ = annual standard deviation (volatility) of the stock price, in percent
> r = annual interest rate
> $\ln$ = the natural logarithm
> e = the exponential function
> N = the cumulative normal distribution function

then

$$C = SN(d_1) - Xe^{-rt}N(d_2)$$

where

$$d_1 = \frac{\ln(S/X) + \left[r + \left(\sigma^2/2\right)\right]t}{\sigma\sqrt{t}}$$

and

$$d_2 = \frac{\ln(S/X) + \left[r - \left(\sigma^2/2\right)\right]t}{\sigma\sqrt{t}} = d_1 - \sigma\sqrt{t}$$

It may not be immediately apparent what the values in the Black-Scholes model represent, but one starting point is put-call parity, discussed in Chapter 15

$$C - P = \frac{F - X}{1 + r \times t}$$

If the underlying contract is a non-dividend-paying stock, the forward price is

$$F = S \times (1 + r \times t)$$

Substituting this into the put-call parity relationship gives us

$$C - P = \frac{S(1 + r \times t) - X}{1 + r \times t} = S - \frac{X}{1 + r \times t}$$

In our examples thus far, we have used simple interest. If, instead, we use continuous interest, rather than dividing by $1 + r \times t$, we can multiply by e^{-rt}. This gives us

$$C - P = S - Xe^{-rt}$$

Because a put can never be worth less than 0, we know from Chapter 16 that the lower arbitrage boundary for a European call option on stock is the greater of either 0 or

$$S - Xe^{-rt}$$

This expression looks similar to the Black-Scholes value for a call option, but without the terms $N(d_1)$ and $N(d_2)$ attached to S and Xe^{-rt}, respectively. What do $N(d_1)$ and $N(d_2)$ represent?

In Chapter 5, we proposed a very simple method for evaluating options by considering a series of underlying prices at expiration and assigning probabilities to each of those prices. Using this approach, the expected value for a call option is the sum of the intrinsic values multiplied by the probability associated with each underlying price

$$\sum_{i=1}^{n} p_i \max(S_i - X, 0)$$

To determine the option's intrinsic value, we combined the underlying price and exercise price into one expression $(S_i - X)$.

The Black-Scholes model takes a slightly different approach by separating the underlying price and exercise price into two distinct components and then asking two questions:

1. If held to expiration, what is the average value of all the stock above the exercise price?

2. If held to expiration, what is the likelihood that the owner of an option will end up paying the exercise price?

If we can answer these questions, the difference between the average value of the stock above the exercise price and the likelihood of paying the exercise price should equal the option's expected value.

To help explain the approach taken by Black and Scholes, let's consider a discrete distribution of stock prices at expiration, but one that more closely resembles a lognormal distribution with an extended right tail. Such a distribution, resulting from a total of 153 occurrences, is shown in Figure 18-1. Using this distribution, how might we evaluate a call option with an exercise price of $12\frac{1}{2}$?

First, we must determine the value of all stock above $12\frac{1}{2}$, that is, the value resulting from all occurrences that fall into troughs 13 through 27. The number of occurrences and the value of the occurrences in each trough are as follows:

Trough	Number of Occurrences	Stock Value
13	11	143
14	9	126
15	8	120
16	7	113
17	6	102
18	5	90
19	4	76
20	3	60
21	2	42
22	2	44
23	1	23
24	1	24
25	1	25
26	0	0
27	0	0
Total	60	987

The average value of all stock above the exercise price of 12½ is the total value, 987, divided by the total number of occurrences, 153

$$987/153 = 6.45$$

Figure 18-1

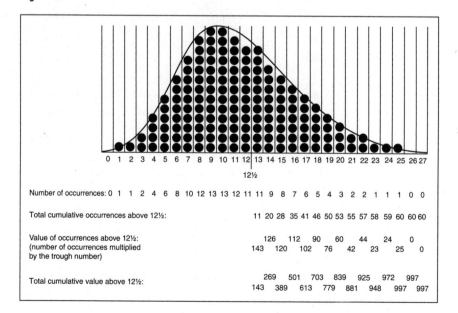

Next, we need to determine the likelihood that we will pay the exercise price of 12½. There are 60 occurrences where the option is in the money (the stock price is above 12½), but there are a total of 153 occurrences. The likelihood that we will pay the exercise price is

$$60/153 = 0.392$$

The average payout resulting from exercise of the option $0.392 \times 12\frac{1}{2} = 4.90$.

In the Black-Scholes model, the average value of all stock above the exercise price is given by $Se^{rt}N(d_1)$, where Se^{rt} is the forward price of the stock. The average amount we will have to pay is given by $XN(d_2)$. The expected value for a call option is the difference between these two numbers

$$Se^{rt}N(d_1) - XN(d_2) = 6.45 - 4.90 = 1.55$$

These terms are slightly different from the terms that appear in the model, $SN(d_1)$ and $Xe^{-rt}N(d_2)$, but we will show shortly how $Se^{rt}N(d_1)$ becomes $SN(d_1)$ and how $XN(d_2)$ becomes $Xe^{-rt}N(d_2)$.

We can confirm that 1.55 is the correct value (with slight rounding error) by returning to our original approach of adding up the intrinsic values multiplied by their probabilities (the number of occurrences divided by 153).

Trough	Intrinsic Value of the 12½ Call	Number of Occurrences	Probability	Option Value
13	0.5	11	0.0719	0.0359
14	1.5	9	0.0588	0.0882
15	2.5	8	0.0523	0.1307
16	3.5	7	0.0458	0.1601
17	4.5	6	0.0392	0.1765
18	5.5	5	0.0327	0.1797
19	6.5	4	0.0261	0.1699
20	7.5	3	0.0196	0.1471
21	8.5	2	0.0131	0.1111
22	9.5	2	0.0131	0.1242
23	10.5	1	0.0065	0.0686
24	11.5	1	0.0065	0.0752
25	12.5	1	0.0065	0.0817
26	13.5	0	0	0
27	14.5	0	0	0
Total option expected value:			1.5489	

This is essentially the approach taken by the Black and Scholes. The primary difference is that the Black-Scholes model, rather than using discrete outcomes as we did, assumes a continuous lognormal distribution.

n(x) and N(x)

Before continuing, it will be useful to define two important probability functions—$n(x)$ and $N(x)$. In this chapter and in previous discussions of volatility, we have often referred to the concept of a bell-shaped, or normal, distribution. Depending on the mean and standard deviation, there can be many different normal distributions, but $n(x)$, the *standard normal distribution*, is perhaps the most common. It has a mean of 0 and a standard deviation of 1. The standard normal distribution, shown in Figure 18-2, also has one very useful characteristic: the total area under the curve adds up to exactly 1. That is, the curve represents 100 percent of all occurrences that form a true normal distribution.

Although the standard normal distribution takes in 100 percent of all occurrences, we may want to know what percent of the occurrences fall within a specific portion of the standard normal distribution. This is given by $N(x)$, the *standard cumulative normal distribution function*. If x is some number of standard deviations, $N(x)$ returns the probability of getting an occurrence less than x by calculating the area under the standard normal distribution curve between the values of $-\infty$ and x, as shown in Figure 18-3. That is, $N(x)$ tells us what percentage of all possible occurrences fall between $-\infty$ and x. Obviously, $N(+\infty)$ must be 1.00 because 100 percent of all occurrences must fall between $-\infty$ and $+\infty$. And $N(-\infty)$ must be 0 because there can be no occurrences to the left of $-\infty$. Because the normal distribution curve is symmetrical, with 50 percent of the occurrences falling to the left of 0 and 50 percent falling to the right, $N(0)$ must equal 0.50. It also follows that the area under the curve between $-\infty$ and x must be equal to the area under the curve between $-x$ and $+\infty$, resulting in this useful relationship

$$N(x) = 1 - N(-x)$$

Figure 18-2 $n(x)$—the standard normal distribution curve with mean = 0 and standard deviation = 1.

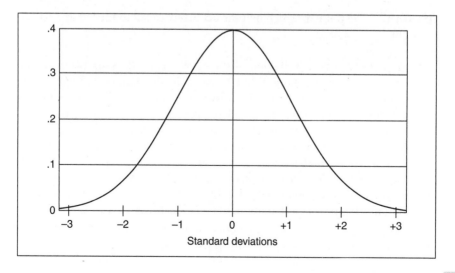

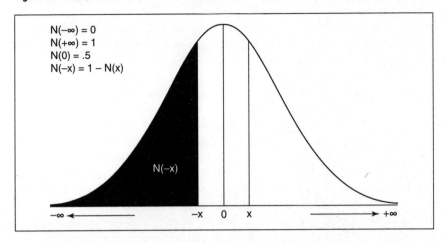

$N(-\infty) = 0$
$N(+\infty) = 1$
$N(0) = .5$
$N(-x) = 1 - N(x)$

$N(-x)$

−∞ ◄——————— −x   0   x   ———————► +∞

The Black-Scholes model makes all calculations using the probabilities associated with a normal distribution. This may seem inconsistent with our assumption that the prices of an underlying contract are lognormally distributed because a normal distribution and a lognormal distribution are clearly not the same. However, by making some adjustments to the value of *x*, we can use $N(x)$ to generate probabilities associated with a lognormal distribution.

It will also be useful to define three numbers used to describe many common distributions:

Mode. The peak of the distribution. The point at which the greatest number of occurrences take place.

Mean. The balance point of the distribution. The point at which half the value of the occurrences fall to the left and half to the right.

Median. The point at which half the occurrences fall to the left and half to the right.

In a perfect normal distribution, all these points fall in the same place, exactly in the middle of the distribution. But consider the distribution in Figure 18-1. The mode, mean, and median of this distribution all fall at different points, as shown in figure Figure 18-4. The mode is approximately 9.3, the mean is approximately 12.7, and the median is approximately 10.5. To make the appropriate adjustments to a lognormal distribution so that we can use the probabilities associated with a normal distribution, we must locate these numbers.

The Black-Scholes model begins by defining the relationship between the exercise price and the underlying price. In a normal distribution, this is simply $S - X$, but in a lognormal distribution, the relationship is

$$\ln\left(\frac{S}{X}\right)$$

Figure 18-4

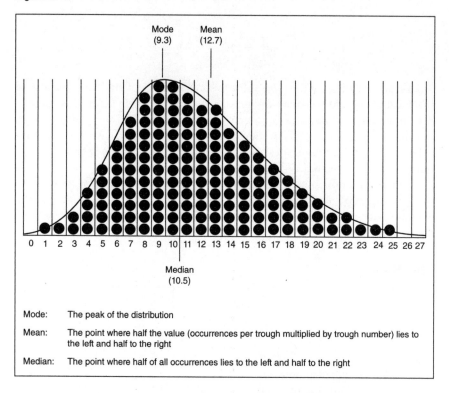

Mode: The peak of the distribution

Mean: The point where half the value (occurrences per trough multiplied by trough number) lies to the left and half to the right

Median: The point where half of all occurrences lies to the left and half to the right

If $S > X$, this value is positive, and the call is in the money; if $S < X$, the value is negative, and the call is out of the money.

Next, because options are valued off the forward price and the forward price is a function of interest rates, we must adjust this relationship by the interest component over the life of the option rt. This gives us[2]

$$\ln\left(\frac{S}{X}\right) + rt$$

The number of standard deviations associated with an occurrence depends on how far the occurrence is from the mean of the distribution. In a normal distribution, the mean, like the mode, is located in the exact center of the distribution. But in Figure 18-4, which approximates a lognormal distribution, with its elongated right tail, we can see that the mean must be somewhere to the right of the mode. How far to the right? This depends on the standard deviation of the lognormal distribution. The higher the standard deviation, the longer the right tail, and consequently, the further to the right we must shift the mean. Mathematically, the shift is equal to $\sigma^2 t/2$. Adding this adjustment gives us

$$\ln\left(\frac{S}{X}\right) + rt + \frac{\sigma^2 t}{2}$$

---

[2] We could in fact drop rt and at the same time replace S with its forward price Se^{rt}. The values are the same: $\ln(S/X) + rt = \ln(Se^{rt}/X)$.

Combining the interest-rate and volatility components gives us the numerator for d_1

$$\ln\left(\frac{S}{X}\right) + \left(r + \frac{\sigma^2}{2}\right)t$$

Finally, we must convert this value to some number of standard deviations. If we know the value of one standard deviation, we can divide by this value to determine the total number of standard deviations. In fact, we know that over any time period t, one standard deviation is equal to $\sigma\sqrt{t}$. If we divide by this value, the result, d_1, tells us, in standard deviations, how far the exercise price is from the mean when adjusted for a lognormal distribution

In the equation shown in Figure 18-5, the calculation of d_1 may seem somewhat complicated, but it is really just a collection of adjustments to the exercise price and underlying price that enable us to use a cumulative normal distribution function to calculate probabilities.

Figure 18-5

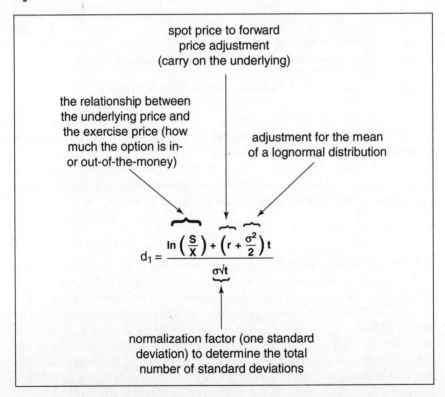

Once we have determined the value of d_1, multiplying the forward price of the stock by $N(d_1)$ gives us the average value of all stock above the exercise price at expiration.

Having calculated the average value of all stock above the exercise price, we still need to determine the likelihood that the option will be exercised. To do this, we need the median of the distribution, the point that exactly bisects the total number of occurrences. In Figure 18-4, we can see that the median in a lognormal distribution falls somewhere to the left of the mean. How far to the left? In fact, the median falls to the left by $\sigma\sqrt{t}$

$$d_2 = d_1 - \sigma\sqrt{t}$$

The value $N(d_2)$ uses the median to calculate the probability of the option being in the money at expiration and therefore being exercised. Multiplying this probability by the exercise price gives us the average amount we will pay at expiration if we own the option

$$XN(d_2)$$

Taking the average value of the stock we will receive at expiration and subtracting the average amount we will pay at expiration gives us the expected value for the call

$$Se^{rt}N(d_1) - XN(d_2)$$

There is still one final step in calculating the theoretical value of a call option, and this step explains how the terms $S^{rt}N(d_1)$ and $XN(d_2)$ become $SN(d_1)$ and $Xe^{-rt}N(d_2)$, which is the way they appear in the Black-Scholes model. The expression $Se^{rt}N(d_1) - XN(d_2)$ represents the expected value of the option at expiration. If we must pay for the option today, the theoretical value is the present value of the expected value. Multiplying the expected value by e^{-rt} yields the familiar form of the Black-Scholes model

$$C = [Se^{rt}N(d_1) - XN(d_2)]e^{-rt} = SN(d_1) - Xe^{-rt}N(d_2)$$

In the original Black-Scholes model, the underlying contract was assumed to be a non-dividend-paying stock. However, since its introduction, the model has been extended to evaluate options on other types of underlying instruments. This is most commonly done by including an adjustment factor b that varies depending on the type of underlying instrument and the settlement procedure for the options. If r is the domestic interest rate and r_f is the foreign interest rate, then

$b = r$ The original Black-Scholes model for options on a non-dividend-paying stock

$b = 0$ The Black model for options on futures

$b = r - r_f$ The Garman-Kohlhagen model for options on foreign currencies

The complete Black-Scholes model, with variations and sensitivities, is given in Figure 18-6.

Figure 18-6 The Black-Scholes model.

If	S = the spot price or underlying price
	X = the exercise price
	t = the time to expiration, in years
	r = the domestic interest rate
	σ = the annualized volatility or standard deviation, in percent

then the value of a European call, C, and the value of a European put, P, are given by

$$C = S\,e^{(b-r)t}\,N(d_1) - X\,e^{-rt}\,N(d_2) \qquad\qquad P = X\,e^{-rt}\,N(-d_2) - S\,e^{(b-r)t}\,N(-d_1)$$

where
$$d_1 = \frac{\ln\left(\dfrac{S}{X}\right) + \left(b + \dfrac{\sigma^2}{2}\right)t}{\sigma\sqrt{t}} \qquad\qquad d_2 = \frac{\ln\left(\dfrac{S}{X}\right) + \left(b - \dfrac{\sigma^2}{2}\right)t}{\sigma\sqrt{t}} = d_1 - \sigma\sqrt{t}$$

The common variations on the original Black-Scholes model are determined by the value of b.

If	$b = r$: The Black-Scholes model for options on stock
	$b = r = 0$: The Black-Scholes model for options on futures where the options are subject to futures-type settlement
	$b = 0$: The Black model for options on futures where the options are subject to stock-type settlement
	$b = r - r_f$: The Garman-Kohlhagen model for options on foreign currencies, where r_f is the foreign interest rate

For options on a dividend paying stock the spot price, S, must be discounted by the value of the expected dividend payments. This can be approximated by setting $b = r - q$, where q is the annual dividend yield in percent. For a more exact calculation we can deduct from S the value of each dividend payment, D, together with the interest which can be earned on that dividend payment to expiration. S is then replaced by $S - \Sigma D_i e^{rt_d}$, where t_d is the time remaining from each dividend payment to expiration of the option.

	Call		Put
Delta (Δ)	$e^{(b-r)t}\,N(d_1)$		$e^{(b-r)t}\,[N(d_1)-1]$
Gamma (Γ)	$\dfrac{e^{(b-r)t}n(d_1)}{S\sigma\sqrt{t}}$	same for calls and puts	$\dfrac{e^{(b-r)t}n(d_1)}{S\sigma\sqrt{t}}$
Theta (Θ)*	$\dfrac{-Se^{(b-r)t}\,n(d_1)\sigma}{2\sqrt{t}} - (b-r)Se^{(b-r)t}\,N(d_1) - rXe^{-rt}\,N(d_2)$		$\dfrac{-Se^{(b-r)t}\,n(d_1)\sigma}{2\sqrt{t}} + (b-r)Se^{(b-r)t}\,N(d_1) + rXe^{-rt}\,N(-d_2)$
Vega**	$Se^{(b-r)t}\,n(d_1)\sqrt{t}$	same for calls and puts	$Se^{(b-r)t}\,n(d_1)\sqrt{t}$
Rho (P)**	$tXe^{-rt}\,N(d_2)$ if $b \neq 0$ $-tC$ if $b = 0$		$-tXe^{-rt}\,N(-d_2)$ if $b \neq 0$ $-tP$ if $b = 0$
Rho$_f$ or Phi (Φ)	$-tSe^{(b-r)t}\,N(d_1)$		$tSe^{(b-r)t}\,N(-d_1)$
Elasticity (Λ)	$\Delta_c\,(S/C)$		$\Delta_p\,(S/P)$

*The theta formula gives the sensitivity of the option to the passage of one year. To express theta values in the more common form of daily decay the theta must be divided by 365.
**The vega and rho formulas give the sensitivity of the option to a one full point (100%) change in volatility (the vega) or interest rates (rho). To express vega and rho values in the more common form of a one percentage point change in volatility or interest rates the vega and rho must be divided by 100.

(continued)

Figure 18-6 (*continued*)

	Call		Put
Vanna	$-e^{(b-r)t} n(d_1) \dfrac{d_2}{\sigma}$	same for calls and puts	$-e^{(b-r)t} n(d_1) \dfrac{d_2}{\sigma}$
Charm	$-e^{(b-r)t}\left[n(d_1)\left(\dfrac{b}{\sigma\sqrt{t}} - \dfrac{d_2}{2t} \right) + (b-r)N(d_1) \right]$		$-e^{(b-r)t}\left[n(d_1)\left(\dfrac{b}{\sigma\sqrt{t}} - \dfrac{d_2}{2t} \right) - (b-r)N(d_1) \right]$
Speed	$-\dfrac{\Gamma}{S}\left(1 + \dfrac{d_1}{\sigma\sqrt{t}} \right)$	same for calls and puts	$-\dfrac{\Gamma}{S}\left(1 + \dfrac{d_1}{\sigma\sqrt{t}} \right)$
Color	$\Gamma\left(r - b + \dfrac{bd_1}{\sigma\sqrt{t}} + \dfrac{1 - d_1 d_2}{2t} \right)$	same for calls and puts	$\Gamma\left(r - b + \dfrac{bd_1}{\sigma\sqrt{t}} + \dfrac{1 - d_1 d_2}{2t} \right)$
Volga (Vomma)	$\text{vega}\left(\dfrac{d_1 d_2}{\sigma} \right)$	same for calls and puts	$\text{vega}\left(\dfrac{d_1 d_2}{\sigma} \right)$
Vega Decay	$\text{vega}\left(r - b + \dfrac{bd_1}{\sigma\sqrt{t}} - \dfrac{1 - d_1 d_2}{2t} \right)$	same for calls and puts	$\text{vega}\left(r - b + \dfrac{bd_1}{\sigma\sqrt{t}} - \dfrac{1 - d_1 d_2}{2t} \right)$
Zomma	$\Gamma\left(\dfrac{d_1 d_2 - 1}{\sigma} \right)$	same for calls and puts	$\Gamma\left(\dfrac{d_1 d_2 - 1}{\sigma} \right)$

A complete listing of all sensitivities and their formulas can be found in *The Complete Guide to Option Pricing Formula* by Espen Gaarder Haug, 2nd Edition, 2007, McGraw-Hill.

A Useful Approximation

A trader might wonder whether it is possible to calculate a Black-Scholes value without using a computer. In general, the answer is no; the computations are just too complex. However, there is one type of approximation that many traders are able to make without too much difficulty.

Suppose that an option is exactly at the money ($X = S$) and that there is one year to expiration ($t = 1$). Suppose also that the interest rate is 0 ($r = 0$) and that volatility is 1 percent ($\sigma = 0.01$). This means that $\ln(S/X) = 0$ and that $\sigma\sqrt{t} = 0.01$. Calculating d_1 and d_2, we get

$$d_1 = \frac{0.01^2/2}{0.01} = 0.005 \quad \text{and} \quad d_2 = \frac{-0.01^2/2}{0.01} = 0.005$$

If we calculate $N(d_1)$ and $N(d_2)$, we find that

$$N(d_1) = 0.501995 \quad \text{and} \quad N(d_2) = 0.498005$$

Because the interest rate is 0, the value of the call option must be

$$(S \times 0.501995) - (X \times 0.498005)$$

If $X = S$, the value of the call is

$$X \times (0.501995 - 0.498005) = X \times 0.003990$$

What does this number tell us? For a one-year European option that is exactly at the forward (i.e., the forward price is equal to the exercise price), for each percentage point of volatility, the expected value for the option is equal to the exercise price multiplied by 0.00399. If the exercise price is 100, the expected value is $0.00399 \times 100 = 0.399$ for each percentage point in volatility.

Why doesn't this value change as we increase volatility? Although the first percentage point of volatility may be worth 0.00399, perhaps the second percentage point is worth either more or less than 0.00399. But recall from Chapter 9 that the vega of an at-the-money option is relatively constant with respect to changes in volatility. Therefore, at a volatility of 20 percent, the value of a 100 call should be

$$20 \times 100 \times 0.00399 = 7.98$$

At a volatility of 35 percent, the value should be

$$35 \times 100 \times 0.00399 = 13.965$$

We also know that the theoretical value of an at-the-forward option is proportional to its exercise price. If the value of a one-year 100 call at a volatility of 20 percent is 7.98, under the same conditions, the value of an at-the-forward 50 call should be

$$20 \times 50 \times 0.00399 = 3.99$$

and the value of a 125 call should be

$$20 \times 125 \times 0.00399 = 9.975$$

We can further refine our approximation if we note that an at-the-money option is made up entirely of time value and that the time value of an option is proportional to the square root of time. If a one-year 100 call is worth 7.98 at a volatility of 20 percent, the same call with six months to expiration ($t = 0.5$) must be worth

$$7.98 \times \sqrt{0.5} = 7.98 \times 0.707 = 5.64$$

Lastly, this is an approximation for the expected value. To determine the theoretical value, we must discount by interest to get the present value. Putting everything together, for an exactly at-the-forward European option, the expected value at expiration is approximately[3]

$$X \times (\sigma \times 100) \times \sqrt{t} \times 0.00399$$

---

[3] To further simplify this approximation, many traders round .00399 to .004. This leads to what is sometimes referred to as the *40% rule*: the expected value of an at-the-forward option is equal to approximately 40% of one standard deviation, where one standard deviation is equal to $F \times \sigma\sqrt{t}$.

and the theoretical value is[4]

$$\frac{X \times (\sigma \times 100) \times \sqrt{t} \times 0.00399}{1 + r \times t}$$

This approximation applies to both calls and puts because under put-call parity, an exactly at-the-forward European call and put must have the same value.

For example, if volatility is 18 percent, what is the expected value of a three-month ($t = \frac{1}{4}$) at-the-forward option with an exercise price of 65?

$$65 \times 0.18 \times 100 \times \sqrt{\tfrac{1}{4}} \times 0.00399 = 65 \times 18 \times \tfrac{1}{2} \times 0.00399 \approx 2.33$$

If interest rates are 4 percent, the option's theoretical value is approximately

$$\frac{2.33}{1 + 0.04/4} = \frac{2.33}{1.01} \approx 2.31$$

Although this is a commonly used approximation, it is only an approximation. As we increase time and volatility, the approximation will actually be slightly greater than the true Black-Scholes value. This is because the vega of an at-the-money option declines slightly as we increase volatility, and this decline is magnified with greater time to expiration. This can be seen in Figure 9-14: the vega of an at-the-money option, although relatively constant with respect to changes in volatility, does in fact decline slightly with increasing volatility. If, in our example, we raise the volatility to 40 percent and increase the time to expiration to two years, the approximation for the expected value is

$$65 \times 40 \times \sqrt{2} \times 0.00399 = 65 \times 40 \times 1.414 \times 0.00399 \approx 14.67$$

while the actual Black-Scholes expected value is 14.48.

The reader who is familiar with the characteristics of a standard normal distribution may already have recognized the significance of the value 0.00399. Referring to Figure 18-2, for a standard normal distribution with a mean of 0 and standard deviation of 1, the peak of the distribution has a value of approximately 0.399 (more exactly, 0.398942). Because a volatility of 1 percent represents 1/100 of a standard deviation, the value from the model is $0.399/100 = 0.00399$.

The Delta

In the Black-Scholes model, the delta of an option is equal to $N(d_1)$. When we defined the delta in Chapter 7, we suggested that the delta is approximately the probability that an option will finish in the money. But we now know that the true probability that an option will finish in the money is equal to $N(d_2)$. Although $N(d_1)$ and $N(d_2)$ are often very close in value, especially for short-term options, $N(d_1)$ (the delta) is always larger than $N(d_2)$.

[4] For a more exact calculation, $1 + r \times t$ can be replaced by e^{rt}.

For a call option that is at the forward, the delta will be greater than 50, even if only slightly. Because we know that

$$\text{Put delta} = \text{call delta} - 100$$

the delta of a put will be less than −50 in absolute value. This means that an at-the-forward straddle will have a positive delta. If a call and put have the same exercise price, at what forward price will the delta of the call and put be identical? This will occur when d_1 is exactly 0. A straddle will therefore be exactly delta neutral when

$$\ln\left(\frac{S}{X}\right) + \left[r + (\sigma^2/2)\right]t = 0$$

Solving, for S, we get

$$S = Xe^{-[r+(\sigma^2/2)]t}$$

For a straddle to be exactly delta neutral, the forward price will be less than the exercise price by a factor of

$$e^{-[r+(\sigma^2/2)]t}$$

As time or volatility increases, the forward price at which the straddle is delta neutral drops further and further below the exercise price—the call goes further out of the money, and the put goes further into the money. With a 0 interest rate, the underlying price at which a 100 straddle will be exactly delta neutral is shown in Figure 18-7. At very low volatilities, the delta-neutral price

Figure 18-7 The underlying price at which a straddle is exactly delta-neutral.

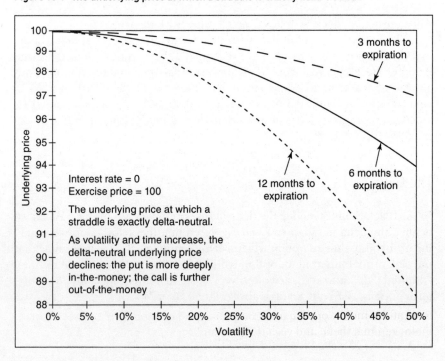

is close to 100. But, at very high volatilities and with increasing time to expiration, the delta-neutral price is well below 100.

The Theta

Of all the sensitivities derived from the Black-Scholes model, the formula for theta is probably the most complex. Depending on the underlying instrument and the option settlement procedure, the passage of time affects option values in three different ways. First, there is a decay in the option's volatility value—as time passes, the distribution of possible prices at expiration becomes more restricted. This is represented by the first term in the theta formula

$$\frac{-Se^{(b-r)t}n(d_1)\sigma}{2\sqrt{t}}$$

Second, for an underlying contract such as stock, the spot price is assumed to move toward the forward price as time passes. This is represented by the second term in the theta formula

$$(b-r)Se^{(b-r)t}N(d_1)$$

Finally, the present value of the option's expected value at expiration is changing as time passes. This appears in the formula as

$$rXe^{-rt}N(d_2)$$

We know from put-call parity that the volatility value for a call and put with identical contract specifications must be the same. The sign of the first component, the decay in volatility value, must therefore be the same for calls and puts. The other two theta components depend on the effects of interest rates and may be either positive or negative depending on the settlement procedure and whether the option is a call or a put.

The decay in volatility value is almost always more important than interest considerations and will tend to dominate the theta calculation. If interest rates are 0 or if options on futures are subject to futures-type settlement, the second and third components in the theta formula will be 0, leaving only the volatility decay component. In this case, the volatility decay component, sometimes referred to as the *driftless theta*, will be the sole factor that determines how an option's theoretical value changes as time passes.

Maximum Gamma, Theta, and Vega

In Chapter 7, we suggested that an option has its maximum gamma, theta, and vega when it is exactly at the money. But, just as we tend to assign a delta of 50 to an at-the-money option, this is only an approximation. Where does the maximum gamma, theta, and vega really occur?

Without going into the mathematical derivation, we can summarize the critical underlying prices S as follows:

Delta of 50:	$S = Xe^{(-b-\sigma^2/2)t}$
Maximum gamma[5]:	$S = Xe^{(-b-3\sigma^2/2)t}$
Maximum theta[5]:	$S = Xe^{(b+\sigma^2/2)t}$
Maximum vega[5]:	$S = Xe^{(-b+\sigma^2/2)t}$

If $b = 0$, the maximum vega and theta will occur at an underlying price that is higher than the exercise price, and the maximum gamma will occur at an underlying price that is lower than the exercise price. Moreover, the maximum vega and theta will occur at the same underlying price. This is shown in Figure 18-8 for a one-year option with an exercise price of 100. If we raise interest rates ($b > 0$), the underlying price at which the maximum theta and vega occur will fall, and the underlying price where the maximum gamma occurs will rise. This is shown in Figure 18-9.

We might also consider what will happen to the vega of an option as we change time. The answer may seem obvious because we previously made the assumption that the vega always increases with time—long-term options are

Figure 18-8 At an interest rate of zero, the underlying price at which the maximum gamma, theta, and vega occur.*

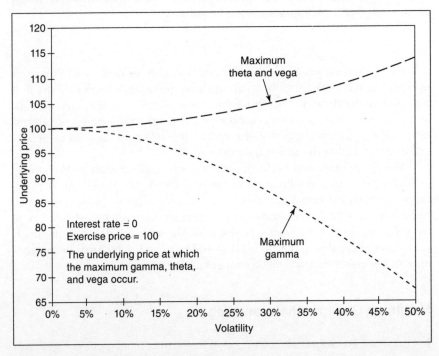

*We can also relate the critical underlying prices to the higher-order risk measures. If we ignore the extremes, where the option is either very deeply in the money or very far out of the money, the maximum gamma will occur when the option's *speed* is 0. The maximum theta will occur when the option's *charm* is 0. The maximum vega will occur when the option's *vanna* is 0.

Figure 18-9 At an interest rate of 4 percent, the underlying price at which the maximum gamma, theta, and vega will occur.

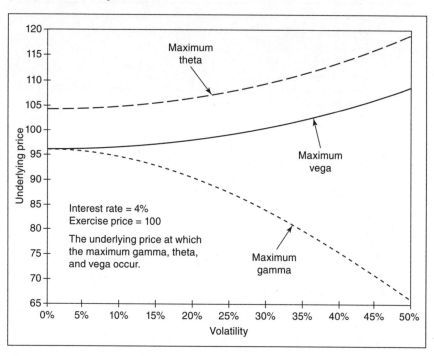

more sensitive to a change in volatility than short-term options. But this is true only if the underlying price is equal to the forward price, as it is assumed to be when evaluating options on futures. If we evaluate a stock option, the forward price for stock is a function of both time and interest rates. If interest rates are greater than 0, and assuming no dividends, as we increase time, the forward price will increase, causing the option to become either more or less at the forward. Because an at-the-forward option tends to have the highest vega, changing time can cause the vega of an option to either rise or fall. This means that under some conditions, it is possible for the vega of a stock option to decline if we increase to expiration. We can see this effect in Figure 18-10.

With an underlying stock price of 100, a volatility of 20 percent, and interest rate of 0, the vega of a 100 call always increases as we increase time to expiration. But as we raise interest rates, there is some point in time at which the opposite occurs—the option's vega begins to decline as we increase time to expiration. At an interest rate of 10 percent, this occurs if there are more than 33 months remaining to expiration. At an interest rate of 20 percent, the critical time is 10 months remaining to expiration.

We can also see where these critical points are by looking at a graph of the *vega decay*, as shown in Figure 18-11. At an interest rate of 0, the vega decay is always positive. At an interest rate of 10 percent, the vega decay is positive with less than 33 months to expiration but negative with more than 33 months. And at an interest rate of 20 percent, the vega decay is positive with less than 10 months to expiration and negative with more than 10 months.

Figure 18-10 Vega as time and interest change.

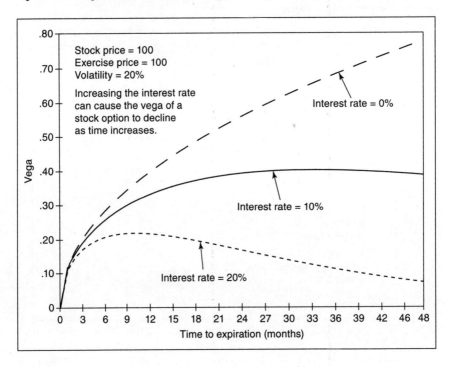

Stock price = 100
Exercise price = 100
Volatility = 20%

Increasing the interest rate
can cause the vega of a
stock option to decline
as time increases.

Interest rate = 0%

Interest rate = 10%

Interest rate = 20%

Vega

Time to expiration (months)

Figure 18-11 Vega decay as time and interest change.

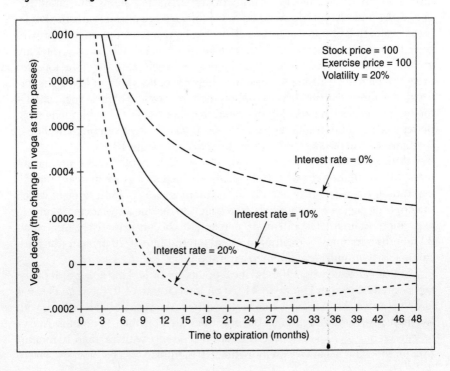

Stock price = 100
Exercise price = 100
Volatility = 20%

Interest rate = 0%

Interest rate = 10%

Interest rate = 20%

Vega decay (the change in vega as time passes)

Time to expiration (months)

19

Binomial Option Pricing

The Black-Scholes model is the most widely used of all theoretical option pricing models. Unfortunately, a full understanding of the model requires some familiarity with advanced mathematics. In the late 1970s, three professors, John Cox of the Massachusetts Institute of Technology, Stephen Ross of Yale University, and Mark Rubinstein of the University of California at Berkeley, were trying to develop a method of explaining basic option pricing theory to their students without using advanced mathematics. The method they proposed, *binomial option* pricing,[1] is not only relatively easy to understand, but the *binomial model* (also known as the *Cox-Ross-Rubinstein model*) that resulted from this approach can be used to price some options (primarily American options) that cannot be priced using the Black-Scholes model.

A Risk-Neutral World

Consider a security that is currently trading at 100 and that, on some day in the future, can take on one of two prices, 120 and 90. Assuming that there are no interest or dividend considerations, would you rather buy or sell this security at today's price of 100?

Instinctively, it seems that one would rather be long this security at a price of 100 than short the security at the same price. After all, the security can go up 20 but down only 10.

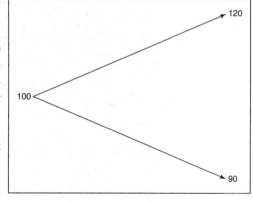

---

[1] John C. Cox, Stephen A. Ross, and Mark Rubinstein, "Option Pricing: A Simplified Approach," *Journal of Financial Economics* 7(3):229–263, 1979.

The decision to go long is probably based on the assumption that the likelihood of the price rising and falling is the same, 50 percent. But why should the probabilities be the same? Perhaps the probability of movement in one direction is greater than the probability of movement in the other direction. Indeed, there should be some probability of upward movement p and downward movement $1 - p$ such that an investor will be indifferent as to whether he buys or sells the security. For an investor to be indifferent, the total expected value must be equal to the current price of 100

$$p \times 120 + (1 - p) \times 90 = 100$$

Solving for p, we get

$$120p + 90 - 90p = 100 >> 30p = 10 >> p = \frac{1}{3}$$

We can confirm that this is correct by doing the arithmetic

$$\frac{1}{3} \times 120 + \frac{2}{3} \times 90 = 40 + 60 = 100$$

If S is the current security price, we can generalize this approach by defining u and d as multipliers that represent the magnitudes of the upward and downward moves. This results in a one-period *binomial tree*:

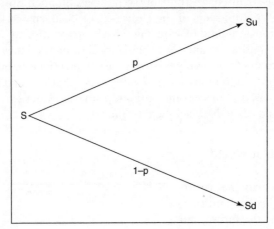

In a *risk-neutral* world,

$$pSu + (1 - p)Sd = S$$

Solving for p,

$$p(Su) + (1 - p)Sd = S >> pu + d - pd = 1 >> p = (1 - d)/(u - d)$$

In our original example, u and d were 1.20 and 0.90, respectively, with p equal to

$$\frac{1 - 0.90}{1.20 - 0.90} = \frac{0.10}{0.30} = \frac{1}{3}$$

What should p and $1 - p$ be for a non-dividend-paying stock? For an investor to be indifferent to buying or selling, the risk neutral probabilities must yield a value that is equal to the forward price for the stock $S(1 + r \times t)$. Therefore,

$$p(Su) + (1-p)Sd = S(1 + r \times t) >> pu + d - pd = 1 + r \times t >> p = \frac{(1+r \times t) - d}{u - d}$$

Valuing an Option

Suppose that we want to value an option using a one-period binomial tree. We know at expiration that an option is worth exactly its intrinsic value, the maximum of $[S - X, 0]$ for a call and the maximum of $[X - S, 0]$ for a put. In a one-period binomial tree, the expected value of a call is

$$p \times \max[Su - X, 0] + (1-p) \times \max[Sd - X, 0]$$

The theoretical value of the call is the present value of the expected value

$$\frac{p \times \max[Su - X, 0] + (1-p) \times \max[Sd - X, 0]}{1 + r \times t}$$

Using the same reasoning, the theoretical value of the put is

$$\frac{p \times \max[X - Su, 0] + (1-p) \times \max[X - Sd, 0]}{1 + r \times t}$$

Suppose that we expand our binomial tree to two periods each of length $t/2$ and also make the assumption that u and d are multiplicative inverses. Then

$$d = 1/u >> u = 1/d >> ud = du = 1$$

This means that an up move followed by a down move or a down move followed by an up move results in the same price. If the magnitudes of the up and down moves u and d are the same at every branch in our tree, then in a risk-neutral world, the probability of an upward move will always be

$$p = \frac{[1 + (r \times t/n)] - d}{u - d}$$

and the probability of a down move will always be $1 - p$.

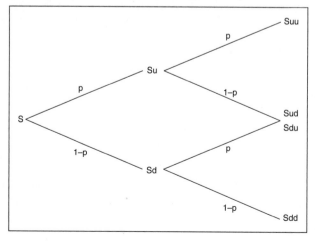

There are now three possible prices for the underlying at expiration—*Suu*, *Sud*, and *Sdd*. There is only one path that will lead to either *Suu* or *Sdd*. But there are two possible paths to the middle price *Sud*. The underlying can go up and then down or down and then up. The theoretical value of a call in the two-period example is

$$\frac{p^2 \times \max[Suu - X, 0] + 2 \times p^2 \times (1-p)^2 \times \max[Sud - X, 0] + (1-p)^2 \times \max[Sdd - X, 0]}{(1 + r \times t/2)^2}$$

The value of a put is

$$\frac{p^2 \times \max[X - Suu, 0] + 2 \times p^2 \times (1-p)^2 \times \max[X - Sud, 0] + (1-p)^2 \times \max[X - Sdd, 0]}{(1 + r \times t/2)^2}$$

Using this approach, we can expand our binomial tree to any number of periods.

If

n = number of periods in the binomial tree
t = time to expiration in years
r = annual interest rate

the possible terminal underlying prices are

$$Su^j d^{(n-j)} \qquad \text{for } j = 0, 1, 2, \ldots, n$$

The number of paths that will lead to each terminal price is given by the *binomial expansion*[2]

$$\frac{n!}{j!(n-j)!}$$

The values of a European call and put are

$$\text{Call} = \frac{1}{(1 + r \times t/n)^n} \sum_{j=0}^{n} \frac{n!}{j!(n-j)!} \times p^j (1-p)^{n-j} \times \max[Su^j d^{n-j} - X, 0]$$

$$\text{Put} = \frac{1}{(1 + r \times t/n)^n} \sum_{j=0}^{n} \frac{n!}{j!(n-j)!} \times p^j (1-p)^{n-j} \times \max[X - Su^j d^{n-j}, 0]$$

A Three-Period Example

Suppose that

$n = 3$
$S = 100$
$t = 9$ months (0.75 year)
$r = 4$ percent (0.04)
$u = 1.05$
$d = 1/u \approx 0.9524$

---

[2] The binomial expansion is sometimes written as $\binom{n}{j}$.

Then the values of p and $1 - p$ are

$$p = \frac{(1 + r \times t/n) - d}{u - d} = \frac{(1 + 0.03/3) - 0.9524}{1.05 - 0.9524} = 0.59$$

$$1 - p = 1 - 0.59 = 0.41$$

The complete three-period binomial tree is shown in Figure 19-1.[3]

Using the three-period binomial tree, what should be the value of a 100 call and a 100 put?

Terminal Price	100 Call Value	100 Put Value	Probability	Number of Paths	Total Probability
115.76	15.76	0	$0.59 \times 0.59 \times 0.59 = 0.2054$	1	0.2054
105.00	5.00	0	$0.59 \times 0.59 \times 0.41 = 0.1427$	3	0.4281
95.24	0	4.76	$0.59 \times 0.41 \times 0.41 = 0.0992$	3	0.2976
86.38	0	13.62	$0.41 \times 0.41 \times 0.41 = 0.0689$	1	0.0689

Figure 19-1 A three-period binomial tree.

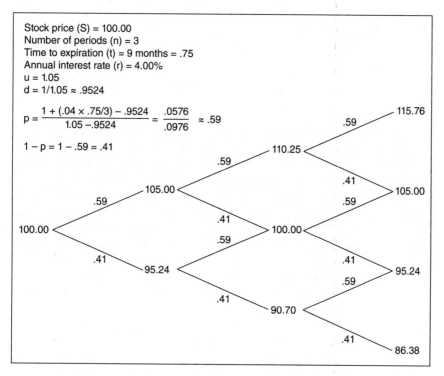

[3] For simplicity, binomial trees are often drawn symmetrically from top to bottom. However, this can be somewhat misleading. If drawn to scale, the branches typically become narrower as we move from top to bottom. We can see this in Figure 19-1: $115.76 - 105.00 = 10.76$ (the top two branches); $105.00 - 95.24 = 9.76$ (the middle two branches); $95.24 - 86.38 = 8.86$ (the bottom two branches). Because $10.76 > 9.76 > 8.86$, the branches must be getting narrower.

The value of the 100 call is

$$\frac{0.2054 \times (115.76 - 100) + 0.4281 \times (105.00 - 100)}{(1 + 0.03/3)^3} = \frac{0.2054 \times 15.76 + 0.4281 \times 5.00}{1.0927} = \mathbf{5.22}$$

The value of the 100 put is

$$\frac{0.2976 \times (100 - 95.24) + 0.0689 \times (100 - 86.38)}{(1 + 0.03/3)^3} = \frac{0.2976 \times 4.76 + 0.0689 \times 13.62}{1.0927} = \mathbf{2.28}$$

If the values for the 100 call and put are correct, they should be consistent with put-call parity

$$C - P = \frac{F - X}{1 + r \times t}$$

We can check this by first calculating the forward price for the stock. Because we are compounding interest over three time periods, the forward price is

$$F = 100 \times (1 + 0.75 \times 0.04/3)^3 = 100 \times 1.0303 = 103.03$$

Then

$$\frac{F - X}{(1 + r \times t/n)^n} = \frac{103.03 - 100}{1.0303} = 2.94$$

which is indeed equal to $C - P$

$$5.22 - 2.28 = 2.94$$

Binomial Notation

When constructing a binomial tree, it is customary to denote each price in the tree as $S_{i,j}$, where $i, j = 0, 1, 2, \ldots, n$. The value of i locates S along the tree moving from left to right. The value of j locates S moving from bottom to top. A five-period binomial tree using this notation is shown in Figure 19-2.

Instead of filling in a binomial tree with the underlying prices $S_{i,j}$ at each node, we can instead fill in the tree with option values, either $C_{i,j}$ for calls or $P_{i,j}$ for puts. Figure 19-3 shows the value of a 100 call at each node along the binomial tree in Figure 19-1. The terminal values $C_{3,j}$ are simply the maximum of either $S_{3,j} - 100$ or 0. For $S_{3,3} = 115.76$, the value of the call $C_{3,3}$ is equal to $115.76 - 100 = 15.76$; for $S_{3,2} = 105.00$, the value of the call $C_{3,2}$ is equal to $105.00 - 100 = 5.00$. For $S_{3,1} = 95.24$ and $S_{3,0} = 86.38$, the 100 call is out of the money, so both $C_{3,1}$ and $C_{3,0}$ are 0.

It's obvious what the value of the 100 call is at expiration, either intrinsic value or 0. But what should be the value of the call at other nodes along the tree? To determine these values, we can work backwards from the terminal values using the probabilities of upward and downward moves and discounting by interest to determine the present value. For example, what is the value of $C_{2,2}$? We know that there is a 59 percent chance that at $S_{2,2}$ the stock will move up in price, in which case the option will be worth 15.76. We also

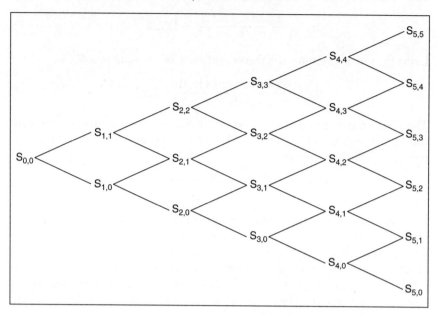

know that there is a 41 percent chance that the stock will move down in price, in which case the option will be worth 5.00. The expected value of the option at $C_{2,2}$ is therefore

$$(0.59 \times 15.76) + (0.41 \times 5.00) = 11.35$$

Figure 19-3 A call value at any point along the binomial tree.

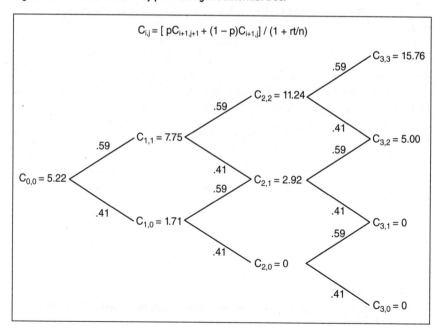

The theoretical value of the option at $C_{2,2}$ is the present value of 11.35

$$\frac{11.35}{1+0.03/3} = \frac{11.35}{1.01} = \mathbf{11.24}$$

Using the same reasoning, the theoretical value of the option at $C_{2,1}$ is

$$\frac{(0.59 \times 5.00) + (0.41 \times 0)}{1.01} = \mathbf{2.92}$$

The value of the option at $C_{2,0}$ must be 0 because either an upward or downward move results in a value of 0. We can express the value of a call at any point along the binomial tree as

$$C_{i,j} = \frac{pC_{i+1,j+1} + (1-p)C_{i+1,j}}{1+r \times t/n}$$

Working backwards along the tree, we come finally to $C_{0,0}$, the option's initial theoretical value. Of course, we already know from our previous calculation that this value is 5.22, so why go through the process of calculating the call value at every point along the binomial tree? The reason for calculating these intermediate values is that they not only enable us to determine some of the risk sensitivities associated with the option, but also, as we will see later, they enable us to calculate the value of an American option.

The Delta

We know the initial value of the 100 call, 5.22. But what is the option's delta at $C_{0,0}$? The delta is the change in the option's value with respect to movement in the price of the underlying contract. We can express this as a fraction

$$\Delta = \frac{C_u - C_d}{S_n - S_d}$$

As we move from $C_{0,0}$ to either $C_{1,1}$ or $C_{1,0}$, the option will go up in value to 7.75 or down in value to 1.71. At the same time, the stock will move up in price to 105.00 or down in price to 95.24. The delta is therefore

$$\frac{7.75 - 1.71}{105 - 95.24} = \frac{6.04}{9.76} = \mathbf{0.62}$$

Using the whole-number format, the initial delta of the 100 call is 62.

We can calculate the delta at every point along the binomial tree by dividing the change in the option's value by the change in the underlying price

$$\Delta_{i,j} = \frac{C_{i+1,j+1} - C_{i+1,j}}{S_{i+1,j+1} - S_{i+1,j}}$$

Figure 19-4 shows the stock price, the value of the 100 call, and the delta of the call at every node along the binomial tree.

In Chapter 8, we showed that the dynamic hedging process enables us to capture the difference between an option's value and its price. We can see

Figure 19-4 Delta of an option using a binomial tree.

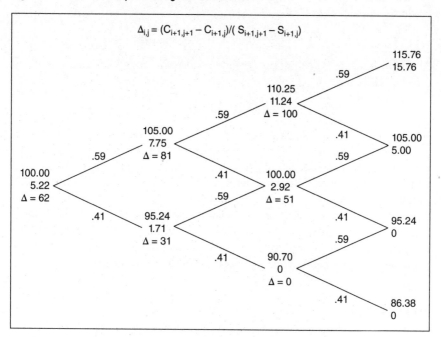

$$\Delta_{i,j} = (C_{i+1,j+1} - C_{i+1,j})/(S_{i+1,j+1} - S_{i+1,j})$$

this same principal at work in the binomial model. Returning to Figure 19-4, suppose that we buy the 100 call at its theoretical value of 5.22 and create a delta-neutral hedge ($\Delta = 62$) by selling 62 percent of an underlying stock contract at a price of 100. What will be the result if we hold the position for one time period?

If the stock price moves up to 105.00, the option will be worth 7.75, resulting in a profit on the option of $7.75 - 5.22 = 2.53$. At the same time, we will lose $0.62 \times (100 - 105) = -3.10$ on the stock position, giving us a loss on the hedge of

$$+2.53 - 3.10 = -0.57$$

If the stock price moves down to 95.24, the option will be worth 1.71, resulting in a loss on the option of $1.71 - 5.22 = -3.51$. At the same time, we will make $0.62 \times (100 - 95.24) = 2.95$ on the stock position, giving us a loss on the hedge of

$$-3.51 + 2.95 = -0.56$$

It seems that we will lose money, either 0.56 or 0.57, regardless of whether the stock moves up or down in price. In fact, both numbers are the same, the difference being due to a rounding error in our calculations (the true delta is 61.88). But this still leaves us with a loss when option pricing theory says we ought to break even.

Recall that when we bought the option and sold stock, the cash flow was a credit to our account of

$$-5.22 + 0.62 \times 100 = +56.78$$

At an interest rate over this time period of 1.00 percent, we are able to earn interest on this credit of

$$0.01 \times 56.78 \approx +0.57$$

Including this in our calculations, we do in fact just break even.

If we go through the delta-neutral rehedging process at every node in the tree, taking into consideration the value of the hedge as well as any interest considerations, regardless of the path the stock follows, at expiration, we will break exactly even. It therefore follows that if we are able to buy an option at a price less than theoretical value or sell an option at a price greater than theoretical value, we will show a profit at expiration equal to the difference between the price at which we traded the option and its theoretical value. This is the principle of dynamic hedging described in Chapter 8.

The Gamma

The gamma of an option is the change in the option's delta with respect to movement in the price of the underlying contract. As we did with the delta, we can express the gamma as a fraction

$$\Gamma = \frac{\Delta_u - \Delta_d}{S_u - S_d}$$

In Figure 19-4, we can see that as we move from $C_{0,0}$ to either $C_{1,1}$ or $C_{1,0}$, the option's delta will either go up to 81 or down to 31. At the same time, the stock will either move up to 105.00 or move down to 95.24. The gamma is therefore

$$\frac{81 - 31}{105.00 - 95.24} = \frac{50}{9.76} = \mathbf{5.1}$$

The initial gamma of the 100 call is 5.1.

We can calculate the gamma at any point along the binomial tree by dividing the change in the option's delta by the change in the underlying price

$$\Gamma_{i,j} = \frac{\Delta_{i+1,j+1} - \Delta_{i+1,j}}{S_{i+1,j+1} - S_{i+1,j}}$$

The Theta

The theta is the change in an option's value as time passes, assuming everything else, including the underlying price, remains unchanged. In a binomial model, at each time period, the underlying price is assumed to move either up or down. The underlying price remains unchanged only after two time periods, when the underlying price either goes up and down or down and up. To approximate the theta, we must therefore consider the change in the option's value over two time periods.

In Figure 19-4, we can see that as we move from $C_{0,0}$ to $C_{2,1}$, the value of the 100 call drops from 5.22 to 2.92, for a loss in value of 2.30. If we want to estimate the daily theta, we can divide by the number of days during this two-period time

$$\frac{0.75 \times 365}{3} = 91.25 \qquad \frac{-2.30}{2 \times 91.25} = \textbf{-0.0126}$$

We can approximate the daily theta at any point along the tree as

$$\frac{C_{i,j} - C_{i+2,j+1}}{t \times 365/n}$$

Vega and Rho

It would be convenient if we could use the same simple arithmetic to calculate the vega and rho that we used to calculate the delta, gamma, and theta. Unfortunately, there is no simple solution to the volatility and interest-rate sensitivities. To determine the vega, we must change the volatility input—we will see shortly how we determine this input—and then see how the option's value changes. To determine the rho, we must change the interest-rate input.

The Values of u and d

We have chosen the upward move u and downward move d so that they form a *recombining* binomial tree. The terminal price for the security is independent of the order in which the price moves occur. Whether the security moves up first and then down or down first and then up, the result is the same

$$u \times d = d \times u$$

If the upward and downward moves were not recombining, the number of calculations would be greatly increased because each node on the binomial tree would yield a completely new set of upward and downward values.

We have also chosen u and d so that they are the multiplicative inverse of each other

$$u \times d = d \times u = 1.00$$

This ensures that if the security makes an upward move followed by a downward move or a downward move followed by an upward move, the resulting underlying price will be same price at which it began. If u and d were not inverses, there would be a *drift* in the underlying price. If, for example, u and d were chosen to be 1.25 and 0.75, then there would be a downward drift because

$$u \times d = 1.25 \times 0.75 = 0.9375$$

In order to calculate the theta, as we did previously, we need to eliminate the drift in the underlying price. This will be true if u and d are multiplicative inverses.

Other than the restrictions that u and d are inverses and result in a drift-less underlying price, we have not specified exactly what the values of u and d should be. It will not come as a surprise that u and d must be derived from the volatility input. If we want binomial values to approximate Black-Scholes values, u and d must be chosen in such a way that the terminal prices approximate a lognormal distribution. We can achieve this by defining u and d as a one standard deviation price change over each time period in our binomial tree

$$u = e^{\sigma\sqrt{t/n}} \quad \text{and} \quad d = e^{-\sigma\sqrt{t/n}}$$

In our three-period example, what volatility does $u = 1.05$ represent? To determine this, we can work backwards to solve for the volatility σ

$$u = 1.05 = e^{\sigma\sqrt{75/3}} = e^{\sigma\sqrt{25}} = e^{0.5\sigma}$$

Taking the natural logarithm of each side, we get

$$\ln(1.05) = \ln(e^{0.5\sigma}) >> 0.0488 = 0.5\sigma >> \sigma = 0.0976 \ (9.76\%)$$

In our three-period example, we used a volatility of 9.76 percent.

Gamma Rent

In theory, every volatility position in the option market represents a tradeoff between the cash flow created by the dynamic hedging process and the decay in the option's value as time passes. A positive gamma, negative theta position will make money through dynamic hedging but lose money through time decay. A negative gamma, positive theta position will perform just the opposite, losing money through dynamic hedging but making money through time decay. Traders sometimes refer to volatility trading as *renting* the gamma, with the rental costs being equal to the theta.

Over a given time period, how much movement is required in the under-lying contract to offset the effects of time decay? We can give an approximate answer by going back to our binomial tree. We know that a delta-neutral position taken at theoretical value will just break even if the underlying contract moves either up by u or down by d. The magnitudes of the u and d are equal to

$$u = e^{\sigma\sqrt{t/n}} \quad \text{and} \quad d = e^{-\sigma\sqrt{t/n}}$$

But these values are equal to a one standard deviation price change over the time interval t/n. Therefore, over any interval of time, the amount of price movement needed in the underlying contract to just break even must be equal to one standard deviation.

The reason that this is only an approximation is that while u and d remain constant, theta changes, sometime very rapidly, as time passes. For very short time intervals or with a great deal of time remaining to expiration, this approximation will be reasonably accurate. However, over longer time intervals or with very little time remaining to expiration, the changes in the theta will cause the approximation to be less accurate.

American Options

Let's go back to our three-period binomial tree in Figure 19-1. But instead of calculating the value of a 100 call, as we did in Figure 19-4, let's work backwards from the terminal prices to calculate the value of a 100 put. The underlying prices, theoretical values, and delta and gamma values for the 100 put are all shown in Figure 19-5. The reader may wish to confirm that the call and put values in Figures 19-4 and 19-5 are consistent with basic principles of option pricing: at every node, put-call parity is maintained; the absolute values of call and put deltas always add up to 100; and the call and put gammas are identical.

If we assume that the 100 put is European and cannot be exercised early, the only reason to calculate the intermediate values is to determine the delta and gamma. But suppose that the 100 put is American. Might there be any reason to exercise the option prior to expiration?

Look closely at the value of the 100 put at $P_{2,0}$ in Figure 19-5. The theoretical value of the put is 8.31. But with an underlying price of 90.70 the put has an intrinsic value of 9.30. If the put is American, anyone holding the put under those conditions will choose to exercise it early. If we are using a binomial tree to evaluate an American option, we might compare the value of the European option with the intrinsic value at each node. If the intrinsic value is greater than

Figure 19-5 The value of a 100 put at any point along the binomial tree.

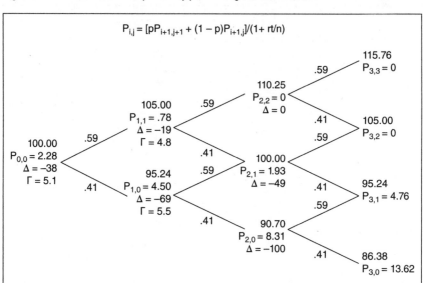

$$P_{i,j} = [pP_{i+1,j+1} + (1 - p)P_{i+1,j}]/(1+ rt/n)$$

the European value, we can replace the value at that node with the option's intrinsic value and then continue to work backwards to determine the option's value at each preceding node. If we replace the value at $P_{2,0}$ with 9.30, the put value at $P_{1,0}$ will be

$$\frac{(0.59 \times 1.93) + (0.41 \times 9.30)}{1.01} = \mathbf{4.90}$$

We need to replace the European value of 4.50 at $P_{1,0}$ with the American value of 4.90.

Finally, the initial value, $P_{0,0}$, is

$$\frac{(0.59 \times 0.78) + (0.41 \times 4.90)}{1.01} = \mathbf{2.44}$$

Because the delta and gamma are calculated from option values at every node, these new values will affect the calculation of the delta and gamma for an American option. The initial delta of the 100 put if it is American is

$$\frac{0.78 - 4.90}{105.00 - 95.24} = \mathbf{-0.42}$$

The delta of the European 100 put was –38, but the delta of American 100 put is –42. The values for an American 100 put at every node are shown in Figure 19-6. Because the delta is affected by the possibility of early exercise, the gamma will also be affected. The gamma for the 100 put is now

$$\frac{-19 - (-79)}{105.00 - 95.24} = \mathbf{6.1}$$

rather than a gamma of 5.1 for the European option.

Figure 19-6 The value of an American 100 put.

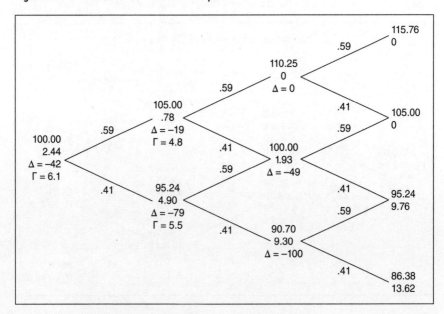

OPTION VOLATILITY AND PRICING

Dividends

How does the possibility of early exercise affect the value of a call? If we look at the call value at every node in Figure 19-4, we find that at no point is it less than intrinsic value. This means that the European and American values must be the same. And, indeed, we know from Chapter 16 that if a stock does not pay a dividend over the life of the option, there is never any reason to exercise an American stock option call early.

But what if the stock does pay a dividend? Suppose that the stock in Figure 19-1 will pay a dividend of 2.00 at some point during the last time period. When a stock pays a dividend, its price typically drops by the amount of the dividend. Consequently, each terminal price in our binomial tree will be reduced by the amount of the dividend,[4] as shown in Figure 19-7. (The terminal values if there is no dividend are shown in parentheses.) If we want to calculate the value of the 100 call, we can use these new terminal prices. Then, as before, we can use the probabilities p and $1 - p$ to calculate the theoretical value and delta of the 100 call at each node of the binomial tree. These values are shown in Figure 19-8.

The value for the 100 call in Figure 19-8 is a European value because we never considered the possibility of early exercise. But look more closely at the value of the call one time period prior to expiration with the stock price at

Figure 19-7 A binomial tree with dividend payment

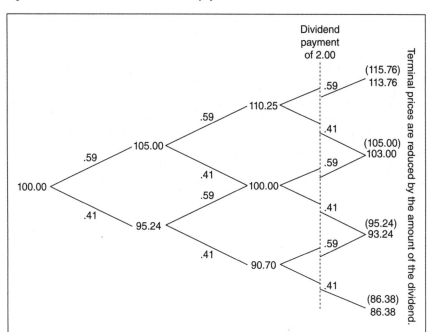

---

[4] For simplicity, we ignore the interest that can be earned on the dividend payment. A more accurate binomial tree should also include this amount.

Figure 19-8 The value of a European call on a dividend-paying stock.

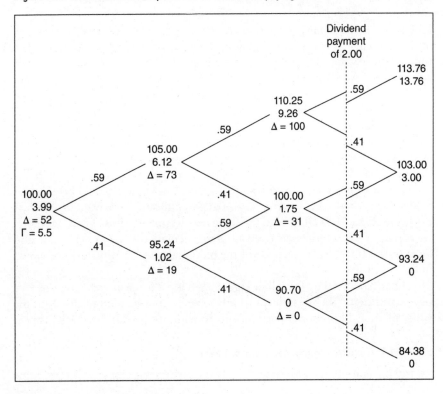

110.25. The theoretical value of the 100 call is 9.26. But, with a stock price of 110.25, the call has an intrinsic value of 10.25. If the call is American, anyone holding the call under these conditions will choose to exercise it early. As we did with an American put, at each node, we can compare the European value of the call with its intrinsic value. If the intrinsic value is greater than the European value, we can replace the value at that node with the option's intrinsic value and then continue to work backwards to determine the option's value at each preceding node. The initial value of the call, $C_{0,0}$, will then be the value of an American call. The complete binomial tree for the American 100 call is shown in Figure 19-9.

If we want to construct a binomial tree for a dividend-paying stock, it might seem that we can simply reduce all stock prices following the dividend payment by the amount of the dividend. In Figure 19-7, where the dividend was paid over the last time period, this reduced the terminal prices by 2.00. But suppose that the dividend is paid during the next-to-last time period, as shown in Figure 19-10. The stock prices at the following nodes are reduced by 2.00. But look at what happens when we continue to calculate stock prices using $u = 1.05$ and $d = 0.9524$. The subsequent stock prices do not recombine. Each node begins a new binomial tree. In our three-period binomial tree, this may not seem like a significant problem. We can still calculate the value of an option using the terminal stock prices (now there are

Figure 19-9 The value of an American call on a dividend-paying stock.

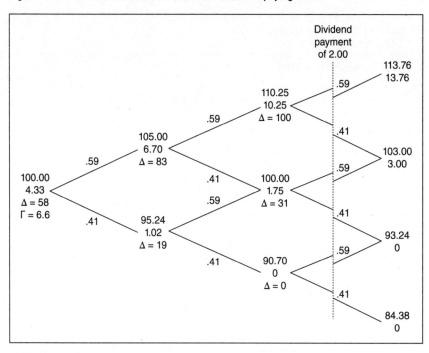

Figure 19-10 The value of an American call on a dividend-paying stock.

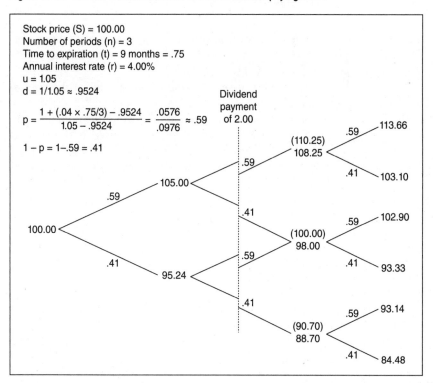

Figure 19-11 A binomial tree with an early dividend payment.

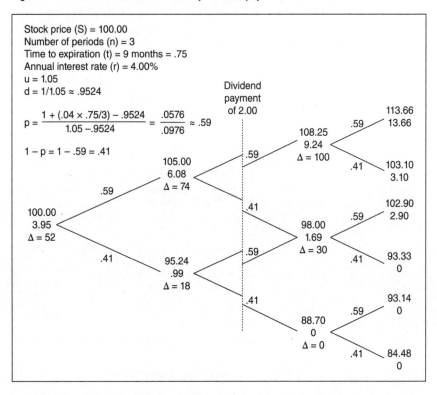

Stock price (S) = 100.00
Number of periods (n) = 3
Time to expiration (t) = 9 months = .75
Annual interest rate (r) = 4.00%
u = 1.05
d = 1/1.05 ≈ .9524

$$p = \frac{1 + (.04 \times .75/3) - .9524}{1.05 - .9524} = \frac{.0576}{.0976} \approx .59$$

1 − p = 1 − .59 = .41

Dividend payment of 2.00

113.66 / 13.66
108.25 / 9.24 / Δ = 100
103.10 / 3.10
105.00 / 6.08 / Δ = 74
102.90 / 2.90
98.00 / 1.69 / Δ = 30
93.33 / 0
95.24 / .99 / Δ = 18
93.14 / 0
88.70 / 0 / Δ = 0
84.48 / 0

100.00 / 3.95 / Δ = 52

six terminal prices instead of four) and then work backward to determine the option's theoretical value. The value for the 100 call using our new binomial tree is shown in Figure 19-11.

What if there are multiple dividend payments over the life of the option? And what if our binomial tree consists of many time periods? Because each dividend payment generates a new set of binomial prices, the number of calculations required to value an option will be greatly increased, perhaps to the point of being unwieldy. This presents a problem to which there is no ideal solution. Perhaps the simplest way to handle dividend payments is to create a complete binomial tree without dividends and then reduce the stock price at each node by the total amount of dividends. An example of this is shown in Figure 19-12, which represents an approximation of the call option value generated in Figure 19-11. Instead of generating new binomial prices after the dividend payment, we have simply reduced all subsequent values by the 2.00 amount of the dividend. We can see that this is only an approximation. The call values in Figure 19-12 tend to be slightly larger than the values in Figure 19-11.

One final comment about the values for p and $1 - p$. We typically expect a probability to fall between 0 to 1.00, that is, somewhere between "no chance" and "absolute certainty." However, this is not necessarily true for p and $1 - p$. Consider the conditions in Figure 19-11:

Stock price $S = 100$
Time to expiration $t = 9$ months
Number of periods $n = 3$
Interest rate $r = 4$ percent
$u = 1.05$
$d = 1/u = 0.9524$

The values for p and $1 - p$ resulting from these values are 0.59 and 0.41, respectively. But suppose that we are in a high inflationary climate and that instead of setting r equal to 4 percent, we set r equal to 40 percent. The new values of p and $1 - p$ will be

$$p = \frac{(1 + r \times t/n) - d}{u - d} = \frac{(1 + 0.1) - 0.9524}{1.05 - 0.9524} = 1.51$$

$$1 - p = 1 - 1.51 = -0.51$$

Thus p and $1 - p$ no longer look like traditional probabilities: p exceeds 1.00, and $1 - p$ is negative. In fact, p and $1 - p$ can fall outside the range for a typical probability. For this reason, they are sometimes referred to as *pseudoprobabilities*.

What is the implication of p being greater than 1.00 and $1 - p$ being less than 0? This means that the potential for movement in the underlying stock is not sufficiently large to offset the interest loss should we buy the stock. In our example with $u = 1.05$, if the stock price always rises over each time period, we will show a profit of 5 percent. But with an interest rate of 30 percent, we

Figure 19-12 The value of an American call on a dividend-paying stock.

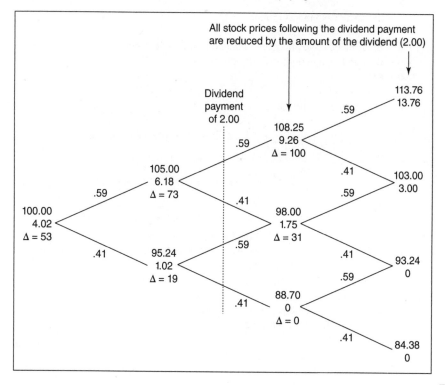

would always be better off leaving our money in the bank and earning interest over each three-month time period of

$$0.30/4 = 7.5\%$$

Of course, if we increase the stock volatility by increasing the value of u, then the potential profit from investing in the stock will go up. If we choose a large enough value for u, the values for p and $1 - p$ will indeed fall between 0 and 1.00. Because the value for u must be greater than $1 + r \times t/n$, with an interest rate of 30 percent, u must be greater than

$$1 + 0.3 \times 0.75/3 = 1.075$$

As we did with the Black-Scholes model, we can use the binomial model to evaluate options on different underlying instruments. The binomial model and its variations are shown in Figure 19-13.

How close are option values generated by a binomial model to those generated by the Black-Scholes model? This question only makes sense for European options because the Black-Scholes model cannot be used to evaluate American options. In our three-period binomial tree, the value of a European 100 call is 5.22, and the value of a 100 put is 2.28. Using the Black-Scholes

Figure 19-13

If	
	S = the spot price or underlying price
	X = the exercise price
	t = the time to expiration, in years
	r = the domestic interest rate
	σ = the annualized volatility or standard deviation, in percent
	n = the number of periods in the binomial tree
	$u = e^{\sigma\sqrt{t/n}}$
	$d = 1/u = e{-}\sigma\sqrt{t}/n$
	$p = [\,(1 + bt/n) - d\,]\,/\,[u - d]$

$$\text{Call} = \frac{1}{(1+rt/n)^n} \sum_{j=0}^{n} \frac{n!}{j!(n-j)!} \times p^j(1-p)^{n-j} \times \max[Su^j d^{n-j} - X,\, 0]$$

$$\text{Put} = \frac{1}{(1+rt/n)^n} \sum_{j=0}^{n} \frac{n!}{j!(n-j)!} \times p^j(1-p)^{n-j} \times \max[X - Su^j d^{n-j},\, 0]$$

The variations on the binomial model are determined by the values of r and b.

If		
	$b = r > 0$:	The binomial model for options on stock
	$b = r = 0$:	The binomial model for options on futures where the options are subject to futures-type settlement
	$b = 0$ and $r > 0$:	The binomial model for options on futures where the options are subject to stock-type settlement
	$b = r - r_f$:	The binomial model for options on foreign currencies, where r_f is the foreign interest rate

(continued)

Figure 19-13 (*continued*)

The value of an option at any node along the binomial tree is
$C_{i,j} = [pC_{i+1,j+1} + (1-p)C_{i+1,j}] / (1+rt/n)$
$P_{i,j} = [pP_{i+1,j+1} + (1-p)P_{i+1,j}] / (1+rt/n)$
The delta of a call (ΔC) or put (ΔP) at any node along the binomial tree is
$\Delta C_{i,j} = (C_{i+1,j+1} - C_{i+1,j}) / (S_{i+1,j+1} - S_{i+1,j})$
$\Delta P_{i,j} = (P_{i+1,j+1} - P_{i+1,j}) / (S_{i+1,j+1} - S_{i+1,j})$
The gamma of a call (ΓC) or put (ΓP) at any node along the binomial tree is
$\Gamma C_{i,j} = (\Delta C_{i+1,j+1} - \Delta C_{i+1,j}) / (S_{i+1,j+1} - S_{i+1,j})$
$\Gamma P_{i,j} = (\Delta P_{i+1,j+1} - \Delta P_{i+1,j}) / (S_{i+1,j+1} - S_{i+1,j})$
The annual theta of a call (θC) or put (θP) at any node along the binomial tree is
$\theta C_{i,j} = (C+_{i+1,i+2} - C_{i,j}) / t$
$\theta P_{i,j} = (P+_{i+1,i+2} - P_{i,j}) / t$

model, the values are 5.01 and 2.05. Both binomial values are greater than the true Black-Scholes values. We can increase the accuracy of the binomial model by increasing the number of time periods. In a four-period binomial tree, the values are 4.79 and 1.84. Figure 19-14 shows the difference between the Black-Scholes and binomial values for the 100 call as we increase the number of time periods from 1 to 10. We can see that the error oscillates between positive and negative, with the absolute value of the error becoming smaller and smaller. Indeed, if we build a tree with an infinite number of time periods, the error will converge to 0. The binomial and Black-Scholes values will be identical.

How many periods should we use in a binomial model? As we divide the time to expiration into smaller and smaller increments, we increase the accuracy. But a greater number of periods also increases the number of calculations, and this number increases exponentially. Given the tradeoff between accuracy and speed, a common choice is often somewhere between 50 and 100 periods.

The accuracy of a binomial calculation can be further increased by taking the average value generated by two periods, sometimes referred to as *half-steps*. For example, the 9-period tree overvalues the 100 call by about 0.07 (Black-Scholes value – binomial value = –0.07), whereas the 10-period tree undervalues the call by about 0.09. If we take the average of the 9- and 10-period values (a 9½-period value), the option is undervalued by only 0.01. The results of this averaging procedure can be seen in Figure 19-14.

Figure 19-14 As we increase the number of periods, the binomial value converges to the Black-Scholes value.

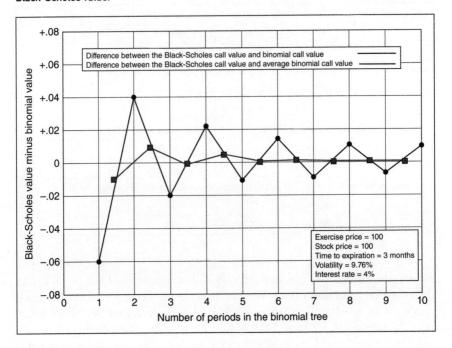

Volatility Revisited

When a trader enters a volatility into a theoretical pricing model, what exactly is he feeding into the model? We know the mathematical definition of volatility—one standard deviation, in percent terms, over a one-year period. Beyond this, we still have the question of interpretation. Does the number represent a realized volatility or an implied volatility? Are we talking about historical volatility or future volatility? Long term or short term? The volatility a trader chooses may vary depending on the answers to these questions.

Consider this situation:

Underlying price = 100.00
Time to expiration = 8 weeks
Interest rate = 0
Implied volatility = 20 percent

Suppose that we buy the 100 straddle at a price equal to its implied volatility of 20 percent, in this case 6.25. The position should be approximately delta neutral because both the 100 call and the 100 put are at the money. After we buy the straddle, implied volatility rises to 22 percent. How are we doing?

We might instinctively assume that the position will show a profit because the increase in implied volatility should be a reflection of rising option prices. Indeed, if there is an immediate increase in implied volatility and all other conditions remain unchanged, the price of the 100 straddle will rise to 6.87, resulting in a profit of

$$6.87 - 6.25 = +0.62$$

But suppose that implied volatility slowly rises to 22 percent over a period of three weeks. Even though the increase in implied volatility will work in our favor, the passage of time will cause the options to decay. In fact, with the underlying contract still at 100.00, the straddle will be worth only 5.43, resulting in a loss of

$$5.43 - 6.25 = -0.82$$

The benefits of rising implied volatility were overwhelmed by the costs of time decay.

Now suppose that instead of rising, implied volatility falls to 18 percent. How will this affect our position? If there is an immediate decline with no changes in any other market conditions, the price of the 100 straddle will fall to 5.62, leaving us with a loss of

$$5.62 - 6.25 = -0.63$$

But suppose that as implied volatility falls to 18 percent, the underlying price is also changing. We are now benefiting from a positive gamma. If the underlying price rises immediately to 105.00, the 100 straddle will be worth 7.09, resulting in a profit of

$$7.09 - 6.25 = +0.84$$

If the underlying price moves in the other direction and falls immediately to 95.00, the straddle will be worth 6.87, now resulting in a profit of

$$6.87 - 6.25 = +0.62$$

The disadvantages of falling implied volatility were more than offset by the benefits of movement in the underlying stock price.

This example illustrate an important principle of option trading:

The longer an option position is held, the more important is the realized volatility of the underlying contract and the less important is the implied volatility. If a position is held to expiration, realized volatility is the only consideration.

We saw this principle at work in Chapter 8 on dynamic hedging. The delta-neutral adjustment process eventually determined whether a position would show a profit or loss, irrespective of any changes in implied volatility. This is not to say that implied volatility is unimportant; prices are always important because they will often determine interim cash flows and capital requirements. But, in order to make sensible trading decisions, we need to know value as well as price. In the final analysis, the value of an option position will be determined by the volatility of the underlying contract.

Determining the right volatility input can be a difficult and frustrating exercise, even for an experienced option trader. The forecasting of directional price movements, either through fundamental or technical analysis, is a commonly studied area in trading, and there are many sources to which a trader can turn for information on these subjects. Unfortunately, volatility is a much newer concept, and there is less to guide a trader. In spite of this difficulty, an option trader must make some effort to come up with a reasonable volatility input if he intends to use a theoretical pricing model to make trading decisions and manage risk.

Historical Volatility

Because the realized volatility over the life of an option will eventually dominate any changes in implied volatility, we will certainly want to give some thought to how we might predict future realized volatility. Such a prediction will often begin by looking at historical volatility data. How should we calculate historical volatility?

We know that volatility represents a standard deviation. Two methods are commonly used to calculate a standard deviation, either

$$\sqrt{\sum_{i=1}^{n} \frac{(x_i - \mu)^2}{n}} \quad \text{or} \quad \sqrt{\sum_{i=1}^{n} \frac{(x_i - \mu)^2}{n-1}}$$

In each case, x_i are the data points, μ is the mean of all data points, and n is the total number of data points. The only difference between the two methods is the denominator, either n or $n - 1$.

If we want to know the standard deviation of an entire population of data points, we can use the first method, dividing by n. This is known as the *population standard deviation*. Suppose, however, that we have a sample set of data points from a larger population, and we want to use this sample to estimate the standard deviation of the entire population. Because our sample is limited, we are likely to miss some of the more extreme data points in the larger population. For this reason, our estimate of the standard deviation for the entire population is likely to be too low. To improve our estimate, we ought to increase the standard deviation calculation. This is commonly done by reducing the size of the denominator from n to $n - 1$, resulting in a *sample standard deviation* of the larger population. Because historical volatility is most often used to estimate a future volatility, historical volatility calculations are most often made using the sample standard deviation, that is, dividing by $n - 1$.

The data points x_i in a volatility calculation are the price *returns*, either the percent change in the underlying price from one time period to the next

$$\frac{p_n - p_{n-1}}{p_n}$$

or, more commonly, the logarithmic change

$$\ln \frac{p_n}{p_{n-1}}$$

Time periods may be any length, but for exchange-traded contracts, returns are usually based on the price change from one day's settlement to the next.

In the standard deviation calculation, μ (the Greek letter mu) is the average of all price returns. Because the volatility is the deviation from average, if a contract goes up 1 percent each day for 10 consecutive days, its volatility over the 10-day period is 0; the price change never deviated from its average. To most traders, this feels wrong. The upward moves of 1 percent ought to represent some volatility other than 0. In fact, most historical volatility calculations use a *zero-mean* assumption: μ is always assumed to be 0 regardless of the actual mean.

When calculating historical volatility, traders typically exclude weekends and holidays, resulting in a trading year of between 250 and 260 days. But one might also calculate volatility using all 365 days, assigning a 0 price change to nontrading days. This method might be appropriate when trying to compare the volatilities of products traded on two different exchanges with different trading calendars. The two methods will obviously yield slightly different historical volatilities. But, if historical volatility is used as a general guideline to future realized volatility, the differences are unlikely to be significant. This can be seen in Figure 20-1, which shows the three-month volatility of the Standard and Poor's (S&P) 500 Index calculated using only trading days (approximately 252 days per year) and using all 365 days.[1] The graphs are almost indistinguishable.

Although daily price returns are most often used to calculate historical volatility, we might instead use weekly price returns. How will this affect the historical volatility calculation? Figure 20-2 shows the three-month volatility of gold from 2001 through 2010 calculated using both daily and weekly price returns. In general, the graphs show similar characteristics, although fluctuations seem to be slightly greater using weekly returns. This is probably due to the smaller number of data points (13 weekly data points rather than 91 daily data points). The greater number of data points will tend to have a smoothing effect. Because the

Figure 20-1 S&P 500 Index three-month historical volatility: 2001–2010.

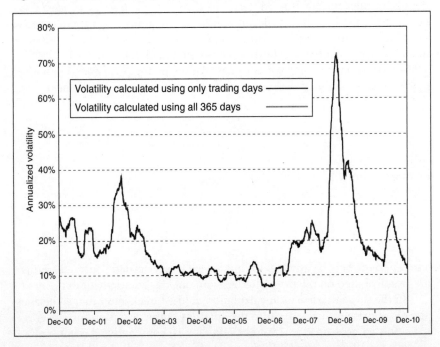

---

[1] Because volatility is always quoted on an annualized basis, whether we calculate historical volatility using all 365 days or only trading days, the standard deviation of price changes must be multiplied by the square root of the number of trading periods in a year. For a 365-day trading year, the standard deviation must be multiplied by $\sqrt{365} \approx 19.1$.

graphs show similar characteristics, we can conclude that if a contract is volatile from day to day, it will be equally volatile from week to week or month to month. Daily returns are used most often in order to increase the number of data points in the volatility calculation and therefore yield a more accurate volatility.

Suppose that the price of a contract fluctuates wildly during a trading day, making dramatic up and down moves, yet finishes the day unchanged. If this is a common occurrence, then using only settlement prices to calculate the historical volatility may result in an incomplete picture of a contract's true volatility. To take into consideration intraday price movement, several alternative methods have been proposed to calculate historical volatility.

The *extreme-value method*, proposed by Michael Parkinson,[2] uses the high and low values during a 24-hour period. This method not only gives a more complete picture of volatility but may also be useful when no definitive settlement prices are available. Using the extreme-value method, the annualized historical volatility is given by

$$\frac{\dfrac{1}{2\sqrt{n\ln(2)}}\sqrt{\sum_{i=1}^{n}\left(\ln\dfrac{h_i}{l_i}\right)^2}}{\sqrt{t}}$$

Figure 20-2 Gold three-month historical volatility: 2001–2010.

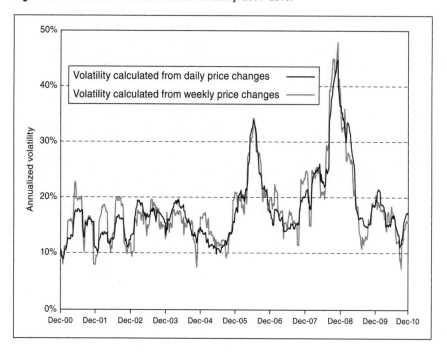

[2] Michael Parkinson, "The Extreme Value Method of Estimating the Variance of the Rate of Return," *Journal of Business* 53(1):61–64, 1980.

where n = number of price returns, h_i = highest price during the chosen time interval, l_i = lowest price during the chosen time interval, ln = natural logarithm, and t = the length of each time interval in years.

An alternative approach proposed by Mark Garman and Michael Klass[3] expands the Parkinson method by also including the opening and closing prices for an underlying contract. Using this method, the annualized historical volatility is given by

$$\frac{\sqrt{\frac{1}{2n}\sum_{i=1}^{n}\left(\ln\frac{h_i}{l_i}\right)^2 - \frac{1}{n}[2\ln(2)-1]\sum_{i=1}^{n}\left(\ln\frac{c_i}{o_i}\right)^2}}{\sqrt{t}}$$

where o_i = opening price at the beginning of trading, and c_i = closing price at the end of trading.

As with the traditional close-to-close estimator, both the Parkinson and Garman-Klass estimators are annualized by dividing by the square root of t, the time between price intervals. (This is the same as multiplying by the square root of the number of time intervals in a year.)

Figure 20-3 shows the three-month volatility of the EuroStoxx 50 Index, a widely followed index of large European companies. The volatility has been calculated using three methods: close-to-close, high-low (Parkinson), and open-high, low-close (Garman-Klass). The last two methods seem to yield a consistently lower volatility than the first method. The explanation probably has to do with the fact that Parkinson and Garman-Klass are used only when markets are open and trading is continuous. But the EuroStoxx 50 Index is not calculated continuously. It is calculated during a period of just under 10 hours, from approximately 9:00 a.m. to 6:50 p.m. European time. During the remaining hours of the day, the volatility of the index is unobservable. Because of this, for contracts that trade only during part of the day, Garman and Klass recommend giving some weight to the close-to-close estimate. One approach is to give the observable volatility (either Parkinson or Garman-Klass) weight proportional to the fraction of the day during which the market is open and give the remaining weight to the close-to-close volatility. This usually means giving greater weight to the close-to-close volatility estimate because many markets are closed more hours than they are open. But the Parkinson and Garman-Klass methods are generally considered more accurate estimates, at least when a market is trading continuously. Thus, it might make more sense to increase the weightings for these estimates and reduce the weightings for the close-to-close estimate. Garman and Klass propose a precise formula for weighting the estimates, but a practical solution might be to simply weight the estimates equally.

Because we have gone into the calculation of historical volatility in some detail, the reader may have been left with the impression that the method

---

[3]Mark B. Garman and Michael J. Klass, "On the Estimation of Security Price Volatilities from Historical Data," *Journal of Business* 53(1):67–78, 1980.

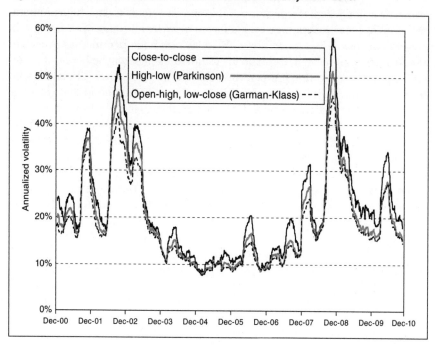

chosen will be an important determinant of whether an option strategy is successful or not. For most traders, though, historical volatility is simply a guideline to what the trader is really interested in—the future realized volatility. Because the results of each method are unlikely to differ significantly, in practice, it probably does not make much difference which method is chosen. It is far more important to be able to interpret historical volatility data rather than to worry about the exact method used.

Some Volatility Characteristics

In Chapter 6, we used the analogy that the volatility in its different interpretations—historical, future, implied—is similar to the weather. The volatility-weather analogy can also help us identify some basic volatility characteristics.

Suppose that we are trying to estimate tomorrow's high temperature, and we have only one piece of information, today's high temperature. What is our best estimate? Because temperatures do not usually change dramatically from one day to the next, our best estimate of tomorrow's high temperature is probably the same as today's high temperature. Temperature readings are said to be *serial correlated*. In the absence of other information, the best guess about what will happen over the next time period is what happened over the last time period. Volatility seems to exhibit this serial correlation characteristic. What will happen in the future often depends on what happened in the past.

Now suppose that we know not only today's high temperature but we also know the average high temperature at this time of year. If today's high temperature is higher than the average, an intelligent estimate for tomorrow's high probably will be lower than today's high. If today's high temperature is lower than the average, an intelligent estimate for tomorrow's high will be higher than today's high. We know that temperatures tend to be *mean reverting*. Volatility also seems to exhibit this characteristic. There is a greater likelihood that volatility, like temperature, will move toward the mean rather than away from it.

We can see the mean-reverting characteristic of volatility if we compare Figure 20-2, the three-month volatility of gold, with Figure 20-4, the price of gold over the same period.[4] Both prices and volatility sometimes rise and sometimes fall. But unlike the price of an underlying contract, which can move in one direction for long periods of time, there seems to be an equilibrium number to which volatility tends to return. Over the 10-year period in question, the price of gold rose from under $300 per ounce to over $1,400 per ounce. Although prices fluctuated, they never again reached the lows of 2001. On the other hand, gold volatility, in spite of dramatic fluctuations between a low of 9 percent and a high of over 40 percent, always seemed to return eventually to the 10 to 20 percent range.

We might conclude from Figure 20-2 that gold tends to exhibit a long-term average or *mean volatility*. When volatility rises above the mean, one can be fairly certain that it will eventually fall back to its mean. When volatility falls below

Figure 20-4 Gold futures prices: 2001–2010.

---

[4]Historical gold volatility in Figure 20-2 and Bund volatility in Figure 20-5 were calculated from settlement prices of the front-month futures contract.

the mean, one can be fairly certain that it will eventually rise to its mean. There is a constant gyration back and forth through this mean.

Mean reversion is a common volatility characteristic of almost all traded underlying contracts. Figures 20-1 and 20-5 show the three-month historical volatility, using daily returns, for the S&P 500 Index and Bund futures from 2001 to 2010. In spite of the dramatic fluctuations, both the S&P 500 Index and Bund futures tend to exhibit a mean volatility to which both contracts tend to return. In the case of the S&P 500 Index, this seems to be somewhere between 15 and 20 percent. In the case of the Bund, a much less volatile contract, the mean volatility seems to be around 5 percent.

In Figures 20-6 through 20-8, we can see more clearly the mean-reverting characteristic of volatility. These graphs show the minimum, maximum, and average realized volatilities for the S&P 500 Index, gold futures, and Bund futures from 2001 to 2010 over time periods ranging from 2 to 300 weeks. For example, in Figure 20-6, if we consider every possible two-week period from 2001 to 2010, we can see that the minimum two-week volatility for the S&P 500 Index was approximately 5 percent, while the maximum two-week volatility was just over 100 percent. The average two-week volatility was approximately 18 percent. For every possible 300-week period, the minimum volatility for the S&P 500 Index was approximately 14 percent, the maximum volatility was 24 percent, and the average volatility was approximately 19 percent. The graphs for the gold futures (Figure 20-7) and for Bund futures (Figure 20-8) show the same

Figure 20-5 Bund futures three-month historical volatility: 2001–2010.

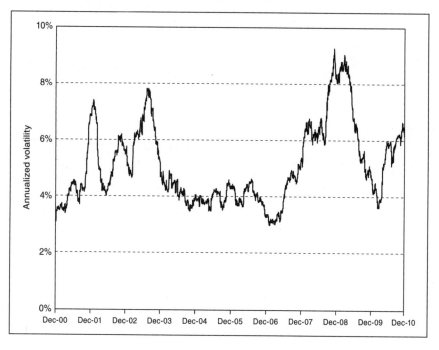

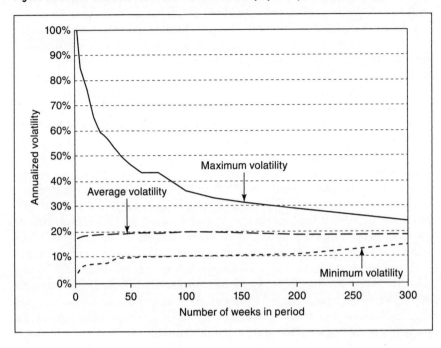

Figure 20-6 S&P 500 Index historical realized volatility by time period: 2001–2010.

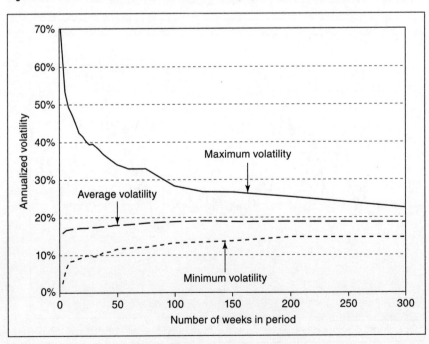

Figure 20-7 Gold futures historical realized volatility by time period: 2001–2010.

Figure 20-8 Bund futures historical realized volatility by time period: 2001–2010.

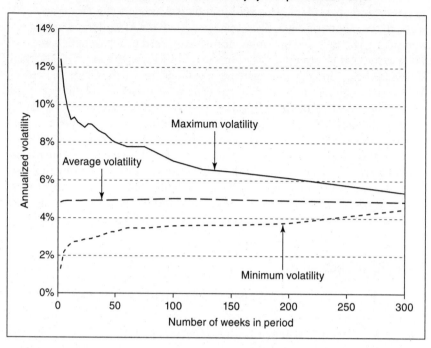

general characteristics. As we increase the length of time over which the volatility is calculated, the results tend to converge to an average or mean volatility.

Graphs similar to those in Figures 20-6 through 20-8 are often used to illustrate the *term structure* of volatility—the likelihood of volatility falling within a given range over a specified period of time. The term-structure graph typically has a conic shape, with greater variations over short periods of time and smaller variations over long periods.[5] Because of the term structure of volatility, it is often easier to predict long-term volatility than short-term volatility. This may seem counterintuitive because we tend to expect greater variability over long periods of time than over short periods. However, volatility can be thought of as an average variability. Over long periods of time, the large and small price fluctuations tend to offset each other, resulting in more stable results.

Because long-term volatility tends to be more stable than short-term volatility, one might assume that it is easier to value long-term options than short-term options. This would be true if all options were equally sensitive to changes in volatility. But we know that long-term options have greater vega values than short-term options—they are more sensitive to changes in volatility. This means that any volatility error will be greatly magnified when evaluating a long-term option. Depending on the time to expiration, the effect of a two or three percentage point volatility error on a long-term option may be greater than a five or six percentage point error on a short-term option.

---

[5] For additional discussion of *volatility cones*, see Galen Burghardt and Morton Lane, "How to Tell If Options Are Cheap," *Journal of Portfolio Management*, Winter:72–78, 1990.

What else can we say about volatility? Looking again at Figure 20-2, we might surmise that volatility has some trending characteristics. From early 2004 through the middle of 2005, there was a persistent downward trend in gold volatility. This was followed by a more dramatic upward trend from the middle of 2005 to the middle of 2006. And from early 2007 through most of 2008, there seemed to be a stepping-stone increase in volatility to a high of over 40 percent. Within these major trends, there were also minor trends as volatility rose and fell for short periods of time. In this respect, volatility charts seem to display some of the same characteristics as price charts, and it would not be unreasonable to apply some of the same principles used in technical analysis to volatility analysis. It is important to remember, however, that although price changes and volatility are related, they are not the same thing. If a trader tries to apply exactly the same rules of technical analysis to volatility analysis, he is likely to find that in some cases the rules have no relevance and that in other cases the rules must be modified to take into account the unique characteristics of volatility.

Volatility Forecasting

How can we use historical volatility data, together with the characteristics of volatility, to predict future realized volatility? Suppose that we have the following historical volatility data for an underlying contract:

6-week historical volatility:	28 percent
12-week historical volatility:	22 percent
26-week historical volatility:	19 percent
52-week historical volatility:	18 percent

We might prefer to look at more volatility data, but if these are the only data available, how should we go about making a volatility forecast?

One possible approach is to simply average all the available data:

$$(28\% + 22\% + 19\% + 18\%)/4 = 21.75\%$$

Using this method, each piece of historical data is given equal weight. But is this reasonable? Perhaps some data are more important than other data. A trader might assume, for example, that the more current the data, the greater their importance. Because the 28 percent volatility over the last six weeks is more current than the other volatility data, perhaps 28 percent should play a greater role in our volatility forecast. We might, for example, give twice the weight, 40 percent, to the six-week volatility but only 20 percent weight to each of the other time periods:

$$(40\% \times 28\%) + (20\% \times 22\%) + (20\% \times 19\%) + (20\% \times 18\%) = 23.0\%$$

Our volatility forecast has increased slightly because of the additional weight given to the six-week historical volatility.

Of course, if it is true that the more recent volatility over the last 6 weeks is more important than the other data, it follows that the volatility over the last 12 weeks ought to be more important than the volatility over the last 26 and 52 weeks. It also follows that the volatility over the last 26 weeks must be more important that the volatility over the last 52 weeks. We can factor this into our forecast by using a regressive weighting, giving more distant volatility data progressively less weight in our forecast. For example, we might calculate

$$(40\% \times 28\%) + (30\% \times 22\%) + (20\% \times 19\%) + (10\% \times 18\%) = 23.4\%$$

Here we have given the 6-week volatility 40 percent of the weight, the 12-week volatility 30 percent of the weight, the 26-week volatility 20 percent of the weight, and the 52-week volatility 10 percent of the weight.

We have made the assumption that the more recent the data, the greater their importance. Is this always true? If we are interested in evaluating short-term options, it may be true that data that cover short periods of time are the most important. But suppose that we are interested in evaluating very long-term options. Over long periods of time, the mean-reverting characteristic of volatility is likely to reduce the importance of any short-term fluctuations in volatility. In fact, over very long periods of time, the most reasonable volatility forecast is simply the long-term mean volatility of the instrument. Therefore, the relative weight we give to the different volatility data will depend on the amount of time remaining to expiration for the options in which we are interested.

In a sense, all the historical volatilities we have at our disposal are current; they simply cover different periods of time. How do we know which data are the most important? In addition to the mean-reverting characteristic, we know that volatility also tends to be serial correlated. The volatility over any given period is likely to depend on, or correlate with, the volatility over the previous period, assuming that both periods cover the same amount of time. If the volatility of a contract over the last four weeks was 15 percent, the volatility over the next four weeks is more likely to be close to 15 percent than far away from 15 percent. Once we realize this, we might logically choose to give the greatest weight to the volatility data covering a time period closest to the life of the options in which we are interested. That is, if we are trading very long-term options, the long-term data should be given the most weight. If we are trading very short-term options, the short-term data should be given the most weight. And if we are trading intermediate-term options, the intermediate-term data should be given the most weight.

Given the serial correlation characteristic of volatility, what volatility should we assign to options that expire in five months if we have only our four historical volatilities: 6-week, 12-week, 26-week, and 52-week volatilities? Because 5 months is closest to 26 weeks, we can give the 26-week volatility the greatest weight and give other data correspondingly lesser weight

$$(15\% \times 28\%) + (25\% \times 22\%) + (35\% \times 19\%) + (25\% \times 18\%) = 20.85\%$$

Alternatively, if we are interested in evaluating 3-month options, we can give the greatest weight to the 12-week historical volatility

$$(25\% \times 28\%) + (35\% \times 22\%) + (25\% \times 19\%) + (15\% \times 18\%) = 22.15\%$$

In the foregoing examples, we used only four historical volatilities. But the more volatility data that are available, the more accurate any volatility forecast is likely to be. Not only will more data, covering different periods of time, give a better overview of the volatility characteristics of an underlying instrument, they will also enable a trader to more closely match historical volatilities to options with different periods of time to expiration. In our examples, we used historical volatilities over the last 12 and 26 weeks as approximations to forecast volatilities over the next six and three months. Ideally, we would like historical data covering exactly six- and three-month periods.

This approach to forecasting volatility is one that many traders use intuitively. It depends on identifying the typical characteristics of volatility and then projecting a volatility over some future period.

The analysis of a data series in order to predict future values falls into an area of study usually referred to as *time-series analysis*. We might wish to apply time-series models to volatility forecasting, but to do so, we need a series of data points where each point is independent of every other point. In our examples, the volatilities we used to make our prediction do not form a true time series because the volatilities overlap and, as such, are not really independent of each other. The 52-week volatility overlaps the 26-, 12-, and 6-week volatilities. The 26-week volatility overlaps the 12- and 6-week volatilities. And the 12-week volatility overlaps the 6-week volatility. But suppose that instead of using as our data points, the historical volatilities, we use the underlying returns. These returns create a true time series to which we might be able to apply a time-series model.

One time-series model often used to estimate future volatility is the *exponentially weighted moving average* (EWMA) *model*. In this model, greater weight is always given to more recent returns, with older returns given progressively smaller weightings. If α is the weighting assigned to each return r, then the estimated variance (the square of the standard deviation) σ^2 over the next period of time is given by

$$\sigma^2 = \alpha_1 r_1^2 + \alpha_2 r_2^2 + \cdots + \alpha_{n-1} r_{n-1}^2 + \alpha_n r_n^2$$

where r_n is the most recent return. The constraints are that all the weightings must add up to 1.00

$$\sum_{i=1}^{n} \alpha_i = 1.00$$

and that the more recent the return, the greater is the weighting

$$\alpha_n > \alpha_{n-1}$$

By choosing a variable λ between 0 and 1.00, the constraints will be met if

$$\alpha_i = \frac{\lambda^{i-1}(1-\lambda)}{1-\lambda^n}$$

As we reduce the value of λ, more recent returns are assigned progressively greater weight—the variance estimate tends to discount the effect of older returns. As we increase the value of λ, the estimate makes less and less distinction between returns—older returns become just as important as newer returns. As λ approaches 1.00 (it can never be exactly 1.00), the weight for all returns converges to a single value, $1.00/n$. A common choice for λ in many risk-management programs is something close to 0.94.

The EWMA model is relatively simple method for predicting volatility. Two factors that it ignores are the likely correlation between successive returns and the mean-reversion characteristic of volatility. The time-series models most often used to forecast volatility were an outgrowth of the *autoregressive conditional heteroskedasticity* (ARCH) *model* first proposed by Robert Engle in 1982.[6] The techniques used in ARCH models have subsequently been refined and extended into what is now commonly referred to as the *generalized autoregressive conditional heteroskedasticity* (GARCH) family of volatility forecasting models. GARCH models consist of three components: a volatility estimate, such as EWMA; a correlation component reflecting the fact that the magnitude of successive returns tends to be correlated (i.e., large returns tend to be followed by large returns, and small returns tend to be followed by small returns); and a mean-reversion component specifying how fast volatility tends to revert to its mean. An in-depth discussion of GARCH models is beyond the scope of this text, but further information on these models is available in most advanced texts on time-series analysis.

Implied Volatility as a Predictor of Future Volatility

If, as many traders believe, prices in the marketplace reflect all available information affecting the value of a contract,[7] the best predictor of the future realized volatility ought to be the implied volatility. Just how good a predictor of future volatility is implied volatility? Although it may be impossible to answer this question definitively, because that would require a detailed study of many markets over long periods of time, we still might gain some insight by looking at sample data.

Figure 20-9 shows the three-month realized volatility (approximately 63 trading days) for the S&P 500 Index and a rolling implied volatility for three-month at-the-money options[8] on the index from 2002 through 2010. However, the values for the three-month realized volatility have been shifted forward so that each data point represents the future realized volatility of the index over the next three months. If implied volatility is a perfect predictor of future volatility, both graphs would be identical, but obviously, this is not the case.

---

[6]Robert F. Engle, "Autoregressive Conditional Heteroskedsticity with Estimates of the Variance of United Kingdom Inflation," *Econometrica* 50(4):987–1000, 1982. Engle was awarded the 2003 Nobel Prize in Economics.
[7]This is known in finance as the *efficient-market hypothesis*.
[8]The three-month implied volatility was calculated by interpolating between the implied volatility of options bracketing three months.

In general, the volatility of the S&P 500 Index tends to lead the implied volatility. If the index becomes more volatile, implied volatility rises; if the index becomes less volatile, implied volatility falls. The marketplace seems to react to the volatility of the index. This was particularly evident during 2008, when implied volatility rose following the dramatic increase in volatility of the index, and in 2009, when implied volatility fell as the index itself became less volatile.

We can do the same comparison using a 12-month period. Figure 20-10 shows the 12-month future realized volatility of the S&P 500 Index (approximately 252 trading days) versus a rolling 12-month at-the-money implied volatility over the same time period. Here the lag is even more evident due to the longer time frame.

Clearly, the implied volatility in our examples did not accurately predict future volatility. But, even if the implied volatility was not a totally accurate predictor, perhaps we can draw some conclusions by looking at the difference between the implied volatility and the future realized volatility. This is shown in Figure 20-11 for both 3- and 12-month options. A positive value indicates an implied volatility that was too low (the future realized volatility turned out to be higher), while a negative value indicates an implied volatility that was too high (the future realized volatility turned out to be lower).

We can see in Figure 20-11 that for much of the period in question, implied volatility seemed to predict a future volatility that was too high by up to 10 percentage points. But there are some dramatic exceptions. During 2008,

Figure 20-9 S&P 500 Index three-month future volatility versus the three-month implied volatility.

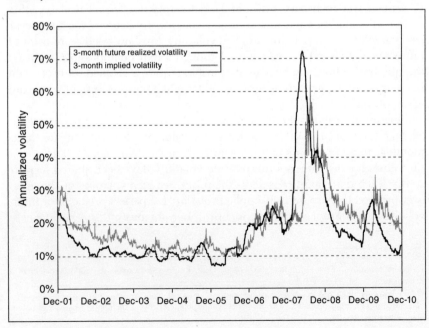

Figure 20-10 S&P 500 Index 12-month future volatility versus the 12-month implied volatility.

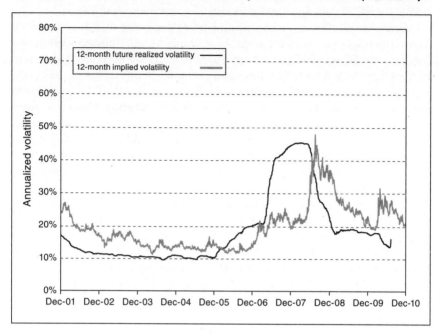

the three-month implied volatility at one point predicted a future volatility that was too low by almost 50 percentage points and at another point predicted a volatility that was too high by 20 percentage points. Admittedly, 2008 was a year

Figure 20-11 Difference between future volatility and implied volatility for the S&P 500 Index.

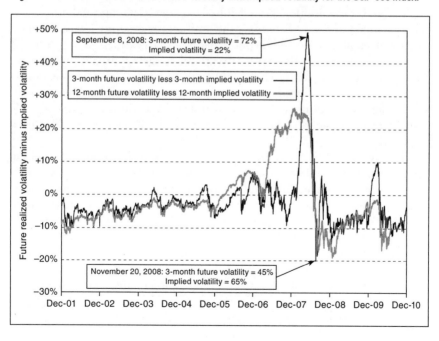

of extremes, but even during other years, a difference of 10 percentage points between implied volatility and future volatility was not uncommon.

Implied volatility is at best an imperfect predictor of future volatility. What else might we conclude from these graphs? Under normal conditions, implied volatility seems to be too high—options tend to be overpriced. Buyers of options may be willing to pay this extra premium in return for the few occasions when implied volatility is dramatically too low and there is a subsequent volatility explosion. This is analogous to insurance. A rational buyer of insurance is aware that the price of an insurance contract is almost certainly higher than its value. Otherwise, the insurance company would have no profit expectation. But buyers of insurance are willing to pay this extra premium for those rare occasions when an unforeseen event occurs and the insurance becomes absolutely necessary.

There are, of course, other reasons why options tend to be overpriced. For the seller of an option, such as a market maker, there may be a cost to replicating the option through the dynamic hedging process, a cost that the market maker is likely to pass on to the customer. Moreover, there may be weaknesses in the theoretical pricing model from which implied volatility is derived. Taken together, these factors may in fact justify the seemingly inflated prices of options in the marketplace.

The Term Structure of Implied Volatility

If held to expiration, the sole determinant of an option position's value is, in theory, the realized volatility of the underlying contract. However, a trader may decide for a variety of reasons that a position should be closed prior to expiration. The position may have achieved its expected profit potential prior to expiration. Or the position, even if it hasn't achieved its expected profit, may have become too risky. Or holding the position may require a large amount of capital, capital that could be put to better use. Regardless of why a trader decides to close out a position prior to expiration, there is usually one primary cause: changes in implied volatility. Although we have emphasized the importance of realized volatility, in the real world of option trading, changes in implied volatility can often make or break a strategy. For this reason, a sensible trader will give some thought to how changes in implied volatility will affect a position.

It may seem that determining the sensitivity of a position to changes in implied volatility is relatively simple. We need only determine the total position vega, which we can do by adding up all the individual vega values. Unfortunately, determining the true implied volatility risk can be significantly more complex. We know that vega values change with changing market conditions, so today's vega may not be tomorrow's vega. Moreover, the vega values across different exercise prices and expiration months may not be a true reflection of implied-volatility risk.

Consider a market where there are three expiration months, all in the same calendar year—March, June, and September. Let's assume that the mean volatility in this market is 25 percent, and although this almost never happens, let's also assume that the current implied volatility for every month is the same, 25 percent.

	March	June	September
Implied volatility	25%	25%	25%

Suppose that the volatility of the underlying contract begins to rise. What will happen to implied volatility? Implied volatility will almost certainly rise, but will it rise at the same rate for each month? If the implied volatility for March rises to 30 percent, will the implied volatility of June and September also rise to 30 percent? Traders know that volatility is mean reverting, and there is a greater likelihood that volatility will revert to its mean over long periods of time than over short periods. Therefore, as we move to more distant expirations, implied volatility is likely to remain closer to its mean, in this case, 25 percent. The new implied volatilities might be

	March	June	September
Implied volatility	30%	28%	26%

Mean reversion will also affect falling implied volatility. If the underlying market becomes less volatile and implied volatility in March falls to 20 percent, the new implied volatilities might be

	March	June	September
Implied volatility	20%	22%	24%

Even if there is a large change in the implied volatility of short-term options, the implied volatility of long-term options will tend to change less because of the mean-reversion characteristics of volatility. Figure 20-12 shows the typical term structure of implied volatility.

The fact that implied volatilities across different expiration months change at different rates can have important implications for risk analysis. Consider an option position consisting of four different expiration months with the following vega values for each month:

	April	June	August	October
Time to expiration	2 months	4 months	6 months	8 months
Total vega	+15.00	−36.00	−21.00	+42.00

What is the implied-volatility risk of the position? We might begin by adding up all the vegas

$$+15.00 - 36.00 - 21.00 + 42.00 = 0$$

With a total vega of 0, it might appear that there is no implied-volatility risk. This, however, assumes that implied volatility will change at the same rate across all months. But we know that this is unlikely. The implied volatility of

Figure 20-12 The term structure of implied volatility.

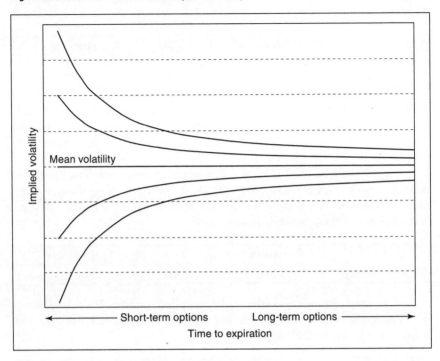

short-term options will tend to change more quickly than the implied volatility of long-term options. Given this, how should we determine our total implied-volatility risk?

Suppose that the mean volatility in this market is 25 percent and that we believe that the term structure of implied volatility is similar to that shown in Figure 20-13. If April implied volatility rises to 28 percent, what will be the profit or loss to the position? If there are two months remaining to April expiration and implied volatility in April rises to 28 percent, we expect June implied volatility to rise to only 27 percent, August implied volatility to only 26.5 percent, and October to only 26.1 percent. Adjusting for the different rates of change, the result is a loss because

$$(3 \times 15.00) - (2 \times 36.00) - (1.5 \times 21.00) + (1.1 \times 42.00) = -12.30$$

And if April implied volatility falls to 22 percent, the result will be reversed; we will show a profit of 12.30. Clearly, the position is not *vega neutral*. We would much prefer implied volatility to fall than rise.

In order to form a more accurate picture of the implied-volatility risk, we must adjust the vega values for each month. We know that for each percentage point change in April implied volatility, June implied volatility will change by

$$2/3 = 0.67$$

Figure 20-13 Relative changes in implied volatility for April, June, August, and October options.

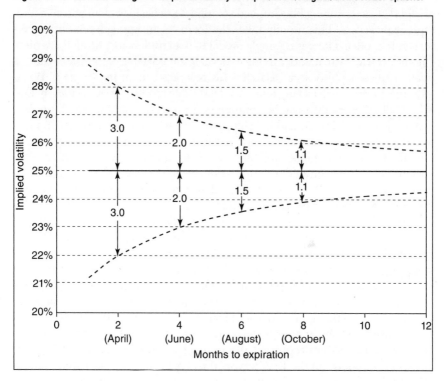

For each percentage point change in April implied volatility, August implied volatility will change by

$$1.5/3 = 0.50$$

And for each percentage point change in April implied volatility, October implied volatility will change by

$$1.1/3 = 0.37$$

If we want to know our total implied-volatility risk in terms of changes in April implied volatility, we can adjust our vega values accordingly

$$\text{June vega} = -36.00 \times 0.67 = -24.12$$
$$\text{August vega} = -21.00 \times 0.5 = -10.50$$
$$\text{October vega} = +42.00 \times 0.37 = +15.54$$

Adding everything up, we can see that we do indeed have a short vega position. For each percentage point change in April implied volatility, the value of the total position will change by

$$+15.00 - 24.12 - 10.50 + 15.54 = -4.08$$

In order to accurately assess implied-volatility risk, a trader will need some method of determining how implied volatilities are likely to change across multiple expirations. This usually takes the form of an implied-volatility term-structure model. There is no single model that all traders use. Models are often "home grown," with a trader trying to develop a model that is consistent with his mathematical sophistication, as well as his experience in the marketplace. Whatever the model, it will usually require at least three inputs: a *primary month* against which all other months will be compared, a mean volatility to which implied volatility tends to revert, and a "whippiness" factor that specifies how implied volatility changes across other expirations with respect to changes in the primary month. The primary month will often be the front month, where trading activity tends to be concentrated. But this is not always the case. In agricultural markets, trading activity is often concentrated in expiration months that fall close to either the planting or harvesting calendar. If this is the case, one of these months may be a better choice as the primary month. Additionally, implied volatility in the front month can be unstable, especially as expiration approaches. It often changes in ways that are inconsistent with the term structure of other expiration months. As a result, many traders evaluate their position in front-month contracts separately from their positions in other months, with the volatility term-structure model applying to all months except the front month. The primary month chosen in this approach will be something other than the front month.

Figure 20-14 shows how the term structure of implied volatility can evolve over time. The values represent the implied volatilities during 2010 of at-the-money options on the EuroStoxx 50 Index for expirations extending out 24 months. Values were calculated at two-month intervals, on the first Friday of February, April, June, August, October, and December. The reader may find it useful to compare the changes in the term-structure graphs with the 30-day historical volatility of the EuroStoxx 50 Index during this period, shown in Figure 20-15. In early February, the term-structure graph was downward sloping: long-term options were trading at lower implied volatilities than short-term options. By April, as a result of declining index volatility, not only had implied volatility declined, but the term-structure graph had inverted and was upward sloping: long-term options were trading at higher implied volatilities than short-term options. After a dramatic increase in index volatility, the June term-structure graph again became downward sloping. Finally, after declining index volatility in the last half of 2010, implied volatilities seemed to settle into a middle area, with a relatively flat term structure.

Note one other important point: the disconnect between the front-month implied volatility and the remainder of the term-structure graph in December. The graph is generally upward sloping, but the front-month implied volatility is still much higher than all other months. This is a common characteristic in many option markets. The front-month implied volatility can often trade in a way that is inconsistent with the term structure of other months.

The term structure in Figure 20-12 is typical of markets where the only factors that tend to affect implied volatility are the recent volatility of the underlying contract and the mean volatility. However, in some markets, there may also be a seasonal volatility factor.

Figure 20-14 Implied-volatility term structure for EuroStoxx 50 Index options during 2010.

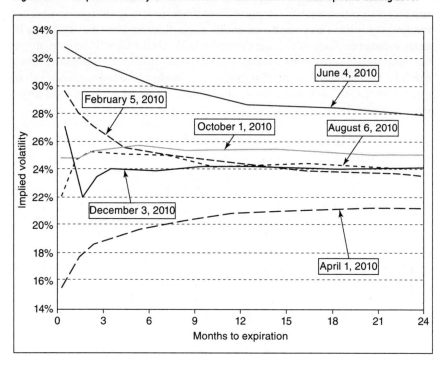

Figure 20-15 EuroStoxx 50 Index 30-day historical volatility during 2010.

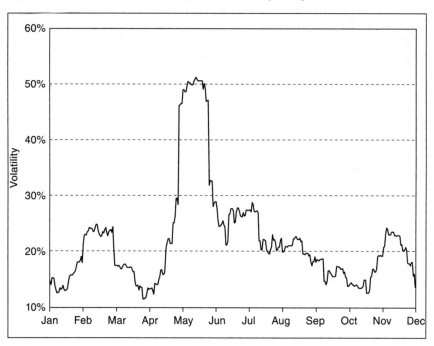

Given the possibility of extremely hot temperatures, as well as droughts, summer expiration months in agricultural markets typically trade at higher implied volatilities than other months, regardless of the time of year. In energy markets where fuel is needed for heating in the winter and cooling in the summer, the possibility of very cold winters and very hot summers may result in some months trading at persistently higher implied volatilities than other months. In such markets, it can be difficult to create a reliable term-structure model.

Figure 20-16 shows the changing term structure of implied volatility for options on natural gas futures during 2009. Although not as obvious as the Eurostox 50 Index in Figure 20-14, we can still detect the tendency of long-term implied volatility to revert to a mean, perhaps around 40 percent. But in addition, there is also a seasonal volatility factor. Note the implied volatility of the October option contract, which has been highlighted with a circle. Regardless of the term structure, October options always seem to trade at an inflated implied volatility. This is perhaps easier to see in Figure 20-17, which shows the average implied volatility of each expiration month during 2009. October clearly carries a higher implied volatility than any other month. The reason for this has to do primarily with the Atlantic hurricane season, which extends from approximately early June to late November, with the height of the season falling in August and September. During this period, any major hurricane can

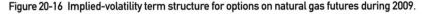

Figure 20-16 Implied-volatility term structure for options on natural gas futures during 2009.

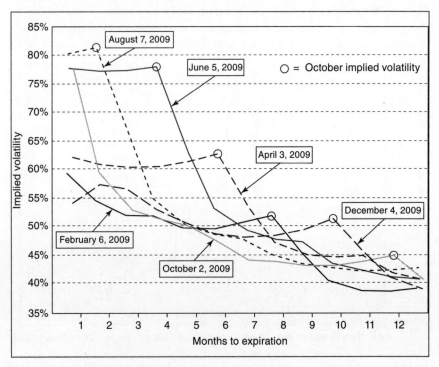

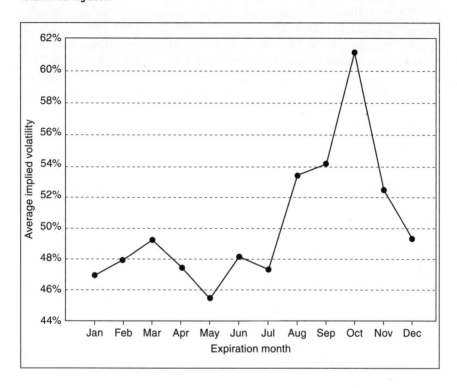

Figure 20-17 Average implied volatility by expiration month of options on natural gas futures during 2009.

disrupt natural gas operations, which in the United States are concentrated along the northern coast of the Gulf of Mexico. October options, which expire toward the end of September, will capture any volatility occurring during the height of the hurricane season. Consequently, October options tend to trade at consistently higher implied volatilities than other months.

Forward Volatility

Let's return to the term-structure graphs of implied volatilities across expiration months shown in Figure 20-14. Can we identify any trading opportunities from these graphs? We might simply decide that implied volatility is either too high, in which case we will prefer to sell options, or too low, in which case we will prefer to buy options. In either case, we can, in theory, capture a perceived mispricing by dynamically hedging the position with the underlying contract. But we might also ask a different question: are any expiration months mispriced with respect to other expiration months? Should we consider some type of calendar spread, selling options in one month and buying options in a different month?

Let's focus on one graph from Figure 20-14, the term structure of Eurostoxx 50 Index options on February 5, 2010. This is shown in Figure 20-18. The large dots represent the at-the-money implied volatilities, with the solid black line representing the best fit generated by a term-structure model. We can see that some contract months seem to deviate from the best-fit line. June 2010 implied volatility falls below the line, whiles September and December 2010 fall above the line. Assuming that each month is in fact trading at the indicated implied volatility,[9] do these deviations represent a trading opportunity? Should we be buying June options and selling September or December options?

One method that traders use to determine the mispricing of a calendar spread is to consider the spread's implied volatility. That is, what single volatility applied to both expiration months will cause the value of the spread to be equal to its price in the marketplace? To better understand this, let's use the volatilities in Figure 20-18 to calculate the prices of several calendar spreads. For simplicity, we will assume that the underlying contract is trading at 100 and that there are no interest-rate considerations. The relevant data is shown in Figure 20-19.

Looking at the February/March calendar spread, the implied volatilities for the two months are 29.61 percent for February and 28.06 percent for March.

Figure 20-18 Implied volatility for at-the-money EuroStoxx 50 Index options on February 5, 2010.

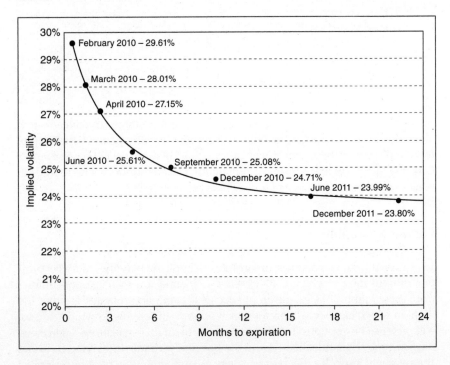

Expiration Month	Time to Expiration (days)	Implied Volatility	Price of the 100 Call	Vega of the 100 Call
February 2010	14	29.61%	2.31	0.078
March 2010	42	28.06%	3.80	0.135
April 2010	70	27.15%	4.74	0.174
June 2010	133	25.61%	6.15	0.240
September 2010	224	25.08%	7.82	0.311
December 2010	315	24.71%	9.14	0.368
June 2011	497	23.99%	11.13	0.461
December 2011	679	23.80%	12.89	0.537

Calendar Spread	Spread Price	Spread Implied Volatility	Spread Vega
February 2010 / March 2010	1.49	25.94%	0.057
March 2010 / April 2010	0.94	24.02%	0.039
April 2010 / June 2010	1.41	21.50%	0.066
June 2010 / September 2010	1.67	23.28%	0.071
September 2010 / December 2010	1.32	22.70%	0.071
December 2010 / June 2011	1.99	21.13%	0.093
June 2011 / December 2011	1.76	22.67%	0.076

The values of the at-the-money calls are 2.31 and 3.80, with a spread value of 1.49. If we evaluate these options using the same volatility, what single volatility will yield a value equal to the price of 1.49? Logically, this volatility has to be less than 28.06 percent because at this volatility the March option is fairly priced, but the February option is too expensive. The entire spread will be worth more than 1.49. We need to reduce the volatility until we find the single volatility that will cause the spread to be worth 1.49. Using a computer, we find that the February/March calendar spread has an implied volatility of 25.94 percent.

We can go through this process for each successive calendar spread, calculating the implied volatility of each spread. These volatilities are shown at the bottom of Figure 20-19. How will these calendar spread implied volatilities look if we overlay them on Figure 20-18? This is shown in Figure 20-20. We can see clearly that the June 2010 options are significantly underpriced in the marketplace compared with nearby expirations, while the September 2010 options are significantly overpriced. If given a choice of strategies, it might make sense to buy the April/June 2010 calendar spread and sell the June/September 2010 calendar spread. Together these spreads make up a time butterfly.

We use these implied volatilities not to determine whether implied volatility in the entire option complex is either too high or too low but rather to determine whether particular months are mispriced with respect to other months.

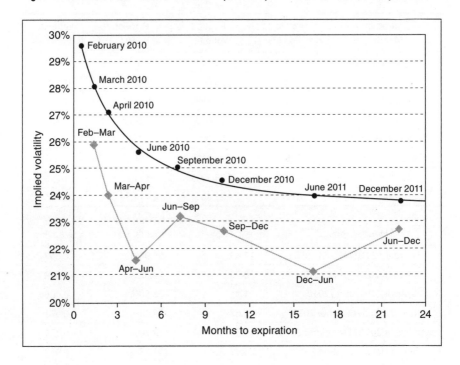

The implied-volatility graph acts as a magnifying glass, enabling us to more easily determine which months are overpriced and which are underpriced.

When the term-structure graph is downward sloping, as it is in Figure 20-20, all calendar spread implied volatilities will fall below the term-structure graph. Alternatively, if the term-structure graph is upward sloping, all calendar spread implied volatilities will fall above the graph. If all implied volatilities fall exactly along the best-fit graph, regardless of whether the graph is upward or downward sloping, the implied-volatility curve will be smooth, suggesting that there are no obviously mispriced calendar spreads.

Determining the exact implied volatility of a calendar spread usually requires a computer programmed with a pricing model. However, it is often possible to estimate the implied volatility of an at-the-money calendar spread if we recall that the vega of an at-the-money option is relatively constant with respect to changes in volatility. Suppose that we know both the prices O_1 and O_2 and the vega values V_1 and V_2 of the two options that make up the calendar spread. The price of the spread is $O_2 - O_1$, and the vega of the spread is $V_2 - V_1$. The implied volatility of the spread, given as a whole number, is approximately equal to the price of the spread divided by its vega

$$\text{Spread implied volicity} = \frac{O_2 - O_1}{V_2 - V_1}$$

This method is not exact because there is likely to be rounding error, and the vega does change slightly as we change volatility. However, this approach may be useful if a trader needs to make a quick estimate of whether a calendar spread is overpriced or underpriced.

The vega values for the individual options, as well as for the various calendar spreads, are given in Figure 20-20. The reader may find it worthwhile to estimate the implied volatility of each spread using this method and then compare the result with the true implied volatility of the spread.

Instead of analyzing the volatility term structure by looking at the implied volatility of successive calendar spreads, we might take a slightly more theoretical approach. Suppose that we have two option expirations, a short-term option expiring at t_1 and a long-term option expiring at t_2. If the implied volatility of the short-term expiration is σ_1 and the implied volatility of the long-term expiration is σ_2, we might ask this question: what *forward volatility* σ_f is the marketplace implying between expiration of the short-term option and expiration of the long-term option?

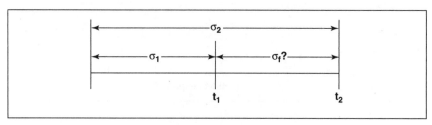

This is analogous to a *forward rate* in an interest-rate market. Given a short-term interest rate and a long-term interest rate, what rate must apply between the two maturities such that no arbitrage opportunity exists? Unlike interest rates, which are directly proportional to time, volatility is proportional to the square root of time. Using this, we can calculate the forward volatility[10]

$$\sigma_f = \sqrt{\frac{(\sigma_2^2 \times t_2) - (\sigma_1^2 \times t_1)}{t_2 - t_1}}$$

We can expand this relationship to any number of volatilities over any number of consecutive time periods. Given forward volatilities σ_i covering the time from t_{i-1} to t_i, the volatility over the entire time period from t_0 to t_n must be

$$\sigma_{t_n - t_0} = \sqrt{\sum_{i=1}^{n} \frac{\sigma_{t_i - (t_i - 1)}^2 \times (t_i - t_{i-1})}{t_n - t_0}}$$

---

[10]Some readers may recognize that the forward volatility calculation results from the fact that the square of volatility or variance σ^2 is directly proportional to time

$\sigma_f^2 \times (t_2 - t_1) = (\sigma_2^2 \times t_2) - (\sigma_1^2 \times t_1)$

Figure 20-21

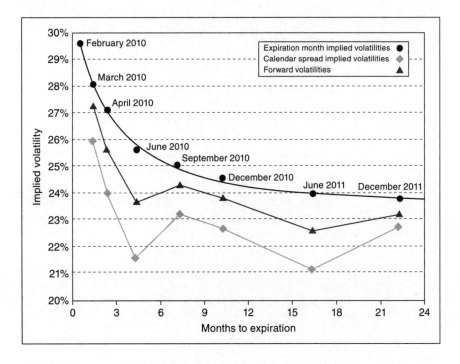

Suppose that we calculate the forward volatilities for the volatility term structure in Figure 20-20. How would this compare with the implied volatilities of the calendar spreads? This is shown in Figure 20-21. The forward volatility graph has the same general structure as the calendar spread graph. Both graphs serve the same purpose—to highlight any mispricing of a particular expiration month.

Every experienced option trader knows that dealing with volatility can be a difficult task. To facilitate the decision-making process, we have attempted to make some generalizations about volatility characteristics. Even then, it may not be clear what the right strategy is. Moreover, looking at a limited number of examples makes the generalizations even less reliable. Every market has its own characteristics, and understanding the volatility characteristics of a particular market, whether interest rates, foreign currencies, stocks, or commodities, is at least as important as knowing the technical characteristics of volatility. And this knowledge can only come from careful study of a market combined with actual trading experience.

Position Analysis

Investors or speculators in option markets often have a particular view of market conditions in terms of either direction or volatility. They attempt to profit from this view through the selection of spreading strategies such as those discussed in Chapters 11 and 12. In Chapter 13, we looked at the risk characteristics of some of these strategies under changing market conditions. Because each spread consisted of a limited number of contracts, it was a relatively simple matter to determine the risks that each spread entailed.

An active option trader, such as a market maker, may build up much more complex positions consisting of many different options across a wide range of exercise prices and expiration months. Unlike simple strategies, where the risks are relatively easy to identify, analysis of a complex position can be particularly difficult because of the many ways in which risks can change as market conditions change. If a trader cannot determine the risks of a position, he will be unprepared to take the necessary action to protect himself when market conditions move against him or to take advantage of his good fortune when market conditions move in his favor.

Before theoretical pricing models came into widespread use, analyzing a complex position made up of many different options was often an impossible task. Even if a trader had some idea of how each option changed as market conditions changed, combining many different options often caused the entire position to change in unexpected ways. Still, if he expected to survive, an intelligent trader needed to make some effort to analyze the position.

In the early days of option trading, one common approach to analyzing risk was to use synthetic relationships to rewrite a position in a more easily recognizable form. If the rewritten position conformed to a strategy with which the trader was familiar, the trader might then be able to determine the risks of the position.

For example, consider this position:

    +29 underlying contracts
    −19 March 65 calls
    +19 March 65 puts

-7 March 70 calls
+49 March 70 puts
-33 March 75 calls
-51 March 75 puts
+30 March 80 calls
+12 March 80 puts

Suppose that the underlying contract is trading at a price of 71.50. What is the delta of this position—positive, negative, or neutral? Without a theoretical pricing model, this may look like an impossible question to answer. And, indeed, without a model, there is no way of knowing the exact delta of the position. But even if we cannot determine the exact delta, perhaps we can determine the direction in which we want the underlying contract to move.

Using synthetic relationships, positions that consist of both calls and puts can be rewritten so that they consist of a single type of option, either all calls or all puts. This can sometimes make a position easier to analyze. Let's take our position and rewrite it so that it consists only of calls, rewriting each put as its synthetic equivalent:

+29 underlying contracts
-19 March 65 calls
~~+19 March 65 puts~~ +19 March 65 calls/-19 underlying contracts
-7 March 70 calls
~~+49 March 70 puts~~ +49 March 70 calls/-49 underlying contracts
-33 March 75 calls
~~-51 March 75 puts~~ -51 March 75 calls/+51 underlying contracts
+30 March 80 calls
~~+12 March 80 puts~~ +12 March 80 calls/-12 underlying contracts

If we total all the contracts, what are we left with?

Underlying contracts	+29	-19	-49	+51	-12	=	0
March 65 calls	-19	+19				=	0
March 70 calls	-7	+49				=	+42
March 75 calls	-33	-51				=	-84
March 80 calls	+30	+12				=	+42

We really have this position.

+42 March 70 calls
-84 March 75 calls
+42 March 65 calls

As complex as the position first appeared, it was simply a long butterfly. And a long butterfly always wants the underlying contract to move toward the inside exercise price, in this case, 75. With the underlying contract currently trading at 71.50, the position must be delta positive. If we had rewritten the position so that it consisted only of puts, the result would have been the same because a call and put butterfly have essentially the same characteristics.

The foregoing example was admittedly created so that when the position was rewritten in terms of synthetic equivalents, its risk characteristics were relatively easy to identify. In reality, the risk characteristics of a complex position rarely fall neatly into place. Analysis of a complex position will almost always require a theoretical pricing model. Even then, the model may not tell the entire story.

Suppose that we have the following market conditions:

Underlying price = 99.60
Time to September expiration = 9 weeks
Volatility = 18 percent
Interest rate[1] = 0

The September 95 put and September 105 call have these risk characteristics:

	Delta	Gamma	Theta	Vega
September 95 put	−25	4.3	−0.019	0.132
September 105 call	25	4.3	−0.019	0.132

What are the risks if we have the following position[2]:

Long 10 September 95 puts
Short 10 September 105 calls
Long 5 underlying contracts

The total risk sensitivities for the position are

Delta: $(10 \times -25) - (10 \times 25) + (5 \times 100) = 0$
Gamma: $(10 \times 4.3) - (10 \times 4.3) = 0$
Theta: $(10 \times -0.019) - (10 \times -0.019) = 0$
Vega: $(10 \times 0.132) - (10 \times -0.132) = 0$

It appears that we have no directional risk (delta is 0), no realized volatility risk (gamma is 0), no risk with respect to the passage of time (theta is 0), and no implied volatility risk (vega is 0). If the position was initiated with some positive theoretical edge and the risk sensitivities associated with the position are all 0, then the position is certain to show a profit. So what's the problem?

The problem is that the delta, gamma, theta, and vega are only measures of the position's risk under current market conditions. But today's market conditions may not be—in fact, cannot be—tomorrow's conditions. Even if the

---

[1] In order to focus on the volatility characteristics of the positions, we assume an interest rate of 0 in this and other examples.
[2] Some readers may recognize this position as a *risk reversal* or *split strike conversion*. More on this in Chapter 24.

underlying price and volatility remain unchanged, time will pass. And we know that the passage of time can change a position's characteristics. Looking at a position's characteristics under current market conditions is only the first step in analyzing risk. We need to ask not only what the risks are right now but also what the risks might be under different market conditions. What will happen if the underlying contract moves up or down in price? What will happen if implied volatility rises or falls? What will happen as time passes?

We can expand our analysis by using what we already know about how risk sensitivities change as market conditions change. Suppose that the underlying price begins to fall. How might our risk change? We know that gamma is greatest for at-the-money options. As the underlying price begins to fall, it is moving toward the lower exercise price, 95, and away from the higher exercise price, 105. The gamma of the September 95 put must be increasing, while the gamma of the September 105 call must be declining. Because we are long the 95 put and short the 105 call, the total gamma position is becoming positive. Moreover, if we have a positive gamma, as the market falls, our position, which was initially delta neutral, will become delta negative.

What if the underlying price begins to rise? Now the market is moving away from 95 and toward 105: the gamma of the September 95 put is declining, and the gamma of the September 105 call is increasing. The entire position is now becoming gamma negative. Consequently, as the market rises, our position will become delta negative.

This seems odd. The position becomes delta negative if the underlying price falls *or* rises. The explanation is the changing gamma: the position becomes gamma positive on the way down but gamma negative on the way up.

Now let's consider what will happen if volatility rises. As volatility increases, the delta of calls moves toward 50, and the delta of puts moves toward –50, while the delta of the underlying contract remains constant at 100. Because we are long puts, now with a delta greater (in absolute value) than –25, and short calls, now with a delta greater than 25, the position is becoming delta negative. If the delta of the September 95 put goes to –30 and the delta of the 105 call goes to +30, the total delta position will be

$$(10 \times -30) - (10 \times 30) + (5 \times 100) = -100$$

In the same way, reducing volatility causes delta values to move away from 50. If the delta of the September 95 put goes to –20 and the delta of the 105 call goes to +20, the total delta position would be

$$(10 \times -20) - (10 \times 20) + (5 \times 100) = +100$$

Summarizing, if volatility rises, we want the underlying market to fall. If volatility falls, we want the underlying market to rise.

What will happen to the position as time passes? Reducing time, like reducing volatility, causes delta values to move away from 50. With no change in the underlying price as time passes, the call and put will move further out of the money. The five underlying contracts will tend to dominate the position, resulting in a positive delta.

We have initially focused on the delta and gamma, but we can also infer what will happen to the theta and vega because these values, like the gamma, are greatest for at-the-money options. If the underlying contract begins to fall, our theta position will become negative (the passage of time will begin to hurt), and our vega position will become positive (we will want implied volatility to increase). If the underlying contract begins to rise, our theta position will become positive (the passage of time will begin to help), and our vega position will become negative (we will want implied volatility to decline). If the underlying price does not change, the gamma, theta, and vega of the position are unlikely to be significantly affected by changes in either time or volatility. We can summarize the effect of changing market conditions on the risk characteristics of the position as follows:

Change in Market Conditions	Resulting Delta Position	Resulting Gamma Position	Resulting Theta Position	Resulting Vega Position
Rising underlying price	Negative	Positive	Negative	Positive
Falling underlying price	Negative	Positive	Negative	Positive
Time passes	Positive	0	0	0
Volatility rises	Negative	0	0	0
Volatility falls	Positive	0	0	0

If a position is not overly complex, a trader may be able to do this type of analysis, first looking at the initial risk sensitivities and then considering how the sensitivities might change as market conditions change. However, a trader can get a more complete picture of a position's risk by looking at a graph of the position's value over a broad range of conditions. Let's do this for the current position:

Long 10 September 95 puts
Short 10 September 105 calls
Long 5 underlying contracts

Figure 21-1 shows the value of the position with respect to movement in the underlying contract. The three graphs represent the value at the current volatility of 18 percent, as well as at volatilities of 14 and 22 percent. From Figure 21-1, we can see the graphic interpretation of delta and gamma. For a negative delta position, the graph extends from the upper left to the lower right—as the underlying price rises, the position loses value. For a positive delta position, the graph extends from the lower left to the upper right—as the underlying price rises, the position gains value. In our example, the position is always delta negative at higher volatilities. Around the current underlying price of 99.60, the position is delta neutral—the graph is exactly horizontal. At lower volatilities, the delta will become positive around the current underlying price.

For a negative gamma position, the graph curves downward, taking on the shape of a frown; price movement in either direction decreases the value of

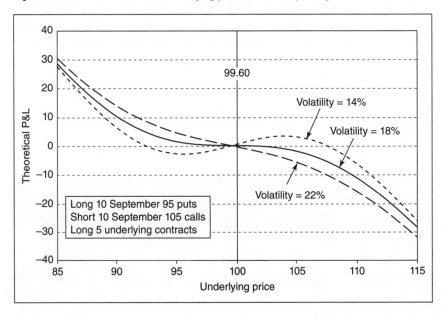

the position. For a positive gamma position, the graph curves upward, taking on the shape of a smile; price movement in either direction increases the value of the position. Our position has a positive gamma below the current price of 99.60 and a negative gamma above 99.60. At lower volatilities, the gamma is magnified (there is greater curvature), while at higher volatilities, the gamma is muted (there is less curvature). The current underlying price of 99.60 is an *inflection point*—the gamma is changing from positive to negative. At this price, the graph is essentially a straight line. The graphic interpretations of a positive and negative delta and gamma are shown in Figure 21-2.

Because gamma and theta are of opposite signs, a positive gamma position will lose value as time passes with no movement in the underlying contract. A negative gamma will gain value. This is shown in Figures 21-3 and 21-4.

Although gamma and theta are always of opposite signs, gamma and vega may be either the same or the opposite. Regardless of whether we have a positive gamma (we want the underlying contract to move) or a negative gamma (we want the underlying contract to sit still), we can have either a positive vega (we want implied volatility to rise) or a negative vega (we want implied volatility to fall). The graphic representations of these positions are shown in Figures 21-5 and 21-6.

It may also be useful to look at graphs of the risk sensitivities as market conditions change. In Figure 21-7, we can see the changing delta as the underlying price and volatility change. Close to the current underlying price of 99.60, raising volatility causes the delta to become negative, while lowering volatility causes the delta to become positive. As we have already seen, if the underlying

Figure 21-2 Positive and negative delta and gamma.

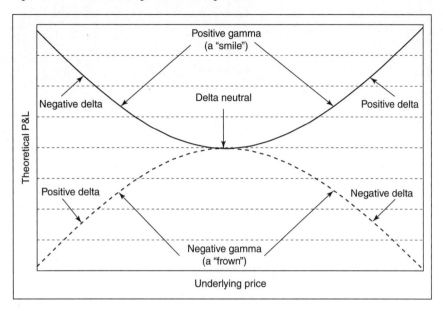

contract either rises or falls, the delta becomes negative. In Figure 21-8, we can
see the changing gamma as the underlying price and volatility change. Close to
the current underlying price of 99.60, the gamma is unaffected by changes in
volatility. The gamma becomes positive if the underlying price falls or negative
if the underlying contract rises.

Figure 21-3 Positive gamma, negative theta position as time passes.

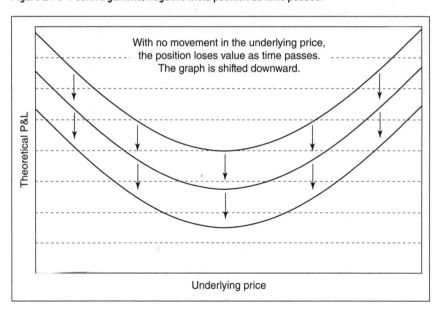

Figure 21-4 Negative gamma, positive theta position as time passes.

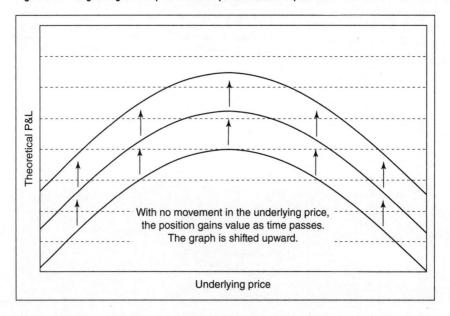

With no movement in the underlying price, the position gains value as time passes. The graph is shifted upward.

Theoretical P&L

Underlying price

In addition to considering the risk sensitivities—delta, gamma, theta, and vega—and the way in which these values change as market conditions change, traders are well advised to look at the *net contract position*. If the market makes a dramatic downward move such that all calls move far out of the money while all puts go deeply into the money, or the market makes a dramatic upward move such that all puts move far out of the money while all calls go deeply into

Figure 21-5 Positive gamma position as volatility changes.

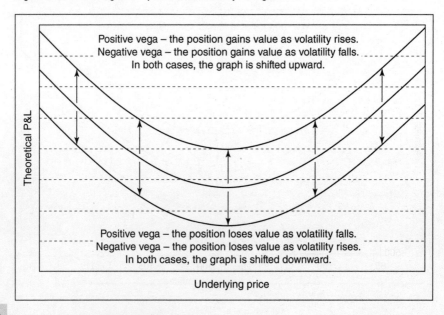

Positive vega – the position gains value as volatility rises.
Negative vega – the position gains value as volatility falls.
In both cases, the graph is shifted upward.

Theoretical P&L

Positive vega – the position loses value as volatility falls.
Negative vega – the position loses value as volatility rises.
In both cases, the graph is shifted downward.

Underlying price

Figure 21-6 Negative gamma position as volatility changes.

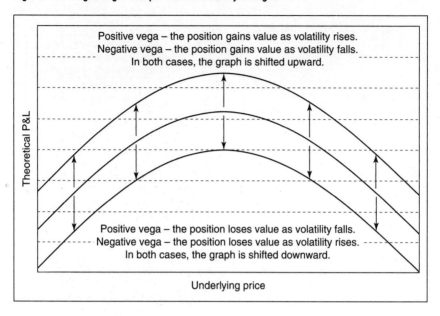

Positive vega – the position gains value as volatility rises.
Negative vega – the position gains value as volatility falls.
In both cases, the graph is shifted upward.

Positive vega – the position loses value as volatility falls.
Negative vega – the position loses value as volatility rises.
In both cases, the graph is shifted downward.

Underlying price

the money, what will be the result? In other words, if the market falls and all puts begin to act like short underlying contracts, or the market rises and all calls begin to act like long underlying contracts, what is the trader left with? In our position, the *downside contract position* is short five. At very low underlying prices, the long 10 September 95 puts together combined with the long 5 underlying contracts will act like a position that is short 5 underlying contracts. The

Figure 21-7 Position delta as the underlying price and volatility change.

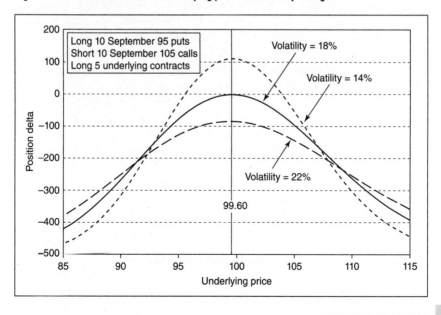

Long 10 September 95 puts
Short 10 September 105 calls
Long 5 underlying contracts

Volatility = 18%
Volatility = 14%
Volatility = 22%

99.60

Figure 21-8 Position gamma as the underlying price and volatility change.

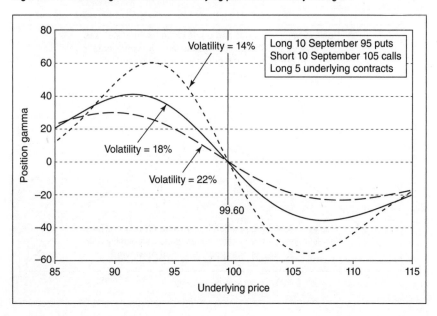

upside contract position is also short five. At very high underlying prices, the short 10 September 105 calls combined with the long 5 underlying contracts will act like a position that is also short 5 underlying contracts. This is apparent in Figure 21-7; the delta approaches −500 in either direction.

The net contract position may sometimes seem irrelevant, particularly if a position consists of very far out-of-the-money options. After all, how likely is it that they will go so deeply into the money that they will act like underlying contracts? But traders have learned, sometimes through painful experience, that big moves occur more often in the real world than one might expect. Extraordinary and unpredictable events—political and economic upheavals, scientific breakthroughs, natural disasters, corporate takeovers—can sometimes cause markets to move dramatically. When this occurs, a trader may find that options that "couldn't possibly go into the money" have done just that.

A trader who is short very far out-of-the-money options may believe that there is so little chance that the options will go into the money that there is no point in buying them back. This may be true, but the clearinghouse will still require a margin deposit for each short option. In order to eliminate this requirement, and perhaps put the money to better use, the trader may want to buy back the options. Of course, he will only want to do this if the price is reasonable. Certainly, the price that the trader will be willing to pay ought to be less than the margin requirement. In the same way, a trader who is long very far out-of-the-money options that he believes are worthless will usually be happy to sell the options at whatever price he can. After all, something is better than nothing, which is what the options will be worth if they expire out of the money.

Very often the price at which traders are willing to buy or sell very far out-of-the money options is less than the minimum price that the exchange normally allows. For this reason, many exchanges permit options to trade at a *cabinet bid*, a bid usually made at a price of one currency unit. For example, if the minimum price for an option on a U.S. exchange is $5.00, an exchange may permit options to trade at a cabinet bid of $1.00. This will allow traders who are either long or short options that they believe to be worthless to remove them from their accounts. The conditions under which cabinet bids are permissible are specified by each exchange.

Now let's consider the more complex position shown in Figure 21-9. The position consists of options that all expire at the same time, but it includes calls

Figure 21.9

Underlying price = 101.25		Time to expiration = 6 weeks		Volatility = 27.00%		Interest rate = 0%		
		Calls				Puts		
Exercise Price	Delta	Gamma	Theta	Vega	Delta	Gamma	Theta	Vega
90	90.9	1.77	−0.0181	0.056	−9.1	1.77	−0.0181	0.056
95	77.1	3.27	−0.0335	0.104	−22.9	3.27	−0.0335	0.104
100	57.2	4.23	−0.0433	0.135	−42.8	4.23	−0.0433	0.135
105	36.3	4.04	−0.0414	0.129	−63.7	4.04	−0.0414	0.129
110	19.5	2.97	−0.0304	0.095	−80.5	2.97	−0.0304	0.095

Option	Position	Delta Position	Gamma Position	Theta Position	Vega Position
90 C	−4	−363.6	−7.08	+0.0724	−0.224
95 C	−12	−925.2	−39.24	+0.4020	−1.248
100 C	+14	+800.8	+59.22	−0.6062	+1.890
105 C	−17	−617.1	−68.68	+0.7038	−2.193
110 C	+12	+234.0	+35.64	−0.3648	+1.140
Call totals	−7	−871.1	−20.14	+.2072	−0.635
90 P	+13	−118.3	+23.01	−0.2353	+0.728
95 P	−20	+458.0	−65.40	+0.6700	−2.080
100 P	−8	+342.4	−33.84	+0.3464	−1.080
105 P	+12	−764.4	+48.48	−0.4968	+1.548
110 P	+8	−644.0	+23.76	−0.2432	+0.760
Put totals	+5	−726.3	−3.99	+0.0411	−0.124
Underlying contracts	+13	1,300	0	0	0
Totals		−297.4	−24.13	+0.2483	−0.759

and puts at five different exercise prices, together with a position in the underlying contract. As before, we assume that the position has some positive theoretical edge. Otherwise, the immediate goal would be to liquidate the position in order to avoid a loss or to alter it in order to create a positive theoretical edge. What are the risks of holding this position?

Beginning with a quick look at the sensitivities, we can see that we are at risk from a decline in the underlying market (negative delta), from an increase in realized volatility (negative gamma), and from an increase in implied volatility (negative vega). Looking only at the delta and gamma, the most favorable outcome seems to be a slow downward move in the underlying market. The least favorable outcome seems to be a swift upward move.

What else can we say about this position? From the negative delta, it's clear that we would like downward movement in the underlying price. But how far down? The current price is 101.25. Do we want the market to fall to 100? To 95? To 90? Perhaps we want an unlimited decline. However, the negative gamma indicates that a swift and violent downward move cannot be good for this position. Taken together with the delta, we can approximate just how far we want the underlying to fall if we realize that *a negative gamma position always wants to become delta neutral.* The profit resulting from a negative gamma position will tend to be maximized when it is delta neutral.

Where will our position be delta neutral if the market starts to fall? For each point decline in the underlying market, we must subtract the gamma, −25.8, from our delta. By dividing the current delta by the gamma, we can estimate that the position is approximately delta neutral at an underlying price of

$$101.25 - (297.4/24.13) = 101.25 - 12.32 = 88.93$$

Of course, this is only an approximation because we are assuming that the gamma is constant, which it is not. An increasing or declining gamma as the underlying price changes will alter our conclusion. However, if we have to make a quick estimate of what we would like to occur, a slow downward move to around 89.00 seems best.

We have also surmised that a swift upward move will hurt this position. Now both the delta and gamma are working against the position. Suppose that the worst happens—the underlying contract suddenly leaps to 150. Will the result be disastrous for us? Here we return to the net contract position: if the market makes a dramatic move such that all contracts move into or out of the money, what are we left with? In a large upward move, all the puts will collapse to 0, while all the calls will eventually begin to act like underlying contracts. Our position is net short a total of 7 calls. But we are also long 13 underlying contracts. This gives us a net upside contract position of +6. If the market makes a really big upward move, we will have a position that is long 6 underlying contracts, giving us a potentially unlimited profit. We can conclude that as the market moves up, at some point our gamma must turn positive, causing the delta to eventually become positive.

The downside contract position is not so favorable. Now all the calls will collapse to 0, while all the puts will act like short underlying contracts. We are net long 5 puts, but we are also long the same 13 underlying contracts. Our net downside contract position is +8. If the market makes a violent downward move, we will have a position that is long 8 underlying contracts, with potentially disastrous results.

Because we are focusing on the risk characteristics of our position, no prices or theoretical values are given for the options in Figure 21-9. We have simply made the assumption that the position has some positive theoretical edge. However, the size of the theoretical edge—how much, in theory, we expect to make with the position if our volatility estimate of 27 percent is correct—can be an important consideration in analyzing the risk of the position. For example, let's assume that the position has a positive theoretical edge of 6.00. If 27 percent turns out to be the correct volatility over the six-week life of the position and we go through the delta-neutral dynamic hedging process,[3] we expect to show a profit of 6.00.

The theoretical edge and vega can help us estimate our volatility risk. From the vega position of -0.759, we know that any increase in volatility will hurt. Consequently, we might ask this question: how much can volatility rise before our potential profit turns into a potential loss? For each percentage point increase in volatility our potential profit will be reduced by the amount of the vega. By dividing the theoretical edge by the vega, we can estimate that the position will break even at a volatility of approximately

$$27.00 + (6.00/0.759) = 27.00 + 7.90 = 34.90\ (\%)$$

Assuming a theoretical edge of 6.00, if volatility turns out to be no higher than 34.90 percent, the position will do no worse than break even. Above 34.90 percent, the position will begin to show a loss. We discussed this concept—the breakeven volatility of a position—in Chapter 7. This can be thought of as the implied volatility of the entire position. It tells us that we have a margin for error of 7.90 volatility points in our volatility estimate. Whether this represents a small or large margin of error depends on the volatility characteristics of this particular market.

How can we increase the margin for error in our volatility estimate? We can do so by either increasing the theoretical edge (without increasing the vega) or by reducing the vega (without reducing the theoretical edge). If we can increase the theoretical edge to 8.00 without increasing the vega, the implied volatility of the position will be

$$27.00 + (8.00/0.759) = 27.00 + 10.54 = 37.54\ (\%)$$

Alternatively, if we can reduce the vega to -0.65, the implied volatility will be

$$27.00 + (6.00/0.65) = 27.00 + 9.23 = 36.23\ (\%)$$

Unfortunately, it may not be possible to do either. In this case, we will have to decide whether the vega risk of -0.759 is reasonable given the potential profit of 6.00.

---

[3] The position is, of course, not currently delta neutral. If we want to dynamically hedge the position, we must begin by offsetting the current delta of -297, perhaps by purchasing three underlying contracts.

We know that the risk sensitivities of the position—delta, gamma, theta, and vega—are likely to change as market conditions change. It is almost impossible to do a detailed analysis of these changes without computer support. However, we may be able to say something about how the delta changes as time and volatility change if we recall that delta values move either toward 50 or away from 50 with changes in time to expiration and volatility.

Consider what will happen if volatility begins to rise. All call deltas will move toward 50 and put deltas toward –50. Because we are net short 7 calls and net long 5 puts, in the extreme, the call delta position will be

$$-7 \times 50 = -350$$

and the put delta position will be

$$5 \times -50 = -250$$

Together with the 13 long underlying contracts, the total delta will be

$$-350 - 250 + 1{,}300 = +700$$

Of course, we would have to raise volatility dramatically for all the deltas to actually approach 50. But, as we begin to raise volatility, the current delta of –297 will become less negative and eventually will turn positive. In a high-volatility market, we will prefer upward movement in the underlying contract.

What about a decline in volatility or the passage of time, both of which will cause delta values to move away from 50? The delta values of out-of-the-money options will move toward 0, while the delta values of in-the-money options will move toward 100. Because we are currently net short 2 in-the-money calls (the 90, 95, and 100 calls) and net long 20 in-the-money puts (the 105 and 110 puts), in the extreme, our total delta will be

$$-200 - 2{,}000 + 1{,}300 = -900$$

If we reduce volatility or time passes, we will prefer downward movement in the underlying contract.

For a new trader, using a basic knowledge of delta, gamma, theta, and vega characteristics to analyze the risk of a position can be a useful exercise. However, when computer support is available, it is almost always easier and more efficient to look at graphs of the position's risk. This has been done for the current position in Figures 21-10 through 21-13.

In Figure 21-10, we can see that at a volatility of 27 percent, the maximum profit on the downside will occur at a price of approximately 95.00, at which point the position delta is 0. This differs considerably from our estimate of 88.93 because the gamma, which was initially –24.13, becomes a much larger negative number as the market drops. The negative delta of –297 is more rapidly offset by the increasing gamma. In Figure 21-12, we see that on the downside, the gamma reaches its maximum of approximately –80 at an underlying price of 93.

If the market moves up, we will initially lose money. But, at an underlying price of 104, the gamma becomes positive. Our negative delta begins to turn

Figure 21-10 Position value as the underlying price and volatility change.

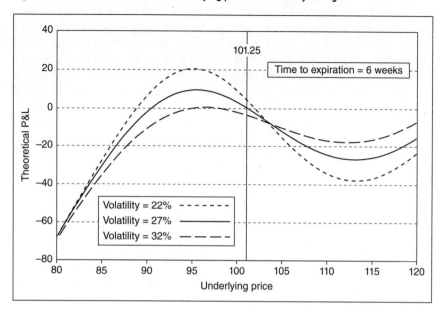

around and at a price of 112 actually becomes positive (Figure 21-11). We will continue to lose money above 112, but at some point the position will begin to show a profit. Figure 21-10 only goes up to an underlying price of 120, but a more extensive analysis would show that at an underlying price of 124, the position will begin to show a profit.

Figure 21-11 Position delta as the underlying price and volatility change.

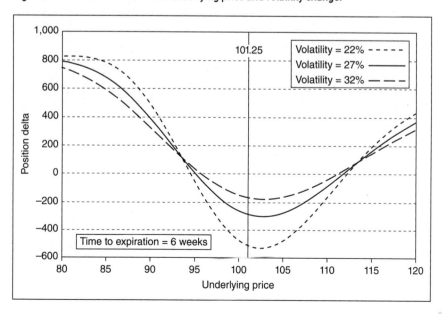

In Chapter 9, we looked at some of the nontraditional higher-order risk measures. Figure 21-12 shows that between the underlying prices of 93 and 114, the position has a positive speed; as the price rises, the gamma increases. Below 93 and above 114, the position has a negative speed; as the price rises, the gamma declines. We can also see that changing the volatility causes the gamma and, consequently, the delta to change at a different rate. Lowering volatility causes the speed to increase, while raising volatility causes the speed to decline.

Figure 21-13 shows the sensitivity of the position to changes in implied volatility, assuming a constant underlying price of 101.25. The position clearly has a negative vega. Any decline in implied volatility will help the position; any increase in implied volatility will hurt the position. Given a theoretical edge, we can estimate the breakeven (implied) volatility for the entire position by dividing the total theoretical edge by the vega. If, for example, we have a total edge of 6.00, we estimated that the position has an implied volatility of approximately 34.90 percent. In fact, we can see in Figure 21-13 that the implied volatility is somewhat higher than 34.90 percent. The six-week graph crosses –6.00, which would exactly offset a theoretical edge of +6.00, at a volatility of approximately 36 percent. The reason the breakeven volatility is greater than our estimate is that the six-week graph has a positive volga—it curves upward slightly. As volatility rises, the vega becomes more positive or less negative. As volatility falls, the vega becomes more negative or less positive. Even though the current volga is positive, we can see that as time passes, the volga of the position becomes slightly negative. The four-week graph is approximately a straight line, while the two-week graph curves slightly downward.

Figure 21-12 Position gamma as the underlying price and volatility change.

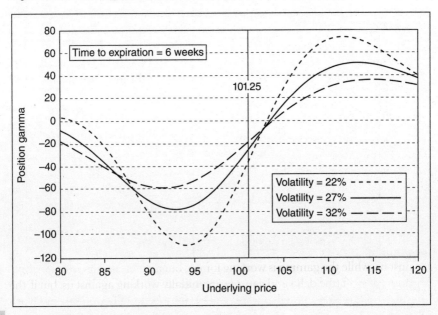

Figure 21-13 Position value as volatility changes and time passes.

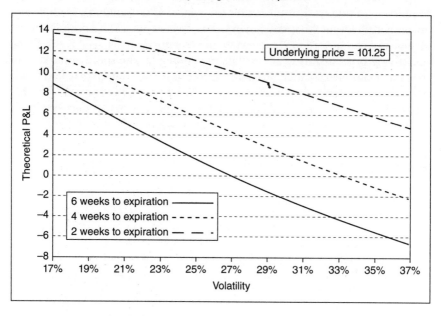

What should we conclude about the position in Figure 21-9? The reason for doing an analysis is to help us determine beforehand what actions to take to either maximize our profits if conditions move in our favor or minimize losses if conditions move against us. We currently have a negative delta. If we wish to maintain a downward bias, then no action is necessary. If, however, we are trading from a purely theoretical standpoint, then perhaps we ought to buy the 297 deltas that we are short. The easiest way to do this is to buy three underlying contracts.

If we maintain our current position and the market begins to decline, what action should we take? If the decline is slow (clearly a very good outcome given our delta and gamma) and there is no increase in implied volatility, perhaps we ought to consider buying puts at lower exercise prices. This will have the effect of offsetting our downside net contract risk and reducing our negative vega while locking in some of the theoretical edge. If, however, the decline is swift, we may have to ignore theoretical considerations and buy puts at the market price. This may be the cost of having a bad position, something that will inevitably occur at some point in every trader's career. If we are forced to buy puts at inflated prices, especially if there is an increase in implied volatility, we may lose money. But if the decline is very swift, the primary objective may be survival. And in the long run, simply surviving, in order to be able to take advantage of those subsequent occasions when conditions work in our favor, can mean the difference between success and failure in option trading.

What action should we take if the market begins to rise? We ought to be prepared for one course of action if the move is slow (the delta is working against us, while the gamma is working for us), but a different course of action if the move is swift (the delta and gamma are initially working against us, but if the upward move is large enough, these numbers may eventually work in our favor).

A detailed position analysis will help us prepare for a variety of changes in market conditions. But no matter how detailed our analysis, we may still encounter situations where we are in uncharted territory. When conditions do change, we can never know for certain how the marketplace will react. If the underlying price begins to rise or fall, depending on the specific market, we may expect implied volatility to change in a certain way. But we may find that it has changed in a completely different way. We may have to accept the fact that our analysis was incorrect and take whatever action we can to reduce our losses or maximize our profits under these new and unexpected conditions.

Some Thoughts on Market Making

In order to ensure liquidity in a market, exchanges may appoint one or more *market makers* in a product. A market maker guarantees that he will continuously quote both a price at which he is willing to buy and a price at which he is willing to sell. As a consequence, a buyer or seller can always be certain that there will be someone in the marketplace willing to take the opposite side of the trade. This does not mean that a customer is required to trade with a market maker. If other market participants are willing to buy at a higher price or sell at a lower price, the customer is always free to trade at the best available price. But by continuously quoting a *bid-ask spread*, the market maker fulfills his role as the buyer or seller of last resort

A market maker must comply with rules established by the exchange concerning the width of the bid-ask spread as well as the minimum number of contracts that the market maker must be willing to trade. If exchange rules dictate that a market maker may quote a bid-ask spread no wider than 2.00, then a bid price of 63.00 for a contract implies an offer price that is no higher than 65.00. Similarly, an offer price of 47.00 implies a bid price that is no lower than 45.00. The market maker may quote a tighter bid-ask spread, for example, 63.50–64.50 in the former case or 45.75–46.25 in the latter, but the spread may be no wider than that specified under the exchange rules.

In addition to quoting a bid-ask spread, a market maker must be willing to trade a minimum number of contracts at the quoted prices. If the exchange minimum is 100 contracts, the market maker must be willing to buy or sell a minimum of 100 contracts at his quoted prices. He may offer to trade more than the minimum, in which case he will usually quote his size along with the bid-ask spread, for example,

63.50–64.50
200 × 200

The market maker is willing to buy at least 200 contracts at a price of 63.50 or sell at least 200 contracts at a price of 64.50. The quoted size need not be balanced:

63.50–64.50
500 × 200

Here the market maker is willing to buy 500 contracts but only willing to sell 200 contracts.

Rules governing the width of a market maker's bid-ask spread usually apply only to the minimum size that the market maker must be prepared to do. If a customer wants to trade a very large number of contracts, a market maker is permitted to widen the spread because of the increased risk associated with the trade. In response to a customer who wants to trade 1,000 contracts, a market maker might quote a spread of 62.00–66.00. To facilitate trading, when a customer has a large order, he will usually indicate that he wants a quote for *size*.

In return for fulfilling his obligations, a market maker will receive special considerations from the exchange. These may come in the form of very low exchange fees or preferential treatment when competing against other market participants. If a customer is willing to sell at the market maker's bid price and two other market participants are also quoting the same bid price, the market maker may be entitled to 50 percent of the order, while the other two bidders may onlybe entitled to 25 percent each.

Unlike investors, speculators, or hedgers, who can choose the strategies that best fit their needs and who can also determine when to enter and exit a market, a market maker has less control over the positions he takes. This does not mean that a market maker is totally at the mercy of his customers. He may be forced to take on a position, but he at least has some choice as to the price at which he does so. Moreover, by adjusting his bid-ask spread, he can to some extent determine the types of positions he acquires. But having done so, he may still find that he has taken on a position that he would prefer not to have.

Although market makers typically represent only a small percentage of option market participants, they can play a crucial role in trading, often determining the success or failure of an exchange-listed product.[4] For this reason, it may be useful to take a closer look at how an option market maker goes about his business.

A successful market maker must ask three questions:

1. What does the marketplace think an option is worth?

2. What do I (the market maker) think the option is worth?

3. What positions am I currently carrying?

The answers to these questions will determine how a market maker prices options and how he manages risk.

The answer to the first question—what does the marketplace think an option is worth?—is the basis for the simplest of all market-making techniques. In this approach, the market maker attempts to profit solely from the bid-ask spread, constantly buying at the bid price and selling at the offer price. No special knowledge of option pricing theory is required, but in order to succeed, the market maker must be able to identify an equilibrium price around which there

---

[4] Customers sometimes believe that market makers "fix" the prices of exchange-traded contracts. This may be true for short periods of time, usually at the beginning of the trading day when very little information is available. Ultimately, however, a market maker's quotes reflect current market activity. A market maker does not set prices any more than a thermometer sets the temperature.

are an equal number of buyers and sellers.[5] If he can correctly determine this equilibrium price, he is in a position to act as a middleman, showing a small profit on each trade while carrying positions for only short periods of time. Of course, the equilibrium price is constantly changing as new buyers and sellers enter the market. Although a market maker will constantly monitor market activity to determine changes in buying and selling pressure, even an experienced market maker will sometimes find, especially in a very fast-moving market, that he has the wrong equilibrium price. When this occurs, he may find that he has either bought or sold many more contracts than he desires.

In addition to profiting from the bid-ask spread, by answering the second question—what do I think the option is worth?—an option market maker will also try to profit from a theoretically mispriced option. The mispricing may be the result of an unbalanced arbitrage relationship, in which case the market maker will attempt to "lock in" the profit by completing the arbitrage. Or the mispricing may be the result of using a theoretical pricing model. In this case, if the market maker buys at a price below or sells at a price above his presumed theoretical value, he can dynamically hedge the position to expiration or until the option is again trading at theoretical value. If his theoretical value is correct, the dynamic hedging process should, in theory, result in a profit.

Once the market maker begins to acquire positions, he must consider the possibility that market conditions might move against him. This brings us to the final question—what positions am I currently carrying? Although there is some risk associated with every position, if the risk becomes too great, an adverse change in market conditions might put the market maker in a situation where he is unable to freely trade and therefore unable to benefit from his position as a market maker. In an extreme case, he may be forced out of business because he is no longer able to fulfill his obligations as a market maker.

A market maker must consider a variety of risks. Initially, he will probably determine a maximum risk he is willing to carry under current market conditions. This may mean limiting the size of his position with respect to the various risk parameters—delta, gamma, theta, vega, and rho. When a limit is reached, the market maker will begin to focus on making markets that will have the effect of reducing his risk. If a market maker is approaching the maximum negative gamma position that he is willing to accept, as he gets closer to this limit, he will increasingly focus on reducing or at least limiting this risk. As a market maker, he still must quote both a bid price and an offer price, but he would much prefer to buy options because this will have the effect of reducing his negative gamma position. Under normal conditions, if asked to make a market, he will likely do so around the presumed theoretical value. If the value of the option is 64.00, he might quote a market of 63.00–65.00, but if the market maker is intent on reducing his negative gamma risk, he will clearly prefer to buy options rather than sell. To reflect this preference, he can adjust his bid-ask spread, perhaps quoting a market of 63.50–65.50. The fact that he has raised both his bid and offer makes it more likely that he will buy options rather than sell. Of course, he

---

[5] A trader who tries to profit solely from the bid-ask spread, buying at the bid price and selling at the ask price without regard to theoretical value, is sometimes referred to as a *scalper*. Scalping is a common trading technique in open-outcry markets.

may still be required to sell if the offer of 65.50 is accepted. But at least he has done so at a more advantageous price.

A market maker must consider not only the risks under current market conditions but also how those risks might change as market conditions change. Suppose that in a rising market the market maker has reached the maximum negative gamma he is willing to accept. However, in analyzing the position, he has also noted that if the underlying contract continues to rise, the gamma risk will begin to decline.[6] If the underlying does move, the market maker may still be hurt because he has a negative gamma position. But he may decide that he can live with this risk because the gamma risk will begin to decline.

In addition to monitoring the various risk sensitivities, a market maker must also intelligently manage his inventory. As conditions change, a position that includes a concentrated risk may evolve into a serious threat to the market maker. Consider a market maker who has the following gamma position spread out over 10 different exercise prices:

75	80	85	90	95	100	105	110	115	120
+110	+425	+300	+68	–2,388	+92	+244	+616	+338	+195

Even if the total gamma risk is relatively small (indeed, the total gamma in this case is 0), the fact that such a large negative gamma is concentrated at one exercise price, 95, is likely to be of concern to the market maker. If these are long-term options, the situation may not be critical today. But as time passes, if the underlying market approaches 95, the position will take on increasingly greater risk. Rather than let this risk increase, an intelligent market maker will focus on spreading out his risk more evenly across exercise prices. In the same way that a wise investor will seek to diversify his risk, a market maker will strive for a similar goal.

In this example, the risk was concentrated at one exercise price. But any concentration of risk at a specific exercise price or expiration date or in terms of a single large risk sensitivity should be a cause for concern. It may not always be feasible because market conditions do not always cooperate, but a market maker's ultimate objective should be to diversify his position as much as possible.

Consider the stock option position shown in Figure 21-14. This position does not fall into any easily recognizable category and represents the type of mixed collection of options that a market maker might accumulate over time as a result of buying and selling by customers.[7] The current market conditions (i.e., underlying share price, time to expiration, implied volatility, and expected dividends) are also shown in Figure 21-14.

To fully analyze the position, we will need to make some assumptions about the term structure of implied volatility. Here we will assume that April

---

[6] In this case, the market maker has a positive speed position. His gamma position becomes more positive or less negative as the price of the underlying contract rises.

[7] An active market maker's position is likely to be much larger than the position shown, with hundreds or even thousands of options at each exercise price. For simplicity, the position shown has been scaled down. But the risk-analysis process will be the same.

Figure 21-14

Underlying share price = 68.76		Interest rate = 4.95%		Expected dividend = 0.58 in 10 weeks	
Time to April expiration = 4 weeks		April implied volatility = 34.27%			
Time to June expiration = 13 weeks		June implied volatility = 33.20%			
Time to August expiration = 21 weeks		August implied volatility = 32.14%			

Exercise Price	April Calls	April Puts	June Calls	June Puts	August Calls	August Puts
55	+77	+47		−103		+32
60	−162	+111	+3	+81	+24	−46
65	+13	−77	+92	−25		
70	+106	−19	−110	−49	−26	−20
75	−8	+122	+86	−2	+8	−25
80	−31	−18	+21		+30	
85	−135	+46	−25	+7	−72	

	Calls	Puts	Delta	Gamma	Theta	Adjusted Vega	Rho
April	−140	+212	−12,615	+504	−2.51	+6.26	−7.50
June	+67	−91	+6,093	+13	−0.62	+0.36	+9.75
August	−36	−59	+3,425	−252	+1.25	−11.19	+10.45
Shares	+3,300		+3,300				
Totals			+203	+265	−1.88	−4.57	+12.70

is the primary month and that the mean volatility for this market is 30 percent. We will also assume that the implied volatility for June changes at 75 percent of the rate of change in April and the implied volatility for August changes at 50 percent of the rate of change in April.[8] We can see that the current implied volatilities are consistent with this term structure:

> April (primary month) implied volatility = 34.27%
>   Difference from the mean = 34.27% − 30.00% = 4.27%
> June implied volatility = 33.20%
>   Difference from the mean = 33.20% − 30.00% = 3.20% ≈ 0.75 × 4.27%
> August implied volatility = 32.14%
>   Difference from the mean = 32.14% − 30.00% = 2.14% ≈ 0.50 × 4.27%

---

[8] We might also make assumptions about the term structure of interest rates, as well as how implied volatility is distributed across exercise prices. In order not to overly complicate the current example, we will assume a constant interest rate across expiration months, as well as uniform implied volatilities across exercise prices. We leave the discussion of *volatility skews* to a later chapter.

Figure 21-15 Position value as the underlying price and volatility change.

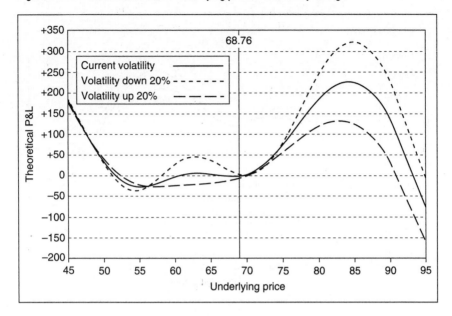

The primary risk characteristics of the position[9]—theoretical profit and loss (P&L), delta, gamma, and vega—are shown in Figures 21-15 through 21-18.[10] From these graphs, it is evident that the risks of the position can change significantly as market conditions change, with the delta, gamma, and vega gyrating between positive and negative. Given this, how should we analyze the position?

A market maker's ultimate goal is to establish positions with a positive profit expectation while intelligently managing risk. Indeed, were it not for the complexities of the marketplace and the unique characteristics of options, a market maker's life might be thought of as quite boring because he is trying to do the same thing over and over:

Get an edge....   Control the risk....
Get an edge....   Control the risk....
Get an edge....   Control the risk....
Get an edge....   Control the risk....

---

[9] In this example, we have assumed that the options are European and have made all calculations using the Black-Scholes model. The risk-analysis process would be the same if the options were American, although the calculations necessarily would have to be made using an American pricing model.

[10] Because of the term structure of volatility, the changes in volatility in Figures 21-15, through 21-18 are expressed in percent terms rather than percentage points. Given our assumptions (i.e., mean volatility = 30 percent, June implied volatility changes 75 percent as fast as April, August implied volatility changes 50 percent as fast as April), a 20 percent increase in volatility from the current levels results in

April: $1.20 \times 34.27\% \approx 41.12\%$
June: $30.00\% + 0.75 \times (41.12\% - 30.00\%) \approx 38.34\%$
August: $30.00\% + 0.50 \times (41.12\% - 30.00\%) \approx 35.56\%$
while a 20 percent decline from the current levels results in

April: $0.80 \times 34.27\% \approx 27.42\%$
June: $30.00\% - 0.75 \times (30.00\% - 27.42\%) \approx 28.06\%$
August: $30.00\% - 0.50 \times (30.00\% - 27.42\%) \approx 28.71\%$

Figure 21-16 Position delta as the underlying price and volatility change.

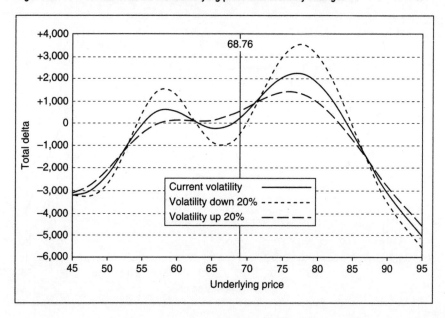

Once a position with a positive theoretical edge has been established, the market maker ideally would like to reduce all risks to 0 without giving up any potential profit. This would be identical to turning the graph in Figure 21-15 into a single horizontal line with a positive theoretical P&L. In reality, with a large and complex position, it is virtually impossible to achieve such a goal.

Figure 21-17 Position gamma as the underlying price and volatility change.

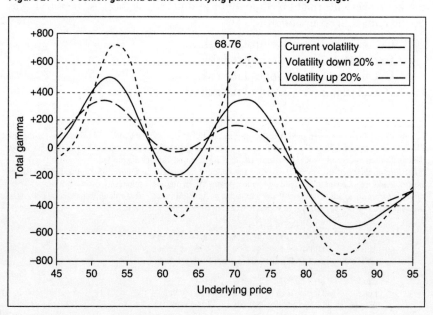

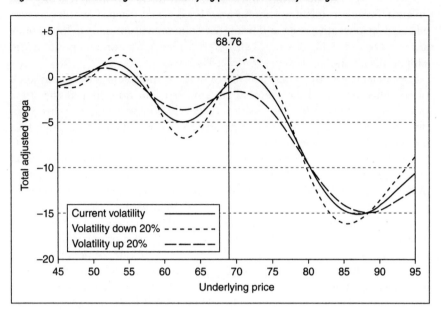

A more practical approach is to ask what changes in market conditions represent the greatest immediate threat to the position and what steps can be taken to mitigate those risks. Even this will depend on many subjective factors: the trader's appetite for risk, his capitalization, the extent of his trading experience, and his familiarity with the market. Unfortunately, there are very few easy answers when it comes to risk analysis.

Some risk limitations will be set by the firm for which the trader works or by the trader's clearing firm. For example, a clearing firm may require that a trader maintain enough capital to withstand a 20 percent move in the underlying contract in either direction. Or the firm may require enough capital to withstand a doubling of implied volatility. If the trader currently has insufficient capital to meet these requirements, he must either deposit additional money with the clearing firm or reduce the size of the position so that it falls within the clearing firm's guidelines.

How should we analyze the risk of the position in Figure 21-14? Risk analysis is important because it enables a trader to plan ahead—to decide what course of action is best—given a change in market conditions. An option trader may have to consider many different market scenarios, but it is often best to begin with three basic questions:

1. What will I do if market conditions move against me?

2. What will I do if market conditions move in my favor? (Risk analysis should focus not only on protecting against the bad things that might occur but also on taking advantage of the good things.)

3. What can I do now to avoid the adverse effects of conditions moving against me at a later time?

What are the bad things that can happen to the position? Clearly, the greatest threat is a violent upward move. Above a stock price of 85, the position will take on a negative delta and from that point on will continue to lose money as the market rises (Figures 21-15 and 21-16). The upside contract position (the sum of all calls and underlying contracts) is −76.

With a current delta of +203, there is also some risk of a declining stock price. This may not be of immediate concern, but note that as the stock price declines toward 62, the position takes on an increasingly negative vega (Figure 21-18). This means that the position is at risk if the stock price falls moderately while implied volatility rises.

In Figure 21-17, we can see that the position has a maximum positive gamma at stock prices of approximately 53 and 72. If the market were to approach either of these prices and remain there, the position would most likely take on its maximum negative theta and consequently begin to decay very rapidly.

Given the various risks, what should be the immediate concern? The answer must necessarily be subjective and will depend on what this trader knows about the characteristics of this stock. If there is some possibility of a really large upward move, for example, the company is a takeover target, it is incumbent on the trader to cover at least some of his upside risk, perhaps by purchasing higher-exercise-price calls. Admittedly, if the prices of the upside calls are inflated because the company is known to be a takeover target, the cost of protecting the upside may be high. But, if a takeover could result in the trader's demise, this may be a price that he will have to pay.

Of course, the trader may believe that a large upward move is so unlikely that he is willing to accept the risk. Then he may want to focus on some of the lesser threats to the position. If he is a disciplined theoretical trader, he may want to cover his current delta position of +203, although this too may represent such a small risk that it is not of immediate concern. Otherwise, he may want to sell approximately 200 deltas in some form—sell stock, sell calls, or buy puts. The last choice, buying puts, especially those with exercise prices of 60 or 65, will have the effect not only of reducing the delta but also reducing the negative vega in the range of 60 to 65. If given the choice, the purchase of April 60 or 65 puts will probably show the greatest benefit to the position. If the stock price does decline to between 60 and 65, these options will be at the money, and at-the-money short-term options have the greatest gamma. As such, they will do the most to offset the negative gamma in this range.

What changes in market conditions might help the position? Below a stock price of 55, the position will take on a negative delta, so a collapse in the stock price will obviously prove beneficial. The downside contract position (the sum of all puts and underlying contracts) is −29. If the stock price should climb toward 85, especially with falling implied volatility, this will also be very favorable. Indeed, almost any decline in implied volatility will help the position, as shown by the vega in Figure 21-18.

Even though time decay may not be an immediate concern, it may still be worth considering how the passage of time will affect the position. The position has a negative theta (consistent with a positive gamma), so the passage of time will work against the position if there is no change in the underlying stock price. The total theta of −1.90 may be small, but note that most of the theta is concentrated in April. And the April position consists of a large long position in April 70 calls. As time passes, the theta of these options, which are close to at the money, will accelerate, causing the position to lose value at an increasingly greater rate. If the market remains close to 70, it is also likely that there will be a decline in implied volatility. Given the position's negative vega, this will work in the position's favor. Still, it may be worth thinking about what action to take if the stock price remains close to 70. The value of the position after the passage of one and two weeks is shown in Figure 21-19.

What else might hurt this position? We have assumed that the stock will pay a dividend of 0.58 in 10 weeks. If the company has not officially announced the dividend, perhaps the actual dividend will be more than or less than this amount. The April options, which expire in four weeks, will be unaffected by a change in the dividend. But how will the overall position be affected? We can run a computer simulation at higher or lower dividend amounts, but perhaps an easier approach is to note that the position is long 3,300 shares of stock. Because we own stock and therefore receive the dividend, any increase in the dividend will cause the position value to rise, and any decrease will cause the position value to fall. The change in value will be approximately equal to the change in the dividend multiplied by the number of shares of stock, in this case, 3,300.

If there is a real possibility that the dividend will be reduced, one way to eliminate the risk is to replace the long stock position with synthetic long stock: sell the stock, and buy calls and sell puts at the same exercise price. This is similar to reducing the risk of a conversion or reverse conversion by turning the position into a box (see Chapter 15).

Figure 21-19 Position value as the underlying price changes and time passes.

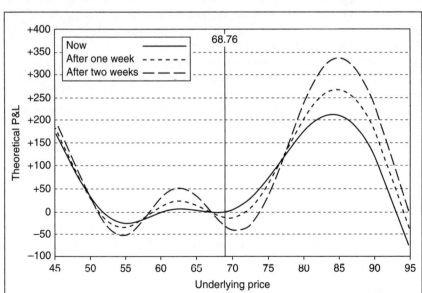

Figure 21-20 Risk sensitivities as the underlying price changes

Stock price	45	50	55	60	65	70	75	80	85	90	95
Theoretical P&L	+179	+32	–25	–1	+4	+5	+74	+182	+221	+131	–76
Total delta	–3,206	–2,306	–14	+533	–232	+571	+2,083	+1,805	–439	–3,092	–5,046
Total gamma	+2	+391	+378	–134	–46	+325	+179	–292	–544	–479	–301
Total adjusted vega	–0.94	+0.86	+0.81	–3.97	–4.01	+0.11	–2.09	–9.68	–14.84	–14.27	–10.70
Total theta	+0.61	–1.06	–1.53	+0.99	+0.51	–2.50	–1.74	+2.91	+6.50	+6.77	+5.18
Total rho	+19	+19	+18	+17	+15	+12	+10	+7	+3	–1	–4
Total vanna	–5	+28	–98	–115	+34	+16	–131	–149	–30	+74	+100
Total charm	–15	–41	+33	+39	–55	–38	+68	+98	+38	–21	–36
Total speed	+45	+77	–90	–63	+81	+34	–82	–84	–14	+32	+34
Total color	–8.00	–4.47	–16.60	–15.53	–12.74	+18.10	+17.62	–5.65	–14.77	–7.36	+.54
Total volga	–0.0004	–0.0008	–0.0023	–0.0005	0	–0.0015	–0.0015	0	+.0002	–0.0009	–0.0017
Total vega decay	+0.037	+0.065	–0.030	+0.092	+0.134	–0.046	–0.0117	–0.035	–0.052	–0.179	–0.247
Total zomma	+10	–8	–28	+24	+21	–26	–22	+15	+27	+13	–1

The total rho of +12.70 also indicates that there is some risk of falling interest rates. For each full-point decline (100 basis points[11]) in interest rates, the position value will fall by 12.70.

It is usually easiest to analyze risk by generating graphs of a position's characteristics, as we have done in Figures 21-15 to 21-19. However, some traders prefer to create a table showing the risk sensitivities at various underlying prices. This has been done in Figure 21-20, beginning with a stock price of 45 and continuing at five-point increments up to a stock price of 95. The table includes not only the traditional risk measures but also the nontraditional higher-order measures discussed in Chapter 9. These higher-order measures can often give a trader a more complete picture of how the risks of his position will change as market conditions change. For convenience, we list these measures below:

Vanna: Sensitivity of the delta to a change in volatility
Charm: Sensitivity of the delta to the passage of time
Speed: Sensitivity of the gamma to a change in the underlying price
Color: Sensitivity of the gamma to the passage of time
Volga: Sensitivity of the vega to a change in volatility
Vega decay: Sensitivity of the vega to the passage of time
Zomma: Sensitivity of the gamma to a change in volatility

[11] Traders commonly express changes in interest rates in *basis points*. One basis point is equal to 1/100 of a percentage point, or 0.0001.

Stock Splits

To conclude our discussion, let's consider one last change in market conditions—a stock split. This often happens when a company wants to reduce its stock price to promote trading in the stock or to encourage wider ownership of the stock. If the stock price remains high, trading activity tends to be limited, with ownership of the stock concentrated in fewer hands.

Suppose that the stock in our example splits 2 for 1, resulting in a new stock price of $68.76/2 = 34.38$. What will happen to the position? Where the trader previously owned 3,300 shares, he will now own $2 \times 3,300 = 6,600$ shares. To maintain the same relationship between each exercise price and the stock price, as a result of the split, the clearinghouse will divide all the exercise prices by 2. The 55 exercise price will become 27½, the 60 exercise price will become 30, and so on. The underlying contract will remain 100 shares of stock, but in order to maintain equity, the clearinghouse will double the trader's position at each exercise price. Instead of being long 77 April 55 calls, the trader will now be long 154 April 27½ calls. Instead of being short 162 April 60 calls, the trader will now be short 324 April 30 calls.

How will the trader's risk position look now? In order to understand what happens, let's consider a simple example. With an underlying stock trading at 60.00, we own a May 60 call with a delta of 50 and a gamma of 5. If the stock splits 2 for 1, our position will now be

	Before Split	After Split
Stock price	60	30
Position	+1 May 60 call	+2 May 30 calls
Underlying contract	100 shares	100 shares
Delta position	+50	+100

Because the option is still at the money, the delta will be 50. But now we own two calls, so our delta position will double to +100.

What about the gamma? Because the gamma is the change in delta per point change in the underlying stock price, if we can determine the new delta position at a stock price of 31, we will know the gamma. Suppose that the stock price rises to 31. This is equivalent to the stock price rising to 62 prior to the split. At a stock price of 62 (prior to the split), our delta position would have been $+50 + (2 \times 5) = +60$. But the stock split caused our delta to double, so the new delta position at a stock price of 31 must be $2 \times +60 = +120$. If the delta rises from 100 to 120 with a stock price change from 30 to 31, the gamma of the position must be +20.

If a stock splits Y for X (each X number of shares will be replaced with Y number of shares), we can summarize the new conditions as follows:

New stock price:	Old stock price $\times X/Y$
New exercise price:	Old exercise price $\times X/Y$
New option position:	Old option position $\times Y/X$

Underlying contract:	Unchanged (100 shares)
New delta position:	Old delta position $\times$ Y/X
New gamma position:	Old gamma position $\times$ $(X/Y)^2$

These calculations hold true as long as the split is Y for 1, where Y is a whole number (e.g., 2 for 1, 3 for 1, 4 for 1, etc.). If Y is not a whole number, the number of shares in the underlying contract may have to be adjusted. For example, using our stock price of 60, what will happen if the stock is split 3 for 2? Now Y is not a whole number because the split is equivalent to 1 ½ to 1. If we own a May 60 call, we can make the following calculations:

New stock price	$60 \times 2/3 = 40$
New exercise price	$60 \times 2/3 = 40$
New option position	$+1 \times 3/2 = +1$ ½ May 40 calls
Underlying contract	Unchanged (100 shares)
New delta position	$+50 \times 3/2 = 75$
New gamma position	$+5 \times (3/2)^2 = +11.25$

The problem here is that the clearinghouse does not allow fractional option positions ($+1$ ½ May 40 calls). In order to eliminate the fraction, the clearinghouse will replace each May 60 call before the split with one May 40 call after the split. At the same time, the underlying contract will be adjusted so that the new underlying contract is equal to the old underlying contract multiplied by the split ratio

$$100 \text{ shares} \times 3/2 = 150 \text{ shares}$$

Using these adjustments, the delta and gamma now make sense. The option is at the money, so it should be equivalent to approximately 50 percent of the underlying contract, or 75 shares. If the stock price rises to 41, equal to a price of 61 ½ before the split, the old delta would have been

$$50 + (1.5 \times 5) = 57.5$$

The option would have been equivalent to 57.5 percent of the underlying contract. Therefore, the new option (the 40 call) should be equivalent to

$$0.575 \times 150 \text{ shares} = 86.25 \text{ shares}$$

As expected, this is the same as the delta (75) plus the gamma (11.25).

What happens to the other risk measures—theta, vega, and rho—if a stock splits? These numbers remain unchanged. The passage of time, changes in volatility, and changes in interest rates have the same effect on a position after a split as before a split. Only the delta and gamma must be adjusted. Indeed, assuming that all other conditions remain unchanged, a stock split has no real effect on a trader's position. It simply results in an accounting change in such a way that equity is maintained. Of course, all other conditions may not

Figure 21-21 The effect of a 2-for-1 stock split.

Underlying share price = 34.38		Interest rate = 4.95%		Expected dividend = 0.29 in 10 weeks	
Time to April expiration = 4 weeks		April implied volatility = 34.27%			
Time to June expiration = 13 weeks		June implied volatility = 32.95%			
Time to August expiration = 21 weeks		August implied volatility = 31.64%			

| | April | | June | | August | |
Exercise Price	Calls	Puts	Calls	Puts	Calls	Puts
27½	154	+94		−206		+64
30	−324	+222	+6	162	+48	−92
32½	+26	−154	+184	−50		
35	+212	−38	−220	−98	−52	−40
37½	−16	+122	+172	−4	+16	−50
40	−62	−36	+42		+60	
42½	−270	+92	−50	+14	−144	

	Calls	Puts	Delta	Gamma	Theta	Adjusted Vega	Rho
April	−280	+424	−25,230	+2,016	−2.51	+6.26	−7.50
June	+134	−182	+12,186	+52	−0.62	+0.36	+9.75
August	−72	−118	+6,850	−1,008	+1.25	−11.19	+10.45
Shares	+6,600		+6,600				
Totals			+406	+1,060	−1.88	−4.57	+12.70

remain unchanged. When a stock splits, we might assume that the dividend also will be split proportionally. But this is not necessarily the case. A stock split often indicates that a company is doing well, and it is not unusual for the split to be accompanied by an increase in the dividend. Any change in the expected dividend will change the value of an option position. Figure 21-21 shows the characteristics of our original position after a 2-for-1 stock split with no change in the expected dividend.

22

Stock Index Futures
and Options

Because stock index futures and options are among the most actively traded of all derivatives, it will be worthwhile to take a closer look at these contracts. Even though the focus of this book is primarily options, stock index futures and options are so closely related, and so many strategies involve both contracts, that it is almost impossible to discuss one without discussing the other. We will therefore include both instruments in our discussion.

What Is an Index?

An *index* is a number that represents the composite value of a group of items. In the case of a stock index, the value of the index is determined by the market prices of the stocks that make up the index. As the stocks in the index rise in price, the value of the index rises; as the stocks fall in price, the value of the index falls. If some stocks in the index rise while others fall, the offsetting changes in stock prices may result in the index itself remaining unchanged, even though the price of every stock in the index may have changed. Although the index is made up of individual stocks, the value of the index always reflects the total value of the stocks that make up the index.

Stock indexes are often classified as being either *broad based* or *narrow based*. A broad-based index is usually made up of a large number of stocks and is intended to represent the value of the market as a whole or at least a large portion of the market. Below are some widely followed broad-based indexes.

Index	Country or Region	Number of Stocks in the Index
S&P 500	United States	500
Nasdaq 100	United States	100
Russell 2000	United States	2,000

(continued)

Index	Country or Region	Number of Stocks in the Index
FTSE 100	United Kingdom	100
Nikkei 225	Japan	225
ASX 200	Australia	200
KOSPI 200	South Korea	200
BOVESPA	Brazil	67
TSE	Canada	60
MSCI EAFE	Australia, Europe, and Far East	1,500
CSI 300	China	300

The designation of an index as broad based can be somewhat subjective. Even if an index is composed of a smaller number of stocks, it may still be considered broad based if the companies that make up the index represent a wide cross section of the economy in a country or region.

Index	Country or Region	Number of Stocks in the Index
Dow Jones Industrials	United States	30
DAX	Germany	30
CAC 40	France	40
Eurostoxx 50	Europe	50
OMX 30	Sweden	30
FTSE MIB	Italy	40
AEX	Netherlands	25
Hang Seng	Hong Kong	30
Sensex 30	India	30
IPC	Mexico	35
Tel Aviv 25	Israel	25
Straits Times	Singapore	30
Swiss Market	Switzerland	20

A narrow-based index is usually composed of a small number of stocks and reflects the value of a particular market segment.

Index	Markey Segment	Number of Stocks in the Index
Dow Jones Transportation	U.S. Transportation Companies	20
S&P Utilities	U.S. Electrical Energy Companies	31

(continued)

Index	Markey Segment	Number of Stocks in the Index
Bank Index	U.S. Banks and Financial Institutions	24
Semiconductor Index	U.S. Semiconductor Companies	30
Oil Service	U.S. Oil Service Companies	15
UK Homebuilders	U.K. Housing Construction	6
EuroStoxx Technology	European Technology Companies	16
FTSE Mining	Worldwide Mining Companies	24

Calculating an Index

There are several methods that can be used to calculate the value of a stock index, but the most common methods focus on either the prices of the stocks in the index or the *capitalization* of the companies that make up the index. To see how these methods work, consider the ABC Index composed of the following three stocks:

Stock	Price	Total Shares Outstanding	Market Capitalization
A	80	100	8,000
B	20	2,000	40,000
C	50	400	20,000

The market capitalization of each company is equal to the stock price multiplied by the number of outstanding shares. This represents the total value of all stock in the company.

If an index is *price weighted*, the value of the index is the sum of the individual stock prices

$$\text{ABC Index (price weighted)} = \sum \text{price}_i = 80 + 20 + 50 = 150$$

If an index is *capitalization weighted* (*cap weighted* for short), the value of the index is the sum of the individual capitalizations

$$\text{ABC Index (cap weighted)} = \sum (\text{price}_i \times \text{shares}_i) = 8{,}000 + 40{,}000 + 20{,}000 = 68{,}000$$

Suppose that the price of Stock A rises 10 percent to 88. How will the value of the ABC Index change if the index is price weighted? The new index value will be

$$88 + 20 + 50 = 158$$

In percent terms, this is an increase of

$$8/150 = 5.33\%$$

We can make the same calculation for the price-weighted index if Stock B rises 10 percent to 22 or if Stock C rises 10 percent to 55. The percent increases in the index are

Stock B: $2/150 = 1.33\%$
Stock C: $5/150 = 3.33\%$

In percent terms, changes in the highest-priced stock, Stock A, have the greatest effect on the value of the index. Stock A has the greatest index *weighting*— it accounts for the largest portion of the index. We can calculate the role that each stock plays in the index by calculating the individual weightings:

Stock A: $80/150 = 53.33\%$
Stock B: $20/150 = 13.33\%$
Stock C: $50/150 = 33.33\%$

We can also calculate the weightings for each stock (with small rounding errors) if the ABC Index is capitalization weighted:

Stock A: $8{,}000/68{,}000 = 11.76\%$
Stock B: $40{,}000/68{,}000 = 58.82\%$
Stock C: $20{,}000/68{,}000 = 29.41\%$

Now Stock B, the stock with the greatest capitalization, has the greatest index weighting.

In a price-weighted index, stocks with the highest price have the greatest index weighting. In a capitalization-weighted index, stocks with the greatest capitalization (stocks with a large number of outstanding shares) have the greatest weighting.

We can also create an *equal-weighted* index where, in percent terms, each stock plays exactly the same role in the index. We can do this by making the initial contribution of each stock to the index identical. For example, suppose that initially the value of our index is

$$\Sigma\,(price_i/price_j) = 1 + 1 + 1 = 3$$

Here each stock contributes exactly 33.33 percent to the index. Of course, if we always divide each stock by itself, the value of the index will never change. But this is only the value when the index is first introduced. Subsequently, as the price of each stock changes, the new price is divided by the old price to determine the new value of the index. If any one stock in the index rises 10 percent, the effect on the index will be the same because

$$88/80 = 22/20 = 55/50$$

If all three stocks rise 10 percent, the new value of the index will be

$$88/80 + 22/20 + 55/50 = 1.10 + 1.10 + 1.10 = 3.30$$

The index will rise exactly 10 percent.[1]

As time passes and some stocks in an equal-weighted index outperform other stocks, the weighting of the stocks will change so that the index will no longer be equal weighted. In order to ensure that each stock in the index accounts for approximately the same value, equal-weighted indexes are periodically *rebalanced*.

Suppose that at a later date the prices of Stocks A, B, and C are 76, 25, and 51, respectively. The value of the equal-weighted index now will be

$$76/80 + 25/20 + 51/50 = 0.95 + 1.25 + 1.02 = 3.22$$

Stock B now accounts for a greater portion of the index than either Stock A or Stock C. To ensure that all stocks again have an equal weighting, the index is now rebalanced

$$76/76 + 25/25 + 51/51 = 3.00$$

Of course, the index value of 3.00 seems inconsistent with the preceding index value of 3.22. In order to generate a continuous index value, the index value after the rebalancing must be multiplied by the percent increase in the index during the previous rebalancing period. In our example, the index after the rebalancing, we must multiply the index value by

$$3.22/3.00 = 1.0733$$

because the index rose by 7.33 percent over the last rebalancing period.

It is a relatively easy task to add up a list of individual stock prices. Consequently, the earliest indexes were price weighted. The Dow Jones Industrial Average, introduced in 1896, is probably the best known of all price-weighted indexes. However, a capitalization-weighted index gives a more accurate picture of each company's value. With the advent of computer technology to make the calculations, most widely followed indexes are now capitalization weighted.

The total capitalization of a company depends on the number of outstanding shares in the company. However, company restrictions may prevent some of these shares from being available for trading. Shares held in the company treasury, by company officers, or in employee investment plans may not be available to the public. The shares that are available for trading are referred to as the *free float*, and it is the number of shares in the free float that typically is used to calculate the value of a capitalization-weighted index.

---

[1] A less common variation on an equal-weighted index involves weighting the stocks geometrically rather than arithmetically. The value of a *geometric-weighted* index made up of n stocks is the nth root of the product of the price ratios. If our ABC Index is geometric weighted, the initial index value will be

$$(80/80 \times 20/20 \times 50/50)^{1/3} = 1.00$$

As the prices of the component stocks change, the value of the index will be

$$[\prod(\text{today's price}_i/\text{yesterday's price}_i)]^{1/n}$$

The Index Divisor

When an index is first introduced, it is common to set the value of the index to some round number. Suppose that we initially want the value of the ABC Index to be 100. To accomplish this, we must adjust the raw index price of either 150 (price weighted) or 68,000 (cap weighted) by using a *divisor* to achieve our target value of 100. Because

$$\text{Raw index value/divisor} = \text{target index value}$$

the divisor must be

$$\text{Divisor} = \text{target index value/raw index value}$$

For our ABC Indexes, the respective divisors are

Price-weighted index: $150/100 = 1.50$
Cap-weighted index: $68,000/100 = 680$

Once the divisor has been determined, all subsequent index calculations are made by dividing the raw index value by the divisor. If the price of Stock B rises to 25, the price-weighted index value, which was initially 100, will now be

$$(80 + 25 + 50)/1.50 = 155/1.50 = 103.33$$

The capitalization of Company B will now be $25 \times 2,000 = 50,000$, and the cap-weighted index value will be

$$(8,000 + 50,000 + 20,000)/680 = 78,000/680 = 114.71$$

It is sometimes necessary to adjust the divisor to ensure that the index accurately reflects the performance of the component stocks. Consider what will happen if Stock A, which was trading at 80, splits 2 for 1. The stock price is now 40, but with 200 shares outstanding.

Stock	Price	Total Shares Outstanding	Market Capitalization
A	40	200	8,000
B	20	2,000	40,000
C	50	400	20,000

If the ABC Index is price weighted, the index value, which was previously 100 (using our divisor of 1.50), will now be

$$(40 + 20 + 50)/1.50 = 110/1.50 = 73.33$$

But is this logical? From the point of view of an investor in Company A, the value of his holdings has not changed, so why should the index value change?

To generate a continuous and logical index value, the index divisor must be adjusted. With a new raw index value of 110 and a target index value of 100 (assuming that no other price changes occurred), the new index divisor will be

$$\text{New divisor} = 110/100 = 1.10$$

When an index divisor is adjusted, the organization responsible for calculating the index will typically issue a press release announcing the new divisor and the reason for the adjustment: "The new ABC Index divisor is 1.10 as a result of the 2 for 1 stock split of Company A."

How will the 2 for 1 stock split affect the divisor in our cap-weighted ABC Index? We can see that the capitalization of Stock A is unchanged at 8,000. Therefore, no adjustment is required. The divisor is still 680.

The component stocks that make up an index are not permanent. A company may cease to exist because it has gone out of business or because it has been taken over by another company. Or a company may no longer meet the criteria for inclusion in an index because its price or capitalization has dropped below some threshold. To maintain a constant number of index components, a company that is removed from an index must be replaced with a new company. This will require an adjustment to the divisor.

Suppose that Company C is replaced in the ABC Index with Company D, currently trading at 75 with 500 shares outstanding:

Stock	Price	Total Shares Outstanding	Market Capitalization
A	80	100	8,000
B	20	2,000	40,000
D	75	500	37,500

The new divisors for ABC Index will be

Price-weighted index:	$(80 + 20 + 75)/100 = 1.75$
Cap-weighted index:	$(8{,}000 + 40{,}000 + 37{,}500)/100 = 855$

Total-Return Indexes

In a traditional stock index, when the price of a component stock falls, the price of the index will fall. This is true even if the price decline is the result of a dividend payout. In a *total-return index*, all dividends are assumed to be immediately reinvested in the index. Consequently, stock price declines resulting from a dividend payout do not cause the index value to decline.

The value of the price-weighted ABC Index composed of our original three stocks with a divisor of 1.50 is

$$(80 + 20 + 50)/1.50 = 100.00$$

If Stock A pays a dividend of 1.00 and opens at a price of 79 on the ex-dividend day, the opening index value will be

$$(79 + 20 + 50)/1.50 = 99.33$$

But if the ABC Index is a total-return index, the opening index value will remain at 100 because the 1.00 decline in Stock A was solely the result of the dividend payout. To maintain an index value of 100, the index divisor must be adjusted to 1.49 because

$$(79 + 20 + 50)/1.49 = 100.00$$

Whenever a component stock in a total-return index pays a dividend, the divisor will be adjusted to reflect the dividend payout.

Although they are less common than traditional indexes, there are some widely followed total-return indexes. The best known of these is probably the German DAX Index. Occasionally, an index, such as the Standard and Poor's (S&P) 500 Index, will be published in two versions, as both a traditional index and a total-return index. The former, however, is much more widely followed.

Impact of Individual Stock Price Changes on an Index

If an individual component stock price changes, how will this affect the value of an index? Suppose that the current value of the price-weighted ABC Index is I. If the price of Stock A (price A) changes by an amount a, what will be the new value of the index? The raw value of the index should rise by a because

$$(A + a) + B + C = I + a$$

In percent terms, the change in the index is a/I. Suppose that we rewrite a/I in a slightly different form

$$a/I = (a/A) \times (A/I)$$

a/A is the percent change in the stock price, while A/I is the stock's weighting in the index. The percent change in the index must therefore be equal to the percent change in the stock multiplied by the stock's weighting in the index. This is true regardless of whether the index is price weighted, cap weighted, or equal weighted.

We can confirm this through an example. Suppose that Stock A in the price-weighted ABC Index, currently trading at 100 with a divisor of 1.50, rises one point. The new index value is

$$(81 + 20 + 50)/1.50 = 151/1.50 = 100.67$$

The weighting of Stock A (before its one-point rise) was 53.33 percent, so the percent change in the index should be

$$0.5333 \times (1/80) = 0.5333 \times 0.0125 = 0.0067$$

From this we get a new index value of

$$(1 + 0.0067) \times 100 = 100.67$$

For the cap-weighted ABC Index, currently trading at 100 with a divisor of 680, the new index value will be

$$[(81 \times 100) + 40{,}000 + 20{,}000]/680 = 68{,}100/680 = 100.147$$

The weighting of Stock A (before its one-point rise) was 11.76 percent, so the percent change in the index should be

$$0.1176 \times (1/80) = 0.1176 \times 0.0125 = 0.00147$$

From this we get a new index value of

$$(1 + 0.00147) \times 100 = 100.147$$

As the price of each stock changes, the new index price is

$$\text{Old index price} \times (1 + \sum \text{percent change}_i \times \text{weight}_i)$$

For a price-weighted index, if we know the index divisor, we can simplify this calculation by noting that the change in the index per one-point move in any individual component is always given by

$$\text{Change in stock price}/\text{divisor}$$

Each 1.00 change in a stock in the price-weighted ABC Index will cause the index to change by

$$1.00/1.50 = 0.67$$

It may seem odd that every point change in a component stock has the same effect on an index. If a component stock rises one point and then rises a second point, the second point will cause a smaller percent increase in the stock price. One might therefore expect the second point to have a smaller effect on the index. But this is offset by the fact that each point increase in the stock also increases the stock's weighting in the index. Taken together, the percent change in the stock and its weighting combine to yield a constant point change in the index.

A trader can occasionally use the foregoing calculations to make a more accurate estimate of an index's true value. Most indexes are calculated from the last trade price of each component stock. But the last trade price may not be an accurate reflection of where the stock is currently trading. Suppose that trading in an index component stock has been temporarily halted.[2] The index value

---

[2] Trading in a stock can be halted for a variety of reasons, but it occurs most often when there is important news pending concerning the company. By halting trading, the exchange hopes to give investors time to absorb the new information and thereby make a better assessment of its impact on the market.

will be based on the last trade price of the halted stock, but this last price may differ significantly from the expected price when trading in the stock resumes.

Suppose that the current value of an index is 1,425.50 and that the last trade price for a component stock is 63.00. However, trading in the stock has been halted pending news that is expected to cause the stock price to rise significantly. Although no one knows the exact price at which the stock will reopen, the indication (very often disseminated by the exchange) is somewhere between 67.50 and 68.00. If the weighting of the stock in the index is 2.5 percent, an index trader might use a price of 67.75 to estimate the new index price when the stock reopens, that is,

$$1,425.50 \times [1 + .025 \times (67.75 - 63.00)/63.00] = 1,428.19$$

Alternatively, the trader may have already determined that each point change in the stock price will cause a change of 0.57 in the index value, yielding a new index estimate of

$$1,425.50 + (4.75 \times .57) = 1,428.21$$

Either estimate will enable the trader to make a more informed decision.

Volume-Weighted Average Price

The index value at the end of a trading day is usually determined by the last price of each component stock when trading closes. But the last trade price may not accurately reflect trading activity in the stock. Suppose that at the close of the trading day the quoted bid-ask spread for a stock is 43.10–43.30 and that the very last trade in the stock was for 300 shares at a price of 43.30. Suppose, however, that just prior to the last trade, 2,400 shares traded at 43.15, and just prior to that, another 1,800 shares traded at 43.10. The last trade of 43.30 seems to be an anomaly, and logic suggests that perhaps one of the other prices ought to be used for the index calculation. To solve this problem, some exchanges use a *volume-weighted average price* (VWAP) over a designated period prior to closing. In our example, if the last three trades during the VWAP period are those just given, the closing price for the stock will be

$$[(300 \times 43.30) + (2,400 \times 43.15) + (1,800 \times 43.10)]/ \\ (300 + 2,400 + 1,800) = 43.14$$

The volume-weighted average price of 43.14 will be used to calculate the index value.

Stock Index Futures

In theory, one can create a futures contract on a stock index in exactly the same way that futures contracts are created on traditional commodities. At expiration, the holder of a long stock index futures position will be required to take delivery of all the stocks that make up the index in their correct proportions. The holder of a short position will be required to make delivery of the stocks.

In fact, no stock index futures contracts are settled through the physical delivery of the stocks that make up the index. Such a process, requiring the delivery of the correct number of shares of many different stocks, would be unmanageable for most clearing organizations. Moreover, settlement might require the delivery of fractional shares of stock, which is not possible. For these reasons, exchanges typically settle stock index futures at expiration in cash rather than through physical delivery of the component stocks.

As with all futures, stock index futures are subject to margin and variation, with a final cash payment equal to the difference between the expiration value of the index and the previous day's futures settlement price. If the index value at the moment of expiration is 462.50 and the preceding day's settlement price for the futures contract was 461.00, the holder of a long position will be credited with a final payment of 1.50. If the value of each index point is $100, the long futures position will be credited with $100 × 1.50 = $150, and the short futures position will be debited by an equal amount. Once this final payment has been made, both parties are *out of the market* and unaffected by any subsequent index movement

What should be the fair price for a stock index forward contract? In Chapter 2, we calculated the forward price for an individual stock by adding the interest costs to the stock price (the cost of buying now) and subtracting the expected dividends (the benefit of buying now)

$$F = S \times (1 + r \times t) - D$$

The forward price for the index can be calculated using the same procedure. We add the interest cost to the current index price and subtract the total dividends that the index components are expected to pay prior to maturity. But unlike an individual stock, where dividends are paid in one lump sum, the dividend payments for an index are likely to be spread out over time. An exact forward price calculation requires us to know the amount of the dividend for each stock, the payment date, and the weighting of the stock in the index. From this, we can calculate the total value of all the dividends, including the interest that can be earned on each dividend payment from the payment date to maturity of the forward contract.

Clearly, calculation of the dividend payout and, consequently, calculation of the forward price can be rather complex. To simplify this calculation, many traders use an approximation by treating the dividend flow as if it were a negative interest rate

$$F = S \times [1 + (r - d) \times t]$$

where d is the average annualized dividend, in percent terms, for the index. If

Current index price = 100.00
Time to maturity of the forward contract = 4 months
Interest rate = 6.00 percent
Average annualized dividend payout = 2.25 percent

the three-month forward price ought to be

$$100.00 \times [1 + (0.06 - 0.0225) \times 4/12] = 100.00 \times 1.0125 = 101.25$$

For long-term forward contracts, this approximation represents a reasonable tradeoff between ease of calculation and accuracy. Unfortunately, for short-term contracts, the fact that dividend payments come in discrete bundles that are spread out unevenly over the life of the forward contract can result in large errors. We can see this in Figure 22-1, which shows the daily dividend payout of the Dow Jones Industrial Index over a three-month period. The total annualized dividend is approximately 2.75 percent, but depending on the time to maturity of a forward contract, this value can either overstate or understate the true dividend payout.

Suppose that a forward contract matures at the end of the three-month dividend cycle. If a position in the forward contract is taken at the beginning of this period, the 2.75 percent estimate of the dividend flow is a reasonably accurate reflection of the actual dividend payout. However, if the position is taken toward the end of the three-month period, after all the dividends have been paid, 2.75 percent is a gross overstatement; the true dividend payout is close to 0. The dotted line in Figure 22-1 shows the true dividend payout, on an annualized basis, from that point in time to maturity. If a position is taken when the dotted line is below 2.75 percent, this estimate overstates the true dividend payout. If a position is taken when the dotted line is above 2.75 percent, this estimate understates the true dividend payout.

Index Arbitrage

In February 1982, the Kansas City Board of Trade began trading futures on the Value Line Stock Index. This was the first exchange-traded stock index futures contract listed in the United States. Two months later, in April 1982, the Chicago Mercantile Exchange began trading futures on the S&P 500 Index.

Figure 22-1 Dow Jones Industrial Index daily dividend payout, October–December 2012.

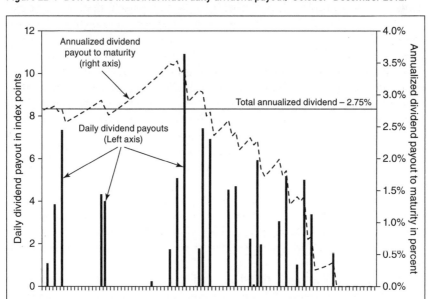

In theory, the price of a futures contract should reflect the fair value of holding the futures contract rather than holding the stocks making up the index. If the futures contract is not trading at fair value, a trader can execute an arbitrage by purchasing one asset, either the basket of stocks or the futures contract, and selling the other. If there are no other considerations, the trader should realize a profit equal to the mispricing of the futures contract. However, this profit will only be fully realized at expiration of the futures contract, at which time the futures contract and index value will converge. At expiration, the value of the futures contract will automatically be settled in cash, but the trader will have to place an order to liquidate the stock position. He will want to do this in such a way that the prices at which the basket of stocks are traded determine the value of the index at the moment of expiration. This can be done by placing a *market-on-close* order, guaranteeing that the last trade price for each stock, which determines the final index value, will be the liquidation price for the trader's stock holdings.

Index arbitrage entails risks similar to any stock futures arbitrage strategy. If the trade has not been executed at a fixed interest rate, any change in rates represents a risk to the position. If dividends have been incorrectly estimated, this will also affect the profitability of the strategy. Moreover, if the strategy involves selling stock short, there may be restrictions that make the strategy impractical. And even if stock can be sold short, the short interest rate may make the strategy unprofitable. This type of strategy, where a trader buys or sells a mispriced stock index futures contract and takes an opposing position in the underlying stocks, is often referred to as *index arbitrage*. Because computers can be programmed to calculate the fair value of a futures contract and to execute the arbitrage when the futures contract is mispriced, such strategies are also known as *program trading*.

With the advent of computer-driven trading, index arbitrage has become an increasingly popular strategy. When a computer detects an index futures contract that is mispriced with respect to the index itself, the computer can send orders to either sell futures contracts and buy the component stocks (a *buy program*) or buy futures contracts and sell the component stocks (a *sell program*). Once the strategy has been executed, it will usually be carried to expiration, at which time the position will be liquidated through a market-on-close order to either buy or sell the component stocks. Initially, exchanges were able to process market-on-close orders resulting from index arbitrage strategies without significant problems. However, as the popularity of program trading increased, exchanges found that as the close of business approached on the last day of trading, they were receiving ever-larger market-on-close orders. These large orders often caused disruptions in the normal trading process, with unexpected jumps in the prices of component stocks. For this reason, many derivative exchanges, at the behest of the relevant stock exchanges, agreed to settle index futures contracts at expiration based on the opening prices of the component stocks rather than the closing prices. This eliminated a last-minute rush to buy or sell stock and enabled stock exchanges to more easily match up buy and sell orders.

Settlement at expiration based on opening prices rather than closing prices is now used for most stock index futures and option contracts. This settlement procedure is sometimes referred to as *AM expiration*. *PM expiration*, where the settlement value is determined by closing prices at the end of the trading day, is still used for a small number of stock index contracts.[3]

Replicating an Index

Sometimes a trader will want to create a holding of stocks that exactly replicates the value of the index. He can do this by holding an amount of each stock in the exact proportion to the stock's weight in the index.

Returning to our ABC Index, we had the following values:

Index Weightings					
Stock	Price	Outstanding Shares	Capitalization	Price Weighted	Cap Weighted
A	80	100	8,000	53.33%	11.76%
B	20	2,000	40,000	13.33%	58.82%
C	50	400	20,000	33.33%	29.41%

If a trader wants to replicate the price-weighted ABC Index, 53.33 percent of his holdings should be in Stock A, 13.33 percent in Stock B, and 33.33 percent in Stock C. If a trader wants to replicate the capitalization-weighted ABC Index, 11.76 percent of his holdings should be in Stock A, 58.82 percent in Stock B, and 29.41 percent in Stock C. If the trader has $100,000 to invest, he needs to hold the following number of shares in each stock:

Stock	Price-Weighted Holdings	Capitalization-Weighted Holdings
A	53.33% × $100,000/80 ≈ 667 shares	11.76% × $100,000/80 ≈ 147 shares
B	13.33% × $100,000/20 ≈ 667 shares	58.82% × $100,000/20 ≈ 2,941 shares
C	33.33% × $100,000/50 ≈ 667 shares	29.41% × $100,000/50 ≈ 588 shares

Because the weighting of each stock in a price-weighted index is proportional to its price, we can replicate a price-weighted index by purchasing an equal number of shares of each component stock. The same, however, is not true for the capitalization-weighted index, where the weighting of each stock is proportional to its total capitalization. In both cases, however, we can confirm that the proper number of shares will replicate a $100,000 investment in the index

$$(667 \times 80) + (667 \times 20) + (667 \times 50) \approx \$100,000 \text{ (price weighted)}$$
$$(147 \times 80) + (2,941 \times 20) + (588 \times 50) \approx \$100,000 \text{ (capitalization weighted)}$$

---

[3] Options on *exchange-traded funds*, which are often designed to mimic a stock index, are subject to traditional PM expiration. The value of the option depends on closing stock prices at the end of trading on expiration day.

Why might someone want to replicate an index? An investor may want to do so in order to earn a return equal to that of the index. This is a common method of diversifying investments. Indeed, the investor may further diversify by replicating several indexes representing various market segments. A trader may also want to replicate an index in order to take advantage of a mispriced arbitrage relationship. If a stock index futures contract is theoretically overpriced, the trader may seek to sell the futures contract and purchase all the component stocks. He will need to do so in such a way that he exactly replicates the index futures contract.

The amount of stock that the trader will need to purchase will depend on the size, or *notional value*, of the futures contract. This, in turn, will depend on the index multiplier that the exchange has assigned to the futures contract. Suppose that our capitalization-weighted index with a divisor of 68,000 is currently trading at 100.00 and that the exchange has assigned a multiplier of $1,000 to each point. The notional value of the futures contract is therefore $100.00 \times \$1,000 = \$100,000$. Given this, it may seem that a trader who is able to sell an overpriced index futures contract can offset this position by purchasing 147 shares of Stock A, 2,941 shares of Stock B, and 588 shares of Stock C. The problem with this approach is that the trader needs to replicate the futures contract, not the actual index. And the futures contract and index may have different characteristics.

To understand why replicating the index will not exactly offset the futures position, consider what will happen over the life of the futures contract while the trader is waiting for expiration, when the futures price and index price will converge. The prices of the stocks will surely fluctuate, resulting in either a profit or loss to his stock position. But this profit or loss will be unrealized because the trader must hold the position to expiration to ensure an arbitrage profit. At the same time, the profit or loss resulting from futures contract will be immediately realized , resulting in a variation credit or debit each day. If there is a variation credit, the trader will earn interest; if there is a variation debit, the trader must pay interest. In either case, the resulting interest will change the arbitrage profit that the trader originally expected. This is another example of settlement risk, which we discussed in Chapter 15. A position that exactly replicates the index is an imperfect hedge against the futures contract because one side is subject to stock-type settlement, while the other side is subject to futures-type settlement. Given this, what should be the correct hedge?

Ignoring dividends, the fair value of a stock index forward contract is

$$F = S \times (1 + r \times t)$$

For each point increase in the index, the index futures contract should rise by $1 + r \times t$. If we think of the cash index as the underlying contract, we can apply the concept of the delta to the futures contract in much the same way we do to an option contract. The delta is the rate at which the value of a contract will change with respect to movement in the underlying contract. If the goal is to be delta neutral, for each futures contract we hold, we must hold an opposing cash index position equal to $1 + r \times t$.

The magnitude of the futures delta will depend on both the amount of time remaining to expiration and the level of interest rates. For a long-term futures contract in a high-interest-rate environment, the required holdings in the component stocks may be considerably greater than the equivalent futures position. As expiration approaches or in a low-interest-rate environment, the futures and stock holdings will be almost identical. Consequently, an index arbitrage strategy requires an adjustment to the stock position as time passes or interest rates change.

Suppose that there are four months to expiration of our ABC Index futures contract and that the annual interest rate is 6.00 percent. If we sell an overpriced futures contract, we must offset this with a long stock holding of $1 + 0.06 \times 4/12 = 1.02$, or 2 percent greater than the holding required for an exact index replication. If a month passes so that there are now only three months to expiration, we should reduce our stock holding to $1 + 0.06 \times 3/12 = 1.015$, or 1½ percent greater than the shares required for an exact index replication. The required holdings for the capitalization-weighted ABC Index are as follows:

Stock	Shares Required to Replicate the Index	Shares Required to Offset a 4-Month Futures Contract	Shares Required to Offset a 3-Month Futures Contract
A	147	$1.02 \times 147 \approx 150$	$1.015 \times 147 \approx 149$
B	2,941	$1.02 \times 2,941 \approx 3,000$	$1,015 \times 2,941 \approx 2,985$
C	588	$1.02 \times 588 \approx 600$	$1.015 \times 588 \approx 597$

A change in interest rates will not only affect the delta of the futures contract but can also affect the profitability of an index arbitrage strategy. If a trader initiates a buy program (i.e., buy stocks, sell futures), he is effectively borrowing cash in order to purchase the stocks. If the cost of funds is tied to a floating interest rate, any rate increase will hurt his position, and any decrease will help. If he institutes a sell program (i.e., sell stocks, buy futures), he is effectively lending cash. Now any rate increase will help his position, and any decrease will hurt it. If the change in interest rates is sufficiently large, an initially profitable strategy might become unprofitable. This is especially true if the program trade consists of long-term futures contracts. In such a case, the interest considerations are magnified because of the greater costs of borrowing or lending over extended periods. In the same way, because of reduced interest considerations, changes in interest rates are unlikely to affect program trades consisting of short-term futures.

We have also assumed that the dividend payout of all the stocks in an index remains constant. But this is not necessarily true. Companies can have good years and bad years, and their dividend policies can change accordingly. In a buy program (i.e., buy the stocks, sell the futures), any increase in dividends will help the position, and any decrease will hurt. In a sell program (i.e., sell the stocks, buy the futures), the opposite is true. In a broadly based index consisting of hundreds of stocks, it is unlikely that a change in the dividend policy of any one company or even several companies will have a significant impact on the profitability of a program trade. But in a narrow-based index consisting of only a few stocks, a change in the expected dividend payout of even one firm can alter the potential profitability of the trade. In such a case, the trader must carefully consider beforehand the possibility of a dividend change for the companies that make up the index.

Bias in the Futures Market

Stock index futures are among the most liquid and actively traded of all futures contracts. These markets enable all types of traders to make decisions based on general market conditions rather than on unique conditions that might affect an individual stock. Most traders believe that the general market is less subject to manipulation than individual stocks and that index markets offer a more level playing field.

One especially active participant in the stock index market is the portfolio manager whose goal is typically to generate a maximum return on capital with a minimum amount of risk. Historically, a portfolio manager has achieved this goal in the equity markets by maintaining a portfolio of stocks that the manager believes will outperform the general market. As the manager identifies new stocks that meet this criterion, he adds them to the portfolio while at the same time selling off stocks that have either met his performance goals or have ceased to perform as expected.

Occasionally, a manager with an equity portfolio may want to protect his holding against an expected short-term decline in the general market. Prior to the introduction of index futures, the only way to do this was to sell off the stocks in the portfolio and then buy them back at a later date. Not only was this time consuming but the transaction costs also tended to reduce the expected profits from the position. But with the introduction of index futures a manager with a broadly based portfolio may decide that his holdings tend to mimic an index on which futures are available. If the manager believes that the characteristics of his portfolio are sufficiently similar to the index, index futures offer a method of hedging the stocks in the portfolio without the time-consuming and costly process of selling each individual stock in the portfolio.

The effect of portfolio hedging strategies on stock index futures tends to result in a one-sided market because the vast majority of equity portfolio managers take long positions in equities. Even if a manager believes that a stock will underperform the market, it is much less common for a manager to sell stock short (sell stock that he does not own) as part of his investment program. Hence, a portfolio manager is almost always trying to hedge a long position in the market. To achieve this, a portfolio manager is most often selling futures contracts. This constant selling pressure tends to depress the price of futures contracts compared with theoretical value.

If there were a sure way to profit from this downward bias in the market, arbitrageurs would take the opposite position in the underlying index. But we have seen that replicating an index with a basket of stocks is not always possible. Moreover, when the portfolio manager protects his long equity position by selling futures, a market maker or arbitrageur ends up taking the opposite position; he is buying futures. If he wants to hedge his position with an underlying basket of stocks, he must sell stocks short. In some markets, the short sale of stock may be prohibited, but even if short sales are permitted, selling stocks short is never as easy as buying stocks. Moreover, the short sale of a stock, as discussed in Chapter 2, may not earn full interest.

Given all these factors, buying and selling pressure in the stock index futures market is not symmetrical. Many more factors seem to result in downward pressure on futures prices than upward pressure. This does not mean that such markets can never become inflated, with futures contracts trading at prices greater than fair value, but this is by far the exception. In stock index markets around the world, there tends to be constant downward pressure on futures prices.

Stock Index Options

There are really two types of stock index options—those where the underlying is an index futures contract and those where the underlying is a cash index. Although they are alike in many respects, they also have unique characteristics that set them apart from each other.[4]

Options on Stock Index Futures

Exchange-traded options on stock index futures were first listed in the United States in January 1983, when the Chicago Mercantile Exchange began trading options on S&P 500 futures contracts. Options on stock index futures are evaluated in the same way as any other futures option. Exercise or assignment results in a futures position, which is immediately subject to margin and variation. The only time exercise or assignment does not result in a futures position is when the options and the underlying futures contract expire at the same time. Because most stock index futures trade on the March-June-September-December quarterly cycle, there are four times each year when stock index futures, options on futures, and options on the cash index all expire at the same time. This *triple witching* typically occurs on the third Friday of the contract month, when all expiring stock index contracts, both futures and options, are settled in cash.

Consider a trader who owns a February 1,000 call on a stock index futures contract. Because February is a serial month (there are no February futures), the underlying contract is the March future. If the March future is trading at 1,025 at February expiration, the trader will exercise the February 1,000 call, resulting in a long March futures position. Unless the trader immediately sells the March future, the position will be subject to a margin requirement that the trader must deposit with the clearinghouse. At the same time, the trader, through exercise, will buy a March futures contract at 1,000. With the futures contract now trading at 1,025, the trader's account will be credited with 25.00 points times the index point value. If the point value is $100, the trader's account will be credited with 25 × $100 = $2,500. In the same way, a trader who is assigned on a February 1,000 call will have a short March futures position. Unless the trader buys back the March future, he will also be required to post margin, and his account will be debited by $2,500. Both the trader who exercises and the trader who is assigned still have market positions. One trader has a long futures position and therefore wants the market to rise. The other trader has a short futures position and therefore wants the market to decline.

---

[4] We might also include options on *exchange-traded funds*. However, exchange-traded funds are issued in shares and therefore tend to trade like individual equity options.

Now consider what will happen at expiration to a trader who owns a March 1,000 call in the same index futures market. Unlike the February option, which is subject to PM expiration (the option essentially expires at the close of business on expiration Friday), the March option is subject to AM expiration because the March future is subject to AM expiration. The value of the March future will be determined by the opening prices of all the component stocks on expiration Friday, and this, in turn, will determine the value of the March 1,000 call. If the call is out of the money, it will expire worthless. If the call is in the money, the exchange will automatically settle all expiring in-the-money options in cash. The trader who owns the call will be credited with an amount equal to the difference between the exercise price and the opening index value times the index multiplier. If the opening index value is 1,040 and the multiplier is again $100, the trader who is long the option will be credited with $4,000. At the same time, the trader who is short the option will be debited by an equal amount. Moreover, once this cash transfer takes place, both traders are out of the market. Whether the index subsequently rises or falls is of no consequence because no market position results from the cash settlement.

Options on stock index futures, like most futures options, are American and therefore carry the right of early exercise. If the options are subject to stock-type settlement, as they are in the United States, there may be some early exercise value over an equivalent European option, as described in Chapter 16, although this extra value will usually be small. If the options are subject to futures-type settlement, as they are on most exchanges in Europe and the Far East, there is effectively no additional value over an equivalent European option.

Options on a Cash Index

The first cash options on a stock index began trading at the Chicago Board Options Exchange (CBOE) in March 1983. The exchange had wanted to list options on one of the widely followed indexes, such as the S&P 500 or Dow Jones Industrials Average, but was initially unable to obtain the rights to trade any of these indexes. As a result, the CBOE decided to create its own *Options Exchange Index* (with ticker symbol OEX) made up of 100 of the largest U.S. companies.[5] Because all individual equity options traded at the CBOE at that time were American, with the right of early exercise, it seemed logical to make OEX options American as well. However, once trading began, it became obvious that the early exercise feature resulted in additional and unforeseen risks and also greatly complicated theoretical evaluation. As a result, all exchange-traded cash index options are now European, with no possibility of early exercise.

---

[5] The CBOE subsequently reached an agreement with Standard and Poor's allowing the exchange to trade options on the S&P 500 Index. As part of the agreement, Standard and Poor's assumed the responsibility for calculating and disseminating OEX values. At the same time, the OEX was renamed the S&P 100 Index, although it still retains its original ticker symbol OEX.

For stock index options on a cash index,[6] no underlying position results from exercise. At expiration, the exchange automatically settles all options in cash, with a cash credit to the purchaser of an in-the-money option equal to the difference between the exercise price and index price and cash debit of an equal amount to the seller of the option. This is the same procedure used to settle expiring futures options when the underlying contract for the option is the expiring futures month. Cash index options are typically subject to AM expiration, with the value of the index, and consequently the value of the options, being determined by the opening prices of all the index components.

How should a trader hedge a position in cash index options? In theory, one might buy or sell all the stocks in the index in the right proportion to hedge such a position. However, this would require trades in many different stocks and, in theory, might require the purchase or sale of fractional shares. Moreover, as the delta of the option position changed, the trader would have to periodically adjust the stock holdings. Given these drawbacks, hedging a position with a basket of component stocks is impractical for most traders. What most traders want is a hedging instrument that is easily traded and correlates closely with the cash index. The contract that meets these requirements is a futures contract on the same stock index as the cash options.

Assuming that futures contracts on an index are available, a trader in a cash index option market will hedge his position with the futures contract that expires at the same time as the options. If no corresponding futures month is available, the nearest futures contract beyond the option expiration is used as the hedging instrument. For index futures trading on the quarterly cycle, we can summarize the underlying hedging instrument as follows:

Cash Index Option Expiration	Hedging Instrument
January, February, March	March futures
April, May, June	June futures
July, August, September	September futures
October, November, December	December futures

Clearly, this is not a perfect solution to the hedging problem because the futures contract and the cash index are not identical. Indeed, a futures contract may trade at a price above or below its theoretical value compared with the cash index. But for most traders, using the futures contract represents a practical solution to the hedging problem.

Even if we use an index futures contract as the hedging instrument, we still need an underlying price to evaluate options. For March, June, September, and December options, if a position is carried to expiration, a trader can be certain

---

[6] Ticker symbols for cash indexes very often end with the letter X, for example, SPX (Standard and Poors 500 Index), DJX (Dow Jones Industrial Index), DAX (Deutsche Aktien Index—the German Stock Index), AEX (Amsterdam Exchange Index), OMX 30 (Stockholm Options Market Index), and ASX 200 (Australian Stock Exchange Index).

that at the moment of expiration the cash value of the index and the value of the corresponding futures contract will converge. Consequently, a trader can treat the futures contract as the underlying contract. Not only does this make practical sense, but it also makes theoretical sense because option values are derived from the forward price of the underlying contract, and the futures contract is simply the traded form of the forward price. Moreover, if both cash options and futures options are available on an index and all options expire at the same time, there is effectively no difference between the options. They will essentially trade at the same prices.[7]

The question of what underlying price to use when evaluating a cash index option is somewhat more complex for serial month options, where there is no corresponding futures month. If December futures are available, we can always price December options using the December futures price. We may also use the December futures contract to hedge an October or November option position if no corresponding October or November futures contract is available. But the October or November forward price will differ from the December forward price, so using the December futures price as the underlying price cannot be correct.

If we assume that the December futures contract represents the correct December forward price, what should be the correct November forward price? We might work backwards because

$$F_{\text{Dec}} = F_{\text{Nov}} \times (1 + r \times t) - D$$

Then

$$F_{\text{Nov}} = \frac{F_{\text{Dec}} + D}{1 + r \times t}$$

However, this requires us to estimate the dividends expected between November and December expirations. An easier method used by most traders is to determine the November forward price implied by option prices in the marketplace. We can do this by observing the prices of a November call and put that are close to at the money and whose prices will consequently be similar and then use put-call parity to calculate the implied forward price. For example,

November 1,000 call = 34.85
November 1,000 put = 29.90
Time to November expiration = 2 months
Annual interest rate = 6.00 percent

Because

$$C - P = \frac{F - X}{1 + r \times t}$$

---

[7] For deeply in-the-money options on futures, which are typically American, there may be a very slight additional early exercise value.

then

$$F = (C - P) \times (1 + r \times t) + X$$
$$F_{Nov} = (34.80 - 29.85) \times 1.01 + 1,000 = 1,005$$

The implied November forward price is 1,005.00.

Now suppose that when we calculate the implied November forward price, the December futures price is 1,010.00. This means that there should be a difference between the November forward price and the December forward price of 5.00. As the price of the December futures contract fluctuates, if we want to calculate theoretical values for November cash options, we can use as the underlying price, the December futures price, less 5.00.

We might also use put-call parity to calculate the implied December forward price. But this is not really necessary because we have the implied December forward price in the form of a December futures contract. Still, we might check to see if December option prices are consistent with the December futures price. If

   December futures price = 1,010
   Time to December expiration = 3 months
   Annual interest rate = 6.00 percent

from put-call-parity we know that the December 1,000 combo (the difference between the prices of the December 1,000 call and 1,000 put) should be

$$C - P = \frac{F - X}{1 + r \times t} = \frac{10}{1.015} = 9.85$$

If the December 1,000 call is trading at a price of 44.60, the December 1,000 put should be trading at a price of 44.60 − 9.85 = 34.75.

	November	December
1,000 call	34.80	44.60
1,000 put	29.85	34.75

The price of the November/December 1,000 roll (i.e., the difference between the December and November 1,000 synthetics) is

$$(44.60 - 34.75) - (34.80 - 29.85) = 9.85 - 4.95 = 4.90$$

23

Models and the Real World

A trader who uses a theoretical pricing model is exposed to two types of risk—the risk that the trader has the wrong inputs into the model and the risk that the model itself is wrong because it is based on false or unrealistic assumptions. Thus far we have focused primarily on the first area, the risk associated with the inputs into the model. A trader will typically deal with this risk by paying close attention to the sensitivities of an option position (i.e., delta, gamma, theta, vega, and rho), thereby preparing to take protective action when market conditions move against him. While any of the inputs into the model may represent a risk, we have placed special emphasis on volatility because it is the one input that cannot be directly observed in the marketplace.

However, an active option trader cannot afford to ignore the second type of risk, the possibility that the assumptions on which the model is based are inaccurate or unrealistic. Some of these assumptions pertain to the way business is transacted in the marketplace, while others pertain to the mathematics of the model.

To begin, we might list the most important assumptions built into traditional pricing models[1]:

1. Markets are frictionless.

   A. The underlying contract can be freely bought or sold, without restriction.

   B. Unlimited money can be borrowed or lent, and the same interest rate applies to all transactions.

   C. There are no transaction costs.

   D. There are no tax consequences.

---

[1] By *traditional pricing model* we mean those that are most commonly used: the Black-Scholes model and its variations or the Cox-Ross-Rubinstein model.

2. Interest rates are constant over the life of an option.

3. Volatility is constant over the life of an option.

4. Trading is continuous, with no gaps in the price of an underlying contract.

5. Volatility is independent of the price of the underlying contract.

6. Over small periods of time, the percent price changes in an underlying contract are normally distributed, resulting in a lognormal distribution of underlying prices at expiration.

The reader may already have an opinion about the validity of these assumptions, but let's consider them one by one.

Markets Are Frictionless

In Chapter 8, we came to the obvious conclusion that markets are not frictionless. The underlying contract cannot always be freely bought or sold; there are sometimes tax consequences; a trader cannot always borrow and lend money freely, nor at the same rate; and there are always transaction costs.

In futures markets, the underlying cannot always be freely bought or sold because an exchange may set a daily price limit beyond which a futures contract is not permitted to trade. When that limit is reached, the market it locked, and trading is halted until the market comes off its limit. If it does not come off its limit, trading does not resume until the next business day.

Even if a futures market is locked, it may be possible for a trader to circumvent the trading restriction. Instead of buying or selling futures contracts, a trader might be able to trade in the cash market. Or the trader might be able to trade a futures spread where one side of the spread is not locked. For example, a trader who wants to buy a June futures contract that is up its allowable limit may be able to buy a June/March spread (i.e., buy June, sell March). If the March futures contract is still trading because it is not up its limit, the trader can then go back into the market and buy back the March futures contract. This leaves him long a June futures contract, which was his original intention. If the underlying futures market is locked but the option market is not locked, a trader might be able to buy or sell synthetic futures contracts.

Trading can also be halted on a stock exchange if a designated stock index either rises or falls during a trading day by a predetermined amount. When this limit is reached, the exchange will halt trading for some period of time. The exchange's *circuit breakers* specify how long trading will be halted for a given percent change in a stock market index

In Chapter 2, we noted that an exchange or regulatory authority may place restrictions on the short sale of stock—the sale of stock that a trader does not actually own. Even if short sales are permitted, there may be restrictions on when such sales can be made. If a trader cannot freely sell stock, put prices will tend to become inflated compared with call prices, and arbitrage relationships, such as conversions and reversals, will appear to be mispriced. Many stock option traders, as a matter of good trading practice, will try to carry some long stock so that they will always be in a position to sell stock if the need arises.

The assumption that a trader can always borrow or lend money freely is a more serious weakness in pricing models. Even if a trader has sufficient funds to initiate a trade, he may find at some later date that he needs additional funds to meet increased margin requirements.[2] If money were freely available, margin would never be a problem. A trader could always borrow margin money and deposit the money with the clearinghouse. Because the borrowing and lending rates are assumed to be the same, and because the clearinghouse, in theory, pays interest on the margin deposit, there would never be a problem obtaining margin money, nor would there ever be a cost associated with it.

In the real world, traders do not have unlimited borrowing capacity. If a trader cannot meet a margin requirement, he may be forced to liquidate a position prior to expiration. Because all models, even those that allow for early exercise, assume that a trader will always have the choice of holding a position to expiration, the inability to meet margin requirements and therefore maintain the position can make the values generated by the theoretical pricing model less reliable. An experienced trader should always consider the risk of a position not only in terms of how much the position might lose in total but also in terms of how much margin might be required to maintain the position over time.

Even if a trader has unlimited borrowing capacity, the fact that for most traders, borrowing and lending rates are not the same can also cause problems with strategies based on model-generated values. A trader who borrows margin money at one rate will almost certainly receive a lower rate when he deposits this money with the clearinghouse. The difference between these rates is something of which the model is unaware. And the greater the difference between borrowing and lending rates, the less reliable will be the values generated by the model.

Although there are occasionally tax considerations, for most traders, these are usually secondary. For a given a strategy, a trader is unlikely to ask himself, "If this trade is profitable or unprofitable, what will be the tax consequences?" Differences in tax consequences rarely make one strategy better than another.[3]

Lastly, the assumption that there are no transaction costs is a serious flaw in the frictionless markets hypothesis. While a strategy may or may not be affected by tax or interest-rate considerations, there are always transaction costs. These costs can come in the form of brokerage fees, clearing fees, or an exchange membership. For some market participants, transaction costs may be

---

[2] The possibility that a trader in a futures option market may also have to come up with additional variation money, as opposed to margin money, after establishing an option position is incorporated into most models. This is why a conversion or reversal in a futures option market may not be delta neutral.

[3] This is not to say that tax consequences are always insignificant. Tax considerations can play a role in portfolio management or in option strategies involving dividends when the dividends are subject to tax rules different from the gains or losses from stock or options.

prohibitive, and a strategy that looks sensible based on model-generated values may not be worth doing when transaction costs are also taken into consideration. Moreover, transaction costs can accrue not only when the strategy is initiated or liquidated but also whenever an adjustment is made. If a strategy will require many adjustments because it has a high gamma and the trader intends to remain approximately delta neutral, the transaction costs can have a significant impact on model-generated values.

Interest Rates Are Constant over the Life of an Option

When a trader feeds an interest rate into a pricing model, the model assumes that this one rate applies to all transactions over the entire life of the option. Whatever cash flows result from an option trade will be either invested, if a credit, or borrowed, if a debit, at one constant rate. In reality, very few traders initiate one trade and simply hold the position to expiration. As traders initiate new positions or close out existing ones, they are constantly borrowing and lending money. Moreover, in futures options markets, traders are subject to changing margin and variation requirements. For all these reasons, most traders require a degree of cash liquidity that is incompatible with borrowing or lending at one fixed rate over long periods of time. To achieve the required liquidity, traders commonly finance their trading activity by borrowing from or lending to their clearing firm at a variable rate. The clearing firm acts as a bank, informing the trader of the effective rate or rates that apply on any given day.

Even if a trader is able to negotiate a fixed rate over some period of time, there is still the problem of determining which of the various rates apply: is the trader borrowing money (a borrowing rate), lending money (a lending rate), or receiving interest on a short stock position (a short stock rebate). In the last case, the rate that the trader receives will often depend on the difficulty of borrowing the stock.

Although changing interest rates will cause the value of a trader's option position to change, interest rates tend to be a lesser risk for most traders, at least for short-term option strategies. The impact of changing interest rates is a function of time to expiration. Because most actively traded options tend to be short term, with expirations of less than one year, interest rates would have to change dramatically to have an impact on any but the most deeply in-the-money options. Changing interest rates become even less of a concern when one considers how much more sensitive option values are to changes in the price of the underlying instrument or to changes in volatility.

This is not to say that a trader should completely ignore interest-rate risk. For stock options especially, raising interest rates raises the forward price, which raises the value of calls and lowers the value of puts. The options that are most sensitive to this change are deeply in-the-money long-term options. Such options will have the greatest interest-rate sensitivity, as reflected by their high rho values. With many exchanges now listing long-term options,

Figure 23-1 Theoretical values as interest rates change.

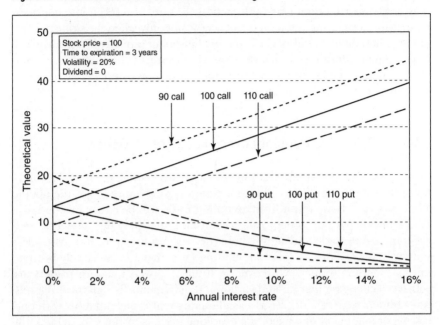

a trader should be aware of the impact of changing rates on such options. Figure 23-1 shows the effect of rising interest rates on long-term stock options. Figure 23-2 shows the effect on rho values for stock options as we increase time to expiration.

Figure 23-2 Rho values as time to expiration changes.

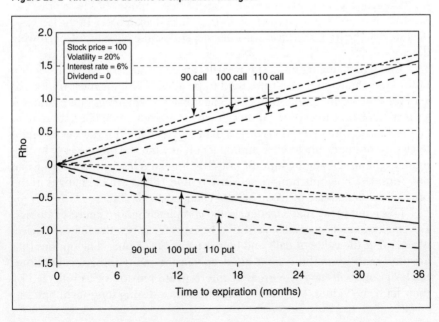

Volatility Is Constant over the Life of the Option

When a trader feeds a volatility into a theoretical pricing model, he is specifying the magnitude and frequency of price changes that will occur over the life of the option. Because these price changes are assumed to be normally distributed, the model recognizes that there will be some number of one, two, three, and so on standard deviation occurrences and that these occurrences will be evenly distributed over the life of the option. Two standard deviation price changes will be evenly distributed among the one standard deviation price changes; three standard deviation price changes will be evenly distributed among the one and two standard deviation price changes; and so on.

In the real world, however, price changes are unlikely to be evenly distributed. Over the life of an option, a trader will encounter periods of high volatility, where large price changes will dominate, together with periods of low volatility, where small price changes dominate. The combination of these high- and low-volatility periods will result in one volatility. But a theoretical pricing model is indifferent as to how the volatility unfolds. The model sees one volatility and evaluates options accordingly.

Figures 23-3 and 23-4 are daily high/low/close bar charts for a hypothetical underlying contract over a period of 80 trading days. Both bar charts represent exactly the same close-to-close realized volatility over the period in question, 28 percent. But the order in which the volatility unfolds is different. In Figure 23-3, volatility is clearly declining, with larger price changes occurring early in the 80-day period and smaller price changes occurring later in the period. In Figure 23-4, the opposite is true. Volatility is rising, with smaller price changes occurring early and larger changes occurring later. The reader may have already guessed that the charts are in fact mirror images of each

Figure 23-3 Falling volatility.

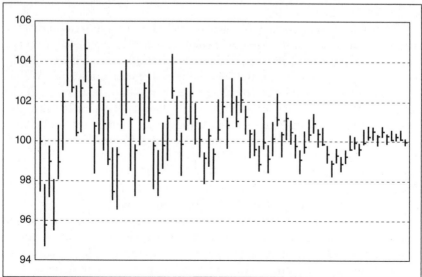

Figure 23-4 Rising volatility.

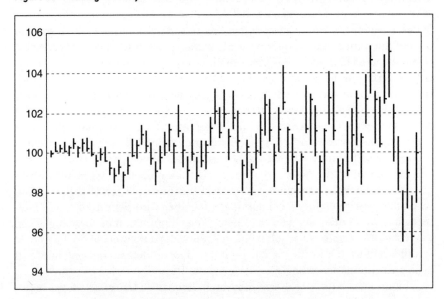

other and therefore must represent the same volatility. Even though the volatility unfolded in two completely different scenarios, in both cases, a pricing model will use the same volatility, 28 percent, to make all calculations.

In both Figures 23-3 and 23-4, the beginning and ending price is 100. Suppose that a trader buys a 100 straddle and assumes, correctly, a volatility of 28 percent. What should this straddle be worth? To simplify the example, let's assume that there are 80 calendar days to expiration and that every day is a trading day (hence no weekends and holidays). To focus only on volatility, let's also assume that the interest rate is 0. Under these assumptions, the Black-Scholes model will generate a value for both the 100 call and put of 5.23, for a total straddle value of 10.46.

Alternatively, suppose that we calculate the value of the 100 call and put by running a simulation of the dynamic hedging process. Using the closing price each day, the number of days remaining to expiration, and a known volatility of 28 percent, we can calculate the delta at the end of each trading day. We can then buy or sell the required number of underlying contracts to remain delta neutral. (This is the same approach used to explain the dynamic hedging process in Chapter 8.) The results of such a simulation show that if the volatility is falling (Figure 23-3), the 100 call and put are worth 2.97 each, for a total straddle value of 5.94. But, if volatility is rising (Figure 23-4), the 100 call and put are worth 6.41 each, for a total straddle value of 12.82. Why do these values differ so dramatically from the Black-Scholes value of 10.46?

A strategy that will be helped by higher realized volatility, such as a long straddle, will benefit most if periods of high in volatility occur when the gamma is greatest. The high gamma will magnify the changes in the delta as the underlying price changes, resulting in greater profit from the dynamic hedging process. Because the 100 straddle is essentially at the money and the gamma of an at-the-money option increases as expiration approaches, any increase in volatility close to expiration will have a disproportionately greater impact on the option's value than a similar increase in volatility early in the option's life. Consequently, the rising-volatility scenario increases the value of the 100 straddle well above the Black-Scholes value. Of course, the higher gamma close to expiration goes hand in hand with a higher theta. With no underlying movement close to expiration, the option will decay at an accelerated rate. Therefore, the falling-volatility scenario has an inordinately negative impact on the value of the 100 straddle, causing the value to fall below the Black-Scholes value.

For out-of-the-money options, the effect is just the opposite. The gamma of an out-of-the-money option is largest early in its life, so a period of high volatility early in the option's life will increase its value. An out-of-the-money option will be worth more than the predicted Black-Scholes value in a falling-volatility scenario and worth less in a rising-volatility scenario. This is confirmed by the results of a dynamic hedging simulation for the 80 put and 120 call. At a volatility of 28 percent, the Black-Scholes values are 0.21 for the 80 put and 0.54 for the 120 call. If, however, volatility is falling, the values are 0.44 and 0.89. If volatility is rising, the values are 0.05 and 0.14.

Option values under our three different volatility scenarios for exercise prices from 70 to 130 are shown in Figure 23-5. With the price of the underlying remaining generally between 95 and 105, options with exercise prices of 95, 100, and 105 are worth more than the Black-Scholes value in a rising-volatility

Figure 23-5 Option values under three different volatility scenarios.

Underlying price = 100
Time to expiration = 80 days
Interest rate = 0
Volatility = 28%

Exercise price:	70	75	80	85	90	95	100	105	110	115	120	125	130
Constant volatility (Black-Scholes) Calls:	30.01	25.06	20.21	15.62	11.48	7.98	5.23	3.22	1.87	1.03	0.54	0.27	0.13
Puts:	0.01	0.06	0.21	0.62	1.48	2.98	5.23	8.22	11.87	16.03	20.54	25.27	30.13
Straddle:	30.01	25.12	20.42	16.24	12.96	10.96	10.46	11.44	13.74	17.06	21.08	25.54	30.26
Falling volatility (Figure 23-3) Calls:	30.04	25.15	20.44	16.00	11.79	7.59	2.97	2.69	2.10	1.43	0.89	0.51	0.27
Puts:	0.04	0.15	0.44	1.00	1.79	2.59	2.97	7.69	12.10	16.43	20.89	25.51	30.27
Straddle:	30.08	25.30	20.88	17.00	13.58	10.18	5.94	10.38	14.20	17.86	21.78	26.02	30.54
Rising volatility (Figure 23-4) Calls:	30.00	25.01	20.05	15.21	10.75	8.97	6.41	3.36	1.29	0.41	0.14	0.05	0.02
Puts:	0	0.01	0.05	0.21	0.75	3.97	6.41	8.36	11.29	15.41	20.14	25.05	30.02
Straddle:	30.00	25.02	20.10	15.42	11.50	12.94	12.82	11.72	12.58	15.82	20.28	25.10	30.04

Using an interest rate of zero, the time premium for a call and put with the same exercise price must be identical. The value of the call and put will differ only by intrinsic value.

market and less than the Black-Scholes value in a falling-volatility market. The opposite is true for exercise prices below 90 or above 110. They are worth more in a falling-volatility market and less in a rising-volatility market.

If an option is held to expiration with no accompanying dynamic delta hedging, the value of the option depends solely on the underlying price at expiration. The option's value is independent of the path by which the underlying contract reaches its terminal value. But the preceding examples make it clear that in a world where a trader dynamically hedges an option position, the value of the option is in fact *path dependent*. Even if we assume a single volatility, the route that the underlying takes can have a significant impact on the value of the option.

Because the value of an option seems to be path dependent, one might conclude that the Black-Scholes model is unreliable. Indeed, for any one random-walk scenario, the value resulting from the dynamic hedging process will almost certainly differ from a Black-Scholes value. But the Black-Scholes model is a probabilistic model. A given volatility will, *on average*, result in a given value for the option. In our example, we considered only two alternative volatility scenarios, where volatility is either rising or falling. But there are an almost infinite number of paths that the underlying price might follow over the life of an option. If we were to generate a large number of random price paths, all with normally distributed price changes and with the same volatility of 28 percent and if we were to then simulate the dynamic hedging process, we would find that, on average, each exercise price is worth something very close to the value predicted by the Black-Scholes model.

Although the Black-Scholes model assumes that prices follow a random walk through time with constant volatility, we might instead assume that volatility is itself random. Several models that assume *stochastic volatility* have been proposed and might, in some cases, be more suitable than a traditional pricing model. At the same time, such models add an additional dimension of complexity to a trader's life and for this reason are not widely used.

Some contracts, by their very nature, are known to change their volatility characteristics over time. Interest-rate products in particular fall into this category. As a bond approaches maturity, the price of the bond moves inexorably toward par. At maturity, regardless of interest rates, the bond will have a fixed and known value. Clearly, one cannot assume that the price of the bond follows a random walk through time. Even if one assumes that interest rates move randomly and that the volatility of interest rates is constant, interest-rate instruments will change their volatility over time because instruments of different maturities have different sensitivities to changes in interest rates. If we take into consideration the fact that interest rates also vary for different maturities, a traditional Black-Scholes type model is obviously not well suited to the evaluation of such products. This has led to the development of special models to evaluate interest-rate instruments.

Trading Is Continuous

To model option values, a model must make some assumptions about how the price of an underlying contract changes over time. One possible assumption is that prices follow a *continuous diffusion process*. Under this assumption, price changes are continuous, with no gaps permitted between consecutive prices. An example of a typical continuous diffusion process might be the temperature readings in a specific location. Although the temperature can change very quickly, there will never be any gaps. If the temperature is initially 25 degrees but later drops to 22 degrees, then at some intermediate time, even if only very briefly, the temperature must have also been 24 degrees and then 23 degrees.

The Black-Scholes model assumes that the underlying contract follows a continuous diffusion process. Trading proceeds 24 hours per day, 7 days per week, without interruption, and with no gaps in the price of the underlying contract. If a contract trades at 46.05 and at some later time trades at 46.08, then at some intermediate time it must also have traded, even if only briefly, at 46.06 and 46.07. If one were to graph with pen and paper the prices of an underlying contract that follow a continuous diffusion process, one would never lift the pen from the paper. An example of this is shown in Figure 23-6a.

If we assume that the underlying contract follows a continuous diffusion process, we can also assume that the dynamic hedging process can be carried out continuously. This is fundamental to capturing an option's theoretical value. The Black-Scholes model assumes that a position can be rehedged to remain delta neutral at every possible moment in time.

A continuous diffusion process may be a reasonable approximation of how prices change in the real world, but it is clearly not perfect. An exchange-traded contract cannot follow a pure diffusion process if the exchange is not open 24 hours per day. At the end of the trading day, a contract may close at one price and then open the next day at a different price. This causes a price gap, something that a diffusion process does not permit. Even during normal trading hours, news might be released, the impact of which can be almost instantaneous, causing the price of a contract to gap either up or down.

Instead of a diffusion process, prices might follow a *jump process*. In a jump process, the price of a contract remains fixed for a period of time and then instantaneously jumps to a new price, where it again remains fixed until a new jump occurs. The way in which central banks set interest rates is typical of a jump process. In the United States, when the Federal Reserve sets the discount rate, it remains fixed until the Fed announces a change. The discount rate then jumps to a new level. A typical jump process, shown in Figure 23-6b, is a combination of fixed prices and instantaneous jumps.

In the real world, prices of most underlying contracts follow neither a pure diffusion process nor a pure jump process. The real world seems to be a combination of the two—a *jump-diffusion process*. Most of the time, trading proceeds normally with no price gaps. Occasionally, though, an unexpected change in market conditions occurs that causes the underlying contract to instantaneously gap to a new price. Such a process is shown in Figure 23-6c.

If a theoretical pricing model assumes that prices follow a diffusion process when in fact they don't, how is this likely to affect values generated by the model? To understand the effect of a gap, consider a trader who sells an at-the-money straddle with the underlying contract trading at 100. How will the trader feel if the underlying contract suddenly gaps up to 105? Clearly, this is not what the trader was hoping for. Such a large move might well be accompanied by an increase in implied volatility, which will also hurt the

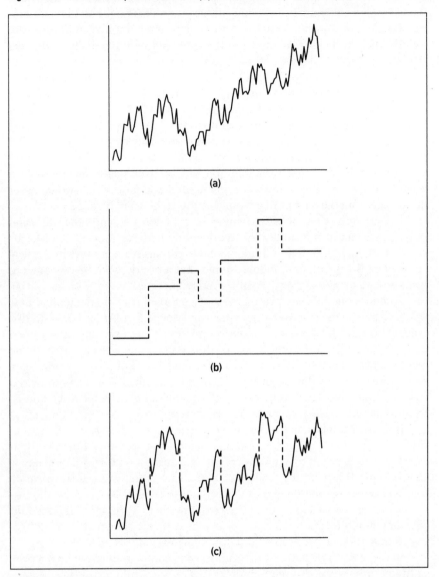

(a)

(b)

(c)

trader's position. But even if implied volatility does not change, because of the negative gamma associated with the short straddle, the large move in the underlying contract will clearly work against the trader. How bad will the damage be? If the options are relatively long term, say, one year, the gap in the underlying price is unlikely to be the end of the world. After all, with one year remaining to expiration, the underlying market could certainly fall back to 100. While the gap has hurt the trader, it is probably not disastrous. But, if the gap occurs with only a very short time remaining to expiration, say, one day, the trader is now in a much worse situation. With only one day to expiration, there is not enough time for the market to retrace its movement. The 100 calls that the trader sold as part of the short straddle will immediately go deeply into the money, acting like short underlying contracts. The straddle may have begun approximately delta neutral, but after the gap, the trader will find himself naked short deeply in-the-money calls, each with a delta of 100. The value of the one-day straddle will increase dramatically compared with the value of the one-year straddle.

The reason the effect of the gap is much greater if the straddle is short term rather than long term is a result of how the gamma changes over time. We know that as expiration approaches, the gamma of an at-the-money option increases, causing the delta to change much more rapidly when the underlying price moves. The dynamic hedging process can reduce some of the damage if the trader is able to buy underlying contracts as the underlying price rises. But a gap is an instantaneous move; there is no opportunity to adjust. The very high gamma, combined with an inability to make any adjustment, makes the consequences of the gap much more dramatic close to expiration.

Not only does the gamma of an at-the-money option increase as expiration approaches, but it also increases as we reduce volatility. Consequently, the impact of a gap will be much greater in a low-volatility market than in a high-volatility market. If we consider these two traits together, we can conclude that at-the-money options close to expiration in a low-volatility market are among the riskiest of options.

Figure 23-7 shows the change in value for a 100 straddle if the market should gap as expiration approaches. The chart shows the change under two

Figure 23-7   Effect of a gap on the value of a 100 straddle.

Underlying price = 100						
Time to Expiration	1 Day	1 Week	1 Month	3 Months	6 Months	1 Year
Implied volatility = 15%						
Initial straddle value	0.63	1.66	3.45	5.98	8.46	11.96
Straddle gamma	101	38	18	11	8	5
Straddle value after a gap from 100 to 105	5.00	5.01	5.58	7.39	9.57	12.90
Increase in value	4.37	3.35	2.13	1.41	1.11	0.94
Implied volatility = 25%						
Initial straddle value	1.04	2.76	5.76	9.97	14.09	19.90
Straddle gamma	61	23	11	6	4	3
Straddle value after a gap from 100 to 105	5.00	5.25	7.20	10.98	14.98	20.78
Increase in value	3.96	2.49	1.44	1.01	0.89	0.88

volatility scenarios, 15 and 25 percent. Note the greater change in the straddle value close to expiration, as well as the greater change in a low-volatility market.

Options have the unique characteristic of automatically and continuously rehedging themselves by changing their deltas as the price of the underlying contract changes. It is this characteristic for which buyers of options are paying. A trader who uses a theoretical pricing model attempts to take advantage of a mispriced option by hedging the option position, delta neutral, with the underlying contract and then manually performing the rehedging process himself over the life of the option. If a model assumes that prices follow a diffusion process, the model also assumes that one can continuously maintain a delta-neutral hedge. But when the market gaps, the assumptions on which the model is based are violated. Consequently, the values generated by the model are rendered invalid. This problem extends to any application that attempts to replicate option characteristics through a continuous rehedging in the underlying market. The proponents of portfolio insurance (see Chapter 17) suffered their greatest setbacks on October 19 and 20, 1987, when the market made several large-gap moves. Because of the gaps, the portfolio insurers were unable to make continuous delta adjustments to their positions. As a consequence, they found that the cost of protection offered by portfolio insurance was much greater than they had expected.

To more accurately evaluate options, a variation on the Black-Scholes model has been proposed that includes the possibility of gaps in the price of the underlying contract. This *jump-diffusion model*, in theory, generates values that are more accurate than traditional Black-Scholes values,[4] but the model is considerably more complex mathematically and also requires two new inputs—the average size of a jump in the underlying market and the frequency with which jumps are likely to occur. Unless the user can accurately estimate these new inputs, the values generated by a jump-diffusion model may be no better—and might be worse—than those generated by a traditional model. Many traders take the view that whatever weaknesses are encountered in a traditional model can be best offset through intelligent decision making based on actual trading experience rather than through the use of a more complex jump-diffusion model.

Assuming that a trader has a delta-neutral position that he intends to dynamically hedge, any gap will have a negative impact on a trader who has a negative gamma position because the trader will not have an opportunity to adjust as the market moves. The same gap will have a positive impact on a trader with a positive gamma position because he will also not have an opportunity to adjust as the market moves. In the latter case, this works to the trader's advantage.

Because a gap in the market will have its greatest effect on high-gamma options, and because at-the-money options close to expiration have the highest

---

[4] A discussion of the jump-diffusion model can be found in most advanced texts on option pricing. For additional information, see Robert Merton, "Option Pricing when Underlying Stock Returns Are Discontinuous," *Journal of Financial Economics* 3(March):125–144, 1976; Stan Beckers, "A Note on Estimating the Parameters in the Jump-Diffusion Model of Stock Returns," *Journal of Financial and Quantitative Analysis*, March 1981, pp. 127–140; and Espen Gaarder Haug, *The Complete Guide to Option Pricing Formulas*, 2nd ed. (New York: McGraw-Hill, 2006).

gamma, it is these options that are most likely to be mispriced by a traditional theoretical pricing model. Consequently, as expiration approaches, experienced traders will tend to rely less and less on model-generated values and more on their own experience and intuition. This is not to suggest that under these circumstances a model is of no value, but one needs to make adjustments when the model is known to be incorrect.

As a result of the gaps that occur in the real world, both a trader's experience and empirical evidence seem to indicate that a traditional model, with its built-in diffusion assumption, tends to undervalue options in the real world. If one compares the average historical volatility of an underlying market with the average implied volatility over long periods of time, the average implied volatility is almost always greater. This seems to indicate that buyers of options are overpaying. Part of this may be due to hedgers willing to pay an additional premium for protective options. But the implied volatility is derived from a theoretical pricing model that does not include the possibility of gaps in the underlying price. The possibility of these gaps tends to indicate that perhaps the values of options are in fact greater in the real world than is predicted by a traditional theoretical pricing model.

We have seen that a gap will have the greatest impact on an option position close to expiration, particularly for at-the-money options because these options have the greatest gamma. From a risk standpoint, this means that it can be very dangerous to sell a large number of at-the-money options close to expiration because any gap in the underlying market can have devastating results. New traders in particular are advised to avoid such positions. No risk manager will appreciate even experienced traders being short large numbers of at-the-money options as expiration approaches.

Expiration Straddles

If it is dangerous to sell at-the-money options close to expiration, perhaps there is some sense in taking the opposite position by purchasing at-the-money options as expiration approaches. This may seem to contradict conventional option wisdom, which focuses on the rapid time decay associated with such options. But there is always a tradeoff between risk and reward. If one sells at-the-money options, the reward may be an accelerated profit if the market doesn't move (high positive theta), but the risk is an increased loss if the market does move (high negative gamma). Because the model does not know about the possibility of a gap in the underlying market, the risk is often greater than the reward. If one sells at-the-money options, the losses from an unexpected gap can more than offset the profits resulting from increased time decay. An experienced trader may therefore take the opposite position by purchasing at-the-money options close to expiration.

This is not to suggest that every time expiration approaches, a trader should buy at-the-money options. As with any strategy, conditions must make the strategy look attractive. But because many traders are intent on selling time premium as expiration approaches, it is often possible to find cheap at-the-money options. Suppose that with three days remaining to expiration, the Black-Scholes model generates a value for an at-the-money call of 0.75. What can we say about this call? Although we may not know the exact value because we don't know the true future volatility, there is high likelihood that in the real world the call is worth more than 0.75 because the model doesn't know about the possibility of a gap in the market. If, on top of this, the call is trading at a price below its model-generated value, say, 0.65, it is likely to be a good buy.

As with any strategy based on volatility, the trader who buys these calls will try to establish a delta-neutral position. Because of the synthetic relationship, if the calls are underpriced, the puts at the same exercise price will also be underpriced. Thus, a logical strategy might be the purchase of at-the-money straddles. This enables a trader to buy both underpriced calls and underpriced puts and to profit if the underlying market gaps either up or down.

In theory, all volatility strategies, including an expiration straddle, ought to be adjusted periodically to remain delta neutral. However, with little time remaining to expiration, the model is not only unreliable with respect to theoretical values, but also unreliable with respect to deltas. Because it is impossible to say what the right delta is, it is also impossible to say what the correct adjustment is. For this reason, traders who buy expiration straddles often abandon any attempt to remain delta neutral and simply sit on the position to expiration. This may not be the theoretically correct way to manage a volatility position, but given all the uncertainties associated with theoretical evaluation as expiration approaches, it may be a practical choice.

Even if a trader carefully chooses his expiration straddles, the great majority of time no gap will occur in the market. In any single case, the trader is more likely to show a loss than a profit. But the primary concern is not the profit or loss[5] from any single trade, but what happens *in the long run*. Returning to the roulette example in Chapter 5, a player who chooses a number at a roulette table can expect to win on average only 1 time in 38. But, if the theoretical value of the bet is 95 cents and the player can buy the bet for less than 95 cents, he expects to be a winner in the long run. Even if he is able to pay a very low price for the bet, say, 50 cents, he still expects to lose 37 times out of 38. But now the bet is very attractive. Even if he only wins 1 time in 38, this will still more than offset the small losses he takes each time he loses. The same logic is true of expiration straddles. A trader may lose several times before winning. But when he does win, he can expect a return that is great enough to more than offset all the small losses.

The fact that an at-the-money straddle may be cheap does not mean that a trader should buy these straddles in large numbers. Such strategies are likely to result in a loss more often than a profit, so an intelligent trader should only invest an amount that he can afford to lose. However, when conditions are right, a trader ought to be willing to make the investment. Even if he loses several times in succession, in the long run, he will encounter gaps in the market or large increases in volatility often enough to make such strategies profitable.

---

[5] This assumes, of course, that the trader is able to absorb the loss and still stay in business for the long run.

Volatility Is Independent of the Price of the Underlying Contract

When a trader feeds a volatility into a theoretical pricing model, the volatility defines a one standard deviation price change at any time during the life of the option regardless of whether the underlying contract happens to be rising or falling in price. If a contract is currently at 100 and we assume a volatility of 20 percent, a one standard deviation price change is always based on this volatility of 20 percent. If, at some later time during the life of the option, the contract should move up to 125 or down to 75, the effective volatility is still assumed to be 20 percent.

In many markets, however, this assumption appears to be inconsistent with most traders' experience. If one were to ask a stock index trader whether his market becomes more volatile when rising or falling, he would probably say that it becomes more volatile when falling. On the other hand, if one were to ask a commodity trader the same question, he likely would give the opposite answer. His market will tend to become more volatile when rising. In other words, the volatility of a market is not independent of the price of the underlying contract. On the contrary, the volatility over time seems to depend on the direction of movement in the underlying contract. In some cases, a trader expects the market to become more volatile if the movement is downward and less volatile if the movement is upward; in other cases, a trader expects the market to become more volatile if the movement is upward and less volatile if the movement is downward.

Because volatility in some markets seems to depend on the direction of price movement in the underlying contract, a further variation of the Black-Scholes model has been proposed. The *constant-elasticity of variance* (CEV) *model*[6] is based on the assumption that volatility changes as the price of the underlying contract changes. Price changes are still assumed to be random in the CEV model, but the volatility, and consequently the magnitude of the price changes, varies with the price of the underlying contract.

Like the jump-diffusion model, the CEV model is both mathematically complex and requires additional inputs in the form of a mathematical relationship between the volatility and price movement in the underlying contract. Given these difficulties, the CEV model has not found wide acceptance among option traders.

Underlying Prices at Expiration Are Lognormally Distributed

In the real world, do prices at expiration form a lognormal distribution? We might try to answer this question by asking how the percent price changes are distributed. If this distribution is normal, the continuous compounding of price changes is likely to result in a lognormal distribution of prices.

Figure 23-8a is a histogram of daily Standard and Poor's (S&P) 500 Index price changes for the 10-year period from 2003 through 2012. Each bar represents the number of occurrences of a given price change rounded to the

---

[6] For information on the CEV model, see John C. Cox and Stephen A. Ross, "The Valuation of Options for Alternative Stochastic Processes," *Journal of Financial Economics* 3(March):145–166, 1976; Stan Beckers, "The Constant Elasticity of Variance Model and Its Implications for Option Pricing," *Journal of Finance*, June 1980, pp. 661–673; Mark Schroder, "Computing the Constant Elasticity of Variance Option Pricing Model," *Journal of Finance* 44(1):211–219, 1989; and Espen Gaarder Haug, *The Complete Guide to Option Pricing Formulas*, 2nd ed. (New York: McGraw-Hill, 2006).

nearest ¼ percent. As one would expect, most of the changes are relatively small and close to 0. As we move away from the 0 in either direction, we encounter fewer and fewer occurrences. The distribution seems to have many of the characteristics of a normal distribution. But is it really a normal distribution, and if not, how does it differ from a true normal distribution?

Figure 23-8 (a) S&P 500 daily price changes: January 2003–December 2012. (b) Crude oil daily price changes: January2003–December 2012. (c) Euro (versus dollar) daily price changes: January 2003–December 2012. (d) Bund daily price changes: January 2003–December 2012.

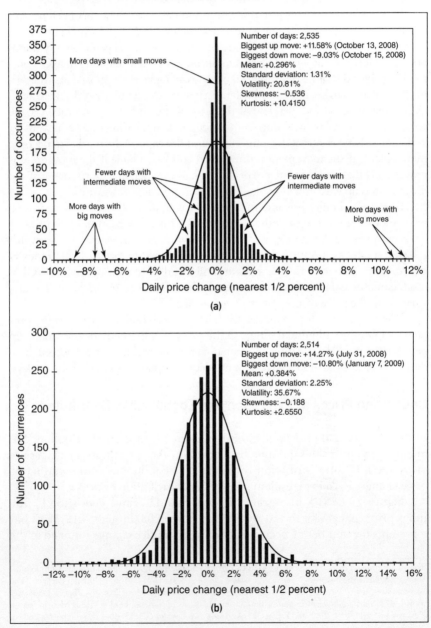

(continued)

Figure 23-8 (*continued*)

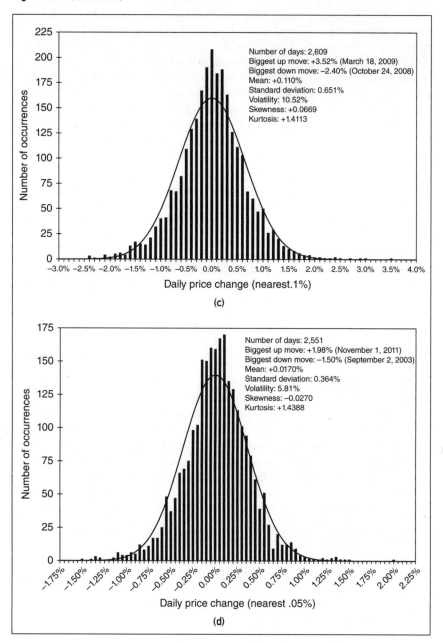

Number of days: 2,609
Biggest up move: +3.52% (March 18, 2009)
Biggest down move: −2.40% (October 24, 2008)
Mean: +0.110%
Standard deviation: 0.651%
Volatility: 10.52%
Skewness: +0.0669
Kurtosis: +1.4113

Daily price change (nearest.1%)

(c)

Number of days: 2,551
Biggest up move: +1.98% (November 1, 2011)
Biggest down move: −1.50% (September 2, 2003)
Mean: +0.0170%
Standard deviation: 0.364%
Volatility: 5.81%
Skewness: −0.0270
Kurtosis: +1.4388

Daily price change (nearest .05%)

(d)

If the frequency distribution conforms exactly to a normal distribution, the tops of the bars should coincide exactly with a true normal distribution. To find out if this is the case, the mean (+0.0296 percent) and standard deviation (1.31 percent) have been calculated for all 2,535 daily price changes over the 10-year period. From these numbers, a best-fit normal distribution has been overlaid on the frequency chart. The actual frequency distribution is similar to the normal distribution, but there are some clear differences. Because the bars representing the small price changes rise above the normal distribution curve, there seem to be more days with small price changes than one would expect from a true normal distribution. Although they are not as obvious, there are also several large price changes, or *outliers*, that rise above the extreme tails of the normal distribution. These outliers seem to suggest that there are more large moves in our frequency distribution than one would expect from a true normal distribution. Finally, in the midsections, between the peak of the distribution and the extreme tails, there seem to be fewer occurrences than one would expect.

One might surmise that the differences in Figure 23-8a between the S&P 500 frequency distribution and the true normal distribution are either unique to the S&P 500 or an aberration of the 10-year period in question, which admittedly included the financial crisis of 2008. However, studies tend to indicate that price-change distributions for almost all exchange-traded underlying markets exhibit characteristics that are very similar to the S&P 500 distribution. There are always more days with small moves, more days with large moves, and fewer days with intermediate moves than are predicted by a true normal distribution. The differences between the actual and theoretical distributions can also be seen in several other histograms covering the same period of time: crude oil (Figure 23-8b), the euro (Figure 23-8c), and the Bund (Figure 23-8d).

Skewness and Kurtosis

Distributions such as those in Figure 23-8a through 23-8d are approximately normal but still differ from a true normal distribution. If one is trying to make decisions based on the characteristics of a distribution, it might be useful to know how the actual distribution differs from the normal. A perfectly normal distribution can be fully described by its mean and standard deviation. But two other numbers, the *skewness* and *kurtosis*, are often used to describe the extent to which an actual distribution differs from a true normal distribution.[7]

The skewness of a distribution (Figure 23-9) can be thought of as the lopsidedness of the distribution, or the extent to which one tail is longer than the other tail. In a positively skewed distribution, the right tail is longer than the left tail. (The lognormal distribution shown in Figure 6-7 is positively skewed.) In a negatively skewed distribution, the left tail is longer than the right tail. A perfectly normal distribution has a skewness of 0. The frequency distribution in Figure 23-8c (euro) is positively skewed, while the distributions in Figures 23-8a (S&P 500), 23-8b (crude oil), and 23-8d (Bund) are negatively skewed.

The kurtosis of a distribution (Figure 23-10) is the extent to which the center of the distribution is either unusually tall or unusually flat. A distribution with a positive kurtosis has a tall peak (*leptokurtic*), whiles a distribution with a negative kurtosis has a low or flat peak (*platykurtic*). A perfectly normal distribution has a kurtosis of 0 (*mesokurtic*).[8]

---

[7] The skewness and kurtosis functions are included in most commonly used spreadsheets. Their formulas can be found in a statistics or probability textbook.

[8] Mathematically, a true normal distribution has a kurtosis of 3. However, as commonly expressed, 3 is usually subtracted from the kurtosis value, so a true normal distribution has a kurtosis value of 0.

Figure 23-9 *Skewness*—the degree to which one tail of a distribution is longer than the other tail.

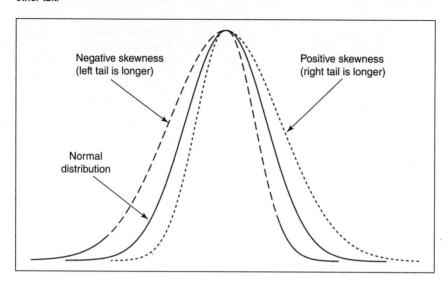

At first sight, a positive kurtosis distribution looks similar to a low standard deviation distribution because both have high peaks. But a distribution with a low standard deviation also has short tails, while a distribution with a positive kurtosis has elongated tails. One might think of a positive kurtosis distribution as a normal distribution where the midsection to the left and right of the peak has been squeezed inward. This forces the peak of the distribution upward and the tails outward. The frequency distributions in Figures 23-8*a* through 23-8*d* all exhibit the same positive kurtosis, which is typical of almost all exchange-traded underlying markets. They have higher peaks (more days with small moves), elongated tails (more days with big moves), and narrow midsections (fewer days with intermediate moves) than are predicted by a true normal distribution. Traders sometimes refer to these as "fat tail" distributions.

The S&P 500 distribution has an unusually large kurtosis value of 10.415. To see the extent to which the tails of this distribution are abnormally fat, we can express the biggest up and down moves in standard deviations and then consider the chances of these moves occurring under the assumption of a normal distribution. The biggest up move in the S&P over the 10-year period was 11.58 percent. With a standard deviation of 1.31 percent, this translates into an 8.84 standard deviation occurrence. The probability of such an occurrence is approximately 1 chance in 2,000,000,000,000,000,000 (2 quintillion, for anyone who is counting). The biggest down move, 9.03 percent, translates into a 6.75 standard deviation occurrence, with a probability equal to approximately 1 chance in 350,000,000,000 (350 billion). Simply put, the likelihood of either of these occurrences is so small that they will essentially never occur.[9]

The kurtosis values for crude oil, the euro, and the Bund are not as dramatic as the S&P 500. But even in these markets under the assumptions of a

---

[9] Nassim Taleb has referred to such unlikely occurrences as "black swans." See Nassim Nicholas Taleb, *The Black Swan: The Impact of the Highly Improbable* (New York: Penguin Books, 2008).

Figure 23-10 *Kurtosis*—the degree to which a distribution has a taller peak and wider tails.

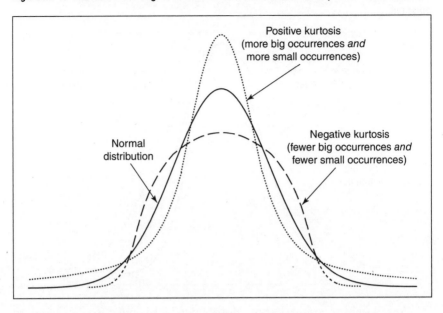

normal distribution, we would expect to see the biggest up and down moves only once in many millions of occurrences. Keeping in mind that the data covered a period of between 2,500 and 2,600 days, we can see how much more often big moves occur are in the real world compared with what is predicted by a normal distribution. The probabilities associated with the largest moves in our sample distributions are shown in Figure 23-11.

Figure 23-11 Probabilities associated with the biggest up and down moves.

Product	One Standard Deviation	Biggest Move in Percent	Biggest Move in Standard Deviations	Probability
S&P 500	1.31%	Up 11.58%	Up 8.84 st. dev.	Too unlikely to calculate
		Down 9.03%	Down 6.89 st. dev.	1 chance in 358,000,000,000
Crude oil	2.25%	Up 14.27%	Up 6.34 st. dev.	1 chance in 8,700,000,000
		Down 10.80%	Down 4.80 st. dev.	1 chance in 1,260,000
Euro	0.651%	Up 3.52%	Up 5.41 st. dev.	1 chance in 31,700,000
		Down 2.40%	Down 3.69 st. dev.	1 chance in 8,900
Bund	0.364%	Up 1.98%	Up 5.40 st. dev.	1 chance in 30,000,000
		Down 1.50%	Down 4.10 st. dev.	1 chance in 48,000

24

Volatility Skews

There are clearly real problems associated with the use of a traditional theoretical pricing model. Markets are not frictionless, prices do not always follow a diffusion process, volatility may vary over the life of an option, the real world may not look like a lognormal distribution. With all these weaknesses, one might wonder whether theoretical pricing models have any practical value at all. In fact, most traders have found that pricing models, while not perfect, are an invaluable tool for making decisions in the option market. Even if a model does not work perfectly, traders have found that using a model, even a flawed one, is usually better than using no model at all.

Still, a trader who wants to make the best possible decisions cannot afford to ignore the problems associated with a theoretical pricing model. Consequently, a trader who uses a pricing model might look for a way to reduce the potential errors resulting from these weaknesses. Initially, one might simply look for a better theoretical pricing model. If such a model exists, it will certainly be worth replacing the old model with the new one. But *better* is a relative term. A model might be better in the sense that it gives slightly more accurate theoretical values. But if the model is extremely complex and difficult to use, or if it requires additional inputs of which a trader cannot always be certain, then the model may merely substitute one set of problems for another. Given the fact that most traders are not theoreticians, a more realistic solution might be to use a less complex model and somehow fine-tune it so that it is consistent with the realities of the marketplace.

A trader trying to compensate for weaknesses in a pricing model might make the assumption that the marketplace is using the same model as the trader and then ask how the marketplace is dealing with the weaknesses in the model. This is somewhat analogous to calculating implied volatility where we assume that everyone is using the same model, that the price of the option is known, and that everyone agrees on all the inputs except volatility. From these assumptions, we are able to determine the volatility that the marketplace is implying to the underlying contract. We can take the same general approach but ask instead what weaknesses the marketplace is implying to the model.

Figure 24-1 shows the implied volatilities across exercise prices for June 2012 FTSE 100 Index[1] options traded on the London International Financial Exchange on March 16, 2012. Calculations were made at the end of the trading day from the average of the bid-ask spread using the Black-Scholes model. It is immediately apparent that implied volatilities vary across exercise prices. If we assume that the exercise price, time to expiration, underlying price, and interest rate are known, the theoretical value of an option in a Black-Scholes world will depend solely on the volatility of the underlying contract over the life of the option. Of course, we won't know what that volatility is until we reach expiration, at which time we can look back and calculate the historical volatility over the 13-week period from March 16 to June expiration. But the FTSE 100 Index can have only one volatility over this period. Because the underlying index is the same for all options, it doesn't make sense in a perfect Black-Scholes world for every exercise price to have a different implied volatility. If the activity in the marketplace were a result of everyone believing in the efficiency of the Black-Scholes model, the selling of overpriced options and the buying of underpriced options would eventually cause every option to have the same implied volatility. Yet this almost never happens in any market.

The distribution of implied volatilities across exercise prices is often referred to as a *volatility skew* or, possibly, a *volatility smile* or *volatility smirk* depending on the shape of the skew. One likely explanation for the distribution of implied volatilities has to do with the way in which options are used as a hedging

Figure 24-1 June 2012 FTSE 100 implied volatilities: March 16, 2012.

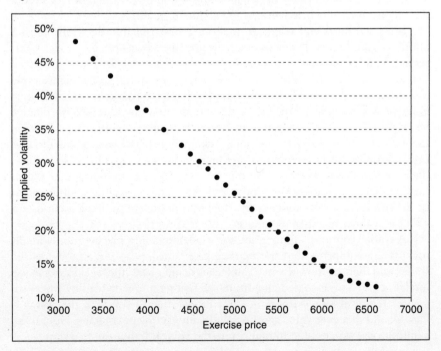

---

[1] The Financial Times Stock Exchange 100 Index (the FTSE 100) is the most widely followed index of U.K. stock prices.

instrument. In the stock market, most investors are long stock[2] and are therefore concerned about a decline in stock prices. The two most common hedging strategies to protect a long underlying position, as described in Chapter 17, are the purchase of protective puts and the sale of covered calls.

If a stock investor decides to purchase a protective put, which exercise price will he choose? An out-of-the-money put costs less than an in-the-money put but also offers less protection against a down move. However, if the investor is so worried about a downward move that he needs the protection afforded by an in-the-money put, he ought to simply sell the stock. The result is that most protective puts are purchased at lower exercise prices.

If, instead, the investor decides to sell a covered call, he will almost always do so at a higher exercise price. This will offer less protection than the sale of an in-the-money call, but presumably the investor holds the stock because he believes that the stock price will rise. If it does rise, he will want to participate in at least some of the upside profit potential. If the stock rises and the investor has sold an in-the-money call, the stock will be quickly called away, limiting any upside profit. The result is that most covered calls are sold at higher exercise prices.

As a result of hedging activity, in the stock option market there tends to be buying pressure on the lower exercise prices (the purchase of protective puts) and selling pressure on the higher exercise prices (the sale of covered calls). This causes the implied volatilities at lower exercise prices to rise and the implied volatilities at higher exercise prices to fall. The resulting skew, such as that in Figure 24-1, is sometimes referred to as an *investment skew*. It occurs in markets in which people freely invest, the most obvious example being the stock market. Traders sometimes describe an investment skew by saying that the "skew is to the puts," indicating that put implied volatilities are inflated. But put-call parity dictates that if a put price is inflated, the call price at the same exercise price must also be inflated, so perhaps it is more accurate to say that the "skew is to the downside."

While investors in the stock market may worry about falling stock prices, in other markets hedgers may worry about rising prices. This is often the case in commodity markets where end users try to protect themselves against rising prices by either buying protective calls at higher exercise prices or selling covered puts at lower exercise prices. In the resulting *demand* or *commodity skew* (there is a demand for the commodity), lower exercise prices have lower implied volatilities, and higher exercise prices have higher implied volatilities. Of course, commodity producers, such as farmers, mining companies, and oil drilling companies, are likely to worry about falling commodity prices, so it might seem that there ought to be equal hedging activity between the longs (producers) and the shorts (end users). But in many markets the end users tend to dominate, perhaps because higher commodity prices, and the concomitant inflationary pressures, are perceived as having a negative effect on the entire economy. Moreover, in some countries, the government has a program of price supports for agricultural products, so growers have less to worry about from falling agricultural commodity prices than end users have from rising prices.

---

[2] There are, of course, investors and traders who take short stock positions, but they are relatively small in number compared with those who are long stock.

Finally, there are markets where both longs and shorts are equally worried. Consider a U.S. company buying goods in Europe that must be paid for on some future date in euros. The company clearly is worried about a rising euro compared with the dollar. At the same time, a European company may buy goods in the United States that must be paid for in dollars. This company is worried about a falling euro compared with the dollar. If both companies choose to hedge their risk in the currency option market, the hedging activity will tend to result in a *balanced skew*, where there is no obvious domination of implied volatilities at either higher or lower exercise prices. This does not mean that implied volatilities will necessarily form a *flat skew*, but the distribution of implied volatilities is likely to be symmetrical around the current underlying price. The three common types of skews are shown in Figure 24-2.

In addition to distortions caused by hedging activity, we also know from Chapter 23 that there are inherent weaknesses in many models. For example, most traders believe that stock markets become more volatile when they are falling and less volatile when they are rising. We also know that an option is most sensitive to volatility changes (it has its highest vega) when it is at the money. If an underlying stock is trading at 100 and the market begins to fall, the vega of the 95 put will rise because it is becoming more at the money. If the market also becomes more volatile because the stock price is falling, this will increase the volatility value of the 95 put. But, if the market begins to rise, the 105 call, even though its vega is rising, will not benefit to the same extent as the 95 put because the market is becoming less volatile. So it should not come as a surprise that the 95 put carries a higher implied volatility and the 105 call a lower implied volatility than expected. This is consistent with an investment skew.

Figure 24-2 (*a*) Investment skew. (*b*) Demand skew. (*c*) Balanced skew.

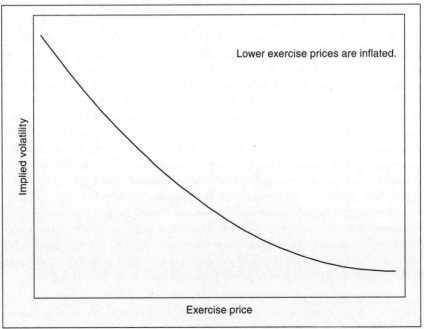

Lower exercise prices are inflated.

Implied volatility

Exercise price

(*a*)

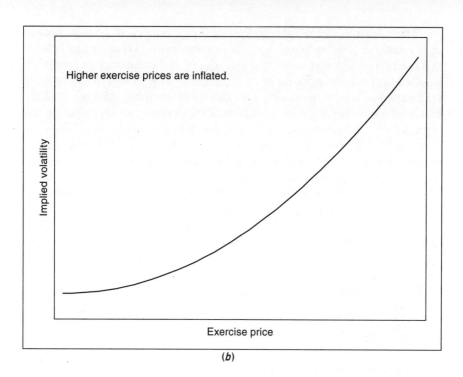

Higher exercise prices are inflated.

Implied volatility

Exercise price

(b)

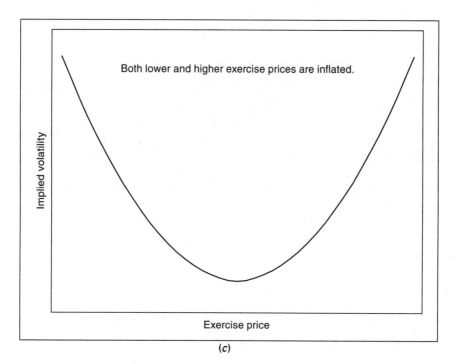

Both lower and higher exercise prices are inflated.

Implied volatility

Exercise price

(c)

The marketplace, like every individual trader, is trying to evaluate options as efficiently as possible given all available information. Whether one believes that markets are efficient or not, one can argue that the marketplace is trying to be efficient. From the wide range of implied volatilities found in almost every option market, we can reasonably infer that the marketplace does not think the Black-Scholes model is perfectly efficient. Unfortunately, trying to identify the source of the inefficiency may not be possible. It might have to do with how options are used in hedging strategies. Or it might have to do with weaknesses in the theoretical pricing model. Whatever the reason, we can make the assumption that at any moment in time the marketplace believes that options are priced efficiently, even if those prices happen to differ from model-generated values.

An option trader using a theoretical pricing model might take the view that the volatility skew contains useful information that can be used in the decision-making process. By treating the volatility skew as an additional input into the theoretical pricing model, the skew becomes an important aid in generating theoretical values and managing risk. Moreover, analysis of the skew can form the basis for a variety of option strategies.

Modeling the Skew

If we want to include a skew in our model, we need to do it in a way that the model understands. This is typically done using a mathematical function that generates a best fit for the skew

$$f(x) = y$$

where y is the implied volatility at each exercise price x. A trader can choose any function that seems to yield a good fit, but many traders use a polynomial function of the form $a + bx + cx^2 + dx^3 + \cdots$. A best-fit function for the implied volatilities in Figure 24-1 is shown in Figure 24-3.

If we think of the skew as an input into the model, then, as with all inputs, we need to ask how changes in the input will affect a position. If we can model possible changes in the skew as market conditions change, we will be in a better position to assess the risk associated with an option position. In particular, as market conditions change, we will want to model both the location and shape of the skew.

Of course, we might take the position that the location and shape of the volatility skew will remain fixed. Under this *sticky-strike* assumption, the current skew determines the implied volatility at each strike regardless of how market conditions change.

Unfortunately, a sticky-strike skew, with its fixed volatilities at each exercise price, is not consistent with the observed dynamics of the marketplace. In most option markets, the skew will shift as the underlying price moves or implied volatility changes. An alternative approach is to use a *floating skew*, where the entire skew is shifted horizontally as the underlying price rises or falls or vertically as implied volatility rises or falls. The shift is equal to the amount of change in either the price or volatility. If the underlying price rises five points, the skew is shifted to the right

Figure 24-3 June 2012 FTSE 100 implied volatilities: March 16, 2012.

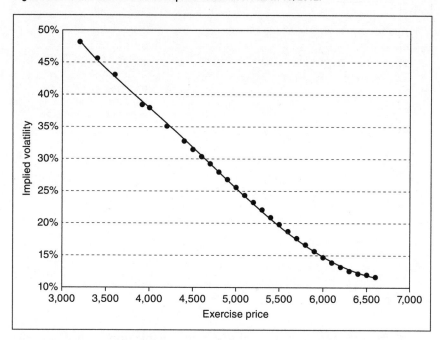

by five points. If implied volatility falls by two percentage points, the skew is shifted downward by two percentage points. This type of skew is shown in Figure 24-4.

Figure 24-4 (a) A simple floating skew as the underlying price changes. (b) A simple floating skew as implied volatility changes.

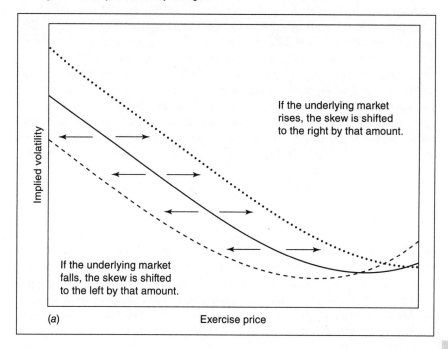

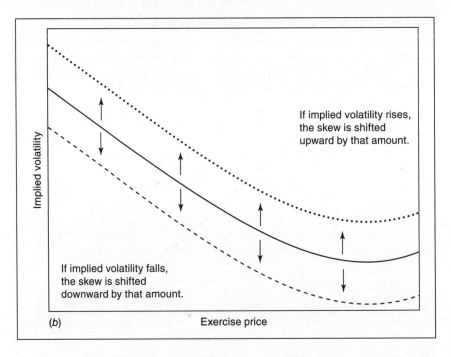

If implied volatility rises, the skew is shifted upward by that amount.

If implied volatility falls, the skew is shifted downward by that amount.

Implied volatility

(b)   Exercise price

Shifting the entire skew might be a reasonable approach if a trader believes that the shape of the skew will remain unchanged regardless of changing market conditions. But is this likely? The implied volatilities at different exercise prices are likely to depend on how the marketplace views the likelihood of either larger or smaller moves in the price of the underlying contract. But all moves are relative with respect to both the underlying price and the time to expiration. In relative terms, a price change of 10.00 is greater with an underlying price of 100 (a 10 percent move) than with an underlying price of 200 (a 5 percent move). In the same way, a 10 percent move is greater over a one-week period than the same 10 percent move over a one-month period.

A first step in adjusting for the relative magnitude of price changes is to express each exercise price along the x axis in terms of its *moneyness*—how far in the money or out of the money the exercise price is as a percent of the underlying price. The 90 exercise price with the underlying price at 100 will have a moneyness of 0.90. This is the same moneyness as the 180 exercise price with an underlying price of 200. We can make a further refinement by expressing each exercise price in logarithmic terms $\ln(X/S)$, where S is the underlying or spot price and X is the exercise price. This is consistent with the assumption that underlying prices are lognormally distributed.

How will the passage of time affect the shape of the volatility skew? Consider a 90 put with the underlying contract trading at 100. As time passes, in relative terms, the 90 put is moving further out of the money. In an investment skew, as the option moves further out of the money, its implied volatility will rise. In a sense, it is moving "up the skew." This will cause the skew to appear more severe as time passes, with lower exercise prices carrying increasingly higher implied volatilities. Higher exercise prices may also be affected by the passage of time because an out-of-the-money call will also go further out of the money.

Depending on the shape of the skew and where an exercise price falls along the skew, its implied volatility may rise, fall, or remain the same. If no adjustment is made, the effect of time passing on the FTSE 100 skew is shown in Figure 24-5.

To compare volatility skews for different expirations, we need to determine theoretically how far in the money or out of the money an option is. Perhaps the easiest way to do this is to express each exercise price in terms of standard deviations away from at the money. Recalling the square-root relationship between time and volatility, and using our logarithmic scale, the number of standard deviations in the money or out of the money for each exercise price is given by

$$\frac{\ln(X/S)}{\sigma\sqrt{t}}$$

with an exactly at-the-money[3] option having a standard deviation of 0. Skews for several FTSE 100 option expirations as of March 16, 2012, are shown in Figure 24-6. When expressed in this format, the skew is sometimes referred to as a *sticky-delta* skew because the delta is an approximation of how far in the money or out of the money an option is.

The skews in Figure 24-6 appear to be similar, but they are clearly not identical. All adjustments thus far have been to the x axis, changing the calibration to more easily compare exercise prices. But we might also adjust the y axis,

Figure 24-5 FTSE 100 option implied volatilities, March 16, 2012 (FTSE = 5965.58).

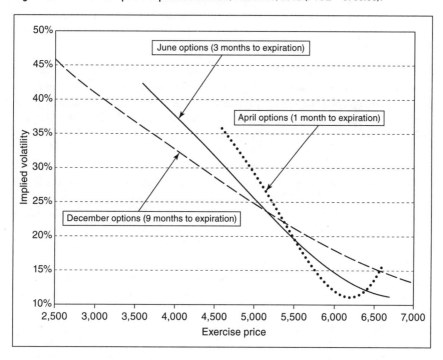

Figure 24-6 FTSE 100 implied volatilities, March 16, 2012.

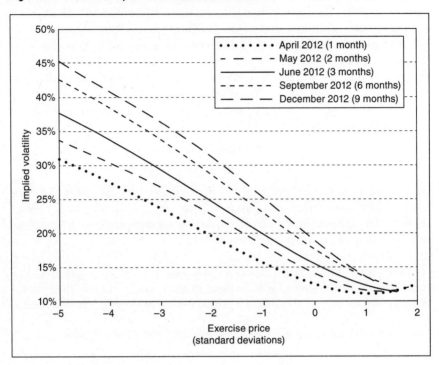

the volatility. When a trader refers to the overall implied volatility in a market, he is almost always referring to the implied volatility of at-the-money options. Whether the implied volatility at any exercise price is high or low will depend on whether it is high or low compared with the at-the-money implied volatility. As a result, many traders recalibrate the y axis in terms of how the implied volatility at an exercise price compares with the at-the-money implied volatility. We can do this by expressing y values as the difference between the implied volatility of an at-the-money option and the implied volatility at each exercise price. If the at-the-money implied volatility is 20 (percent) and the implied volatility at an exercise price is 25 (percent), the y value is $20 - 25 = -5$. If the implied volatility at a different exercise price is 18 (percent), the y value is $20 - 18 = 2$.

This method may be satisfactory if implied volatilities remain relatively constant, but suppose that the at-the-money implied volatility doubles from 20 to 40 percent. We might also expect the volatility at each exercise to double. An exercise price that previously had an implied volatility of 25 percent will now have an implied volatility of 50 percent, and an exercise price that previously had an implied volatility of 18 percent will now have an implied volatility of 36 percent. We can better calibrate the y axis by expressing the volatility at each exercise price as a percent of at-the-money implied volatility. With an at-the-money implied volatility of 20 percent, an implied volatility of 25 percent would be expressed as $25/20 = 125$ percent. An implied volatility of 18 percent would be expressed as $18/20 = 90$ percent. And an implied volatility equal to the at-the-money implied

Figure 24-7 FTSE 100 implied volatilities, March 16, 2012.

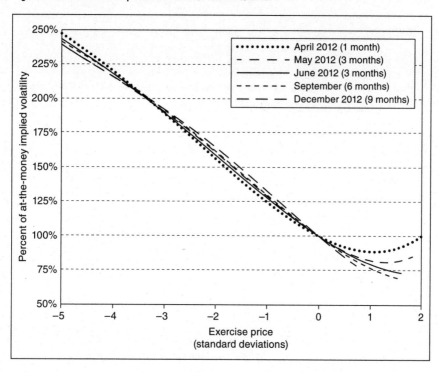

volatility would be expressed as $20/20 = 100$ percent. In Figure 24-7, the y axis for the sample FTSE 100 skews has been recalibrated using this approach.

Figure 24-7 is typical of many stock indexes, exhibiting a very pronounced investment skew, with lower exercise prices significantly inflated compared with higher exercise prices. A different set of skews, for wheat options, is shown in Figure 24-8. In this example, the skews exhibit more curvature but with higher exercise prices somewhat more inflated, as is often the case with a demand or commodity skew. The skews also seem to exhibit less consistency across different expiration months than the FTSE 100. While skews in a financial product tend to be similar across expiration months, skews in a commodity market can often vary across different expirations, perhaps owing to seasonal volatility considerations or because of short-term supply and demand imbalances.

The foregoing method of modeling a skew is used by many traders but is in no way meant to be definitive. Adjustments are often required to prevent the model from generating illogical volatilities or theoretical values. For example, as we reduce volatility, an out-of-the-money option goes further out of the money because it is a greater number of standard deviations away from the underlying price. But in an investment skew, as a put goes further out of the money, it's volatility is rising—it is "climbing the skew." If the skew is sufficiently steep, the increase in volatility may in fact cause the theoretical value of the put to rise. This is inherently illogical because we expect all option values to decline if we reduce volatility.

Figure 24-8 Wheat implied volatilities, January 27, 2012.

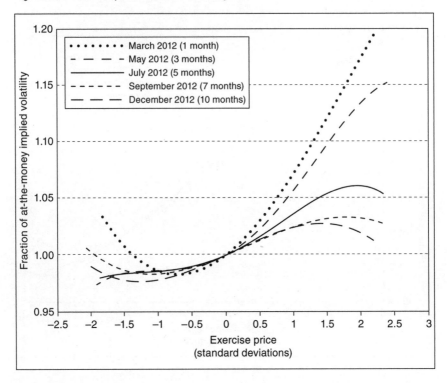

Skewness and Kurtosis

The shape of the skew is not constant. As market conditions change, option prices will also change, often causing the shape of the skew to change. Two common changes have to do with the tilt and curvature of the skew. The tilt, which defines how much the implied volatilities of lower exercise prices differ from the implied volatilities of higher exercise prices, is often referred to as the *skewness*. This follows logically from the definition of skewness in Chapter 23 (see Figure 23-10). If the probability distribution has a longer left tail (negative skewness), there is greater likelihood of large down moves, resulting in greater demand for lower exercise prices. If the distribution has a longer right tail (positive skewness), there is greater likelihood of large up moves and, consequently, greater demand for higher exercise prices. Examples of positive and negative skewness are shown in Figure 24-9.

The curvature, or *kurtosis*, defines how much the implied volatilities of both higher and lower exercise prices are inflated compared with the at-the-money implied volatility. This also follows logically from the definition in Chapter 23 (see Figure 23-11). If the probability distribution has "fat tails," there is a greater likelihood of large moves in either direction. Consequently, there will be a greater demand for out-of-the-money options (positive kurtosis). Examples of increasing positive kurtosis are shown in Figure 24-10.[4]

---

[4] Because all exchange-traded markets seem to exhibit positive kurtosis, we ignore negative kurtosis skews.

Figure 24-9 Skewness.

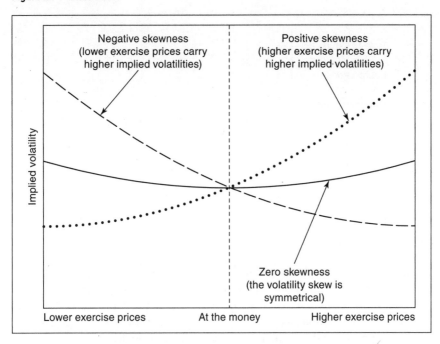

We might think of the skew as an input into a theoretical pricing model (Figure 24-11), but the skew is input into the model as a formula rather than as

Figure 24-10 Kurtosis.

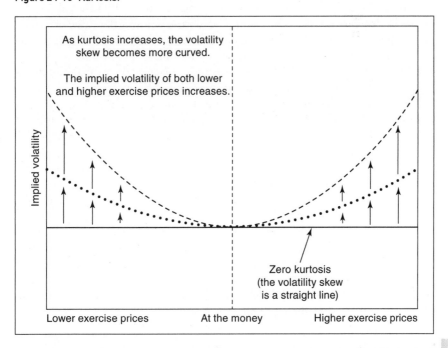

Figure 24-11 The skew as a model input.

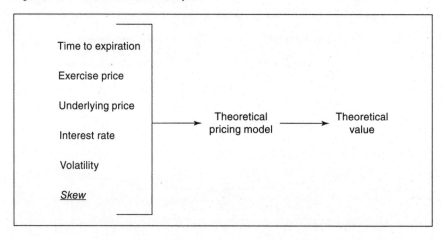

a single number. As with any input, it will be useful to determine how sensitive an option value or option position is to changes in the shape of the skew.

The sensitivities associated with a skew will depend on the skew model that is used. For example, let's assume a very simple second-degree-polynomial model where the volatility y at an exercise price x is given by

$$y = a + bx + cx^2$$

In this model, the value of a is the base volatility, usually the implied volatility of the at-the-money options. The values of b and c represent the skewness and kurtosis, respectively, of the volatility skew. We can raise or lower the value of a as implied volatility rises or falls. We can raise or lower the value of b to increase or decrease the skewness. And we can raise or lower the value of c to increase or decrease the kurtosis. b can be either positive or negative depending on whether higher or lower exercise prices are inflated. For exchange-traded markets, the value of c is almost always positive because the probability distributions of these markets always exhibit some fat-tail characteristics.

The sensitivity of an option's theoretical value to a change in skewness or kurtosis will depend on how the option's value changes as we raise or lower the value of b and c. If raising the value of b by one unit will cause the option to fall by 0.15, then the option has a skewness sensitivity of −0.15. If raising the value of c by one unit will cause the option to rise by 0.08, the option has a kurtosis sensitivity of 0.08. For active traders who carry very large option positions, the skewness and kurtosis sensitivities can represent significant risks and, as with all risks, must be monitored to ensure that that they remain within acceptable bounds.

The units used to express skewness and kurtosis sensitivity will depend on how the skew model has been constructed. Most traders choose a unit that represents a common change in the skewness and kurtosis values. For example, if the value of b commonly ranges from 0.20 to 0.40, a logical unit for b might be 0.01. If the unit value is an unwieldy number, the value can be adjusted by including a multiplier. If the unit value for b is 0.001 but we wish to express the unit value as a whole number, we can use a multiplier of 0.001 to yield a unit value of 1. The model will then be expressed as

$$y = a + 0.001bx + cx^2$$

If we raise the skew value of b by 1, we are really raising it by 0.001. The same approach can also be used to express c in simple units.[5]

In most skew models, the at-the-money exercise price acts as a pivot point so that an option that is exactly at the money has a skewness and kurtosis sensitivity of 0. Options that are in the money or out of the money can have either a positive or a negative skewness sensitivity. If we increase the skewness input, the volatility of higher exercise prices will rise, whiles the volatility of lower exercise prices will fall. Consequently, higher exercise prices will have positive skewness sensitivity values, and lower exercise prices will have negative sensitivity. If we increase the kurtosis input, the volatility of options at both higher and lower exercise prices will rise. Consequently, any option that is not exactly at the money will have a positive kurtosis sensitivity.

Which options are the most sensitive to changes in skewness and kurtosis? There is no definitive answer because it depends on the volatility characteristics of the market as well as the skew model that is used. But in many skew models puts with deltas of –25 and calls with deltas of +25 tend to have the greatest skewness sensitivity. For this reason, a common measure of skewness is the difference between the implied volatility of the –25 delta put and the +25 delta call. There is no similar benchmark for kurtosis, but for many models, puts with deltas of approximately –5 and calls with deltas of +5 tend to have the greatest sensitivity to a change in kurtosis.

Skewed Risk Measures

How we model the volatility skew also will affect the risk measures generated by a model—the delta, gamma, theta, and vega. Look again at Figure 24-4a, where the floating skew is shifted either right or left as the underlying price rises or falls. As the skew is shifted, the volatility at some exercise prices will rise, while the volatility at other exercise prices will fall. This change in volatility can cause an option's value and its risk sensitivities to change either more or less than expected if there were no skew.

For example, consider an out-of-the-money put with a delta of –20. Ignoring the gamma, if the underlying price rises 1.00, we expect the option value to decline by 0.20. But in an investment skew, such as in Figure 24-4a, as the underlying price rises, the volatility of an out-of-the-money put will rise as it moves further out of the money. If the option has a vega of 0.10 and the shift in the skew causes the implied volatility of the option to rise 0.5 percent, the higher volatility

---

[5] When traders use the terms *skewness* and *kurtosis* (or *skew* and *kurt* for short), it is not always clear whether they are referring to the inputs into the model (the values of b and c in our example) or the sensitivity of the option's value to a change in these inputs. Typically, a trader will refer to the sensitivities as the option's skewness or kurtosis. Or the trader will refer to his skewness and kurtosis position: the sensitivity of his entire position to a one-unit change in the skewness or kurtosis inputs.

will cause the option's value to rise by $0.5 \times 0.10 = 0.05$. Consequently, the option will only decline by 0.15, a decline of 0.20 due to a change in the underlying price combined with an increase of 0.05 due to the increase in implied volatility. The option has a *skewed* or *adjusted delta* of −15.

The inclusion of a volatility skew in a pricing model will affect the calculation of all option risk measures and can greatly complicate a trader's ability to manage risk. For many traders, it may be best to keep things simple, perhaps using a skew model to generate theoretical values while using a traditional model to calculate the delta, gamma, theta, and vega. For an active trader who carries large option positions, calculating accurate skewed sensitivities becomes much more important because the total value of the position can change very quickly as market conditions change. Financial engineers at professional option trading firms are often responsible for developing methods to accurately calculate theoretical values and risk sensitivities using a volatility skew model. But even the most sophisticated model is unlikely to generate values that exactly model option prices under all market conditions. A model can help, but it will always have limitations.

By combining the volatility term structure across expiration dates with the volatility skew across exercise prices, we can form a *volatility surface*. While sometimes difficult to visualize, a volatility surface may enable a trader to more easily see the basic volatility characteristics of an option market. The more exercise prices and expiration dates that are available, the more accurate will be the volatility surface. Sample volatility surfaces for the FTSE 100 options and wheat options are shown in Figures 24-12 and 24-13. At the time, the FTSE 100 Index was trading at 5,966, and the front-month wheat futures contract was trading at 647.

Figure 24-12 FTSE 100 volatility surface, March 16, 2012.

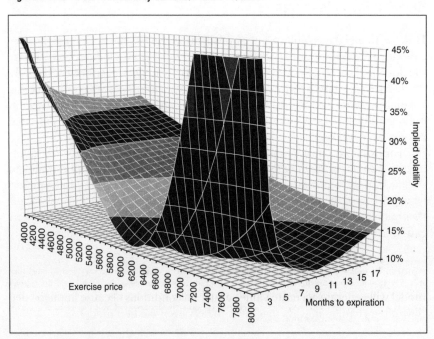

Figure 24-13 Wheat volatility surface, January 27, 2012.

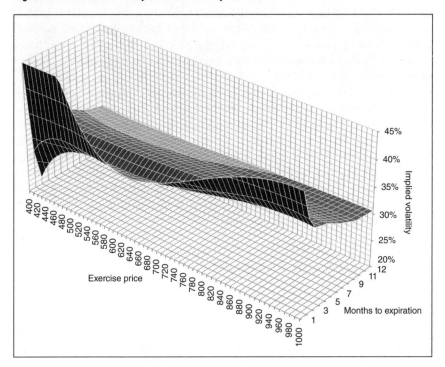

Shifting the Volatility

Traders have long noted that in many option markets, implied volatility tends to change as the price of the underlying contract changes. Some markets exhibit a direct relationship between movement in the underlying price and changes in implied volatility: when the underlying price rises, implied volatility tends to rise; when the underlying price falls, implied volatility tends to fall. This is typical of markets with a demand skew, such as agricultural and energy products. Other markets may exhibit an inverse relationship: when the underlying price rises, implied volatility tends to fall; when the underlying price falls, implied volatility tends to rise. This is typical of markets with an investment skew, such as stock and stock index markets.

For purposes of both option evaluation and risk management, many traders will attempt to incorporate this characteristic into an option pricing model. One possible theoretical solution is the CEV model referred to in Chapter 23. But this model can be mathematically complex and requires additional inputs, all of which make it difficult to use. Alternatively, many traders simply use a "home grown" model that shifts the volatility up or down in a way that is consistent with the observed volatility characteristics of a market. However, no model will generate accurate values under all conditions because implied volatility often changes in ways that seem to defy even the best model.

A shift in volatility can also affect the risks associated with a position. Consider a trader who buys an at-the-money straddle. Ignoring interest considerations and slight adjustments for a lognormal distribution, the trader's position is approximately delta neutral: the call has a delta of 50, and the put has a delta of −50. But delta neutral means that the trader has no particular preference for market movement in one direction or the other. Is this really true? If this position is taken in a stock index market, the trader actually has a preference for downward movement because he prefers higher volatility, something that is more likely to occur in a falling market. Even though the position may be delta neutral in a theoretical world, in the real world, it is delta negative. On the other hand, if this position is taken in a commodity market, where the market is likely to become more volatile when prices rise, the trader really has a positive delta position. Of course, it may be difficult to determine the real-world delta of either position. That will depend on how fast volatility rises or falls as the underlying price changes. But in neither case is the position truly delta neutral.

Skewness and Kurtosis Strategies

Just as a trader may have an opinion about the direction of movement in a market (delta strategies) or about implied and realized volatility (vega and gamma strategies), a trader may also have an opinion about the shape of the volatility skew. We can see in Figure 24-14 that, depending on the type of skew and whether a trader expects the skew to become steeper or flatter, the trader will want to buy lower

Figure 24-14 (*a*) Declining skewness. (*b*) Increasing skewness.

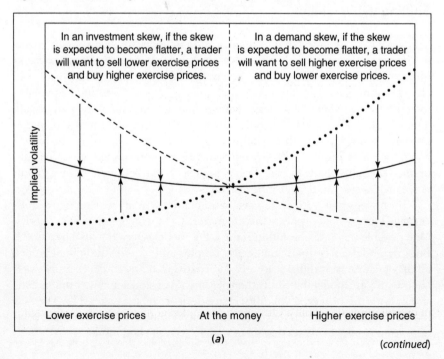

In an investment skew, if the skew is expected to become flatter, a trader will want to sell lower exercise prices and buy higher exercise prices.

In a demand skew, if the skew is expected to become flatter, a trader will want to sell higher exercise prices and buy lower exercise prices.

Implied volatility

Lower exercise prices   At the money   Higher exercise prices

(*a*)

(continued)

Figure 24-14 (*continued*)

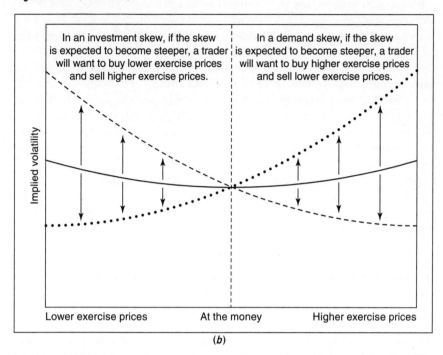

In an investment skew, if the skew is expected to become steeper, a trader will want to buy lower exercise prices and sell higher exercise prices.

In a demand skew, if the skew is expected to become steeper, a trader will want to buy higher exercise prices and sell lower exercise prices.

Implied volatility

Lower exercise prices   At the money   Higher exercise prices

(*b*)

exercise prices and sell higher exercise prices, or vice versa. This is most commonly done using out-of-the-money options, very often 25 delta calls and –25 delta puts because these options tend to be most sensitive to changes in the slope of the skew.

If a skew trade is not hedged, the position will clearly have a positive delta (long calls and short puts) or negative delta (long puts and short calls). A trader who wants to focus solely on "buying skew" or "selling skew" must offset the delta position, most commonly with an opposing delta position in the underlying contract. When this is done, the entire strategy is usually referred to as a *risk reversal*. With the underlying contract trading at a price close to 100, the following are typical risk reversals (delta values are in parentheses):

> +10 June 95 puts (–25)
> –10 June 105 calls (+25)
> +5 underlying contracts

or

> –30 December 90 puts (–15)
> +30 December 110 calls (+15)
> –9 underlying contracts

In these examples, the calls and puts have the same delta, but this is not a requirement. More commonly, calls and puts are chosen with the same vega values.[6] This ensures that the position is vega neutral at inception and therefore primarily sensitive to changes in the slope of the skew rather than changes in overall implied volatility. Of course, as market conditions change, the delta,

---

[6] A risk reversal that is vega neutral will tend to be gamma neutral, although this will not always be the case. A trader may have to decide whether it is more important for the risk reversal to be vega neutral or gamma neutral.

gamma, and vega of the position will almost certainly change. When this occurs, a trader will have to decide whether to maintain the position and, if so, how best to manage the delta, gamma, and vega risk. The risk characteristics of a typical risk reversal were discussed in Chapter 21.

Just as a trader may have an opinion about skewness, the slope of a volatility skew, a trader may also have an opinion about kurtosis, the curvature of a volatility skew. If the kurtosis is expected to increase, the prices of options at both lower and higher exercise prices will increase. A trader will therefore want to buy strangles by purchasing both out-of-the-money calls and out-of-the-money puts. If the kurtosis is expected to decrease, option prices at both lower and higher exercise prices will decline. A trader will then want to sell strangles by selling both out-of-the-money calls and out-of-the-money puts. This is shown in Figure 24-15.

If a trader "buys" kurtosis by purchasing strangles or "sells" kurtosis by selling strangles, the position will also be sensitive to overall changes in volatility because the position will have a very pronounced positive or negative vega. Even if the trader is correct in his assessment of kurtosis, the position can be negatively affected by overall changes in implied volatility. If the trader wishes to focus solely on kurtosis, he will need to neutralize his vega position without changing the kurtosis of the position. Because at-the-money options are neutral with respect to kurtosis, a trader can achieve this by taking an offsetting vega position in at-the-money straddles. Assuming that the selected strangles and straddles are delta neutral, the entire position will also be delta neutral. With the underlying contract trading at a price close to 100, the following are typical kurtosis positions (vega values are in parentheses):

Figure 24-15 Rising and falling kurtosis.

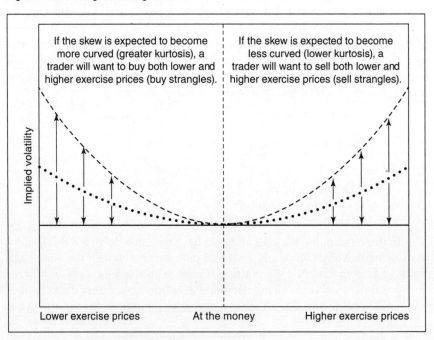

Long strangles:	+35 June 90 puts (0.11)
	+35 June 110 calls (0.12)
Short straddles:	−20 June 100 calls (0.20)
	−20 June 100 puts (0.20)

or

Short strangles:	−26 December 80 puts (0.08)
	−26 December 120 calls (0.09)
Long straddles:	+10 December 100 calls (0.22)
	+10 December 100 puts (0.22)

If a kurtosis position is made up of a strangle that has exactly half the vega of the straddle, a vega-neutral position will consist of two strangles for each straddle. When done in this 2 × 1 ratio, the position is sometimes referred to as a *dragonfly*.

An opinion about skew and kurtosis can also be incorporated into other strategies. Consider the skews in Figure 24-16 on the same underlying product but for different expiration months. If a trader has no opinion on whether either skew is mispriced individually but believes that the skews are mispriced with respect to each other, a logical strategy might be to take a skew position in one expiration month and an opposing skew position in the other month. For example, a trader might buy out-of-the-money puts in June and sell out-of-the-money puts in March. At the same time, the trader might sell out-of-the-money calls in June and buy out-of-the-money calls in March. The trader has, in effect, bought put calendar spreads and sold call calendar spreads. If the skew is the only consideration (the trader has no opinion on whether implied

Figure 24-16 Buying and selling skew in different expiration months.

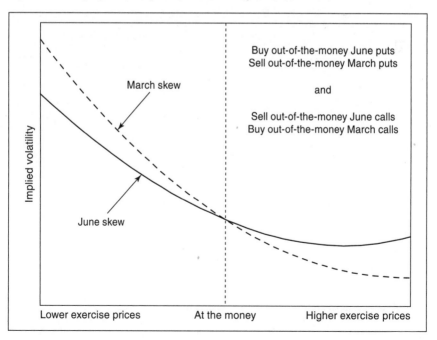

volatility is high or low), the trader will try to take a position that is vega neutral by choosing calendar spreads that have approximately the same vega. Any residual deltas can be hedged away with the underlying contract.

If, in addition to an opinion about the skew, a trader also has an opinion about the relative implied volatility in different expiration months, he can take this into consideration when choosing a strategy. If a trader believes that implied volatility in June is low compared with implied volatility in March, the trader will consider buying calendar spreads—buy June options and sell March options. If, at the same time, the trader also believes that the skews are mispriced with respect to each other, as in Figure 24-16, he will choose calendar spreads that take both relationships into consideration. Now he will want to buy put calendar spreads—buy out-of-the-money June puts and sell out-of-the-money March puts. By doing so, the trader takes advantage of both implied volatility and skew. Note that the trader will avoid call calendar spreads because the volatility and skew will tend to offset each other. The June calls are too expensive with respect to skew, but the March calls are too expensive with respect to implied volatility. If the trader believes that June implied volatility is high compared with March, now he will choose to sell call calendar spreads because the June calls are too expensive with respect to both implied volatility and skew.

The same approach can be used when kurtosis in two different expiration months seems to be mispriced, as shown in Figure 24-17. Now a trader might consider buying June strangles and selling March strangles. If this is a simple kurtosis strategy within a single expiration month, it will be necessary to offset the vega by purchasing at-the-money straddles. But a trader can avoid this complication by choosing strangles in the two different expiration months that have approximately the same vega values. This ensures that the entire strategy is sensitive only

Figure 24-17 Buying and selling kurtosis in different expiration months.

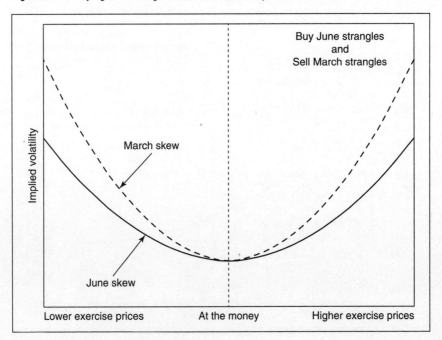

to changes in kurtosis. If, at the same time, June implied volatility seems low compared with March, the strategy has an added advantage. June options are cheap compared with March options with respect to both volatility and kurtosis.

Implied Distributions

In a perfect Black-Scholes world, the prices of the underlying contract are assumed to be lognormally distributed at expiration, and every option with the same expiration date ought to have the same implied volatility. The fact that options across different exercise prices have different implied volatilities must mean that the marketplace believes that the distribution of underlying prices at expiration is not lognormal. Exactly what probability distribution is the marketplace implying to the underlying contract at expiration? We can estimate this implied distribution by looking at the prices of butterflies in the marketplace.

At expiration, a butterfly has a minimum value of 0 if the underlying price is at or outside the wings and a maximum value of the amount between exercise prices if the underlying price is exactly at the body, or midpoint, of the butterfly. At expiration, the 95/100/105 butterfly (i.e., buy a 95 call, sell two 100 calls, buy a 105 call) will have a minimum value of 0 if the underlying price is at or below 95 or at or above 105, a maximum value of 5.00 if the underlying price is exactly 100, or some amount between 0 and 5.00 if the underlying price is between 95 and 100 or between 100 and 105.

Suppose that exercise prices at five-point intervals are available extending from 0 to infinity:

..., 70, 75, 80, 85, 90, 95, 100, 105, 110, 115, 120, 125, 130,...

What will be the value of the position at expiration if we buy every five-point butterfly?

···	+1 70 call	+1 75 call	···	+1 115 call	+1 120 call	···	
···	−2 75 calls	−2 80 calls	···	−2 120 calls	−2 125 calls	···	
···	+1 80 call	+1 85 call	···	+1 125 call	+1 130 call	···	

Regardless of the underlying price at expiration, the entire position will always have a value of exactly 5.00. As a result, if we add up the prices of all the butterflies, the total value must be 5.00.[7]

Suppose that we make the assumption that the only prices that are possible at expiration are prices that are equal to an exercise price

..., 70, 75, 80, 85, 90, 95, 100, 105, 110, 115, 120, 125, 130,...

The probability of each underlying price occurring must be equal to the price of that butterfly, where the inside exercise price is equal to the underlying price divided by 5.00. If the price of the 75/80/85 butterfly is 0.15, the probability of an underlying price of 80 at expiration must be

$$0.15/5.00 = 0.03 \ (3\%)$$

---

[7] If we include interest rates, and the options are subject to stock-type settlement, the total will be the present value of 5.00.

Figure 24-18 Butterfly values and probabilities.

Exercise price:	75	80	85	90	95	100	105	110	115	120	125	130	135
Call value:	25.00	20.04	15.20	10.71	6.88	3.98	2.06	0.95	0.39	0.15	0.05	0.01	0
Butterfly value:	0.04	0.12	0.35	0.66	0.93	0.98	0.81	0.55	0.32	0.14	0.06	0.03	0.01
Price probability:	0.008	0.024	0.070	0.132	0.186	0.196	0.162	0.110	0.064	0.028	0.012	0.006	0.002

If the price of the 90/95/100 butterfly is 0.50, the probability of an underlying price of 95 at expiration must be

$$0.50/5.00 = 0.10 \ (10\%)$$

Figure 24-18 shows a series of call values together with the resulting butterfly values for our series of exercise prices.[8] The probability associated with each underlying price is determined by dividing the butterfly value by the total value of all butterflies, which we know must be 5.00. (The reader may wish to confirm that all the butterfly values do indeed sum to 5.00 and that the probabilities sum to 1.00, or 100 percent.) The underlying prices and their associated probabilities are shown in Figure 24-19. Note that these values form a probability distribution that is skewed to the right. This should come as no surprise because the values were derived from the Black-Scholes model, which assumes a lognormal distribution of underlying prices.

Figure 24-19 A discrete probability distribution implied from the prices of butterflies.

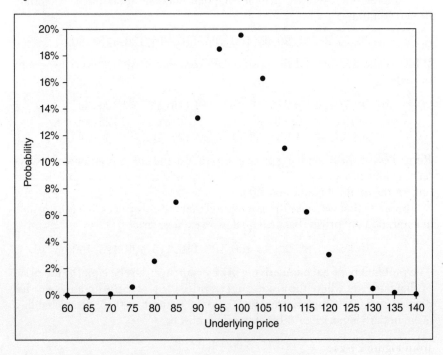

---

[8]The values in Figure 24-18 correspond, approximately, to Black-Scholes values using an underlying price of 100, three months to expiration, a volatility of 20 percent, and an interest rate of 0.

Figure 24-20 A continuous lognormal probability distribution implied from the prices of butterflies.

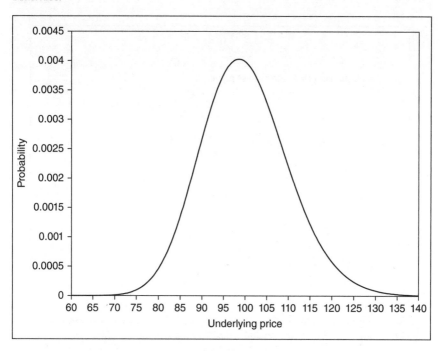

Of course, the distribution in Figure 24-19 is only an approximation because it includes a limited number of underlying prices. A more exact distribution requires us to consider more and more exercise prices. We can do this by reducing the width of the butterflies. Instead of using increments of 5.00, we might use increments of 2.00, 1.00, or 0.50. Indeed, if we use increments that are infinitesimally small, the butterfly values will enable us to construct a continuous probability distribution. Figure 24-20 shows the probability distribution with the increment between exercise prices reduced to 0.10. With such a small increment, the distribution appears almost continuous.

How does the distribution implied by option prices compare with a traditional lognormal distribution? The implied distribution will change as option prices change, so there cannot be one implied distribution under all market conditions. But we might get some sense of the distribution that the marketplace is implying by using the prices of butterflies generated by a volatility skew to derive a distribution and comparing it with a Black-Scholes distribution with a constant volatility. In Figure 24-21, we have taken the volatility skew for the FTSE 100 options shown in Figure 24-3 and created two distributions, one from the prices generated from the skew and one from prices generated from a constant volatility across every exercise price. What can we infer from Figure 24-21?

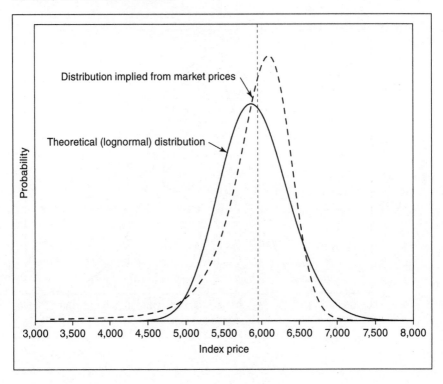

Figure 24-21 Three-month price distribution implied from FTSE 100 option prices, March 16, 2012 (FTSE 100 Index = 5,965.58).

Compared with a traditional lognormal distribution, the marketplace seems to be implying the following:

1. A greater probability of a small to intermediate upward move

2. A greater probability of a large downward move

3. A smaller probability of a small to intermediate downward move

4. A smaller probability of a large upward move

This implied distribution is typical of most stock index markets, and many of these points seem to be consistent with the S&P 500 histogram in Figure 23-8a. There do seem to be more small moves in the real world than is predicted by a theoretical distribution. There also seem to be more large downward moves and fewer intermediate downward moves. But the histogram also shows more big upward moves, which is not consistent with the implied distribution.

Figure 24-22 shows the three-month distribution implied from the prices of options on wheat futures on January 27, 2012. This implied distribution seems to conform more closely to a theoretical lognormal distribution than

Figure 24-22 Three-month price distribution implied from wheat option prices, January 27, 2012 (with three-month wheat futures at 661.75).

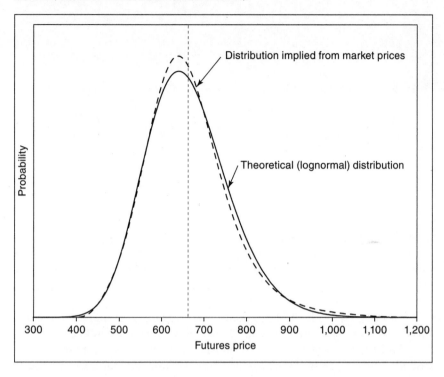

does the distribution in the FTSE 100 example. However, the marketplace is still implying more small moves, slightly fewer intermediate upward moves, and slightly more large upward moves than a true lognormal distribution.

Of course, Figures 24-21 and 24-22 are snapshots of markets at one moment in time, and it would be unwise to draw any sweeping conclusions from these examples. Nonetheless, it can often be useful for a trader to compare his opinions about a probability distribution with that implied by prices in the marketplace. If there is a clear disagreement, it may point the way to a potentially profitable strategy.

25

Volatility Contracts

Volatility contracts have been one of the major success stories in the derivatives market. They enable market participants to pursue strategies that were previously either impossible or, even under the best conditions, difficult to execute. But volatility contracts have unusual characteristics, and any trader hoping to make the best use of these contracts must be fully familiar with these characteristics.

Prior to the introduction of options and option pricing models, there was no effective way for a trader to capture volatility value or to profit from a perceived mispricing of volatility in the marketplace. Once listed options were introduced, however, it became possible to use the implied volatility in an option market to determine how the marketplace was pricing volatility. In Chapter 8, we showed that a trader could then capture a volatility mispricing by either buying or selling options and dynamically hedging the position over the life of the option.

This all sounds very good in theory, but in the real world, things are not so simple. Even if we are somehow able to look into the future and determine the true volatility of the underlying contract over the life of the option, the actual results of any single dynamic hedging strategy will almost certainly differ from the results predicted by the theoretical pricing model. This is often due to the weaknesses in traditional theoretical pricing models, many of which we touched on in Chapter 23:

> The order in which price changes occur can affect the results of a dynamic hedging strategy.
> If gaps occur in the underlying price, it may not be possible to buy or sell the underlying contract in a way that is consistent with the dynamic hedging process.
> The returns for an underlying contract may not be normally distributed.

In addition to weakness in the model, the costs of dynamically hedging a position may be significant. Each time the position is rehedged, a trader may have to give up the bid-ask spread, and there will also be brokerage and exchange fees. These costs will certainly reduce, and may even erase, any expected profit.

Even if one is interested in trading volatility, the drawbacks of using a dynamic hedging approach will often deter a trader from using options to trade volatility. To overcome this obstacle, traders have sought a less complicated method of implementing volatility strategies. This has led to the development of volatility contracts, contracts that enable a trader to take a position on volatility without going through a complex and costly dynamic hedging process. At expiration, the value of these contracts depends solely on a relatively straightforward volatility calculation.

There are two primary types of volatility—realized volatility and implied volatility. Consequently, there are two types of volatility contracts. *Realized volatility contracts* settle into the realized volatility of an underlying contract over a specified period of time. *Implied volatility contracts* settle into the implied volatility of options on an underlying contract on a specified date.

Realized Volatility Contracts

At expiration, the value of a realized volatility contract is equal to the annualized standard deviation of logarithmic price returns over the life of the contract. The returns are typically calculated from daily settlement prices on the primary exchange on which the contract is traded. This means that the annualization factor will depend on the number of trading days in a year on that particular exchange. If there are 252 trading days, the settlement volatility will be

$$\sqrt{252 \sum_{i-1}^{n} \frac{\ln(x_i)^2}{n}}$$

where each data point x_i is equal to the daily price returns p_i/p_{i-1} (today's settlement price divided by yesterday's settlement price), and n is the number of trading days in the calculation period.

There are two points of particular note. First, the expiration value represents the true volatility over the calculation period rather than a volatility estimate. We therefore use the population standard deviation rather than the sample standard deviation, dividing by n rather than $n-1$. Second, the volatility calculation is independent of any trend in prices. We therefore assume a 0 mean, using $\ln(x_i)$ for each data point rather than $\ln(x_i) - \mu$. These calculation conventions are common to most realized volatility contracts.

The profit or loss at expiration for a realized volatility contract will depend on the price at which the initial trade was made, the notional amount of the trade, and the value of the contract at expiration. If the buyer of a realized volatility contract enters into the trade at a price of 20 percent with an agreed-on notional amount equal to $1,000 per volatility point and the realized volatility over the calculation period turns out to be 23.75 percent, the buyer will show a profit of

$$\$1,000 \times (23.75 - 20.00) = \$3,750$$

If the realized volatility turns out to be 18.60 percent, the buyer will show a loss of

$$\$1,000 \times (18.60 - 20.00) = -\$1,400$$

Realized volatility contracts are most often traded in the off-exchange market, with banks and proprietary trading firms acting as market makers.[1] Quotes for realized volatility contracts typically include a price, quoted in volatility points, and a volatility exposure, quoted as *notional vega*. A market maker who offers a quote for realized volatility of 19.50 –20.50 for $10,000 notional vega is willing to buy the contract at a volatility of 19.50 percent and sell the contract at a volatility of 20.50 percent, with every volatility point having a value of $10,000. In the same way, a client may put in an order to buy $25,000 notional vega at 30. The client is prepared to pay a volatility of 30 percent, with every volatility point having a value of $25,000.

In these examples, the price of the volatility contract was quoted in volatility points and settled in volatility points. In fact, most realized volatility contracts are settled in *variance points*, where variance is equal to the square of volatility

$$\text{variance} = \text{volatility}^2 \quad \text{and,} \quad \text{conversely,} \quad \text{volatility} = \sqrt{\text{variance}}$$

For this reason, realized volatility contracts are often referred to as *variance contracts* or, more commonly, *variance swaps*.

Why settle a volatility contract in variance points rather than volatility points? As we shall see later, for purposes of hedging a volatility contract, it is much easier to replicate a variance position than a volatility position. Additionally, the reader may recall from the discussion of forward volatility in Chapter 20 that variance has the very desirable characteristic that it is proportional to time. If the variance over some time period t_1 is equal to σ_1^2 and the variance over a second successive time period t_2 is equal to σ_2^2, then the variance over the combined time periods is

$$\frac{\left(t_1 \times \sigma_1^2\right) + \left(t_2 \times \sigma_2^2\right)}{t_1 + t_2}$$

This means that variance contracts can be easily combined to cover consecutive time periods, even if the time periods are not of equal length.

For example, if the annualized volatility over a two-month time period is 25 (expressing the volatility in points) and the annualized volatility over the following one-month time period is 22, the annualized variance over the entire three-month period is

$$\frac{\left(2/12 \times 25^2\right) + \left(1/12 \times 22^2\right)}{3/12} = \frac{\left(2/12 \times 625\right) + \left(1/12 \times 484\right)}{3/12} = 578$$

If a volatility contract is quoted in volatility points with a notional vega amount, but settlement is in variance points, how much is each variance point worth? Without going into the mathematics, by convention, each variance point is equal to the notional amount divided by twice the volatility price

$$\text{Value per variance point} = \frac{\text{vega notional}}{2 \times \text{volatility price}}$$

---

[1] When a contract is traded between private parties without an exchange as an intermediary, the possibility of one party defaulting on its obligations adds an additional risk dimension to the trade. Counterparty risk can be an important consideration in the off-exchange market.

If the buyer of a volatility contract pays 20 for \$10,000 vega notional, but the contract is settled in variance points, each variance point has a value of

$$\$10,000/2 \times 20 = \$250$$

If the realized volatility over the life of the contract turns out to be 19 percent, the buyer will show a loss of

$$\$250 \times (19^2 - 20^2) = \$250 \times (361 - 400) = \$9,750$$

If the realized volatility over the life of the contract turns out to be 23 percent, the buyer will show a profit of

$$\$250 \times (23^2 - 20^2) = \$250 \times (529 - 400) = \$32,250$$

Because variance is the square of volatility, if a contract is settled in variance points, the value at settlement can quickly escalate with higher volatilities. If a single dramatic event occurs that causes the underlying contract to make an unexpectedly large move, resulting in a volatility over the calculation period of 50, the profit to the buyer in our example will be

$$\$250 \times (50^2 - 20^2) = \$250 \times (2,500 - 400) = \$525,000$$

Of course, the seller will have an equal loss. Indeed, the seller of a variance swap may not be willing to take on the risk of a one-time dramatic event that causes volatility to skyrocket. Many variance swaps therefore have a cap that limits the expiration value of the contract. If the contract trades at a price of 20 and has a volatility cap of 40 (equal to a variance of 1,600), no matter how high volatility goes, the profit to the buyer and risk to the seller can never be greater than

$$\$250 \times (40^2 - 20^2) = \$250 \times (1,600 - 400) = \$300,000$$

Caps are most common for variance swaps on individual stocks, where a one-time event can result in a dramatic increase in volatility. Caps are less common for variance swaps on broad-based indexes, where a one-time event affecting one index component is unlikely to have a correspondingly large effect on the volatility of the entire index. Of course, variance swaps are primarily an off-exchange product. The buyer and seller of the swap are free to negotiate any contract specifications, including a cap, that are mutually agreeable to both parties.

Implied Volatility Contracts

Realized volatility is an important consideration in option pricing, but it is something that cannot be directly observed, at least at any given moment in time. When option traders talk about volatility, they are most often referring to implied volatility, which is something that can be observed. The implied volatility is a consensus, derived from the prices of options in the marketplace, of what the volatility of the underlying contract will be over some period in the future. Because option prices can be observed at any moment in time, implied volatility at any moment can likewise be observed.

In the early days of exchange-traded options, the concept of implied volatility was not well understood, at least not among most nonprofessional traders. However, as option trading increased in popularity, all market participants, both professional and nonprofessional, began to pay closer attention to the implied volatility in option markets. As a means of promoting a better understanding of options and as an aid to both traders and end users, exchanges began disseminating implied volatility data. With growing public interest in options, these numbers began to appear with increasing frequency in financial news reports.

There are, of course, many different implied volatilities. Not only are there many different underlying markets, but for each underlying, there are many different exercise prices and expiration months. What exchanges wanted was one number that reflected the general implied volatility environment. This led the Chicago Board Options Exchange (CBOE) to focus on the implied volatility of a broad-based index, specifically its most actively traded product, the Options Exchange Index, with ticker symbol OEX. In 1993, the CBOE began disseminating values for the volatility index (VIX), a theoretical 30-day implied volatility calculated from the prices of options on the OEX. The VIX eventually developed into a widely recognized financial indicator not only in the option community but also in the financial world in general. Other exchanges have followed suit by creating volatility indexes of their own, but the VIX remains the best known of all implied volatility indexes.

As the VIX became more widely recognized, the CBOE began to consider the possibility of creating a tradable contract based on the VIX. This necessitated two major changes in the index. The first change had to do with the underlying contract. Initially, VIX values disseminated by the CBOE were derived from the prices of OEX options. However, the CBOE subsequently introduced options on the Standard and Poor's (S&P) 500 Index, with ticker symbol SPX, and these eventually replaced the OEX as the exchange's most actively traded index product. That, combined with the fact that the S&P 500 was a much more widely followed index than the OEX, led the exchange in 2003 to begin calculating the VIX from the prices of S&P 500 options rather than OEX options.

The second change had to do with the calculation method. The original VIX was calculated from calls and puts at the two exercise prices that bracketed the index price—essentially the at-the-money options. For a given expiration month, the call and put implied volatilities at each exercise price were averaged, and these were then weighted by the difference between the exercise price and the index price to yield an implied volatility for that expiration month. In order to determine a theoretical 30-day implied volatility, the two near-term expiration months were weighted to derive a final value.[2] An example may help to clarify the methodology.

Assume that the index price is 863.40 and that the two exercise prices that bracket this number are 860 and 870. Assume also that the nearest option contract, Month 1, has 14 days remaining to expiration and that the second option

---

[2] For a description of the original VIX methodology, see Robert Whaley, "Derivatives on Market Volatility: Hedging Tools Long Overdue," *Journal of Derivatives*, Fall 1993, pp. 71–84.

contract, Month 2, has 42 days remaining. Implied volatilities for the two exercise prices in each month are as follows:

	Month 1		Month 2	
	860	870	860	870
Call	22.16	21.48	20.13	19.93
Put	22.21	21.44	20.17	19.94

The average implied volatilities for each exercise price and month are

Month 1:   860 $(22.16 + 22.21)/2 = 22.185$
                 870   $(21.48 + 21.44)/2 = 21.46$
Month 2:   860 $(20.13 + 20.17)/2 = 20.15$
                 870   $(19.93 + 19.94)/2 = 19.935$

The implied volatility in each month is the interpolated implied volatility between the two exercise prices—the implied volatilities weighted by their distance from the index price. The closer the exercise price is to the index price, the greater is the weighting:

Month 1: $22.185 \times (870 - 863.40)/10 + 21.46 \times (863.40 - 860)/10$
                 $= 22.185 \times 0.66 + 21.46 \times 0.34 = 14.6421 + 7.2964$
                 $= 21.9835$
Month 2: $20.15 \times (870 - 863.40)/10 + 19.935 \times (863.40 - 860)/10$
                 $= 20.15 \times 0.66 + 19.935 \times 0.34 = 13.299 + 6.7779$
                 $= 20.0769$

The VIX value is the interpolated implied volatility between the two expiration months—the implied volatilities weighted by how close their expirations are to 30 days. The closer to 30, the greater the weighting. With expirations of 14 and 42 days, the final VIX value is

$$20.0769 \times (30 - 14)/28 + 22.2785 \times (42 - 30)/28$$
$$= 20.0769 \times 0.5714 + 22.2785 \times 0.4286$$
$$= 11.4725 + 9.5479 = 21.0204$$

The final VIX value disseminated by the exchange is the calculated VIX value rounded to two decimal points, in this case 21.02.

When the exchange began planning for trading in VIX-related products, there were two major objections to the original calculation methodology. First, any exchange-traded product has to have a very well-defined value on which everyone can agree. If there are significant disagreements as to the value of a contract, especially at expiration, some traders will feel that they are being treated unfairly. This will certainly inhibit trading in the product and might, in some situations, lead to legal action against the exchange. The original VIX calculation required a theoretical pricing model to determine implied volatilities. This in itself can result in disagreements. Which model should be used? The Black-Scholes model? The binomial model? Some other more exotic model? (Recall from Chapter 22 that the OEX is an American option, carrying with it the right of early exercise.) Even if there is general agreement on an appropriate model, there may be disagreements as to the inputs into the model. What interest rate ought to be used? What dividend assumptions should be made? The exchange concluded that if it wanted to introduce trading in VIX-related products, it would be necessary to improve on the existing calculation methodology.

The second objection had to do with the fact that only at-the-money options were used to calculate VIX values. As traders became more knowledgeable about options, the volatility skew, or smile, became increasingly important in describing the volatility environment and in determining appropriate strategies. Traders wanted an implied volatility index that would encompass not only the implied volatility of at-the-money options but also the implied volatility across a broad range of exercise prices.

The VIX calculation methodology that was eventually chosen to replace the old methodology was suggested in a research paper from Goldman Sachs published in 1999.[3] The paper essentially asked this question: is it possible to create an option position that will capture the true volatility of the underlying contract under all possible volatility scenarios?

In theory, if we want to take a volatility position, we can either buy options (a long volatility position) or sell options (a short volatility position) and then dynamically hedge the position to expiration. For example, we might take a long volatility position by purchasing one or more at-the-money options and selling a delta-neutral amount of the underlying contract.[4] By periodically rehedging the position to remain delta neutral, we will capture the volatility value of the underlying contract.

This all sounds very nice in theory, but it almost never works out exactly as expected. Perhaps the greatest drawback to the strategy is the fact that exposure to the volatility of the underlying market, as measured by the vega, will change over the life of the strategy. An option's vega value is greatest when the option is at the money, but even if we begin by purchasing at-the-money options, the options will almost certainly not remain at the money. As the underlying price rises or falls, the options will either go into the money or out of the money, and the vega of the position will decline. This was discussed in Chapter 9 and is shown again in Figure 25-1.

If we want to create a long volatility position, we want a constant exposure to volatility regardless of changes in the price of the underlying contract. We might try to accomplish this by purchasing options across a broad range of exercise prices. In this scenario, shown in Figure 25-2, one exercise price will always be at the money. Unfortunately, this will still not result in a constant vega exposure because at-the-money options with higher exercise prices have greater vega values than at-the-money options with lower exercise prices. If we add up all the vega values in Figure 25-2 at each underlying price, the total vega will be lower at lower underlying prices and higher at higher underlying prices.

---

[3] Kresimir Demeterfi, Emmanuel Derman, Michael Kamal, and Joseph Zou, "More than You Ever Wanted to Know about Volatility Swaps," Goldman Sachs Quantitative Strategies Research Notes, New York, March 1999.

[4] This is essentially equivalent to buying at-the-money straddles.

Figure 25-1 The vega (volatility sensitivity) of an option.

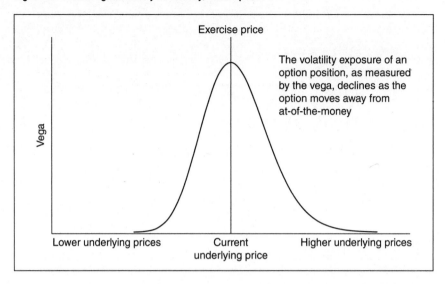

To achieve a constant volatility exposure, we need to buy more options with lower exercise prices and fewer options with higher exercise prices. How many options at each exercise price should we buy? It turns out that the proper proportion of each exercise price needed to create a position with constant volatility exposure is inversely proportional to the square of the exercise price

$$1/X^2$$

The result of doing this is shown in Figure 25-3.

Figure 25-2 Volatility exposure if we purchase one option at each exercise price.

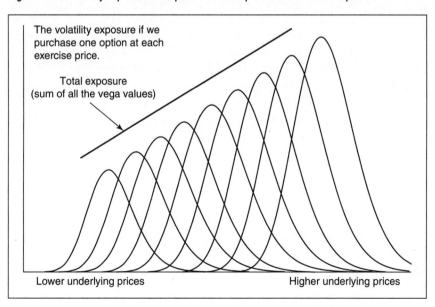

Figure 25-3 Purchasing $1/X^2$ options at each exercise price.

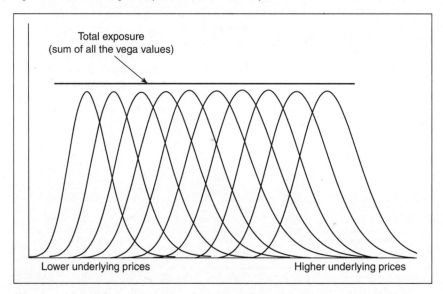

Of course, to exactly replicate a volatility position, we would have to pur-chase options, in the correct proportion, at every possible exercise price—essentially an infinite number of options. Exchanges, however, only list a finite number of exercise prices. Still, it might be possible to use the exercise prices that are listed to create a position that closely approximates a theoretically con-stant volatility position. This is the basis for the VIX calculation methodology used by the CBOE.

Essentially, the value of the VIX is the cost of purchasing a strip consist-ing of options at every available exercise price. Because the VIX represents a 30-day implied volatility, the value of the VIX is derived from strips of options in the two monthly expirations that bracket 30 days. The values of the strips are then weighted by how close each expiration is to 30 days. Without going into the complete derivation of the VIX,[5] there are some important aspects that are worth pointing out:

1. The value of the VIX is derived from the volatility value (time value) of the options in the underlying index, not the intrinsic value. There-fore, only the prices of out-of-the-money options (compared with the forward price) are used.

2. The (implied) forward price for the index is determined using put-call parity for the closest-to-the-money exercise price.

3. The option value used at each exercise price is the average of the quoted bid price and ask price.

---

[5] For a detailed description of the VIX calculation methodology, see "The CBOE Volatility Index," available at: https://www.cboe.com/micro/vix/vixwhite.pdf.

4. When two exercise prices with a nonzero bid are encountered, no lower exercise prices for puts or higher exercise prices for calls are included in the calculation

5. Because only a finite number of exercise prices are available, the contribution of each option to the final VIX calculation is adjusted based on the distance between consecutive exercise prices. The greater the distance between exercise prices, the greater is the weighting in the index for a specific option.

Note that the VIX calculation depends only on the prices of options—no theoretical pricing model is required. Other than option prices, the only other required input is an interest rate, which is necessary to determine the index forward price under put-call parity as well as the interest cost of purchasing the options. For this, the CBOE uses the risk-free rate—the U.S. Treasury bill rate with maturity closest to the option expiration. Otherwise, calculation of the VIX is relatively straightforward.

Because the VIX represents a theoretical 30-day implied volatility, traded contracts on the VIX typically expire 30 days prior to expiration of the options used to calculate VIX values, usually the third Wednesday of the previous month. VIX January contracts expire 30 days prior to expiration of February SPX options; VIX February contracts expire 30 days prior to expiration of March SPX options; and so on.

With exactly 30 days remaining to expiration of SPX options, the value of the VIX at expiration is determined solely by the prices of SPX options in the expiration month. For purposes of settlement, rather than using the average of the bid and ask, the expiration value of the VIX is calculated from the actual opening trade prices of SPX options on expiration Wednesday. The trade prices are determined through a *special opening rotation* where standing buy and sell orders are automatically matched to determine one opening trade price for each option. If no trade takes place for an option, the price used for that option reverts to the average of the bid and ask. This procedure can sometimes cause unusual jumps in the VIX value at expiration. If all options trade at the ask price on the opening (a *buy print*), the expiration value is likely to be higher than expected. If all options trade at the bid price on the opening (a *sell print*), the expiration value is likely to be lower than expected. Immediately after the VIX expiration value is determined by the special opening rotation, calculation reverts to its normal methodology using the average of the bid-ask spread.

Some VIX Characteristics

While volatility is, in theory, independent of the direction in which the underlying contract is moving, in the real world, traders have long recognized that some markets tend to become more volatile as the underlying price rises, while other markets tend to become more volatile as the underlying price falls. There is a widely held belief that stock index markets exhibit the latter characteristic. It should therefore not come as a surprise that the VIX is generally negatively correlated with the S&P 500 Index. When the index falls, the VIX tends to rise; when the index rises, the VIX tends to fall. This inverse correlation between changes in the S&P 500 and changes in the VIX for the 10-year period from 2003 to 2012 can be seen in Figures 25-4 and 25-5. Figure 25-4 confirms the tendency of S&P 500 prices and VIX prices to move in opposite directions. Figure 25-5 shows the strong inverse correlation value of −0.7444 between percent changes in the values of the two indexes. Figure 25-5 also includes a best-fit line for the two sets of values: the percent change in the VIX is approximately 5.7 times greater than the percent change in the S&P 500, but in the opposite direction.

Given the apparent inverse correlation between the S&P 500 Index and the VIX, one might wonder whether this is actually supported by market data. If the VIX rises, will the S&P 500 Index become more volatile? If the VIX falls, will the index become less volatile? Because the VIX represents a 30-day implied volatility, if the marketplace is correct, whenever the VIX rises, the next 30 days ought to be more volatile than the previous 30 days, and whenever the VIX falls, the next 30 days ought to be less volatile than the previous 30 days. The more the VIX rises or falls, the greater should be the change in realized volatility. The actual results over the sample 10-year period are shown in Figure 25-6.

If there is a correlation between changes in the VIX and changes in realized volatility, it is not apparent from the data. Sometimes the VIX rises and sometimes it falls, but there is no obvious increase or decline in volatility over

Figure 25-4 S&P 500 and VIX prices: 2003–2012.

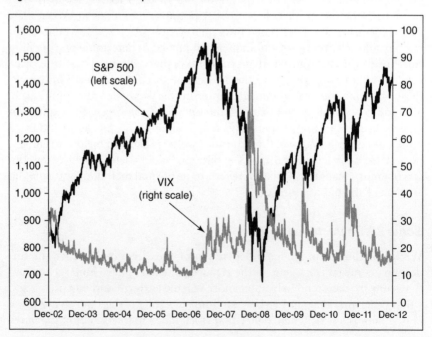

Figure 25-5 Daily S&P 500 Index changes versus daily VIX changes: 2003–2012.

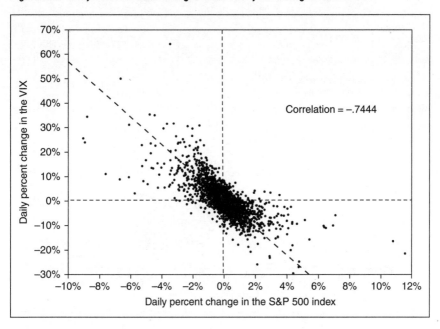

the following 30-day period. (There is a very small but probably insignificant positive correlation of +0.1561.) Therefore, one might conclude that the VIX has no predictive value as an indicator of rising or falling realized volatility. Perhaps what drives the VIX is not the expectation of future realized volatility, but

Figure 25-6 Does a change in the VIX predict a change in realized volatility?

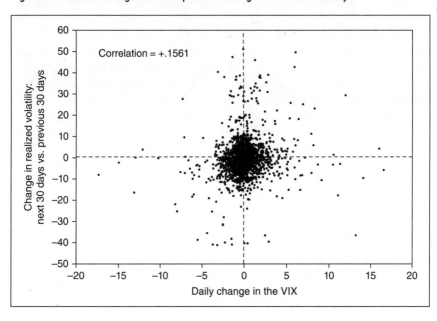

Figure 25-7 Are falling stock markets more volatile than rising markets?

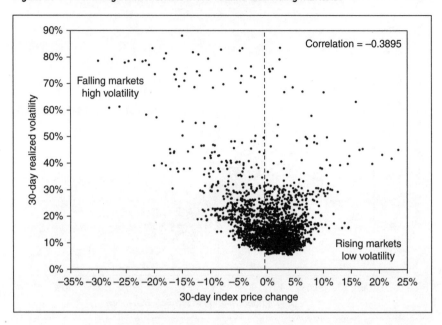

the desire to buy protection in a falling stock market. In a falling market, more hedgers enter the market, and they are often willing to pay higher prices for protective options without regard to considerations of realized volatility. They are driven by the fear of further declines in the market. For this reason, the VIX is sometimes referred to as the *fear index*.

We have also noted the widely held belief that stock index markets tend to become more volatile as the underlying price falls and less volatile as the underlying price rises. We might ask whether this assumption is borne out by the available data. Figure 25-7 shows the change in the price of the S&P 500 Index over a 30-day period compared with the realized volatility over the same period. If the conjecture is true, more data points ought to fall in both the upper left portion (a falling index together with higher volatility) and the lower right portion (a rising index together with lower volatility).

Here there is some reason to believe that falling stock markets do indeed tend to be more volatile than rising stock markets. We can see from the sample period (2003–2012) that there are more high-volatility occurrences to the left of the 0 line and more low-volatility occurrences to the right of the 0 line. There is a moderate inverse correlation of –0.3895.

Trading the VIX

As with all indexes, the VIX is composed of components, with each component having a weight within the index

$$\sum (\text{weight}_i \times \text{component}_i)$$

An index can often be replicated by purchasing all or a large number of the index components in the correct proportion. This is commonly done in the stock index market to create a portfolio that tracks an index or as part of an arbitrage strategy. But unlike a stock index, it is not easy to replicate the VIX. As options go into and out of the money, the index components and their weights within the index are constantly changing. For most traders, the only practical method of buying or selling the VIX is through its derivative products: futures and options or products linked to these contracts. Because the VIX itself cannot be easily bought or sold, VIX derivatives do not always track the index or perform as expected, and new traders are often surprised by the results of VIX-related strategies.

VIX Futures

The CBOE began trading VIX futures contracts (with ticker symbol UX or VX depending on the quote vendor) in 2004. The futures contracts settle into the value of the VIX at the opening of trading on expiration Wednesday, with each volatility point having a value of $1,000.

VIX futures have unusual characteristics when compared with more traditional futures markets, and traders who enter the VIX futures market for the first time are often surprised and frequently disappointed at the results of a VIX futures strategy. There are two primary reasons for this. First, VIX futures exhibit a term structure, which can affect how futures prices change as market conditions change. Second, unlike a position in other futures markets, an underlying position in the VIX cannot be easily replicated. In a stock index futures market, a trader can replicate an underlying index position by buying or selling the component stocks. In a physical commodity futures market, a trader can replicate a long underlying position by purchasing the commodity. But for most traders, replicating an underlying VIX position directly using options from which the index is calculated is usually not a practical choice.

VIX futures tend to reflect the term structure of implied volatility in the S&P 500 discussed in Chapter 20 and shown in Figure 20-13. Most often VIX futures exhibit a contango (upward-sloping) relationship, where long-term maturities trade at higher prices than short-term maturities. A typical VIX contango structure, for futures during August 2012, is shown in Figure 25-8. Although less common, VIX futures can also exhibit a backward (downward-sloping) relationship. Such a structure for futures prices one year earlier, in August 2011, is shown in Figure 25-9. Figure 25-10 shows the VIX moving from contango to backward during the financial crisis in the latter half of 2008.

When VIX futures are in a normal contango relationship, as in Figure 25-8, if there is no change in market conditions, as time passes, the futures contract will move down the term-structure curve, gradually losing value as time passes. How does this affect trading decisions in the VIX futures market?

Logically, a trader will want to buy a futures contract when he believes that the futures price will rise and sell a futures contract when he believes that the price will fall. Most traders assume that when an underlying index rises or falls, futures contracts on that index will also rise or fall, and this is generally

Figure 25-8 VIX futures in contango (upward sloping).

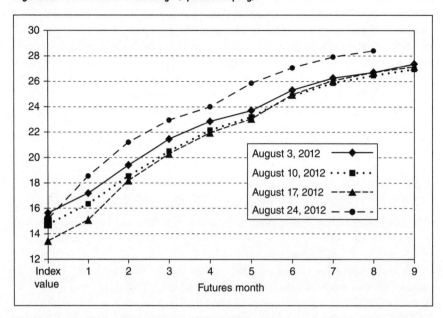

true of the VIX—when the index rises, VIX futures rise; when the index falls, VIX futures fall. Most traders also assume that when an index rises or falls, futures prices will rise or fall by approximately the same amount. But VIX futures prices reflect where the marketplace thinks SPX implied volatility will be at maturity of the futures contract. Implied volatility, as reflected in the

Figure 25-9 VIX futures in backwardation (downward sloping).

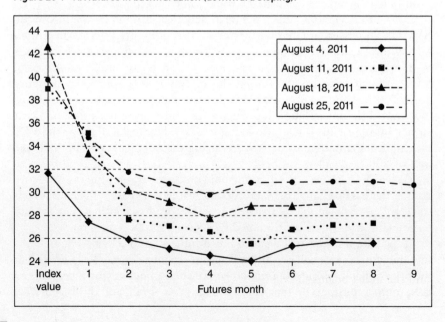

Figure 25-10 VIX futures moved dramatically from contango to backward during the financial crisis in late 2008.

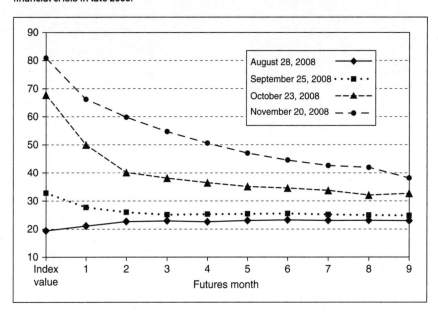

index value, may be high or low today. If, however, the marketplace believes that implied volatility will change between now and expiration of the futures contract, the futures contract will be priced accordingly. A trader will be disappointed indeed if he buys a VIX futures contract, sees an increase in the index, but finds that there is no corresponding increase in the futures price.

Suppose that VIX futures are in a normal contango relationship and that a trader believes that there is likely to be a rise in the value of the VIX in the near future. If he buys a futures contract and the expected increase in the VIX occurs, what will be the result? The trader might assume that the futures price will increase by the same amount as the index, but this will not necessarily be true. If the increase in the VIX occurs well before expiration of the futures contract, the futures price may rise much less than the index price. Such a scenario is shown in Figure 25-11. Over a four-day period in July 2011, the index value rose from approximately 19.4 to 23.7, an increase of 4.4 index points. But over the same period, the front-month August futures contract, with approximately three weeks remaining to expiration, rose only 2.0, from 19.3 to 21.3. Indeed, over the last two days, even though the index rose from 23.0 to 23.8, futures prices hardly changed at all. A trader who owned an August futures contract would have shown a profit because the futures price rose. But seeing the increase in the VIX value without a similar increase in the futures price, the trader would almost certainly have been disappointed at the result.

A similar situation can occur if VIX futures are in a backward structure and the index begins to fall. Figure 25-12 shows the change in VIX prices over a four-day period in December 2008. During this period, the VIX fell

Figure 25-11 VIX futures prices do not change as quickly as the index.

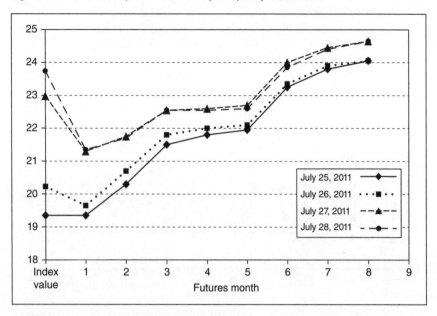

from approximately 52.4 to 44.9, a decline of 7.5 index points. But the front-month January futures price fell only 5.0, from 52.4 to 47.4. A trader who sold January futures would likewise be disappointed with the results.

In a traditional futures market, where it is usually possible to take a long or short position in the underlying index or commodity, futures prices must

Figure 25-12 VIX futures prices do not change as quickly as the index.

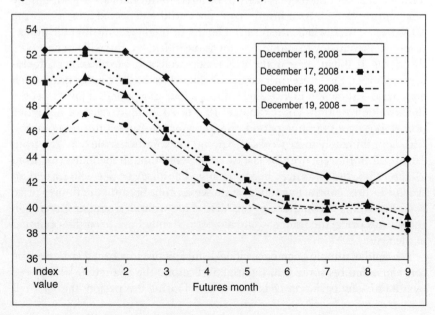

change at approximately the same rate as underlying prices. If this were not true, there would be an arbitrage opportunity available. In a stock index market, if the futures price rises faster than the index price, traders will sell the futures contract and buy the component stocks; if the index rises faster than the futures price, traders will buy the futures contract and sell the component stocks. A trader can hold both positions to maturity, knowing that at maturity the index and futures prices must converge. Unlike a stock index, though, the VIX is not easily tradable. Consequently, VIX futures prices need not change at the same rate as the index. If the index price rises or falls, VIX futures may not rise or fall by the same amount. Indeed, futures prices might not change at all.

At expiration, the price of a VIX futures contract will settle into the index value regardless of any term-structure considerations. Therefore, the closer the futures contract to expiration, the more closely it will respond to any change in the index value. A change in the index value at expiration will be reflected immediately in the futures price.

Given the foregoing discussion, when choosing a simple futures strategy, a trader should always keep the following in mind:

1. When the VIX term structure is contango, as time passes with no change in the index value, VIX futures prices will inevitably decline.

2. The price of a VIX futures contract will almost never change as quickly as the index price.

3. Futures prices and index prices must converge at futures expiration.

4. For most traders, replicating the index is not a realistic choice. Therefore, futures prices must often be evaluated independent of the index price.

Because of its unusual characteristics, trading VIX futures may sound complex. But VIX futures are not necessarily more complex than other futures markets. They are simply different, and a trader must recognize these differences. Buying a VIX futures contract can be profitable if a trader believes that an increase in the index value will occur, especially if the increase occurs close to expiration, or if the trader believes that there will be a large increase in the value of the index, perhaps resulting in an inversion of the term-structure curve from contango to backward. In the same way, selling a VIX futures contract can be profitable if a trader believes that a decline in the index value will occur close to expiration or if the trader believes that there will be a large decline in the value of the index, perhaps resulting in an inversion of the term structure from backward to contango. But in both cases the trader must also temper his expectations, knowing that the change in the futures price will almost always be less than the change in the index price.

Instead of simply buying or selling a single futures month, a trader might consider a futures spread, buying one futures month and selling a different month. VIX futures spreads, like individual futures, are sensitive to the term structure of the futures market. In the unlikely situation where the term structure is a straight line with constant slope, regardless of whether futures prices rise or fall, the spread value will remain unchanged. Even if both futures contracts lose value as time passes (a contango term structure) or gain value as time passes (a backward term structure), their relationship will remain constant. They will lose or gain value at exactly the same rate. If, however, the term structure is curved, a much more common situation, the short-term futures contract will change value more quickly than the long-term futures contract. Under these conditions, if the shape of the term structure remains unchanged, the purchase of a long-term futures contract and the sale of a short-term future contract will be profitable in a contango market, and the purchase of a short-term futures contract and the sale of a long-term future contract will be profitable in a backward market. Examples of this are shown for a contango market in Figure 25-13.

Of course, it is unlikely that the term structure will remain constant. As market conditions change, the structure can alternate between contango and backward, with varying degrees of curvature for each structure. Because a short-term futures contract will almost always change more quickly than a long-term contract, if a trader believes that a contango structure will become less curved or will move toward a backward structure, the sale of a futures spread (i.e., sell long term, buy short term) is likely to be profitable. If the trader believes that a backward structure will become less curved or will move toward a contango structure, the purchase of a futures spread (i.e., buy long term, sell short term) is likely to be profitable. These two scenarios are shown in Figures 25-14 and 25-15.

Figure 25-13 A futures spread in a contango market.

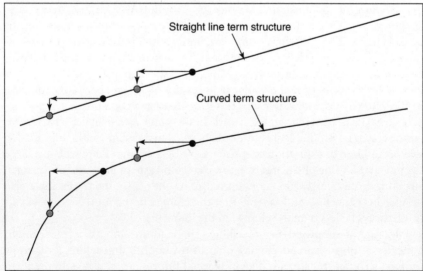

Figure 25-14 A futures spread when the term structure moves from contango toward backward.

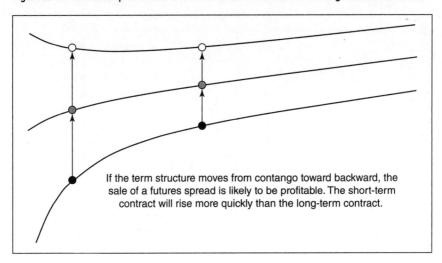

If the term structure moves from contango toward backward, the sale of a futures spread is likely to be profitable. The short-term contract will rise more quickly than the long-term contract.

VIX Options

The CBOE began trading VIX options in 2006. The options are European (no early exercise) and settle into the value of the VIX at the opening of trading on expiration Wednesday, with each volatility point having a value of $100.

Compared with other financial indexes, the VIX is highly volatile. From Figure 25-4, it's evident that the VIX can double or even triple in price over short periods of time. The volatile nature of the VIX is confirmed in Figure 25-16, the 50- and 250-day volatilities of the VIX from 2003 to 2012. Over the 10-year sample period, the 50-day volatility occasionally reached highs of almost 200 percent, while it rarely fell below 50 percent. A trader might assume that options on the VIX will be priced accordingly, with implied volatilities that

Figure 25-15 A futures spread when the term structure moves from backward toward contango.

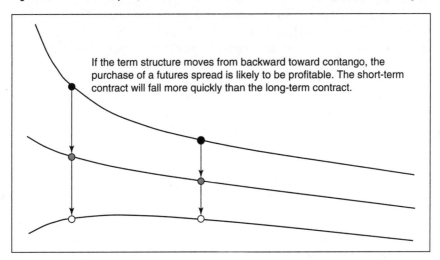

If the term structure moves from backward toward contango, the purchase of a futures spread is likely to be profitable. The short-term contract will fall more quickly than the long-term contract.

Figure 25-16 VIX 50- and 250-day historical volatility: 2003–2012.

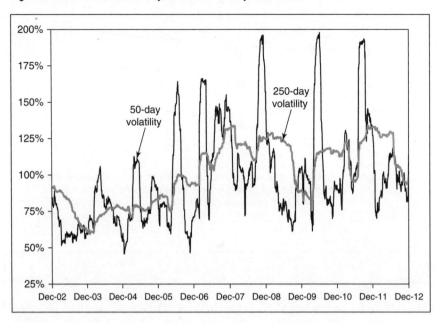

reflect the highly volatile nature of the index. This would be true if one could hedge a VIX option position with the VIX. But because the index itself cannot be easily bought or sold, the instrument that is most commonly used to hedge a VIX option position is a VIX futures contract. VIX futures, however, are less volatile than the index because futures prices tend to change at a slower rate than the price of the index. Figure 25-17 shows the 50-day volatility of the index compared with the same 50-day volatility of the first three futures months. Rarely is the front-month futures contract as volatile as the index. Moreover, back months become progressively less volatile, reflecting the converging term structure of the index.

Just as a VIX futures trader is likely to be disappointed when a futures contract fails to move as much as the index, a VIX options trader is likely to be disappointed when the value of an option does not react to the full volatility of the index. For a theoretical trader who follows a dynamic hedging procedure, expectations about VIX volatility should focus on the volatility of the futures contract used to hedge the option position, not the volatility of the index.

Not only do VIX options tend to carry lower implied volatilities than one would expect from the volatility of the index, but the distribution of implied volatilities differs significantly from other option markets. The price of a traditional stock or commodity can, in theory, rise without limit. Moreover, over long periods of time, there is an expectation that the prices of many traded stocks and commodities will appreciate, with longer time periods accompanied by greater appreciation. This is the philosophy behind long-term investing. But, unlike the price of a stock or commodity, over any given period of time, there are practical limits beyond which implied volatility is unlikely to go. An option trader would be surprised indeed to see implied volatility in a stock

Figure 25-17 Fifty-day historical volatility of the VIX and the first three futures months.

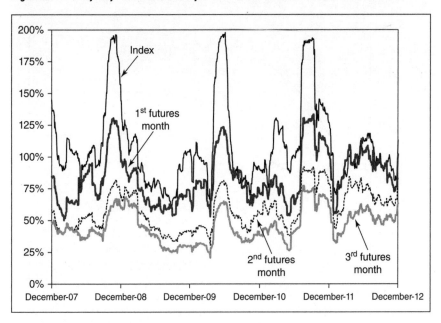

index market fall below 5 percent, no matter how long he observed the market. A trader would likewise be surprised to see implied volatility rise above 100 percent. Moreover, the value of the VIX is influenced by the mean reverting characteristics of volatility. When the VIX is at a very low level, there is a greater likelihood that it will rise; when it is at a very high level, there is a greater likelihood that it will fall. Consequently, expectations about VIX prices will differ from expectations about the price of traditional underlying contracts. These expectations are reflected in the volatility skew, the distribution of implied volatilities for VIX options across exercise prices.

The volatility skews for VIX options on March 19, 2012, are shown in Figure 25-18. The shape of these skews is considerably different from the skew for a typical stock or commodity. With some variation, in most stock and commodity option markets, exercise prices that are farther away from the current underlying price tend to carry increasingly higher implied volatilities—hence the term *volatility smile*. But, for VIX options, the implied volatility of lower exercise prices drops off very quickly. While higher exercise prices carry higher implied volatilities, at some point on the upside, implied volatilities stop increasing and tend to flatten out. Rather than being a smile, the shape of the skew might be described as a half frown.

VIX options seem to be implying a price distribution that is different from a traditional stock or commodity. Using option prices and the butterfly approach described in Chapter 24, we can construct an implied price distribution for the VIX. This distribution is shown in Figure 25-19 for June options on March 19, 2012 with approximately three months remaining to expiration. At the time, June VIX futures were trading at 23.95. Compared with a traditional lognormal distribution, the left tail is much more restricted, reflecting a belief that there is almost no chance that the VIX will be below 10.00 at June expiration. The right

Figure 25-18 VIX option implied volatility skews, March 19, 2012.

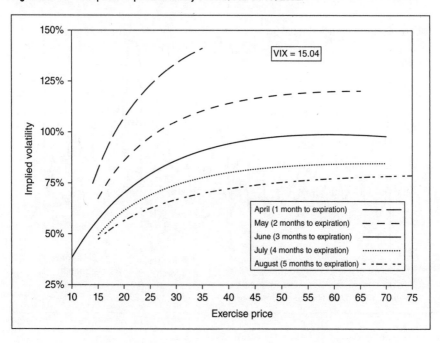

tail is also more restricted, perhaps reflecting a belief that large upward moves are less likely than in a lognormal distribution. Although it may be difficult to discern from the graph, the marketplace also seems to be implying a slightly better chance of a very large upward move at the far end of the right tail.

Figure 25-19 Three-month price distribution implied from VIX option prices, March 19, 2012 [with the three-month (June) future at 23.95].

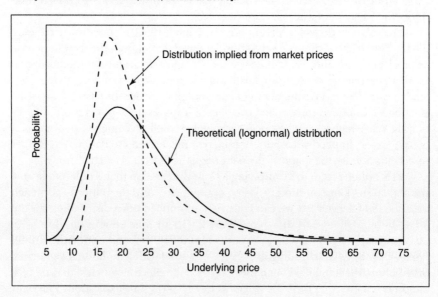

Replicating a Volatility Contract

Even though replication of a realized variance or VIX position is not a practical choice for most traders, in theory, it is possible to create such a position. How can this be done?

Suppose that a trader sells a realized variance contract at a volatility of 20 (percent), equal to a variance of $20^2 = 400$. If the actual realized volatility over the life of the contract is greater than 20 percent, the trader will lose money; if the actual realized volatility is less than 20 percent, the trader will make money. How can a trader hedge this position? A variance position can be replicated by purchasing a strip of options across all exercise prices. To create a position with a constant-variance exposure, it is necessary to purchase $1/X^2$ (where X is the exercise price) of each option. Then, by dynamically hedging the entire position in order to remain delta neutral throughout the life of the variance swap, the total value of the strategy will exactly match the actual realized variance of the variance contract.

It may seem that a volatility position can be replicated using the same approach. But the fact that volatility is the square root of variance means that if the variance exposure is constant, the volatility exposure cannot be constant. Let's return to an earlier example where a realized volatility contract with a vega exposure of $10,000 was purchased at a price of 20. We can compare the outcomes in two different cases. In the first case, the contract is settled in variance points, with each point having a value equal to the notional vega divided by twice the volatility price: $10,000/(2 \times 20) = \$250$. In the second case, the contract is settled in volatility points with each point have a value of $10,000.

Realized Variance	Variance P&L	Realized Volatility	Volatility P&L
250	−$37,500	15.81	−$41,900
300	−$25,000	17.32	−$26,800
350	−$12,500	18.71	−$12,900
400	0	20	0
450	+$12,500	21.21	+$12,100
500	+$25,000	22.36	+$23,600
550	+$37,500	23.45	+$34,500

At a realized variance of 400 (a realized volatility of 20), the variance P&L and the volatility P&L are the same. However, as the difference between the contract variance price of 400 (a volatility price of 20) and the realized variance increases, the difference between the variance P&L and volatility P&L increases.

A strip of options done in the correct proportion of $1/X^2$ yields a constant exposure to variance. But the same strip of options does not yield a constant exposure to volatility. As realized volatility rises or falls, a trader who uses a strip of options to hedge a volatility position cannot be certain that the strip will exactly offset his position. This uncertainty makes it difficult to hedge volatility exposure, which is why such contracts are usually settled in variance points.

In our example, if the trader can create the hedge that replicates a long volatility position at a price of 19 (percent), the trader will have a certain profit in the form of an arbitrage. He has a short volatility position at a price of 20 (a variance of 400) and a long variance position at a price 19 (a variance of 361). If the contract is settled in variance points, he must show a profit of $39 \times \$250 = \$9,750$.

If a trader buys the entire strip of options in order to achieve a constant-variance exposure, how can he determine the volatility value of the strip? Did he buy the strip at a volatility of 19 percent, or 20 percent, or 21 percent, or some other volatility? The methodology used by the CBOE to calculate the VIX is essentially a way of turning the cost of the strip into a volatility value. This is analogous to taking the price of an option and turning it into an implied volatility. The VIX methodology takes the prices of all the options in the strip and turns them into an implied volatility position, but one with constant-variance exposure.

At expiration, the value of a VIX contract is determined by a single strip of SPX options that expire 30 days in the future. But the VIX represents a constant 30-day implied volatility, and prior to expiration, there are no options that expire in exactly 30 days. Consequently, two strips of options that bracket 30 days are required to calculate the VIX, with appropriate weighting of each strip to yield a 30-day implied volatility. In theory, each strip must be dynamically hedged to remain delta neutral. But VIX replication requires the purchase of one strip and the sale of the one strip, and it turns out that gamma values of each strip will approximately offset each other. With a total gamma close to 0, no delta-neutral rehedging is necessary. The position can be carried to expiration of the VIX contract, at which time the long-term strip can be closed out at the option market prices that will determine the expiration value of the VIX.

Unfortunately, there are several problems with this strategy. When the long-term strip is closed, a trader will also want to close the short-term strip. However, while the long-term strip is closed by the special opening rotation on VIX expiration Wednesday, the short-term strip actually expires on either the Friday immediately preceding or immediately following VIX expiration. If the options that make up the short-term strip expire on the Friday after Wednesday VIX expiration, the trader can try to close the short-term strip himself on expiration Wednesday. But in order to do so, he will have to give up the bid-ask spread on every option, and this can be costly. If the options that make up the short-term strip expire on the Friday prior to Wednesday VIX expiration, the trader will have to carry a naked position in the long-term strip for an additional five days. This can also be costly. How can the trader deal with the risk that the short- and long-term strips do not expire at the same time? Unfortunately, there is no good solution to this problem, which is one reason why replicating the VIX is so difficult.

An additional problem arises because the value of the VIX is calculated from the prices of out-of-the-money options. If a trader replicates the VIX by buying one strip and selling another, some of the options that were previously out of the money will almost certainly go into the money over the life of the strip. To have a position that is equal to the VIX value at expiration, the in-the-money options must be converted to out-of-the-money options. We know from synthetics that an in-the-money option hedged with an underlying contract is equivalent to an out-of-the-money option of the opposite type. Therefore, for each option that is in the money, a trader can buy or sell, as necessary, one underlying contract. When the entire position, including the underlying contracts, is closed at expiration, it will exactly equal the expiration value of the VIX. The only problem with this approach is that there is no easily traded underlying for SPX options because the underlying consists of a basket of the 500 stocks that make up the S&P 500. If there are S&P 500 futures available that expire at the same time as the VIX, the futures can be used as a proxy for the underlying contract. Otherwise, a trader may have to create a proxy underlying, perhaps in the form of combos (i.e., long call/short put or short call/long put, with the same exercise price) expiring at the same time as the short-term strip.

While a professional derivatives trading firm might in some cases seek to replicate a realized variance or VIX contract in the option market, for most traders, given the complexities, replicating these contracts is not a realistic possibility.

Volatility Contract Applications

Certainly the most common use of VIX and variance contracts is to speculate on volatility. A trader who has an opinion on whether realized volatility will rise or fall can speculate by buying or selling a variance swap. A trader who has an opinion on whether implied volatility will rise or fall can speculate by buying or selling a VIX contract. In the latter case, a trader can speculate directly on implied volatility by trading VIX futures or speculate on VIX volatility by trading VIX options.

Volatility contracts can also be used as a hedging instrument. Market makers and hedge fund managers sometimes acquire volatility positions, perhaps unintentionally, as a result of their market activities. If they want to hedge away some of this volatility risk, variance and VIX contracts offer a simple way of doing this. A trader who has a realized volatility position, either a positive or negative gamma, can trade variance contracts to hedge his realized volatility risk. A trader who has an implied volatility position, either a positive or negative vega, can trade VIX contracts to hedge his implied volatility risk.

In addition to hedging a volatility position, VIX contracts can sometimes be used as a hedge against a market position, especially a market position that approximates a broad-based portfolio. Because there is an inverse correlation between movement in the stock market and changes in implied volatility (see Figures 25-4 and 25-5), a portfolio manager who is long equities might take a long position in the VIX by either buying VIX futures, buying VIX calls, or selling VIX puts. If stock prices decline, there is an expectation that implied volatility will rise, and the resulting increase in value of the VIX position will offset at least some of the losses in the stock market.

Although volatility contracts are used most often to address direct volatility concerns, market participants sometimes take on indirect volatility positions, positions that have volatility implications that are not immediately apparent. For example, an option market maker typically profits from higher option trading volume. But higher volume is often the result of higher volatility. When there is greater volatility, there is greater demand for options. As such, the market maker has an indirect long volatility position. He would like volatility to increase not because he has intentionally taken a long volatility position but because he is in a business where higher volatility tends to result in higher profits. To hedge this indirect long volatility position, market makers sometimes take a short volatility position in volatility contracts, most commonly the VIX. Of course, the market maker is really hedging trading volume, and he should not take such a large VIX position that his attention is diverted from his primary market-making activities.

Another type of indirect volatility position is one in which a portfolio manager is required to periodically rebalance a portfolio. There is a cost to the rebalancing process, and the cost is typically higher in times of high volatility when bid-ask spreads tend to widen. The portfolio manager therefore takes on a short volatility position as the rebalancing period approaches. He can hedge this short volatility position by taking a long volatility position in the VIX.

Finally, there are some positions that are taken in the option market that are not usually thought of as volatility positions but that have volatility implications. Perhaps the most common option hedging strategy is the covered call, the sale of call options against a long underlying position. Consider a portfolio manager who sells index calls against a broad-based portfolio of stocks. What are his goals? First, he wants the value of his portfolio to increase. Second, he wants to outperform some benchmark against which his performance is measured, perhaps a broad-based index such as the S&P 500.

If the manager sells calls against his portfolio holdings and the market rises, he will achieve his first goal because the portfolio will increase in value. But, if the market rises too far, eventually the calls he sold will be exercised, limiting the upside profit potential. If the market continues to rise, he will fail in his second goal because the benchmark index will eventually outperform the portfolio.

If the manager sells calls against his portfolio and the market declines, he will achieve his second goal of outperforming the index because he will have taken in premium through the sale of calls. But, if the decline is great enough, he will fail in his first goal because the covered calls offer only a partial hedge against a declining market.

From the portfolio manager's point of view, the covered call strategy will perform best, and he will achieve both his goals when the market either doesn't move or moves very little. The portfolio will increase in value as a result of the premium received for the covered calls. And the portfolio will outperform a benchmark index that consists only of stocks. If the portfolio manager wants the market to sit still, he has a short volatility position. He can hedge away some of the risk of a short volatility position by taking a long VIX position, usually by buying VIX futures.

A Final Thought

Because the use of a theoretical pricing model requires a trader to make so many different decisions with respect to both the inputs into the model and the reliability of the assumptions on which the model is based, a new option trader may feel that making the right decisions is either an impossible task or simply a matter of luck. It is true that a trader using a model will almost certainly be wrong about at least some of the inputs into the model, and luck undoubtedly does play a role in the short run. But in the long run traders who are willing to put in the effort required to understand how a model works, including its strengths and weaknesses, always seem to come out ahead. Experienced traders know that under most conditions, using a model, with all its problems, is still the best way to evaluate options and manage risk.

Regardless of whether a model is simple or complex, a trader who uses a model needs to have faith in the model. Otherwise, why use a model at all? Indeed, for traders who are not mathematically proficient, using a model is often a leap of faith. But having faith in a model does not mean having blind, unquestioning faith. If a model returns values that are clearly inconsistent with common sense, or if market conditions are changing so quickly that it is impractical to use the model in its current form, a trader may have to decide whether to adjust the model, if that is possible, or simply to stop using the model. Although we have emphasized the importance of models, trading is both an art and a science. Experienced traders know that there are times when it is perhaps best to put the model aside and make decisions based on other intangible assets, whether intuition, "market feel," or experience. A trader who slavishly uses a model to make every trading decision is heading for disaster. Only a trader who fully understands what a model can and cannot do will be able to make the model his servant rather than his master.

Glossary of Option Terminology

This glossary includes option-related terms as they are most commonly used. However, the reader should be aware that option terminology is not uniform. Traders may sometimes refer to different strategies or option characteristics with the same term. They may sometimes refer to the same strategy or characteristic with different terms.

All or None (AON)   An order that must be filled in its entirety or not at all.

American Option   An option that can be exercised at any time prior to expiration.

Arbitrage   The purchase and sale of the same or closely related products in different markets to take advantage of a price disparity between the two markets.

Asian Option   See *Average Price Option*.

Assignment   The process by which the seller of an option is notified of the buyer's intention to exercise. The seller is required to take a short position in the underlying position in the case of a call or a long position in the case of a put.

At the Forward   An option whose exercise price is equal to the forward price of the underlying contract. Sometimes referred to as *At-the-Money Forward*.

At the Money   An option whose exercise price is equal to the current price of the underlying contract. On listed option exchanges, the term is more commonly used to refer to the option whose exercise price is closest to the current price of the underlying contract.

Automatic Exercise   The exercise by the clearinghouse of an in-the-money option at expiration unless the holder of the option submits specific instructions to the contrary.

Average Price Option   An option whose value at expiration is determined by the average price of the underlying instrument over some period of time. Also known as an *Asian Option*.

Backspread   A spread, usually delta neutral, where more options are purchased than sold, where all options are the same type and expire at the same time.

Backward   A futures market where the long-term delivery months trade at a discount to the short-term delivery months.

Barrier Option   A type of exotic option that will either become effective or cease to exist if the underlying instrument trades at or beyond some predetermined price prior to expiration.

Bear Spread   Any spread that will theoretically increase in value with a decline in the price of the underlying contract.

Bermuda Option   An option that can be exercised prior to expiration, but only during a predetermined period or window. Also known as a *Mid-Atlantic Option*.

Binary Option   An option that, if in the money at expiration, makes one predetermined payout. Also known as a *Digital Option*.

Box   A long call and short put at one exercise price, together with a short call and long put at a different exercise price. All options must have the same underlying contract and expire at the same time.

Bull Spread   Any spread that will theoretically increase in value with a rise in the price of the underlying contract.

Butterfly   The sale (purchase) of two options with the same exercise price, together with the purchase (sale) of one option with a lower exercise price and one option with a higher exercise price. All options must be of the same type, have the same underlying contract, and expire at the same time, and there must be an equal increment between exercise prices.

Buy/Write   The purchase of an underlying contract together with the sale of a call option on that contract.

Cabinet Bid   An option price that is smaller than the normally allowable minimum price. On some exchanges, a cabinet bid is permissible between traders desiring to close out positions in very far out-of-the-money options.

Calendar Spread   The purchase (sale) of one option expiring on one date and the sale (purchase) of another option expiring on a different date. Typically, both options are of the same type, have the same exercise price, and have the same underlying stock or commodity. Also known as a *Time Spread* or *Horizontal Spread*.

Call Option   A contract between a buyer and a seller whereby the buyer acquires the right, but not the obligation, to purchase a specified underlying contract at a fixed price on or before a specified date. The seller of the call option assumes the obligation of delivering the underlying contract should the buyer wish to exercise his option.

Cap   A contract between a borrower and a lender of floating-rate funds whereby the borrower is assured of paying no more than some maximum interest rate for borrowed funds. This is analogous to a call option where the underlying instrument is an interest rate on borrowed funds.

Charm   The sensitivity of an option's delta to the passage of time.

Chooser Option   A straddle where the owner must decide by some predetermined date whether to keep either the call or the put.

Christmas Tree   A spread involving three exercise prices. One or more calls (puts) are purchased at the lowest (highest) exercise price, and one or more calls (puts) are sold at each of the higher (lower) exercise prices. All options must expire at the same time, be of the same type, and have the same underlying contract. Also known as a *Ladder*.

Class   All options of the same type with the same expiration date and same underlying instrument.

Clearinghouse   The organization that guarantees the integrity of all trades made on an exchange.

Clearing Member   A member firm of an exchange that is authorized by the clearinghouse to process trades for its customers and that guarantees, through the collection of margin and variation, the integrity of its customers' trades.

Collar   A long (short) underlying position that is hedged with both a long (short) out-of-the-money put and a short (long) out-of-the-money call. All options must expire at the same time. Also known as a *Cylinder*, *Fence*, or *Range Forward*.

Color   The sensitivity of an option's gamma to the passage of time.

Combination (Combo)   A two-sided option spread that does not fall into any well-defined category of spreads. Most commonly, it refers to a long call and short put or short call and long put, which together make up a synthetic position in the underlying contract.

Compound Option   An option to purchase an option.

Condor   The sale (purchase) of two options with different exercise prices, together with the purchase (sale) of one option with a lower exercise price and one option with a higher exercise price. All options must be of the same type, have the same underlying contract, and expire at the same time, and there must be an equal increment between exercise prices.

Contango   A futures market where the long-term delivery months trade at a premium to the short-term delivery months.

Contingency Order   An order that becomes effective only on the fulfillment of some predetermined condition(s) in the marketplace.

Conversion   A long underlying position together with a synthetic short underlying position. The synthetic position consists of a short call and long put, where both options have the same exercise price and expire at the same time. Sometimes referred to as a *Forward Conversion*.

Covered Write   The sale of a call (put) option against an existing long (short) position in the underlying contract.

Cylinder   See *Collar*.

Delta (Δ)   The sensitivity of an option's theoretical value to a change in the price of the underlying contract. Also known as the *Hedge Ratio*.

Delta Neutral   A position where the sum total of all the deltas add up to approximately 0. Under current market conditions, the position has no preference as to the direction of movement in the underlying market.

Diagonal Roll   See *Time Box*.

Diagonal Spread   A long option at one exercise price and expiration date, together with a short option at a different exercise price and expiration date. All options must be the same type. This is the same as a calendar spread using different exercise prices.

Digital Option   See *Binary Option*.

Dragonfly   A long (short) straddle, together with two short (long) strangles at the same exercise price, where all options expire at the same time and have the same underlying contract. The exercise price of the straddle will usually fall as close as possible to the midpoint between the exercise prices of the strangles.

Dynamic Hedging   A process in which the underlying contract is periodically bought or sold in order to maintain a desired position in a market. Dynamic hedging is most often used to maintain a delta-neutral option position.

Efficiency   A number that represents the relative risk and reward of a potential option strategy. The risk and reward are typically represented by the total gamma, theta, and vega of the strategy. The efficiency is generated by dividing one sensitivity by another.

Elasticity   The percent change in an option's value for a given percent change in the value of the underlying instrument. Sometimes referred to as an option's *Leverage Value*. The elasticity is sometimes denoted by the Greek letter *Lambda* (Λ).

Eurocurrency   Currency deposited in a bank outside the currency's home country.

Eurocurrency rate   The interest rate paid on currency deposited in a bank outside the currency's home country.

European Option   An option that may only be exercised at expiration.

Exchange Option   An option to exchange one asset for another asset.

Ex-Dividend   The first day on which a dividend-paying stock is trading without the right to receive the dividend.

Exercise   The process by which the holder of an option notifies the seller of his intention to take a long position in the underlying contract in the case of a call or a short position in the underlying contract in the case of a put.

Exercise Price   The price at which the underlying contract will be delivered in the event an option is exercised. Also known as the *Strike Price*.

Expiration (Expiry)   The date and time after which an option may no longer be exercised.

Exotic Option   An option with nonstandard contract specifications. Sometimes referred to as a *Second-Generation Option*. Exotic options are usually traded in the over-the-counter (off-exchange) market.

Extrinsic Value   See *Time Value*.

Fair Value   See *Theoretical Value*.

Fence   See *Collar*.

Fill or Kill (FOK)   An order that will automatically be canceled unless it can be executed immediately and in its entirety.

Flex Option   An exchange-traded option where the buyer and seller are permitted to negotiate the exact terms of the option contract. Typically, this includes the exercise price, the expiration date, and the exercise style (either European or American).

Floor   A contract between a borrower and a lender of floating-rate funds whereby the lender is assured of receiving no less than some minimum interest rate for loaned funds. This is analogous to a put option where the underlying instrument is an interest rate on loaned funds.

Forward Contract   An agreement between a buyer and a seller to exchange money for goods at some later date. At maturity, the buyer is obligated to take delivery and the seller is obligated to make delivery.

Forward Conversion   See *Conversion*.

Forward Price   The price that the buyer of a forward contract agrees to pay at maturity of the contract.

Forward Start Option   An option that becomes effective only on some future predetermined date.

Front Spread   A spread, usually delta neutral, where more options are sold than purchased, where all options are the same type, and all expire at the same time.

Fugit   Assuming that all market conditions remain unchanged, the expected amount of time remaining to optimal early exercise of an American option.

Futures Contract   An exchange-traded forward contract.

Futures-Type Settlement   A settlement procedure used by commodity exchanges whereby an initial margin deposit is made but under which no immediate cash payment is made by the buyer to the seller. Cash settlement takes place at the end of each trading day based on the difference between the original trade price or the previous day's settlement price and the current day's settlement price.

Gamma (Γ)   The sensitivity of an option's delta to a change in the price of the underlying contract.

Good 'til Canceled (GTC)   An order that remains active until it can either be executed or is canceled by the customer.

Guts   A strangle where both the call and the put are in the money.

Haircut   On a securities exchange, money that a professional trader is required to keep in his account in order to cover the risk of his position. Haircut requirements are normally determined by the regulatory authority under which the exchange operates.

Hedge Ratio   See *Delta*.

Hedger   A trader who enters the market with the specific intent of protecting an existing position in an underlying contract.

Horizontal Spread   See *Calendar Spread*.

Immediate or Cancel (IOC)   An order that will automatically be canceled if it cannot be executed immediately. An IOC order need not be filled in its entirety.

Implied Volatility   Assuming that all other inputs are known, the volatility that would have to be input into a theoretical pricing model to yield a theoretical value that is identical to the price of the option in the marketplace.

In-Option   A barrier option that becomes effective only if the underlying instrument trades at or through some predetermined price prior to expiration. Also known as a *Knock-In Option*.

In-Price   The price at which the underlying instrument must trade before an in-option becomes effective.

In the Money   An option that has intrinsic value greater than 0. A call option is in the money if its exercise price is lower than the current price of the underlying contract. A put option is in the money if its exercise price is higher than the current price of the underlying contract. An option may also be *In the Money Forward* if it has intrinsic value greater than 0 when compared with the forward price of the underlying contract.

Index Arbitrage   A strategy which attempts to profit from the relative mispricing of options, futures contracts, or the component stocks which make up a stock index.

Intermarket Spread   A spread consisting of opposing market positions in two or more different underlying securities or commodities.

Intrinsic Value   For an in-the-money option, the difference between the exercise price and the underlying price. Out-of-the-money options have no intrinsic value. An option whose price is equal to its intrinsic value is said to be trading at *Parity*.

Iron Butterfly   A long (short) straddle, together with a short (long) strangle, where all options expire at the same time and have the same underlying contract. The exercise price of the straddle is located at the midpoint between the exercise prices of the strangle.

Iron Condor   A long (short) strangle with narrower exercise prices, together with a short (long) strangle with wider exercise prices, where all options expire at the same time and have the same underlying contract. The narrower strangle is centered between the exercise prices of the wider strangle.

Jelly Roll   See *Roll*.

Kappa (K)   See *Vega*. The Greek letter kappa is sometimes used to denote an option's exercise price.

Knock-In Option   See *In-Option*.

Knock-Out Option   See *Out-Option*.

Ladder   See *Christmas Tree*. Alternatively, a type of exotic option whose minimum value increases as the underlying contract goes through a series of predetermined prices, or rungs, over the life of the option.

Lambda (Λ)   See *Elasticity*.

LEAP (Long-Term Equity Anticipation Security)   A long-term (usually more than one year) exchange-traded equity option.

Leg   One side of a spread position.

Leverage Value   See *Elasticity*.

Limit The maximum allowable price movement over some time period for an exchange-traded contract.

Limit Order An order to be executed at a specified price or better.

Local An independent trader on a commodity exchange. Locals perform functions similar to market makers on stock and stock option exchanges.

Locked Market An exchange-traded market where trading has been halted because prices have reached the limit permitted by the exchange.

Long A position resulting from the purchase of a contract. The term is also used to describe a position that will theoretically increase (decrease) in value should the price of the underlying contract rise (fall). Note that a long (short) put position is a short (long) market position.

Long Premium A position that will theoretically increase in value should the underlying contract make a large or swift move in either direction. The position will theoretically decrease in value should the underlying market fail to move or move very slowly. The term may also refer to a position that will increase in value should implied volatility rise.

Long Ratio Spread A spread where more options are purchased than sold.

Lookback Option An exotic option whose exercise price will be equal to either the lowest price of the underlying instrument in the case of a call or the highest price of the underlying instrument in the case of a put over the life of the option. A lookback option can also have a fixed strike, in which case its value at expiration will be determined by the maximum underlying price in the case of a call or the minimum underlying price in the case of a put over the life of the option.

Margin Money deposited by a trader with the clearing house to ensure the integrity of his trades.

Market-if-Touched (MIT) A contingency order that becomes a market order if the contract trades at or beyond a specified price.

Market maker An independent trader or trading firm, usually appointed by an exchange, that is prepared to both buy and sell contracts in a designated market. A market maker is required to quote both a bid and offer price in his designated contract.

Market-on-Close (MOC) An order to be executed at the market price at the close of that day's trading.

Market Order An order to be executed immediately at the current market price.

Mark-to-market A method of valuing a position based on the current market price of all contracts which make up the position.

Married Put　A long (short) put together with a long (short) underlying position.

Mid-Atlantic Option　See *Bermuda Option*.

Midcurve Option　In futures option markets, a short-term option on a long-term futures contract. Midcurve options are most common in euro-currency futures markets, such as Eurodollars and Euribor.

Naked　A long (short) market position with no offsetting short (long) market position.

Neutral Spread　A spread that is neutral with respect to some risk measure, most commonly the delta. A spread may also be lot neutral, where the total number of long and short contracts of the same type are equal.

Not Held　An order submitted to a broker but over which the broker has discretion as to when and how the order is executed.

Omega (Ω)　The Greek letter sometimes used to denote an option's elasticity. An alternative to lambda (Λ).

One-Cancels-the-Other (OCO)　Two orders submitted simultaneously, either of which may be executed. If one order is executed, the other is automatically canceled.

Order Book Official (OBO)　An exchange official responsible for executing market or limit orders for public customers.

Out of the Money　An option that currently has no intrinsic value. A call is out of the money if its exercise price is more than the current price of the underlying contract. A put is out of the money if its exercise price is less than the current price of the underlying contract. An option may also be *Out of the Money Forward* if it has no intrinsic value when compared with the forward price of the underlying contract.

Out-Option　A type of barrier option that is deemed to have expired if the underlying instrument trades at some predetermined price prior to expiration. Also known as a *Knock-Out Option*.

Out-Price　The price at which the underlying instrument must trade before an out-option is deemed to have expired.

Out-Trade　A trade that cannot be processed by the clearinghouse due to conflicting information reported by the two parties to the trade.

Overwrite　The sale of an option against an existing position in the underlying contract.

Parity　See *Intrinsic Value*.

Phi (Φ)   For foreign-currency options, the sensitivity of the option's value to a change in the foreign interest rate. Sometimes referred to as Rho_2.

Pin Risk   The risk to the seller of an option that at expiration will be exactly at the money. The seller will not know whether the option will be exercised.

Portfolio Insurance   A process in which the quantity of holdings in an underlying instrument is periodically adjusted to replicate the characteristics of an option on the underlying instrument. This is similar to the delta-neutral dynamic hedging process used to capture the value of a mispriced option.

Position   The sum total of a trader's open contracts in a particular underlying market.

Position Limit   For an individual trader or firm, the maximum number of open contracts in the same underlying market permitted by an exchange or clearinghouse.

Premium   The price of an option.

Program Trading   An arbitrage strategy involving the purchase or sale of a stock index futures contract against an opposing position in the component stocks that make up the index.

Put Option   A contract between a buyer and a seller whereby the buyer acquires the right but not the obligation to sell a specified underlying contract at a fixed price on or before a specified date. The seller of the put option assumes the obligation of taking delivery of the underlying contract should the buyer wish to exercise his option.

Range Forward   See *Collar*.

Ratchet Option   A type of exotic option whose minimum value is determined by the underlying price at a series of predetermined time intervals over the life of the option.

Ratio Spread   Any spread where the number of long market contracts (long underlying, long call, or short put) and short market contracts (short underlying, short call, or long put) are unequal.

Ratio Write   The sale of multiple options against an existing position in an underlying contract.

Reversal   See *Reverse Conversion*.

Reverse Conversion   A short underlying position together with a synthetic long underlying position. The synthetic position consists of a long call and short put, where both options have the same exercise price and expire at the same time. Also known as a *Reversal*.

Rho (P)   The sensitivity of an option's theoretical value to a change in interest rates.

Risk Reversal   A long (short) underlying position together with a long (short) out-of-the-money put and a short (long) out-of-the-money call. Both options must expire at the same time. Also known as a *Split-Strike Conversion*. The position is equivalent to a *Collar*.

Roll   A long call and short put with one expiration date, together with a short call and long put with a different expiration date. All four options must have the same exercise price and the same underlying stock or commodity. In slang terms, sometimes referred to as a *Jelly Roll*.

Scalper   A floor trader on an exchange who hopes to profit by continually buying at the bid price and selling at the offer price in a specific market. Scalpers usually try to close out all positions at the end of each trading day.

Second-Generation Option   See *Exotic Option*.

Serial Option   On futures exchanges, an option expiration with no corresponding futures expiration. The underlying contract for a serial option is the nearest futures contract beyond the option expiration.

Series   All options with the same underlying contract, same exercise price, and same expiration date.

Short   A position resulting from the sale of a contract. The term is also used to describe a position that will theoretically increase (decrease) in value should the price of the underlying contract fall (rise). Note that a short (long) put position is a long (short) market position.

Short Premium   A position that will theoretically increase in value should the underlying contract fail to move or move very slowly. The position will theoretically decrease in value should the underlying market make a large or swift move in either direction. The term may also refer to a position that will increase in value should implied volatility fall.

Short Ratio Spread   A spread where more options are sold than purchased.

Short Squeeze   A situation in the stock option market, usually resulting from a partial tender offer, where no stock can be borrowed to maintain a short stock position. If assigned on a short call position, a trader may be forced to exercise a call early to fulfill his delivery obligations, even though the call still has some time value remaining.

Sigma (σ)   The commonly used notation for standard deviation. Because volatility is usually expressed as a standard deviation, the same notation is often used to denote volatility.

Specialist   A market maker given exclusive rights by an exchange to make a market in a specified contract or group of contracts. A specialist may buy or sell for his own account or act as a broker for others. In return, a specialist is required to maintain a fair and orderly market.

Speculator   A trader who hopes to profit from a specific directional move in an underlying contract.

Speed   The sensitivity of an option's gamma to a change in the underlying price.

Spread   A long market position and an offsetting short market position usually, but not always, in contracts with the same underlying market.

Split-Strike Conversion   See *Risk Reversal.*

Stock-Type Settlement   A settlement procedure in which the purchase of a contract requires full and immediate payment by the buyer to the seller. All profits or losses from the trade are unrealized until the position is liquidated.

Stop-Limit Order   A contingency order that becomes a limit order if the contract trades at a specified price.

Stop (Loss) Order   A contingency order that becomes a market order if the contract trades at a specified price.

Straddle   A long (short) call and a long (short) put where both options have the same underlying contract, the same expiration date, and the same exercise price.

Strangle   A long (short) call and a long (short) put where both options have the same underlying contract, the same expiration date, but different exercise prices.

Strap   An archaic term for a position consisting of two long (short) calls and one long (short) put where all options have the same underlying contract, the same expiration date, and the same exercise price.

Strike Price (Strike)   See *Exercise Price.*

Strip   An archaic term for a position consisting of one long (short) call and two long (short) puts where all options have the same underlying contract, the same expiration date, and the same exercise price. Alternatively, in Eurocurrency markets, a series of futures or futures options designed to replicate the characteristics of a long-term interest-rate position.

Swap   An agreement to exchange cash flows. Most commonly, a swap involves exchanging variable-interest-rate payments for fixed-interest-rate payments.

Swaption   An option to enter into a swap agreement.

Synthetic   A combination of contracts that together have approximately the same characteristics as some other contract.

Synthetic Call   A long (short) underlying position together with a long (short) put.

Synthetic Put   A short (long) underlying position together with a long (short) call.

Synthetic Underlying   A long (short) call and short (long) put where both options have the same underlying contract, the same expiration date, and the same exercise price.

Tau (τ)   The commonly used notation for the amount of time remaining to expiration. Some traders also use the term to refer to the sensitivity of an option's theoretical value to a change in volatility (equivalent to the vega)

Term Structure   The distribution of implied volatilities across different expiration months in the same underlying market.

Theoretical Value   An option value generated by a mathematical model given certain prior assumptions about the terms of the option, the characteristics of the underlying contract, and prevailing interest rates. Also known as *Fair Value*.

Theta (Θ)   The sensitivity of an option's theoretical value to a change in the amount of time remaining to expiration.

Three-Way   A position similar to a conversion or reversal but where the long or short position in the underlying instrument has been replaced with a very deeply in-the-money call or put.

Time Box   A long call and short put with the same exercise price and expiration date together with a short call and long put at a different exercise price and expiration date. This is simply a roll using different exercise prices. Also known as a *Diagonal Roll*.

Time Premium   See *Time Value*.

Time Value   The price of an option less its intrinsic value. The price of an out-of-the-money option consists solely of time value. Also known as *Extrinisic Value* or *Time Premium*.

Time Spread   See *Calendar Spread*.

Type   The designation of an option as either a call or a put.

Underlying   The instrument to be delivered in the event an option is exercised.

Vanilla Option   An option, usually exchange traded, with standardized and traditional contract specifications as opposed to an exotic option.

Vanna   The sensitivity of an option's delta to a change in volatility.

Variation   The daily cash flow resulting from changes in the settlement price of a futures contract.

Vega.   The sensitivity of an option's theoretical value to a change in volatility. Also known as *Kappa*.

Vega Decay   The sensitivity of an option's vega to the passage of time.

Vertical Spread   The purchase of an option at one exercise price and the sale of an option at a different exercise price where both options are of the same type, have the same underlying contract, and expire at the same time.

Volatility   The degree to which the price of a contract tends to fluctuate over time.

Volatility Skew   The tendency of options at different exercise prices to trade at different implied volatilities. Also known as a *Volatility Smile*.

Volatility Smile   See *Volatility Skew*.

Volga   The sensitivity of an option's vega to a change in volatility. Also known as *Vomma*.

Vomma   See *Volga*.

Warrant   A long-term call option. The expiration date of a warrant may under some circumstances be extended by the issuer.

Write   To sell an option.

Zero-Cost Collar   A collar where the prices of the purchased and sold options are equal.

Zomma   The sensitivity of an option's gamma to a change in volatility.

B

Some Useful Math

The mathematical functions and calculations referred to in this text are included in almost all commonly used spreadsheets, and for most traders, it is not necessary to know exactly how the calculations are made. Of far greater importance is the ability to interpret the numbers that result from the calculations.

For the reader who is interested, a detailed discussion of these mathematical concepts can be found in any good statistics or finance textbook. For convenience, we include an overview of these concepts and applications.

Rate-of-Return Calculations

An interest rate is the most common rate of return. The total interest can be computed in three ways: simple, compound, and continuous. If

r = annual interest rate
t = time to maturity, in years
n = number of compounding periods per year
PV = present value of an investment
FV = future value of an investment
$\ln(x)$ = natural logarithm
$e^x = \exp(x)$ = exponential function [(note that the natural exponential function and natural logarithm are inverses, that is, $\ln(e^x) = e^{\ln(x)} = x$)]

then, for simple interest,

$$FV = PV \times (1 + r \times t)$$
$$PV = FV/(1 + r \times t)$$
$$r = (FV/PV - 1)/t$$
$$t = (FV/PV - 1)/r$$

for compound interest,

$$FV = PV \times (1 + r \times t)^{nt}$$
$$PV = FV/(1 + r/n)^{nt} = FV \times (1 + r/n)^{-nt}$$
$$r = [(FV/PV)^{1/nt} - 1] \times n$$
$$t = [\ln(FV/PV)/\ln(1 + r/n)]/n$$

and for continuous interest,

$$FV = PV \times e^{rt}$$
$$PV = FV/e^{rt} = FV \times e^{-rt}$$
$$r = \ln(FV/PV)/t$$
$$t = \ln(FV/PV)/r$$

Because volatility is a continuously compounded rate of return, we can use the exponential and logarithmic functions to do similar calculations for volatility. If

t = time to expiration, in years
F = a forward price after the period of time t
σ = annual volatility or standard deviation
X = an option's exercise price

then a price range of n standard deviations is

$$F \times e^{-n\sigma\sqrt{t}} \text{ (down } n \text{ standard deviations)}$$
$$F \times e^{n\sigma\sqrt{t}} \text{ (up } n \text{ standard deviations)}$$

The number of standard deviations required to reach an exercise price is

$$\ln(X/F)/\sigma\sqrt{t}$$

Normal Distributions and Standard Deviation

If

x_i = each data point
n = number of data points
σ = standard deviation or volatility
μ = average or mean

then the mean or average μ is

$$\mu = \frac{1}{n} \sum_{i=1}^{n} x_i$$

When calculating the standard deviation from the entire population, σ is given by

$$\sigma = \sqrt{\frac{1}{n} \sum_{i=1}^{n} (x_i - \mu)^2}$$

When estimating the standard deviation from a sample of the entire population, σ is given by[1]

$$\sigma = \sqrt{\frac{1}{n-1} \sum_{i=1}^{n} (x_i - \mu)^2}$$

The normal distribution curve $n(x)$ is given by

$$n(x) = \frac{1}{\sigma \sqrt{2\pi}} e^{-(x-\mu)^2 / 2\sigma^2}$$

In a standard normal distribution, $\mu = 0$ and $\sigma = 1$.

Many of the measures associated with a distribution are derived from a group of numbers called *moments*. In general, the jth moment m_j about the mean μ of a distribution is given by[2]

$$m_j = \frac{1}{n} \sum_{i=1}^{n} (x_i - \mu)^j$$

From the second, third, and fourth moments, we can calculate the skewness and kurtosis of a distribution

$$\text{Skewness} = \frac{m_3}{m_2 \sqrt{m_2}}$$

$$\text{Kurtosis} = \frac{m_4}{m_2^2}$$

A perfectly normal distribution has a skewness of 0 and a kurtosis of 3. To normalize the kurtosis such that a normal distribution has a kurtosis of 0, it is common to subtract 3

$$\text{Kurtosis} = \frac{m_4}{m_2^2} - 3$$

Figure B-1 shows calculation of the mean and standard deviation for the pinball distribution in Figure 6-2. The steps required to calculate the skewness and kurtosis would require an inordinate amount of space. However, the relevant values, including the first three moments, are

$$m_2 = 9.0291 \quad m_3 = 1.1095 \quad m_4 = 222.7640$$
$$\text{Skewness} = 1.1095/(9.0291 \times \sqrt{9.0291}) = +0.0409$$

(The right tail of the distribution is very slightly longer than the left tail.)

$$\text{Kurtosis} = (222.7640/9.0291^2) - 3 = -0.2675$$

(The peak of the distribution is slightly lower and the tails slightly shorter than a true normal distribution.)

---

[1] The sample standard deviation is sometimes denoted with s (instead of σ).
[2] In the same way we calculate a sample standard deviation by dividing by $n-1$, we can also calculate sample moments by dividing by $n-1$ rather than dividing by n.

Figure B-1 Calculation of the mean and standard deviation for the distribution in Figure 6-2.

Trough number	Number of occurrences	Total value		Deviation from the mean	Deviation squared	Deviation squared times occurrences
0	0	0		−7.4935	56.1525	0
1	2	2		−6.4935	42.1655	84.3310
2	2	4		−5.4935	30.1785	60.3570
3	4	12		−4.4935	20.1915	80.7660
4	5	20		−3.4935	12.2045	61.0225
5	6	30		−2.4935	6.2175	37.3050
6	9	54		−1.4935	2.2305	20.0745
7	10	70		−0.4935	0.2435	2.4350
8	11	88		+0.5065	0.2565	2.8215
9	9	81		+1.5065	2.2695	20.4255
10	7	70		+2.5065	6.2825	43.9775
11	5	55		+3.5065	12.2955	61.4775
12	3	36		+4.5065	20.3085	60.9255
13	2	26		+5.5065	30.3215	60.6430
14	1	14		+6.5065	42.3345	42.3345
15	1	15		+7.5065	56.3475	56.3475
	77	577				695.2440

Mean = 577/77 = 7.4935

Population standard deviation = $\sqrt{695.2440/77}$ = 3.0049

Sample standard deviation = $\sqrt{695.2440/76}$ = 3.0246

Volatility

Volatility is usually calculated as a sample standard deviation. It is also common to assume a mean of 0. The estimated annualized volatility is then given by

$$\sigma = \sqrt{\dfrac{\dfrac{1}{n-1}\displaystyle\sum_{i=1}^{n}(x_i)^2}{\sqrt{t}}}$$

where $x_i = \ln(p_n/p_{n-1})$ = natural logarithm of the current price p_n divided by the previous price p_{n-1} and t = the time interval, in years, between price changes.

If the underlying contract is a stock, in theory, the price returns x_i should be adjusted to reflect the forward price of p_{n-1} over each time period. However, unless interest rates are very high or the stock will pay a dividend, using the actual price rather than the forward price is unlikely to significantly alter the results.

The volatility calculation for the stock option example in Figure 8-1 is shown in Figure B-2. Because price changes were observed at seven-day intervals ($t = 7/365$), to annualize the volatility, it was necessary to divide by $\sqrt{7/365}$. The calculation represents the population standard deviation (dividing by n rather than $n-1$) and is based on the actual mean of the price changes.

We might also calculate the volatility assuming a 0 mean or use an estimated standard deviation. The various results are as follows:

Population standard deviation, actual mean:	37.62%
Population standard deviation, 0 mean:	37.88%
Estimated standard deviation, actual mean	39.65%
Estimated standard deviation, 0 mean:	39.93%

There is very little difference between the calculations made from the actual mean and a 0 mean. The estimated standard deviation is always greater than the population standard deviation.

Figure B-2 Volatility calculation for the stock option example in Figure 8-1.

Stock price	Logarithmic return	Deviation from mean	Deviation squared
97.70			
99.50	+.018256	+.012152	.000148
92.75	−.070250	−.076355	.005830
95.85	+.032877	+.026773	.000717
96.20	+.003645	−.002460	.000006
102.45	+.062946	+.056842	.003231
93.30	−.093555	−.099660	.009932
91.15	−.023314	−.029419	.000865
95.20	+.043473	+.037369	.001396
102.80	+.076805	+.070701	.004999
103.85	+.010162	+.004058	.000016
	Sum of the returns		**Sum of the squared deviations**
	+.061045		.027140
	mean return = .006105		

Annualized volatility

$$= \sqrt{(.027140/10)}/\sqrt{7/365}$$

$$= .052096/.138485$$

$$= .3762 \ (37.62\%)$$

Index

Naked position, 164, 209, 547
Narrow based stock index, 441–442
Natural gas futures, 403–404
Natural longs and shorts, 321
Negative dividend risk, 279
Negative gamma position, 106–107, 230,
    414–418, 421
Negative interest rates, 83
Negative theoretical edge, 118
Negative time value, 109–110
Negative vega, 230, 236
Negative volga, 236
Net contract position, 417
Neutral hedge. *See* Riskless hedge
Neutral spread, 210, 547
New York Mercantile Exchange, 29
Nominal value. *See* notional value
Nonsymmetrical strategies, 185
Normal distribution, 69–73, 75–77,
    480–481, 554–556
Not held, 209, 547
Notional value, 6, 455
Notional vega, 513

OBO. *See* Order book official
OCO. *See* One-cancels-the-other
OEX. *See* Options Exchange Index
Omega (Ω), 154, 547
One-cancels-the-other (OCO),
    209, 547
Open interest, 5
Open position, 5
Opening trade, 5
Option pricing, 32–36, 62, 90–91,
    338–339, 358
Option replication. *See* Portfolio insurance
Option risk analysis, 116
Option-pricing theory, 119
Options Clearing Corporation, 10, 36
Options Exchange Index (OEX),
    459, 515
Order book official (OBO), 547
Orders, submitting spread, 208–209
OTC. *See* Over-the-counter market
Out of the money, 33–35, 93, 135–136,
    419–420, 423, 470–471, 547
Outliers, 481
Out-option, 547
Out-price, 547
Out-trade, 547
Over-the-counter (OTC) market, 19
Overwrite, 324, 547

Paralysis through analysis, 118
Parity. *See* Intrinsic value
Parity graphs, 38–51
Parkinson, Michael, 384
Partial derivatives, 100
Path dependent, 471
Phi (Φ), 112
Physical commodities, 2, 14–15
Physical settlement, 7–8
Physical underlying, 30–31
Pin risk, 274–275
P&L. *See* Profit and loss
Plain-vanilla-interest-rate swap, 5
Population standard deviation, 382
Portfolio insurance, 335–337
Portfolio manager, 333–334, 336, 537
Positive dividend risk, 279
Positive gamma position, 106–107, 415
Premium, 4
Price changes, 479
    individual stock, 448–450
    in lognormal distributions, 84
    underlying, 141–142, 145–146,
        149–150
    volatility and observed, 80–81
Price distribution, 73
Price movement, 65, 72–75
Price volatility, 82
Price weighted index, 443–445, 449,
    454–455
Pricing, of American options,
    309–317
Pricing models, 62, 338–339
    American, 309
    entering skew into, 489–494
    European, 309, 377
    volatility skew in, 499
    weaknesses, 484–485
Probabilistic model, 471
Probabilities, 4, 376, 483
    delta and, 104–106
    expected value, 53–54, 59–60
    models and, 56–57
    symmetrical distribution of, 60
    theoretical values in, 54–56
Probability functions, 344
Profit and loss (P&L), 46–51, 124, 125, 133
Program trading, 453
Protective options, 323–324, 327, 329
Protective put, 486
Protective value, 308
Pseudoprobabilities, 376

About the Author

Sheldon Natenberg began his trading career in 1982 as an independent market maker in equity options at the Chicago Board Options Exchange. From 1985 to 2000, he traded commodity options, also as an independent floor trader, at the Chicago Board of Trade.

While continuing to trade, Mr. Natenberg has also become active as an educator. In this capacity, he has conducted seminars for option traders at major exchanges and professional trading firms in the United States, Europe, and the Far East. In 2000, Mr. Natenberg joined the education team at Chicago Trading Company, a proprietary derivatives trading firm.